The Complete Indoor Gardener

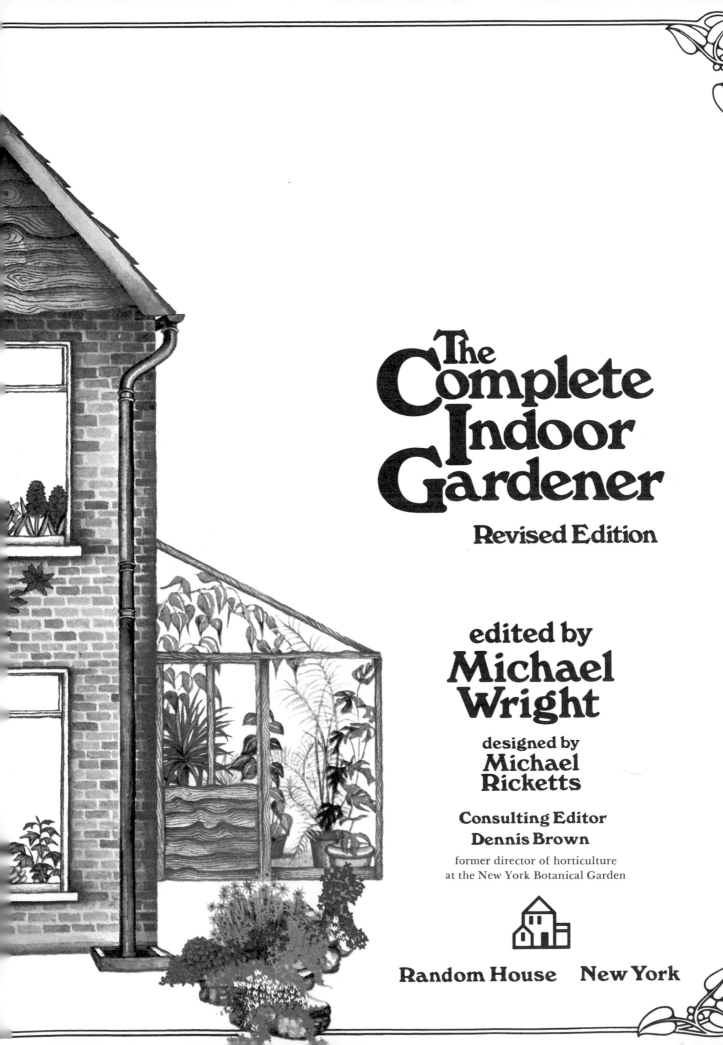

The Complete Indoor Gardener

Revised Edition

edited by
Michael Wright

designed by
Michael Ricketts

Consulting Editor
Dennis Brown
former director of horticulture
at the New York Botanical Garden

Random House   **New York**

Conceived and designed by New Leaf Books
Ltd, 2 Motcomb Street, London SW1

Manufactured in the United States of America
9876543

Library of Congress Cataloging
in Publication Data

Main entry under title:
The Complete indoor gardener.

Bibliography: p.
Includes index.
1. Indoor gardening. 2. House plants.
3. Container gardening. 4. Plants, Ornamental.
I. Wright, Michael, 1941–
SB419.C54 1979   635.9'65   79–4799
ISBN 0–394–50748–7
ISBN 0–394–73813–6 pbk.

The Complete Indoor Gardener

1: Creating your indoor garden

2: Plants to grow in your home

3: Plants for indoors and out

4: Outdoor gardening – without a garden

Contents

Welcome to the world of indoor gardening. We hope that you will find plenty in these pages to interest you, that you will find *The Complete Indoor Gardener* both a fascinating book to browse in of a winter's evening and a valuable reference work for years to come.

You will discover, as you browse, that we have rather stretched the meaning of the word 'indoor' in the title. When we first conceived the book, we felt that there was a great need for an attractive gardening book for anyone without a real garden, but that to restrict ourselves to the growing of plants literally inside the home would meet only part of the need. There are plenty of people who would like also to grow things in window boxes, or on a few square yards of balcony or flat roof, or perhaps on an area of concrete just outside the door – on a patio, terrace or basement area, perhaps.

These are the neglected areas of gardening literature, and that is why this book deals with such places as well as the growing of indoor plants. We only stop short where the real garden – with its lawns and flower beds – begins. So we genuinely feel that we have something to offer you whoever you are – beginner or green-fingered expert – and wherever you live – in a single room or a penthouse, in the most modest terraced house or in a spacious home standing in its own grounds.

Finding your way around
Apart from its scope, the major difference between *The Complete Indoor Gardener* and other gardening books lies in the way it is organized. You will find that each two-page spread of the book forms a self-contained unit, covering one topic or one aspect of a topic. You can read all about bottle gardens, for example, on pages 32 and 33, while pages 106 and 107 deal with how to grow bulbs. The whole book is divided up in this way into a total of 110 sections. These, as you can see from the contents list, are in turn grouped into eight major parts.

The Complete Indoor Gardener is a book for the person who is just as interested (or even more so) in the appearance and decorative effect of his plants as in the actual growing of them. So, when you read the parts of the book specifically describing the plants and their treatment, you will find that they are not, as in most gardening books, arranged alphabetically or (except for such natural groups as the palms) in their botanical families. Instead, they are grouped together according to their characteristics and decorative uses. That is why the houseplants with huge leaves are all on pages 40 and 41, while brilliantly coloured kinds are on pages 46 and 47, and so on.

Of course, dividing the plants into categories like this is bound to be a bit arbitrary in some cases, but it seemed to us to be of more practical use, and cross-references deal with plants that could logically be placed in two or more groupings. Finally, if you want to find out about a particular plant whose name you know, you will find a comprehensive index of common and botanical names at the back of the book. There is also a separate index of general topics, which includes general plant groupings.

Those Latin names
Which brings us to the problem of botanical names – some of them Greek, actually, rather than Latin – which many people feel are used by gardening writers and nurserymen alike purely to confuse. Just the opposite is the case. If we were to use nothing but the everyday common names – particularly where houseplants are concerned – there would be no end of confusion, particularly since this book is being read in many countries. For the plant that answers to the name of devil's ivy in Britain is called the pothos in the US, but call it *Scindapsus* and you stand a good chance of being understood in both countries. In the same way, the American patient Lucy changes her name to busy Lizzy on crossing the Atlantic, but in both places she answers to the name of *Impatiens*. And when, in the name of marketing, commercial growers (or their advertising agencies) coin 'common' names for plants that have never before been given them, things tend to become even more confused.

That is why we have primarily used botanical names in this book, giving the better known common names where appropriate and indexing all the common names we could find. This is not to say the botanists are blameless where confusions arise. You will find a number of plants in these pages that have more than one botanical name, either through accident or through a deliberate change. But at least these are comparatively few and are to be found in reference books, so that any problem or confusion is quite easily sorted out.

Writing botanical names
The botanical name is printed in italic type. The first name (which is always given a capital letter) is the *genus* name (plural *genera*). One genus can include a large number of different plants, but they are – at least in the eyes of botanists – fundamentally similar. Examples of genera are *Ficus* (the figs), *Philodendron* and *Chrysanthemum*. The different plants within a genus are called *species*, and their names come after the genus name: *Ficus radicans* (trailing

fig), *Ficus diversifolia* (mistletoe fig) and so on. To save space, and so long as no confusion can arise, the genus name is often abbreviated after the first time it occurs in a particular section of the book: *Ficus radicans, F. diversifolia*.

You will sometimes see a third name, after the genus and species names. This happens where a species has two or more forms that are not different enough to be classed as separate species, but are nevertheless distinct; the leaf or flower colour may be different, for example. Where these occur naturally, in the wild, they are termed *subspecies* or *varieties*, and the extra name is printed in italics.

Introduction

The plants
You will find literally hundreds of species, varieties and hybrids in the pages that follow. Sometimes you may get annoyed when you cannot find a plant that is described and that takes your fancy. Worse still (but unfortunately all too possible), your local nurseryman may never have heard of it.

For this, we can only apologize in advance, for not all the plants mentioned are easily available in all countries. If you have problems finding what you want locally, we can only suggest that you try some of the specialist growers listed at the end of the book. Houseplants are booming all over the world, and nurserymen are introducing new kinds all the time (while quietly dropping some that failed to live up to their early promise). We have tried to include all the indoor plants you are likely to come across, and some that should appear before too long. But we also have to apologize for any new introductions that we have not covered.

Among outdoor plants, we have had to be more selective, as there are very many hundreds of possible candidates. The contributor of this part of the book, Mrs Frances Perry, has chosen something over 200 kinds that are particularly suitable for growing on window ledges, patios, terraces and similar places.

Bear in mind with the outdoor plants that there will be considerable variations in size and performance according to the growing position, soil, temperature and so on; the figures given are only approximate. Also, while all the recommended plants should flourish in cool temperate regions, including most of the British Isles, and most of them in warmer places, too, people in areas of more extreme climate – such as north-eastern Scotland, Scandinavia, alpine areas and north-eastern North America – will have to be more choosy. In the index of plant names you will find an indication of the plants' hardiness.

One final apology is due to those readers who speak English but live outside Britain: You will find some 'Britishisms' that sound strange to you. Probably the commonest are the word peat where in North America you would talk of peatmoss, and the recommendation to use John Innes potting mixtures. The former you have now been told about, while the latter is explained on page 218. The other major problem – that of differing common names for plants – is covered by the index, so we hope that this minor communication breakdown will not put you off sharing with us the fun of indoor gardening.

From all the people who helped to create *The Complete Indoor Gardener*, good growing!

The most commonly grown form of trailing fig, for example, has variegated leaves – that is, they have green and cream patches – and its full name is *Ficus radicans variegata*. You will often come across the varietal names *variegata* and *tricolor*, the latter usually meaning that the plant's leaves have reddish patches or tinges, as well as light-coloured parts.

If the third name is in quotation marks, but is not printed in italics, this means that the variety arose first in cultivation, not in the wild, and it is termed a *cultivar* (*culti*vated *va*riety). An example is the sturdy modern variety of the rubber plant, *Ficus elastica* 'Robusta'. Hybrids – new kinds of plants raised by cross-breeding existing kinds – are often written in the same way, but here the hybrid name simply follows that of the genus; examples are *Fuchsia* 'Thalia' and *Agapanthus* 'Headbourne Hybrids'. Such named hybrids are commonest among outdoor plants, bulbs and flowering pot-plants. A hybrid may also be indicated by an ×, however, as in *Billbergia × windii*. Finally, common names are always printed in roman (upright) type, without capital letters except where a proper name is involved (as in the Norfolk Island pine).

1 Creating your indoor garden

The most exciting part of indoor gardening is the selection and arrangement of house-plants so that they complement your design scheme and help to create an interesting, decorative interior.

Whether you have nothing more than a row of pots on a window sill or a comprehensively stocked conservatory, with skill and imagination you can make an effective display.

In the next 20 pages you will find a combination of stimulating ideas and practical advice that will help you develop this skill.

Plants for a purpose

There are big houseplants and small. There are slender, graceful specimens, and kinds that spread out bushily. Some ramble and tumble, while others – given a chance – will climb for the ceiling. There are plants with brilliant flowers, and kinds whose primary attraction is their foliage. Some have leaves painted brilliantly with colour; others are cool and subtle shades of green. Many have handsome, glossy foliage with a texture like polished leather. Some are like velvet, while a few kinds have delicate leaves that are almost transparent.

There is an enormous and increasing range of kinds that you can buy from plantsmen, garden centres and exotic plant nurseries. The pages that follow are crammed with them, and if you do not know very much about houseplants the choice can be pretty bewildering. This is all the more true if you have in mind the finished effect that you want, in interior design terms, and are faced with a number of rather similar young specimens that give only the merest hint of their future potential.

We have tried to help by grouping the plants together in a logical way in the descriptions starting on page 34. Rather than dealing with them in alphabetical order of their names or in botanical families, as most houseplant books do, each two-page spread of this book describes a number of plants that have some basic characteristics in common. For example, all those plants with particularly big leaves are described on pages 40 and 41, so if you feel that this is the kind of plant you need to decorate a particular room, turn to those pages.

In some cases, plants have been grouped on a botanical basis, but this is only where the layman will be just as familiar with the plants' characteristic form as the botanist. Palms, ferns and cacti are examples, and the members of groups like this not only look somewhat alike but also generally need much the same treatment. If you do want to find out about a particular plant whose name you know, you will find a comprehensive index of plant names at the end of the book. As a further aid to selecting the plants you want, the chart on pages 242 and 243 summarizes the characteristics and needs of the better known types of indoor plants.

If, however, you have only a hazy idea of the kinds of plants you want for a particular situation, the information given here will guide you. Remember that houseplants are tools of the interior designer, and you should, for best results, choose plants to fulfil a particular purpose. Buying a plant on impulse simply because you like it, and then trying to find somewhere to put it, is rarely so satisfactory. In just the same way, you should take into account plants' needs – in terms of their physical environment – both when choosing and positioning them. You will find much information on these subjects in the pages that follow, dealing with individual plants, while the final part of the book, which starts on page 214, goes into more technical details about the care and cultivation of your plant collection.

Decorative-leaved plants
To make a permanent houseplant, any plant should have attractive leaves, but some types have particularly decorative leaf patterns or colourings. Such plants may seem rather overpowering if you use too many of them, but a few can form a focal point to a group of plants, or in some cases to a whole room **left**.
Plants with particularly bright leaf colourings are described on page 46, while those with patterned leaves are on page 48. There are also some brightly coloured or patterned specimens among the large-leaved plants described on page 40. In addition, there are a number of brightly coloured *Dracaenas* and *Cordylines* (page 44), bromeliads (page 72) and fancy-leaved geraniums (page 104), while many other plants have variegated varieties.

14

Plants to stand alone

It is always tempting to buy large specimen plants **left**, **above** and **above right** that have an immediate impact, and in the right setting such plants can be most impressive. A number of houseplants will reach tree-like proportions given time, notably members of the fig family, which includes the rubber plant, *Ficus elastica* (see page 36). Others include the palms (page 43) and those plants, such as the larger *Dracaenas*, that look rather palm-like but are not true palms (page 44).

If you prefer bushier types, there are various foliage shrubs (page 38) and large-leaved plants (page 40) that make substantial specimens. These are all grown primarily for their foliage, but there are also some substantial flowering indoor shrubs (pages 88 and 102). Roses (page 75) can also be grown indoors.

Climbers and trailers

Plants that ramble over a table or shelf, tumble from a suspended pot **left**, or climb up canes or other supports, can be extremely useful in many situations. Effective room-dividers, for example, can be made with climbing foliage houseplants (page 50), while trailing foliage plants (page 52) are ideal for edging a plant display table. Most flowering climbing plants (page 86) are best grown in a porch, conservatory or garden room, but some that can also be used in the home are described on page 84.

Smaller plants

Big, spectacular specimens have their valuable uses, but so do much more insignificant plants – the kind you might stand on a window sill **right**. You will find a selection of smaller-leaved foliage plants on page 54, while many of the trailing plants (page 52) are also quite small, as are the ivies (page 50) and some of the decorative-leaved plants on pages 46 and 48. For shady positions where the atmosphere can be kept moist and preferably fairly cool, ferns (page 56) are ideal, while there are also some dwarf ferns specially suited to growing in glazed cases (page 58). For some small flowering plants see pages 76 to 79, while on page 110 you will find details of some of the smallest bulbs. Finally, most cacti and succulents (pages 60 to 71) are quite small and compact.

Plants with flowers

However attractive their leaves may be, virtually no permanent foliage houseplants can challenge the beauty and impact of colourful flowers. A room filled with flowering pot-plants would be rather overpowering, but a few choice specimens can provide a valuable splash of colour against a framework of foliage **below left**.

They range from annuals that can be raised easily from seed (page 78) and herbaceous pot-plants (page 80), through a number of climbing and trailing types (pages 84 to 87) to flowering shrubs (pages 88 and 102, the latter including plants that can be moved outdoors in summer).

Among the kinds that have foliage of permanent interest all year round are the bromeliads (page 72) and some of the African violet family (page 76), as well as some other handsome types described on page 74. Particularly useful are plants that flower in winter (page 82) and those with fragrant flowers (page 90). Given care, many cacti and succulents (pages 60 to 71) can be brought into flower, while even orchids (pages 92 to 99) can be kept and flowered indoors. Geraniums (page 104) and begonias (page 116) are favourites for both indoors and out, while bulbs (pages 106 to 115) include a great range of familiar and less well known flowers, all of which will bring bright colour and beauty to your home.

Plants in interior design

An interior without living greenery is rather like a meal without salt or spices – it may serve its basic purpose, but is dull and uninspiring. Plants bring vitality and visual excitement to a room. They serve as much more than ornaments, thanks to the added dimension brought by their living, growing, ever-changing character and their subtle variations in tone and texture.

But to incorporate plants into an interior design scheme in a really effective way is a demanding as well as an exciting aspect of indoor gardening. As room dividers or screens, or as focal points within an interior, the plants become an integral part of the visual whole, highlighting or modifying architectural features. So it is essential to take into account the characteristics of both the plants and the room if you are to make the best use of either.

Design guidelines

Many varieties of indoor plants can be used very effectively in interior design; ultimately the choice depends on the imagination and inspiration of the gardener, and on whether conditions meet with the plant's requirements (see page 220). Nevertheless, it is a good idea to take some basic guidelines into consideration when buying plants.

Foliage varieties whose appearance does not change radically from season to season are usually the best choice for permanent plants. Shape, leaf form and texture must be distinctive, so that the plant creates a definite effect. And the amount of pruning, cutting back and general care that will be required should also be taken into account when plants are to be permanently on view in a living room. Like fine furniture, they look their best only if they are properly cared for and kept in good condition.

The relationship between a plant's size and the scale of the room in which it is to grow is all-important. A fully-grown *Ficus benjamina* (weeping fig) will dwarf a cottage drawing-room; a solitary fern adds nothing to a spacious, open-plan modern interior.

Matching leaf forms and plant shapes to architectural style is another factor. Traditional rooms usually require plants with comparatively delicate foliage: *Rhoicissus rhomboidea* (Natal vine, or grape ivy) and ferns, for example. Spacious, high-ceilinged interiors can be exceptions, however, and often provide settings suitable for larger tropical plants such as *Dracaenas*. Small-leaved plants can also be displayed attractively in modern interiors, but the stark lines of contemporary architecture provide an ideal background for the distinctive leaves of tropical varieties such as *Monstera deliciosa* (Swiss cheese plant, or split-leaf philodendron) and *Ficus elastica* (the rubber plant).

Most plants are seen to best advantage against plain backgrounds, but varieties with strong foliage forms can be effectively displayed against patterns – provided there is a definite contrast between the size of the leaves and the motifs in the pattern. The leaves of *Schefflera actinophylla* (umbrella tree) will relieve the fussiness of a small-patterned wallpaper or fabric; the delicate foliage of an asparagus fern contrasts well with large, abstract designs. But never try to display a plant with vividly coloured or patterned leaves against an equally bold wall covering; the effect will be sheer visual chaos.

Using plants purposefully

Open-plan interiors are very much a feature of modern homes, and indoor plants can be used effectively to separate the various living areas. Free-standing plants – *Ficus benjamina*, for example, or climbers such as *Philodendrons* or *Rhoicissus rhomboidea* trained on canes – will create a visual division in their own right, and are especially suitable where a token separation, between living area and dining area, for example, is required. Plants used in this way should be tall but not spreading.

Alternatively, plants may be trained over a room-divider or screen. A light specimen – a small-leafed ivy (*Hedera*) for example – will give visual continuity to the areas concerned, while a denser plant such as a *Philodendron* will provide a more complete separation. The latter might be used in a bedsitting room to screen the sleeping area from living quarters. Plants may climb upwards from floor level, or cascade from a container placed on top of the divider. A selection of climbing and trailing plants is given on pages 50 to 53.

Floor-level plant boxes housing a varied group of specimens (see page 20) define the areas within an interior without detracting from its spaciousness. They are especially useful in smaller houses, for instance to indicate the entrance area if a front door opens directly into a living room, or to divide living-room from dining-room.

Contrasting the shape and outline of indoor plants with the dominant lines of an interior can alter a room's scale. A high-beamed ceiling is 'lowered', for example, if hanging baskets (page 128) are suspended from the beams. And a spreading *Monstera deliciosa* or *Philodendron* will detract from vertical lines so that a high-walled interior seems more compact.

Brightening dull spots

An empty wall becomes a decorative asset if it is used as a background for a distinctively foliaged specimen such as the 'silhouette plant' (*Dracaena marginata*), trailing plants such as *Plectranthus oertendahlii* cascading from wall brackets, or climbers such as *Philodendrons* trained on poles. Stairways are often visually 'dead' areas that can usefully be treated in this way.

An unused fireplace is another decoratively dead area that can be enlivened by plants. The scale of the hearth and mantelpiece are important. A small fireplace provides a distinctive setting for a single plant such as a maidenhair fern (*Adiantum*); a larger specimen such as a *Pteris* fern, a dwarf palm, a *Hydrangea*, or a group of foliage and flowering plants, are more suitable for a bigger fireplace. It is essential to block off the chimney

A number of quite simple guidelines will help you make the most effective use of your houseplants. **above** If you have big, bold, architectural interiors, use equally big and bold plants. **below 1** A tiny plant, however pretty, is completely lost in a large room. **2** Make purposeful use of existing features, such as fireplaces, mantelpieces and bays. **3** Do not be afraid to cut back your larger plants when they grow out of scale. **4** Choose plants in relation to their backgrounds, to avoid clashes. **5** Bring variety with unusual features like hanging baskets. **6** Use plants to enliven dull areas, such as hallways.

before arranging the plants, however, to prevent draughts. Crumpled newspaper pushed up out of sight makes an effective temporary blockage.

The imaginative use of plants will also transform alcoves, niches and dull corners into positive decorative assets. Alcoves and niches should be treated as design areas in their own right, and painted or wallpapered to provide settings for a particular plant or group of plants. Unfortunately, these areas are usually dark and generally not conducive to plant growth, a disadvantage they share with fireplaces and, often, plant boxes. One solution is to use plants such as *Sansevierias*, *Philodendrons*, *Aspidistras*, ferns, palms or the tougher *Dracaenas* that enjoy (or at least will survive in) these conditions. Colour can be provided by introducing flowering plants or cut flowers in season.

Alternatively, you can choose plants largely for their appearance and display them only for short periods. Specimens shown in adverse conditions will need a long resting period, and you will have to ensure that replacement plants are always on hand. It is possible to arrange a rota of plants, possibly of the same type, and move all specimens to different parts of the home once a month.

Dramatic spotlights will enhance the plants' appearance and back-lighting can be extremely effective with, for example, a Boston fern (*Nephrolepis*). But you can only rely solely on artificial lighting if a proper growth light is used, or if you rotate the plants to better lit positions

regularly. More information about growing plants under artificial light is given on pages 234 and 235.

Windows: link with outdoors

Bay windows, architectural features of many older houses, can be used to good effect by the indoor gardener. They are ideal sites for plants that flourish in cold night conditions: *Azaleas*, cyclamen and *Primulas*, for instance. An additional advantage is that they protect plants to some extent from the heat inside a room. Arrangements may range from simple window-sill groupings to window gardens with plants such as *Chrysanthemums*, poinsettias (*Euphorbia pulcherrima*) or cyclamen arranged on transparent supports (see page 22).

Plant stands (see page 18) supporting similar or blending specimens, or tall plants such as *Dracaenas*, will extend the window display into the room if they are placed on either side of the bay window. Or the severe lines of the window frame can be softened by trailing plants – a small-leaved ivy or ivy-leaved geranium (*Pelargonium peltatum*), for instance.

If a living-room opens out onto a patio or roof garden, or if french windows lead into a garden, a sense of spaciousness and unity is created by visually linking the interior with the exterior. This may be achieved by matching outdoor plants with similar indoor specimens. Hardy palms on a roof garden may be echoed by a *Howeia belmoreana* (Kentia palm) indoors, for instance; and *Hedera canariensis* (Canary Islands ivy) is an impressive outdoor wall plant that can be linked with indoor ivies. Many bulbs grow indoors as well as out. These and other dual-purpose plants will be found in the part starting on page 118.

To help unify the interior and exterior schemes, similar containers should be used in the garden and in the house. And if a room opens onto a roof garden it is also worth considering whether the same flooring material can be used in both areas to provide a further link.

All around the home

Indoor plants need by no means be confined to the living-room. Ferns, for instance, relieve the usually stark and hygienic lines of a bathroom, and flourish in its warmth and humidity. The gracefully spreading shape of a *Howeia belmoreana* contrasts with the functionalism of a modern kitchen.

On a staircase, climbers such as *Fatshedra lizei* will disguise shabby balustrades, and enliven a stark stairwell. Climbing plants such as ivies, entwined around a hall window, brighten an entrance hall, often the Cinderella room in a house. *Philodendrons*, *Ficus elastica* and palms will add a luxurious air. And for those with enough space, a large-scale indoor garden (see page 28) could provide a focal point for the whole house.

The enormous range of indoor plants available today means that there is a variety for virtually any design purpose. Study their possibilities and their cultural needs. Used sparingly, and with imagination, they will dramatically accent and enhance every interior.

Displaying your houseplants

The successful use of indoor plants in an interior design scheme depends on the skill with which individual specimens or groups of specimens are displayed. Arranging plants so that their unique characteristics of shape, habits of growth, foliage forms and colours, flowers and size can be fully appreciated is challenging and creative. Done well, it makes all the difference between having a nondescript collection of plants and something that really adds to the appearance of the setting.

A cardinal rule is that each plant or group of plants should form a focal point within an interior. And they must be used with restraint. In the first flush of enthusiasm it is only too easy for the novice indoor gardener to add and add to a collection until individual specimens are lost in an amorphous mass of greenery, overflowing from window sills, table tops, alcoves and niches.

Plants must blend happily with other specimens in an interior, and with the furnishings and character of the room. When choosing specimens for a free-standing display in the centre of the room, remember that they will be more closely linked with the carpet or flooring, and surrounding furniture, than with walls or curtains. More information about selecting plants for specific interiors is given on page 16.

Combining statuary or a painting with plants will create an unusual decorative accent. *Hederas* (ivies) are effective against a smooth marble surface, for instance, and the trees in a painting might be echoed by a plant in the foreground. The flowers and foliage of smaller specimens such as cyclamen or *Azaleas* are enhanced if they are reflected by a polished table top or some other glossy surface. A mirror backing adds an extra dimension to a display, and simultaneously enlarges the interior.

Supports and containers

Two basic guidelines should be taken into consideration when choosing plant supports and containers: They must blend with interior furnishings; and, although they are an integral part of a display, they must not detract from the plants. Provided these rules are observed, there is an enormous range of choice. Modern plant supports include glass-topped wrought-iron tables, slatted or plain wooden tables, and pedestals. Clay, earthenware and china containers blend well with most interiors.

Victorian pieces are especially suitable for period interiors. Wooden or metal jardinieres, tiered plant stands, and aspidistra stands were specifically designed for displaying plants. But many other pieces of Victorian or even 'junk' furniture can be used to support plants. Whatnots, wash-stands, and corner cupboards are examples; the bloom of old polished wood blends attractively with delicate foliage.

Unusual containers include wicker baskets, brass saucepans, fire buckets, and even decorative bird cages. A Victorian soup tureen is the ideal container for delicately foliaged plants such as ferns. Metal containers, with their glow-

ing patina, blend well with modern and period interiors. Colourful patterned containers should really be used only for plants with strong foliage forms – *Schefflera actinophylla* (umbrella tree) for instance. If a more delicate plant in a gay container is essential to an interior scheme, choose a pot with colours that blend with foliage or flowers.

Whatever kind of decorative container you choose, it is usually best to have the plant itself growing in an ordinary flower-pot, and to stand this in the container, preferably filling the gap with damp peat or sphagnum moss to hide the flower-pot. If you do want to plant directly in the decorative container, make sure that it has drainage holes and that the material it is made of will not affect the plant.

Plant accents

An impressive mature specimen of a large tropical plant is often arresting enough to stand in its own right. A *Ficus benjamina* (weeping fig) is dramatic in front of a picture window, for instance. But smaller specimens may be dwarfed by their surroundings, and grouping plants, either of the same or different species, is one of the most creative aspects of indoor display. Suggestions for arrangements are given on page 20.

When planting a combination grouping it is a good idea to select a support or container that blends with the predominant specimen in the group. The final choice will, of course, depend on the effect that you want to achieve, but it

is sensible to bear some basic guidelines in mind when choosing.

Best suited to modern interiors, both the larger tropical plants, such as *Ficus elastica* (rubber plant) and *Monstera deliciosa* (Swiss cheese plant, or split-leaf philodendron), and smaller specimens such as some of the *Dracaenas* blend best with linear, modern containers. Stainless steel, earthenware and wood are among the best materials. Palms have period associations, and are often attractively displayed in Edwardian or Victorian containers. Wicker baskets can also be used for palms.

Trailers and climbers

The attraction of trailing plants lies mainly in their cascading foliage, and

above left For instant impact, choose an impressive container with an equally impressive plant – this one is a mature bird's-nest fern (*Asplenium nidus*). A much more modest way of achieving impact, however, is with a skilfully arranged group, such as that **below left,** which includes a small specimen of the same fern, together with an ivy and a golden *Tradescantia*. A larger group, such as the *Dieffenbachias* **above** makes an effective room-divider. For smaller displays, the choice of container is particularly important. **top** The 'old-fashioned' look of this *Begonia* suits very well the setting of pewter and old oak. **below** A simple window feature is formed by a busy Lizzie (*Impatiens*) in a copper pot-holder. **below right** The cascading foliage of a spider plant (*Chlorophytum*) looks splendid against a Victorian aspidistra stand.

ideal supports include pedestal or console tables, or tiered constructions such as plant stands, shelved corner cupboards, or tiered tables that allow foliage to fall natural from one level to another. This applies whether trailers are used alone or in groups with other species. They can often be combined attractively with more compact specimens; ivy blends well with *Saintpaulias* (African violets), for example.

In wall-holders and hanging baskets, trailers will add decorative interest to a blank wall, which will itself emphasize their trailing foliage. Climbing specimens may be trained over netting attached to walls; or on moss sticks or canes if a more compact effect is required (see page 225). Trailing and climbing plants are also ideal subjects for screens (see page 16).

Although many of these plants need room to spread if they are to show to best advantage, a carefully pruned ivy or *Philodendron scandens* (sweetheart vine) is attractive if it is simply trained to tumble over the side of a small clay or earthenware container.

Compact plants and ferns
To be decoratively effective, smaller specimens should be displayed singly or in deliberately massed arrangements. A single African violet in a wicker or china basket, lit by a reading lamp or spotlight, can make a focal point in an interior scheme. But a group arrangement of the same plants on a plant stand, pebbled tray or plant table is dramatically effective.

These and many other small flowering plants, such as cyclamen, get the attention they deserve if they are used for table decoration, and a massed arrangement will form a dramatic centrepiece to a dinner table. When using small plants in a combined arrangement make sure the proportions are balanced, however, or the smaller specimens may be overwhelmed by plants that are only slightly larger.

More exotic plants such as cacti and succulents are best displayed against a linear background – on a modern coffee table, for instance, or in a plant trough. Select a container with clean curves that echo the lines of the plant or plants. Grey-green succulents such as *Gasteria* harmonize well with the glow of pewter.

Smaller specimens look attractive in tiny, unusual containers: *Echeveria elegans* or a small *Sedum* in an egg cup, for instance.

Ferns may be displayed singly, or massed together for traditional effect. Boston ferns (*Nephrolepis exaltata*), for example, are attractive on a Victorian plant stand. Their delicate foliage usually blends best with period containers, but they also look good in hanging baskets (see page 57).

Seasonal flowering plants
Colourful seasonal plants such as *Azaleas*, tulips, hyacinths, daffodils and geraniums (*Pelargoniums*) are most effective when massed together, with or without foliage plants, on a window sill, in a window garden, or on a plant table. A plant trolley (or painted tea trolley) laden with a mass of colourful blooms is a dramatic accent to any room – and has the added advantage that it can be moved around at will.

Flowering plants can also be introduced into groups of foliage specimens, to add a natural splash of seasonal colour. *Azaleas*, cyclamen and poinsettias are especially useful for brightening a winter-time interior (see page 82). As an alternative, you can create a *pot-et-fleur* arrangement (see page 21), in which seasonal cut flowers are combined skilfully with a group of permanent foliage plants.

The sparse foliage of many heavy-headed blooms such as *Chrysanthemums* and carnations (*Dianthus*) may detract from their appearance if they are seen at eye-level. Supported on a low plant table or coffee table, or in containers placed on a pebbled floor tray, they are seen to their best advantage, from above. A floor tray is also ideal for small orange and other *Citrus* trees.

Special features
In addition to the more everyday arrangements of plants discussed here, you will find a number of special ways of cultivating and displaying plants in the following pages. An interesting feature that can be used in almost any room is a terrarium (see page 30) or its very popular variant, the bottle garden (see page 32). Both these are not only attractive in their own right, but also create the humid conditions in which many plants thrive. A terrarium can be built in to a bay window, and this and other ideas for using windows creatively for displaying plants are given on page 22.

With these and all kinds of plant display, you should be prepared to experiment and try out new ideas. Try not to do the obvious thing of placing plants in the middle of a shelf or table, or in the corner of the floor. Move them around and consider how their new positioning affects the appearance of the room – and vice-versa. Look out for new and unusual containers in junk shops, hardware stores and so on. Consider the relationship of plants, containers and settings, and bear in mind the suggestions given here. But, most important of all, do not be hidebound by these or any other rules.

Plant groups and jungles

Large, specimen houseplants are impressive but expensive, yet lesser specimens and smaller plants tend to look rather pathetic standing alone on a shelf or table. You will create much more impact by grouping such plants together to make a kind of indoor jungle.

There are many ways of doing this, from simply arranging a number of individually potted plants in a group – either free-standing or arranged on a gravel tray – to creating semi-permanent mixed plantings in large troughs or bowls. The overall size and complexity of the scheme depends only on your pocket and the needs of the setting, but there is one basic rule that you should always try to follow: Choose, as far as possible, plants that are compatible in their light, warmth and water needs. So long as you make the right choice in this respect, plants in a group will usually flourish far better than similar specimens growing alone.

Choosing the container

An enormous range of containers can be used for indoor plant groups, from plastic imitation baskets a few inches across to large troughs sunk permanently into the floor. In between are many decorative containers in such materials as earthenware and stoneware, plastic and glass-fibre, wood and wrought iron. There are bowls, tubs, urns and troughs. Purpose-made containers can also be constructed of wood, using a square or oblong shape for the corner or side of a room, or a narrow trough where the plants are to form a room-dividing screen.

Drainage and leakage are always problems to consider. Plants appreciate good drainage, but furnishings need protection. If the whole container can be stood on a waterproof tray, or if potted plants are to be stood on individual saucers inside the container, then there is no problem. Otherwise, make sure that the container itself is waterproof, and have a good layer of drainage material at the bottom. If you construct your own container from wood, a cheap and effective waterproof liner can be made with heavy-gauge plastic sheeting.

Choosing compatible plants

A surprising number of plants that would seem quite alien do in fact get along surprisingly well together if a little thought is given to their needs before planting. Sun-loving cacti, for example, should not be planted with *Philodendrons* that require very much less light. And it would be inadvisable to incorporate cyclamen demanding fresh air and light with *Marantas* that need warmer and much more shady conditions. Apart from such obvious incompatibilities, however, there is little to restrict your choice of plants.

Experience shows that varying moisture requirements is not the super-difficult problem that it is usually made out to be. For example, *Sansevierias* grow best in light, dry and warm conditions, but are tough enough to withstand very different treatment provided the conditions do not become too wet and cold. With mixed plantings soil

Ways of forming groups
For maximum flexibility, place free-standing plants in individual saucers or on a tray of gravel. Then plants can easily be rearranged or replaced if they fade. For a more permanent, but still changeable, arrangement, plunge the individual pots in moist peat **right**. This is excellent for combating the dry conditions of most centrally heated rooms. Plunge the pots to the rims only, so that you can check the water needs of each plant. In fact, such groupings plunged in peat will tend to become semi-permanent, as the plant roots find their way out of the bottom of the pots and into the peat. Plants often grow extremely well this way. For even more permanent groupings, plant directly in potting mixture **above**. Use a free-draining mix containing a good proportion of fresh sphagnum peat. If there are no drainage holes, incorporate a two-inch bottom layer of gravel or crocks mixed with lumps of charcoal. To finish the surface, pebbles are better than gravel, as they let you see when watering is needed.

left This 'jungle' is dominated by a *Neanthe* (*Chamaedorea*) *bella*. The other palm is a *Cocos weddeliana*, and it also includes *Pteris* and *Nephrolepis* ferns and a variegated ivy. **above** A tall *Ficus benjamina*, a *Sansevieria* and a *Fatsia japonica* make a simple but effective group. **above right** The tall plant in this tub is a *Dracaena marginata* and that with mottled leaves a form of *Dieffenbachia*.

below left Small gift arrangements like this (which includes an African violet) often have inadequate drainage; you may have to drill holes in the bottom and use a drip tray. If such a group becomes untidy or choked, or if one or more plants die, be prepared to replant in a new container. **below** Mixed plantings can vary widely in size. These containers incorporate automatic watering devices.

probably late in the season, when they have stopped growing for the winter, or in the spring just prior to new growth appearing. You may be able to propagate new plants from the prunings (see page 228).

Replanting will usually mean removing the container to an outhouse where the inevitable mess will not matter too much. The group should then be watered in order to minimize root damage when the plants are removed and their roots carefully teased apart. When you have separated the plants, remove all dead leaves and examine all the plants for pests or disease (see page 232), paying particular attention to the undersides of the leaves.

In replanting, you may find that you can incorporate some of the original plants with some newcomers in the old container. Or it may be easy to replant all the plants in a new, larger trough. Alternatively, it may be possible to divide some of the plants to make two or more smaller specimens. You can pot these plants up separately, or you may even have enough for a whole new indoor jungle.

conditions should always be on the dry side, as excessive moisture that cannot drain away will inevitably result in root damage. And this will later be reflected in a general poor appearance of all the plants in the grouping.

From the visual point of view, try to choose plants that give a variety of size, form and texture – although, at the other extreme, groups of several plants of the same kind can look very effective. Some ideas for group plantings are illustrated, but when creating your own arrangements remember to allow a reasonable space between each plant to permit natural growth. As a result, the group will probably have a rather thin appearance at first, but this is inevitable if it is to take on a natural look in time.

Care and maintenance

If the container used for a group planting has no drainage holes, it is vital to make sure that you never overwater the potting mixture. In fact, it is best to err on the dry side, and a moisture meter can be extremely useful – particularly if it has a long probe so that it gives a reading low down in the container.

Generally speaking, plants grouped in containers grow very much better and more rapidly than plants in individual pots, so it becomes necessary from time to time to prune back the more vigorous plants, or even to replant the whole group. Pruning of the purely foliage plants such as *Ficus benjamina* and *Rhoicissus rhomboidea* can be tackled at almost any time. But the best time is

Pot-et-fleur arrangements

For the ever-increasing number of flower arrangers – who invariably love their plants as well – a pot-et-fleur arrangement provides the best of both worlds. It consists of a permanent arrangement of plants in a trough or similar container with one or more spaces where a small flower vase is sunk almost to the rim in the potting mixture or peat. It is best to put a pinholder or a block of flower arranger's foam plastic in the vase.

It is then up to the skill of the flower arranger to improve the appearance of the overall display by introducing just a few seasonal flowers in the flower-holder. In similar

fashion you can use flowering pot-plants, such as small *Chrysanthemums* and poinsettias, as temporary splashes of colour to improve the appearance of plant arrangements that are otherwise composed almost entirely of greenery.

Garden in a window

The chances are that even the most avid indoor gardener began his hobby in a very small way, growing one or two pot-plants on a window sill. Given the right kind of attention, window sills are an ideal place to grow a wide range of houseplants, providing that prime need of all plants – light. Sometimes, indeed, there is too much of this commodity for certain plants – some prefer very dim conditions – but it is always possible to shade excess light, whereas to boost that of a gloomy area is much more difficult.

There are, in fact, many ways of using windows for growing plants – from standing a solitary pot on a sill to building up a comprehensive collection in an elaborate built-on structure. Installing shelves across the window or a permanent trough on the sill greatly increases your scope – though at the expense of some of the room's daylight, of course. A bay window – particularly the rectangular rather than curved type – gives perhaps the greatest scope with the minimum of structural work.

Other glazed areas in the home also offer exciting possibilities for growing plants – from porches, well lit hallways and full-length French windows to stair-wells, corridors and other places lit from above by skylights. With carefully chosen groups of plants, these can be made into eye-catching features.

The plant window

The most elaborate way of using a window for growing plants is to turn it into the kind of window garden that is a focal feature of many homes on the continent of Europe, particularly in Holland, Germany and Scandinavia. It usually consists of a single, large plate-glass window with an extra-large concrete sill. This may be equipped with a drain, being shaped like a huge shallow sink. There may also be a water point nearby to make watering easy or allow automatic watering (see page 237).

The whole of the base of such a plant window can be strewn with shingle, which is kept wet to maintain humidity. The main snag is that a window garden is soon liable to become filled with vegetation, so it must be seen as primarily a place for plants and not for letting in

light! Depending on its aspect, it will accommodate any plant that can be grown on a window sill, plus very many greenhouse plants that will enjoy the humid conditions.

Another type of plant window – which dates back to the last century – consists of a glass case built out and on to an existing window. Brackets mounted below the outside window ledge support the case, which takes the form of a tiny lean-to greenhouse (or, if you prefer, a built-on terrarium). The original window glass and frame may be left in position, or it may be best to remove the window altogether. If the inner window is left, the plant window is like a miniature conservatory; it should be fitted with vents, and special care must be taken with shading if necessary.

You may need official building permission before building a plant window of this type; check before starting work. Choose the construction materials to blend with those of the house and make sure that it does not protrude too far. It must be strong enough to support numerous pot-plants when watered, as well as shelving of plate glass. Exposed plant windows of this type may get chilly;

left Windows crammed with potted plants can brighten the dingiest surroundings, while for the real enthusiast, a glazed plant window **above** provides a miniature conservatory.

electric tubular heaters, thermostatically controlled, are the best solution.

A bay or bow window can also be partitioned off to isolate it from the room, and fitted up as a window garden. The advantage of isolating a plant window like this is that you can maintain a high level of humidity. At the same time, you can keep the temperature above room level, so that really exotic and 'difficult' plants can be grown.

Places for tall plants

Hallways, porches, stair-wells and other places lit by full-length windows or skylights all give the advantage of height. Any plant that reaches grand proportions looks very effective wherever its height can be appreciated, and palms, *Grevilleas*, *Scheffleras* and many other large houseplants are ideal for such places. Under skylights, where the light comes from directly overhead, most plants grow happily, forming neat, symmetrical specimens. Hanging baskets

Plants on window sills
above The simplest window sill display is to have the plants lined up in ornamental pots. They are best planted in ordinary flower-pots, plunged in damp peat in decorative outer pots. These latter can range from genuine antiques to purpose-made pot-holders of pottery, plastic or metal. Cover the sills with a water- and scratch-resistant material if you value your decorations. Plate glass is excellent, but you can use laminated plastics.
above right A better but more elaborate arrangement is to obtain a fitted trough covering the entire sill. This can be ornamented, and should be filled with peat and the pots plunged. If you are likely to change the plants frequently, however, it is better to avoid any plunge material to prevent mess. Hide the pots with moss.

Larger-scale fittings
right A window can sometimes be fitted with tiered shelves to accommodate more plants. Again, plate glass is the best material, and can be supported on brackets. Small trailing plants like *Campanula isophylla* are ideal here.
below You may be able to plant still more plants just

below the window sill in plant stands in the form of ornamental troughs. These are often made in wrought iron. These lowermost plants can be made to obscure the pots of those on the window sill, so that ornamental pot-holders are not needed. Finally, you could hang small hanging baskets or pot-holders from the ceiling.

can also be effective under skylights, but use non-drip containers (see page 128).

Climbers such as *Hederas* (ivies) and some *Philodendrons* can be grown a considerable distance up stair-wells. You may also be able to grow climbers around a window, the plants being given large pots stood on the floor at the side. Morning glory (*Ipomoea*, or *Pharbitis*) is very successful grown this way.

In porches, some of the more hardy climbers, such as the beautiful *Lapageria rosea*, with its large white, pink or crimson flowers, can be grown. If you have a large porch, you can equip it with shelving to accommodate a large plant collection. If glassed-in, it can be used in much the same way as a small lean-to greenhouse – and for the same types of plant. One word of warning, however: Porches may be prone to chilly draughts, so beware of introducing particularly tender specimens.

Choosing the plants
You should always take the particular environment into account when choosing plants, and this is particularly true for windows, porches and the like. Before choosing consider how much sunshine or daylight the situation receives, and how high the temperature will rise in full sun. (Use a maximum-minimum thermometer; see page 236.) The ideal window site is one receiving some sunshine for part of each day. If there is too much sunlight, and the temperature soars too high, it is best to fit some form of shading; venetian blinds are excellent,

but external canopy blinds are the best.

For a window receiving a lot of sun, try such plants as cacti and succulents, *Beloperone guttata* (shrimp plant), *Cobaea scandens*, geraniums (*Pelargoniums*), *Nerines* and *Sansevierias*. Sunless or overshadowed windows that are also cool need such plants as *Acorus gramineus*, *Araucaria excelsa* (Norfolk Island pine), *Asparagus* ferns, *Aspidistras*, *Cissus antarctica* (kangaroo vine), *Fatshedra*, *Fatsia japonica* (false castor-oil plant), *Soleirolia*, formerly *Helxine*

(baby's tears), ivies (*Hederas*), *Philodendron scandens* (sweetheart vine), *Primulas* and *Saxifraga sarmentosa* (mother of thousands). If, on the other hand, the shady window is warm owing to room heat, most of the sub-tropical shade-lovers will thrive, including *Aglaonemas*, *Aphelandras*, *Begonias*, *Calatheas*, *Chlorophytum* (spider plant), *Codiaeums* (crotons), *Dieffenbachia* (dumb cane), *Dracaenas*, *Fittonias*, *Hoyas*, *Marantas* and *Peperomias*.

Apart from the light level, draughts may be a problem – particularly in porches, hallways and stairways. Avoid draughty places for most of the sub-tropicals, or try to stop chilly air currents with glass screens and so on. If they are unavoidable, choose hardy or almost hardy plants, such as hardy ferns and palms, *Cissus antarctica*, *Fatsia japonica*, ivies and *Stenocarpus sinuatus*. Another problem may be fumes from cooking, smoking or open fires. Plants with fine and delicate foliage are particularly at risk, so avoid these.

Apart from the plants mentioned here, there are many more that will thrive in your window garden, as you will see in the following two sections of this book. Always try to achieve variety and contrast – cool and subtle shades of green acting as a foil for the brilliantly-coloured specimens. Many kinds can be permanent residents, but bringing in temporary flowering specimens will give you interesting seasonal variations. Then your windows can become glazed gardens of beauty at all seasons.

The garden room

If you were to cross the old-fashioned conservatory with the modern patio, and make sure that the end result had all the creature-comforts for everyday living and relaxation, the result might well be the ideal garden room. A place intermediate between house and garden, it is a room in which plants can flourish and yet can be lived in without the feeling that the plants are crowding you out.

Warm without being too humid, the garden room generally doubles as a sun-lounge in cool climates. Designed with plenty of glass, it traps the meagre sun to give something approaching Mediterranean or Californian conditions for a good part of the year. For best results, of course, it should face the mid-day sun, and – given good siting and design – it may well become the most popular room in the house for all the family.

Aspect and arrangement
Sometimes a garden room is designed and constructed as part of the house when it is built. More frequently it tends to be added on as an afterthought, and many prefabricated do-it-yourself structures are sold by the makers of garden buildings, greenhouses and the like. These are usually quite easy to erect, but some have design faults, as explained below.

It is not essential to have a garden in which to build a garden room, provided of course that you have enough space on which to site it. You can even build it above ground level, on a flat roof or wide balcony, provided local building laws permit. (This is something that should always be checked before planning a garden room or extension of any kind.) Nevertheless, the favourite site is undoubtedly at ground level against a sunny wall where french or casement doors can lead directly from the house into the garden room. Remember, though, that even with a glass roof the garden room will inevitably obstruct some light from the adjoining room.

On the garden side, it is much nicer if doors lead from the garden room onto a patio or terrace, and from there to the garden proper. A paved area of some kind is very desirable since it allows you to sit in the open but to retreat easily and quickly into the garden room should the weather change. A garden room so designed will make it much easier to enjoy functions like barbecues, sunbathing and outdoor meals even in areas with an unsettled climate. Wide-opening garden room doors – possibly folding right back in concertina fashion – make for the most versatile arrangement, and also allow you to move furniture in and out onto the terrace easily.

Design and materials
Unfortunately, many garden rooms of the prefabricated type are badly designed. They may look good at the start, but quickly deteriorate. Be very cautious if much plastic is used in the construction. Plastic, being soft, is likely to be abraded by wind-blown grit and lose its clarity. Some plastics become brittle on prolonged exposure to sunshine. None have the solar heat-trapping effect of glass, nor do they retain warmth so well.

Glass is also more pleasing aesthetically and easier to clean without scratching.

For a garden room that is also to be used as a sun-lounge, you should of course have the panes of glass as large as possible. But remember that you will not get much of a sun-tan behind ordinary glass, as it absorbs most of the rays that pigment the skin. So sun-lovers should have the room designed with large doors opening to the outside so that they can sunbathe in direct sunlight but with side protection from winds. Plenty of glass may be splendid for letting the sun in, but if you prefer some privacy choose half-glazing or fit curtains – preferably made from damp-proof fabric such as synthetics or glass-fibre.

A transparent roof is, however, always advisable. It need not be clear, so long as it lets in good light. For safety reasons, a glass roof should be reinforced with wire. Then tiles, guttering, ice or snow falling from the upper roof are less likely to come crashing through. Make sure that the garden room roof slopes enough to shed fallen leaves and so on, which look unsightly and obscure the light. A flat roof may also accumulate a lot of snow, and is likely to drip condensation on the occupants of the room.

Condensation drip is a common fault with garden rooms. Be particularly wary of corrugated plastic roofing with an insufficient slope. In winter and in certain weather conditions, such a structure can be impossible to occupy because of water dripping from the roof corrugations. It is particularly tiresome if oil heaters are used, since every gallon of oil produces another gallon of water, in the form of vapour, when it burns. In such a case, the only solution is to keep down humidity as much as possible and increase ventilation.

Flooring is another important consideration. For comfort's sake, the floor should be warm and dry. Timber boarding or similar material, with a ventilation space below, is excellent. However, you may prefer tiles, and some extremely decorative – if expensive – ceramic floor tiles are available. At even greater expense, these can be combined with underfloor heating cables if you have a solid concrete base. More economically, concrete can be covered with one of the modern cushioned vinyl decorative coverings. These are remarkably hard-wearing, and resist spilled water and dropped flower-pots. Alternatively, for a more natural look, use cork tiles sealed with polyurethane varnish.

Heating and furnishings
Unless you live in a warm climate, even the most sunny garden room will probably need some artificial heating. If possible, extend the home central heating system. Whatever system you adopt, try not to increase the atmospheric humidity; a warm, damp atmosphere may be enjoyed by many plants, but it is not pleasant to live in. So it is best to avoid oil-burning heaters unless there is efficient ventilation and a good slope to the roof. Electric heating tubes, convectors and fan-heaters are good but expensive to run.

Furniture made from natural materials – such as wood, bamboo, wicker and the like – usually blends well into the garden room. Being light, it can also be moved outside easily. Decorative cast iron (or imitations in aluminium or plastic) may be preferred, but this tends to fit better into a conservatory (see page 26) than into a modern garden room. Beware of introducing ordinary home furniture; if the atmosphere is too damp, or there is much spillage of water when watering the plants, polished surfaces can be ruined. If you want some kind of floor covering, it is best to use plastic matting or polypropylene carpet. Rush mats usually blend well, but tend to go mildewed if conditions are damp.

Take care not to crowd out the room with plants, and make sure that there is plenty of space for people to move about and recline in comfort. You may like to construct permanent raised beds or the

like for plants to be plunged in peat (as described for plant groups on page 20). Generally, however, it is better to have the plants in movable troughs or pots – self-watering for preference (see page 236) – on stands, and on shelving around the room. It is then much easier to change the decor or move furniture about. You can usually have hanging and wall containers, provided that the roof will take the weight, but these should be of a type designed to prevent dripping and to be easy to water (see page 128).

Choosing the plants

Since for living comfort the room should be bright, sunny and usually airy, choose plants that will thrive in these surroundings. Those demanding a moist atmosphere are best avoided. Plants liking the most light can be set nearest the glass. Find places at the rear of the room and under tables or shelves for those preferring less light. If there is space, one or two tall specimen plants like palms grown from the floor to the roof will add charm and character.

In the following two sections of this book you will find details of many plants that can be grown easily in garden rooms. Consult, too, the plant selection chart on pages 242 and 243. Apart from many of these houseplants and dual-purpose plants, a number of kinds that are more commonly grown in the greenhouse should thrive, including *Acacias*, *Eucalyptus*, *Jacaranda mimosaefolia*, *Musa ensete* (dwarf banana) and *Ricinus communis* (true castor-oil plant), as well as dwarf conifers, potted roses and many garden annuals and half-hardy annuals.

Among specialist collections, cacti and succulents have ideal conditions in a garden room, although cacti should generally be moved to cooler quarters in winter (see page 63). The plants can be grown in pans set on shelves, or grouped together to form cactus gardens, with pieces of stone and rock added to form miniature landscapes. Some bonsai may also do well in the garden room, provided that they are watered properly and put in the open from time to time. Remember, though, that these are basically hardy plants that need airy conditions, so consult a specialist supplier before choosing (see page 182).

The knack of successfully furnishing a garden room with plants is to provide a decorative living backdrop for the family's leisure pursuits without letting the plants obtrude. It should extend your life and enjoyment without making you a horticultural slave. For, unlike a conservatory, a garden room is a place where people, not plants, come first.

The romantic conservatory

The conservatory is a place of romance, elegance and, perhaps, a little mystery. It is an all-year-round exotic garden, a place that differs fundamentally from the garden room in that, although it can be used to some extent as a living area, there is never any doubt that plants predominate over people. It differs, too, from the ordinary greenhouse in that it is a show place and ought never to be used for such mundane things as propagation or raising seedlings. Plants are displayed there – having preferably been grown to the flowering stage in a greenhouse – but they should be removed as soon as they begin to fade. Permanent residents ought to be beautiful the year round, and some of them can become almost part of the structure by growing up the roof supports and columns. There may be pools, fountains or other water effects, and the structure itself is nearly always impressive – even awe-inspiring.

The historic conservatory

A genuine conservatory is now an antique to be preserved wherever possible. It had two ancestors – the orangery and the first greenhouses. Orangeries were really large garden buildings with huge windows built to overwinter citrus trees – among the first tender evergreens introduced to northern European gardens – that were stood outside in tubs and pots during the summer. However, more sophisticated orangeries were used to grow other plants, such as *Camellias*, and sometimes were ornamented with statues and used as sitting-out places. The early greenhouses, on the other hand, were more mundane affairs. Heated by baskets of burning charcoal, they were used in Britain and elsewhere for such things as cucumber-growing.

In 1844, the great palm house at Kew Gardens in England was built, and from then on the conservatory gained steadily in popularity, to reach a peak late in the nineteenth century. Fuel and servants were cheap, so the structures could be elaborate and spacious, and a high temperature could be maintained. Nurserymen sent plant-collectors to the ends of the earth, and conservatory collections of tropical plants were proudly shown off to visitors. Guests might be received in the conservatory and afternoon tea served there.

The erection of the Crystal Palace in London for the 1851 exhibition, and of the enormous temperate house at Kew in 1862, did much to publicize the delights of the conservatory in Britain, and the features of these buildings were often copied on a small scale. Conservatories were generally very ornate and used small panes of glass, often including coloured glass to form patterns and sometimes pictures in the manner of stained-glass windows. There would be domes, gables, ornamental ironwork.

The modern conservatory

Conservatories in such grand manner are now, alas, almost a thing of the past. The heating and manpower involved in their upkeep is beyond all but the very wealthy, the public institution or the botanic garden, particularly as an ex-

tensive range of greenhouses is needed to keep such a place stocked with display plants all the year round.

On a considerably more modest scale, however, the conservatory can be reproduced. There are firms that will build custom-made structures of period design – though generally from wood rather than the traditional cast iron. In its simplest form, the conservatory need be nothing more, structurally, than a lean-to greenhouse used for display rather than raising plants, and entered through glazed doors from the home as for a garden room. You could even adapt a narrow (but well lit) passageway or a large porch or other structure to serve as a conservatory.

Remember when building or adapting a conservatory that an environment most suited to the plants is the first consideration. It is most economical to have a 'cool' collection, for which a minimum winter temperature of about 7°C (45°F) is ideal. The best way to provide heating is to extend the home central heating system. Otherwise, you will have to use a standard type of greenhouse heating, but avoid introducing ugly heater fans, pipes or radiators if possible. Whatever form of heating is used, it should if possible have independent thermostatic control. Automatic ventilation is also an advantage; for some more details of this and other conservatory equipment, together with hints on conservatory management, see page 237.

If you choose your plants correctly, it does not matter much if the conserva-

tory receives no sun at all. But a sunny conservatory may have to be shaded in summer to keep down the temperature. Slatted exterior blinds are best for this, but you can create much natural shade by the generous planting of interior climbers against the glass.

The atmosphere of a conservatory has to be kept far more humid than that of a garden room. If there is a fair area of staging strewn with moisture-retaining material, or built-up plunge beds of damp peat, this may be enough to maintain humidity by evaporation of the moisture. However, in summer a certain amount of damping-down – splashing of water on the floor – may be necessary. For this reason it is best if the floor is partially paved or tiled, with areas – such as under the staging – of soil covered with shingle. The point is that, after damping-down, any impermeable floor may become puddled – very undesirable when a conservatory has direct access to the house. If you prefer tiled or mosaic flooring for large areas, it is advisable to include drains so that water can run away.

Display and furnishings

Since the aim in a conservatory should be to create the illusion of plants in natural settings, the selection and display of plants needs special care. Always hide pots from view if possible. It is useful to have tiered staging – a step-like arrangement of shelves instead of the normal benches. Then the flowers and foliage of the plants on one step can be made to obscure the pots on the step

Modern conservatories
The modern conservatory can attempt to reproduce the grandeur of its Victorian ancestor, or be no more than an adapted greenhouse. The wood-framed conservatory **left** comes into the former group, the aluminium-framed lean-to **below** into the latter. The small but elegant type **above** is designed in the manner of a summerhouse, while even a narrow porch **right** can serve the purpose of a conservatory.
bottom However big or small, using tiered staging and climbers will help to create an effective display.

above. In this way you can create magnificent banks of flowers. Sphagnum moss or pieces of bark are also useful for obscuring flower-pots, or these may be plunged in small raised beds of peat.

Such displays should always be eye-catching, but they need constant attention since many of the plants are at their best for relatively short periods. Just as important are the 'framework' plants – the large specimens and climbers that give the conservatory its overall character. What can be done much depends on the size of the conservatory. If it is large enough to have columns or posts these make excellent supports for climbers, which often seem to become part of the structure when mature. They should be trained as naturally as possible, and any ties wires, and so forth, well obscured.

Larger plants such as shrubs and small trees can be grown in large pots. Sometimes large jardiniere-type pots in Victorian design can be obtained and used to blend with the conservatory structure. Italianate or other decorative pots may also be suitable; otherwise it is better to obscure the pots with moss or cork as already described. Permanent beds were often made in the original conservatories, and the plants grown in soil. In the modern version this is best avoided, and pots plunged in peat beds. Should anything go wrong it is much easier to replace plants, and large volumes of soil will not have to be moved or sterilized if there is trouble from pests and diseases.

Furniture of wood or wicker can be used, as in a garden room, but beware of

rot and mildew in the damp atmosphere. Probably the best type of conservatory furniture is the ornate cast iron type or its imitations in aluminium or plastic. As well as tables, chairs and benches, beautiful plant stands and troughs are available in these materials. In a large conservatory, stone seats and similar furniture can be used as permanent fixtures, and even garden arches erected. Statues and garden ornaments were common in Victorian conservatories.

In some cases aviaries and aquaria can be found a place in conservatories. Much depends on the conditions of temperature and humidity maintained, and if in doubt you should consult a veterinary expert. Remember that many pesticides used on plants are extremely poisonous to animals and fish. The conservatory may also be used to display wardian cases (see page 30) and possibly terrariums where plants requiring warmer conditions can be grown. With care, artificial light can be used both for the plants and for general night-time illumination (see page 234).

Choosing the plants
All plants commonly grown in greenhouses will feel at home in a conservatory, with the possible exception of those demanding very sunny and bright conditions. Evergreen foliage plants are best for permanent planting, and many suitable subjects will be found in the next part of this book. Colourful foliage plants, such as *Coleus*, *Cineraria maritima*, *Amaranthus*, and *Begonia rex*, can be brought in as temporary residents to enhance floral displays. Ferns, tree ferns, cycads and palms were frequently found in the old conservatories. Bromeliads and other epiphytic plants can be displayed on a tree branch covered with moss (see page 73).

Always try to include some scented plants, such as *Jasminum polyanthum* – a vigorous climbing jasmine – and, if there is room, *Luculia gratissima*, which grows to the size of a small tree and becomes covered with phlox-like, intensely fragrant flowers. Plants with scented foliage (see page 91) can also be included. Climbers are usually indispensable for giving a professional touch and making the structure 'marry' with the plants. Such plants as *Abutilon megapotamicum* (a climbing form of flowering maple), *Lapageria rosea* (Chilean bellflower), *Passifloras* (passion flowers), variegated ivies, *Philodendrons* and others are easy climbers. Sometimes roses and *Fuchsias* can also be trained up into the roof.

Hanging baskets should be used freely if possible; they are particularly suitable for a conservatory with a high roof. *Fuchsias* of the pendulous type grow particularly well in conservatories when displayed in baskets, creating glorious patches of colour. For temporary colourful display, plants like *Calceolarias*, *Cinerarias*, *Salpiglossis*, *Schizanthus*, *Streptocarpus*, *Azaleas*, gloxinias, spring and summer bulbs and many more can be used. Brought into their display positions just as the buds are showing colour, they will ensure that the conservatory is cheerful all year round.

Plants at work

Houseplants today are less and less restricted to houses. There has been a tremendous upsurge in the use of living plants and flowers in beautifying offices, hotels and almost all public buildings. Whether the result of a lone secretary making a single-handed attempt to brighten up her surroundings with a pot-plant, or of a deliberate policy decision by a company to enhance the entrance-hall of its prestige office building with an elaborate plant arrangement, the green invasion has reached the commercial world in force. Surprisingly enough, it is even extending to the industrial world, and as factory conditions improve, more and more of them are being decorated with vegetation.

The reasons are many, but the restfulness of natural greenery and the ability of plants to break up and counteract the harsh lines of modern office buildings and their furnishings must be high on the list. As more company managers realize how much better their employees work in pleasant – even landscaped – surroundings, so office plants are changing from being a 'prestige' luxury to a psychological necessity. What is more, they can have important utilitarian functions, acting as screens and pleasant dividers for open-plan office areas.

Conditions and care
Ideally, office plants need much the same conditions as any plants indoors: reasonable light, fresh air (but not draughts), steady warmth in the region of 18°C (64°F) and careful attention in respect of watering. Unfortunately, the conditions in many work-places are often far from ideal. Lack of light is not often a problem in modern buildings – though baking-hot sun streaming through large windows may be. Even more harmful is excessive heat from central heating, combined with dry air and tobacco smoke. Finally, the plants may have to contend with the dregs from coffee cups – or even alcohol at the office party.

Very little can be done about the last two problems, while the only effective answer to other adverse conditions is to choose tough plants in the first place. Gay and exciting though *Codiaeums* (crotons), *Dracaenas* and *Calatheas* may be, it is much more sensible and practical to choose more durable plants at the beginning. Watch how they respond to the conditions and treatment for a few months before trying more exotic kinds.

Watering is much less of a problem these days, thanks to self-watering containers that have a water reservoir in the base. Nylon wicks carry moisture up into the potting mixture as needed, and the only attention necessary is to top up the reservoir every two to three weeks. Containers of this kind are available in many shapes, sizes, colours and styles that will suit almost any office interior.

Even with such aids, however, a maintenance arrangement with a commercial office plant contractor is the best way to keep any large group of plants in good trim. It is certainly better than relying on the uncertain knowledge and erratic attention of one of the staff or the office cleaner. Two kinds of contract are

generally available. The contractor either supplies the plants on hire and keeps them in good condition, replacing them as necessary. Or he simply maintains – usually by weekly visits – plants owned by the company.

Choosing the plants
The first rule when acquiring office plants is to choose mature plants growing in at least five-inch pots. These will settle down in the new environment much better than young plants in very small pots – which have a high mortality rate in office conditions. Secondly, avoid plants that prefer cool conditions – such as *Cissus antarctica* (kangaroo vine) and ivies. Geraniums (*Pelargoniums*), on the other hand, thrive in warmth and can withstand considerable drought; they do need plenty of light, however.

For grander displays, varied groupings of houseplants are often created, but in lofty, spacious areas it is equally effective to use large individual specimens or groups of several plants of a single kind. Large *Schefflera actinophylla, Monstera deliciosa, Philodendron hastatum* and – where a large plant of more spreading habit is wanted – *Philodendron bipinnatifidum* are among the very best. When available, *Pandanus veitchii* and *Pandanus sanderi* (screw-pines) are also superb when placed in splendid isolation; but they have viciously saw-edged leaves, so position them out of the way of passers-by.

For single-species groups, *Sansevieria trifasciata laurentii* can be extremely effective if a number of mature plants with leaves three to four feet tall are grouped together. Many of the taller-growing *Dracaenas* are also useful in the same way, and the spiky leaves of *Dracaena marginata* can be very handsome in well lit areas. If possible, choose plants of varying heights; multi-headed specimens can be particularly effective.

When designing mixed plantings, remember that a hotch-potch of different plants seldom looks as good as the same container planted with fewer, more mature plants. Three or four well established plants will usually be enough to create a striking effect. For a simple arrangement in a container two feet in diameter, for example, you need little more than a four-foot *Ficus benjamina,*

a two-foot *Sansevieria trifasciata laurentii* and a spreading *Fatsia japonica* some 12 inches tall. The last is one of the most useful and durable of all indoor plants. For filling in around the base of other plants, *Chlorophytum capense variegatum* (*C. comosum*; spider plant) is a useful alternative to the *Fatsia*, but it is best to use two or three specimens to achieve the same effect.

There are any number of variations that you can employ when arranging plants in containers, of course, and some more ideas will be found on page 20. The most important requirement is to ensure that the composition has a well balanced look, and that plant sizes and heights are in proportion to the dimensions of the tub or trough.

Special features

One good way of counteracting the dryness and stuffiness of office air is to grow small plants in a terrarium (see page 30). If closed, this will need very little attention. Elaborate built-in kinds with artificial lighting can be made into effective features for foyers and entrance halls.

Plants form an important feature of modern office interior design. A glazed entrance **above** is one of the best places for houseplants that like light and air, but by providing artificial light — if necessary, day and night — some kinds can flourish in open-plan offices **right,** making for a greatly improved working environment.
far right One aid to solving the maintenance problem is to use self-watering containers. **below** To create a really big impression, a large-scale indoor garden can be built in a foyer. This one is lit by skylights.

Bottle gardens are equally easy to maintain, but smaller (see page 32).

Few things are as soothing and tranquil as the sound of running water, and, where space permits, an indoor garden that has water as its main attraction will make a really dramatic yet restful effect in an office entrance or hotel foyer. Plants reflected in the water will add an extra dimension to the display. But first make sure that there will be no problems with condensation. In fact, of course, dry air is a more common problem, and the presence of water will help to counteract this. See page 177.

Finally, however grand or modest the office planting scheme, the important thing to realize is that plant life should not be used simply to conceal unsightly objects or to brighten up darker areas. To be seen at their best, plants ought to have prominent positions in reasonably good light where they can be admired and set off to best advantage. If the prospect is of the plants being put in an ill-lit, poorly ventilated and inadequately heated corner, it is quite frankly better not to bother, as the chances of them surviving are poor.

29

Terrariums and plant cases

In 1834 there appeared in the *Gardener's Magazine* an article that marked the start of one of the most extraordinary of horticultural fashions. It described how a London doctor, Dr Nathaniel Ward, grew rare and delicate plants – ferns particularly – in small glass cases rather like miniature indoor greenhouses. As described in more detail on page 59, fern cases – or wardian cases, as they were generally known – were soon to be found in many elegant drawing rooms, and ferns became among the most popular of all house and garden plants.

The fashion declined in the last quarter of the 19th century, and today very few genuine wardian cases can be found, even in antique shops. But a modern version has appeared and is finding favour with a new generation of indoor gardeners. Known variously as the terrarium, plantarium or plant case, it can vary from a modest jam-jar housing a single plant, through converted fish-tanks to an elaborate, purpose-built miniature greenhouse tacked on to the window of a house (see page 22). A simple kind ideal for growing small ferns is shown on page 58, while the ever-popular bottle garden (see page 32) is really only another variation on the terrarium theme.

Nor is the modern terrarium gardener restricted to growing ferns, though many of these do thrive enclosed in glass. Given enough warmth, tropical and sub-tropical foliage plants of all kinds – many of them extremely difficult as houseplants – can be used, as can many kinds of flowering plants, so long as you can easily reach inside to remove dead flowers. African violets (*Saintpaulias*) and their relatives are easy and cheap terrarium subjects, while many of the smaller orchids will also thrive. At the other extreme, an interesting project for a young gardener is to create a woodland terrarium using wild woodland plants such as mosses (see page 203).

How terrariums work

There is no real mystery behind the modern popularity of growing plants in glass cases: they are an ideal means of countering the hot, dry atmosphere of

centrally heated homes, which is so harmful to so many plants. Inside the glass confines of the terrarium is built up a humid microclimate that, combined with adequate heat, suits very well the more tender houseplants whose natural home is the steamy jungle.

In fact, the community within a terrarium is almost completely self-supporting, its physical ingredients being cycled and recycled by the plant life. Water in the potting mixture at the bottom is taken up by the plants and given off as vapour from their leaves. Together with water evaporated directly from the soil, this condenses in droplets on the glass walls and roof, to run back down to the soil. The atmosphere inside also remains in balance, the plants absorbing oxygen at night and giving off carbon dioxide, reversing this process in daylight.

Even within a completely sealed glass case, then, a group of plants can thrive with almost no attention. On the other hand, if the case has an opening to the air, you will have to water the plants occasionally – though usually far less often than normal potted plants. Some people use open-topped tanks like fish-tanks without any cover, and while this does increase the humidity around the plants to some extent, the result is not so much a terrarium as a certain kind of plant holder. The same applies to giant brandy snifters, which make decorative containers for African violets.

Of course, there are some plants – desert cacti and succulents, in particular – that abhor dampness for any length of time, as it very quickly makes them rot. Some people grow these in open-topped glass cases, but since they are essentially

Planting and maintenance

Always make sure the container is thoroughly clean before planting, and select your plants to suit its shape and size, ensuring that they all like similar conditions. With a very large terrarium, you may prefer to stand potted plants on a tray of damp sand, but direct planting is generally necessary. In this case, a drainage layer of gravel mixed with charcoal lumps (or charcoal lumps alone) is essential; it should be an inch deep in small terrariums, two inches in large. Then add twice that depth of moist potting mixture – preferably John Innes 1, or some other kind not too rich in fertilizer,

mixed with some extra peat. When planting, allow room for the plants to grow; otherwise the terrarium will become so crowded that you cannot see the individual specimens. After planting, the potting mixture should always remain slightly moist, and with closed terrariums there should be slight condensation on the inside. If condensation is excessive, leave the lid off for a few days to let it dry out; if there is no condensation, water very carefully with a fine spray. Two final rules: Always remove dead foliage and flowers. And watch out for any pests or diseases, and treat immediately.

Plants for larger terrariums

Botanical name	Common name	Remarks
Aglaonema spp		Choose small varieties
Aphelandra squarrosa	Zebra plant	Yellow bracts; vigorous
Begonia masoniana; B. rex	Iron-cross begonia	Beware mildew with B. rex
Calathea spp		Beautiful but tender
Carex morrowi		Grassy
Chlorophytum comosum	Spider plant	Plantlets on runners
Cordyline 'Rededge'		Small Dracaena
Dionaea muscipula	Venus fly-trap	Insectivorous bog plant
Dracaena marginata tricolor		Slow-growing
Drosera spp	Sundews	Insectivorous bog plants
Epiphyllum hybrids	Orchid cacti	Large flowers
Episcia cupreata		Flowering trailer
Ficus diversifolia	Mistletoe fig	Bushy; berries
Philodendron melanochryson		When small
Pleomele reflexa	Song of India	Slow-growing Dracaena
Rhoeo discolor		Purple undersides to leaves
Saintpaulia ionantha	African violet	Good under artificial light
Scirpus cernuus	Dwarf bullrush	
Sinningia speciosa	Gloxinia	Flowering; has dormant period
Smithiana hybrids	Temple bells	Flowering; have dormant period
Sonerila margaritacea		Very difficult
Stromanthe amabilis		Attractive leaves
Syngonium podophyllum	Goosefoot plant	Climber
Tillandsia spp		Bromeliad
Zygocactus truncatus	Christmas cactus	Winter-flowering

See also pages 33, 59 and 96 to 99.

Kinds of terrariums

The most elaborate type of terrarium **far left** can be a permanent fixture in a room. With built-in artificial lighting and heating, and a sliding glass door, it can house a wide range of foliage and flowering houseplants. Much less elaborate models may consist of converted fish-tanks **far left below** or various glass containers **below left,** including cheese-dish covers and laboratory jars. A bell jar **right** can hold a single plant, while various purpose-built terrariums are available. The one **below** is plastic, but has adjustable air vents.

fresh-air plants it is much better to use open pans, troughs or pots. Don't use a terrarium just for the sake of it; use it to grow plants that will really benefit from its environment.

Terrarium containers

From a jam-jar to a giant brandy snifter, from a fish-tank to a genuine antique wardian case, there is virtually no limit to the kind of container that you can make into a terrarium. There are only two important limitations: the glass should be clear, so that the plants can get all the light they need – and can be seen. And, to preserve your furnishings, it should not leak at the bottom; if necessary use special aquarium-sealing paint on the inside.

A further point, as explained above, is that the terrarium should preferably have a closed or almost closed lid. If possible, this should slope, so that condensed water runs down rather than dripping in large drops on the foliage. If a horizontal lid is essential, wiping it regularly will prevent too much damage – though you will have to water the plants more frequently in order to make up for the water wiped off. If you are fitting a lid to a tank, or are making your own complete terrarium, remember that

water runs much more freely down glass than plastic, so use the latter only if it is absolutely essential.

As explained on page 58, a glass dome or case placed over (but just inside the rim of) a trough or bowl in which the plants are grown is an alternative type of terrarium. Such a case may be purpose-made, or you could use a large glass cheese-dish cover. A laboratory equipment supplier may have alternatives, including the large all-glass tanks used to preserve specimens in school biology laboratories. These are often much more attractive than metal-framed fish-tanks. An alternative might be to cut the top off a large wine or other jar. At the opposite extreme, an antique curio cabinet can be used to house plants, with due care to prevent leakage or water damage to the cabinet frame itself.

Apart from such adaptations, specially made terrarium containers are sometimes available – particularly in the United States, but increasingly in other countries. Hesitate before buying one of these, though. Is it big enough, or the right shape for where you want to put it? Is it made of glass or plastic? Would it not be more fun to adapt some other container or even to build (or have built) a terrarium from scratch? The most

elaborate purpose-built structure can have all kinds of refinements, like a pitched roof, a door in the side, air heating cables (see page 227) and artificial lighting (see page 234). This really is going to extremes, certainly, but the result will be a genuine miniature conservatory or tropical greenhouse in your living room, and the ability to grow a fine range of really exotic small plants.

Choosing the plants

There are several general rules to bear in mind when stocking a terrarium. First, pick plants that all enjoy broadly the same conditions, and in particular moisture-loving types. Second, keep in mind the size of the terrarium; you do not want to have to prune back a quick-growing specimen too often, although some small plants can of course be included in even a large terrarium.

The table on page 33 lists a number of plants suitable for bottle gardens, and these of course can also be grown in other kinds of terrariums. Most kinds of ferns (see pages 56 to 59) are also suitable, together with many of the smaller-growing orchids (see pages 96 to 99). In addition to all these, the table on this page gives some suggestions for larger terrarium plants.

Gardens in bottles

The bottle garden is an elegant variation of the terrarium and wardian case (see page 30). Given an interesting bottle – and there is no need to restrict yourself to the ever-popular carboy – it makes an attractive feature in almost any room. It has the same fascination as a ship in a bottle. 'How did the plants get there?' is the perennial question fired at the owner. Bottle gardens can be bought ready-planted, but it is much more fun and not too difficult to do it yourself.

Just like a terrarium, a well designed bottle garden is completely self-supporting. Moisture given off by the plants' leaves condenses on the inside of the glass, runs down to the soil at the bottom and is absorbed again by their roots. At night, the plants give off carbon dioxide and absorb oxygen, reversing the process in daylight. This means that the bottle garden forms a balanced community, and can be completely closed with a stopper. Once established, such a bottle garden needs little more than warmth, light and a periodic inspection to see that all is well. Even an unstoppered bottle garden will need watering only rarely, making it ideal for an office.

Inside the bottle, the humid conditions are ideal for many houseplants – so much so, in fact, that you must be careful to choose slow-growing types, or the container will soon become choked with vegetation. Even slow-growing plants do grow, of course, so start with small specimens and do not crowd them too much. This is even more important than with an openable terrarium.

Bottle-gardening tools

If your bottle garden has too narrow a neck to get your hand inside, you will need a set of tools **right** with long handles for planting and maintenance. It is easy to make suitable tools, using canes or stiff wire for the handles.

Use an ordinary table fork and spoon to make a bottle-garden fork and spade. These can be used together to lower plants into the bottle, or you can use a length of wire with its end twisted into a loop. The latter tool can also be used to remove plants you want to change. A cork or cotton reel on a cane is useful for packing down the soil around a plant's roots. Use a razor blade stuck into the end of a cane for pruning and cutting off dead leaves, and remove these pieces from the bottle with a sharp spike. Even better, you may be able to make a tool rather like an elongated clothes-peg. The final tool that is useful for keeping your bottle garden attractive is a piece of sponge fixed to a length of stiff wire; this can be bent as necessary and used to clean down the inside of the glass.

Filling

After thoroughly washing out your bottle, use a wide funnel and cardboard tube to pour in a two-inch layer of charcoal lumps. This provides drainage and keeps the garden 'sweet', preventing growth of algae. Then pour in two to three inches of dry potting mixture. 'One-sided' bottles need more mixture at the back.

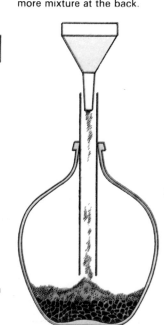

Planting

A weak potting mixture, such as the kind normally used for seeds, is best; use a peat-based type plus sand. Plant near the edge first. Scoop out a depression. With spoon and fork or a special wire tool, lower a plant into position. Cover the roots and firm down the soil around them.

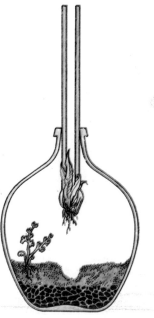

Maintenance

After planting, water enough to make the soil moist, not wet, using a spray if possible. A closed bottle never needs rewatering, an open one only rarely. The correct amount of water gives only moderate condensation inside the glass. Remove dead leaves and weeds promptly, and watch for pests and diseases.

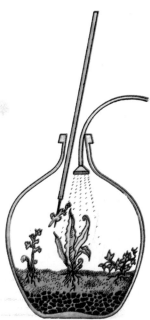

Bottle garden containers

When choosing a bottle suitable for planting, the only limit is in your own imagination. From flagon cider bottles to huge industrial chemical jars, the most utilitarian glass containers can be used, so long as they are reasonably transparent – green glass is unsuitable – and so long as they can be cleaned of their former contents. Goldfish bowls of various shapes are ideal for single specimens, while a hunt round a junk shop will often turn up other suitable containers. You may be lucky enough to find an antique wasp-catcher, which looks like a bulbous bottle on short legs with a small hole in the bottom. Even a decanter can be planted with a miniature plant, while garden centres often sell containers specially for bottle gardens.

Planting schemes
left Inside view of a bottle garden, in this case a huge industrial acid bottle. At the far end, the bromeliad is a hybrid, *Cryptobergia rubra*. In front of it is a *Maranta leuconeura kerchoveana* (with dark markings) and an *Episcia cupreata* (with red undersides to the leaves). On the right is a mat of tiny-leaved *Selaginella apus*, and in front of this a *Maranta leuconeura erythrophylla* and a *Peperomia caperata* (with crinkled leaves). The ivy is *Hedera* 'Adam'.

Replanting
A well balanced bottle garden with slow-growing plants should need little attention for years. Control the more vigorous plants by pruning. Removing plants intact is more difficult than planting, but it can be done with a bent-wire tool. Loosen the roots, then hook the plant out roots first.

above There are many varied containers that you can use to make a bottle garden, so long as you choose carefully the plants to put in them. The cider flagon on the left contains a small-leaved ivy, *H.* 'Lutzii' and a *Saxifraga sarmentosa tricolor*. The latter grows more slowly than the normal *S. sarmentosa* (mother of thousands), but still needs regular pruning. In the jar on the right are (from left to right) a *Selaginella apus*, a *Sansevieria hahnii variegata*, and a *Fittonia verschaffeltii*. The *Fittonia* and the larger, all-green variety of the *Sansevieria* also form part of the scheme in the large carboy. This also contains the large-leaved *Maranta leuconeura erythrophylla*, a small *Cryptanthus acaulis*, the small-leaved croton, *Codiaeum variegatum pictum*, and a *Pilea mollis*.
right An African violet (*Saintpaulia*) thrives in a humid atmosphere, and is ideal for growing in a glass container. But you must be able to remove the flowers, so use a goldfish bowl or something similar.

Planning
right top For a bottle garden to be seen from all sides, plant taller specimens in the centre and low-growing plants around them. The soil should be more or less level.
right bottom If it will be seen from only one side, bank up the soil at the back of the bottle and position the larger plants there.

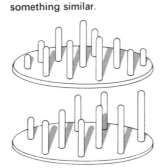

Bottle garden plants
All the smaller ferns and most selaginellas (see pages 56 to 59) are ideal for bottle gardens, plus the following:

Botanical name	Common name	Remarks
Acorus gramineus		Grass-like
Begonia boweri; B. rex (small-leaved sorts)		Beware mildew with *B. rex*
Cocos (Syagrus) weddeliana	Dwarf coconut palm	Use small plant
Codiaeum variegatum (smallest sorts)	Croton	For large bottles
Cryptanthus spp	Earth-stars	Small bromeliad
Dracaena godseffiana; D. sanderiana		For large bottles
Ficus pumila; F. radicans variegata	Creeping fig; Trailing fig	Prune regularly
Fittonia argyroneura; F. verschaffeltii		Attractive leaves
Hedera helix (small-leaved variegated sorts)	English ivy	Prune regularly
Maranta leuconeura vars	Prayer plant	For large bottles
Neanthe bella (Chamaedorea elegans)	Dwarf palm	Use small specimen
Sansevieria hahnii		Small *Sansevieria*
Pellionia pulchra		Prune regularly
Pilea cadieri nana; P. mollis	Aluminium plant; 'Moon Valley'	Prune regularly

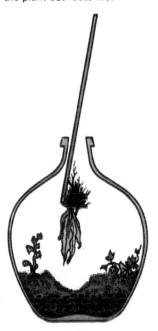

Herbs in jars
A fun idea for a sunny kitchen window sill is to grow your own herbs in individual bottles. Wide-necked jars are needed, so that you can get scissors in to harvest the crop. Sweet jars or large storage jars with ground-glass lids are ideal. You can buy small plants, putting one in each jar as for a decorative bottle garden. Or you can grow the herbs from seed, sowing only a few seeds in each jar. Parsley, thyme, chives, savory – all these and more can be grown in this way. More vigorous types such as sage can be grown from cuttings until they out-grow the container. Then they must be removed and new cuttings taken.

2 Plants to grow in your home

There are hundreds of kinds of plants that
you can grow indoors, ranging from
Victorian favourites that are coming back
into fashion to new discoveries only now
becoming available from nurserymen.
With the information presented in the pages
that follow you can choose the types that
will suit your home conditions and your
design scheme. You will find tall, majestic
trees and modest types ideal for a window
sill, kinds that are grown simply for their
foliage and others with attractive flowers.
For the enthusiast there are cacti and
orchids – and many, many more.

Handsome indoor trees

Even the plainest room is brought to life by living greenery, and the quickest cure for a large, stark, inhuman interior is to introduce one or two specimen indoor trees. Chosen carefully, they can have as much impact as a fine piece of furniture or a painting, and even in the more modest indoor home garden a tall specimen plant gives emphasis and scale.

Mature palms are very popular today for this purpose (see page 42), but there are a number of other houseplants visually powerful enough to stand on their own in a large empty space. In their natural environment these form substantial trees, and the best of them have the same visual effect – scaled down – when grown indoors. They will, in fact, attain a considerable size after a number of years of indoor growth, but with their roots confined to pots they grow far less vigorously than in the wild. If they do begin to outgrow their setting, most of those described here except the Norfolk Island pine (*Araucaria excelsa*) will come to no harm if excessive growth is pruned back. So there is no need to worry that they will drive you from house and home!

A more serious problem is cost and availability. There is always a demand for really large specimen plants of this kind for the interior landscaping of hotels and offices, so you usually need to order them from the grower well in advance of delivery. And since they take a lot of growing space in the greenhouse, they cannot be cheap. Younger plants are easier to find and cheaper to buy – but of course you will have to wait for them to become mature specimens.

Araucaria
One of the most handsome of all indoor trees is the Norfolk Island pine, *Araucaria excelsa*. As the common name suggests, it comes from an island not far

Araucaria excelsa

from New Zealand. It has branches arranged in tiers that radiate from a central stem so that they make an extremely elegant shape. The branches and stem are all covered with pale green leaves rather like pine needles. The plant is at its most attractive when between three and six feet in height; after

that it becomes much coarser in appearance. Unfortunately, pruning can only ruin the plant.

It needs good light and cool conditions – about 13°C (55°F). If it does not have even, all-round light, turn it regularly so that growth is symmetrical. Err on the side of dryness when watering, particularly in winter. Young plants are not difficult to raise from seed.

Cussonia; Schefflera
Three rather similar plants, all of which reach a substantial size quite quickly, are *Cussonia spicata*, *Heptapleurum arboricola* (sometimes sold as *Schefflera venulosa erystrastachys*) and *Schefflera actinophylla* (commonly known as the umbrella tree but also called *Brassaia actinophylla*). They all have palmate leaves that radiate like fingers of a hand from the end of the leaf stalk. The *Cussonia* grows very rapidly and may

Schefflera actinophylla

Heptapleurum arboricola

be the ideal plant for filling a gap quickly. Be careful when moving it, though; the stems snap very easily.

The umbrella tree is possibly the most attractive of all the larger indoor foliage plants, combining elegance and impact. It is not difficult to manage. When indoor trees reach seven-inch and larger pot sizes they will benefit from being potted into Potting Mixture no. 3. As small plants, however, they prefer a more peaty mixture.

The *Heptapleurum* is a comparative newcomer as a commercial houseplant, but it is an attractive and surprisingly durable plant. With leaves that are similar in shape to those of the *Schefflera* but much smaller, it has the advantage of growing well either large or small. Allowed its head, it forms a stately tall specimen, but if the growing tip is removed it becomes a very attractive but more shrubby plant.

Ficus elastica
The rubber plant, *Ficus elastica*, needs little introduction as it is undoubtedly the best-known tree-like houseplant. The best current variety is the large-leaved *F. elastica* 'Robusta', which is a great improvement over *F. elastica* 'Decora', itself an improved variety introduced after World War II.

All rubber plants of this type need a temperature in the region of 13°C (55°F) to thrive, and good light while remaining protected from direct sunlight. Excessive watering is the main reason for failure, so allow the root system to dry out a little between waterings.

Most rubber plants are allowed to grow as stately single stems, but it is not difficult to make large plants bush out into a more tree-like shape. When they are about six or seven feet high, cut off the growing point with a sharp knife to encourage the development of side-shoots. While the roots are confined to a pot it will take anything from 10 to 15 years to produce a reasonable rubber plant tree. But given better conditions, with more room for root growth, development would be more rapid.

It is wishful thinking to expect similar tree-like results from any of the variegated rubber plants that are sometimes available. They are both more tender and slower-growing than the all-green varieties, and need warmth, good light and careful watering. The hardiest and easiest variety to manage is 'Europa', whose leaves are mottled with cream and two shades of green. It also suffers less from browning of the leaf edges, which afflicts all the varieties in time and for which there seems to be no cure. Older varieties include 'Doescheri', whose leaves have light and dark green patches, ivory edges and (when young) a pink tinge; 'Schryveriana', with cream-edged leaves with cream and dark green mottlings; and the all-too-rare 'Tricolor', which has leaves mottled with yellow, pale green and dark green.

right From left to right are *Ficus benghalensis*; *Ficus elastica* 'Robusta'; *Ficus elastica* 'Schryveriana'; *Ficus benjamina* (in front of the table); and *Ficus lyrata*.

Other large-leaved Ficus

Of the other large-leaved members of the fig family, the easiest to obtain are *F. benghalensis* (the Bengal fig or banyan) and *F. lyrata* (the fiddle-leaf fig). The latter is much more popular, having large leaves shaped like the body of a violin. But it is also the more difficult to care for in average indoor conditions. A temperature of not less than 19°C (66°F) is needed, and the growing position should be shaded from direct sunlight. To obtain maximum growth it is best to plant *F. lyrata* in a large indoor garden filled with a good depth of Potting Mixture no. 3.

The same may be said for *F. benghalensis*, which is a very strong-growing plant that will attain tree dimensions in as little as four years, given good conditions. A drawback with this plant is that the leaves (rather like a rubber plant's in shape) are covered in a natural downy material that gives them a permanently dusty appearance. Spraying the leaves with white oil used at a rate of three to four fluid ounces to one gallon of water will greatly improve their appearance.

Smaller-leaved Ficus

The Moreton Bay fig (*F. macrophylla*) and the peepul tree (*F. religiosa*) are not much used by the commercial nurseryman, and are difficult to obtain. These plants are, in fact, at their best when grown as more compact shrubs rather than as large trees. This will entail removing their growing points when they have attained a reasonable height. Loss of some of the leaves during the more difficult winter months is almost inevitable, and will be more marked if the root system remains excessively wet.

Undoubtedly the most popular of all the smaller-leaved ficus trees, *F. benjamina* (the weeping fig) is also the most easily obtained. It is not impossible to grow this plant to a height of twelve to fifteen feet, although it may take as many years. By this time the trunk will have taken on a silver birch appearance that is most attractive. Oddly enough, as the plant matures and attains a reasonable height, it seems much easier to care for, and will tolerate quite harsh cutting back with no apparent ill effects. By tying a supple young stem down with stout twine, the main stem may be encouraged to grow horizontally; the resulting plant looks particularly effective growing over an indoor pool.

Other kinds

A number of *Dracaenas* and similar plants can reach tree proportions in time (see page 44). Much the same applies to some of the larger shrubs described on page 38, including *Grevillea robusta* and *Dizygotheca elegantissima*.

Bushy foliage plants

Where the need is simply to fill a large space with greenery, there are a good collection of indoor shrubby plants available, generally at quite reasonable cost. They in fact fulfil much the same purpose as hardy shrubs for the garden. They are durable, and have leaves of interesting shapes, colours and textures. They form useful bulky shapes as whole plants, and can generally be kept pruned or clipped to a reasonable size or be allowed to grow to large dimensions.

They are, in fact, good general-purpose houseplants that are much used by commercial horticulturalists for displays and decorations of various kinds. Such plants as *Fatsia japonica*, *Grevillea robusta* and the *Pittosporums* are particularly useful as 'working plants'. They will look good and withstand wide ranges of temperature – from the draughty entrance of a hotel to the hot and stuffy atmosphere of an overheated room or a cold and miserable marquee. If the grower who depends on his plants for a living can rely on them, so clearly can the amateur at home.

Dizygotheca; Grevillea

Two graceful shrubs that can be grown from seed with little difficulty in warm conditions are *Dizygotheca elegantissima* (also known as *Aralia elegantissima* and commonly called the false aralia) and *Grevillea robusta* (the silk oak of Australia). Both have delicate, feathery leaves that are rather like those of some ferns (although the false aralia's are dark reddish-brown).

Both will develop into plants of considerable size if their growing tips are not removed at an early stage in order to check upward growth. The false aralia will, in fact, take on tree proportions. Unfortunately, as it does so the leaves become much coarser and the appearance is generally far from elegant. Shaded, moist, draught-free conditions will suit it best, with the temperature maintained at around 20°C (68°F).

Euonymus japonicus aureo-picta

The silk oak, on the other hand, will fare very much better if the conditions are cool and light, and no harm will be done if the plant spends the summer season out of doors. To get the best out of these plants it is essential that the root system at no time becomes excessively dry. (But beware of overwatering, too.) Regular feeding of established plants is also a must, and annual potting on in the spring is advisable. Use a rich potting mixture such as no. 3.

Eriobotrya; Euonymus

When shopping for indoor plants, there is no need to restrict yourself completely to plants suitable purely as houseplants. You can sometimes select kinds that may be planted out in the garden when they have lost their attraction indoors. *Eriobotrya japonica* (loquat) and *Euonymus japonicus* are two such plants. Both require cool, light conditions when used as potted plants. Outdoors the loquat will need the protection of a sheltered wall in colder areas. Not many houseplant growers sell these, but they are usually obtainable from shrub nurseries and garden centres.

There are several varieties of *Euonymus* with variegated leaves from one to three inches long. The *Eriobotrya* has much larger leaves – up to 12 inches long – that are a beautiful grey when young.

Fatsia; Fatshedra

Equally at home in cool indoor positions and also outdoors where winter conditions are not too harsh are the false castor oil plant, *Fatsia japonica* (sometimes sold as *Aralia sieboldii*) and a hybrid derived from it, *Fatshedra lizei*.

Like the true castor oil plant (*Ricinus communis*), *F. japonica* has large, dark green palmate leaves with seven to nine pointed lobes. It is one of the most useful of all indoor plants. Exceptional plants may reach a height of some eight to ten feet in as many years, but they usually remain much more compact. They like cool conditions – around 13°C (55°F) – and annual potting on when small. (Use Potting Mixture no. 3.) But once plants are in 10-inch pots, they can be sustained for several years by regular feeding during the growing season.

The variegated form of *F. japonica*, with whitish patches on the leaves, is a particularly fine plant. But it is more difficult to obtain and more expensive than its plain relative. It also needs a slightly higher temperature and more

Dizygotheca elegantissima

Grevillea robusta

Fatshedra lizei

careful watering if browning of the leaf edges is to be avoided.

F. lizei is a man-made hybrid between an ivy (*Hedera*) and *F. japonica* – hence the name *Fatshedra*. Hence, too, its leaf shape and habit. It has leaves similar in shape to those of *F. japonica* but about half the size. It tends to grow tall, and can be trained up pillars or staircase handrails. Or it can be kept more compact by regularly removing the growing tips. This plant also has a variegated form, but it is much more difficult to keep in good order. Both types are liable to be damaged by leaf-cleaning agents.

Ficus diversifolia

Not in the least like other *Ficus* in appearance, *Ficus diversifolia* (the

Fatsia japonica

Podocarpus macrophyllus Maki

mistletoe fig) has small, rounded leaves that are dull in appearance and not particularly attractive. However, at a very early age yellow-tinged berries are produced – in profusion on healthy plants – and these are the principal attraction. Keeping the growing tips pinched out regularly will result in a neat and decorative plant that will be a continual source of interest.

To do well, this plant should have light, moist conditions where the temperature does not drop below 19°C (66°F). Lower temperatures result in a plant of hard, less-attractive appearance. When potting on the potting mixture should be fairly light; for example, two parts of no. 3 and one part sphagnum peat. Potting on is only necessary every second year, however – and even less frequently for mature plants.

Pittosporum

Pittosporums are much underrated as pot plants, but the foliage of these evergreens (most of them indigenous to Australia and New Zealand) is much used by florists when preparing flower arrangements and displays. The leaves are glossy and leathery, rather like small rhododendron leaves.

Pittosporum tobira and *P. undulatum* are both fairly tough plants that do well in cool, airy conditions and are excellent subjects for large conservatories. There is also a variegated form of *P. tobira*. Possibly the best form for indoor use is *P. eugenoides variegatum*, which makes

an attractive bush and is not demanding in respect of care and attention – in fact, it seems capable of enduring quite harsh treatment and still regaining its attractiveness when conditions improve.

Podocarpus

Podocarpus macrophyllus Maki (southern yew) forms a compact bush that may

Ficus diversifolia

be clipped to shape at almost any time, and makes an excellent terrace plant during the summer months in colder areas. The leaves are slender and leathery, yellowish-green on top and bluish-green underneath. Large tubs will eventually be required and it is important that the no. 3 potting mixture is free-draining, with a layer of crocks in the bottom. The container should be in proportion to the size of the plant, as small plants in large containers seldom seem to do well.

Stenocarpus

The Australian native evergreen tree *Stenocarpus sinuatus* (wheel of fire) gets its common name from the way the orange-red flowers seem to explode into a much brighter red as they mature. Unfortunately, this is a pleasure reserved for those who see the plant develop in its natural environment.

When grown as a pot plant it has attractive, glossy leaves (rather like deeply-cut oak leaves) that vary in shading from plant to plant. In fact, leaves on the same plant may have many different shades. As a young plant (raised from seed) it is particularly colourful, but loses much of its attractiveness as it ages. Older plants are also more difficult to maintain in good condition; ensuring free drainage is beneficial. The only heat it needs is enough to protect it from frost, and like many other large indoor shrubs can take a 'holiday' outdoors in warm weather.

39

Plants with giant leaves

When you have been collecting and growing all kinds of foliage and flowering plants for many years, it is not necessarily the most exotic and colourful that give the greatest pleasure. More often than not the eye will be attracted by leaves that have a pleasant shape and are a cool, soothing green colour. In this respect, many members of the aroid family come into their own – plants such as the *Philodendrons*, *Monsteras* and *Syngoniums*, all of which are related to the arum lily. Some of these have leaves that are (for houseplants) huge: up to 24 inches across in some cases. Others are of more manageable size in the average home.

On the other hand, there are a number of large-leaved houseplants that have interesting leaf patterns and colourings, and are not plain green. These give a dramatic focal point to any large group of plants, and they are much used for big indoor plant arrangements.

Aspidistra

As its ability to survive in dark, draughty Victorian drawing rooms shows, the 'cast-iron plant' is, indeed, pretty tough. The original *Aspidistra lurida* (from China) has long been superseded by its

Caladium hybrids

Aspidistra eliator

Japanese cousin, *A. eliator*, with its long, lance-shaped dark green leaves. There is also a variegated form of *A. eliator*, with ivory stripes, but it is very difficult to obtain. Either may produce small purplish flowers at soil level.

Excessive sun and over-watering should be avoided, and also cleaning of the leaves with leaf-cleaning agents. Above all, do not keep it in too large a pot; it flourishes best when pot-bound.

Caladium

The tough leaves of the *Aspidistra* are in complete contrast to those of *Caladium* hybrids, some of which are translucent. Others have vivid green, red and cream colourings on the large arrow-head leaves, which vary in length from nine inches to more than two feet. In fact, there are scores of varieties of *Caladium*, though not all are easily available and those that can be bought generally come as unnamed mixed tubers. One of the best and most easily available, however,

is *C. × candidum*, which has green-veined white leaves.

Plants that are bought in leaf in spring should be kept moist and warm – 20°C (68°F) – with high humidity for best results. These are never more than temporary houseplants, however, and the foliage will die down in middle to late summer. After this, keep the tubers dry and warm until early the following spring, when they should be started into growth in moist peat at about 21°C (70°F). Then pot into a peaty mix.

Dieffenbachia

The *Dieffenbachias*, commonly known as dumb canes, include a wide range of superb plants, all of upright habit with large, attractively marked leaves. The odd common name comes from the paralysing effect of the sap on one's speech. Should it get into the mouth, the tongue swells up, rendering one speechless. So it is as well to keep these plants away from children.

In recent years the compact, speckled-leaved *D. arvida* 'Exotica' has – thanks to its durability and ease of handling – become one of the most popular of the more exotic indoor plants. It seems to survive quite happily in conditions where most other *Dieffenbachias* would die overnight. Among other kinds, *D. picta*, *D. amoena*, *D. sequina* and a number of others make substantial plants in three to four years from first potting. There are many mutants of *D. picta*, and the creamy-yellow leaves of the variety known as 'Rudolph Rhoers' is quite the best.

Apart from 'Exotica', all *Dieffenbachias* demand agreeably warm, draught-free, moist conditions and a reasonably peaty potting mix. Mature plants produce uninteresting arum-like inflorescences that are best removed as they appear. New plants can be propagated

Dieffenbachia arvida 'Exotica'

by cutting plant stems into sections a few inches long and rooting in boxes of warm, moist peat (see page 228).

Monstera

Monstera deliciosa, the Mexican breadfruit, is commonly known as the 'Swiss cheese plant' because of the slits and holes in its leaves. It is an old favourite among houseplants. In favourable conditions it may develop into a plant ten feet high and the same across in as many years, but such growth would not be expected in most home conditions. Here, growth is less free and the actual leaf size smaller than in a conservatory (where leaves two feet across may be produced). Nor is it likely to fruit – which is a pity, since the pulp of the fruit has a delicious 'fruit-salad' flavour.

Like most aroids, *M. deliciosa* likes a free-draining potting mixture containing a good proportion of both peat and coarse sand. Many ready-mixed peat-based types are suitable; the main need

40

is to prevent waterlogging, which causes rotting of the roots. Aerial roots will appear from the stem; as they become long enough encourage them to grow into the pot of growing mixture.

M. deliciosa 'Borsigiana' has smaller but similarly shaped leaves that are carried on stems that tend to grow in a much more erect fashion. As with other

Monstera deliciosa 'Borsigiana'

climbing aroids, it grows best against a support that will retain moisture. A simple support of this kind can be made by wrapping wet sphagnum moss around a stout wooden stake; the aerial roots will root into it if the moss is kept moist (see page 225).

M. deliciosa is often wrongly referred to as *Philodendron pertusum* or *Monstera pertusa*, and Americans know it as the split-leaf philodendron. *P. pertusum* is a similar but smaller plant.

Philodendron

Among the larger-leaved *Philodendrons* there are many plants invaluable to the interior decorator. Some are squat, with low-growing rosettes of beautifully fresh-coloured green leaves, while others in their native environment or a large conservatory would, with little encouragement, entwine their aerial roots around the nearest tree or support and set about climbing to the top. Grow them all in the kind of potting mixture described above for *Monstera deliciosa*.

Philodendron bipinnatifidum

Among the larger low-growing types for pot culture, *P. bipinnatifidum* is one of the very best, with its deeply incised leaves, rather like hands with many fingers. Like all the *Philodendrons* mentioned here, it will thrive in really warm temperatures – never less than 20°C (68°F) – and high humidity, although it is not so fussy as some. Feed it little and often and avoid exposing to bright sunlight. Where there is ample ceiling height it is also the perfect subject for a really large hanging basket; so located it also takes up less of the valuable space that a plant of eight-foot spread would normally demand.

Also particularly fine – more of the connoisseur's plant – is *P. wendlandii*, which has broad spear-shaped leaves formed in the fashion of a shuttlecock. Where *P. bipinnatifidum* will tolerate less than perfect conditions, do not neglect *P. wendlandii*, as loss of only a few leaves will ruin the overall appearance of the plant.

The more tidy *Philodendrons* are also useful in plant collections where greenery with interesting shape is a useful foil for more colourful front plants. With arrow-shaped leaves that may range from one to two feet in length and that have a rosy tint when young, there is *P. erubescens*. Of similar shape and a better copper-red colouring is the variety 'Burgundy'. Both are climbers, and like other climbing members of the genus will do well with a mossed support, as described for *Monsteras*. Among the other climbing arrow-leaves, the most widely available plant is *P. hastatum*, which is very similar to a plant popular in Europe in recent years, *P.* 'Tuxla'.

Particularly beautiful, but all too rare, is *P. elegans*. This is another climber, but has delicately fingered, palm-like leaves. Equally beautiful in a different way are *P. andreanum* and *P. melanochryson*. Both have superb velvety-green leaves that hang vertically, but they are smaller and more heart-shaped in the latter plant. It is also

Philodendron melanochryson

easier to keep than the former, which (like *P. elegans*) will test the skill of the most accomplished indoor gardener.

Syngonium

If you want to accommodate climbing aroids in a smaller room, the *Syngoniums* will be useful. They are less invasive than other aroids and have more colourful

Syngonium podophyllum

foliage. But the leaves have a similar arum shape. In fact, the common name of the most popular type – *S. podophyllum* – is goosefoot plant. (It is also often sold under the name *Nephthytis*, however.) Treat it in the same way as the climbing *Philodendrons*; it will especially like a damp mossed support.

Tetrastigma

The final large-leaved plant comes from the vine family. It is *Tetrastigma voinierianum*, which is an excellent backing plant that will grow at a prodigious rate in suitable conditions. The conditions suggested for the larger *Philodendrons* will suit it very well. Not a very attractive plant alone, it needs regular potting on into no. 3 mixture in order to keep the masses of roots under some control. Its strong tendrils entwine themselves around any support, so there is little need for any tying in. The leaves – each up to six inches long – have a natural dusty appearance and should not be cleaned or rubbed.

Tetrastigma voinierianum

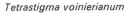

The elegant palms

Of all indoor plants, palms are the epitome of elegance. They seem almost to be more at home in the foyer of a large Victorian hotel – with the tinkling of a pianist and guests drinking tea from bone china cups – than in the jungles where they grow wild. But if palms suit the formality of nineteenth-century elegance, they fit equally well into ultra-modern design schemes.

As a result, the demand for palms, after a lull when they were out of fashion, has been growing strongly once again. Unfortunately, most palms are relatively slow-growing, and nurserymen have not been able to keep up with the demand for the larger varieties, and prices are high.

On the other hand, palms are generally quite tolerant plants that do not need much attention. Although they come from sunny places, most of them – *Howeias* in particular – do not mind shade, although growth is improved if they are placed in or near a window. They will also put up with cool winter temperatures – down to 7°C (45°F) or even lower in some cases. They will not grow much in winter gloom, and need no feeding and little water at this time, though their roots should remain damp. In spring and summer, however, they should be watered freely and fed about once a month. All palms like a damp atmosphere; spray their leaves regularly.

Palms are quite happy in pots that seem rather small for the size of the plant, and they do not need potting on until root growth begins to push the plant out of its pot – perhaps every three years for a large specimen, more often for a vigorously growing younger plant. Do not use too rich a potting mixture: Mix no. 2 or a peat-based type, preferably with sand added to improve drainage. The mixture should be packed very firmly into the pot.

Although there are many species of palms suitable for growing in the house or conservatory, the range of choice is not wide for most amateur growers. With the rebirth of interest in palms, however, some nurserymen are introducing more unusual varieties. Also, it is often possible to get seeds of rarer types from botanical seedsmen. These are best germinated in a propagator and, given moist, warm conditions – 24°C (75°F) if possible – they should germinate in four to six weeks.

Chamaerops
The European fan palm, *Chamaerops humilis*, is the only palm to grow wild in Europe. Although a Mediterranean species, it will stand temperatures only just over freezing point. Both it and its even more hardy Chinese cousin, *Chamaerops excelsa* (more properly called *Trachycarpus fortunei*), have fan-shaped leaves on stalks that can grow several feet in length. Young indoor specimens are much smaller, however, and do not have the trunk of the mature plant.

Cocos
Perhaps the prettiest of all dwarf palms easily available for indoor gardeners, *Cocos wedelliana* is a relative of the coconut palm. It is more properly called *Syagrus wedelliana*, but is normally sold as *Cocos*. It has attractive, feathery leaflets even when small. It is not easy to keep for long, however. Give it plenty of water and a minimum winter temperature of 15°C (59°F) – more if possible – and you may be lucky.

Howeia
The closely-related *Howeia forsteriana* and *H. belmoreana* are the commonest large indoor palms today. These are the Palm Court palms, and can be bought in many sizes from two-foot youngsters to splendid specimens 10 or 12 feet tall. They come from the Lord Howe Islands in the Pacific; hence their name. Hence, too, the other name they are often given, *Kentia* – that of the islands' main town.

Both species are long-lasting and shade-tolerant, though they should have plenty of water in summer. They like a winter temperature of 13°C (55°F), *H. forsteriana* being the more tender. It is also the faster-growing, but is not quite so attractive as *H. belmoreana*. The latter has very gracefully drooping leaflets, whereas those of *H. forsteriana* are larger and stand out more rigidly.

Neanthe
The plant commonly sold as *Neanthe bella* or *Chamaedorea elegans* is properly called *Collinia elegans*. It comes from Mexico, and is one of the best known and easiest dwarf palms to grow. From a six-inch seedling, it will in a few years reach a height of 18 inches, with individual leaflets four to six inches long. Unfortunately, as it grows the leaflets become rather large and coarse, and the plant loses the elegance of its youth. This palm needs less winter moisture and less feeding than most, and does not mind a dry atmosphere.

Phoenix
As shown on page 198, the date palm, *Phoenix dactylifera*, can be grown from a date stone. It is slow-growing at first, consisting of little more than a single thick, grass-like leaf, but forms a reasonable specimen in three or four years. It soon grows more rapidly, however, and is liable to outgrow most rooms in 10 to 15 years. It has stiff, prickly leaves and will stand quite low temperatures. Rather similar in appearance are two dwarf members of the same genus that are sold as houseplants. They are *P. canariensis* from the Canary Islands and the soft-leaved and more delicate-looking *P. roebelenii* from India. They both grow more slowly than *P. dactylifera* – particularly the more tender *P. roebelinii*.

Other palms
There are many other palms that could be grown indoors, but are difficult to obtain in some countries. The South American *Chamaedorea erumpens*, for example, is available in the US but not so easily in Europe. It is known as the bamboo palm because of its cane-like stems. Rather similar are *Crysalidocarpus lutescens* from Madagascar and *Chamaedorea costaricana* from South America. Among the palms with fan-shaped leaves are *Rhapis excelsa* and its smaller relative *R. humilis*, both from Asia, *Latania borbonica* from Madagascar and *Livistona chinensis* from Asia. *Reinhardtia gracilis*, the window palm, is an attractive dwarf type.

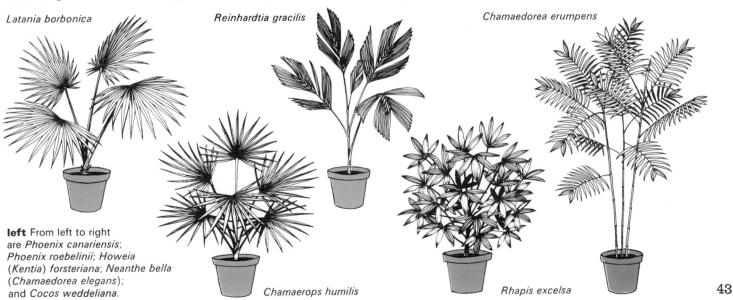

Latania borbonica   *Reinhardtia gracilis*   *Chamaedorea erumpens*

left From left to right are *Phoenix canariensis*; *Phoenix roebelinii*; *Howeia* (*Kentia*) *forsteriana*; *Neanthe bella* (*Chamaedorea elegans*); and *Cocos weddeliana*.

Chamaerops humilis   *Rhapis excelsa*

The 'palms' that aren't

A lot of plants that have no botanical right to the name are commonly called palms, for the very good reason that they do in a way resemble true palms. With its elegant, ringed trunk surmounted by a tuft of slender, pointed leaves, for example, a mature *Dracaena marginata* looks a good deal more like a desert island palm tree than do most proper palms grown as houseplants. The reason is, of course, that the latter have virtually no trunk in the sizes normally seen indoors.

Like the graceful palms, these impostors have a stark beauty that has particular appeal to the architectural mind. Plants of this kind seem to lend themselves to the severe contours and colour schemes of modern buildings.

Some of the *Dracaenas* are particularly useful in this context. Whereas most indoor plants have little attraction once they have shed their lower leaves, the more stately of the *Dracaenas* acquire a new elegance when only a tuft of leaves is left at the top and the attractive stem is exposed. In this respect *D. marginata* is one of the best examples, and plants that have had their growing tops removed to allow development of several growing heads can have a fascinatingly exotic look. *Dracaena fragrans* (and its many varieties) and *D. draco* (the dragon tree) are similar, but of much more robust appearance.

These houseplants that resemble palms are a diverse collection originating from many parts of the world, but the genus *Dracaena* is well represented. So is the closely-related genus *Cordyline*. (So closely are they related, in fact, that the names are used almost interchangeably by some growers and sellers of houseplants.) There are other kinds of palm-like plants, but these are the most important for indoor gardeners.

Cordylines

Native to New Zealand, where it may grow to a height in excess of thirty feet, *Cordyline australis* and the similar *C. indivisa* (both also called *Dracaenas*) will survive outdoors in more moderate areas. It is much more likely, though, that you will see these plants as compact,

Cordyline terminalis 'Firebrand'

From left to right are *Dracaena fragrans* 'Massangeana'; *Dracaena marginata*; and *Dracaena deremensis* 'Bausei'.

low-growing shrubs with long, narrow leaves radiating from a central stem. All the *Cordylines* require light, warm and moist conditions, but these two are among the easiest to care for.

Far and away the most popular commercial plant among the more tender *Cordylines* is *C. terminalis* 'Firebrand' (marketed by many growers of exotic plants as *Dracaena terminalis*), which has cerise, purple and green leaves, and a clean, upright habit of growth. Other varieties, with different leaf colourings, are also available from time to time. For healthy development, the plants need lightly shaded, reasonably warm conditions where the temperature is maintained at about 19°C (66°F). The potting mixture should be moist, though not permanently saturated. The use of soft (or rain) water is an advantage.

Being somewhat delicate, it is almost inevitable that *C. terminalis* 'Firebrand' will in time shed its lower leaves, and it is not often possible to grow one to a height of more than 2½ to 3 feet indoors before it dies off completely. However, the exciting and colourful early growth makes it well worth purchasing and replacing every second year or so.

Having similar colouring but much smaller leaves and a more compact appearance, *C.* 'Rededge' (also called *Dracaena* 'Rededge') is a more recent introduction and is, if anything, a slightly more difficult plant to care for in the home. Growing conditions and treatment are almost exactly those described for *C. terminalis* 'Firebrand'. Both will require a good proportion of peat in the potting mixture when potting on in the spring.

Tough Dracaenas

For harsh conditions where plants must endure a little neglect, *Dracaena marginata* should be high on the list, as it will tolerate many variations and still survive. Removal of the growing point when the plant is about three feet in height will induce it to branch, improving its appearance as a result. At a height of about five feet this plant may show the odd characteristic of oozing a sticky substance from its topmost leaves so that they stick tightly together. This prevents the natural upward growth of the plant, resulting in the growing top snapping off.

The variegated form of *D. marginata*, sometimes sold under the name of *D. m. tricolor*, must be one of the most exciting foliage plants to be introduced in recent years. Its foliage is predominantly cream in colour, but is suffused with pink, giving the plant a very rich, almost

Dracaena marginata tricolor

glowing appearance. It seems very tolerant of average room conditions, but is not as tough as the original. For both these plants good light is important, and try to avoid cold, wet winter conditions.

On stouter trunks, *D. draco*, the dragon tree of the Canary Islands, requires similar treatment and is a particularly durable plant. It is not suited to confined space, however. In the same category is *Yucca aloifolia*, sometimes called Spanish bayonet, which has very sharp and spiteful pointed leaves that should be kept well out of harm's way. Both are good conservatory plants.

More tender Dracaenas

What could sound more exotic than the song of India? This is the English name for the plant generally known as *Pleomele reflexa variegata* but which is now officially included in the genus *Dracaena*. The name is as fascinating as the plant itself, with its clusters of six-inch-long

Pleomele reflexa variegata

golden leaves – each with just a touch of green – on top of many branching stems. It will give a completely new dimension to any group of plants. Regardless of the growing conditions, loss of the lower leaves will be inevitable. If conditions are light, warm and on the dry side, the song of India can be a pretty durable plant. One drawback is its painfully slow rate of growth, but a plant ten feet tall and perhaps 15 years old is a handsome sight indeed.

With similar-shaped leaves that are mostly grey and white in colour, *D. sanderiana* has a more erect habit and is much freer-growing than the *Pleomele*. Growing more quickly, it is also more freely available, and it is best to choose a pot planted with three or four small plants, as this will provide a fuller and more attractive display. As *D. sanderiana* ages the plant tends to become leggy and unattractive, so is not usually worth keeping for more than about three years indoors. Growing conditions should be lightly shaded and moist, at a temperature of not less than 19°C (66°F). Use Potting Mixture no. 3 with a little extra peat when potting on biennially.

Much more effective as a single plant is *D. deremensis*. Retaining its lower leaves is a distinct advantage as these are most attractive and may be 18 inches in length on mature plants. Follow the growing instructions advised for *D. sanderiana* and endeavour to provide a moist atmosphere around the plant. There are many excellent varieties: 'Warneckii' has sword-shaped leaves that are greyish-green with a white band on either side. In 'Bausei' the leaves are margined green, with a broad band of startling white in the centre. 'Rhoers Gold' has older leaves almost identical to 'Warneckii', but the young leaves are a handsome pale yellow colour.

The broad, straplike leaves of *D. fragrans* are predominantly mustard yellow in colour, and the plants require more space in which to mature, but the

Dracaena sanderiana

same growing conditions will suit them. These *Dracaenas* produce what promise to be exotic and spectacular flower clusters when they reach a height of some five to six feet, but they are not in the least attractive as they open, and are best cut off. After flowering in this way, the plants will branch naturally at the top, giving them a more tufted and often more attractive look. Among the varieties of *D. fragrans* are 'Massangeana', 'Lindenii' and 'Victoria', the latter being much the most colourful and by far the most difficult to care for.

Other palm-like plants

The screw-pines (*Pandanus*) are superb individual plants that are all too scarce. *P. veitchii* is one of the most easily obtained species, and has green and white striped leaves. These are rather like giant pineapple leaves (hence the name; the 'screw' part comes from the corkscrew form of the mature tree's trunk). The leaves are saw-edged, but are not very harmful if the plant is treated with a little respect. *Pandanus* are durable plants needing the same treatment as *Dracaena marginata*.

Very easy but slow-growing is the so-called elephant-foot or pony-tail plant,

Pandanus sanderi

Beaucarnia recurvata. The first name comes from the bulbous trunk base, the second from the crowning tuft of narrow leaves. It likes good light but is otherwise undemanding. The swollen trunk stores moisture – a sign that it will withstand considerable drought.

Finally among the plants that look like palms are two extremely ancient groups of plants that date back beyond the age of dinosaurs: the cycads and the tree ferns. *Cycas revoluta* (the sago palm) is extremely slow-growing and is seen at its best in the warm houses of botanic gardens. Try to grow it only if you have patience and the warm, steamy conditions it needs. Some tree ferns, such as *Cibotium schiedei* from Asia, *Cyathea dealbata* from New Zealand and *Dicksonia antarctica* from Australia are tougher but are rarely seen for sale. You may be able to grow them from spores obtainable from a botanical seedsman, however (see page 56). If you succeed, you will have beautiful and unusual plants – not palms, but with much the same grace.

45

Plants with colourful leaves

Since houseplants are bought for decoration, it is no surprise that commercial growers offer a wide range of plants with attractively marked or coloured leaves. Those that rely for their appeal on vivid leaf colourings are described here, while pages 48 and 49 cover mainly those with other attractive markings.

Unfortunately, it would be foolish to suppose that all the available fancy-leaved plants will flourish permanently in the home. This is where the owner of a well-stocked conservatory or greenhouse has a considerable advantage. He can bring his more delicate plants into the house for a short period and then return them to the conservatory's more congenial atmosphere before they come to too much harm. For only a few days in adverse conditions can prove fatal to the more delicate subjects, and among these are a number of coloured- and fancy-leaved types. So when these are indoors, watch carefully the temperature and humidity (see page 220), and site them out of draughts.

Begonia

Taken all round, there are few groups of plants that can compare with the *Begonia rex* for their variations of leaf colouring, be it a single leaf or a complete plant. The varieties of rex begonias are legion and it is only possible to describe a few.

With dark-veined silver leaves, *B. rex* 'Fairy' is an excellent choice, and there is a similar but more miniature variety that is flushed with pink and named (for some unaccountable reason) 'Shirt-sleeves'. With serrated leaf edges, 'Hélène Teupel' is reddish-brown in colour, with silver markings. One of the larger types, and a most spectacular plant, is 'Bettina Rothschild', which is frequently given the common name 'blaze of fire', as the foliage seems to glow when the light catches it at the right angle.

These varieties are seldom offered for sale as named plants, and when they are there is much confusion over naming. But when selecting named or unnamed plants it is often better to choose the more miniature forms as the larger leaves are more easily damaged and seldom seem so attractive. Mildew is a problem in damp conditions (see page 233), and some varieties tend to become leggy after a year or two. Benlate will check the mildew, but there is little one can do about the legginess other than replace the plant. Fortunately, it is easy to propagate from leaf cuttings (see page 228).

By potting plants on into slightly larger containers as the roots become pot-bound, many of the larger-leaved sorts will make plants that are as much as three feet across. A fifty-fifty potting mixture of Mix no. 3 and peat should be used when potting on.

Codiaeum

There is some controversy, but it is usually accepted that the *Codiaeum* (commonly known as the croton or Joseph's coat) is indigenous to Sri Lanka (Ceylon). But whatever its original home may be, it is now well established as the most colourful shrub in every tropical country of the world. It is also the prime standby of almost every plant decorator, whether he is a consultant interior designer or he works for the local parks department.

There seems to be no limit to the range of colours – from yellow and pale green through orange and red to almost black – that one might find in a collection of croton plants, and a single leaf will often defy description. The leaf shapes, too, are more varied than in any other group of houseplants. Many new introductions appear on the scene, but the tried and trusted older sorts still easily hold their own, and it is difficult to do other than list a few favourites.

If you want a type for growing on to become a specimen plant, few can compare with *Codiaeum variegatum* 'Reidii', which has large oblong leaves in many shades of red and orange. When confined to a pot it will grow to a height of ten feet and a breadth of six to seven feet. Having trilobed leaves of bright yellow veined with green, the variety 'Eugene Drapps' will grow to similar dimensions in agreeable conditions.

Possibly the best of all in respect of colour, durability and general appearance is the old favourite 'Mrs Iceton', which has comparatively small oval leaves and just about every colour imaginable. Quite often these fine old plants go unnoticed by the commercial grower until they are 'resurrected' and given a change of name, hence the fact

Begonia rex varieties

that 'Mrs Iceton' masquerades today under a number of other names.

The narrow-leaved crotons are also interesting, and the best choice here would be 'Warrenii', a useful display plant that does not have the heavy appearance of most of its relations. 'Golden Ring' has similar narrow leaves, but as the name suggests these are distorted into a spiral – not especially attractive, though it does add some interest to the collection.

In very warm, very moist, very light

Codiaeum variegatum 'Pennick'

conditions, with ample feeding and potting on into Potting Mixture no. 3 when necessary, the majority of crotons will grow quite rapidly. Nevertheless, it may take up to twenty years to produce one of the size mentioned above, and during all that time there should be no neglect in the way of temperature, watering and feeding.

Potting must be done with more firmness than for other indoor plants, and the potting mixture should be well drained. Thereafter plants must be kept moist, as any drying out will inevitably result in loss of leaves, and full sun is essential if plants are to retain their vivid colouring. In poor light they quickly revert to green and do less well. Cuttings of almost any size can be rooted at any time of year, but they must have a temperature in the region of 24°C (75°F) to have a reasonable chance.

Coleus
More often than not, the more colourful the plant, the more problems there are likely to be in its cultivation. But the *Coleus*, or flame-nettle, is both brilliantly coloured and easy. Like a good sire at the racing stud, *Coleus blumei* has given its name to many fine plants, all with foliage much more colourful than the bronze-red leaves of the original. Colourings vary from red and bronze to brown and purple, all patterned with yellows, whites and shades of green. The leaves are nettle-like, with serrated edges. The whole plant forms a bushy sub-shrub.

For the most part, the *Coleus* hybrids

Coleus blumei

are relatively easy to care for, and do perfectly well out of doors in milder weather. Cuttings root with little difficulty and, once rooted, regular potting on into Mixture no. 3 should not be neglected. Regular feeding of mature plants is also advisable. Growing tips should be regularly pinched out to keep plants bushy, compact and attractive. New plants can also be raised easily from seed. This is sold in mixtures, and you can then propagate the best forms by cuttings.

Fittonia
The patterns on the leaves of *Fittonia argyroneura* and *F. verschaffeltii* (red and silver respectively) are often likened to fish-bones. Both plants are colourful and low-growing, with paper-thin leaves, but are among the most difficult to keep in good order. Cold and wet conditions are almost instant death to them, and cold water on their leaves will soon result in failure. Protect them from direct sunlight, and when potting ensure that the mixture is very peaty. The best place to grow them indoors is in a draught-free glass case, or terrarium (see page 30), or in a bottle garden (see page 32). *F. argyroneura* 'Nana', a small-leaved form, is much easier to keep, however.

Fittonia verschaffeltii

Hypoëstes; Saxifraga
An inexpensive way of getting together a collection of houseplants is to raise a few of the more common sorts from seed (see also page 78). One such plant could be *Hypoëstes sanguinolenta*. Not a very interesting plant, it is unusual in that its dark green leaves have pink spots. The stems are wiry and growth fairly quick; prune it regularly to keep it tidy.

Saxifraga sarmentosa (also called *S. stolonifera*, mother of thousands or strawberry geranium) is equally easy, and is

Hypoëstes sanguinolenta

simply propagated by pinning down the young plantlets that are freely produced from the parent on runners much like strawberry runners. Root and grow them on in a peaty potting mixture and they will be little trouble in a warm room. The plant has pretty, rounded leaves with pale green vein markings. The variety *tricolor* has attractive red, cream and green variegations, but is more tender and more difficult to root.

Rhoeo
A plant that looks rather like a cross between a bromeliad (see page 72) and a young *Dracaena* or *Cordyline* (see page 44) is *Rhoeo discolor*. The stiff, fleshy, pointed leaves radiate out from a short central stem. They are dark green on top, purple underneath; and the plant looks most striking as a solo specimen. It likes lightly shaded, warm conditions. The potting mixture should not be allowed to get too wet in winter.

Other kinds
A number of other plants with coloured leaf markings are described on the next two pages, as they are varieties of plants that do not have such brilliant colourings. Among other houseplants with coloured leaves are a number of *Dracaenas* and *Cordylines* (see page 44), the *Caladiums* with their huge leaves (see page 40) and some of the *Tradescantia* family (see page 53). The fancy-leaved varieties of *Pelargoniums* (geraniums; see page 104) also make attractive pot plants for a sunny window sill.

Plants with patterned leaves

Apart from the brightly coloured plants described on the previous two pages, there are many houseplants whose leaves have equally attractive, if more muted, markings. These are all good subjects for grouping in displays – on a table or in an alcove, for example. While such a collection would look rather cluttered if composed entirely of plants with patterned leaves, such plants add variety and interest to a group of greenery.

Aglaonema

Most *Aglaonemas* have blotched or mottled leaves, though not all of them are particularly colourful – or even interesting. *A. commutatum* and *A. modestum* (Chinese evergreen), for example, have little excitement compared to others in the group. Producing small, compact plants, *A. costatum* has a prominent ivory-white midrib to its leaves, which are predominantly green with interesting white speckles. *A. pictum* has more attractive mottling and is a slightly more vigorous grower, but it lacks the attractive midrib. Quite the most colourful and possibly the freest growing is *A. pseudobracteatum*, which has very attractive cream and green variegated leaves. When

Aglaonema 'Silver Queen'

well grown, this may attain a height of three feet or more. It is not easy to find, however, and is prone to mealy bug infestation (see page 232).

For many years *A. robelinii* enjoyed reasonable popularity, but in recent years has been superseded by a similar though more attractive plant, *A.* 'Silver Queen'. This has lance-shaped silver-grey leaves that may range from 6 to 18 inches in length, and will develop into a huge clump of a plant if conditions are favourable. All the *Aglaonemas* need to be grown at a temperature of not less than 16°C (61°F), and must be kept moist and shaded.

Begonia

The fibrous-rooted begonias seem to offer an even wider selection of different kinds than *Begonia rex* (see page 46), and they are very much more varied in their appearance. Also many of them flower profusely. In this category the best-known is probably *B.* 'President Carnot', which has silver-speckled brown leaves and large clusters of pendulous flowers. Growing to a height of four to five feet

Begonia masoniana

and much fuller in appearance, *B. haageana* also flowers freely during the summer months. In hanging baskets both *B. richmondensis* and *B. glaucophylla* do well; the latter has beautiful orange-red flowers from late winter.

In the more miniature size range there are *B. boweri*, with striking green markings in its leaves, and *B. sutherlandii*, with small, pale green leaves and small orange flowers. The latter is an easy window plant that dies down in winter, when it should be kept dry. It also develops tiny tubers from which one may easily propagate new plants – one very good reason for the popularity and wide distribution of this variety.

B. masoniana (the iron cross begonia) is a plant that has enjoyed considerable popularity in recent years. It has leaves with a dull gold tinge and a distinctive German 'iron cross' marking. Warm, moist conditions are needed for most of the begonias, and they will all prefer some protection from direct sunlight.

Calathea; Ctenanthe

The conditions surrounding a plant play an important part in success or failure, and one would need virtually perfect con-

Calathea insignis

ditions in order to produce quality plants of *Calathea zebrina*. When well managed this is a truly spectacular plant with light and dark emerald-green leaves that have a velvet sheen. Temperatures of not less than 19°C (66°F) are a must, as are a peaty potting mixture and extreme care when watering. Use tepid water – never too much – and keep the area surrounding the plant permanently humid.

Just a little less difficult, but by no means easy, *C. mackoyana* (the peacock plant, sometimes sold as *Maranta mackoyana*) is one of the most beautiful foliage plants in cultivation today. Grown by a true expert this can attain a height of four feet and have leaves a foot or more in length and six inches in width. Impossible, some may feel, when they view their own miserable specimens, but nurserymen specializing in only this and one or two similar types do achieve the most incredible results.

The colours and patterns in the leaves are equally incredible – almost to the point where one leans forward to touch the leaves just to make sure that they are real. They are paper-thin and transparent in parts, other parts being dark green on the upper surface and reddish-purple

Calathea mackoyana

underneath. As a result, the dark green parts look reddish when light shines through, whereas the rest is a silvery colour. And all this forms an intricate pattern rather like the leaves of a plant!

A little less trying is *C. picturata*, which has a dark green leaf margin and the entire central area silver. The reverse of the leaf is an interesting maroon colour. The easiest *Calathea* to care for is *C. louisae*. Unfortunately, it is also the least attractive, having dull green leaves with only a little central variegation.

Closely related to the *Calatheas* (and often sold under that name since their own is so unpronounceable) are the *Ctenanthes*. Of these, *C. lubbersiana* and *C. oppenheimiana tricolor* are the best known and most easily available. Both have attractively marked leaves, rather like those of *Calatheas*, and *C. lubbers-*

Dracaena godseffiana 'Florida Beauty'

iana is one of the most durable of the group. The second, however, is very much a plant for the experienced grower with favourable conditions at his disposal, as it abhors wet and inadequately heated premises. It demands warmth and humidity.

Dracaena

Attractive markings or variegations can make an otherwise rather boring plant into a subject full of interest. A good example is the contrast between the dull green, rather uninteresting *Dracaena godseffiana* and the cultivated variety of the same plant known as 'Florida Beauty'. The latter has its oval, dark-green leaves thickly covered in cream-coloured spots. (Its form is quite unlike that of other *Dracaenas*, incidentally.)

Given good light and a temperature in the region of 17°C (63°F), *D. godseffiana* 'Florida Beauty' will make one of the most attractive of indoor plants that will in time grow to a height of six feet or more. It can be propagated by cuttings. Preferably put several cuttings in one pot and remove their growing tips. Avoid overwatering in winter.

Maranta; Stromanthe

Closely related to the *Calatheas*, but generally easier to grow, the *Marantas* mentioned here abhor above all any exposure to direct sunlight. This is particularly true of *M. leuconeura erythrophylla*. This takes on a most dejected appearance in the sun; otherwise it is a particularly fine indoor plant. Yet it is a most exotic-looking plant that would suggest a delicate constitution, with olive green principal colouring, interesting red veins and for good measure pale blotches on the leaves. Room conditions where it can enjoy reasonable warmth will suit it well. Feed it occasionally and pot on into a very peaty mixture (one of the soilless preparations, for example) in the spring of every second, or even every third year.

Equally easy and long-suffering is *M. leuconeura kerchoveana*. This plant has two common names: rabbits' tracks, because the dark blotches on the pale green leaf background are said to resemble rabbits' paw-marks; and prayer plant, because the leaves fold together like hands in prayer as darkness des-

cends. *M. l. kerchoveana* is one of the most tolerant of houseplants, though it does appreciate a humid atmosphere; so plunging its pot in damp peat will be beneficial.

M. leuconeura massangeana, like the previous two plants, is a variety of *M. leuconeura* – itself not very interesting and seldom offered for sale. And, although *M. l. massangeana* is offered from time to time, it is really only the expert who should try to grow it indoors or in the conservatory. It is a squat plant, with a shorter distance between the leaf joints than the other two varieties, and the main attraction is the very fine herringbone pattern of veins on the leaves. Its essential needs are humidity, warmth and careful watering.

Stromanthe amabilis, another relative of the *Calatheas* and *Marantas*, is also a

Maranta leuconeura kerchoveana

Maranta leuconeura erythrophylla

Stromanthe amabilis

squat plant, having leaves of a metallic colour with interesting markings. *S. sanguinea* has larger lance-shaped leaves. The undersides are a deep maroon colour. Both *Stromanthes* need the same growing conditions as the *Marantas*.

Sonerila

When you know all there is to know about indoor plants and you are seeking a challenge to demonstrate your prowess, then is the time to attempt *Sonerila margaritacea*. This must rank as one of the most difficult of them all. Its leaves are oval in shape and the plant overall has a beautiful silvery appearance. It seldom grows to more than one foot in height. Keep it warm, maintain a humid atmosphere and water carefully; good luck!

Ivies and other leafy climbers

The exotic and colourful plants that are difficult to grow have their important part to play in a collection of indoor plants. But so do the more mundane ivies, vines and similar plants, which are easier to care for, easier to handle, and faster growing. Vast numbers of them are bought each year, and they undoubtedly appeal to the person who wants plants that will not present too many problems.

In fact, four of them – *Cissus antarctica* (the kangaroo vine), *Hedera canariensis* (Canary Islands ivy), *Philodendron scandens* (sweetheart vine) and *Rhoicissus rhomboidea* (Natal vine or grape ivy) – are probably never out of the top twenty most popular houseplants the world over. None of them have flowers, none have colourful foliage, and none have intricate leaf patterns or shapes, although their glossy foliage is attractive. Their inborn toughness must have a lot to do with their popularity.

The majority of the plants described here will climb or trail, according to need, but it is more usual to see the larger-leaved types, in particular, climbing walls, trellises and suchlike. When tying in these climbing plants it is important to ensure that the string is not too tight, as this will almost certainly lead to sweating and eventual damage.

Cissus; Rhoicissus

Cissus antarctica (kangaroo vine) has glossy green leaves, oval in shape and serrated along their edge. A natural climber that will attach itself to the support provided by means of tendrils, it does best in cool conditions in the region of 13°C (55°F). In very hot rooms the leaves seem to dehydrate as they shrivel up and die. Once established in a ten-inch pot and fed regularly, the kangaroo vine seems to fare very much better than when confined to a smaller pot.

Whatever else may be said of *C. striata*, there can be no complaints about its rate of growth. The individual leaves are the smallest of the *Cissus*, but this is no drawback as they are produced in great profusion. Due to its untidy habit and its prodigious rate of growth, not many are offered for sale by commercial growers. Cool conditions will suit them; in milder areas they will survive out of doors.

A plant for the ambitious, *C. discolor* should not be confused with the other members of its genus, as it is a very much more difficult plant to care for, even in the most agreeable greenhouse conditions. It is sometimes seen in hanging baskets, but is a natural climber and has the most colourful leaves imaginable: green, white, crimson, purple – to name but a few of the colours. Also, the undersides of the leaves are rich crimson. In the words of a Victorian writer, 'It is perhaps the most exquisitely coloured variegated plant . . . in cultivation.' A minimum temperature of not less than 19°C (66°F) should be the aim, with moist surroundings that are shaded but not too dark. It also needs an open, free-draining potting mixture.

Rather similar in appearance to *C. antarctica* and one of the toughest of all foliage pot plants is *Rhoicissus rhomboidea* (Natal vine or grape ivy). It is the

Rhoicissus rhomboidea

ideal plant for almost any indoor location: hot or cool, moist or dry, it seems to matter little. The three-sectioned glossy leaves – somewhat smaller than the kangaroo vine's – should be cleaned at times. The form 'Jubilee' has slightly larger and much darker leaves, while 'Ellen Danica' has maple-like leaves.

Cissus antarctica

Dioscorea

Dioscorea discolor (variegated yam) grows from a tuber, and produces paper-thin leaves as it climbs any available support. The attractively mottled leaves may grow to some eight inches in length, but this would happen only in ideal conditions. The plant sheds its leaves in winter, when the tuber should be kept warm and dry. It is essential that the tuber should be started into growth in spring in a very warm propagating bed, as it is very reluctant to get under way in less agreeable conditions.

Gynura

A vigorous grower on a par with *Cissus striata* is the *Gynura* (sometimes called the velvet plant). Two species are occasionally available: *G. aurantiaca* and *G. sarmentosa*. The latter is the smaller and more agreeable of the two. Both have wine-red leaves that are covered in purple hairs. They are very eye-catching when the light strikes them at the right angle – hence the common name. Both

Gynura sarmentosa

are vigorous growers and need no special attention; one major drawback is that their flowers smell abominably and must be removed as they appear. The plants should be trained to a framework to keep them reasonably tidy.

Hedera

The *Hederas* are the true ivies, and you can have them green or variegated, with pointed or cristate leaves, slow or fast growing – there seems no limit to the range available. Most have the common name of English ivy (*Hedera helix*), and do well in cool positions that are reasonably well lit and not too damp – a nice fresh, airy atmosphere, in fact. Having outstayed their welcome indoors they may be planted in the garden to provide ground cover under shrubs, or against a wall that they may climb.

Against a wall, one of the most attractive is *H. helix* 'Jubilee' (also known as 'Golden Heart'), which surprisingly does not do so well or look nearly so pretty as a pot plant. Another tough one for outdoor window boxes is the grey and green variegated variety 'Glacier'. 'Heisse' is very similar but a little less tough. The green forms are also surprisingly popular, and the best of these varieties are 'Chicago', 'Pittsburgh' and 'Shamrock'.

Hedera canariensis variegata; H. 'Heisse'

Philodendron scandens

Senecio macroglossus variegatus

Slower growing and a little more difficult to care for are the reasonably new cultivar 'Goldchild', the exquisite small-leaved 'Adam' and (with naturally arching stems) 'Little Diamond'. The last two have grey and white variegations.

Perhaps even more popular as a houseplant is *H. canariensis*, the Canary Islands ivy, which has larger leaves than English ivy. They are all-green in the basic species, but the much more popular *H. canariensis variegata* has an attractive green, silver-grey and white colouring. 'Maculata' has more speckled variegations and is less hardy, while 'Gold Leaf' has very large, dark green leaves with pale yellow centres.

All of these thrive in cool conditions, as recommended for *Cissus antarctica* (see above). As with all *Hederas*, however, new growth will have to be tied in as there are no convenient tendrils. The plants will, nevertheless, attach them-

selves to walls and pillars by means of the adventitious roots that develop along the stem just below the leaves. Growing against a damp wall in the conservatory they can be most impressive. In very dry and hot conditions browning of leaf edges presents problems. This is mainly due to minute red spider mites on the reverse of the leaves (see page 232). A regular drenching spray with a suitable insecticide on the underside of the leaves will deter, if not eradicate them completely. *H. canariensis* is also an impressive outdoor wall plant and is perfectly hardy in areas with a moderate climate.

When potting on, all the ivies will do well in Potting Mixture no. 3 with a little extra peat added; cuttings will also root readily into the same medium.

Philodendron

With its heart-shaped leaves and tough constitution, *Philodendron scandens*

(sweetheart vine) is one of the most popular of all houseplants. It likes moderately warm conditions – about 16°C (61°F) – and a fair amount of moisture, though it does not mind dry air so much as other *Philodendrons* (see page 41). It climbs vigorously, though cutting back weak growth will make it bush out. Clean the mid-green leaves from time to time. *P. oxycardium* is very similar.

Piper

Also with heart-shaped leaves – but this time bronze-green with pink mottling – *Piper ornatum* (ornamental pepper) is, however, much more demanding. Although easier to manage than *Cissus discolor* (see above), it should have the same growing conditions. So should its relative *P. nigrum*, which is not particularly attractive, but is interesting because of the freely produced clusters of green berries. These turn red and then black; dried, they are in fact peppercorns.

Senecio

With leaves similar to the small *Hederas*, *Senecio macroglossus variegatus* (Cape ivy) is a pleasant, free-growing plant. It will attain a height of some four feet when grown in a pot before it becomes ragged and loses its appearance. The leaves have a waxy feel to them that in fact makes it easily distinguishable from the true ivies. The small, daisy-like flowers with yellow centres are attractive but not plentiful. The green leaves of *S. mikanioides* (German ivy) provide an excellent contrast, and this plant is equally easy to care for. Cuttings root readily, so older plants that have become untidy are easily replaced. Greenfly can be a bothersome pest, however (see page 232).

left The leaves of some popular varieties of ivy: **1** *Hedera* 'Chicago'; **2** *H.* 'Chicago Variegata'; **3** *H.* 'Adam'; **4** *H.* 'Green Ripple'; **5** *H.* 'Mini Green'; **6** *H.* 'Eva'; **7** *H.* 'Little Diamond'; **8** *H. canariensis variegata*.

51

Trailing foliage plants

For putting the finishing touches to displays of houseplants, for edging the plant table indoors or in the conservatory, for running an attractive tumbling river of greenery along a window ledge, for creating an eye-catching eye-level display in a hanging basket: this is where small foliage plants with a naturally trailing habit come into their own, and there are a great many suitable kinds. The humble *Tradescantia* (wandering Jew or wandering sailor) is frequently dismissed as too common, but it can be an excellent plant when well grown. There are also many others, however, ranging from *Soleirolia* with its minute green leaves to *Scindapsus aureus*, which can on occasion be encouraged to climb to a height of six feet.

Since the greatest space available in any room or conservatory is above your head, why not make maximum use of it by introducing trailing plants in hanging baskets and other attractive containers (see page 128)? They will do nothing but enhance the surroundings. But remember that developing an attractive hanging basketful of plants is a slow process. It is important that all the growing tips of young plants should be periodically nipped out to promote a more shapely and fuller display. Then your basket will not have that thin, bedraggled look that is so unsightly.

Ceropegia

For small pots suspended at about eye level, *Ceropegia woodii* (hearts entangled) can be a lot of fun. Its leaves are rather sparse and are carried on wiry stems that either dangle over the edge of the pot or creep over the surface of the potting mixture. The real attraction is in their heart shape and fleshy, puffed-up appearance; their colouring is a speckled grey-green. Reasonable warmth and a little shade are needed, with watering that is not too heavy-handed.

Ficus

The soft-green matted leaves of *Ficus pumila* (creeping fig) can be particularly pleasing to the eye when seen nestling down amid a galaxy of colour from other exotic plants, and this is the sort of plant that does much by way of contrast in a display. Very different from most other houseplant *Ficus* (see page 36), it has small one-inch leaves. It is a plant that can be put to many uses, but is at its best when rambling over a moist pebble surface, rooting at every joint.

Equally adaptable, but a little more difficult to care for, is *F. radicans variegata*, which has wiry stems and beautiful white and green variegated leaves. This can be encouraged to grow in a hanging basket, but is usually better when its pot is placed on a moist pebble or peat surface. Excessive drying out of the root system of either of these *Ficus* will almost inevitably result in the leaves shrivelling and dying off.

Soleirolia

Soleirolia soleirolii (known as mind-your-own-business in Britain, but as baby's tears in America) is a pretty little green plant with minute leaves. The English common name is derived from the fact that the inquisitive finger that prods at the plant leaves a tell-tale hole for all to see. To grow it, just put a few pieces in a pot in the warm, water them and they will make lovely mounds of soft greenery for the window sill.

Pellionia

For damp, warm conditions *Pellionia daveauana* and the more compact and better form *P. pulchra* are fine in-filling plants and, with careful attention to watering, they can be encouraged to make interesting and colourful hanging basket subjects. Both are natural creepers that become untidy in time, but, since the plants root as they make their way over damp peat or similar material, they are not difficult to cut into sections and pot separately, thus renewing your stock. The better type is mainly green and silver-grey in colour, with rounded one-inch leaves, but in some circumstances it will produce an extraordinary range of colouring on the same plant. Alas, the cuttings taken from these more exciting pieces seldom retain their interesting colours as they grow.

Pilea

Another plant with at least two interesting common names is *Pilea microphylla* (also called *P. muscosa*, but commonly known as the gunpowder plant or artillery plant). It has fleshy stems, moss-green, fern-like leaves and inconspicuous flowers. The interest mainly lies in the flowers. When the pollen is dry, these seem to explode and scatter clouds of pollen in all directions. Surprisingly, however, it has not become very popular as a houseplant.

Another of the creeping pileas that you may come across is *P. nummularifolia* (known in the US as creeping Charly), which is also useful for growing in hanging baskets. It has yellowish-green rounded leaves about $\frac{3}{4}$ inch across. Both plants do well in moderate conditions, needing little special treatment.

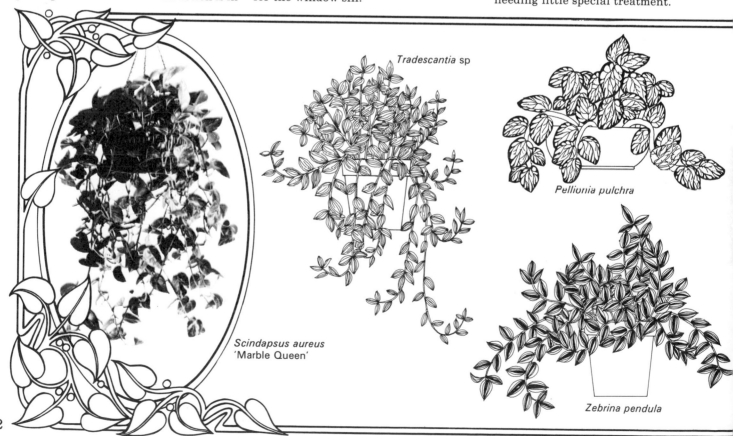

Scindapsus aureus 'Marble Queen'

Tradescantia sp

Pellionia pulchra

Zebrina pendula

Scindapsus

Shade and warmth – not less than 20°C (68°F) – are the essential requirements for *Scindapsus aureus*, a plant that is known in the US as the pothos, but is also called the ivy arum. The last name is apt, since it is a member of the arum family (the aroids), and it can climb quite sturdily to six feet. It is normally seen as a much more modest plant, however, and is best as a natural trailer. The leaves are roughly heart-shaped, about three inches long and green in colour with mustard-yellow markings. There is also a form called 'Marble Queen' that has white and green variegations. This is much sought-after but is not an easy plant to care for. Both must have a peaty potting mixture and moist surroundings, with humidity and shade.

Tradescantias and similar

This is by far the largest group described here because, apart from the true *Tradescantias* – named after John Tradescant, once Charles I of England's royal gardener – there are many related plants in cultivation. In addition, a number of quite unrelated ones look or grow in a very similar way, and need much the same conditions. *Tradescantias* are, of course, known as wandering Jews or wandering sailors, but the same names are often applied indiscriminately to other members of the group. *Tradescantias* are also called spiderworts.

None of these plants are very difficult to grow, and all will need reasonable light, a temperature in the region of 13°C (55°F) and moist rather than saturated conditions. Feed them regularly when established, and when propagating be sure to put several cuttings in each potful of Mixture no. 2. The same mix will suit them all for all purposes.

The original wandering Jew is *Tradescantia fluminensis*, with its fine silver variegations, but there are very many other types, including a 'Golden' variety. Even among the silvers there are superior plants such as *T.* 'Quicksilver'. There are also plants that have predominantly gold, pink and brownish-purple colouring, as in *T.* 'Purpurea' (also called *Zebrina purpusii*).

The main problem with growing any of these is keeping the plants looking attractive and full. So many appear leggy and unkempt simply because of the old belief that if neglected they will better retain their variegated colouring. This is nonsense. Give them a good, light position and feed and pot them well, and they will be much more rewarding. What about the green leaves that may appear? The answer is that these should be removed as soon as they are seen so that only the more attractive foliage is allowed to grow.

Among the close relatives of the *Tradescantias*, *Zebrina pendula* has the slightly broader leaves of *T.* 'Purpurea', and also has a short leaf stalk attaching the leaf to the stem, whereas the true *Tradescantias* have none. This plant is a perfect example of 'cheap and cheerful', and it really does make an excellent indoor plant in all sorts of locations. The reverse side of the leaf is purple and the colour of the leaf surface may vary considerably depending on the growing conditions. Leaves of really healthy plants have a lovely silver sheen.

Also part of the same family, *Commelina benghalensis* has fleshy leaves that are a pale grey-green in colour and are striped and edged with white, while *Cyanotis somaliensis* is a small creeper with soft, hairy foliage – which is why it is sometimes called 'pussy ears'. The leaves are bright green with small purple markings. *Callisia elegans* (*Setcreasea striata*), on the other hand, has olive-green leaves that are attractively striped, and is compact and of neat appearance. The undersides of the leaves are purple, and it has insignificant white flowers.

A grass that is often mistaken for a *Tradescantia* is *Oplismenus hirtellus variegatus* (also called *Panicum variegatum*). This can be very invasive, so only a little should be used as it will quickly fill its allotted area. The thin, narrow leaves are attractively marked in white with a trace of pink. The catmint, *Glechoma hederacea variegata* (also known as *Nepeta* or ground ivy) has an unpleasant odour when handled, but is otherwise a useful plant that will ramble about under the tabling in the conservatory, trail over the edge, or make a fine hanging basket. Untidy growth can be chopped back.

Other ramblers

Two useful cream and green variegated *Peperomias* are *P. glabella* and *P. scandens*, both of which will do well in reasonable light allied to even temperatures in the region of 18°C (61°F). Both have the fleshy leaves typical of *Peperomias* (see page 54). Another plant that may be persuaded to climb, but is much happier and more attractive when given a little freedom, is *Rubus reflexus pictus*. To some eyes it is an attractive indoor plant, with its bright green lobed leaves blotched in maroon. But it is on the whole rather coarse and needs frequent cutting back to keep it under control.

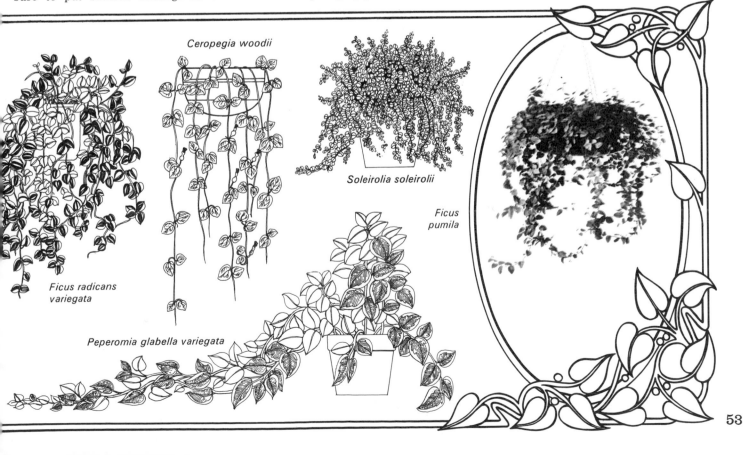

Ceropegia woodii

Soleirolia soleirolii

Ficus pumila

Ficus radicans variegata

Peperomia glabella variegata

The smaller-leaved plants

Even the most disinterested indoor gardener usually has a few plants on a window sill, and this is where the compact plants described on these two pages come into their own. They are the sort of subjects that fit happily into most locations with need for little more than an attractive pot cover or holder to make them complete. Also, many of these are very useful for arranging in small groups.

Even in the most agreeable conditions, these plants will remain neat and compact over a long period with need for little more than general attention in the way of watering and feeding. Potting on should be needed no more than once every second year. For almost all of them a potting mixture comprised of two parts Mixture no. 3 plus one part sphagnum peat will be suitable.

Plants with grassy foliage

A number of popular houseplants have narrow, grass-like leaves that are excellent for giving plant collections with more conventional rounded leaf shapes a more interesting appearance. *Acorus gramineus variegatus*, for example, has stiff, erect green and off-white leaves that sprout from rhizomes. It prefers to be very wet, and will happily stand in water. It is, in fact, hardy outdoors in many areas. A little taller-growing, with similar leaves that are of more delicate appearance, *Carex morrowii variegata* does equally well indoors, but should not be kept quite so wet.

Much more popular is *Chlorophytum comosum* (the spider plant) with broader grassy leaves that arch gracefully and are variegated cream and green. Mature plants produce young, perfectly formed plantlets on the ends of long stalks. These improve the appearance of the plant, and are a ready-made source of propagating material. This one is an exception to the rule given above; it should be potted on annually into Potting Mixture no. 3 without the extra peat. Keep it moist and in good light.

The umbrella plant (*Cyperus alternifolius*) is by far the largest overall of the plants described here. It is, however, one of the easiest of pot plants to grow, and yet seems to be much neglected by commercial growers of indoor plants. From green clusters of narrow, pointed leaves, 'umbrellas' sprout to a height of

Cyperus alternifolius

Chlorophytum comosum

little more than two feet when the roots are confined to pots.

Warm, shaded, very moist conditions are essential, and annual potting on into Potting Mixture no. 3 is advised. These are ideal plants for bordering indoor water garden features (see page 177). Propagation is simply a matter of dividing the matted roots into sections.

For actually standing in the water of more extensive water gardens, the papyrus, *C. papyrus* – similar in shape with stems seven feet in height – is an ideal subject requiring similar conditions.

Another interesting plant is *Scirpus cernuus*. It resembles a miniature bulrush and has glossy green, rounded stems that hang over the pot rather than remaining more conventionally erect. If kept moist in light shade it is little bother.

Peperomias

There exist hundreds of kinds of *Peperomias*, many of them with thick, fleshy leaves, but not all make desirable houseplants and only a few are commonly available from commercial growers. All of them will do well in good light but with some protection from direct sunlight. Persistent watering that does not allow the roots to dry out a little between each application will be harmful.

The dark green and heart-shaped leaves of *Peperomia caperata* are a perfect foil for more colourful plants. Its leaves are deeply ridged, so adding to the attraction, and the plant remains compact. When it becomes old and untidy, new plants can be raised by rooting individual leaves in a peaty mixture in warm conditions. There exists a much more scarce variegated form that is also more difficult to increase, as cuttings with short pieces of stem attached are essential. Simple leaf cuttings of the variegated type root with reasonable satisfaction, but all new growth is green rather than variegated, so it is

Peperomia magnoliaefolia

pointless to propagate them in this way.

With metallic grey colouring, *P. hederaefolia* grows in the same compact fashion and is, if anything, less difficult to care for. An added attraction here are the greenish catkin-like flowers that appear when the plant is quite small.

Surely the most popular of the *Peperomias* is *P. magnoliaefolia*, with altogether larger and more fleshy leaves that in good light are a bright cream and green colouring. In poor light the leaves take on a tired appearance and lose much of their bright colour, however. It is sometimes an advantage to pot this plant into one of the soilless mixes. Cuttings are taken using a piece of stem with two or three top leaves attached, or a piece of stem with a single mature leaf.

Even more attractive to many eyes than any of the above is *P. sandersii* (also known as *P. argyreia*, but given the common names watermelon peperomia and rugby-football plant). Its smooth, dark green leaves have silver bands. They grow up to four inches long and are heart-shaped. Of similar shape but coloured bluish-green with dark veining are the leaves of *P. marmorata*.

In complete contrast are the small *P.* 'Princess Astrid', with profuse dainty waxy-green leaves; *P.* 'Aztec Gold', with pale green ridged leaves suffused with gold; and *P. obtusifolia* in its various forms, which have large, fleshy, reddish-

tinged leaves that are near spatulate in shape. The latter is a larger and more robust plant than any of those previously mentioned. Finally, and of quite different habit, there is *P. scandens*, a trailer described on page 53.

Pileas

Almost as profuse as the *Peperomias* in the number of species available as houseplants are the *Pileas*, which are members of the nettle family. To make a good job of growing *Pileas* it is important not to leave the same tired old plants in the same pots year after year. Grow fresh ones from easily rooted cuttings – several to a pot is best – and throw away the parents. All *Pileas* should be well fed when they are actively growing, and potted on into Potting Mixture no. 3 as needed. (For descriptions of trailing kinds not covered here, see page 52.)

Best known of the group is probably *Pilea cadierei* (aluminium plant), which has fleshy stalks and leaves that are attractively coloured in shades of silver and green. It will grow quite rapidly and become untidy in favourable conditions, so it is important to remove the growing tips regularly and to cut it back occasionally. For indoor decoration the variety *P. cadierei nana*, with identical colouring but more compact, has largely superseded the original form.

Pilea 'Bronze' (also dubbed 'New Silver' and silver-leaf *Pilea*) is, on the whole, not a particularly attractive plant, and does not stand up well to room conditions, but it is interesting in showing another variation in *Pileas*. The quilted leaves are dull bronze-green in colour, with a lighter silver centre that is attractive in healthy plants growing in a moist, warm, lightly shaded environment. Not dissimilar in colouring, but without the silver, *P. involucrata* (also known as *P. spruceana*) has smaller oval leaves that invariably have tiny bluish-pink flower clusters in their axils. The last, if several cuttings are rooted in the pot, will also develop into a much more compact and attractive plant.

P. mollis (also known as *P.* 'Moon Valley') is a fairly recent introduction. Its leaves are similar in shape to those of a nettle, are wrinkled all over, and in mature plants may reach a size of some four inches by three. The colouring is a

Pilea cadierei

Pilea mollis

pleasing dull gold on emerald green and looks especially fine in a group of mature plants – perhaps five in a ten-inch dish.

Tolmeia

The final plant in this selection recommended for the window sill is *Tolmeia menziesii*, commonly known as the pick-a-back plant. The latter name comes from the way the leaves produce young plants at their base, and seem to carry them. When large enough, these plantlets can be removed and propagated. The leaves are a fresh green colour. They are covered in down, and are lobed and toothed. The plant is hardy outdoors, but forms a compact houseplant – not beautiful but certainly interesting.

Peperomia caperata

Peperomia hederaefolia

Peperomia sandersii

The graceful ferns

Most ferns are decorative and undemanding. They are grown for the grace and beauty of their fronds, which more than compensates for the lack of flowers. There is a very wide range, from the stately, slender blade of the hart's-tongue (*Scolopendrium vulgare*) to the fragile, lacy beauty of the maidenhair (*Adiantum capillus-veneris*). Yet when compared with the rich, exotic appearance of many other kinds of houseplants, almost all ferns create an air of relaxation and delicacy.

Many ferns can be grown indoors or in a conservatory. Since their natural home is in shady places, they should be kept away from too much sun, and can be positioned almost anywhere in the room except on a sunny window sill. They look at their best when a number of ferns are grouped together in individual pots or planted in one container.

In a garden room or shaded conservatory, the whole staging can be devoted to groups of varied types of ferns, making a delightful feature. If the plants' pots are plunged in peat, so that only the foliage shows, a pool can be introduced, with miniature aquatics (as for a miniature garden; see page 194), adding to the attraction and increasing humidity. The front of the staging can be clothed with *Selaginella krausiana* and its golden form, *S. krausiana aurea* – both charming, fern-like trailing plants that will intermingle happily.

Cultivating ferns

Ferns should be watered regularly, but should never be allowed to become waterlogged, as this may cause rotting of the roots. Humidity is essential for their wellbeing, and you can provide this in a heated room by plunging each pot in a larger container of damp peat, or by standing it on a saucer of pebbles or gravel that is kept constantly wet. For a group of ferns, you can use a gravel tray or a trough. All the ferns recommended here will grow well in a minimum temperature of 10 to 13°C (50 to 55°F), although some can, in fact, stand even colder conditions. No fern can survive for long in hot, dry air.

Potting on can usually be carried out once a year, preferably at the beginning of the growing season (see page 218), but if the roots are not completely filling the pot just remove the surface layer of soil and add a top-dressing of fresh potting mixture. A good general mixture can be made up of one part good loam, two parts leaf-mould or peat and one part coarse sand, with some small pieces of charcoal added. If you want to use a ready-made potting mixture, choose a peat-based type with added coarse sand or mix equal parts of Potting Mix no. 2 and peat.

Moss will sometimes grow on the surface of the ferns' pots. This is decorative and gives the impression of dampness below, but it may be misleading and is best removed. You should then prick over the surface to allow air in, and add more potting mixture if necessary. If the fronds of your ferns develop a poor colour, this may be an indication that they are getting too much light. But if the ferns are in shade, then the cause may be lack

The tree fern **above** – graceful but sturdy – contrasts with the small species **above right** – an *Adiantum* flanked by two *Pteris*.

of nutrient, and a little bonemeal can be used to improve the health of the plants.

Propagation of ferns

The simplest way to increase your fern collection is by dividing thick clumps or cultivating offsets (see page 228). Some ferns send out rhizomes which root and grow new plants. Others produce little bulbils on the fronds, and these grow into young plants with roots; they can then be detached and planted elsewhere.

Growing ferns from spores is not difficult, and may be the only way to acquire the more unusual kinds. You can also collect spores from your own plants. They are generally formed on the under-surface of the fronds, though there are a few, such as the hard fern (*Blechnum spicant*) and the parsley fern (*Cryptogramma crispa*) that have separate spore-bearing fertile fronds. When ripened, the spores can be gently shaken off into a paper bag and put aside to dry. They should then be sown in moist (but not saturated) sterilized potting mixture in a sterile container. Spread the spores very sparsely, cover the container with glass and put it in a shady position.

The larger ferns

One of the ferns that, as mentioned above, develop bulbils on the fronds, from which new plants can grow, is *Asplenium bulbiferum*, known in the US as the mother spleenwort. It has much divided fronds 12 to 18 inches long that taper to a point, and makes an interesting and unusual houseplant. Its relative *A. nidus* (the bird's-nest fern) is better known and quite different. The fronds are lance-shaped, completely untoothed and bright green in colour. It grows up to three feet.

The pinnae (the individual small leaves making up the fronds) of *Cyrtomium falcatum* are a dark, glossy green, and are shaped rather like holly leaves, though without the spines – hence the common name holly fern. The fronds grow one to two feet long. One of the best indoor ferns for growing in pots or hanging baskets is *Nephrolepis exaltata* in

its various forms. It is often known as the sword fern because of the long, tapering fronds, which may grow up to three feet long. The variety 'Bostoniensis', commonly known as the Boston fern, is one of the most popular, with its feathery leaves. In the variety 'Whitmannii' the fronds are bipinnate – that is, small, feathery fronds branch out on either side of each stem.

Platycerium bifurcatum (sometimes called *P. alcicorne*, and commonly known as the staghorn fern) is epiphytic, and looks at its best when growing attached to a piece of wood or cork, with peat and sphagnum moss around the roots, and hung from a pillar or wall in a conservatory. It also thrives in baskets or shallow pans, however. The main fronds are two to three feet long, broad and ribbon-like for half their length but then dividing sharply so that they look like antlers. Other, smaller fronds are also formed, which cling to the supporting bark.

The soft shield fern, *Polystichum setiferum divisilobum*, is exceptionally handsome. It has dense, plume-like fronds that are much divided and taper to a point. They may grow up to three feet long. The hart's-tongue fern, known botanically as *Scolopendrium vulgare* or *Phyllitis scolopendrium*, is a stately plant

Asplenium nidus

Nephrolepis exaltata 'Whitmannii'

Asparagus plumosus

Asparagus meyeri

with smooth, bright green blades up to 18 inches long. It is rather variable in shape, some forms having terminal crests and others undulating edges to the fronds.

Smaller kinds

All the ferns described above make substantial plants. Among the smaller types that do well in groupings, some of the most beautiful are the maidenhair ferns, *Adiantum capillus-veneris* and other species of *Adiantum*. With their fragile-looking fronds on slender stems forming sprays of characteristic small fan-shaped leaves, they are immediately appealing. Unfortunately, they are not very easy to keep indoors, and need a fairly light position with plenty of humidity. They do not like water sprayed directly on the fronds, however. Somewhat similar to the *Adiantums* is the button fern, *Pellaea rotundifolia*, whose small, dark green leaves are round rather than fan-shaped.

Platycerium bifurcatum

A good plant for a hanging basket is *Davallia bullata*, the squirrel's-foot or ball fern. This has finely divided fronds up to ten inches long. About the same size is *Polypodium vulgare* (the adder's fern), but its leaves are leathery and dark green, cut almost to the mid-rib. There are several very decorative forms, some crested and some with the pinnae divided at the tips.

One of the easiest and most widely grown small indoor ferns is *Pteris cretica*, the ribbon or brake fern. The leaves are long, narrow and ribbon-like, much divided at the ends and crested in some forms. There are also variegated forms. Slightly larger, but with narrower leaves, is *P. multifida*, the spider fern. Its stems rise vertically about nine inches and then branch out into pendulous, fan-shaped sprays, making it a very handsome plant.

Although several of the above – particularly the *Adiantums* and *Pellaea* – do well in fern cases, terrariums and larger bottle gardens, there are also several kinds of truly miniature ferns that are ideal for such closed cases. They grow only three or four inches tall, and thrive in the humidity of a closed glass case. They are described on page 59, with the article on wardian cases.

Other fern-like plants

It is quite common to find plants that look to the layman exactly like members of one group, but are classified quite differently by botanists. Such plants include the so-called asparagus ferns, which are not ferns at all but members of the lily family. Best known – and perhaps the most widely grown 'fern' of all – is *Asparagus plumosus*, commonly known as the lace fern, the feathery fern or simply the asparagus fern. It is often used by florists in making up buttonholes and other small flower arrangements, and is an easily grown houseplant. It has delicate, hair-like leaves and

sometimes produces small white flowers, followed by black berries.

Also widely used by florists is *A. medeoloides* (*A. asparagoides*), commonly known as smilax. It is a trailing plant with small, bright green leaves. *A. sprengeri* (emerald-feather) is naturally a climber, but it can be grown and trimmed to cascade over a bowl or basket. Its leaves are coarser than those of the other asparagus ferns. The least fern-like of all is *A. meyeri*, whose leaf-clad stems look rather like a lot of miniature cypress trees arching out from the centre.

Much closer to the ferns, botanically speaking, are the *Selaginellas*, pretty plants with bright green foliage. *Selaginella apus* forms small hummocks of greenery that will spill over the edge of the pot. As mentioned earlier, *S. krausiana* and the golden-leaved variety *S. krausiana aurea* have trailing stems, and are excellent for hanging baskets or the front of plant tables or staging. They like the same conditions as indoor ferns – damp, shade and moderate warmth.

57

Dwarf ferns and fern cases

Miniature ferns and the related *Selaginellas* are among the most exquisite plants to be found in nature: so graceful and delicate in form, so soothing to tired minds in their serene beauty and wonderfully varied tones of green. Unhappily, they originate in the main in sheltered, damp places and are difficult to grow out of their natural habitat.

The best solution, if you want to grow these delightful plants, is to use a closed glass case, a modern version of the wardian case so popular in Victorian times that is, in fact, a simple kind of terrarium (see page 30). Here, the miniature ferns will flourish in a humid atmosphere protected from draughts and sudden fluctuations of temperature. Indeed, with such a fern case it is possible to cultivate some of the most delicate of all ferns, such as the filmy ferns whose natural home is in the saturated atmosphere of a cave or near a waterfall. Such plants will shrivel in hours in the dry atmosphere of a normal room.

As well as wardian cases, ornamental bowls covered with glass domes were also very popular in Victorian times, and such domes can sometimes be found in antique shops. Wardian cases themselves largely went out of fashion in Britain in the last quarter of the nineteenth century, and few genuine examples remain. A simple modern alternative is not difficult to construct, however, as is shown. Alternatively, it is possible to adapt an aquarium tank or some other kind of glass case.

Planning the garden

If you use a glass dome, the bowl in which the plants grow should be of slightly larger diameter, so that the rim of the dome rests within that of the bowl, to conserve moisture. This is very important. If the dome rests outside the container, the moisture that condenses on the inside of the glass will not run back down to the soil. Again, if you use the kind of glass case shown the glass must rest just within the sides of the container.

With either of these kinds of fern case, or with one that has a door, both the planting and the subsequent care of the garden is much easier than with a narrow-necked bottle garden (see page 32). Such easy access means that some shade-loving flowering plants can be included. But it is very important to remove faded flowers, for if these are left a fungus called botrytis can develop on the decaying blooms. This is not only unsightly but if left unchecked may spread, with devastating results.

If you have no time to attend to this need, then it is best to limit the garden to non-flowering plants. Some suitable kinds are described on the next page. A few pieces of rock, carefully positioned, will show the plants to advantage. A small pool can be decorative, and also adds humidity to the atmosphere; it can be constructed as for a miniature trough garden (see page 194).

Filling and planting

The base of the container should be covered with drainage material that

includes 25 per cent small pieces of charcoal. Cover this with a layer of peat, and then add potting mixture; Mixture no. 2 is suitable. Water moderately and allow to settle. Next, position the rocks and, if you have one, the pool. Then introduce the first plants.

A modern fern case
A fern case is best made of glass – not plastic – as condensed moisture adheres to the latter and does not run freely. The simple design illustrated **left** has a narrow frame of metal or wood. The glazed roof should slope at an angle of about 60°, with the highest side at the front to give an unimpeded view of the plants. Also, the sloping roof encourages the condensed moisture to run down. With a flat-topped case, the condensation tends to gather on the under-surface and fall in large drops on to the plants – which is not good for them. If you cannot have a fern case constructed specially, you can use an aquarium tank with a sheet of glass on top. But it is then important to lift this occasionally and wipe the water droplets from the glass. This may reduce the humidity within the tank; if necessary syringe the plants from time to time.
below left A simple and decorative alternative to a specially made glass case is a bell-jar with a round bowl. A miniature rose can be planted as well as ferns.

If you are using a round bowl, place the taller plants towards the centre, but for a rectangular fern case they should be at the back, allowing room for them and their roots to grow. Then position the low-growing plants and add more potting mixture. The final level of this should be just below the top of the container so that moisture running down the glass does not spill over the sides.

The next essential is to balance the moisture content – that is, to ensure a proper cycle of humidity that will condense and run down to the roots. It is difficult to estimate the amount of moisture needed, but you should first moisten the potting mixture and syringe the plants lightly, and then place the cover in position. If after a few days there is a great deal of condensation on the glass, then the atmosphere is saturated, and the glass should be propped up to allow a little air in and some of the moisture to evaporate. Alternatively, if there is no water condensing on the glass, then the plants can be syringed again until a proper balance has been achieved. This is shown by the presence of just a slight film of moisture on the inside of the glass.

Once planted and balanced, fern cases and domes can be left indefinitely. The only attention necessary is to remove dead flowers if there are any, and perhaps to prune any foliage that has grown excessively. Act quickly if you see any sign of pests or diseases, but so long as none of these appear your glazed fern garden should be a source of great pleasure for many years.

Miniature ferns

There are many beautiful small ferns suitable for growing in a fern case or under a glass dome. They include most of the smaller of the kinds described on page 57, together with some truly miniature species that grow only a very few inches high.

Asplenium fontanum (the smooth rock spleenwort), for example, is a beautiful but rare little fern. Its lance-shaped fronds are about one inch across at the centre, and it grows three to four inches tall. *A. ruta-muraria* (the wall rue spleenwort) is somewhat like the maidenhair fern (*Adiantum capillus-veneris*; see page 57) in form, but the fronds are tough and leathery and a very dark green. It grows up to three inches high. *A. trichomanes* (the maidenhair spleenwort) is an engaging little evergreen. The stems are stiff and black; they have a tendency to remain after the older green pinnae (leaves) have fallen, and should be cut off. It is two to four inches high. Resembling the above, but more lacy, is *A. viride* (the green spleenwort). It is bright green, including the stems, and the pinnae are deeply notched. It reaches a height of two to six inches.

Blechnum penna-marina is a small edition of *B. spicant* (the hard fern; see page 56), with a creeping underground stem. It is one of the few ferns that have separate fertile fronds. These rise well above the barren fronds, unlike other ferns, which bear the spores on the under-surface of all fronds. It grows two to four inches high. *Ceterach officinarum* (the scaly spleenwort) has rather thick fronds, not deeply divided. The backs of these are covered with brown scales, hence its popular name of rusty-back. It grows three to four inches tall. *Woodsia alpina* is a rare little fern of unusual beauty, with narrow fronds. The pinnae are rather widely spaced, alternate and lobed. The plant reaches a height of up to six inches.

Other miniature plants

If you wish to grow plants other than ferns in a small glazed case, some of the most attractive suitable types are the following: *Acorus gramineus pusillus*, a minute rush two inches tall; *Hedera* 'Green Feather', a tiny, very slow-growing ivy with slender, pointed lobes; *H.* 'Très Coupé', which is even smaller and has leaves that are even more finely divided; *Selaginella apus*, which has a cluster of minute, fan-shaped fronds and is almost ethereal in its delicacy, forming a dense hummock of brilliant green about one inch high; and *S. emiliana*, which grows erect, six to ten inches high, and is much branched and fern-like in habit, and exquisite.

Ceterach officinarum

A fern column

A fern column can be an interesting and attractive feature for anyone who has patience and deft fingers. It can be constructed to suit one of the tall glass domes (which were used in the last century to cover waxed flowers or stuffed birds) in a slightly larger-diameter bowl. Make a tube of wire mesh to suit the size of the dome, allowing space for the ferns to grow. Secure it to the bowl, possibly with cement. Using a cardboard or stiff paper tube and a funnel, pour a little charcoal, mixed with peat-based potting mixture, into the base of the wire mesh column. Dampen this and plant the first fern through the mesh. Add more potting mixture and then plant the next fern at right angles and higher up. Syringe and firm down. Add more potting mixture and then the next fern, damping and firming at each stage, until the whole column is planted. Finally, fill the surround at the base of the column with peat and charcoal, and add more ferns or moss; syringe thoroughly and cover with the glass dome.

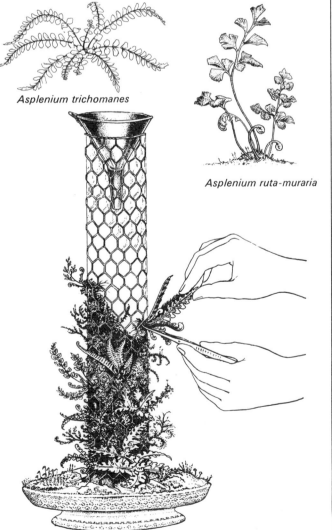

Asplenium trichomanes

Asplenium ruta-muraria

Dr Ward's experiments

Although Dr Nathaniel Ward was not the first person to use small glazed cases for growing plants, it was the publicity given to his experiments that popularized the idea. As a result, elaborate 'wardian' cases became fashionable items of furniture.

In a book of his published in 1842, Dr Ward tells how he tried to grow ferns in his garden in the area of the London Docks. As none of them survived, he came to the conclusion that they could not live in the smoky atmosphere, so he gave up in despair. Ward was also a keen entomologist, however, and one day early in 1830, wishing to observe the development of a hawk moth, he buried the chrysalis in some moist earth in a bottle, which he sealed with a lid. A few days later he noticed some vapour in the bottle which condensed and ran down the sides into the earth, thus keeping the amount of moisture constant.

Before the moth emerged, Ward was astonished to see that a seedling fern was growing in the bottle. Fascinated by the spontaneous growth of the fern, he left it undisturbed in the bottle, where it flourished for nearly four years without any water being added or the cover removed. From his observations he deduced that ferns need a humid atmosphere and protection from smoke and draughts. To prove his theory he constructed numerous fern cases – like miniature greenhouses – of varied shapes and sizes, and experimented with a wide range of ferns and other plants.

He was able to record remarkable successes. The most spectacular was his Killarney fern (*Trichomanes speciosum*). This is one of the filmy ferns that usually grow in caves, where the atmosphere is consistently moist. It is so delicate that its fronds are almost transparent, and shrivel in dry air. Ward relates his success with this very lovely but difficult plant, which was much admired by many people who visited him to see it.

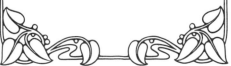

Flowers of the desert

Whether you love them or hate them, find them repulsive or fascinating, there is no doubt that cacti represent a striking example of nature's ability to adapt. Except in a few primitive kinds, the leaves of normal plants are reduced to spines and the stems thickened to provide an enormous water reservoir. Both help the plant to withstand desert drought, and some cacti also have protective layers of white hairs.

Not all cacti bear spines, but all have woolly or hairy tufts called areoles. Sometimes these are more like bristles, but in most varieties they have the appearance of felt. They are only found on true cacti, and similar-looking plants that do not have them are succulents (see page 68). Where cacti do have spines, these grow from the areoles, and some species also have tiny barbed glochids.

In spite of the extraordinary environment that has influenced their development, cacti make some of the best houseplants. They will tolerate terrible treatment for years and yet still produce flowers when they get going again. It is a complete myth that cacti flower only once in a hundred years; provided they are healthy, nearly half of all the species commonly grown will produce flowers by the end of their third year if you follow the simple rules explained opposite. Some of the taller candelabra-type cacti and the prickly pears will, however, take longer.

The only conditions that cacti really will not tolerate are damp cold. They need to be kept indoors or in a heated greenhouse during the winter in cold regions. During the summer, however, they can safely be put outdoors on a rockery or other sunny place.

Forest cacti

Quite different – both in appearance and needs – from the desert cacti described above are the epiphytic types that come from the forests of Brazil. In nature they live on tree branches. Best known are the Easter cactus (*Schlumbergera*), Christmas cactus (*Zygocactus*) and orchid cacti (*Epiphyllum* hybrids). They have no spines, and the 'leaves' are in fact succulent, flattened stems. Unlike desert cacti, they enjoy shady conditions and some water in winter; for more details, see page 67.

Parodia sanguiniflora

Cactus characteristics

Areoles occur on all cacti; they are small tufts – usually felt-like, but sometimes woolly or bristly. In many cacti, the flowers grow from the areoles. Most have spines growing from them – often a strong central spine and smaller radial ones. In prickly pear cacti, there are also small hooked hairs called glochids; these frequently stick into fingers. Some cacti are ribbed, or have tubercles. They vary widely in overall shape.

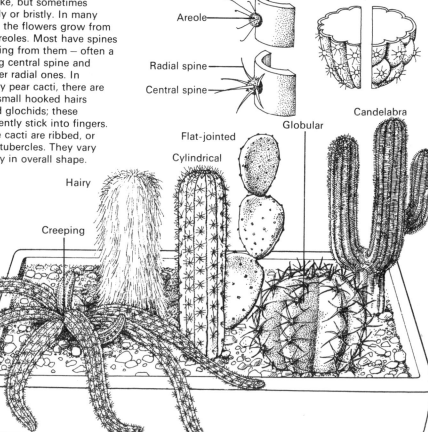

Epiphyllum 'Midnight'

Cultivating cacti

Indoors, grow your cacti on a window sill, where they can easily get their three main needs: sunshine, light and air. Ventilation is essential, as fresh air is the one thing really plentiful in the desert; so open the windows whenever possible. Temperature does not matter much in summer, but it is essential that desert cacti are rested in winter at a maximum temperature of 6°C (43°F), on a cool bedroom window sill, perhaps.

Equally essential if your cacti are to have any chance of flowering the next summer is a complete lack of water in autumn and winter. The exact period varies with climate, but in northern Europe best results come from giving no water at all from the third week in September until the third week in March. They will shrivel and look terrible, but this is how to ensure summer success.

Also important, however, is correct watering in summer. In the wild, cacti send their roots out over a wide area, but when grown in a pot these grow downwards. It is important therefore to water the plants thoroughly when the potting mixture is dry rather than to give them a little at a time. In this way, the water will reach the deep young roots, and also sour patches that might kill the plants are prevented from building up. The best way of watering cacti is to plunge the pots until the bubbles stop, and then allow them to drain.

Whatever potting mixture you use, it must be free-draining. Mix equal parts of sterilized garden soil, coarse silver sand and peat, adding ½ teaspoonful of powdered chalk or crushed egg-shells to each seven-inch pot.

Strange-shaped cacti

In some strains of cacti a genetic mutation occurs that gives them a grotesque appearance. They may grow in a wavy form (known as christate varieties) or develop a proliferation of branches (monstrose varieties). These cacti are not diseased. They are frequently grafted on to other cacti, and unusually-shaped specimens are highly valued. One of the most frequently seen types is *Cereus peruvianus monstrosus* (see page 63). A christate cactus is shown below.

A christate variety of *Mila* sp

A cactus garden above Planting a cactus bowl, try to think four years ahead; do not crowd the cacti. This prevents air circulation and also lets disease spread very easily. It is best to use a few large stones to fill in the gaps; they can be removed as the plants grow. Culture is just the same as for pot-grown plants, but very good drainage is essential.

Cacti from seed
With mixed packets, first separate the large seeds from the small. Sow in a moist mixture of two parts loam to one part peat and one part coarse sand. Mix the small seeds with a little fine sand and just sprinkle the mixture on top of the soil. Sow the larger ones separately, covering them with about ⅛ inch of fine sand. Put the tray or pan in a warm, light place, and cover with a sheet of glass. Keep moist, and water with weak copper sulphate to suppress algae. Remove the glass when the seedlings are clearly visible. When the seedlings are large enough to handle without damage, transplant into cactus potting mixture. Use a knitting needle as a dibber,

Grafting cacti
Cacti are sometimes grafted onto a different rootstock — particularly if they are naturally pendant, as with *Epiphyllums* and other epiphytic cacti, or if they do not develop strong roots of their own. The Hibotan varieties of *Gymnocalycium mihanovichii* **right** come into this category, as do most christate cacti. Grafting is not difficult to perform.

and plant them ½ inch apart. Grow on until they are touching. Then transplant into very small pots, and eventually into two-inch pots. In the early stages, do not rest the cacti in winter.

Cacti from cuttings
Take cactus cuttings in spring, using a sharp knife. With a clearly jointed cactus, take off a joint and slice off the lower part about a quarter the way up from the base. This gives a larger area for roots to develop. With globular cacti that make offsets, simply remove an offset. Lightly dust the cut with powdered charcoal and allow it to dry for three days. Then insert it in the soil used for cactus seed, but provide bottom heat.

Pests and diseases
Mealy bugs and scale insects are the commonest cactus pests; both can be controlled with malathion (see page 232). More serious are cactus diseases, generally caused by fungi. The main sign is a brown, often mushy, patch. Unfortunately, however, the fungus first attacks the watery tissues between the central core of the cactus and the skin, and then spreads outwards; the plant may be killed before you notice it. Good culture is the best preventive, since it is difficult for the fungus to attack a healthy plant; however, modern systemic fungicides such as Benlate can do a great deal to help. It is a good idea to water your cacti with this occasionally.

Tall-growing cacti

Cacti with true leaves

The most primitive of all cacti are the Pereskieae, and they hardly look like cacti at all. Two varieties are commonly offered for sale, and are both easily recognized by their perfectly ordinary leaves. *Pereskia grandifolia* has green leaves, and a flower and spiny stem like those of a dog rose. *P. aculeata rubescens* (*P. godseffiana*) has golden leaves with a faint reddish tinge. Both kinds require slightly more warmth in winter than most cacti, and will also need some shade from direct sunlight in summer to prevent scorching of the leaves. *P. aculeata* is often used as grafting stock for some of the epiphytic cacti (see page 67). The leaves of some varieties fall during the resting period, but this can be overcome by keeping them a little warmer. Unlike other cacti, they should not be allowed to dry out in winter.

Prickly pears

The Opuntieae, commonly known as prickly pears, is one of the best known cactus families, largely because of the small bristles at the base of the spines. These easily become detached and stick

Opuntia sp

to fingers and clothing. Known as glochids, they can cause considerable irritation. If you get a lot stuck to your fingers, the best remedy is to apply a thin layer of rubber solution glue and rub it off when dry – and the glochids with it. Soap and water will also do the trick, but more slowly.

Although the best known prickly pears are the flat-jointed ones, the family also includes cylindrical types. Within this broad division there are more than ten separate genera. The best known species of flat-jointed prickly pears is undoubtedly *Opuntia microdasys* (sometimes called bunny-ears cactus in the US) and its various varieties. *O. microdasys albispina* has white polka-dot-like areoles surrounding the spines and *O. microdasys rufida* has reddish ones. There is also a common hybrid between *O. microdasys* and *O. cantabrigensis* which has the latter's hardiness and the honey-coloured areoles farther apart than in the true species.

O. leucotricha has a very dark green skin, white spines and glochids with attractive long white bristles. *O. ficus-indica* also has a very dark skin but is notable for its lack of spines. Another kind that may be confused with *O. ficus-*

Opuntia microdasys rufida

indica is *O. monacantha*; this has only one large spine on each of the comparatively distant areoles, which are set on glossy green stems. Its variegated form, *O. monacantha variegata*, is one of the very few naturally occurring variegated cacti. The pads here are tinged with red, and the whole plant has a rather sickly appearance; as if to bear this out, considerable care is needed in its cultivation and it is very slow-growing. *O. tuna* is more frequently found in its monstrose form, *O. tuna monstrosa*. This is known as 'Maverick' in the US; it makes an attractive, relatively spineless, clumping plant with cylindrical ovate joints.

When confronted with a plant that appears to be a prickly pear, it may be best to disregard the first half of the name on the label and to try to find a second half that corresponds. This is because botanists have renamed many of the plants once called *Opuntia*. A good example of this is *Brasilopuntia brasiliensis*, which many growers still sell as *Opuntia brasiliensis*. This makes a dwarf plant with very thin joints; those farthest from the trunk are broadly oblong while those nearer the trunk are circular. The spines are few, and the plant branches freely, eventually producing attractive white flowers.

The cylindrical-jointed opuntias are sometimes scarcely recognizable as members of the family, and generally produce a few rudimentary leaves on the young growth which fall off with age. If in

Opuntia tuna monstrosa

doubt about a species you can always try touching the bristles to see if they detach easily on to your finger. If they do there is a very good chance of it being an opuntia, even if it doesn't look like a prickly pear. A good example of this is *Austrocylindropuntia cylindrica* (formerly known as *Opuntia cylindrica*). At first sight, this looks more like one of the candelabra-type cacti (see below). It is easily distinguished from the candelabra-types, however, by the ¼-inch-long leaves that appear at the top of the stems and fall off as the plant grows. *A. salmiana* is similar but with much thinner stems with a faintly purplish tinge. This is one of the most rewarding of all opuntias to grow as it flowers when comparatively young. The normal variety offered for sale has a yellowish flower that is red on the outside, but there is also an attractive white-flowered variety, *A. salmiana albiflora*. *A. subulata* is another commonly seen plant.

Brasilopuntia brasiliensis

It is popular with nurserymen since by cutting off the main stem an inch or so above the soil the plant may be induced to branch easily and prolifically – and the piece cut off can be propagated.

Of the *Cylindropuntias*, *C. tunicata* is sometimes offered for sale. This is a vicious plant with two-inch spines that have a white papery sheath that comes off when the spines are handled. Finally among the cylindrical cacti there is a somewhat rare species called *Pterocactus kuntzii* (sometimes sold as *P. tuberosus*). This is unusual because of its tuberous root, from which the numerous prostrate branches grow. It is difficult to grow in a pot and it is best to graft it.

Candelabra cacti

Of the three main cactus tribes, by far the largest is the Cereeae. The main difference between these and the other kinds – the Pereskieae and Opuntieae – is the more-or-less complete absence of rudimentary leaves or glochids. So big is the group, however, that it is divided up into seven sub-tribes, and the 'candelabra' cacti form one of these sub-tribes. The descriptions that follow, incidentally, refer to plants between two and five years old – which may differ

Austrocylindropuntia subulata

widely in appearance from a mature wild specimen. For example, *Carnegiea gigantea* when sold as a small pot-plant looks very different from the enormous plants seen in Arizona desert photographs. For this cactus is the giant saguaro, the state emblem of Arizona.

The botanical name of the candelabra cacti is Cereanae, which comes from the Greek word for torch. Generally speaking, even young specimens exhibit this upright cylindrical appearance with the exception of the saguaro mentioned above, which usually appears to be more spherical. The plants are some of the most easily raised cacti from seed and a certain amount of indiscriminate hybridization has occurred, particularly between *Cereus peruvianus* and *C. jamacaru*. *C. peruvianus* is the species most commonly seen in collections. It has blueish-green stems with four or five ribs that are deeply divided at the top of the plant but flatten out towards the base. *C. jamacaru* is frequently sold as *C. peruvianus*, but the true species differs in having numerous radial spines (*C. peruvianus* normally has only six) and in having more closely set areoles when young. As mentioned on page 61, there are several monstrose varieties of *C. peruvianus*, including *C. peruvianus monstrosus* (often labelled simply *C. monstrosus*) and *C. peruvianus monstrosus minor*.

All the candelabra cacti mentioned so far have somewhat sparse spines, but

Cereus peruvianus

another well known group within the Cereanae are the old man cacti. The true old man cactus is *Cephalocereus senilis*. This is very slow growing indeed, and is covered by long, white silky bristles which should be carefully washed in weak soapy water if they become matted. They should then be combed out and the excess soap rinsed off thoroughly. Very similar are *Cephalocereus palmeri* (*Pilosocereus palmeri*), *Espostoa lanata* and *Oreocereus celsianus*. *C. palmeri* differs from all of them in that the long white bristles hang along the edges of the ribs only, and do not cover the entire body. *E. lanata* has fairly fine hairs which seem to grow more in a spiral than the somewhat coarse hairs of *C. senilis*, which hang downwards. *E. lanata* also has a few spines on the younger growth at the top of the plant. *O. celsianus* is fairly heavily armed with spines, particularly on the younger growth.

Cephalocereus senilis

Cleistocactus straussii could easily be confused with the old man type of cactus, but although apparently just as white from a distance, on closer inspection the whiteness is clearly caused by spines rather than bristles. This is an attractive, comparatively fast-growing variety warmly recommended to the beginner. Species of *Lemaireocereus* are quite often seen, but apart from *L. marginatus*, which has closely set areoles with white felt down the ribs, they are mostly difficult to overwinter.

A very wide range of species and hybrids are sold under the name of *Trichocereus pasacana*, but they are generally quite squat when young, only growing taller when four to five years old. *Myrtillocactus geometrizans* is a very commonly seen species with handsome grey-green stems banded darker where the new growth appears. It branches freely even when quite young. If allowed to get too cold in winter, brownish scaly patches may develop on the stem, but these are not harmful and it is best to leave them on.

Climbing and crawling cacti

The species described previously are all basically self-supporting, but the Hylo-

Myrtillocactus geometrizans

cereanae are climbers or crawlers, and many of them will make aerial roots for clinging to supports if they are given the opportunity. The stems tend to be weak and bend easily. If grown in a pot, they usually need staking; otherwise you can grow them actually in the ground in a conservatory or greenhouse, and train them up against the wall. All these cacti have beautiful flowers, generally produced at night.

The species most often seen is the rat's-tail cactus, *Aporocactus flagelliformis*, which has long, thin, trailing stems that produce pink flowers. This species likes plenty of sun. It has a tendency to rot back and does better when grafted on to another climber, *Hylocereus undatus*. In fact *H. undatus* and the bristly *H. trigonus* are both more commonly used as grafting stock than sold as plants in their own right. The stems are distinctive on account of their dark green, chunky triangular shape. They branch freely. One of the most famous of this group of cacti is the 'queen of the night', *Selenicereus grandiflorus*. This is a nocturnal flowerer, and has enormous, heavily scented white flowers. It will flower more readily when planted up against a wall rather than when in a pot. If you are doubtful about the amount of heat available, however, you could try *S. pteranthus*, the 'princess of the night', which is reputedly hardier. *S. boeckmannii* produces its white, heavily scented flowers when quite young.

Selenicereus sp

63

The 'hedgehog' cacti

There are two large groups of cacti whose botanical name comes from the Greek word *echinos*, meaning *hedgehog*. Although most cacti could be compared to hedgehogs, these plants have a particularly rotund and prickly appearance. They are the *Echinocereanae* and the *Echinocactanae*. In the first group the flowers come from the side of the plant, while the *Echinocactanae* produce their flowers from the new growth at the top.

The Echinocereanae

These are among the easiest cacti to flower, and make an ideal starting point for the novice anxious to have some flowers even on quite young plants. The true *Echinocereus* are distinguished by their green stigmas (the central part of the flower to which the pollen grains adhere), and the one most commonly found for sale is *Echinocereus fitchii*. This is at first a solitary, upright plant not unlike a *Cereus* (see page 63), but it will branch from the base with age. The stems are fairly well covered by short, spreading spines. The most important feature is the flower, which is produced even on two-year-old plants from woolly areoles near the top of the stem. It is a magnificent pink colour and up to $3\frac{1}{2}$ inches in diameter. There is considerable variation in the plants sold under this name, as much cross-hybridization has been tried by nurserymen.

E. salm-dyckianus is another attractive member of the family; it is sometimes known as the strawberry cactus. This lacks the dense spine covering, and has orange flowers on older plants. *E. enneacanthus* is also quite often found in garden shops, and has spreading spines and notches on the ribs above the areoles; it should not be confused with *E. stramineus* (sometimes called *Cereus stramineus*), which has much longer central spines up to $3\frac{1}{2}$ inches in length, at first brown but becoming white with age. Generally *Echinocereus* prefer a slightly more open potting mix than most cacti, with extra fine sand.

Rebutias are among the best loved cacti, and it is so easy to get them to flower that they are indispensable to every collection. Because of their popularity, growers have extensively cross-hybridized the various kinds, and a detailed description of them all would be tedious and unnecessary here. They are almost all more or less globular in shape, and produce their flowers in a ring round the base of the plant. Colours range from white and pink, through lilac and violet, to red, orange and yellow. The first sign of flowering is the presence of red pimples amongst the basal spines, and no water should be given until these appear. When the buds are about $\frac{1}{10}$ inch long you can start watering and give the plant warmth.

Aylostera deminuta is very similar to the *Rebutias*, and produces a ring of fiery-orange flowers about half way up the stumpy stems, which form dense clusters at soil level. *Lobivia densispina* (*L. famatimensis*) is not as commonly seen as it should be. The name comes from the country of origin, Bolivia, and this species has been extensively hybri-

Rebutia sp

Echinocereus fitchii

Lobivia densispina

Setiechinopsis mirabilis

dized to produce flowers in every hue of red, pink and orange. They appear from woolly areoles on the plant's side.

Pseudolobivia kratochvilleana (also called *Echinopsis kratochvilleana*) and *P. aurea* (*Lobivia aurea*) are both near relatives to the *Lobivias*, but have much larger flowers on longer stems. The

former is white, occasionally tinged with pink, and the latter a magnificent golden-yellow. Finally there is *Setiechinopsis mirabilis*. This is a strange species, with brownish-purple stems. It seldom lives long in cultivation, but is easy to raise from seed. The nocturnal flowers are freely produced on quite young plants.

The Echinocactanae

This group also includes some very free-flowering species. Generally, water should be given before the buds are really conspicuous, as soon as the weather begins to get warmer, but *Parodia chrysacanthion* can get its first water before most other varieties at the beginning of spring. Although the yellow flowers of this plant are rather small, and are almost lost among the spines at the top of the plant, they are freely produced at a time when little else in the cactus collection is in flower.

P. sanguiniflora produces rather larger scarlet flowers in great profusion towards the middle of the summer. Each areole has a central hooked spine, and so do those of *P. gracilis*, which has the merit of producing its smallish orange flowers throughout the latter part of the summer, and *P. mutabilis*, with larger yellow or orange flowers produced somewhat earlier.

Most large cactus collections have a specimen of *Notocactus leninghaussii*, which has a fairly dense covering of silky golden spines. These more than make up for its reluctance to flower when young. (A plant less than nine inches high seldom if ever produces flowers.) It also has an infuriating habit of growing so fast that it bursts open down the sides, so try not to rush it with overwatering or feeding. The other *Notocactus* flower when a lot younger; among those with comparatively few spines are *N. submammulosus pampeanus*, which flowers easily, and *N. ottonis*,

Notocactus submammulosus pampeanus

Gymnocalycium quehlianum

Parodia mutabilis

which quickly starts to make clusters around the base. It is a good idea to remove some of these offsets and grow them on, as the large plants frequently rot back in cultivation. *N. tabularis*, *N. concinnus* and *N. apricus* all have a more dense covering of spines.

Notocactus do not make ideal plants for people who go out to work as they need bright sunlight to open the flowers and are really only at their best for a few hours either side of midday. The flowers, although mostly large, are not very freely produced and only last a day.

Many of the *Gymnocalyciums*, on the other hand, produce flowers right through the summer. The best of these is undoubtedly *Gymnocalycium damsii*, which has a pale green body with flattish

Astrophytum myriostigma

ribs, and produces attractive white flowers. *G. mihanovichii* has pale diagonal flecks on the ribs and a greenish flower, but the variety more commonly seen today is the so-called Hibotan variety *G. mihanovichii friedrichii rubrum*. In these plants, the plant bodies are bright scarlet (see the photograph on page 61). They are invariably grafted onto another cactus body, and are unlikely to flower. They need rather more warmth and water in winter than other cacti – about 10°C (50°F) – and need plenty of light if the natural green colour is not to return. *G. quehlianum* is another good variety with large white flowers with a red throat. *G. bruchii* (*G. lafaldense*) is also frequently offered for sale; it makes a fairly small plant with pink flowers.

Echinocactus grusonii, the golden barrel cactus or mother-in-law's armchair, is a spectacular plant once it is five or more years old. It then starts to produce flatter spines and acquires its characteristic globular shape. Although unlikely to flower, it is extremely resilient and will tolerate years of neglect.

Some of the most curious of all cacti are the bishop's-cap cacti, *Astrophytum myriostigma*, and *A. ornatum*. The former is almost completely spineless but the dark green bodies are heavily flecked with small white pimples in some varieties. It is not easy to flower in the home, but will do so with care. This is not so with *A. ornatum*, which will only flower when five years old or more. The true *A. ornatum* has the white flecking in diagonal stripes, but there are a large number of variants often known as 'Baguine's Hybrids' which were first raised during the nineteenth century and which flower more readily. The spines of these hybrids are not nearly so pronounced as those of the true *A. ornatum* species.

Ferocactus wislizenii is very commonly seen, as are one or two other species, such as *F. electracanthus*. *Ferocactus* all have extremely vicious spines and are a danger to horses in the wild since they tend to get lodged inside the hoof. The spines are produced on prominent bulges on the ribs, and are frequently attractively coloured when young, although when old they turn a drab straw-grey colour. These plants seldom flower in cultivation, but they

Hamatocactus setispinus

are relatively easy to raise from seed. Like *Echinocactus grusonii* they will tolerate a great deal of neglect.

Hamatocactus setispinus is a must for every cactus collection. Not only does it freely produce large yellow flowers with a red throat during the latter part of the summer, but when these are gone they leave large red berries on the plants. This is another variety which is easily raised from seed, especially if it is fresh, and the plant can be induced to flower within two years of sowing.

Some of the most fascinating shapes for cacti are found among the *Stenocactus*. These have deep wavy-edged ribs, looking as though a learner had driven a plough over them. The two best kinds to start with are *Stenocactus hastatus* and *S. zacatecasensis*. The former has yellow flowers, and the latter white flowers tinged with pink, produced freely on plants of four or more years of age. **65**

Mamillarias and forest cacti

The group of cacti known botanically as the Coryphanthanae form one of the most easily recognised cactus families. Its members differ from all others in having large protuberances called tubercles all around the stem rather than just on the ribs. Another distinguishing feature is the way the flowers appear from between the areoles, on the tubercles, whereas in other groups they appear from the areoles amongst the spines. The tubercles are especially prominent, and the name of the largest genus in the group, the *Mammillarias*, comes from the Latin word for *breast*.

The *Mammillarias* are not by any means the only cacti in the group, however, and a very good plant for the beginner is *Thelocactus bicolor*. Although very slow-growing and a shy flowerer, it has attractively coloured spines (which vary from yellow at the tip, through white to a red base) which have given it the name rainbow cactus. There is also a variety called *T. bicolor tricolor*, in which the red section is even more marked.

Although *Mammillarias* are among the easiest plants to grow, they are also particularly susceptible to fungal attacks, and it is a good idea to knock the plants out of their pots regularly during the growth period to inspect the roots. If they are white at the tips then everything should be all right, but if they are brown you should immediately suspect a fungus attack. In the latter case, it would be a sensible precaution to remove one or more of the offsets that are freely produced, and to root them, meanwhile drying out the parent plant carefully in a warm place. One other good idea is to start the plants into growth by watering them a little earlier than other cacti and to start their dormancy period a little later.

Mammillaria itself is such a large genus, and the individual species within it are so similar, that it is easiest to divide them into two groups – those that exude a milky sap when pierced and those that do not.

Watery-sap Mammillarias
These varieties are generally the ones most susceptible to disease, but also include most of the prettiest kinds. *Mammillaria microhelia* is a particularly attractive small variety, with spines arranged like little suns, and creamy-yellow flowers. *M. microheliopsis* is similar, but has a pinkish grey tinge on the central spine on each tubercle.

M. schiedeana is a very pretty, low-growing, clump-forming species, but is a little delicate and normally must be grafted; so too must *M. plumosa*, which has unique feather-like spines completely covering the small, dark green body. *M. prolifera* is rather similar, but is strong enough to grow on its own roots and the spines lack the feather-like appearance of *M. plumosa*. The plant body is also more freely clustering; it produces very large numbers of offsets, so the plant can build up a fairly dense clump even when quite young. The flowers are small and greenish-yellow, but it has attractive large red seed pods.

Mammillaria bocasana

Mammillaria bombycina

M. decipiens and *M. camptotricha* are both similar in having comparatively long spines almost completely covering the body. *M. camptotricha* has much longer spines but is a more shy flowerer. *M. bocasana* is another of the *Mammillarias* with a fairly dense, woolly covering. It is not unlike *M. prolifera*, but is much larger and has pink seed pods, not red. It is a fairly reliable flowerer.

M. heeriana does not form clumps as readily as the other varieties, and tends to form a more elongated, cylindrical body. It freely produces red flowers, which come well through the spines (which are of a dark red colour) in a circle about two-thirds of the way up the plant. Although by far the most commonly sold cactus, *M. zeilmanniana* is also the most susceptible to fungal attacks. It produces a complete ring

white flowers. Partly because it is so suited to modern centrally heated homes, growers have hybridized it with the less tolerant *M. zeilmanniana*, so that some of the plants sold as *M. wildii* do in fact have pinkish flowers.

Finally in this group, *M. bombycina* is one of the most beautiful *Mammillarias*. It not only has an attractive grey-haired covering, but produces red flowers on plants four years of age or more. The central spine on each tubercle, which is hooked, is also frequently tinged red, adding to its attractions.

Milky-sap Mammillarias
As mentioned earlier, these varieties tend to be tougher than those in the previous section, and also have a thicker skin. *M. hahniana* is commonly called the old lady cactus, because of its long,

Mammillaria heeriana

of violet flowers each spring even on quite young plants, but seems to be at its most susceptible at the beginning and end of the growth period. There is also an attractive white-flowered variety, *M. zeilmanniana alba*, which seems to be slightly hardier.

If you have problems in providing a cool enough place to over-winter your cacti, but still want to have some in flower in the summer, one of the best choices is *M. wildii*. This has a dark green body and the true species has

white, woolly hairs, which are freely produced from between the tubercles. In the end, these spread all round the plant rather like those of *Cephalocereus senilis* (see page 63). *M. parkinsonii* bears a superficial resemblance when young, but although quite a lot of wool is produced it never attains the length of that in *M. hahniana*.

M. heyderi is one of the most attractive species of *Mammillaria*, and is also extremely free-flowering, sometimes even blooming twice in the same year.

66

Mammillaria parkinsonii

The adult form is elongated, but younger plants are somewhat flattened. The white flowers tinged with green project between the large tubercles. It is one of the earliest varieties to flower.

Within the group of plants sold commercially as *M. magnimamma* or *M. centricirrha* (they are both in fact the same) there is a very great variety. Some bear more resemblance to *M. compressa*, and look as though someone had trodden on them. Those with a great deal of wool in the axils probably should be labelled *M. nejapensis*, which has yellowish flowers, or *M. collinsii*, which is a rather shy flowerer. *M. uncinata* is very similar but has a short central hooked spine about $\frac{1}{2}$ inch in length on each tubercle, and cream-coloured flowers.

Cacti of the forests

The final major group of cacti are quite different from all the rest, in both appearance and treatment. They are commonly called leaf cacti, because the plant bodies are flattened; these leaves are, however, actually stems. The large flowers are produced either from notches in these stems or from their tips. By far the best known kind is the Christmas cactus, *Zygocactus truncatus*.

This and its relatives are epiphytic – that is, they grow on forest trees in their natural habitat. For this reason, they are often grafted onto a terrestrial rootstock when cultivated. Unlike other cacti, they do not need a winter resting period; some of them in fact flower at this time. You should treat them just like any other houseplant, although the

Zygocactus truncatus

Epiphyllum 'Sunburst'

group known as the Rhipsalidanae need much more warmth and humidity all the year round than the larger Epiphyllanae. Both groups grow better in a potting mixture that contains some sphagnum moss or very coarse peat to give it an open texture.

Zygocactus truncatus, the Christmas cactus, is particularly suited to grafting, and has attractive pendulous green branches which are covered with salmon-pink trumpet-shaped flowers in mid-winter. There is also an almost white variety called *Z. truncatus delicatus*, a pink variety called 'Margrit Koeniger' and a most attractive orange one called 'Weihnachtsfreude'. It is a good idea to put *Zygocactus* outside in a shaded position during the warm summer months so as to ripen the stems. *Schlumbergera gaertneri*, commonly called the Whitsun cactus or Easter cactus, is similar in its requirements and colouring, but flowers, as its names imply, in the spring.

A great deal of hybridization has been carried out to produce the varieties commonly sold as *Epiphyllums*. These have magnificent flowers ranging in colour from deep crimson through pink to white. A great deal of effort has gone into finding a yellow one, but so far without success. *Epiphyllums* tend to make rather large plants, and the beginner with limited space available would do better to buy a plant of *Nopalxochia phyllanthoides* 'Deutsche Kaiserin', which is frequently sold as an

Epiphyllum but makes a much more compact plant with pale pink flowers.

The Rhipsalidanae are generally more difficult to care for than the Epiphyllanae described above, and will definitely do better in a humid greenhouse. They need some shade in the summer, and should not be allowed to dry out in the winter. The most frequently seen variety is *Rhipsalidopsis rosea*. This makes an attractive hanging plant with small, pale pink flowers. *R. rosea* is not an easy plant and tends to shrivel unaccountably. A number of hybrids exist between it and *Schlumbergera gaertneri*.

Two true *Rhipsalis* can be grown in the home: *Rhipsalis houlletiana*, which has pendulous branches with wavy edges, and *R. paradoxa*, with three-ribbed, chunky branches, and ribs on alternate side on each branch. Both have white flowers, but these appear only on well established specimens of the latter plant.

Nopalxochia 'Deutsche Kaiserin'

Simply grown succulents

Succulents, like the cacti they often resemble, have a particular fascination for many people. Besides exotic shapes, many of them have fascinating, subtle leaf colouring and colourful flowers. Some, such as the *Echeverias* and *Sempervivums* (houseleeks), could well provide an interesting collection of plants on their own, without any other plants being needed to add to the interest. Others include such well known houseplants as *Sansevierias* and *Kalanchoës*.

The more easily available succulent plants are described on these two pages. For some more unusual kinds, see pages 70 and 71.

Cultivating succulents

The basic difference between succulents and cacti is that the latter always have tufts of hair, felt or bristles known as areoles (see page 60). They need slightly different growing conditions, though most succulents are quite easy to care for. Generally speaking, they require a very light position, but plants in the plant room or conservatory will be better for some protection from strong sunlight. Though there are exceptions, the potting mixture should generally be kept moist during the growing summer months of the year, and very much on the dry side during winter. (But, unlike cacti, they do need some water in winter.) It is also particularly important to ensure that the potting mix contains a good amount of coarse sand that will assist drainage, as waterlogging of the root system can prove particularly harmful.

When potting on, most plants will look very much better if they are put in shallow, rather than deep pots. There are exceptions, however, such as *Lithops* (see page 70), which have long tap roots that need deeper pots. The best time for potting most of them on is the spring, and the new pot should be only a little larger than the old, since small plants in large pots inevitably do less well.

A temperature in the region of 16°C (61°F) will suit most succulents during the summer months, and in winter the temperature can drop as low as 9°C (48°F) – or even lower if you can be sure that there is a minimum of moisture in the atmosphere. In winter it is especially important to remember that wet and cold conditions together can spell death to the majority of potted plants, particularly those of a succulent nature. Circulation of good, clean fresh air is another cheap commodity that these plants will appreciate much more than a stuffy atmosphere, so adequate ventilation during suitable weather conditions is essential.

On the whole, succulent plants are best treated as temporary room plants that should spend the greater part of the year in the generally better light conditions of a garden room, conservatory or greenhouse. The fascinating *Sempervivums* will in fact do very much better if they can spend their entire existence out of doors on a terrace with the occasional protection of a sheet of glass to keep off the worst of the weather. Only a day or two indoors in an inadequately lit room will be enough for them to lose all their lustre.

Sansevieria trifasciata laurentii

Sansevieria hahnii 'Golden'

Rosette-forming plants

The small spatulate leaves of *Aeonium tabulaeforme* combine to form a perfect rosette as they radiate outwards. It is an interesting plant that is pale green in colour and produces yellow flowers. It is best to raise new plants each year, either from seed or from leaf cuttings. The latter should be allowed to dry for a day after removal from the plant before they are inserted in a peat and sand mix in warm conditions. *A. arboreum* is more erect-growing to a height of some three feet, and produces rosettes at the top of slender stems; there is also a form with coppery-coloured leaves.

With their neat, uncluttered appearance, subtle glaucous-grey colouring and attractive flowers, the *Echeverias* in their many forms deserve to be very much more popular. Easy to care for, most form into rosettes of fat little leaves that are extremely neat in appearance, and there are a great number of kinds to choose from. *Echeveria harmsii* (better known as *Oliveranthus elegans*) has rather open rosettes and colourful, lantern-like flowers that are red outside and yellow in. This species is frequently offered by commercial growers, so it is more freely available than most. At the other end of the scale, *E. setosa* has stemless rosettes of red-tipped green leaves that are covered in attractive white hairs. Clusters of yellow-tipped vermilion flowers grow on short stems.

Easy to care for in room conditions, the *Hawarthias* if anything require less space than the *Echeverias*. They also have rosette-forming leaves with interesting colours and patterns; the flowers are small and inconspicuous. The rosettes of the *Sempervivums* (houseleeks) are produced in great profusion, and crowd together to make attractive hummocks of colour. As the common name suggests, in *Sempervivum arachnoideum* (cobweb houseleek) the leaves look as if they are covered in cobwebs. (See page 165.)

Stiff-leaved kinds

Probably the best known of all succulent plants is mother-in-law's tongue (*Sansevieria trifasciata laurentii*, known in the US as the snake plant), which is grown in millions annually and is quite one of the toughest of all indoor plants. It needs little more to do well than good light, a reasonable temperature and roots that are kept almost permanently dry. New plants can be made by cutting away the young plants that grow up on rhizomous roots at the base of the parent plant; allow the cuttings to dry at the severed end before putting them into small pots of Potting Mixture no. 1 in a very warm place.

Less well known and quite different in appearance is *S. hahnii*, which forms low rosettes not unlike that of the *Aloes* (see below). Particularly attractive is the variety 'Golden'. *S. hahnii* needs similar treatment to *S. trifasciata laurentii*.

Equally tough are the *Aloes*, many of which form rosettes and have vicious spines and sharp points to their leaves. *Aloe variegata* (partridge-breasted aloe) is probably the best known, and has attractively marked overlapping leaves.

Echeveria derenbergii

There are a great number of other *Aloes* to choose from, many of them much too large for the average home, but ideal for terraces where they can be placed away from the flow of humanity. Commonly known as the century plant, *Agave americana* (and its various forms) is possibly the best known of the tough and rather similar *Agaves*, many of which produce very spectacular flower spikes from one to forty feet in height. Some of them die after flowering.

Other common succulents
Like the *Echeverias*, the *Crassulas* in their varied form and colour could well form the basis of a more specialized

Agave botterii

Aloe variegata

collection. *Crassula argentea* forms a compact and attractive small tree and has green leathery leaves; it is also very easy to manage. For the more experienced grower *C. (Rochea) falcata* (scarlet paint-brush) has leathery leaves and clusters of rich red flowers on stout six-inch stems. *Faucaria tigrina* (tiger's jaw or tiger's chaps) is a stubby plant with thick fleshy leaves that have long hairs on their inside edge, giving the plant a tiger's-jaw appearance. The yellow flowers are an additional interest.

Kalanchoës, particularly *Kalanchoë blossfeldiana* 'Vulcan', are grown in vast quantities by nurserymen, and are best grown on a light window sill until they are no longer attractive. Then it is best to throw them away, as they seldom make attractive plants in their second year. Young plants form at the tips and along the edges of leaves of *K. diagremontiana* and *K. tubiflora*, making them extremely easy to propagate – so easy, in fact, that left on the greenhouse tabling, plantlets form and fall off, rooting into the gravel- or peat-covered surface. As a result of this habit, the former plant is known as mother of thousands, a name it shares with *Saxifraga sarmentosa* (see page 47). A final worthwhile *Kalanchoë*, shrubby and upright, is *K. beharensis*, which is quite slow-growing.

All the smaller succulents are ideal for arranging in dish gardens, and there are a number of *Sedums* (stonecrops) that are perfect for this purpose. With green to brown ovoid leaves that resemble small beads when they fall from the plant (these pieces root readily), *Sedum stahlii* (coral beads) has yellow flowers and is easy to manage. Hardy out of doors in many areas, *S. sieboldii medio-variegatum* has glaucous leaves with cream-coloured centres. It is much used as a potted plant by European nurserymen. The pink flowers are not very attractive, but the colourful foliage more than compensates. The plant dies down in winter and can be propagated by division.

Kalanchoë blossfeldiana 'Vulcan'

Some unusual succulents

Lithops spp

and spectacular the flowers or foliage then the more interesting the plant is likely to be. The living stones are the exact opposite, in that the less conspicuous and less easy to detect they are, then the more they are likely to fascinate the grower and his friends.

Colours are mainly grey-green to reddish-brown, and when placed amongst pebbles of similar colouring *Lithops* can be very difficult to detect. There are many species to choose from, and their flowers are mainly white or yellow in colour. The plants form into small clumps, and seldom attain a height of more than two inches, so these could also prove useful and interesting for the grower who is faced with the eternal problem of limited space for all the plants he wants to grow.

Pleiospilos bolusii

Another South African succulent, *Rhombophyllum nelii* (commonly known as elk's-horn) has spreading, lobed leaves that resemble elk's-horns as they grow to varying heights. The foliage is grey-green in colour, and the freely produced flowers are yellow and daisy-like. The plant is easily raised from seed.

Larger plants
Needing much more space than the above to allow for growth that may reach anything from three to ten feet in height, *Adenum multiflorum* (impala lily) is nevertheless an attractive succulent deciduous shrub with a thick trunk. Its crimson-edged white flowers are funnel-shaped. The sap is poisonous. *A. obesum* has a more spreading habit. It also develops an interesting trunk and has pink-edged carmine flowers. It is commonly named the desert rose.

Among the *Cotyledons* there are many plants with surprisingly attractive foliage. *Cotyledon undulata* has wedge-shaped leaves that, like those of most of the other *Cotyledons*, are covered in down, adding to the attraction. While the plant colouring overall is silver-grey, the topmost edge of the leaf is crimped and white in colour. The flowers are orange to red, but the leaves are the main attraction. The plant grows to about one foot in height.

The *Euphorbias* include many, many

Rare and unusual plants – so long as they are also attractive – are doubly fascinating to the keen grower, but they do need searching out. Among the succulents covered on these two pages, for example, few are offered on the general market, and most can be bought only from specialist growers. Another excellent way of obtaining such unusual plants is to join the local and/or national society concerned – this applies to orchids or geraniums just as much as to succulents. You can then usually acquire both plants and seed at reasonable cost – or even for nothing or on exchange with other members. Also, competitions add an incentive to one's plant-growing, and visiting the homes of other members enables comparisons and exchanges to be made.

Small kinds
Among the unusual succulents that grow to a height of only a couple of inches is *Anacampseros rufescens* (also known as *A. arachnoides grandiflora*). This plant has spiralling rosettes of small fleshy leaves that are green on top and purple on the reverse, with white 'cobwebs' in the leaf axils. The deep pink flowers open only in sunlight.

Conophytum giftbergensis is a South African native forming neat green globes with dark spots. The globes are split at the top, and from the split appear yellow flowers with a deeper golden centre. *C. griseum* (silver stars) is rust-coloured with dark spots, and bears a profusion of white daisy-like flowers. These compact little plants are ideal where space is limited.

Quite different in habit, *Cyanotis kewensis* and *C. somaliensis* are both succulent members of the *Tradescantia* family (see page 53), and are equally easy to care for. The former has leaves that are covered by an attractive woolly brown hair, and the latter has a covering of white hair. Their flowers are small and insignificant; blue on the former, purple and orange on the latter.

Among the most fascinating of all the succulents are the so-called living stones (*Lithops*). Most plants are grown for their distinctive qualities; the more colourful plants, from the lowly *Euphorbia splendens prostrata* (commonly known as the crown of thorns) and the completely non-succulent poinsettia (see page 82) to majestic tropical trees that could only be grown indoors in juvenile form. The crown of thorns (often labelled *E. millii splendens* and most commonly sold in the variety 'Bojeri') is, in fact, not at all unusual. With its many thorns, its small oval leaves and its small, bright red flowers, it is one of the easiest succulents to manage, and is freely available. There is, however, a very similar plant with yellow flowers, *E.* 'Tananarive', that is much more unusual and a little more difficult to care for. Particular care is needed when watering.

One of the more tree-like *Euphorbias* that is excellent in difficult situations is *E. tirucali* (milk bush). It has pencil-thick, glossy green leaves, and will in time develop into a tree of some thirty feet in height. But it can be trimmed back to more manageable size at almost any time. In complete contrast, *E. obesa* develops into a small spherical dome that is rust coloured and not unlike a sea anemone or a tubby cactus. It has quite minute flowers.

Euphorbia splendens 'Bojeri'

Euphorbia tirucali

Senecio (Kleinia) nerifolia

Growing to a height of some 15 inches, *Senecio (Kleinia) articulatus* (candle plant) has oddly jointed, pale grey stems and darker green leaves that are divided into three. Its stems also have slightly darker stripes, and the flowers are a yellowish-white colour. *S. stapeliaeformis* (*Kleinia stapeliaeformis*) is a plant that will more often be seen on sale as *Kleinia* rather than *Senecio*, which is now the proper name. Easy to care for, having purple and silver, angled fleshy stems and dark green leaves, it is short lived. The flowers are scarlet. Cuttings a few inches in length will root readily in summer if allowed to dry before planting.

Finally, there are a group of plants – the *Stapelias* – with a very unpleasant characteristic, as is indicated by the common name of carrion flower. Although the flowers are exotic in appearance, they have an abominable smell. The object is to attract blow-flies to transfer pollen from one flower to another. Many of these flowers are quite spectacular,

Euphorbia obesa

and those of *Stapelia gigantea* are up to 18 inches in diameter; from such a flower the smell is offensive to say the least! So either remove all flower buds or stand your plant outdoors when in flower.

Probably the starfish flower (*S. asterias*) and the star flower (*S. variegata*) are the most popular species. Both are very easily raised from cuttings that should be allowed to dry off for a day or two after removing from the plant. Potting on is only necessary when growth has completely crowded the pot and is growing over the side.

71

The fascinating bromeliads

Many houseplants originate in tropical lands, but – with the possible exceptions of orchids and cacti – none appear quite so exotic as the bromeliads. With their rosettes of leaves forming a natural vase for catching and holding rainwater, they look every bit the jungle inhabitants they are. The pineapple is the only member to have any commercial importance outside the decorative plant market, and all the bromeliads come from tropical America. Their appearance becomes even more fascinating when the flowers appear, generally surrounded by bracts in incredible colours.

Many bromeliads are epiphytes that attach themselves and thrive on the most meagre foothold. They get both food and water from what falls into the vase, and the roots are primarily used to anchor the plant to its support. This is one reason why they are so happy in the home or conservatory growing on 'trees' specially made for this purpose (see opposite). In fact, the foliage of many kinds – *Tillandsias* in particular – is often much improved when growing in this way. A few, however, are terrestrial (ground-living).

In spite of their exotic appearance, bromeliads are not difficult to grow. The main need is to keep the vase of the epiphytic kinds filled with water, changing this water from time to time. The root system, on the other hand, should be kept only slightly moistened; avoid permanent saturation at all costs. Feeding is not important, but very weak liquid fertilizer may be added to the water in the vase or – probably better still – a foliar feed may be applied to the leaves (see page 222). The terrestrial types, on the other hand, should be fed and watered like normal houseplants.

As the roots have very little real function in the epiphytes, the actual mixture in the pot is not very important. However, it must be open and free draining, so mixes containing lots of peat, moss, leaf-mould, osmunda fibre and suchlike are ideal. The best method of propagation is to remove mature side shoots from larger plants with as much root as possible, and pot them up.

In the home, bromeliads present few problems provided they have reasonable light and warmth. Although they will tolerate considerable temperature variation with no apparent ill effect, they fare better in a steady temperature in the region of 19°C (66°F). The only pests likely to be encountered are scale insects on the leaves and mealy bug in the roots; both can be cleared by three or four applications of malathion at regular intervals. Use as a drench in the pot for the bug, and (wearing rubber gloves) wipe scales off with a malathion-soaked sponge.

Of the plants themselves, there is a vast number; it has been estimated that there are somewhere in the region of 2,000 species in 45 genera. Alas, only a minute proportion can be purchased by the ordinary man in the street, and these are the plants that the commercial nurseryman can grow and handle economically. A few specialist growers do, however, handle some rarer kinds.

Aechmea

The *Aechmeas* are all rosette-forming plants, mostly with colourful bracts that will last for many months. After flowering, the parent rosette will fade and die; it should then be cut away to

Aechmea rhodocyanea (A. fasciata)

allow the new shoots that will by then have appeared at the base to take over. These new shoots can be left attached to grow on together, or they may be removed and potted separately; but they will take several years to flower again.

Aechmea chantinii (sometimes labelled *Billbergia chantinii*) has upright leaves with an olive-green base and attractive, irregular cross-bands of silver. The bracts are red, tipped with yellow, and there is an added bonus in the brilliant red bract leaves. The best known *Aechmea* is *A. rhodocyanea* (also known as the urn plant, *A. fasciata* or

Ananas bracteatus striatus

Billbergia rhodocyanea), which has broader leaves, a fuller appearance and a wide variation of leaf colouring, but is predominantly grey-green with horizontal grey bands. The large conical rosette of bracts is pink and the small flowers blue. *A. fulgens* is a smaller plant bearing brilliant red bracts and leaves that are a dusty grey colour. *A. fulgens discolor* has olive-green leaves with maroon-purple under-sides.

Ananas

The ordinary pineapple, *Ananas comosus*, is a terrestrial bromeliad of upright habit with dull grey-green leaves, viciously spined along their edges. The main interest is in the pineapple fruit produced like a large drumstick from the centre of the rosette. It is possible to grow your own from the tuft of leaves on a pineapple fruit (see page 200).

Much more spectacular in every way is *A. bracteatus striatus* (sometimes known as *A. comosus variegatus* or the ivory pineapple), which is very much larger and will need a slightly heavier potting mixture (incorporate some Potting Mixture no. 3) to prevent overbalancing. The leaves may attain a length of three feet, and the edges are wickedly barbed. They are superbly coloured, however, in rich green and cream, and older plants are often suffused all over with a rich reddish-pink that gives the plant an incredibly exotic appearance. And that's not all; the fruit – on a three-foot stem – is a fantastic red, and it bears a succession of intense blue flowers.

Billbergia

Among the easiest bromeliads to grow are the *Billbergias*, which, alas, have flower bracts that last for only a very short time. The best known is *Billbergia nutans* (angel's tears or queen's tears), which has narrow, dull-grey leaves and short-lived drooping flowers that are pink and green. A plant of better appearance, *B. × windii* has green leaves some 15 inches in length and flowers that

Billbergia × windii

are pale green, with a touch of blue and colourful yellow stamens. The pink bracts are much larger than in *B. nutans*. *B. decora* is more of an aristocrat, and has tubes of elegant leaves two feet or more in height that are brownish-green and speckled in white. The exotic pendulous inflorescence has large pink bracts and green flowers.

Cryptanthus

For dish gardens and small indoor garden effects, few plants are better than the *Cryptanthus*, the majority of which resemble starfish and are commonly known as earth-stars. They are ter-

Cryptanthus bromelioides tricolor

Neoregelia carolinae tricolor

Vriesia

Another genus offering many spectacular plants, both for their flowers and for their foliage, are the *Vriesias*. The bright red bracts of *Vriesia splendens* are sword-shaped – hence the common name flaming sword – and remain colourful for many weeks; the flowers are yellow. The green leaves are distinctively marked with deep purple horizontal bands that gradually disappear as the bract emerges from the vase. Both *V. fenestralis* and *V. hieroglyphica* are majestic plants. The former has green leaves covered in a network of fine lines. The latter is often referred to as the 'king of the bromeliads', and has beautiful hieroglyphic markings.

restrial, and most form flat rosettes of leaves that are thick at their base and taper to a point. The flowers are insignificant, but many have fascinating leaf colourings. *C. acaulis* has fleshy leaves of soft green, while *C. acaulis* 'Rubra' is reddish-brown. *C. bivittatus* is striped light and dark green, and *C. fosterianus* – one of the largest – has a leaf pattern not unlike that of a pheasant's feather, and is mainly reddish-brown. A more erect plant, *C. bromelioides tricolor* is the most freely available. The leaves are cream and green, suffused with pink.

Guzmania

The *Guzmanias* include a number of striking plants and for foliage few can better *Guzmania musaica*, which produces a large rosette of broad reddish-

Guzmania monostachya

brown leaves that are white-mottled; the flower spike is insignificant. *G. zahnii* is a spectacular plant which has strap-like olive-green leaves and a sturdy, nine-inch-long inflorescence with pink and yellow bracts and white flowers. The bracts remain colourful for several weeks.

Neoregelia; Nidularium

Neoregelia and *Nidularium* are similar in that they both produce flat-growing rosettes and have stemless flowers that remain about the water level in the vase. *Neoregelia carolinae tricolor* is the most impressive, with mature plants reaching a diameter of some thirty inches. The green leaves are variegated cream and pink, and just prior to producing flowers the short leaves at the edge of the vase turn a brilliant red. The flowers are blue

and comparatively insignificant. *Neoregelia spectabilis* has metallic-green leaves that turn purple at their base as the plant flowers. The main attraction, however, is the leaf tips, which are red in colour and resemble a painted fingernail – hence the common name it is given: fingernail plant.

Nidularium fulgens also has brilliant red bracts in the centre of the rosette of bright green shiny leaves. The small flowers are violet-blue. In *Nidularium innocentii*, the bracts are coppery-red, but the green leaves are flushed with purple on top and wine-red underneath.

Tillandsia

Ideal for the bromeliad tree, the *Tillandsias* all make comparatively small rosettes, with recurving leaves on most,

Vriesia splendens

many of them tapering off into thin curls. Many are quite minute plants, such as *Tillandsia ionanthe*, with rosettes little more than three inches in width, green leaves and delightful blue flowers. *T. cyanea* is one of the most spectacular, with reddish-brown leaves and a flat oval bract that is clear pink and some six inches long. Its flowers are large, violet in colour and borne on either side of the bract.

Making a bromeliad tree

Find a stout tree branch with a number of firm smaller branches attached. Fasten it to a pillar in a conservatory; or attach it to a firm base, such as a box of concrete, that is light enough to allow mobility. Remove the plants from their pots and firmly wrap the root ball in wet sphagnum moss. Place the plants in natural positions, such as on forks or curves in the branches, and fasten in position with green plastic-coated wire. Thereafter, spray the moss regularly with tepid water to make sure that the roots do not dry out excessively. *Tillandsias* and *Cryptanthus* are probably the best kinds.

Handsome leaves, exotic flowers

Spathiphyllum wallisii

Aphelandra squarrosa 'Brockfield'

There are a number of house and conservatory plants that defy categorizing as either 'foliage' or 'flowering' types. Of course, all the plants grown mainly for their flowers do also have leaves, but these are often not particularly attractive. Some, however, both bear beautiful flowers and have foliage as handsome as that of any 'foliage' plant. Some *Begonias* (see page 48) rate highly in this respect, but the few kinds described on this page are particularly striking.

Anthurium; Spathiphyllum
Related to the arum lily, and with rather similar spathe flowers, the grand and exotic *Anthurium andreanum* must rate as one of the most exciting of all warm conservatory plants. Its mature leaves are large and of elongated heart shape, and the flower spathes are brilliantly coloured in shades of red, pink, and a very pleasing white. A firm spadix extends up from the base of the spathe. The better known and more compact *A. scherzerianum* (flamingo flower) produces many more smaller leaves per plant, and has flowers that are mostly soft red in colour. The spadix curls.

Both plants like an agreeably warm and humid atmosphere and watering with rain water. They should be potted into a peaty mixture when the plants are transferred to larger pots about once every other year. Cut flowers will last for several weeks in water.

With white flowers of similar shape and leaves that are less leathery and more plentiful, there are a number of *Spathiphyllums* that are reasonably easy room plants to care for. Ideally, conditions should be similar to those suggested for *Anthuriums*, but they will, without undue harm, tolerate lower temperatures of around 16°C (61°F). The two plants most likely to be found are *Spathiphyllum wallisii*, which is of compact habit, and *S.* 'Mauna Loa', which is larger and a little more difficult to care for.

Aphelandra; Sanchezia
With colourful white-veined leaves and topped with showy long-lasting bracts, there are a number of varieties of *Aphelandra squarrosa* (sometimes named tiger plant or zebra plant). They are mostly a little difficult to manage in normal room conditions, but are well worth the extra care that is needed. Best known is probably *A. squarrosa louisae*, which produces a cluster of golden-yellow bracts that last over a long period, and *A. squarrosa* 'Brockfeld', which has larger but fewer flower bracts, but compensates for this by having more attractively marked foliage. *A. squarrosa leopoldii* has more slender elliptic leaves and reddish stems topped by yellow flowers in dull red bracts.

All varieties need light shade, a temperature of not less than 19°C (66°F), and a permanently moist environment, as any drying out of the potting mixture will inevitably result in loss of leaves. Neglect of regular feeding will also be harmful. Pot on into slightly larger pots using Mixture no. 3 each spring. Plants seldom look attractive for more than three years indoors, but new plants can easily be reared from cuttings.

Sanchezia nobilis glaucophylla belongs to the same family as the *Aphelandra*, and needs similar growing conditions. It attains a height of some four feet, and has large, tough, lance-shaped leaves with yellow veins, and yellow flowers.

Ardisia
Very much a plant for the patient grower, *Ardisia crispa* (also known as *A. crenula*) is a compact shrub that will in time reach a height of about four feet. Its leaves are elliptical, tough and glossy-green in colour. Clusters of pink-flushed white flowers appear in winter and are followed by masses of scarlet berries. These may well last throughout the year and are the plant's principal attraction. No more than average conditions are required, but growth will be less dismal in a temperature of around 21°C (70°F).

Strelitzia
Easily the most exotic-looking of all the flowers covered here, *Strelitzia reginae* is commonly known as the bird-of-paradise flower. The name comes from the flower bracts, which are an incredible galaxy of colour that embraces brilliant orange, red and tongues of the most vivid blue. The flowers are large and stiff-stemmed, and the leaves tough, oblong and a glaucous colour.

In spite of its exotic appearance, it is a far from difficult plant that will grow in what would seem disagreeable conditions with no apparent discomfort. Given good light, reasonable warmth and normal watering and feeding, it could almost be described as a beginner's plant. It is also comparatively easy to grow from seed, but you will have to be patient over several years before the first, flamboyant flowers appear.

Strelitzia reginae

Growing roses indoors

Rosa 'Garnette Red'

Rosa 'Baby Masquerade'

Roses are probably the most popular of all garden plants, and yet few people attempt to grow them indoors. This is a great pity, since an indoor rose produces the most exquisite blooms, given the right conditions and treatment.

Being vigorous and hardy outdoor plants, roses' prime needs are plenty of light, water and food, and reasonably cool, airy conditions. A stuffy, dim, overheated room will not suit them; the stems will grow spindly and weak, and the leaves will drop. But they should thrive in a sunlit, airy porch, garden room or conservatory – or, of course, in a greenhouse, where millions of roses are grown for the florist trade. And smaller varieties will do well on a sunny window sill. Even in such surroundings, however, no rose will make a permanent houseplant; it must always have an outdoor 'rest' for part of the year.

Varieties to try

All but the most vigorous kinds of roses (species, varieties and hybrids of *Rosa*) can be grown indoors, so long as they are chosen carefully for their setting. Climbing roses make splendid subjects for training up the back wall of a conservatory or its pillars, for example, but are too vigorous otherwise. They are best planted permanently in a bed of rich soil. For garden rooms and porches, the smaller-growing bush and standard (tree) roses can be grown in pots and forced for early blooms. Choose Hybrid Tea types if you want exquisite large flowers, Floribundas for clusters of medium-sized flowers or Polyanthas if you prefer masses of smaller blooms.

Miniature roses that grow only 8 to 12 inches tall are ideal for window sills, but in between these and the normal bush roses are a group specially suited to life indoors. These are the Garnette varieties, which were first bred in Germany and probably have a longer flowering period than any other rose. They

form compact, bushy plants about 1½ feet tall, and have small double flowers borne in trusses.

Cultivation

If you want to force rose bushes into bloom in the spring, work needs to start in the autumn. Pot young plants of bush or standard varieties in eight- or nine-inch pots, miniatures in four- or five-inch. Use a rich potting mixture such as Mix no. 3, and pack it down very firmly around the roots. Water the plants and stand them outdoors until midwinter. If possible, sink the pots in soil; otherwise, use a peat mulch to prevent them freezing solid.

In midwinter, prune the bushes. Cut out any weak shoots and then cut the other stems back to just above the third or fourth strong bud above the base. The plants can then be brought indoors. Ideally, their temperature should be increased slowly over the next few months from about 5°C (41°F) at night and 8°C (46°F) in the day in midwinter to about 13°C (55°F) at night and 18°C (64°F) in the day in late spring. Otherwise, choose a cool, well lit place.

During this growth period, the potting mixture should be kept quite moist. Once buds begin to form, liquid fertilizer should be given every week to ten days. Spraying of the foliage is essential to maintain humidity. This treatment should be continued through the flowering season, which extends into early summer. Remove all dead blooms and watch out for pests and diseases, using a systemic insecticide or fungicide if necessary (see pages 232 and 233).

When the plants stop flowering, move them outdoors and again, if possible, sink the pots in soil. Water them regularly in dry weather, and remove any flower buds that appear. If you want to force them again, repot them with fresh potting mixture in the autumn. Alternatively, remove the top inch or two of

Rosa 'Ena Harkness'

potting mixture and replace with fresh. Then, in midwinter, prune and bring them into growth indoors once again. Do not expect your plants to respond well to this treatment more than two or three times, however. After this, plant them permanently outdoors.

Roses to grow in pots

Hybrid Tea: 'Alpine Sunset' (cream*); 'Drambuie' (deep amber); 'Ena Harkness' (red*); 'King's Ransom' (yellow*); 'Madame Butterfly' (pale pink*); 'Maturity' (deep pink*); 'Ophelia' (silvery-pink*); 'Sylvia' (pink*); 'Worthwhile' (buff-yellow)

Floribunda: 'Cairngorm' (apricot*); 'Edith Dennett' (salmon-pink*); 'Fleur Cowles' (pink*); 'Isis' (white*); all Garnette varieties

Polyantha: Most, including: 'Cecile Brunner' (pink); 'Paul Crampel' (orange-red); 'Perle d'Or' (yellow)

Miniature: 'Baby Gold Star' (yellow); 'Baby Masquerade' (crimson and gold); 'Cinderella' (pink); 'Coralin' (coral)

Climbing: 'Compassion' (yellow-orange); 'Dreaming Spires' (gold*); 'Golden Ophelia' (gold*); 'Marechal Niel' (yellow)

Miniature climbing: 'Pink Cameo' (pink); 'Showoff' (buff-orange)

Varieties marked with an asterisk are scented.

The African violet family

Among the flowering plants that can make a permanent home indoors, no single family is so important as the Gesneriaceae, or gesneriads. Most of them are relatively small plants, but all have attractive foliage and colourful, exquisite flowers. Foremost among them are the African violets (*Saintpaulias*) and gloxinias, closely followed by *Achimenes*, commonly known as the hot water plant, and *Columnea*. The last, like three other important members of the family – *Aeschynanthus*, *Episcia* and *Hypocyrta* – are natural trailers, and all four are dealt with elsewhere, on pages 84 and 85.

All the gesneriads need warm, shaded and moist conditions in which to grow. The trick is to strike a happy balance. The gloom of an ill-lit room with few windows is not the answer, as reasonable light is essential if the plants are to do at all well. On the other hand, ensure that they are not subjected to strong, direct sunlight. Even this statement must be qualified, however, for some types – African violets in particular – will tolerate surprisingly sunny locations unharmed, so long as water is kept off the flowers and leaves. These soon scorch in the sun if wet patches remain.

African violets

Without any doubt, the worldwide favourite of all the gesneriad family – and perhaps among all houseplants – is the African violet (*Saintpaulia ionantha*). The main reason for its popularity is undoubtedly its ability to flower freely throughout the year – although summer and autumn are the best seasons – together with its compactness and brilliant colouring. It was discovered in the mountains of East Africa in 1892, and yet its possibilities as a houseplant were only realized in the 1920s.

There are a seemingly endless number of varieties of African violets, with more being added all the time. Some remain in favour for a reasonable length of time while others rapidly disappear. Blue in its many shades is the principal flower colour, but there are also whites, pinks, reds and bicolours, and single and double forms. The list of names is positively bewildering and looking through a specialist catalogue suggests that finding new names for new introductions must present a considerable problem for the raiser! Although the flowers are, of course, the main attraction, the leaves are also appealing. Heart-shaped, slightly fleshy and a deep green colour on top, with a velvety texture, they are a dark maroon underneath in some varieties.

The fact that there are so many commercial growers and individuals prepared to spend a deal of time hybridizing these enchanting little plants is in itself a considerable advantage to the grower of one or two plants on his or her window sill. The individual flowers and trusses of flowers have improved out of all recognition in recent years, but added to this there has been a considerable step forward in developing a tougher strain of *Saintpaulia*. As a result there is very much less need for the intensive

Saintpaulia ionantha varieties

care – almost incubator treatment – that was at one time needed to achieve real success with them indoors. However, it must be added that there is still a marked improvement in performance if they are grown in a terrarium equipped with sophisticated lighting and heat and humidity controls (see page 30).

Agreeably warm conditions with temperatures of not less than 19°C (66°F) are desirable, as consistently low temperatures will inevitably result in a droopy, stunted and lifeless appearance. Adequate light is also essential, and the plants will be much improved both in appearance and in overall performance if they can be placed under some form of artificial light in the evening. Take care, though, not to have strong lights too close to the plants, or there will be a danger of scorching both the foliage and the flowers.

Offering advice to the beginner on the watering of almost any plant presents many difficulties, as there is no definite rule that one can state as a guide. However, saturated root conditions cause more plant fatalities than any other single fault, so it is wise to err on the dry side when wielding the watering can. This is certainly so with *Saintpaulias* – always let the plants dry

out a little between each application. Never use cold water, and make sure that water never gets on to the leaves or flowers, as these are very easily marked – particularly if the plants are subjected to direct sunlight while they are still wet.

Potting on is only necessary about every second year, and the new container must be only a little larger than the old. A peaty potting mixture is essential, and should you have facilities for making your own potting mixture, a suitable mix can be achieved by reversing the amounts of peat and loam, so providing a much lighter composition (see page 218). Otherwise use a commercial peat-based mix or a special *Saintpaulia* mix. Do not firm it down when potting.

Too frequent potting on is not a good idea. The reason is that plants tend to grow much more vigorously in a new mix that is to their liking, and while they are actively growing in this way they tend to produce far fewer flowers. When the pot is well filled with roots, almost all potted plants will produce flowers more prolifically. Reluctant plants can also be encouraged to flower by keeping the roots a little drier than normal, or by feeding them with a fertilizer that contains a high proportion of phosphates; high-nitrogen fertilizers tend to encourage more leaf development at the expense of flowers (see page 222).

African violets are not difficult to grow from seed, needing a germination temperature of 18 to 21°C (64 to 70°F). Favourite plants can be propagated by division, but by far the easiest way is to take leaf cuttings (see page 228). These root very easily in a mixture of peat and sand at about 20°C (68°F), or even with the ends of the stalks simply stood in water.

To do well with African violets, the really important consideration is to ensure that your plants have a light, warm and reasonably moist situation in the home, as they positively abhor conditions that do not provide these needs.

Gloxinias

Second only to the African violet among the gesneriad family is the gloxinia, known botanically as *Sinningia speciosa*. With its large, dark green, velvety leaves and large bell-shaped flowers, it is altogether a more flamboyant plant. It is also one of the easiest summer-flowering plants to care for, and one of the most colourful. The flowers may be violet, purple, crimson, scarlet, pink or white, with many bi-coloured forms.

Plants are easily raised from seed, thinly sown in a warm temperature in spring, and gradually potted on into slightly larger containers as they fill their pots with roots. The use of an open, peaty potting mixture is essential. They in time form tubers that may be kept from year to year by allowing the plants to dry out after they have lost their attraction. Store the tubers in warm, dry conditions, and start them into growth in the spring by half burying them in moist peat in a warm position. Pot them into a more substantial mixture when the tubers have developed a number of new leaves. Plants may also be increased by means of leaf cuttings from healthy plants (see page 228).

Sinningia speciosa (gloxinia) varieties

Other gesneriads

Among the other members of the gesneriad family, the best known is the *Achimenes*, of which there are many species and varieties from which you can choose. They grow about 9 to 12 inches high, with widely flaring trumpet flowers in a wide range of colours. The flowering period extends from early summer until autumn.

These plants have rhizomes formed like the overlapping sections of a pine cone, and new plants can be raised by peeling these sections off and planting them individually in moist peat in a warm place. The common name of *Achimenes* – hot water plant – comes from the fact that if you plunge the rhizome into hot water before planting and bringing into growth – at the end of winter – it will develop leaves much more quickly. New plants also grow from seed sown in early spring, or from cuttings from young shoots taken at the same time. Provided they are kept moist, reasonably warm

Smithiana hybrids

Achimenes hybrid

and fed, these are among the easiest of indoor plants to care for.

With similar scaly rhizomes, *Kohleria* does not need the hot water treatment to accelerate growth. Otherwise, it should have similar treatment to *Achimenes*, but is a much bolder plant that will grow to three feet or more. The flowers are again trumpet-shaped, and there are varieties in various red, pink and orange colourings.

Smaller than the *Kohlerias*, but also of upright habit, are three more members of the family: *Gesneria* (which, of course, gave its name to the whole family), *Rechsteinera* and *Smithiana* (commonly known as temple bells). They all have clusters of narrow tubular or bell-shaped flowers in brilliant colours – mainly reds – and flower in the autumn. They are tuberous – like gloxinias – but need a temperature of about 21°C (70°F). In other respects, they can be treated in the same way as gloxinias (see above). By starting *Gesnerias* into growth in early summer, however, they will flower in winter.

The final important gesneriad apart from those described on page 84 is the *Streptocarpus*, commonly known as the Cape primrose. The rather coarse leaves are almost stemless, and the trumpet-shaped flowers grow from stems rather like those of primroses. There are many

Streptocarpus hybrid

fine varieties with flowers of white, pink, red, violet or blue, and they flower over many months in warm, lightly shaded conditions. They can be raised with equal ease from either seed or cuttings. Start off in Potting Mixture no. 1, progressing to no. 2 and no. 3 as they grow. They give little trouble. **77**

Easy pot-plants from seed

Certainly the cheapest way to build up a colourful collection of pot-plants is to grow your own from seed. A number of favourites can be grown very easily this way, following the general instructions given on page 226.

As will be seen, some flower only a few months after sowing; others can be grown on over winter to make handsome large specimen plants for the spring display. In a few cases, either annual or biennial treatment can be given depending on the time of sowing and when you want the plants to flower. Some of the plants, although flowering the first year like an annual, can be saved for subsequent years and are perennial by nature. Of all the easily grown pot-plants, *Calceolarias*, *Cinerarias*, *Salpiglossis* and *Schizanthus* are probably the most exotic and showy.

Cineraria; Calceolaria

Cinerarias cover themselves with daisy-like flowers in every possible colour-shade except yellow. Dwarf Multiflora types are neat and compact, with blooms more profuse, than in the large-flowered kinds. The latter are splendid for exhibition and shows. A taller Stellata type with starry flowers is available, and also double-flowered forms such as 'Gubler's Double'. The

Cineraria Multiflora hybrids

double types are limited in colour range and flower less freely.

The seed is best sown in early summer, but earlier sowings will give plants flowering in midwinter. Transfer seedlings to 2½-inch pots, and pot on to final five-inch pots. Only frost-free conditions are necessary over winter. There should be good light; but *Cinerarias* do not like brilliant sunshine or high temperatures, which cause them to wilt. Keep a careful watch for attack by greenfly (aphids; see page 232).

Calceolarias (whose full name is *Calceolaria × herbeo-hybrida*) have a particularly exotic appearance, with pouch-shaped flowers in a wide range of colours and shades with the exception of blue. The flowers are often splashed or speckled with contrasting colours, giving a very gay effect. They can be grown in much the same way as *Cinerarias*, and again there are small-flowered Multiflora and giant-flowered types. Recently F1 hybrids have been introduced. These are neat and compact, and flower very soon after sowing, being especially suited for winter pot-plants. The stems of the

Calceolaria hybrids

larger hybrids should be tied to a cane for support. Both stems and foliage are often very brittle and careful support is particularly necessary when the masses of flowers are borne.

Excellent for window boxes or for summer flowering in pots, as well as for planting in the open garden, are the new F1 hybrids derived from *Calceolaria integrifolia*. These have smaller flowers than other *Calceolarias*, in brilliant yellow, and can be grown as annuals.

Schizanthus; Salpiglossis

Schizanthus (butterfly flower) hybrids have graceful ferny foliage and a profusion of flowers that resemble exotic butterflies. They come in every possible colour and combination, and are often prettily marked. There are dwarf and taller large-flowered varieties. Sowings can be made at two periods: in autumn for growing on the plants over winter to give a magnificent spring display, and from very early spring to early summer for summer and autumn flowering.

The autumn-sown plants will need stopping – by removing the growing tips – from time to time to induce bushy growth with lots of side shoots. This is done first when the plants are seedlings and again after the side shoots have grown several inches. The shoots formed can again be stopped so as to get more and more – each will eventually bear masses of blooms. No further stopping should be done from late winter so that the flower buds can form. Spring-sown plants can be stopped once, but some of the dwarf varieties such as 'Hit Parade'

Schizanthus hybrids

can be left alone. Autumn-sown plants will need at least a seven-inch pot for final flowering. Plants for summer require four- to five-inch pots. Keep winter plants frost-free, and all plants slightly shaded when flowering. They may need canes for support.

A great advance has recently been made by the development of F1 hybrid *Salpiglossis* such as 'Splash'. The plants are shorter, more sturdy, and more vigorous than the older ordinary hybrids. The flowers are marvellous – freely borne, trumpet-shaped and having rich colours usually veined with gold.

As with *Schizanthus*, sowings can be made in autumn and early spring. In this case only one stopping is necessary when the seedling is a few inches tall, although plants to be grown on over winter can be stopped a second time if desired. Also like *Schizanthus*, the plants need canes for support. Generally five- to six-inch pots are big enough for flowering plants. *Salpiglossis* are almost hardy and sometimes perennial, but you will get the best results by treating them as annuals or biennials.

Quick-flowering annuals

One of the fastest-flowering plants from seed is *Cuphea ignea* (commonly known as the Mexican cigar-plant). This often

Salpiglossis hybrids

produces its first quaint flowers as a seedling. They are tubular and scarlet with black tips. It then goes on to flower as it develops until finally the fully grown plant is covered in flowers. This species is the best *Cuphea*, making a neat, shrubby plant needing only a 3½-inch pot.

A charming plant for shallow half-pots (where it may need support with a few twiggy sticks), or sometimes for hanging containers, is *Lobelia tenuior*. This resembles the well-known garden *Lobelias* except that the flowers are very much larger and a rich blue colour. To encourage bushy plants stop the seedlings when about three inches high. Several can be put in each seven-inch half-pot. Since the plant is rather tender, sowing is best left until the warmer weather of

Cuphea ignea

spring arrives. Another blue-flowered favourite, the blooms being of unusual shape, is *Torenia fournieri* (wishbone flower). This can also be left for late sowing if the weather is cold. It can also be grown in half-pots or in hanging containers, although it is less suitable than *Lobelia tenuior*.

Yet again grown in a similar way is the sweetly fragrant *Exacum affine*, which is also bluish-purple. In warmth this will continue flowering well into winter and it will fill a greenhouse or room with its scent, although the flowers are neither large nor showy – although quite pretty. Some new dwarf varieties have recently appeared – but they may have lost scent. Yet other modern varieties are fragrant, however, so seek a reliable seedsman's advice or choose older strains.

Garden annuals

Most of the popular garden annuals can be grown in pots, given bright airy conditions, but some are specially suited for indoors, like the *Schizanthus* and *Salpiglossis* already described. Double *Petunias* make fine specimens with huge clove-scented blooms often bi-coloured pink or red and white. Single Grandiflora *Petunias* also make fine pot-plants with large trumpet flowers, sometimes with frilled edges. The variety 'El Toro', an F1 hybrid, is outstanding for its vivid red colour and velvety texture.

There are also some fine pot-plants among the *Begonia semperflorens* varie-

Torenia fournieri

ties, of which there are now many (see page 116). Most of the F1 hybrids can be recommended. The large-flowered types like 'Muse Rose' and those with variegated foliage, such as 'Colour Queen', are especially suited to pots. Another special favourite is *Phlox drummondii*, which can also be sown in autumn for overwintering and subsequent spring flowering. Seeds of these neat compact phloxes can be bought in separate or mixed colours.

Celosia plumosa, known as Prince of Wales' feathers, is a neat pot-plant with very decorative feathery plumes. The best varieties are coloured in rich gold or brilliant red, and there are also some dwarf kinds growing only about 10 to 12 inches tall instead of the usual 1½ to 3 feet. *Celosia cristata* (cockscomb), with its strange velvety combs in various colours, probably looks more effective when viewed close-up in pots than when bedded outdoors. The dwarf variety 'Jewel Box' is recommended.

Annuals or perennials

A number of extremely good plants can be grown to flower very quickly, like annuals, but can be saved for flowering in subsequent years if desired. Sometimes

Exacum affine

the plants with the best flowers or colours can be saved and the rest discarded, depending on the space available.

One of the most important is *Gerbera*, now available in the form of hybrids all of which flower well the first year of sowing. These are eagerly sought by flower-arrangers because the blooms are excellent for cutting, and the large daisy-shaped blooms come in the most unusual subtle colour shades of great beauty. There are also double and semi-double forms, such as 'Thurman's Double', but these are not really so graceful as the single kinds. Sow as early in the season as possible and pot on to five-inch pots for flowering. In cool conditions flowers are often produced throughout the winter months as a bonus to the main summer display.

Celosia plumosa

Lantana hybrids have flowers resembling those of *Verbena*. The newer hybrids are dwarf and have mixed colours. Sow the seed again as early in the season as possible in a temperature of about 20°C (68°F), and pot on to five-inch pots.

One of the most remarkable plants to be introduced recently is the F1 hybrid *Hibiscus* 'Southern Belle'. From an early sowing, growth is amazingly rapid and in about five months or less the plants will have reached a height of four feet, and be bearing the most enormous poppy-shaped flowers – often 12 inches across. The colours are carmine, rose-pink, or white with carmine centres. The flowers last only about two days but are freely borne. At the end of the season the plants can be cut back and kept almost dry over winter. They usually grow up again the following year, but the finest plants are raised by annual sowing.

Lilies have a reputation for taking a long time to flower from seed. *Lilium formosanum* is a remarkable exception – it flowers as an annual very easily. The variety to get is 'Pricei', which grows two to three feet tall in pots. Sow early and you can expect beautiful fragrant white trumpet blooms during summer. About five seedlings can be given an eight- to ten-inch pot the first year. It is well worth saving the bulbs that will have formed by winter. These can be potted separately early the following season, and even better blooms will be produced in late summer.

Gerbera hybrids

Flowering herbaceous pot-plants

Permanent houseplants – both flowering and foliage-only types – form the basis of any indoor plant collection, but it is useful to have others that, though only temporary, provide a colourful and spectacular display. Herbaceous flowering pot-plants come into this category, and form a kind of part-way stage between the permanent houseplants and a vase of cut flowers. They include such favourites as carnations, *Chrysanthemums* and *Impatiens* (busy Lizzies), but there are many other, less well known types that will reward you with brilliant blooms.

All the following grow well in standard potting mixtures (see page 218). Generally, keep them on the dry side in winter, but water well when they are in active growth.

Carnations

Carnations (classified botanically as *Dianthus*) do not make ideal pot-plants because they usually grow tall and need careful support. However, the exquisite flowers are great favourites for year-round availability and cutting. Although some carnations, such as the 'Chabaud' type, can be taken up from a garden border, potted, and flowered indoors in winter, it is far better to obtain Perpetual Flowering varieties. These are sold by specialist nurseries as named varieties and they give huge, wonderfully coloured blooms that are usually sweetly fragrant.

The plants can be bought as rooted

Dianthus (Perpetual carnation varieties)

cuttings in winter and early spring, but fully grown plants in five-inch pots can also be obtained. Young plants must have the tops snipped off when they have grown about ten pairs of leaves. All side shoots that grow out afterwards must also be 'stopped' in the same way, when about five pairs of leaves have been formed. To avoid all shoots flowering at the same time, stop the fastest-growing shoot first and the others at staggered intervals. Each shoot will bear a number of buds, but only one should be allowed to develop. Remove others at as early a stage as possible.

In the meantime pot on as required into five- or six-inch pots. Keep the potting mixture nicely moist. It is important to remember that carnations

Chrysanthemum 'Lilian Hoek' (Spray variety)

must have plenty of light and air. Only frost-free winter conditions are needed.

Particularly good for pots, but with smaller flowers, are the American Spray carnations. These should not have any buds removed, but should otherwise have similar treatment. In all cases the plants should be carefully supported with canes, or special shop-bought carnation supports made from wire, from an early stage. Otherwise there is a danger of the stems snapping.

Chrysanthemums

Nowadays most *Chrysanthemums* sold as houseplants arrive as short-stemmed flowering specimens in pots or bowls. These have usually been tricked into low growth by treatment with special dwarfing chemicals. They may further have been induced to flower out of season by using artificial light to give them short 'days' and long 'nights'.

These plants can be saved and grown on, but they will grow to a considerable height and will flower from late summer to autumn. If there are several plants to a container they should be separately potted after flowering. The top growth can be cut off and the plants kept only slightly moist over winter. When growth begins in spring it is best to remove shoots and use them as cuttings (see page 228), discarding the old roots.

All the larger-flowered *Chrysanthemums* have to be stopped: If left alone they will form a single bud at the top of the stem; this never develops and should be removed to encourage side shoots to form. These will produce buds that flower, but they can be further stopped if desired to obtain more side shoots and more buds – which will of course give smaller flowers.

Types with single blooms are much easier to grow, requiring little stopping. Of special interest are the recently introduced 'Mini-Mums' developed by the Wye College of Horticulture, Eng-

land. These grow only eight inches high and have single flowers in a wide colour range. They make excellent pot-plants needing only 3½-inch pots. 'Charm' *Chrysanthemums* can be grown from seed and are single-flowered types again needing little stopping. These, too, are low-growing and of bushy habit.

All *Chrysanthemums* are best grown in the open, or on a balcony, until the flowers are almost ready. They can then be taken into a cool, well lit room or conservatory to give the blooms weather protection only. Apart from the small varieties mentioned above, the plants ultimately need eight- to nine-inch pots, and should be given a rich potting mixture and be well fed. A stout supporting cane must also be provided for the taller-growing varieties.

Handsome evergreen foliage

A number of herbaceous pot-plants have year-round foliage as well as attractive blooms. *Clivia miniata* (Kafir lily), for example, has bold strap-shaped leaves and bears a number of large trumpet flowers held erect on stout stems. These

Vinca rosea 'Little Pinkie'

are very showy and usually a bright orange colour. The roots are fleshy, and flowering sized plants need eight- to ten-inch pots. The blooms appear from spring to summer, and a temperature of only about 4°C (39°F) is needed in winter.

Vinca rosea (Madagascar periwinkle) has glossy foliage and pretty starry flowers in carmine or white with carmine centres. This can be raised from seed and often flowers the same year. Grow in five-inch pots finally. *Heliconia* is best

Clivia miniata

obtained in the form of dwarf hybrids. Seed is available, although this way it takes about 3 years for blooms to appear. The plants are rather like a small-scale *Strelitzia* (see page 74). The foliage is particularly attractive and tropical-looking, and plants can be kept in seven- or eight-inch pots. Both *Vinca* and *Heliconia* need a winter minimum of at least 7°C (45°F) and may flower from spring till autumn.

Deciduous types

Agapanthus (African lily) is a particularly good tub plant for the terrace or cold conservatory; see page 149. The same applies to *Hedychium gardnerianum* and other species of *Hedychium*, popularly called gingers. The flowers are formed on spikes, usually yellow or white, and are very fragrant. *Hedychiums* flower in late autumn.

Asclepias curassavica (blood flower) has heads of flowers of unusual form, in bright orange-red, from late summer to autumn. After flowering it can be cut back to encourage compact growth the following year. A good plant for the cool

Hedychium gardnerianum

conservatory, it may retain its foliage, but should still be cut back.

Almost hardy is *Nierembergia caerulea*, which can also be cut back at the end of the season. This neat little plant is best grown in a shallow half-pot, and flowers from summer to autumn. The best variety is 'Purple Robe' with purple *Campanula*-like flowers. Also hardy but best protected from frost is *Dicentra spectabilis* (bleeding heart), again a very neat subject. The foliage is pretty, as are the rose-red heart-shaped dainty flowers borne in very early summer. Don't be surprised if this plant dies down soon after flowering – it is quite natural.

There are a number of *Mimulus* species and hybrids, but those derived from *Mimulus moschatus* (musk) are very easy

Asclepias curassavica

from seed. These can be grown in five-inch pots of moist potting mixture. They should be given good light or they will become straggly. The early summer flowers are exotically blotched in shades of red on yellow. Some people prefer to raise them as annuals from seed, but any particularly fine-coloured forms can be saved and grown on as perennials.

Kinds for shade

The *Primulas* are among the plants that prefer a position without too much light; they are covered on page 83. In the same category, *Heliotropium peruvianum* (heliotrope or cherry pie) is well known for its characteristic scent. The variety 'Marine' has a compact habit and deep violet flower clusters. *Trachelium coeruleum* has heads of massed tiny flowers in lavender blue and is very attractive. Both heliotrope and *Trachelium* can also be grown in a fairly sunny place provided quick changes are not made, and both flower from spring to summer. *Rehmannia angulata* produces hundreds of tubular scarlet flowers with orange dots from spring to summer, and is a real delight. All the above plants can be grown from seed if preferred and should be ultimately given five-inch pots.

Nertera granadensis (bead plant) earns its common name from the multitude of bright orange berries, the size of beads, with which it covers itself. These often last well into winter indoors. Only frost-free conditions are necessary since the

Heliotropium peruvianum hybrid

plant is almost hardy. It is best grown in half-pots because it is very low-growing. A tiny miniature, with flowers resembling minute foxgloves, is *Tetranema mexicana* (Mexican foxglove). This needs only a 2½- to 3½-inch pot. The foliage forms a neat rosette and the flowers are purple.

With the exception of *Nertera*, all the shade plants under this heading should have a winter minimum of about 7 to 10°C (40 to 50°F).

For sunny windows

Two plants that will not open their lovely daisy-like flowers unless given a very sunny position are *Gazania* and *Venidio-arctotis*. They both have beautifully rich colourings covering almost every possible shade except blue, and need only frost protection in winter. *Gazanias* are sold as hybrids and *Venidio-arctotis* is a cross between *Venidium fastuosum* and *Arctotis grandis*.

An interesting everlasting is *Limonium (Statice) perezii*, which often flowers in winter. It has large clusters of flowers ranging from lavender to vivid blue. *Incarvillea delavayi* has rose-pink trumpet

Gazania hybrid

flowers at the beginning of summer. Both these two can be grown from seed.

Plants for anywhere

Perhaps the most popular of all flowering pot-plants are the *Impatiens* hybrids, of which there are now very many. Well known as busy Lizzies, the best forms are the dwarf compact types. The flowers come in shades of red, salmon and cream to white, and there are some bicoloured forms. The finest plants – for flower-size, free-flowering, and habit – can be had from a good strain of seed. Thereafter, the best of a batch can be very easily multiplied from cuttings.

Also easy from seed are *Oxypetalum (Tweedia) caeruleum*, with sprays of starry pale blue flowers and grey-green foliage; *Celsia arcturus*, which has spikes of rich yellow flowers; and *Pentas*, which should be bought as dwarf hybrids and again have starry flowers in many colours. All these do well in a position that is free from frost in winter.

Requiring warmth in winter, but remarkable for its long flowering period, is *Globba winitii*. This has fleshy roots, long green leaves, and magenta and yellow flowers. Busy Lizzies can usually be best grown in 3½-inch pots, but the others described under this heading need the five-inch size.

81

Pot-plants for winter colour

In the gloomy days of winter, few things bring more cheer than a handsome and colourful pot-plant. Most foliage house-plants are of course available at this season of the year, just as at any other. But there are a number of plants with attractive flowers or fruit that appear solely in winter, and these are grown and sold in great numbers. With Christmas making this the busiest season of the year for gift plants, it is no surprise that nurserymen in Europe, North America and Japan have bred some exquisitely coloured kinds.

Christmas is also responsible for converting many people to the hobby of growing houseplants. Many of the gift plants simply survive – or, if they happen to be treated in the right way, thrive – for varying periods before dying and being thrown away. But in some cases, the recipient decides to find out more about his plant and how to help it survive for another season – and another indoor gardener is born.

A point to remember if you are buying one of these delightful winter-flowering plants as a gift is that they are not all easy to keep in good condition for long. Most of them, for example, like cool, airy conditions, and will not thrive in a stuffy, overheated room. So try to choose a gift to suit the environment it will have to inhabit.

Apart from the winter-flowering plants described here, there are a number of others covered elsewhere in this book. Among them are the 'Gloire de Lorraine' *Begonias* (see page 117); *Zygocactus* (the 'Christmas cactus'; page 67); *Kalanchoë* (page 69); and a number of orchids (pages 92 to 99). Bulbs are of course commonly forced into winter bloom (see page 107).

Azaleas and heathers
Indian azaleas – which are generally labelled *Azalea indica*, although the correct name is *Rhododendron simsii* – are grown in vast numbers and many var-

Rhododendron simsii (*Azalea indica*) varieties

Rhododendron (*Azalea*) 'Kirin'

ieties for winter colour indoors. The plants are woody, with masses of rich, dark green leaves. The flowers – single or double – come in many shades of white, pink, orange or red. Also available from time to time are the more compact Kurume azaleas, such as 'Kirin' and 'Hinomayo', with their smaller blooms.

If bought in bud, azaleas will bloom for many weeks in a cool, well lit room, provided their most important need – adequate watering – is not neglected. Indeed, the best simple advice is to give them a daily plunge in a bucketful of water until all the air bubbles escape from the pot. During the summer months the plants may be put outdoors, where they will require less water but should not dry out; they will also benefit from regular spraying of the foliage. Rainwater is best. When potting on, use a mixture of peat and leaf-mould. The Kurume types are hardy in slight frost,

but Indian azaleas should come under cover in the autumn.

In the same family as the azaleas – and needing the same cool, light conditions – are the winter-flowering heathers, or Cape heaths: *Erica gracilis*, with its masses of small dark pink flowers, and *E. hiemalis*, with tubular rose-pink flowers that are tipped with white. These should also be kept moist and frost-free, but after flowering indoors are not usually worth keeping.

Cyclamen
Thanks to its fresh, clean beauty, the florist's cyclamen, *Cyclamen persicum*, still holds its own in Christmas popularity in many countries, in spite of competition from other seasonal plants. Most cyclamen bought at this season will have been raised in cool, well aired and lightly shaded greenhouses from seed sown 12 to 15 months earlier. To keep the plants in a good state indoors, similar conditions are needed; at all

Cyclamen persicum varieties

costs avoid hot, dry, airless surroundings. Do not over-water, but the potting mixture should not dry out completely.

After flowering, when the plants naturally die down, allow their pots to dry out, and store them in a cool but frost-free place until new growth appears in midsummer. Then repot them in new potting mixture in the same pots, and put them in a fairly warm place to allow good leaf growth. Then gradually reduce the temperature to the ideal winter level of about 13°C (55°F). However, you will usually get better results by raising fresh plants from seed sown in autumn at about 24°C (75°F). When potting on the seedlings, use Potting Mixture no. 2 with a little extra peat added.

Poinsettias
The poinsettia – known botanically as *Euphorbia pulcherrima* – has long been the traditional Christmas plant in the United States, where it is often planted with small ferns. It now also seems to have the edge over the cyclamen in some other countries. It is an altogether more showy plant, bushy and well clothed with lush green leaves in properly grown specimens. The actual flowers are small and insignificant, but are surrounded by bracts the same size as the normal leaves

Euphorbia pulcherrima varieties

but vividly coloured – generally red, but pink or white in some varieties.

At one time, poinsettias were among the most troublesome of indoor plants, rapidly dropping their leaves. But modern varieties – particularly the Anglo-American 'Mikkelrochford' and the Norwegian 'Annette Hegg', both with dark red bracts – are much more tolerant of room conditions. Nevertheless, they still need good light and a temperature maintained around 16°C (61°F), and the roots should not be kept saturated for long periods. They are also more compact and easily managed than earlier varieties, as they will bush out evenly if the tops of young plants are nipped out when about five inches high. Commercial growers also use a chemical to reduce the amount of stem between leaves.

Eventually, most of the leaves will drop and the plant becomes unattractive. Then you can cut the stems down to four or five inches from the previous year's growth, and keep it dry and warm until new growth appears. Once a fair number of leaves have developed, pot on into fresh Potting Mix no. 2, begin gradual watering, and put it in a favourable growing environment. To get the plant to flower, it must be kept in no more than normal daylight – positively no artificial light in the evening from early autumn. In fact, flowering can be induced at any season if it is kept in the dark for 14 hours out of every 24 for at least a month. New plants can be raised from early summer cuttings.

Closely related, but with narrow leaves

Euphorbia fulgens

and masses of small flowers with bright red bracts, is the spurge, *E. fulgens*. This is also a winter-flowering shrub needing a light, warm position. Like the poinsettia it has a resting period after flowering.

Primulas

During the winter months, many kinds of *Primulas* are available as flowering pot-plants – all of them a fresh-looking reminder of spring. *Primula × kewensis* has yellow flowers, but is not a particularly pleasing plant. *P. malacoides* (fairy primrose), in many shades of lilac and rose-pink, is much more dainty. *P. sinensis* is available in many colours, along with *P. obconica*. The last has robust foliage and strong flower stems, but causes an irritating rash in some people who touch the plant – or, in a few cases, if they are merely in the same room. As a result it is sometimes known as the poison primrose.

All the *Primulas* are perennial, but much better results will be achieved in-

Primula × kewensis

doors by raising new plants from freshly sown seed. This is reasonably easy, though the seed is extremely small and needs careful handling. To have flowers in winter, sow the seed in early spring.

For colourful fruit

There are many varieties of *Capsicum annuum* (Christmas pepper), all having attractive chilli fruits in many colours carried above the rather weak foliage. They are colourful and interesting plants

Capsicum annuum

Solanum capsicastrum

that do best in cool, light conditions; avoid saturation when watering. To raise your own plants, sow fresh seed in the spring and pot on the plants into Potting Mixture no. 2 or 3.

Needing similar conditions, *Solanum pseudocapsicum* (Jerusalem cherry) and *S. capsicastrum* (winter cherry) both bear round orange or yellow berries on smallish plants. These abhor heavy shade, excessive heat and gas – any of which will almost inevitably result in loss of leaves and berries. The berries are not cherries at all, and are poisonous – so keep them well away from children. New plants can be raised from seed sown in spring, as for *Capsicums*. The growing points of early shoots should be removed to promote a bushier appearance and the maximum number of berries.

More winter-flowering shrubs

Apart from azaleas and winter heathers (see above), several other shrubs can come into flower during the winter months. *Acacia armata* (kangaroo thorn) bears rich yellow heads of flower in late winter on dense green foliage. It flowers freely as a small plant. For the conservatory, where it can be planted out to grow against a wall, the long-lasting, fragrant flowers of *A. pubescens* (a form of mimosa) and its feathery green foliage can be particularly pleasing as spring approaches.

Bouvardias are attractive evergreen shrubs whose fragrant pink, white or red flowers persist well into winter. They need good light and cool conditions; use Potting Mixture no. 3 when potting on. Prune hard when they finish flowering.

The cool, light conditions needed for the above will also suit the many *Camellias* that are available as potted flowering plants. Superb single and double flowers set off against dark green ovate leaves are the attraction here. The flowers are in shades of pink, red and white. If at all possible, use rainwater for watering. They are lime-haters, so pot on into a lime-free version of Potting Mixture no. 3 (see page 218). After flowering, they can be moved outdoors.

83

Colourful climbers and trailers

With more and more people rediscovering the delights of the conservatory – or its modern equivalent, the plant room – there is an ever-increasing need for the more exotic flowering plants to act as colourful living furniture. Many of the trailing and climbing plants described on these two pages will flourish in such an environment, provided it is adequately heated in winter, but it would be foolish to choose indiscriminately.

You can provide only one set of growing conditions in a small area, so select your plants accordingly. A warm room shaded from the sun will need quite different plants from a room that is light, airy and poorly heated. Of course, it is often possible to provide protection for shade-loving subjects in one corner of the conservatory. But temperature differences are more difficult to achieve in a small room, though a small heated plant case or terrarium (see page 30) can be provided for delicate smaller subjects.

Some of the less vigorous kinds can also be grown as houseplants if the right conditions can be achieved. Trailers are often easier here – *Hypocyrta glabra* (the clog plant) is a popular houseplant, for example – but some climbers can be trained on canes, trellis or wire hoops. *Hoya carnosa*, for instance, sometimes flowers as a very small plant.

Trailers for warmth and shade

Almost all the epiphytic plants are seen at their best when they are suspended in mid-air, be they in a hanging basket or a suspended pot. Or, more like their natural habit, they can be attached to a piece of bark that is in turn hung from the wall or ceiling. The three types mentioned here will all be at their most spectacular if they are suspended at about eye level so that their stems droop down, showing off their striking flower colouring. All will do perfectly well in hanging baskets filled with a potting mixture containing a liberal amount of peat. Putting several plants, rather than a single specimen, in each basket will provide a much more exciting effect when flowers appear.

Aeschynanthus (*Trichosporum*) *lobbianus* has elliptical leaves that are dark green on healthy plants, but the colour may vary to pale green where plants have been exposed to too much light. The spectacular flowers are in shades of glistening red with a yellow throat. As a result, it is sometimes called the lipstick plant.

The flowers of the *Columneas* are generally less spectacular than the foregoing, but what they lack in this way they more than make up for in numbers. One of the best known and probably the easiest to care for is *Columnea × banksii*, which produces masses of small ovate leaves on stiff stems, and has attractive reddish-orange flowers. Its ease of propagation from cuttings is reason enough for its popularity. *C. microphylla* has much smaller leaves that are soft to the touch and lack the rigidity of the former plant's, but it is interesting nevertheless, with dull red flowers that have a tinge of yellow in the tube. Where there is ample head room that will permit growth to

trail for some five to six feet, an ideal subject is *C.* 'Stavanger'. This variety has flowers three inches long and colouring that embraces fiery red, orange and a touch of yellow for good measure.

The *Columneas* will all flower better if the potting mixture is kept a little drier than normal just prior to their natural flowering time, which starts in spring. They enjoy damp, shaded conditions, and an average temperature of 19°C (66°F), but will do well enough in lower temperatures provided they are kept on the dry side.

In the same environment, *Episcias* will also do perfectly. There is a wide choice of these delightful little plants which, besides bearing small though attractive flowers, have the added bonus of pleasing foliage. *Episcia cupreata* (flame violet) is one of the best known, and causes little bother. It has coppertinged leaves that are soft and hairy, and orange-yellow single, tubular flowers. There are almost a score of attractive mutants of *E. cupreata* that could form an interesting plant collection alone.

Strong climbing subjects

For summer splendour in the conservatory, the most colourful climber must be the *Bougainvillea*, although the winter appearance, when the woody branches are denuded of foliage, is not at all attractive. The brilliant purple flowers

Columnea × banksii

Bougainvillea sp

of *Bougainvillea glabra* are probably the best known, but there are now many other kinds, with more attractive colouring, that are equally easy to care for. Another old favourite is *B. × buttiana* 'Mrs Butt' (known as 'Crimson Lake' in the US), which is freer growing and

Episcia cupreata

Hoya carnosa variegata

flower panicles age the colours change.

In winter the roots of *Bougainvillea* should be kept dry and the plant reasonably warm. When new growth is evident early in the spring normal watering should begin. If necessary, the plant can be potted on, once it has made a good amount of leaf, to a slightly larger container, using Potting Mix no. 2. The pot must be well drained. In summer the principal need is for good light, reasonable warmth and airy conditions, with occasional feeding. Thereafter, it is simply a question of tying in the normally vigorous growth and sitting back to admire what is usually an abundance of brilliant colour. Mealy bug (see page 232) can be a problem, particularly in more inaccessible high branches, but not many problems arise otherwise if growing conditions are agreeable.

For the light, airy situation, the azure-blue flowers of *Plumbago capensis* can be a real joy. Its cultivation is not difficult if, instead of growing conventionally in pots, plants can be planted out in a narrow border in the conservatory where they have a freer root run. It is commonly called the Cape leadwort.

The heavily scented tubular white flowers of *Stephanotis floribunda* will provide an added interest to the conservatory collection and, once settled in, the plant is not too much of a problem. Keep it on the dry side in winter, when

loss of some leaves is inevitable, and treat the troublesome and messy mealy bug pest as soon as it is seen, since otherwise it is difficult to reach amongst the twisting stems of the plant. In late summer, following flowering, fairly harsh pruning is usually needed to keep excessive growth under control.

Similar treatment is needed for *Hoya carnosa* (the wax flower) which, if anything, is a more rampant grower. The main attraction here is the jewel-like, waxy flower clusters that hang on short stalks. There are also two variegated varieties, however, that also have attractive fleshy leaves: one gold and green, the other green with pink edges that fade to a creamy colour. Much more compact, but with similar pendulous wax flowers, is the superb *H. bella*. This is one for the expert, however, needing warm, shaded conditions. It does best in a basket.

A truly rampant climber that will take the place over if not kept under strict control is *Passiflora caerulea* (passion flower). It will, in fact, grow outdoors in many areas. Growth will be less vigorous – and the plant will flower more freely – if the roots are confined to a pot that would seem too small for the top growth of the plant. The flowers are quite unique, and their various parts were used by early Christian missionaries to South America (where the plant originated) to illustrate the biblical story of the crucifixion – hence the common name. In *P. caerulea* they are predominantly white and bluish-purple, and three inches across. In the variety 'Constance Elliott', however, they are all-white, and other species have flowers of similar shape but other colourings – though purple, blue and white predominate.

Some other kinds

Trails of white star flowers some three feet in length are not impossible with *Campanula isophylla* (star of Bethlehem) when growing in a pot as small as five inches in diameter. The secret is to keep it light and cool, well watered and fed during the summer months, and to cut it back almost to the bone for its winter rest. Pot into fresh Potting Mixture no. 3 when new growth is evident in spring. *C. isophylla* 'Mayii' has hairy leaves and blue flowers; it is a more difficult subject needing extra warmth.

The glossy-green, fleshy-leaved *Hypocyrta glabra* (also known as *H. radicans* or the clog plant) bears masses of orange flowers in the spring, and thrives in reasonable light and warmth. It is an excellent basket subject, and likes shaded, humid conditions.

For almost any position in a wide assortment of conditions, *Plectranthus oertendahlii*, and its variegated form, will give little trouble. It is another trailer, and besides attractive veined foliage the flowers of palest pink are an added attraction. Keep it moist, well fed, lightly shaded and reasonably warm. In similar conditions *Lotus berthelotti* (winged pea) will also do well. Although its growth is more untidy, the scarlet butterfly flowers are attractive.

bears larger flowers that are crimson in colour, as the American name indicates. A popular European variety in recent years has been 'Kiltie Campbell' which, like a number of other excellent cultivars, originated from Kenya. Colouring is in many shades of orange; as the

Passiflora caerulea

Flowering conservatory climbers

When it comes to choosing plants for a glazed plant room – whether it be the traditional kind of conservatory, a modern-style sun-lounge or merely a lean-to greenhouse attached to the house – the choice is enormous. For here we are in the realm of greenhouse plants, rather than houseplants that will tolerate more trying conditions.

Many of those included here are dual-purpose plants that may climb of their own accord, may be encouraged to do so by tying in, or may trail over the edge of the plant room table or from hanging baskets. Some are quick-growing, invasive plants that need ample headroom to be seen at their best. These may also need periodic pruning, and, where the ceiling is low, overhead trellis or wires may be necessary for attachment. Most will also need good light in order to flourish, but also some protection from strong sunlight.

Not all the plants in this section are compatible in every way, but the majority can be grown in reasonably cool conditions – particularly during the winter, when the temperature can be lowered to about 10°C (50°F) for most. For many, drier root conditions in winter are essential, and this is a distinct advantage where lower temperatures prevail. Most of these plants will grow much more freely – and be a good deal less bother to care for – if they can be planted in large beds of potting mixture. There are exceptions, but in the main Mix no. 3 will give excellent results, and a little added charcoal will prevent the mixture turning sour. Whether in pots or beds, adequate drainage is essential. The potting mixture should be firm but not rammed down hard.

Finally, with all these climbing plants it is particularly important to keep a watchful eye open for pests, as these are difficult to control once they have established themselves in the twining branches of more inaccessible specimens.

The pea family
The climbing peas (members of the Leguminosae) provide many of the tougher rambling plants for clothing the walls and ceilings of plant rooms. In the main they are reasonably easy to manage. *Chorizema cordatum* has spiny, heart-shaped leaves and orange-red flowers with a yellow blotch at their base. Native to Australia, where it has the common name of flame pea, the branches are thin and wiry. It is not difficult; water well and allow to dry a little before watering again.

Clianthus puniceus (parrot's bill) is an all-purpose plant that can be used as a climber, border or basket plant. It is attractive, with fern-like foliage and scarlet flowers not unlike the claws of a lobster. There are also white and rose-coloured forms. Growing to a height of some three feet, *C. formosus* (*C. dampieri*, or glory pea) is a much more difficult plant in the early stages of its growth. This is because it does not do particularly well on its own root system, and needs to be grafted on to young plants of *Colutea arborescens*. While the graft is establishing a temperature of not less than 21°C (70°F) must be maintained. When obviously established, the temperature can be gradually reduced to about 14°C (57°F). The principal attraction here is the pendulous racemes of scarlet pea-shaped flowers with a dark purple blotch at their base. It can also be grown as a hanging basket or border subject in the conservatory.

Bearing masses of violet flowers with yellow spots, *Hardenbergia monophylla* (*H. violacea*, or coral pea) is an easy plant that will reach a height of some ten feet. Any pruning that is necessary should be tackled in late winter and, when required, potting on should be undertaken at the same time.

The flowers of *Swainsonia galegifolia*, another Australian native, are mainly purplish-red, though they also come in other colours. They provide a welcome splash of summer colour. The plant will appreciate a sheltered, sunny position out of doors in warmer areas. New plants may be raised from cuttings a few inches in length taken in the spring, or from seed soaked in warm water for an hour or two before being sown shallowly in Potting Mixture no. 1.

Easy kinds from seed
Although not many of the climbing plants described on these two pages are available from commercial growers, many of them are easily raised from seed; and all of the following are. For best results, use fresh seed from a reliable supplier and sow in Potting Mixture no. 1 at about 19°C (66°F) (see page 226). Young plants should be protected from strong sunlight.

The tuberous-rooted *Antigonon leptopus* (coral vine) is a showy climber with arrow-shaped leaves on winding stems. It bears racemes of rose-pink flowers, and prefers light, cool, evenly moist conditions. Having kidney-shaped leaves, *Aristolchia elegans* (calico flower) grows to about ten feet and needs light shade and some humidity. The flowers consist of a dull yellow tube and purple cup, the inside of which is marked in white.

Cobaea scandens (cups-and-saucers) gets its common name from the cup-and-saucer appearance of the purple flowers that appear in summer. Though perennial, it is much better to grow this fast-growing plant as an annual and to raise fresh plants each year. It can be grown out of doors in summer, and adapts to many differing conditions in the plant room, but prefers light, cool conditions. Immediately after flowering, the shoots of the deciduous climber *Mandevillea suaveolens* (Chilean jasmine) should be pruned hard to within a few buds of the base. The bright green leaves are heart-shaped and borne on twisting stems, and the delightfully scented flowers appear in summer. Avoid wet conditions in winter. *Manettia inflata* has thin, almost thread-like stems and fleshy green leaves, from the axils of which individual tubular flowers are produced. These are a bright, waxy yellow with scarlet bristles at their base. The plant should be lightly pruned after flowering.

Maurandia erubescens (also called *Asarina erubescens*) is commonly named the creeping gloxinia because of the similarity in the large trumpet-shaped flowers. The plant blooms over a long period and has interesting twining flower stalks. Black-eyed Susan (*Thunbergia alata*) is one of the best known climber/trailers in this section, and has orange or yellow flowers with dark purple centres that are colourful for much of the year. Avoid the temptation to overpot, and guard against saturated conditions.

Needing slightly warmer conditions, *Oxypetalum caeruleum* (also called *Tweedia caerula*) is also less free growing. It produces fragrant blue flowers in summer. Best results may be achieved by sowing seed direct into the plant-room border or into the pots where the plants are intended to grow. Morning glory (*Ipomoea purpurea* or *Pharbitis purpurea*) has deep-purple, funnel-shaped flowers that individually last for only a few hours each morning, but there is a

Ipomoea purpurea 'Wedding Bells'

continual fresh supply. It is a free-growing climber that is also available in many other colours. When sowing, put several seeds in a small pot so that the potful is progressively potted on as required. There are also some excellent related perennial species available for the warmer plant room.

Some other kinds
Cestrum purpureum (also called *C. elegans*) has dull-green leaves and attractive pendulous clusters of wine-red flowers. It attains a height of about ten feet and can be increased by means of cuttings. Also propagated from cuttings taken in summer, *Solanum jasminoides* has woody stems and star-shaped white flowers tinged with blue. *S. seaforthianum* has purple flowers with yellow anthers, followed by scarlet fruits. Free-flowering in the spring, *Streptosolen jamesonii* is a rambling shrub with oddly wrinkled leaves. Its flowers are tubular and bell-shaped, and orange in colour. All these plants are members of the potato family, Solanaceae.

The pendulous, rose-crimson bell flowers of *Lapageria rosea* are among the most beautiful of all climbing plants; the leaves are ovate and leathery. A free-draining peaty potting mixture is most essential for this subject, and the growing temperature should be in the region of 13 to 16°C (55 to 61°F). It is commonly called the Chilean bell-flower.

High temperatures between 16 and 21°C (61 and 70°F) are required for *Beaumontia grandiflora* (herald's trumpet). The large ovate leaves may be eight inches long, and the large, dark-throated, white trumpet flowers are a special feature of this plant. But it is a subject that requires that little extra care in order to do well.

Pyrostegia ignea (*Bignonia venusta*) is a natural climbing shrub with self-clinging tendrils and clusters of bright red-orange flowers that are tubular in shape and borne in clusters. The leaves are oblong and pointed. This will tolerate quite severe pruning in late winter, when all weak growth should be completely removed.

Thunbergia alata varieties

Indoor flowering shrubs

Indoors, as in the garden, shrubby plants that bear colourful flowers are an essential part of any balanced plant collection. The plants covered here are a varied selection. All are decorative. Most will happily spend the warm summer months outdoors, perhaps on a sheltered terrace or balcony; some of the most suitable types for this treatment are described on pages 102 and 103. Some of the flowering shrubs – notably *Gossypium*, the cotton plant – have important commercial uses.

Not all these plants are suitable for anything other than ideal conditions indoors, but all will do well in a conservatory or greenhouse. If you can raise them under glass, any of them can be brought into the home for periodic display. In their natural environment many will develop into substantial shrubs or small trees, but with their roots confined to pots the rate of growth is considerably reduced. Careful pruning will also help to keep them within bounds, and will result in more compact and attractive plants.

The mallow family

The most important commercial decorative plant in the mallow family is undoubtedly *Hibiscus rosa-sinensis* (rose of China or Chinese hibiscus), of which there are many cultivars. The majority have large single flowers – though there are also doubles – in many shades of yellow, orange and red. Plants may be allowed to dry out and shed their leaves in winter, or they may be kept watered, so retaining their leaves. Individual flowers last for little more than one day, but they are produced in great profusion, so there is a continual supply throughout the summer months. Reasonably light, airy conditions are an essential requirement, together with ample water and feeding while the plants are actively growing.

The variety *H. rosa-sinensis Cooperi* is an equally easy, bolder plant with white and green variegated foliage. The small red flowers are less conspicuous than in the type, but it will develop into a superb plant if it has a reasonable space in which to grow.

Also in the same family are the *Abutilons*, commonly known as the flowering maples because of their leaf shape. There are a number of kinds available, and possibly *Abutilon striatum thompsonii* is both the most attractive and the most readily available. It has the typical 'maple' leaves – dark green with yellow

Abutilon sp

mottling – and bell-shaped flowers that are salmon-orange in colour. Raised in spring from seed or cuttings, it is easily managed in warm, light conditions.

Cotton plants, *Gossypium herbaceum* and *G. hirsutum*, are not difficult to raise from seed sown in warm conditions in the spring. Transplant singly into small pots filled with Potting Mixture no. 2 as the plantlets become large enough. They like a temperature in the region of 19°C (66°F), and good light. The leaves are palmate, and the flowers an attractive yellow – a paler shade in the latter species. After flowering, fruit capsules form, and these eventually burst to expose fluffy balls of cotton fibres.

The pea family

A space-filler that may attain a height of some twenty feet when in a large pot, *Albizzia julibrissin* (silk tree) is easier to handle as a much smaller subject. It is not difficult to raise from seed in spring in warm conditions. In smaller pots, the plants can be kept at a more reasonable height, so new plants should not be needed each year. The acacia-like foliage makes an attractive foil for other plants.

The evergreen shrub *Cassia fistula* (pudding-pipe tree) does best in a free-draining potting mix in moderate warmth. It is the producer of medicinal senna pods. *Caesalpinia sepiaria* is a rambling shrub with masses of small leaves and upright yellow flowers that eventually form curved pods. Provide reasonable light and place the plant out

Hibiscus rosa-sinensis varieties

Gossypium hirsutum

Pachystachys 'Lutea'

of doors in summer in more temperate climates; prune only sufficiently to retain its shape.

There are many fine species of *Cytisus* (broom) that form very colourful potted plants, and *Cytisus canariensis* (the genista of the flower trade) is one of the best. It may grow to some six feet in height. Re-pot in Mixture no. 2 or no. 3 in late spring. To retain better shape and a more manageable plant that will also flower more freely, it should be pruned hard after flowering.

Poinciana (Caesalpinia) pulcherrima is a tropical shrub with leaves not unlike those of the mimosa and showy orange-red racemes of flower. It requires the same treatment as *C. sepiaria*.

The spurge family
This family offers many surprises, none greater than the *Acalyphas*, of which two are occasionally available: *Acalypha hispida* and *A. wilkesiana*. The former is variously known as red-hot cat's-tail or the chenille plant; its main attraction is the pendulous, beetroot-red flowers that are rather like cats' tails and are freely produced in summer. The coppery-red foliage of *A. wilkesiana* is especially attractive on more mature plants. Both plants do best in agreeably warm conditions – in the region of 19°C (66°F) – where the atmosphere is kept humid by frequently moistening the area around the plant. Keep a watchful eye for red spider mite (see page 232).

Bract-forming plants
There are a number of indoor flowering shrubs that form colourful bracts around their flowers. All of those described below need warm, lightly shaded and moist conditions to succeed, but given these requirements will develop into quite spectacular plants.

As its common name suggests, the bracts of *Beloperone guttata* (the shrimp plant) are a pinkish colour, and they do look remarkably like shrimps. In the early stages of growth, the growing tips should be regularly pinched out and the early flowering bracts should also be removed. This will promote more vigorous leaf growth and a more compact plant. To keep your plant healthy and on the move, feed it regularly and pot on into Mixture no. 3. Straggly growth can be pruned to shape when the plant is not in flower.

A very fine variety with lime-green to yellow bracts is sometimes available. It is sold as *B.* 'Lutea' or *B.* 'Yellow

Queen', and is a little more difficult to care for than *B. guttata*. But in conditions to its liking it forms a much larger and more spectacular plant.

Crossandra infundibuliformis is a little more difficult to manage, and will demand all the cultural suggestions mentioned earlier, with an important addition: very careful watering that ensures that the roots are kept evenly moist, avoiding extremes of wet and dry. The bracts are a dark salmon colour and the leaves a glossy green – an added attraction in any plant. There is also a cultivar of more compact habit named 'Mona Wallhed'.

In recent years *Pachystachys* 'Lutea' has come to the fore as an interesting and floriferous plant that produces an endless succession of golden yellow bracts throughout the summer months. These rise above the plain green foliage. Ample moisture and regular feeding are essential, as is annual potting on into Potting Mix no. 3. The pot must be adequately drained. Non-flowering cuttings root readily in warm conditions at almost any time of the year in a mixture of peat and sand.

Some evergreens
Fragrance is always an attraction in plants, and among the longest-flowering fragrant shrubs that can be grown indoors are the *Boronias*. These compact plants from Australia need warm, lightly shaded and moist conditions. There are a number of species, any of which will be rewarding, including *Boronia denticu-*

lata, *B. elatior*, *B. megastigma* and *B. serrulata*.

The purple, fragrant flowers of *Brunfelsia calycina* are borne on compact plants from late winter until autumn. *Brunfelsias* need warmer conditions – some 20°C (68°F) – in order to do well. Pot on into Mixture no. 3 fairly firmly after flowering. *Fabiana imbricata* bears white flowers in early summer. It may grow to a height of some eight feet, and needs to be kept on the dry side in winter, in cool conditions. Requiring a peat and leaf-mould potting mixture, *Gordonia axillaris* also produces white summer flowers and may attain a height of as much as 15 feet.

Beloperone guttata

Fragrant indoor plants

Even the most beautiful foliage or flowering plant is somehow lacking if it has no scent. This is even more true indoors than in the garden, of course – hence the attraction of fragrant cut flowers. Unfortunately, there are not very many fragrant houseplants, but those described here are renowned for their fragrant flowers or foliage. All are very decorative and perennial by nature. With a few exceptions they are easy to grow, some soon flowering from seed.

Calonyction

The climber *Calonyction aculeatum* is commonly called the moonflower because the large white convolvulus-like flowers open at dusk. They are intensely fragrant and will fill a room or conservatory with a lily-like scent. The stems are usually long enough for cutting, and a pink variety is sometimes available.

The seed can be sown as early in the season as convenient and germinates best if soaked overnight in water before sowing. Pot on to seven-inch pots, in which the plants will bloom the first year. Give them a cane to climb up. The species is perennial and is best eventually given a permanent position in, say, a lean-to conservatory so that the fragrance can penetrate into the house. The ultimate height is from 10 to 12 feet.

Citrus

Oranges, lemons, limes and other *Citrus* plants all have strongly fragrant flowers, usually star-shaped, white, and of waxy texture. Most of the fruit you buy is from plants that do not come true from seed, and if you start from pips you must not be surprised if the resulting plants flower poorly or not at all. The fruit, if any, may also be nothing like you expect. However, the most likely pips to experiment with are from lime (*Citrus aurantifolia*), lemon (*C. limon*) and grapefruit (*C. paradisi*). Lemons are indeed almost hardy in frost-free places, and the other

species only need a cool place in order to make fine plants after a few years.

Pot on the seedlings as the roots fill their pots. Ultimately provide small tubs or large pots. The plants do best if stood out in the open in summer and given protection indoors for the winter. Small tubs can be mounted on wheels so that they can be pushed into an orangery or conservatory conveniently in autumn. Most *Citrus* grow very well and vigorously in the generally used potting mixtures, such as no. 2.

If space is limited, dwarf varieties can be grown. There are dwarf lemons, such as the ponderosa lemon, but *Citrus mitis* (the calamondin orange) is one of the most widely grown. The fruit is about the size of a walnut and can be preserved in syrup. The flowers are very freely produced, sweetly scented and very pretty. This particular species prefers an acid potting mixture. If other species seem to develop yellowed foliage it may also be advisable to water with a solution made up by dissolving a pinch of aluminium sulphate in a pint of water. This will help make the soil acid, but the treatment is not always necessary.

Coffea

The coffee plant, *Coffea arabica*, is easy to grow from fresh (unroasted) beans. These germinate if immersed in moist peat in a warm place. The seedlings should be potted on and will grow well in congenial warmth. The plants have attractive glossy foliage, and if the temperature can be kept up they will grow to the size of small bushes and produce masses of white, very fragrant flowers. These are followed by red berries that contain coffee beans.

Cyphomandra

The tree tomato, *Cyphomandra betacea*, is usually grown in the mistaken belief that the fruit can be used in the same way as tomatoes. Actually the plant is

quite different, and the fruit from plants grown in the non-ideal conditions of rooms and conservatories is of poor quality. However, the attractive flowers have a pleasant fragrance. Sow the seed in spring and grow on the plants to five-inch pots. Overwinter in a minimum temperature of about 10°C (50°F), keeping the plants slightly moist. Early the following spring pot on to eight-inch pots. The plants may then flower, but usually this takes about three years from seed – by which time the plants will probably be three to four feet tall.

The flowers are pinkish in colour and borne in racemes. The fruits that follow are like plum-shaped tomatoes and at their best have an intense tomato flavour. As grown outdoors in places like New Zealand they are delicious, but tend to be 'woody' when grown indoors. The foliage sometimes has an unpleasant smell if bruised, and it attracts greenfly (aphids; see page 232) – so preventive spraying with a safe insecticide is advisable.

Datura

The plant commonly known as angel's trumpet is *Datura suaveolens*. This is best seen when it has become established to form a very small tree, although it will flower from two to three years after sowing the seed. It bears very large, white, lily-like trumpet flowers which hang down from the stems most beautifully and have an intense lily-like fragrance. Best results are had in a warmish greenhouse or conservatory, or a room where the air does not become too dry. Plants can be flowered in ten-inch pots, and subsequently should be given small tubs or larger pots if possible. Water freely in summer but less in winter.

Daphne

Several slightly tender species of *Daphne* are well known to gardeners, and most can be grown even better in a frost-free greenhouse or conservatory. The most

Citrus sp

Citrus sinensis

Datura suaveolens

popular is *Daphne mezereum*, which has flowers from pink to red on leafless branches from late winter to spring. However for a cool conservatory or room the species *D. odora* is recommended. This has purplish flowers with a strong spicy aroma, also from winter to early spring. An interesting variety called 'Aureomarginata' is also sometimes available. This is very decorative,

Daphne odora

with creamy-white margins to the leaves, and it is slightly hardier than the species.

All *Daphnes* tend to dislike lime or chalk. Pot them in a lime-free potting mixture, or leave out the chalk from formulae you make yourself (see page 218). Note that *Daphne* berries are poisonous although often decorative – so see that children do not swallow them.

Gardenia

Making an exquisitely scented buttonhole flower, *Gardenia jasminoides* is unfortunately not one of the easiest in this group to grow. The variety 'Florida' makes a neat pot-plant, but for success two levels of temperature are really

Gardenia jasminoides

needed: for active growth 16 to 26°C (60 to 80°F), and in winter about 10°C (50°F). When flowering, the plants should be kept cool and water applied cautiously. When the plants are growing actively the air should be kept warm and humid, and water given freely, with frequent overhead spraying with tepid water. Old

plants frequently fail to flower well and are best discarded. It is an advantage to mix some crushed charcoal with the potting mixture.

Jasminum

Not all species of jasmine are scented. The easiest and most powerfully fragrant for a cool conservatory, or for growing in pots in cool rooms indoors, is *Jasminum polyanthum*. Once established this can grow so vigorously that it would smother everything else in a conservatory unless kept severely checked. Since it becomes covered with wonderfully fragrant white flowers in early spring, you may be reluctant to prune drastically. Nevertheless, plants given permanent positions

Jasminum polyanthum

must be kept under control. As young plants the species can be trained up and down canes inserted in quite small pots.

Luculia

The species *Luculia gratissima* is not well known but is easy to raise from seed. It can be flowered in ten-inch pots, but is most impressive if room can be found in a cool conservatory. There it will grow to an appreciable size, even to form a small tree. When bearing its showy rose-pink flowers in winter, it is a wonderful sight – and the fragrance is fantastic! To grow it to a fair size use a small tub. The roots can be kept slightly pot bound with advantage in this case. Water well in summer, prune to shape in winter, and from then on keep fairly dry until growth commences again.

Scented-foliage plants

Among the plants with scented foliage rather than flowers, the best known are probably the scented-leaved geraniums (see page 105). Most *Eucalyptus* are fairly hardy, but a species ideal for indoors that is not suitable for chilly

places is *Eucalyptus citriodora*. This can be grown from seed and makes a very attractive foliage plant. Its leaves give a strong lemon scent when gently rubbed.

Myrtles have very aromatic foliage as well as attractive flowers and usually decorative fruits. They are ideal for cold conservatories or where only frost protection is possible, but they usually grow to a considerable size eventually.

Eucalyptus gunnii

The common myrtle is *Myrtus communis*. This can be grown in pots, where growth can be confined to a spread and height of about two to three feet. There are also some particularly compact varieties available. The foliage is shiny and charming flowers appear in summer.

Lippia citriodora, also known as *Aloysia citriodora* or lemon scented verbena, is an old favourite of cold conservatories. It is not notable for showy flowers, although these are pretty – tubular and pale mauve – and appear in late summer. The long pale green leaves are very strongly lemon-scented, and this is particularly intense when the leaves are crushed. The plant should be cut back to

Myrtus communis

the old wood in late winter, and the young growth should be 'stopped' from time to time (by pinching out the growth points) to induce bushy habit. If this is not done the plant can become very straggly. When grown in a greenhouse or conservatory the temperature should not fall below freezing in winter.

Orchids, the ultimate exotics

Of all the flowering plants that can be grown in the home or conservatory, none have quite such an aura as orchids. Ever since Victorian days, when rich amateurs paid small fortunes for rare specimens brought from the mountains and jungles of far-distant lands, they have represented the summit of horticultural luxury. And even today the orchid houses of the world's great botanical gardens attract admiration and awe.

As a result of this attitude, very many people are afraid to grow orchids indoors, believing them to be difficult and expensive. In fact, just the opposite can be the case. Many kinds do admittedly need hot, steamy, jungle-like conditions, but many others are as easy to cultivate as plenty of the plants sold specifically as houseplants. They have their own particular likes and dislikes, certainly; and these are often different from the needs of other houseplants. But there is no great difficulty in meeting their requirements in most homes.

Equally, the idea that orchids are expensive has elements of both truth and myth. A unique and beautiful hybrid may cost many hundreds of pounds, but there are plenty of beautiful subjects available for a tiny fraction of this price. One reason is new methods of propagation, which have made it possible to grow literally thousands of plants from a single small cutting. So for much less than £5 you can buy a plant that would have been auctioned a hundred years ago at a hundred times the price.

The diversity of orchids

Making up one in seven of all the world's flowering plant species, it is not really surprising that the orchid family contains some fascinating subjects. There are minute blooms that need studying with a magnifying glass, and others a foot across. There are some with solitary blooms on single stems, some with tall spikes of flowers, and some with dozens of clustered tiny blooms. Some live naturally thousands of feet above sea level, while others inhabit low-lying steamy swamps. There are hardy wild orchids in most parts of Europe and North America, while an Australian type lives totally underground. Some orchid blooms are beautifully scented, while others have no fragrance at all and some stink foully.

In all there are probably some 25,000 distinct orchid species, and as a result of their unique ability to hybridize, both in the wild and in cultivation, more than 50,000 hybrids are known. Even among members of the same species there may be wide variation.

What makes orchids different

Part of the mystique of orchids undoubtedly arises from the odd appearance of the plants. Very many have thick, fleshy swollen parts at the base of the stems. These are known as pseudo-bulbs, and act as food and water storage organs for periods of drought.

Perhaps the greatest single characteristic that makes orchids different from all other plants, however, lies in the way the flower is built. There are always three sepals and three petals, but one of

Orchids and science
Science has greatly aided the orchid collector and grower. **above** John Lindley was the most eminent Victorian orchid botanist, and the systematic arrangement of orchids into genera and species is still based on his classification. This, in turn, has been the basis on which growers have been able to hybridize orchids. Equally important for the

successful grower has been an understanding of the plants' structure and function. **above** Orchids are unique in having swollen parts at the base of the stems called pseudo-bulbs **1**, which store water. As the plant grows, new pseudo-bulbs are formed, and the old back-bulbs **2** wither. The orchid flower always has three petals **3** and three sepals **4**. One of the petals is enlarged to form the lip or labellum **5**, just above which is the column, the combined pistil and stamens.

CYPRIPEDIUM FAIRRIEANUM

The variety of orchids
Some orchids are terrestrial species – that is, they live naturally on the ground. An example is *Paphiopedilum* (*Cypripedium*) *fairrieanum* **above**. Others are epiphytic, living on tree-branches and similar places, like *Miltonia spectabilis moreliana* **below**. Orchid flowers also vary widely in shape, size and number, as the illustrations here and opposite show.

PL. XXVII. MILTONIA SPECTABILIS MORELIANA (½ G.)

the petals is always modified in a particular way. In the *Cypripediums* and *Paphiopedilums*, for example, it is a shoe-shaped pouch – hence the common name slipper orchid. Or it may be in the form of an apron (as in *Miltonias*, or pansy orchids) or a lip (as in the *Odontoglossums*, *Cymbidiums* and – most flamboyant of all – the *Cattleyas*). Usually this third petal has a different colour pattern from the others, and may even be the largest part of the flower (as in *Brassavola digbyana*).

The reproductive mechanism of the orchid flower is also unique. In place of the normal separate male and female parts – the stamens and pistil – there is a single structure called the column. So different is this from the arrangement in other flowers that it was not until the middle of the last century that orchids' method of reproduction was properly understood – a vital first step to producing hybrids. In fact, the first successful orchid hybridization was performed only in 1854, and by the end of the century there were a mere 90 or so known hybrids.

The orchid hunters

By this time, orchid-collecting had become a big business. Long before – as early as the seventeenth century – orchids had been brought into Europe from the tropics by seamen and others. But the then 'methods' of cultivation were often lethal. It was only when cast iron pipes became available – allowing greenhouses to be heated with hot water from boilers – that the commercial cultivation of orchids developed.

From the early 1830s, dedicated and informed men were sent out to the tropics to collect orchids and other plants. They worked either for wealthy private patrons or, like the Lobb brothers sent out in 1840 and 1843 by James Veitch, for commercial nurserymen. During the 1850s, a stream of collectors poured into the tropics of Asia and the Americas, working for nurserymen in various European countries. The stream became a torrent in the 1890s – the hey-day of Frederick Sander, the giant among Victorian orchid dealers.

In some cases, the collectors were brutally ruthless, taking every sample of particular plants that they could find – tens of thousands in some cases – or taking just a few and destroying all others to preserve their rarity. At one auction, Sander offered 40,000 specimens of *Paphiopedilum spicerianum*. At others, a single specimen of an extreme rarity might fetch thousands of pounds.

This, the golden age of orchid hunting, came to an end with the start of World War I. But it was just after the war – in 1922 – that an American scientist called Lewis Knudson discovered how to grow orchid plants from seed in sterile flasks of nutrient jelly without the fungal growth usually needed. This enabled orchid seedlings to be grown by the thousand – and, with mass production, prices began to tumble. Then, after World War II, George Morel, a French scientist, discovered how to propagate hundreds of plants from a tiny cutting taken from the tip of a growing shoot. This method of 'meristem' propagation means that 'copies' of new

and beautiful hybrids can be produced in unlimited numbers – far more than by old methods of dividing whole plants.

Living with orchids

If propagating methods have advanced, the cultivation of orchid plants in a living room is no modern development. These exciting plants were cultivated successfully well over a hundred years ago in numerous European and North American homes. Even in those days, when home heating was mostly by open coal fires, enthusiasts grew and flowered their orchid plants with as much success as today's home gardeners. There were fewer varieties to be tried, of course, and a preponderance of the easiest-to-grow plants. There were very few hybrids, in particular, but the species were much more numerous.

With the advent of centrally heated homes, thermostatically controlled, and modern methods of lighting, many kinds of orchid thrive at least as well in a living room as a greenhouse. For suggestions of good kinds to try, see pages 96 to 99. Even with easy types, you need to choose the growing position carefully, of course, and provide the conditions your plants enjoy. But this is not particularly difficult if you follow the hints on pages 94 and 95. In fact, having your plants close at hand rather than in a possibly remote greenhouse makes control over the conditions – particularly the vital factor of lighting – easier. And, of course, you have the supreme advantage of having your collection of unique and beautiful plants close at hand to admire.

Cymbidium hybrid

Oncidium varicosum

Paphiopedilum praestans

Growing orchids indoors

Most people are unjustifiably scared of growing orchid plants, particularly if they have no greenhouse or conservatory. In fact, if you take a little trouble to give them the conditions they like – in other words, conditions as close as possible to those in their natural home – orchids are a good deal less trouble than many other plants. However, the fact that almost all cultivated orchids – even the hybrids – originate in the forests and mountains of tropical and subtropical regions means that suitable conditions are not always easy to achieve.

Careful choice of the varieties to grow is the first requirement, for it is obviously very difficult to keep a type that needs steamy jungle conditions in your living room. Even among the plants recommended on pages 96 to 99 there is considerable variation in needs, and these individual quirks are explained with the plant descriptions.

Basic requirements

In spite of these variations, however, there are basic requirements common to all orchids – principally heat, humidity and light. And the most important factor is light. The intensity of light that orchid plants receive in the wild varies widely from the Amazon forests to the Colombian Cordilleras and the foothills of the Himalayas. But all tropical and subtropical regions have at least 10 and usually 14 hours of daylight every day of the year. So if you can give your plants at least ten hours of light daily – if necessary boosting natural light with artificial – this will go a long way towards achieving good growing conditions. Remember, however, that exposure to light for more than 16 hours a day may prevent orchids flowering. Also, except in winter in cool temperate regions, direct, unshaded sunlight is too over-powering for most orchids. Wherever your orchids grow, turn the pots occasionally so that illumination is even.

The second factor is warmth, which is closely linked with humidity: in general, the higher the temperature, the higher the humidity should be. Most of the orchids recommended for indoor growing like an average day-time temperature of 20 to 21°C (68 to 70°F) in summer and 15 to 18°C (59 to 64°F) in winter – with the night temperature about 5°C (10°F) lower. This night-time drop is most important, and if necessary you should move your plants to a cooler part of the home at night.

The best way of achieving good humidity is to stand your plants just above a tray of wet gravel over a heat source, such as a radiator (see the next page). The heat evaporates the water, and the vapour envelops the plant in a congenial atmosphere. If in doubt, use a hygrometer to gauge humidity, and give your plants an occasional fine mist with a syringe. A humidity level of 50 per cent is usually enough.

Linked with humidity is the problem of ventilation. Orchids abhor cold draughts – like many houseplants – but they like a nicely buoyant, fresh atmosphere. Ventilation is particularly important when growing orchids in a closed

Providing orchids' needs
Light Give your plants ample daylight, but shade them from strong, direct sunlight. You can boost natural light with artificial (see opposite).

Air Keep your orchids out of draughts, but make sure that they have a fresh, buoyant atmosphere. If necessary, use a small fan to circulate air in an enclosed space.

Water If in any doubt, use a moisture meter to check on the potting mixture, as overwatering is fatal. Most orchids need water only when the mixture is almost dry.

Warmth It is essential to ensure that your plants have enough warmth. Standing them on a tray on a window sill above a radiator is generally the best solution.

Humidity Just as vital as warmth is adequate humidity. Grow your plants in a glass case, or stand them on inverted pots over a tray of gravel that is always kept wet.

The plants illustrated **above** are (left to right) *Paphiopedilum insigne*, the dwarf *Sophronitis coccinea* (*S. grandiflora*) and *Paphiopedilum venustum*.

terrarium; if this does not have adjustable louvres, a tiny fan can be positioned at the bottom.

The watering of orchids is an art, and more plants suffer through over-watering than from drought. Modern orchid potting mixtures, containing a high proportion of fir bark for some genera, is deceptive since the surface appears dry when in fact the middle and lower parts are very wet. The best advice is to use a moisture meter and only give water when actually needed. Use rainwater or the water collected when you defrost your refrigerator, but allow refrigerator water to reach room temperature before use. Distilled water can also be used. Much less water is needed in the cooler, darker conditions of winter than in the warmth of summer.

Also feed your plants only in summer, when there are plenty of hours of light. Artificial fertilizers benefit some genera, but should only be given well diluted.

Apart from these specific hints, remember that orchids are much like human beings, and thrive in clean surroundings. Remove any weeds you find growing on the potting mixture. Also remove any old, dead leaves and back-bulbs. (Healthy back-bulbs can be used for propagation.) Use stakes to support the heavy flower heads of plants like *Cattleyas*, *Paphiopedilum* hybrids, *Cymbidiums* and *Odontoglossums*; tie the flower stems with raffia when still in the bud stage. The pendulous types, such as many miniature *Cymbidiums* and some *Odontoglossums*, should not of course be interfered with – the all-too-common sight of a pendulous *Cymbidium* flower staked to grow upwards is uncanny.

Finally, remember that putting the plants outdoors during the warmer days of summer will make their life much easier, for the sun, rain and fresh air will work wonders. Orchid plants grown outside in clean air will tolerate extremes of temperature and other conditions that would set them back severely indoors.

Growing positions

You can, of course, grow orchids anywhere in the home that has adequate light, warmth and humidity, but the most convenient place for many people is a wide window sill – preferably one that does not receive direct sunlight. The window should be draught-free – double-glazed for preference – and an adjustable blind helps to control lighting. If there is a radiator underneath, heating problems are probably solved, but you must control the humidity.

The best way is to place a metal or plastic tray on the sill, filled about an inch deep with shingle or gravel. Keep this constantly wet. Place the plant pots on inverted flower-pots to keep their bases from direct contact with the wet material and to allow them more air. A group of plants will in any case create a more humid atmosphere than a solo specimen, and these can be grouped in plastic, metal or wooden planter troughs. Some versions have a canopy housing one or two fluorescent light tubes.

Best of all for the smaller-growing kinds is a glazed terrarium complete with louvres or a fan for ventilation, and fluorescent lighting in the roof (see page 234). With artificial lighting and heating, a cellar is an ideal place to grow orchids, if you bring them out into the living room for display and put them outdoors in summer.

below Taller-growing orchids, such as this *Odontoglossum grande*, can stand on a window sill, the pot in a container of damp peat.

Pots and potting

Various containers can be used for orchids: pots of clay or plastic (preferably the black type), wooden boxes or baskets, rafts made with slabs of wood or fibre, or simply a chunk of osmunda or tree fern. The potting mixture used for orchids is quite different from normal houseplant mixes, and can be obtained from specialist nurserymen. It is usually based on shredded fir bark, but osmunda fibre is best and live sphagnum moss is an excellent addition. Many modern mixes contain plastic chippings.

Repot each spring, using a pot big enough for just one more pseudo-bulb to grow. Tease out all the old fibre from the roots. Remove any dead roots. Carefully pack new potting mix between and around the roots. Crock the pot for drainage. When growing orchids indoors it is best not to pack the potting mixture down too firmly. When using a chunk of wood, fibre or osmunda, pack potting mixture in and around the roots and strap the plant to the slab with copper wire or nylon string.

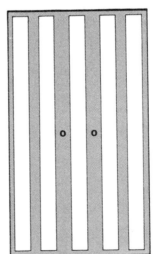

Artificial lighting

Controlled manually or with a time-switch, artificial lighting is invaluable for boosting or completely replacing natural daylight.
above A simple stand with one or two fluorescent tubes is excellent for growing small orchids, such as the *Cattleya*, *Miltonia* and *Paphiopedilum* hybrids shown. In larger installations, a combination of fluorescent tubes – 'cool white', 'daylight' or 'Gro-Lux' – and ordinary incandescent bulbs will ensure that your orchids grow and flower well. Try using 25- or 40-watt incandescent bulbs spaced evenly between long tubes, which should be about four inches apart. The best combination is about 10 watts of incandescent lighting for every 100 watts of fluorescent.
left above To ensure even illumination it is best to construct a battery of five to eight tubes and their accompanying bulbs. Use clear plastic sheeting to filter out the harmful ultra-violet rays, and **left** place the lamps at least four inches (and preferably six inches) above the foliage.

Brassavola digbyana fimbripetala

If you are embarking on the adventure of growing orchids indoors, and are consulting the catalogues of some specialist nurserymen, you may well be confused at the range of species and hybrids offered. There are literally thousands in cultivation, and they are generally catalogued for greenhouse cultivation in 'cool', 'intermediate' and 'hot', 'stove' or 'East India' sections. These of course refer to the temperature and humidity needs of the particular plants which, as explained on page 94, go hand in hand.

Indoors, the easiest conditions to reproduce are usually those of the cool or intermediate house, needing minimum winter temperatures of 10°C (50°F) and 13°C (55°F) respectively, and the plants described here and on pages 98 and 99 fall into those categories. They are also the parts of a grower's catalogue it is best to consult, although it may also be possible to grow some small hothouse types in a heated glass case. The recommendations include a number of large plants well suited to standing free in an alcove or on a window-sill tray, and also some smaller-growing types good for closed glass cases or terrariums.

Most of the kinds described are species. These are generally cheaper than the hybrids, and it would be impossible to mention more than a tiny fraction of the named hybrids that could be grown. If you want to cultivate some hybrids, it is best to discuss your needs with a specialist grower.

Brassavola

Brassavola digbyana (also known as *Rhyncolaelia digbyana*) is related to, among others, the *Cattleyas*, *Laelias* and *Sophronites*, and has been much used with these in hybridization. *B. digbyana* itself has a pale greenish-white flower with a magnificently fringed lip, and this latter feature turns up in many bi- or trigeneric hybrids such as the *Brasso-cattleyas* and *Brassolaeliocattleyas*, which come in many colourings. A quadrigeneric hybrid called *Potinara* has *Cattleya*, *Brassavola*, *Laelia* and *Sophronitis* in its make-up. The species and the various hybrids all like growing conditions similar to those of *Cattleyas* (see below).

Cattleya

Central and South American in origin, *Cattleyas* are among the most popular of all orchids. The flowers are generally large, often fragrant, and have a broad, tongue-shaped lip that may have a frilled or fringed edge.

Cattleyas are divided into two groups. The first, which includes most of the hybrids, consists of the so-called labiate or unifoliate plants, which have single leaves growing from each pseudo-bulb. The orchids in this group, which is named after *Cattleya labiata*, discovered in Brazil in 1818, are generally larger than those in the second section. These are the bifoliate *Cattleyas*, whose flower spikes rise from the pseudo-bulb between paired leaves.

C. labiata itself has five-inch-wide flowers of bright rose suffused with mauve, and leathery leaves up to 12 inches long. *C. dowiana* is another member of the labiate group, and its flower spike bears up to six yellow blooms with large crimson-purple lips streaked with gold. *C. dowiana aurea* has even more gold in the lip, and flowers in late summer and autumn.

Among other labiate *Cattleyas* are *C. gaskelliana*, *C. mossiae*, *C. trianaei* and *C. warscewiczii*. The flowers of *C. gaskelliana* are variable, but often amethyst-purple suffused with white; the lip has an area in a deeper shade of this colour. The plant blooms during summer. *C. mossiae* has eight-inch-wide flowers. They are rose-purple, sometimes deeply coloured, but often pale to almost white. It blooms in spring and early summer.

The flowers of *C. trianaei* have the same colour variations as *C. mossiae* but are slightly larger – up to nine inches wide. One of the finest orchids of the labiate group is *C. warscewiczii*. Its flower, which normally appears in high summer but sometimes earlier, is a delicate rosy-mauve and may be up to 11 inches wide.

All these beautiful, if somewhat large, orchids, need plenty of light with warmth during the day and a fall in temperature of 6 to 8 deg C (11 to 14 deg F) at night. A buoyant atmosphere is necessary, and humidity should always be high except when the plant is flowering, when excess moisture will cause spotting on the blooms and will shorten their life. So it is a good idea to move the plant during the flowering period to a cooler and drier situation. Plants should be repotted every two years or so, when they may be divided if necessary. An open potting mixture is needed; modern ones are usually based on fir bark.

Of the bifoliate group, larger plants include *C. loddigesii*, which can grow to 12 inches in height. It bears delicate

Cattleya 'Gwen Turner'

rosy-lilac flowers during late summer and early autumn. *C. aclandiae* has yellow-green blooms with black or purple contrasts, and flowers in late summer and autumn. It can be grown in a perforated pan or a basket. Although some people find it difficult to cultivate in a greenhouse it is included here because of its neat, small habit.

C. aurantiaca is a small bifoliate *Cattleya* which can be grown in a closed glass case or terrarium. It bears 6 to 12 small brilliant orange-red flowers during summer and autumn. In its natural state it often grows on bare rock and is exposed to extremes of temperature. *C. 'Gwen Turner'* is a related hybrid. Other bifoliates suitable for small growing cases include the dwarf *C. luteola*, which bears two to five pale yellow flowers, each two inches wide, during early winter, and *C. maxima*, a spring-flowering plant that bears many rose-purple flowers about five inches wide.

Coelogyne

One of the easiest orchids to grow indoors is *Coelogyne cristata*. A native of the lower Himalayas, where it grows at 4,500 to 7,000 feet, it thrives in cool conditions. It has up to seven pure white, yellow-centred flowers, three to four inches wide, that droop from pendulous spikes about six inches in length. It blooms in late winter and early spring. Watering should be liberal during

Brassolaeliocattleya 'Enid Oppenheim'

Cattleya 'Queen Sirikit'

growth, and gradually tapered off towards autumn. *C. cristata* grows best in six-inch perforated pans filled with a potting mixture of sphagnum moss peat, sphagnum moss and plastic chippings. It dislikes being disturbed by repotting, and does best in a crowded pot.

Cymbidium

Cymbidium devonianum is a spring-flowering miniature orchid with drooping flowers in colours varying from olive-green with purple spots to yellow-buff with purple streaks. It should be watered regularly when new growth emerges from the base of the pseudo-bulb, but allowed to become fairly dry between waterings. When you do water, saturate the pot. A well-drained potting mixture of fir bark, live sphagnum moss and some agent to keep it open, such as charcoal or plastic chippings, is required. *C. devonianum* can be put outside during the summer.

Cypripedium

The name *Cypripedium* is nowadays used indiscriminately for members of four genera of slipper orchids: the true *Cypripediums*, which are native to North America and include some beautiful but difficult garden plants; the *Selenepediums* and *Phragmipedilums*, both from South America; and the *Paphiopedilums*. These last come from Asia, and are the plants most commonly known as *Cypripediums*.

Laeliocattleya 'Golden Hind'

They are by far the most important and widely seen of the group; see page 98.

Dendrobium

Although many of the 1,500 or so species of *Dendrobiums* are purely of scientific or botanical interest, many are attractive and can be cultivated. The flowers – and, in fact, the whole plants – vary widely in form, the flower lips sometimes bearing extraordinary fringes. All the *Dendrobiums* mentioned here are from Asia, and need plenty of water during the annual growth period, but this should be tapered off when the new growth matures. An open, well-drained potting mixture is required.

A small-growing species, *Dendrobium aggregatum* bears drooping clusters of about six primrose-yellow blooms, each two inches wide. It is best grown on a plain block of maple, elm, or other wood, and will flower annually during spring if it is suspended in good light. It needs cool surroundings after the growth period. Also spring-flowering, *D. chrystoxum* has golden-yellow flowers on drooping stems. It grows best on a raft or block of wood.

D. fimbriatum bears pendulous sprays of 12 to 20 orange-yellow flowers. The variety *D. fimbriatum oculatum* has orange-yellow flowers two to three inches wide; the base of the lip is fringed and its centre is blotched with maroon. It is shorter than *D. fimbriatum*, and more suitable for indoor growing. Like *D. chrystoxum*, both flower in spring.

Epidendrum

The *Epidendrums* include some brilliant and showy orchids that are extremely rewarding to grow. *Epidendrum radicans*, also known as *E. ibaguense*, from Guatemala, bears clusters of brilliant red flowers, 1 to 1½ inches wide, throughout the year. It grows best in conditions that

give it room to spread – against a pillar, for instance, when it will climb to six or seven feet. It should be watered, thoroughly, only when the potting mixture is almost dry.

E. vitellinum, which comes from high in the mountains of Mexico, bears bright red blooms with an orange-yellow lip. They appear in autumn and winter. It will thrive in slightly cooler conditions than *E. radicans*, and needs even less

Dendrobium fimbriatum oculatum

watering when the pseudo-bulb has reached its full size. It can be grown with advantage in a basket or raft suspended in good light. Both species need an open, well drained potting mixture.

Laelia

Tropical epiphytic orchids from Central and South America, *Laelias* are closely related to *Cattleyas* (see above). *Laelia pumila* was first discovered in Brazil growing on trees at an elevation of about 2,500 feet. It is a dwarf, compact plant bearing one, or occasionally two, four-inch-wide flowers that appear during autumn. The sepals and petals are bright rose-purple, and the lip is deep crimson with yellow keels. The varieties *L. pumila dayana* and *L. pumila praestans* are also rose-purple. The white *L. pumila alba* is more rare and has been used with *Cattleyas*, *Brassavolas* and *Sophronites* to produce hybrids.

L. jongheana also bears rose-purple flowers. The collector who discovered this species died shortly afterwards, and the first plant, sent to a Monsieur de Jonghe in Brussels, disappeared for some years. It flowered for the first time in cultivation in 1872. *L. gouldiana* is a natural hybrid between *L. anceps* and *L. autumnalis*. It bears a spike of about five rose-pink flowers, each about three inches wide, during late autumn and early winter.

These plants can all be grown either in a glazed case or free-standing. A potting mixture of sphagnum moss peat and live sphagnum moss kept open by plastic chippings is required. Keep the mixture pleasantly moist at all times, and give the plants as much light as possible. It is important to ensure that there is a difference of about 8 deg C (14 deg F) between day and night temperatures.

Orchids to grow 2

Lycaste

Natives of tropical America, many *Lycastes* are ideal houseplants. Watering should be liberal during the summer growing season, but reduced as the leaves dry off. During late autumn and winter give only enough moisture to prevent the pseudo-bulbs from shrinking. *Lycastes* need a potting mixture of sphagnum moss peat, live sphagnum moss and plastic chippings.

Lycaste aromatica, a Mexican species, has one orange-yellow bloom, $1\frac{1}{2}$ inches wide, to each spike. A well grown plant, however, will bear many of these aromatic, long-lasting flowers. *L. cruenta*, from Guatemala, is similar to *L. aromatica*, with orange-yellow petals, spotted red at the base, and green sepals; but the flowers are larger – $2\frac{1}{2}$ inches wide – and have no scent. They may appear at any time of the year, but usually during spring and early summer.

L. deppei has three- to four-inch flowers with ivory-white petals and pale green sepals spotted with carmine. It blooms in spring and early summer. *L. skinneri*, also known as *L. virginalis*, is a larger plant with five- to seven-inch-wide white petals strongly tinted with rose, and white sepals flushed with pink. The flowers appear at any time during the year. The leaves are 15 to 20 inches

Lycaste aromatica

long. There were 16 distinct varieties in cultivation in 1894, of which only the rare pure white *L. skinneri alba* remains.

Miltonia

The large, flat, pansy-like flowers of the hybrid *Miltonias* – commonly known as the pansy orchids – come in a range of brilliant colours. They grow best in a potting mixture of sphagnum moss peat and live sphagnum moss kept open with plastic chippings. Watering should be selective and restrained, but the mixture should always be slightly moist. Flowers start blooming on small plants only two or three years old, and increase in size and number as the plants become older and bigger.

Miltonia spectabilis is a Brazilian orchid with white or cream flowers, three inches wide, sometimes touched with rose at the base of the petals. It flowers from middle to late summer. *M. spectabilis moreliana* is a dramatic variation, being plum-coloured with a rose-purple lip (see the illustration on

Miltonia 'Red Knight'

page 92). *M. roezlii*, from Colombia, has a flower spike bearing two to five sweetly scented white blooms, each $3\frac{1}{2}$ to 4 inches across, with a purple blotch at the base of the petals. It flowers from late spring to early summer.

Most modern hybrid *Miltonias* are a result of breeding from *M. roezlii* and another Colombian species, *M. vexillaria*, which has pale rose-mauve, or sometimes white, flowers with yellow veining on the lip. However, several interesting hybrids have recently been made from Brazilian species. Their colours vary, but are generally bluish-pink to deep red. There are also yellow and green examples. Hybrids usually bloom from spring to mid-summer.

Although *Miltonia* blooms will last for upwards of a month on the plant, the Colombian ones wither quickly when cut. Young plants bearing one or two flowers should be given a little extra warmth.

Odontoglossum

Native to Central and South America, *Odontoglossums* are named from the Greek words for *tooth* and *tongue* because their lips bear tooth-like projections. They have been popular with growers and hybridizers from the early days of orchid-growing. As well as the following species, the smaller-growing hybrids are also good indoor subjects.

Odontoglossum grande is one of the easiest orchids to grow indoors on a window sill. Originating in Guatemala, it is the largest and most colourful of the genus, and is commonly known as the clown orchid. It bears cinnamon-brown

Odontoglossum hybrid

and yellow six-inch-wide flowers, up to seven on a spike, generally in winter (see the photograph on page 95).

O. citrosmum is a delightfully scented Mexican species, first discovered growing in profusion on oak trees at the beginning of the nineteenth century. In its natural state it has more than 30 blooms on each pendulous spike, but cultivated plants usually have only five to ten pink flowers, each about $2\frac{1}{2}$ inches wide. It blooms during spring.

O. cervantesii has white flowers with chocolate streaks at the base of the petals. Although first found in Mexico it grows over a wide area including Guatemala. *O. hallii* is a spring-flowering orchid, first discovered growing at an elevation of 8,000 feet by a Colonel Hall. Its flowers are yellow and chestnut brown, and up to four inches wide.

Odontoglossums need surroundings that are airy, moist and on the cool side, with plenty of light in winter. You should shade them heavily in hot summer weather, however. There is no resting period, and the potting mixture should always be kept slightly moist.

Oncidium

Originating in the American sub-tropics, *Oncidiums* bear eye-catching blooms on branching stems, and are very rewarding

Oncidium ornithorynchum

to grow. In *Oncidium ornithorynchum* each spike bears a veritable cloud of $\frac{3}{4}$-inch-wide rose-lilac flowers, usually in autumn. *Oncidiums* need plenty of watering in summer, but very little in winter.

Paphiopedilum

The tropical *Paphiopedilums*, formerly called *Cypripediums*, are popularly known as the slipper orchids because of the characteristic shape of the lip. Generally there is only one flower on a stem, which rises from the middle of new growth. However, there are exceptions with three or four flowers to a stem.

The species described below, and also many of the *Paphiopedilum* hybrids, make good houseplants because they need less light than most other orchids. They like a potting mixture of sphagnum moss peat, sphagnum moss and plastic chippings. Equal proportions of chopped osmunda fibre and sphagnum moss were used in the past, and if good osmunda fibre is available this is still the best mixture. However, a degree of

Paphiopedilum 'Harrow'

skill is necessary in using it for potting. The natural home of the *Paphiopedilums* is in the monsoon belt, and most species should always be kept moist. They are terrestrial plants, and like to be grouped.

Paphiopedilum barbatum has three-inch-wide flowers on a 9- to 12-inch stem. The dorsal sepal is white with purple lines radiating from a green base. The lip is deep brownish-purple, and the plant has tessellated (patterned) leaves. It blooms in summer. *P. callosum*, from Thailand, is similar to *P. barbatum*, with wide white blooms striped with purple and green, and tessellated leaves which should be misted daily in hot weather.

P. delenatii bears delicate pink flowers that are notable for their perfume, making the plant unique among *Paphiopedilums*. Its flowering period is generally during summer, but can vary. It was introduced from Indo-China in the early

Paphiopedilum spicerianum

1930s, and was rare for many years, but has since been propagated.

Once very rare and consequently expensive, *P. fairieanum* is now easily available. It grows wild in the Himalayas, and its name comes not from its discoverer, but from the owner of the first cultivated specimen, a Mr Fairie of Liverpool, who paid over £1,000 for the plant in 1857. A dwarf orchid which flowers from late summer to autumn, it is one of the best for home growing. The stem is four to six inches high, and the flower about three inches wide. It boasts a delightful dorsal sepal with a white background streaked and tessellated in purple, and a touch of green at the base. The petals, shaped like a buffalo's horns, are white, lined with purple (see the illustration on page 92).

P. philippense, from the Philippines, has a white dorsal sepal with symmetrical brown-purple stripes, and ribbon-like petals five to six inches long. Although it comes from one of the hottest regions of the tropical world, it can be grown in the living room provided the temperature is about 21 to 24°C (70 to 75°F), with humidity kept as high as possible. It is worth the effort because it is a most attractive species.

P. spicerianum, from Assam, has a pure white dorsal sepal with a clearly indented vertical 'rib' and a green and red area at the base. The petals are similarly ribbed, and are yellowish-green spotted with red. The origin of this very pretty species was secret for some time. As with many other orchids, however, it is now available at a reasonable price.

All the above are small plants well suited to terrarium culture. Among the larger *Paphiopedilums*, *P. hirsutissimum* is a Himalayan species introduced into Europe in 1857. Its four-inch-wide flow-

ers have dark purple petals with blackish hairs, and the dorsal sepal is blackish-purple on green. The leaves are attractively tessellated.

P. insigne, discovered in northern India in about 1820, has a white dorsal sepal with an apple-green base and brownish-purple spots. Its many varieties have made this species extremely popular. Today the most common is *P. insigne sanderae*, which has a white dorsal sepal with a yellowish-green base, and yellow petals.

F. W. Burbage, a Victorian writer, said of it: 'In a window, or in a well lighted sitting-room, it is perfectly at home, and, with proper attention as to watering and sprinkling occasionally to rid the leaves of dust, increases in size, and flowers regularly every winter. It is not particular as to compost; it will grow in loam, peat, common garden soil, peat fibre and bone dust, peat loam and sand, loam and dried cow manure, peat fibre and horse droppings, sphagnum moss and charcoal, and, finally, coconut fibre surfaced with growing *Selaginella krausiana*. It is most vigorous in constitution, and so defies all bad and indifferent culture, growing even under no special culture of any kind.'

Another larger plant, *P. venustum* is a native of north-eastern India. The white dorsal sepal is symmetrically striped with green or purple, the petals spread themselves horizontally, and the yellowish lip is veined with green. As a bonus, the leaves are prettily marbled in light green on dark green, so the plant is attractive even when not in flower.

Zygopetalum

The 20 species of *Zygopetalum* are native to Venezuela, Colombia, Brazil and the Guianas. *Zygopetalum mackayi* is now frequently seen in cultivation. It bears three-inch-wide yellow-green flowers, blotched with purple, during autumn and winter. They are delicately scented. *Z. mackayi* is best grown in an alcove, or free-standing.

Zygopetalum mackayi

3 Plants for indoors and out

You can grow daffodil and tulip bulbs
indoors in bowls, or you can grow them
outside in a tub, window box or flower bed.
These are the dual-purpose plants, useful
both as houseplants and flowering pot-
plants and (at least in the warmer seasons)
for outdoors.

Apart from all sorts and sizes of bulbs,
corms and tuberous plants, there are dual-
purpose flowering shrubs and two worldwide
favourite indoor/outdoor plants:
geraniums and flowering begonias. They
are all covered in this part.

Dual-purpose flowering shrubs

Dual-purpose plants that can be grown both outdoors and in are particularly valuable, and most of the plants described here are adaptable in this way. A few are hardy enough to be grown permanently outdoors where winters are not too severe; thus plants can be given a permanent outdoor home when too big for the house, while providing cuttings for new indoor specimens. Others when grown in tubs can be used for garden-room or conservatory decoration in the winter and transferred to a terrace or patio for the summer season.

Not many of the plants described on these two pages are sold by houseplant nurseries. In some cases, however, shrub nurseries will supply them. Apart from the plants described here, you will find other indoor flowering shrubs, many of which can spend part of the year outdoors, on pages 75 (roses), 82 and 83 (winter-flowering kinds), 84 to 87 (climbing and trailing shrubs), 88 and 89 (indoor flowering shrubs) and 90 and 91 (fragrant types).

Moisture-loving kinds

Hardy outdoors in many areas (where they need a moist, shaded position) the *Astilbes* (often erroneously sold as *Spiraea*) are also sold as colourful pot-plants in spring. The foliage is fern-like, and the plumes of flowers come in many shades of white through pink to red. To force as pot-plants, *Astilbe* roots should be dug up in early autumn and potted after splitting into manageable

Astilbe sp

pieces; use Potting Mix no. 3 with the addition of a little extra peat. Cover the pots of root with peat, and protect from frost until midwinter. Then gradually introduce the plants to slightly warmer conditions until a temperature of about 16°C (61°F) is being maintained. When growth appears, water freely and when in full leaf give regular applications of liquid fertilizer. Having outlived their decorative value indoors, the plants should be gradually hardened off prior to planting out in the garden again in a position with moist soil.

Belonging to the same family, the *Hydrangea* is one of the most spectacular spring-flowering plants, and is available in many shades of white, pink and red. Blue shades are also available; these

Hydrangea macrophylla Hortensia variety

plants have been chemically treated by the grower with a blueing powder that increases the acidity of the potting mixture, but it is not effective on white varieties. In order to retain blue colouring when the plants are planted in the garden after flowering indoors, it is essential that the soil should have a high level of acidity.

Cool, light conditions are required when growing *Hydrangeas* as pot-plants, and cuttings taken from blind shoots in late summer produce the best flowers. After flowering, all weak growth and shoots that have flowered should be pruned out. While in active growth it is important that the roots do not at any time dry out. Having shed their foliage naturally, the plants should be placed in a cool, frost-free place until growth buds appear again. Then they may be gradually introduced to warmer temperatures until something in the region of 16°C (61°F) is being maintained. Many European nurseries specialize in producing plants with a single stem and one spectacular flower head, but it is possible after many years of careful culture to obtain multi-head plants with a hundred blooms or more.

Summer terrace plants

Many of the flowering shrubs that make good tub subjects for the terrace or patio in summer are happiest in cool, fairly dry winter conditions indoors, with plenty of light. Among them is *Abelia*

Abelia grandiflora

grandiflora, with pink or white flowers in summer, and *Callistemon citrinus* (the bottle-brush). The latter has fascinating scarlet flower spikes shaped like bottle-brushes, and makes an excellent show when planted or positioned against a wall. Its growth will need tying in, however. From *Capparis spinosa* capers are obtained; they are the pickled flower buds. The plant needs cool conditions, and in midsummer bears white flowers.

For a sunless aspect that is moist and cool there are a number of varieties of *Cassiope*. They bear white flowers. The tallest reaches a height of some 12 inches while others, such as *Cassiope hypnoides*, are quite prostrate. *Choisya ternata* has white flowers in midsummer and will often oblige with a second flush later in the year; average conditions will suffice. Needing cool, light conditions and rainwater when watering, *Leschenaultia biloba* is a compact shrub bearing blue flowers in summer.

Warm winter conditions – about 18°C (61°F) – are needed for *Jacarandra acutifolia*. This is decorative as a small plant, and produces blue flowers when a mature plant of ten feet or more in height. Also needing a little extra warmth, *Lagerstroemia speciosa* has rose-purple summer flowers over a long period. *Melaleuca huegelii* is a spreader that attains a height of some six feet and bears clusters of creamy white flowers; it is native to Australia. Attractive red berries follow the white summer flowers of *Nandina domestica* (heavenly

Callistemon citrinus

bamboo); the attractive stems have pinnate leaves that take on a pleasing red shade in late summer.

A spreading South African shrub, *Polygala myrtifolia grandiflora* has purple spring flowers and grows to about five feet in height. It requires good light. The South African national flower, *Protea*, produces exotic flowering bracts in a wide range of colours. Related to the *Protea*, *Leucospermum nutans* makes a densely foliaged bush about four feet in height. It bears yellow-orange flowers some four inches across.

The pomegranate, *Punica granatum*, provides a compact, small-leaved shrub that bears pendulous orange flowers. However, it would be wishful thinking to expect a crop of edible fruit as the small

Punica granatum

Clerodendrum thomsonae

musk) is ideal. Brown-spotted yellow flowers are produced throughout the summer. Warm, lightly shaded and moist conditions are necessary. Clusters of white flowers spotted with purple are also a feature of *Jovellana sinclairii*.

Fuchsias

Finally among the adaptable flowering shrubs that can be used indoors and out are the brilliant *Fuchsias*. Few plants can compete with them in respect of ease of culture and profuse flowering over a very long period that begins in early spring and continues until autumn. There are many varieties to choose from in a wide range of colours. Some are best suited to hanging basket work, some as climbers against a wall and some as attractive bushes, while there are those that are hardy outside all the year round in many places. The latter may be seen as hedges, small trees or as miniature plants. A visit to any nursery specializing in *Fuchsias* will more than satisfy the demands of anyone wishing to set up a collection of these most useful of all potted flowering plants.

To get the best out of your *Fuchsias*, adequate light is most essential, but some sun protection should be given. Keep them well watered, fed and potted on while they are in active growth. It is important to use a good potting mixture (no. 3 for preference) in pots that are well drained, and to keep the plants growing strongly.

fruits seldom mature on pot-grown plants. The plants are slow-growing and require no special treatment. *P. granatum nana* is a dwarf variety that grows only about three feet tall.

An attractive mixture

Seen at its best when grown as a climbing wall plant, *Clerodendrum thomsonae* is an attractive plant with profuse red-centred white flowers. They are borne in clusters throughout the spring and summer months. In dry conditions, the plant will shed its leaves in winter and start into growth again in early spring. Another handsome wall subject

is *Fremontia californica* (*F. mexicana*), which attains a height of about ten feet and has attractive yellow flowers.

Sparmannia africana is a graceful indoor shrub with a number of common names. One is African hemp. Another, African wind-flower, comes from the way in which the white flower opens outwards when affected by the slightest breeze. It is easy to care for, needing lots of moisture, and grows quickly.

For a well-watered hanging basket, or for creeping unhindered over the conservatory tabling and among other plants in a large container, *Mimulus moschatus* (also called *M. diplacus* or

Protea cynaroides

Fremontia californica

Fuchsia hybrids

Geraniums, the easy favourites

Geraniums and pelargoniums (botanically speaking, all *Pelargoniums* and only distantly related to the plants known botanically as *Geraniums*) are grown in almost every corner of the world, from Alaska to Australia. They flourish almost everywhere, and are among the most popular of all plants for growing both in and out of doors. They are easy to grow and to propagate from cuttings or, in some cases, from seed.

Geraniums have no dormant period, and modern varieties will flower non-stop for nine or ten months of the year, so long as they are free from frost and have ample light – full sun if possible – and a little water. They grow happily and decoratively in tubs and troughs on terraces or balconies, in wall pockets and hanging baskets, in pots outdoors or on indoor window sills. They can live for months under conditions of drought, thanks to their semi-succulent stems, but seldom survive more than five days if waterlogged. Humid heat (particularly at night) also does not suit them well. They prefer a well drained medium loam soil, or one of the peat-based potting mixtures (see page 218).

There are literally thousands of named varieties of geraniums, ranging from three-inch dwarfs and rambling trailers to bushes and tree-like standards several feet tall. Flower colours embrace a wide range from white through pinks and oranges to purples, reds and near blacks. But there is no true blue. Some kinds have interestingly marked leaves, while another group give off varied perfumes when their leaves are brushed. When choosing named varieties it is best to consult a specialist grower's catalogue.

Zonal geraniums

Although the Zonal group strictly includes many of the plants described under other headings (such as fancy-leaves, Irenes and Deacons), there are also thousands of cultivars that cannot be included in any other section. Botanically they are classed as *Pelargonium × hortorum*; they are, in fact, the plants

Pelargonium 'Prince Regent' (Zonal)

known simply as 'geraniums'. The term Zonal comes from the leaf markings of many varieties, which are shaped like a horseshoe – hence the alternative name of horseshoe geraniums.

Many are purely bedding varieties that can be used in patio flower beds, but the group also includes a vast number of novelties that are often grown as pot-plants for indoor use, for the show bench or for flower arrangements. F1 hybrids offered by seedsmen are also Zonals. Raised in a warm greenhouse, they will flower profusely the first year.

Fancy-leaf varieties

Strictly speaking, these form a sub-group of the Zonal pelargoniums. Most of the older kinds have small, insignificant flowers, the main beauty being in the foliage. New strains now have larger and more impressive flowers in a greater range of colours.

The leaf colouring may be a simple white or cream edging to a mid-green leaf, or the most complicated pattern of reds, greens, yellows and browns, all intermingled and overlaid to provide a natural kaleidoscope of colour. As with all geraniums, fancy-leaves require adequate light if they are to flower properly, but they still develop their attractive foliage even in poor light conditions.

Pelargonium 'Mrs Henry Cox' (fancy-leaved)

The leaf colouring can be affected by feeding as well as by the quality of the light. A plant that is fed with a high-nitrogen fertilizer (see page 222) will lose much of its brilliance and revert to almost pure green. One fed with a high-potash feed, on the other hand, will produce intense leaf-colouring at the expense of growth. Similarly a plant in bright light will have poor leaf markings, whilst one in partial shade will have better leaf colours but fewer flowers.

Some fancy-leaves will grow no taller than 18 inches, whilst in the correct environment others will make a plant several feet high. Some people use the variety 'Caroline Schmidt' as a standard, with a head five feet high and three feet wide, carrying dozens of blooms. Fancy-leaf varieties make good edging plants and add colour to hanging baskets or urns, and some make excellent pot-plants. An example of the latter is 'Mrs Henry Cox', whose foliage is perhaps the most brilliant of all the group, being basically

yellow with red, green and brown areas and overlays. The flowers are single and salmon-pink.

Ivy-leaf varieties

These geraniums, classified as *Pelargonium peltatum*, have shield-shaped fleshy leaves on trailing stems. They will not climb of their own accord, but can be trained to many attractive forms, either upwards, against trellis screens or walls, or trailing as for hanging baskets, tubs,

Pelargonium 'L'elegante' (ivy-leaved)

window boxes and wall pockets. In warm climates they are often grown among the branches of trees, and they also make excellent ground-cover plants. Most varieties make attractive pot-plants for growing indoors, and will flower throughout the year if given a well-lit position.

Ivy-leaf geraniums all benefit from hard pruning at the beginning of the season to force an abundance of side breaks. This makes a bushier plant with more flowers. There are over 200 varieties in cultivation. Flower forms include singles, doubles and semi-doubles, and the colour range is similar to that for other groups except that there is no orange shade.

Regal pelargoniums

Often simply called 'pelargoniums', Regal varieties are known in the US as show pelargoniums or Martha Washington geraniums; the botanical name is *Pelargonium × domesticum*. These have larger petals than other types, and a papery leaf that is always a plain green colour. Useful for most purposes, Regal pelargoniums are particularly suitable as centre-pieces in hanging baskets, urns and tubs, surrounded by complementary shades of miniatures and ivy-leaves. They are also favourite pot-plant subjects, and can often be seen in the windows of country cottages and the foyers of hotels.

Modern varieties will bloom out of doors throughout the summer, and indoors for over nine months of the year if given proper attention. Few of the older strains, on the other hand, can be flowered for more than two months in the summer, so it is important to choose carefully. There are more than 1,000 varieties in cultivation in colours ranging from

Pelargonium 'Aztec' (Regal)

pure white through every shade of pink, red and mauve to near-black. Most of the flowers are either bi- or tri-coloured.

Other colourful kinds

Apart from the well known groups of geraniums described above, there exist a number of special kinds, some of them old and well established, others recent introductions. They are all very useful for special purposes. The greatest range is among the miniature and dwarf types. These are ideal for window boxes, rockeries and wall pockets, and for edging bowls and troughs. Heights vary from about three to nine inches, and there are more than 500 varieties in cultivation. Flowers may be either single or double, in every shade from pure white to deep purple, the leaves pea-green to near

Pelargonium 'Deacon Sunburst'

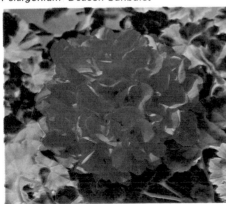

black, with and without zoning. Although mostly Zonals, there are a few miniature Regals, but these all have flowers in shades of purple and white.

The Deacons represent an entirely new strain of geranium, having a compact, bushy habit with no tendency to sprawling. Under correct conditions they will carry several heads of flower at the same time throughout the year. They are unique in that the size of the plant can be regulated to a large extent by the size of pot. For example, a plant in a four-inch pot will grow to a spherical shape about eight inches in diameter, whereas one in

Pelargonium 'Stellar Cathay'

a 15-inch pot will make a bush nearly four feet across. The flowers are semi-double, in colours ranging from white to dark red.

Modern semi-doubles originating in the US, Irene varieties have a compact, bushy habit if well grown. Their height is 12 to 18 inches, and they usually carry four to five flower heads at the same time in constant succession. Used mainly for outside bedding and as centre-pieces in ornamental bowls and tubs, colours range from white through pink and salmon to dark red.

Rosebud geraniums are attractive novelties at their best as specimen pot-plants grown indoors. There they will reach 15 to 18 inches in a normal season under reasonable conditions. The flowers resemble tiny half-opened rosebuds, and each flower stem carries a mass of these.

Introduced into Europe from Australia in 1966, Stellar geraniums have star-shaped foliage with or without zoning. The flowers may be either single or double. The lower petals are broad and wedge-shaped, the upper petals sharply forked and much narrower. In their native conditions they will grow to five

Pelargonium 'Firedragon' (Zonal cactus-type)

feet or more, but in cool temperate regions seldom make more than 18 inches in an average year. Stellars make an ideal centre-piece for large tubs and raised beds, and are very good as pot-plants. The long stems are useful for flower arrangements.

Scented-leaf geraniums

Quite different from other geraniums, the scented-leaf types are usually grown for their perfume, which is released when the foliage is gently brushed or disturbed. The flowers (with very few exceptions) are rather insignificant. Scented-leaf geraniums are widely grown as houseplants for the blind, but can also be planted outside. Some will become quite massive if left untrained; so for indoor use severe pruning is essential. There are about 50 species and varieties in cultivation, with a great assortment of perfumes, ranging from rose and mint to lemon and spice. Probably the strongest-scented is 'Mabel Grey', with a citron or verbena fragrance.

Growing beautiful bulbs

Few plants give bigger dividends for a small outlay than bulbs. Planted correctly and at the right season, they never fail to provide a brilliantly decorative display, and yet by midsummer have died down and disappeared, leaving the ground free for succeeding plants.

They can also be used in a variety of situations, and are particularly attractive grouped in open places between shrubs. Many of the smaller kinds are suited to the rock garden, creating bright spots of colour from midwinter on. Grass – even the most minute patio lawn – provides an ideal natural setting for crocuses, baby *Narcissi*, aconites and fritillaries, while tulips, hyacinths, daffodils and *Narcissi* in particular make excellent bedding subjects for raised beds, small borders or squares of earth between paving slabs.

Bulbs also force satisfactorily in pots and bowls to provide flowers indoors in the winter months when little else is in character. The colours are exciting and the shapes varied, while – for added measure – many varieties of bulbs possess a delightful fragrance.

Bulbs can be bought in great variety. Some of them are old favourites – of which exciting new varieties are constantly being produced – while others are less well known, though often equally worthwhile. They are described in detail on the following pages. For the well known favourites, such as daffodils and tulips, see pages 108 and 109. Miniature kinds are covered on pages 110 and 111, while pages 112 and 113 deal with various unusual and interesting kinds. Finally, the large, exotic kinds – such as lilies and *Hippeastrums* – are described on pages 114 and 115.

Bulbs outdoors

Most outdoor bulbs are planted in late summer or early autumn. There are a few exceptions, like autumn crocus (*Crocus speciosus* and others), *Fritillaria imperialis* and *Lilium candidum*, all of which need to be planted in midsummer. A few others require spring planting, and with bedding tulips it is advisable to wait until late autumn or early winter, when fire disease (which can destroy tulips) is less active.

Choose an open, sunny position for display kinds, and always use top quality bulbs. Although some of the hardier sorts, such as *Narcissi* and snowdrops, seem to thrive on neglect, even these do better in good soil than poor. With flowers 'on show' in prominent positions, good conditions are essential. The soil should be rich yet well drained. Hyacinths and tulips appreciate manure but it must be well matured. Work some of this eight to ten inches down so that the roots have to go after it, and every other season scatter a dressing of bonemeal (four ounces per square yard) over beds where the soil is not normally changed.

Plant bulbs with a dibber or trowel. If the first is used make sure that the base of the bulb rests on the soil at the bottom of the hole and is not left hanging. The best depth of planting varies according to the kind of bulb and type of soil. There is no hard and fast guide, although somewhere between two and three times the height of the bulb is a good rule of thumb. Plant the bulbs deeper in light soils than heavy ones.

Bulbs can be used outdoors in tubs, strawberry pots, sink gardens, window boxes and other containers, also in raised beds and mini-lawns. In the latter

Planting schemes for spring

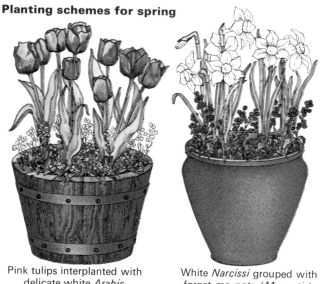

Pink tulips interplanted with delicate white *Arabis*

White *Narcissi* grouped with forget-me-nots (*Myosotis*)

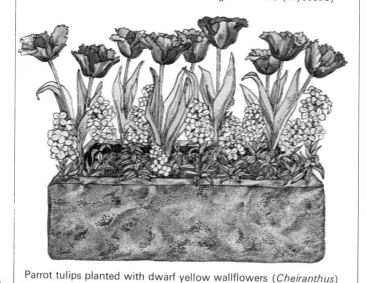

Parrot tulips planted with dwarf yellow wallflowers (*Cheiranthus*)

Unusual ways with well known bulbs

106

case, or to create natural effects among shrubs, scatter the bulbs and plant them wherever they happen to fall.

After flowering, bulbs in turf and permanent beds can be left to die down naturally. Container-grown and formal bedding sorts, however, must make room for other plants. Lift these and plant them closely together in a spare bed or tub of potting mixture, water and leave them to die down. Do not cut off the foliage prematurely, as the leaves are needed to build up a food supply for the next season. Once the leaves are dead, lift and clean the bulbs, and store them in a cool, dry place until planting time comes round again. Although they will not be so good the second season, the flowers are useful for mixed bedding or cutting purposes.

Bulbs indoors

Bulbs which force well include hyacinths, double tulips, daffodils, crocuses, lilies and lily of the valley. Many of the smaller kinds, like snowdrops, and also bulbous irises, resent too much heat and are best 'grown cool'. This entails planting them in pots or pans of sandy potting mixture and growing them along in a cold frame or greenhouse. They will still flower well ahead of garden specimens, and can be taken indoors for display.

If you want early displays of daffodils, *Narcissi*, hyacinths and so on, buy specially prepared bulbs. Nurserymen prepare forcing bulbs by subjecting them to hot and cold temperature changes – techniques that naturally make them more expensive. The bulbs should be firm and solid, and free from bruises or mildew stains.

There are various ways of growing them, bulb fibre (composed of peat, oyster shell and charcoal) being the cleanest and most popular potting mixture. Certain *Narcissi* and crocuses can be grown on pebbles or in bulb glasses with water. Hyacinths do exceptionally well on wet newspaper pellets, and tulips and daffodils in a light soil potting mix.

If bulb fibre is used, dampen it first and half fill the bowls. Stand the bulbs close together, but not touching, and work more bulb fibre between them. Do not 'screw' them into position as this consolidates the material so that the roots cannot penetrate downwards; instead they turn upwards and out of the tops of the bowls. When finished, the necks of hyacinths, *Narcissi* and *Amaryllis* will protrude, but all the other bulbs should be completely covered.

Next, wrap the bowls in black plastic sheeting and stand them outdoors on a hard surface. Cover them with six inches of sand, ashes or leaves, and leave them alone for eight or nine weeks. If you have no garden, or even a balcony or terrace, or if you live in an exceptionally cold district where frost persists, you should keep them indoors but in a dark, cool place. Temperatures at this stage should not exceed 4°C (40°F).

Take them out of this 'plunge' when the pots are full of roots and the shoots around one inch high. Keep them in a cool – about 10°C (50°F) – but light place. For an interesting effect, sprinkle the tops of the bowls with grass seed. Water when necessary. Gradually, the leaves will elongate and the flower buds show, and at this stage they can go into the living room at about 18°C (60 to 65°F) to flower. By this time the grass seed will have sprouted and will make a pleasant green background for the bulbs.

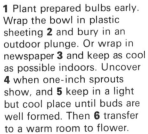

Forcing spring bulbs

1 Crocuses and certain *Narcissi* like 'Cragford' and 'Soleil d'Or' will grow on pebbles. Half fill a saucer or bowl with these, wedge the bulbs in position, stand in a light place and keep a little water always at the base of the container.
2 Bulb glasses for hyacinths and crocuses show the roots growing and are fun for children. Wedge the bulbs in the necks of the glasses with water nearly – but not quite – up to their bases. Soft water with a few lumps of charcoal is preferable.
3 For a grand display plant daffodils in layers in a deep container – a row of bulbs, then bulb fibre, then more bulbs until the pot is full.

When they come to flower the stems will be of different lengths, those at the bottom being shortest, so a tall mass of blooms is produced.
4 Many bulbs make a good display in strawberry pots or in the smaller tulip and crocus pots. All have holes around the sides; plant one large bulb or several small in each, and more in the top. Watch for drying out of the potting mixture.
5 Grow hyacinths on newspaper. Dampen them and break up into nut-sized pellets. Place in bowls, but do not press down or the material will go like papier mâché. Set bulbs in position and grow on as when using bulb fibre.

1 Plant prepared bulbs early. Wrap the bowl in plastic sheeting **2** and bury in an outdoor plunge. Or wrap in newspaper **3** and keep as cool as possible indoors. Uncover **4** when one-inch sprouts show, and **5** keep in a light but cool place until buds are well formed. Then **6** transfer to a warm room to flower.

Everybody's favourite bulbs

The most popular bulbs, corms and tubers are those which are easiest to grow and readily available. They are usually showy – even flamboyant – yet reliable in all soils. They include such plants as daffodils, tulips, irises and hyacinths, which are grown in their millions in all parts of the world.

The Dutch are the biggest producers of these bulbs, and by scientific methods of heat control the growers can alter their flowering seasons so that they bloom anywhere in the world at the appropriate time of year. Many of the following can be forced for early blooms if specially treated (see page 107), and all are suitable for growing in beds or in containers of various kinds.

Gladiolus

Gladioli are favourite summer cut flowers which can also be forced for out-of-

Gladiolus Grandiflorus hybrids

season blooms. Rich soil with good drainage, and full sun are essential. They are not frost-hardy, so cannot be planted until spring. They should then be set three inches deep and six to eight inches apart. The main groups are the large flowered Grandiflorus hybrids, those with hooded top petals called Primulinus, and the smaller Butterfly and Miniature strains.

When autumn frosts cut the foliage,

Hyacinthus orientalis 'Blue Jacket'

the corms can be lifted, dried and cleaned, and then stored in an airy frost-proof room until spring. The small cormlets around the bases of the old ones can be grown on for propagation.

Dwarf *Gladioli* of the *Gladiolus* × *colvillei* type are attractive in pots of well drained, rich loamy soil. Plant three to a six-inch pot, one inch deep.

Hyacinthus

Sweet-scented hyacinths (*Hyacinthus orientalis* cultivars) are top favourites for forcing in bowls, but are also much used for window boxes, containers and bedding. Plant the bulbs three to four inches deep in autumn and then scatter a little bonemeal over the soil. They grow 12 to 18 inches high and have a wide colour range. Blues, pinks and white are the commonest, but there are also yellow and orange varieties.

Iris Xiphium hybrid

Roman hyacinths (*H. orientalis albulus*) are smaller and earlier, with white to light blue flowers. They are often forced for midwinter indoor display.

Iris

The bulbous irises include many suitable for small patio gardens. The season starts with the winter-flowering two-inch *Iris histrioides* 'Major', whose china-blue flowers even brave snow. *I.*

Narcissus triandrus 'Thalia'; *Iris reticulata*

danfordiae is yellow and the same height, and later comes *I. reticulata*, which is deep blue with gold markings but pale blue or purple in its varieties (six to eight inches). Plant all these two to three inches deep.

The Dutch, Spanish and English bulbous irises (members of the so-called Xiphium group) grow 1½ to 2 feet tall, and come in a good range of colours – from blue, mauve and yellow to white. They make good cut flowers and should be planted in autumn three inches deep in sun and good soil.

Narcissus

Narcissi (which include daffodils as well as the plants commonly called *Narcissi*) are perhaps the easiest of all bulbs for cool climates. Extreme heat is fatal, though; they never grow and soon fade away. On the other hand, the flowers and foliage of *Narcissus tazetta* forms like 'Paper White' – which are excellent, along with many others, for forcing – may be damaged by frost.

Outdoor daffodils like a fairly stiff, fertile soil, which must be moist during the growing season. Bulbs should be planted in autumn four to six inches deep (deeper in light soils), though the smaller species and hybrids should be only two to four inches deep. Container-grown bulbs should be lifted after flowering and treated as described on page 107, but naturalized specimens can go untended for years except for the occasional autumn top-dressing of bonemeal.

Yellow is the predominant colour, often teamed with gold, white, pink or red, but brown and green varieties have been bred. There are eleven divisions of *Narcissi*, graded according to colour, size of trumpet and other characteristics. These include large and small cupped *Narcissi*, doubles, jonquils (with bunches of blooms on every stem), sweet-scented poet's *Narcissi* and many species.

The smaller sorts, which grow only a few inches tall, are attractive in pots, window boxes, rock pockets and mini-lawns. Most flower in early spring and include *Narcissus asturiensis* (*N. minimus*), the smallest, only three to four inches high with well defined trumpets; *N. bulbocodium* (hoop petticoat), six inches or less with flared trumpets and much reduced perianth segments; *N. cyclamineus* and its hybrids, four inches, with long narrow trumpets and perianth segments flaring back like a donkey's ears; and the tiny angel's tears *Narcissi* (*N. triandrus albus*), white to cream and 6 to 12 inches tall.

Tulipa

Few bulbs are more adaptable and brilliant than tulips, which come in a wide range of colours, from purest white to almost black (in fact, a dark purple). There are singles and doubles, self-coloured and bi-coloured forms. Among the vast number of types suitable for containers or bedding, the season opens with the Early Single varieties (12 to 15 inches); followed by Early Doubles (10 to 12 inches) and then the Mendels and Triumphs; the shapely Darwins and Parrots (the latter with fringed petals

Ranunculus asiaticus double-flowered hybrids

Narcissus 'Paper White' **left** is one of the Tazetta group, and is among the earliest of all the *Narcissi* to flower. Planted in late summer, it will bloom indoors very early in the winter. It is also extremely easy to grow, needing no soil – simply stand the bulbs on wet pebbles or gravel – and not needing to be kept in the dark in the early stages of forcing. Simply stand the bowls of bulbs on a window sill in a cool room, and bring them into the warmth of a living room when the flower buds are well formed.

and strange colour streaks) and the waisted Lily-Flowered types – all around two feet; and also such breeds as Cottage (up to three feet), Late Doubles, Multi-Flowered and Broken.

All the above should be planted in late autumn (to avoid the risk of the bulbs contracting fire disease), in well drained soil and sun. For details of dwarf tulips see page 113.

Other spring-bloomers
Anemones (wind flowers) greet the spring with starry flowers and deeply cut leaves. The tuberous roots of the St. Brigid and de Caen types of *Anemone coronaria* (the former semi-double, the latter single) grow around 12 inches tall, and have brilliant flowers of many colours. These are excellent for cutting. Plant the tubers two to three inches deep in late autumn, late spring and again in summer to obtain a succession of bloom. These plants require well drained soil and plenty of sun.

The three-inch, blue-flowered *A. blanda* needs a sheltered site and well drained soil. It blooms in early spring, and white, deep pink and purple forms are available. *A. nemorosa*, with its white single and double flowers, does best in light shade. It grows to three to five inches. The six-inch, blue-flowered *A. apennina* is a charmer for naturalizing in grass or between shrubs. Plant all these smaller sorts two inches deep.

Muscari (grape hyacinths) are easy bulbs for edging beds, naturalizing in grass or growing around trees and ornaments. The flowers are bunched – like grapes – on six- to eight-inch stems. Starch from the bulbs was once used to stiffen linen – hence their other name of starch lilies. *Muscari armeniacum*, whose flowers are blue, and its varieties 'Heavenly Blue' (a particularly rich blue) and 'Cantab' (sky-blue) are the commonest kinds, together with *M. botryoides* (china blue) and *M. botryoides* 'Album', which is white. Plant the bulbs three inches deep in autumn.

Valuable for cutting as well as for outdoor decoration are the tuberous-rooted 'buttercups' derived from *Ranunculus asiaticus*. These have showy, round double or semi-double yellow, red, orange and pink flowers on 9- to 12-inch stems in the 'Turban' and 'French' strains. Plant the tubers, with the protruding claws downwards, two to three inches deep in autumn or early spring.

Shade-tolerant types
Convallaria majalis (lily of the valley) is frequently included in bulb lists because its rhizome tolerates similar lifting, storing and forcing. See page 162.

Scillas are the woodland bluebells of England (*Scilla non-scripta*, also known as *Endymion*) and Spain (*S. (E.) hispanica*). When grown in moist leafy soil or between shrubs they colonize readily from seed and offsets, flowering in late spring. The flowers of the Spanish bluebell are larger than the English, and blue, white and pink forms occur. They grow up to nine inches tall, and should be planted two to four inches deep.

Anemone St Brigid hybrids

Muscari armeniacum

Scilla non-scripta

Dwarf bulbs and corms

Tiny bulbs – ranging from the common crocus and snowdrop to the less well known *Sternbergia* and *Ipheion* – have a great many uses for those with little or no garden space. The elfin faces of winter aconites, snowdrops and crocuses, peeping from small rock pockets or tiny patio flower beds, bring welcome spots of colour to the gloom of winter.

In a patio garden, even a minute patch of grass can be planted with a few baby daffodils, snowdrops or early crocuses. Many dwarf bulbs – especially *Sternbergias* and *Zephyranthes* – grow happily at the foot of sunny walls. Or they can be planted in small raised beds, protected if necessary in winter with a frame of glass. The baby bulbs are ideal, too, for growing in window boxes, in containers to stand on balconies or window sills, or mixed with dwarf shrubs in sink gardens or tubs.

Most need good drainage with plenty of water during the growing season. In cold districts they can be satisfactorily flowered in pans of gritty potting mixture, topped with pebbles or granite chippings and grown along in a cold frame or unheated greenhouse. Early autumn is the best time to plant, unless otherwise stated.

The commoner kinds

Chionodoxa luciliae (glory of the snow) has charming starry blue flowers with white centres, several clustering together on four-inch stems. *C. sardensis* is a richer blue. Grow them in groups and plant three inches deep in full sun. They flower very early.

The ever-popular crocuses are ideal for planting in grass, in containers, or in small beds or rock pockets, although sun is necessary for the blooms to open to their fullest extent. The colours are varied but particularly rich in purples, mauves, yellows and whites.

There are three main groups: winter-flowering sorts like *Crocus imperati*, *C. chrysanthus*, *C. etruscus*, *C. sieberi* and *C. tomasinianus*; spring-bloomers, which include the large-flowered Dutch crocus – *C. neapolitanus* (*C. vernus*) and its hybrids – which are useful for forcing; and the autumn-flowering kinds like *C. sativus* (the source of saffron), *C. kotschyanus* (*C. zonatus*) and the mauve *C. speciosus*. The first two groups should

Colchicum speciosum 'Album'

be planted in early autumn and the last in midsummer, all three inches deep.

Eranthis are cheery winter-bloomers with golden, buttercup-like flowers, backed by ruffs of green scalloped leaves. *Eranthis hyemalis* is the well known winter aconite, but *E. × tubergenii* has larger flowers. Plant two inches deep in light shade. Where the establishment of dormant roots fails to produce results, try moving plants that are already in flower. This is invariably successful.

Although snowdrops (*Galanthus*) are generally known as winter-bloomers, there are also autumn-flowering kinds like *Galanthus nivalis reginae-olgae*. On the whole the genus favours fairly heavy soil, provided it is well drained, and they are not averse to chalk. Plant the little bulbs two to three inches deep in sun or semi-shade. *G. nivalis* (the common snowdrop, also known as fair maids of February) grows to six inches and has a number of varietal forms, including a double. *G. elwesii* is a fine large-flowered species six to ten inches tall.

Late-blooming types

Colchicums are often misnamed autumn crocus or meadow saffron, for the flowers of the smaller kinds do somewhat resemble those of crocuses. However, they belong to the lily family, whereas crocuses are related to irises. The two are quite different in leaf, *Colchicum* foliage being large and coarse. It appears in spring, the flowers in late summer.

The large flowers are white or mauve to purple, and may be plain or chequered. The 10- to 12-inch *Colchicum speciosum* flowers a little later than the four-inch *C. autumnale* (naked boys) and its varieties. 'Water-lily', an especially fine form of the former, has double rosy-lilac flowers. Suitable for sun or shade, they all do best in light, well drained soil. Plant the tubers three inches deep in midsummer. There are also spring-flowering species, such as *C. luteum*, but these are less common.

Sternbergia lutea, the fall daffodil, in fact looks like a yellow crocus when it blooms in late autumn. The leaves are long and narrow and the overall height about six inches. The species will only flourish in well drained soil in a sheltered spot where sun can bake the bulbs. *S. sicula angustifolia* is a little hardier.

Zephyranthes candida (flower of the wind) must have sun, shelter and well drained soil. In cool climates it is best grown in pots. In late summer the beautiful white, starry flowers are borne on 6- to 12-inch stems above a carpet of grassy leaves. Plant the bulbs four inches deep and increase by offsets.

Other small bulbs

Bulbocodium vernum, with purplish crocus-like flowers, and *Puschkinia scilloides*, the striped squill, which has white flowers striped with blue, are both small enough for sink gardens. The former has flowers that appear at ground level in early spring. It is sometimes called the red crocus, or the meadow saffron of spring, and may be listed as *Colchicum vernum*. Plant both bulbs two inches deep in autumn.

Erythroniums are charmers for moist spots in light shade. They flower in spring with bunches of nodding 'Turk's cap' flowers and plain or mottled leaves. Plant them four inches deep in cool leafy or peaty soil. *Erythronium californicum* (trout lily) has cream flowers with darker eyes on 12-inch stems, and mottled foliage. The blooms of *E. dens-canis*, the dog's-tooth violet, vary from white to pink, mauve or purple. It too has chocolate-blotched leaves and grows eight inches tall. *E. tuolumnenso* is distinguished by plain green leaves, and bears several golden-yellow flowers on stems 12 inches or more in height.

Chionodoxa luciliae

Eranthis hyemalis

Crocus speciosus

Scilla peruviana

Allium cernuum

Cyclamen neapolitanum

Dwarf daffodils
There are many dwarf forms of *Narcissus*, which are charming in pots or window boxes, at the front of miniature borders or in small patches of grass. They need moist soil and plenty of sun. The number of species is limited, but many hybrids have been bred. Most flower in early spring. The smallest include *Narcissus asturiensis* (*N. minimus*), a perfect dwarf trumpet daffodil, *N. triandrus albus* (angel's tears) and *N. bulbocodium* **left** – all less than six inches tall. Slightly larger are *N. cyclamineus* and *N. pseudonarcissus*.

Ipheion uniflorum is the correct name for a plant variously referred to as *Milla*, *Triteleia* or *Brodiaea*. It makes a splendid edging plant for spring borders and rose beds, with masses of dark green, grassy leaves and saucer-shaped, sweetly scented flowers on six-inch stems. Colours vary from lilac to deep blue. Plant four inches deep and give it a sunny situation.

Scilla bifolia, the twinleaf squill, often has more than the two leaves its name indicates. The best forms have turquoise-blue flowers, but pink and white forms are common. It blooms in spring, on eight-inch stems, as the snow melts. More vigorous is *S. sibirica*, a Russian species with violet or prussian-blue drooping florets on eight-inch stems. The variety 'Atrocoerulea', often known as 'Spring Beauty', is earlier and more robust than the type.

Among the summer-flowering species is *S. peruviana*. Named for a ship, not the country, it is native to central Mediterranean regions. This bears broadly conical heads of tightly packed, lilac-blue, starry flowers, and has a large bulb, up to two inches across. Plant all these *Scillas* three inches deep in sun and well drained soil. (For blue-bells, also classified as *Scilla*, though properly *Endymion*, see page 109.)

For dryer spots
Dwarf cyclamen are very long-lived, especially where the corms are left undisturbed and can bake in the summer sun. They colonize readily from seed and are suitable for rock pockets, pans or for growing under trees. Plant shallowly, first covering the tubers with leafy compost, and repeat this dressing annually after growth has died down.

Winter-blooming cyclamen include *Cyclamen coum*, with dumpy magenta

Oxalis adenophylla

flowers on three-inch stems. *C. × atkinsii* is similar but with marbled leaves. *C. neapolitanum*, with beautiful silver-marked leaves, has large, flat tubers with both shoots and branches projecting from their upper surfaces. It is important not to break these when planting and to set the tubers the right way up – that is, with the domed, smooth side downwards. The species flowers in autumn, with white to carmine scented flowers. (See also page 82.)

Other plants with tuberous roots which tolerate fairly dry conditions in summer include *Corydalis solida*, with racemes of purple flowers in late spring, and *C. lutea*, yellow-flowered and up to one foot tall. There is also *Oxalis adenophylla*, which may not be hardy in all situations. This forms mats of silvery, clover-like leaves, topped by inch-wide, pale pink flowers with white eyes. They appear in early summer. Plant these in sun or light shade, covering shallowly.

Several smaller members of the onion family are pretty in summer, particularly *Allium beesianum*, with bright blue or white flowers (eight inches tall), *A. cernuum*, with white to pink to red umbels of nodding flowers (8 to 12 inches) and *A. moly*, the lily leek, rich yellow and six to ten inches high. All these like sun and good drainage.

111

Some unusual bulbs

It is always fun to try growing something new, and most of the bulbs mentioned here are not very commonly grown. This is partly because they are neither as robust nor as prolific as the more usual types, so care must be taken to site them in sheltered places. But they are well worth trying if you want a change from the daffodils, crocuses, *Gladioli* and other well-loved bulbs.

Many of these off-beat bulbs come from places like South Africa and the Himalayas, where conditions are very different from those in Europe and most of North America, and they may need special conditions. Dry soil during dormancy is a common requirement. This is difficult in areas of high winter rainfall, but can be overcome by covering them with glass or polythene sheeting. Alternatively they can be grown in containers where conditions can be controlled. But a few like moist soil.

For hot, dry situations

Amaryllis belladonna blooms in late summer, but is inclined to be temperamental over flowering unless the bulbs are kept dry in winter. Accordingly they should be given a hot, dry spot, preferably against a warm wall. The rosy-red and sweetly scented trumpet flowers appear bunched at the tops of the 12- to 18-inch stems, with the strap-shaped leaves following in spring. There are varieties with white or pink flowers, both with yellow throats.

Babianas are suitable for pot work indoors or can be planted outdoors in spring. Plant them six inches deep in

Babiana varieties

well drained soil. The cup-shaped flowers, frequently fragrant, come in brilliant colours on ten-inch stems.

Brodiaeas and *Calochortus*, both from California, need similar treatment. *Brodiaea californica* has umbels of pink to violet, trumpet-shaped flowers on one-foot stems. *B. laxa* is deep blue and 12 to 18 inches tall, *B. pulchella* (*B. congesta*) violet and one foot. All are summer-blooming, and are frequently listed in bulb catalogues under the names *Triteleia*, *Dichelostemma*, *Brevoortia* and *Hookera*.

Calochortus (butterfly lilies) are beautiful bulbs with grassy leaves and saucer-shaped flowers in striking colours. *C.*

Lachenalia aloides variety

venustus bears three-inch-wide blooms of white, cream or yellow marked with blotches of crimson. They are borne on 12-inch stems. *C. uniflorus* (cat's ears) is lilac-blue, six inches tall and summer-blooming. Plant the bulbs three inches deep – on a layer of sand – and keep them dry when dormant.

Ixias (corn lilies) are not very hardy, so they are best grown in pots of sandy soil or in sunny, sheltered beds with protection in winter. They flower in spring, carrying several dainty star-like blooms on thin, wiry stems. The colours are varied – sea green in *Ixia viridiflora*, but cream, white and red, violet, or purple with darker centres in the mixed strains offered by bulb merchants.

Lachenalias are called Cape cowslips because they come from South Africa and their tubular flowers are borne in bunches like the European cowslip (*Primula veris*). *Lachenalia aloides* (also known as *L. tricolor*) has green flowers edged with red and yellow, or bright gold in the variety 'Nelsonii'. Both grow about 12 inches tall and have mottled leaves. *L. bulbiflora* (*L. pendula*) has plain leaves with purple, green and yellow flowers. For best results plant the bulbs in rich soil in mid-summer, five or six to a five-inch pot, and grow under

Tigridia pavonia

glass at about 13°C (55°F). They flower in early spring.

Tigridias (tiger flowers) need similar cultural treatment to *Gladioli* (see page 108), except that water should be withheld once the foliage withers because they are rather more tender. The four-inch cup-shaped flowers are quite distinctive, with three large petals and three smaller spotted petals looking rather like a tiger's face. They are orange-scarlet, spotted with crimson, in *Tigridia pavonia*, but cultivars with orange, yellow, white, pinkish-crimson and mauve flowers are common.

Veltheimia capensis is an ideal plant for indoor gardening, as it is easy and decorative even when out of flower. The oblong leaves are bright green with crisp curly edges, and the strawberry-pink flowers grow in dense drooping heads at the tops of 18-inch stems. They look something like *Aloes* or red-hot pokers (*Kniphofias*). Often winter-blooming under glass, they are not hardy outside in Britain or many parts of Europe or North America.

Spring-blooming kinds

The fritillaries (*Fritillaria*) form a large family with many species. The most spectacular is *Fritillaria imperialis*, the crown imperial, which grows two to three feet tall. The stems terminate in a tuft of leaves like the top of a pineapple. Just beneath these the large and showy orange-scarlet or golden flowers are arranged in pendulous whorls. The bulbs should be planted in midsummer six inches deep in full sun. Put them at an

Fritillaria meleagris varieties

angle on a layer of sand, and pack them round with more sand, giving them well drained but moist soil.

F. meleagris, the snake's head fritillary, will grow in grass or borders in sun or light shade, but needs moist soil. The 12-inch stems terminate in large, pendant, bell-like flowers that may be white or purple-chequered. *F. latifolia* is similar but much smaller, growing to only about six inches. Its round, bell-shaped flowers vary from yellow to a dark reddish-purple.

Hermodactylus tuberosus (also known as *Iris tuberosa*) is the widow iris, so-called because of its strange, iris-like flowers of greenish-yellow and black-

Tulipa 'Heart's Delight' (Kaufmanniana hybrid)

purple. It blooms in spring in sheltered spots, or can be forced in pots. It grows one foot tall.

Other unusual spring-bloomers include the tulip species and their direct hybrids, most of them much smaller than the common hybrid tulips described on page 108. Among the more interesting kinds are *Tulipa tarda*, which is yellow with white-tipped petals, several appearing on each four-inch stem; *T. sylvestris*, yellow and 12 inches tall; *T. praestans*, orange-scarlet and 16 inches tall; *T. kaufmanniana* and its hybrids, the water-lily tulips, of various colours but mainly reds, yellows and whites, which are about eight inches tall; *T. fosteriana*, brilliant scarlet and 8 to 24 inches tall; and *T. greigii*, with chocolate-striped leaves and orange-scarlet flowers, eight to ten inches tall.

Summer-bloomers

Most *Alliums*, which are close relatives of the onion, will grow in ordinary soil in sun or light shade. Among the most spectacular is *Allium christophii* (*A. albopilosum*), with large heads of violet-blue flowers that can be dried for winter decoration. It grows one to two feet tall. Others include *A. oreophilum* (*A. ostrowskianum*), with huge umbels of rosy blossoms on six- to nine-inch stems, and *A. karataviense*, with huge white heads of flowers, like footballs, up to a foot in circumference. The beautiful bright blue *A. beesianum* likes a cool, moist position, whereas *A. caeruleum*, also blue, needs dryness and full sun; it grows one to two feet tall.

Crocosmia masonorum from South Africa is hardier than its near relatives, the *Montbretias*, and is more attractive. It is a striking plant with clusters of large, reddish-gold, tubular flowers carried on stiff 12- to 18-inch stems, and flat leaves something like those of *Gladioli*.

Among the bulbs that bloom in early summer, *Sparaxis tricolor* hybrids, or harlequin flowers, are well worth trying. Their blooms are vividly coloured in orange, red, pink and purple, and have prominent dark throats; they grow on 15- to 18-inch stems. Another is *Tritonia crocata* (blazing star), with fan-like leaves which resemble those of *Freesias* (see page 115) and cup-shaped coppery-orange flowers with yellow bases. These

Sparaxis tricolor hybrids

grow on one-foot stems. Grow both of these plants as for *Ixias* (see above).

For wetter spots

Several bulbs thrive in heavier soil and wetter situations. They include *Schizostylis coccinea*, commonly known as the Kafir lily, a name it shares with *Clivia miniata* (see page 114). This blooms in late summer with several scarlet flowers on 12- to 18-inch stems, or a softer pink in the variety 'Viscountess Byng'.

The *Ornithogalums*, particularly *Ornithogalum umbellatum*, the star of Beth-

Ornithogalum thyrsoides

lehem, like moist conditions and light shade. This species has clusters of white flowers, striped with green, in early spring. *O. nutans* has greenish flowers. The chincherinchee (*O. thyrsoides*) is more tender and should be grown in pots or treated like *Gladioli* (see page 108).

Camassias are North American plants and flower in early summer. Plant them four to five inches deep in borders or grass. The leaves are lax and strap-shaped, the starry flowers growing in long spikes. *Camassia cusickii* is pale blue, while *C. leichtlinii* varies from white to blue, or double creamy-yellow in the variety 'Plena'. All grow around three feet tall. *C. quamash*, one to two feet tall, has edible bulbs and deep blue to white flowers. It is commonly known by its American Indian name, quamash.

Apart from these, most *Leucojums* (snowflakes) like cool, moist, peaty soil. They are very similar to snowdrops (*Galanthus*) except that all the petal parts are the same length, instead of alternately long and short. They bloom at various times of the year. *Leucojum vernum*, the spring snowflake, grows eight inches tall; its blooming improves when naturalized for several seasons. *L. aestivum*, the summer snowflake, grows up to two feet, and is good for cutting. *L. autumnale* blooms in autumn on eight-inch stems. Unlike the others, it needs good drainage.

113

The exotic bulbs

Any unusual plant makes a talking point in the patio-garden or home. Or it can be used for an accent position, such as by the side of a wrought iron gate or in a large tub by a pool. The more spectacular bulbs are ideal for such uses. Some are appreciated for their size, others for their rich fragrance, and yet others for their unusual habit.

Not all of the plants described here are in fact bulbous in a strict botanical sense – some have corms, tubers or rhizomes – but they are all alike in having underground storage organs and periods of dormancy. Bulb merchants group such plants collectively under the umbrella title of bulbs, and they generally need much the same treatment.

With the exception of the lilies, none of the following are reliably hardy in cool temperate climates. Some must be wintered away from frost, and it would be advisable to grow certain others all the time under glass. This of course does not apply in warm climates.

Lovely lilies

Lilies are the aristocrats among bulbs, beautiful in flower, good for cutting, sweetly scented and including kinds for sun or shade. They can be grown cool in pots for indoor display, while some kinds can be forced gently (see page 107).

Some lilies are stem-rooters, and produce roots above the bulb as well as below; so these have to be planted deep enough to allow for this growth. Others, like the white madonna lily (*Lilium candidum*), only have basal roots. These need very little covering, although others in this section may require deeper planting. Check such points with your supplier before planting. All lilies appreciate leafy, humus-type soil; some will tolerate lime, others hate it.

Hardiest and easiest outdoors are the European sorts like *L. martagon* (with maroon or white blooms), *L. pyrenaicum* (yellow, spotted with black) and *L. monadelphum* (clear yellow with black spots). Among the oriental species is the splendid *L. auratum*, with immense flowers up to a foot across, white, streaked with gold and crimson; *L. henryi*, orange; *L. regale*, richly scented and creamy-white; *L. speciosum*, with white or crimson reflexed flowers; and the fiery-gold *L. tigrinum*, the tiger lily.

Lilium candidum

Zantedeschia aethiopica

Hybrid lilies are sold as garden or pot-plants, and are more disease-resistant – especially the Mid-Century group, the de Graaf lilies and the Preston and Bellingham hybrids. The best kinds for forcing are the Mid-Century hybrids, *L. auratum*, *L. speciosum*, and *L. longiflorum* (the Easter lily, with white, heavily fragrant blooms that – in spite of the name – appear in summer).

Long-flowering exotics

Agapanthus are used freely in tropical gardens, but in cooler climates are usually grown in conservatories or in tubs that are stood outside for the summer flowering season. *Agapanthus africanus* (*A. umbellatus*) has strap-like leaves and immense umbels of funnel-shaped, light to deep blue or white flowers on two- to four-foot stems. Very similar and slightly hardier is *A. campanulatus*, whose variety 'Isis' has beautiful lavender-blue flowers.

Light, well drained soil is needed by all *Agapanthus*, with a mulch or feeds in summer and a position in full sun. But withhold water during dormancy. A race known as 'Headbourne Hybrids' is hardier than most and can be grown outdoors in various parts of North America and Europe (including Britain). Keeping the roots protected and dry in winter (with straw and polythene) is the ingredient for success. (See the illustration on page 149.)

Zantedeschia aethiopica (trumpet lily, calla or arum lily) is a long-flowering South African with smooth, arrow-shaped leaves and large, white, trumpet-shaped flowers that first appear in spring. Other species come in other colours, for example gold in *Z. elliottiana*, lemon-yellow in *Z. pentlandii* and white, pink, wine-red and almost black in *Z. rehmannii*. The last is often known as *Richardia*.

A form of *Z. aethiopica* called 'Crowborough' is hardy in many parts of Britain. When in doubt, however, grow *Zantedeschias* in large pots of rich soil, water freely in summer, and aim at winter temperatures around 10°C (50°F).

Bulbs for pots

Clivia miniata is a favourite cottager's plant and a robust grower, with strap-shaped leaves and huge flower heads of

Freesia hybrids

Hippeastrum hybrid

orange-red and yellow trumpets (see illustration on page 80). It flowers best when pot-bound, so only repot occasionally, but give regular liquid feeds.

Freesia refracta and its hybrids are sweetly scented spring-bloomers with tubular flowers on slender, wiry stems. Colours vary from white to yellow and gold, also pink to red and mauve. Semi-doubles and doubles are also available. The bulbs are planted in late summer, five or six to a five-inch pot of good potting mixture. Bury them one inch deep and keep them cool – about 5°C (41°F) – until growth starts; then increase warmth gradually.

Haemanthus katharinae carries round heads of spiky, pinkish-red flowers – like

Haemanthus multiflorus

catherine wheels – on one-foot stems. It blooms in spring, whereas the quite distinct *H. albiflos* flowers in autumn with a large, white, stamen-filled bloom resembling a paint brush. Both should be rested after flowering and should ideally be grown at 13 to 16°C (55 to 61°F).

Hippeastrums (commonly but incorrectly known as *Amaryllis*) are favourite pot-plants, ideal for indoor cultivation. They have large, striking, trumpet-shaped flowers on two- to three-foot stems in white, pink, scarlet or deep red shades. There are varieties that will bloom at almost any season.

Plant the huge bulbs four to six months before the flowering season, first soaking them in tepid water. Pot them individually in five- to seven-inch pots, with half their bulk exposed. Use a potting mixture of loam, leaf-mould and sand, or Mixture no. 2. They should be kept in a light place to flower, with a minimum temperature of 13°C (55°F). When the foliage starts to yellow, water should be reduced and the pots turned on their sides to dry until the next year.

Sprekelia formosissima is the Jacobean lily, and grows about one foot high with one, or occasionally two, large, deep crimson, orchid-like flowers. These may be five inches across. Rest in winter and restart in spring for summer flowers.

Vallota speciosa (Scarborough lily) is a delightful subject for late summer. When pot-bound it flowers very freely, the two-foot stems carrying many brilliant scarlet, trumpet blooms. Reduce water when the foliage dies.

Some hardier types

A number of the exotic, showy bulbs can be grown outdoors in sheltered situations. Among them is *Crinum × powellii*, an impressive member of the *Amaryllis* family with large, fragrant, pink or white trumpet-shaped flowers. These appear on two- to three-foot stems in late summer. The extremely large bulb needs to be partially exposed. It needs a warm, sheltered position and plenty of room. It can be grown in a tub filled with good, rich potting mixture.

Dracunculus vulgaris, the dragon arum, is a curious aroid from southern Europe with a fleshy, spotted, three-foot stem, handsome, deeply divided leaves and very large maroon-purple flowers. These may be a foot long and eight inches across, but after several days smell badly and then attract flies. These act as pollinators. It has a large round tuber which should be planted in a warm, sunny situation. It is summer-flowering.

Eremurus (foxtail lilies) are stately herbaceous perennials with octopus-shaped tubers which should be planted six to eight inches deep and packed around with sand. The impressive spikes are studded with small starry flowers. *Eremurus stenophyllus* (*E. bungei*) has gold and deep pink hybrids on two- to three-foot stems. *E. olgae*, which is pink or white, is four feet tall. The 'Shelford Hybrids' – up to six feet tall – come in white, yellow, orange and pink, and *E. robustus*, a soft pink colour, grows up to six to ten feet.

Galtonia (*Hyacinthus*) *candicans* is attractive in late summer, when planted near brightly coloured perennials like *Kniphofias* (red-hot pokers). The spikes of white, drooping bells are good for cutting, growing 2 to 2½ feet tall. Plant the bulbs six inches deep in sun or a lightly shaded position.

Nerines have umbels of white, pink or red lily-like flowers – without the leaves – in late summer. These are good for cutting, growing 12 to 15 inches tall. Generally they are grown in pots with the bulbs partially exposed, but *Nerine bowdenii* tolerates a little frost and may be grown outside in sunny, sheltered spots. *N. sarniensis* (known as the Guernsey lily, although it comes from South Africa) is deep rose-pink. *N. flexuosa* has up to 12 blooms on a stem.

Crinum × powellii

Brilliant flowering begonias

If it is a splash of intense colour that you need – to brighten up a room, conservatory, window box or patio – there are few plants that rival the flowering begonias. The lustre of their dazzling reds, pinks, golds, yellows and whites is superb. The main snag is that many types are more happy as greenhouse and outdoor subjects than as houseplants. Given careful cultivation, however, most can be grown successfully in the home.

Another thing that sometimes puts off the beginner is the bewildering range of types. There are literally hundreds of species of begonias, and although only a small number have significance for gardeners, many of these have been crossed and re-crossed to produce an enormous number of hybrids. Add to this the fact that many almost identical hybrids bear different names, and confusion is natural. In fact, however, there are only three major groups of begonias that the gardener need bother with: those with fibrous roots, those that form round, fleshy tubers, and those that spread by means of horizontal underground stems, or rhizomes.

The rhizomatous kinds include the *Begonia rex* varieties, grown mainly for their richly coloured foliage, and the less showy North American species such as *B. boweri* and its many forms. These and other foliage begonias – generally the easiest of the group to grow indoors – are described on pages 46 and 48.

Tuberous-rooted begonias

These are probably the best-known kinds of begonias, and they have been bred in a wide range of forms, all classified under the name *B. × tuberhybrida*. Like other begonias, these have separate male and female flowers on the same plant. The male ones are generally double, but not the female, and removing the latter (easily recognized by the seed capsule behind the petals) encourages the males to grow even larger.

The varieties with the largest flowers are sometimes termed Grandiflora, and these make handsome pot plants. The Pendula begonias have a naturally trailing habit ideal for hanging baskets and window boxes, while the Multifloras with their small, single flowers and the larger-flowered Multiflora Maxima types with sprays of double blooms make compact plants ideal for small patio beds. The newer Bertini Compacta varieties also belong in this group, all of which are summer-flowering. By growing them under artificial light and adjusting the length of 'day' and 'night', however, they can be brought into flower at virtually any season – though this is a task for the real enthusiast (see page 234).

Fibrous-rooted begonias

These are very varied, and include the small-flowered wax begonias, *B. semperflorens*, which are raised from seed every year by the million for summer bedding. They are good for patios and window boxes, and come in various shades of red, pink and white. As the name suggests, they can bloom almost all round the year, given the right conditions. Like almost all begonias, they are killed by frost, but a few in a pot will decorate a window sill all through winter.

An unnamed double tuberous begonia of perfect shape

Begonia × tuberhybrida Pendula varieties

Begonia × tuberhybrida 'Wedding Day'

Begonia 'Scarlet Bedder' (Bertini Compacta)

Begonia 'Colour Queen' (fibrous-rooted hybrid)

Begonia 'Fireglow' (Rieger hybrid)

Begonia semperflorens varieties

Also fibrous-rooted are two groups of truly winter-flowering begonias, both based on *B. socotrana*. These are the well-known 'Gloire de Lorraine' type – very similar in appearance to *B. semperflorens* – and the rather less popular Hiemalis hybrids. The latter are rather similar to the summer-flowering tuberous hybrids, but somewhat smaller. Probably related to these, but blurring the distinction between the tuberous and fibrous-rooted types, are the recently-introduced Rieger begonias. These were bred in Germany as houseplants, and will flower virtually all the year in conditions of low heat, light and humidity.

A final important fibrous-rooted group are the cane-stemmed, or 'angel-wing', begonias typified by *B.* × 'Lucerna'. These have long-pointed leaves that look rather like wings. They are generally tall plants that bear pendulous clusters of summer flowers.

Cultivating begonias

Begonias can be obtained as mature plants, seedlings, seeds or (in the case of tuberous types) dormant tubers. Tubers are easier to grow than seeds and should be started into growth in early spring at a temperature of about 16°C (61°F). Bury the tubers completely in shallow trays of moist potting mixture. Transplant them into pots when two or three inches high, and remove the first two or three flower buds to strengthen the plants. Restrict the large-flowered kinds to one or two shoots, but encourage several shoots from each tuber with the Pendula types by pinching out the tips when the shoots are three to four inches long.

Begonia seed is very fine, and is difficult to spread evenly. So mix it with some silver sand. Then sprinkle this mixture on the top of a pan of potting mixture, but do not cover it with extra soil. Sow in winter or early spring at 16 to 19°C (61 to 66°F), and keep them moist until they germinate. Many begonias can also be propagated by cuttings – stem cuttings for the tuberous kinds and leaf-stem cuttings for the winter-flowering ones (see page 228).

Begonias grow well in any normal potting mixture, but be sure never to overwater them. It is best to let the mixture get fairly dry and then give it a good soaking; do not leave the plants standing in a saucer of water, however. The main problem with growing most flowering begonias indoors is lack of humidity. The tuberous types, particularly, tend to drop their buds and flowers in protest. If, therefore, you want to grow them as houseplants, stand the pots on a tray of wet gravel or plunge them in damp peat. They will also do well in a terrarium – or, of course, in a conservatory where a large plant collection maintains high humidity. The cane-stemmed and winter-flowering begonias are less demanding, but almost all kinds need good light. Strong direct sunlight will burn their leaves, however, so shade them in the height of summer.

Once the fibrous-rooted begonias have finished flowering, they should be discarded, but tuberous kinds can last many years. Lift them carefully in the autumn, and put them in a cool, dry place to die down. When the foliage has withered, remove the stems and store the tubers in dry peat or sand in a cool but frost-free place. Then, when spring comes again, they can be brought into growth to yield another year's brilliant display.

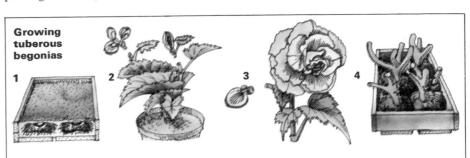

Growing tuberous begonias

1 Plant the tubers in early spring, hollow side up.
2 Remove early buds for vigorous growth. **3** Remove the small female flowers to ensure large male blooms. **4** After top growth dies down, store tubers in a cool, dry place.

4 Outdoor gardening -without a garden

There is no need to have vast, rolling acres in order to grow an attractive range of outdoor plants. With the smallest patio, terrace or yard you can create an oasis of greenery and brilliant flowers growing in pots, tubs and other containers. Or you can brighten your surroundings with window boxes. Perhaps you can display plants on a balcony or create a roof garden.
This part of The Complete Indoor Gardener will show you how.

Gardens on concrete and stone

Many small gardens are short on soil, particularly the back gardens or yards of terrace houses in urban areas. Even where there is soil this may be too poor to support plants, especially if a previous tenant has concreted all or part of its surface. In such cases it is a Herculean task to break the concrete, cart it away (in some cases unavoidably through the house) and replace it with soil. It may also be necessary to garden on stone or concrete in an inner courtyard; and certainly it is essential on roofs, balconies, verandahs and similar places.

Problems and possibilities

There are advantages and disadvantages with this form of gardening, and the challenge is to make virtue out of necessity. On the credit side is the fact that one can build the garden on several levels. This always creates interest – particularly for those with ground floor or basement apartments, for they get a more dramatic view. There are several ways of altering levels. The most impressive method is to build up the part of the garden farthest from the house and connect it to the lower level with one or more shallow steps.

This back area should be about one foot higher than the rest and have a base of hardcore, with paving slabs or crazy paving on top. Holes can be left to take soil for small trees or for the part submergence of deep containers. If the steep part is finished off with a dry-stone wall, various rock plants can be inserted to trail down over its edge (see page 126). Alternatively it can be left with a level course of bricks or a coping.

Other ways of raising levels include using containers of varying heights and having window boxes or raised flower beds. Among other advantages, stone-paved gardens are dry to walk on and do away with weed problems. Also, through this use of plant containers, the whole design and layout can be easily changed from time to time.

On the debit side there may be excessive exposure to the elements. Wind and sun can soon dry out shallow containers, and excessive shade (from nearby buildings) can draw up plants or prevent flowering. On the other hand, the site may be too open, with little privacy, or the aspect grimy and depressing.

The plan

It may seem pretty daunting to attempt to create a beautiful patio garden out of a dingy back-yard, but try to look beyond the immediate problems to the possibilities of the site. Start by standing with your back to the house and studying the view outwards; this, after all, is the aspect you will see most of the time. Which features are worth preserving? What should be masked?

Shabby existing flooring can be smartened up with a layer of plain or coloured tiles, or thin paving. Old surround walls are often sooty or discoloured. Paint them over with a light colour-wash to create an immediate effect of brightness and at the same time destroy hibernating pests in their crevices. The house may also benefit from this treatment. Gaily

painted shutters make small windows look larger, and flower boxes – with trailing greenery and blossoms – enhance the effect.

Judiciously sited, climbing plants can be made to hide many ugly features. Trellis fixed in front of walls can be used to support a wide range of plants, particularly climbing roses, *Clematis*, trumpet vines (*Campsis radicans*) or even peach trees in sunny situations, with honeysuckles (*Lonicera*), climbing nasturtiums (*Tropaeolum*) and climbing *Hydrangeas* in shade. Don't plant these too close to the wall, however, or the roots will become too dry. Leave a 9- to 12-inch gap, so that you can reach behind to prune, mulch, feed and water.

Ugly existing trees which are difficult to fell can be used as plant props. Remove the branches and train *Clematis* and climbing roses (they do well together) or *Hydrangeas* up the trunk. Three stout poles, arranged wigwam-fashion and tied at the top, provide a cheap support for the same kinds of plants.

Window boxes are not solely for window sills. Staggered at different heights on a blank wall they can transform a bleak scene and also provide growing areas for culinary herbs. Use grass as an amenity, sowing seed to provide an edging for a raised flower bed or around tree trunks for a green undercarpet.

Special features
Exploit garden furniture, statuary, odds and ends of containers and the like. An old hay manger or even an old-fashioned

With imagination, even the most cramped and unpromising paved area can be transformed with plants in containers. **left** Make walls an asset by suspending hanging baskets from brackets and growing climbers on trellis. Where there is room, introduce interesting plant containers and furniture **top right** or items of sculpture **right** and **far right**. It is always worthwhile paying attention to the actual paved surface, which can have an interesting texture or be interplanted with grass or trailers **below right**.

fire grate fastened to a wall makes a superb plant-holder. Make inner linings of plastic netting for these to hold the soil and plants. Small pools with fountains and cascades are easy to install and pleasant to listen to on a hot day. They bring birds to the garden, and since the same water can be used over and over again are economical to run (see pages 170 to 177).

Dark corners can be highlighted with containers full of flowers in season. Tubs, strawberry pots, old wash coppers, water filters, horse troughs and sinks all have their uses. If a large old mirror is fixed to a back wall immediately behind a colourful flower border, it will reflect the scene and give the appearance of going on and on. This makes the garden seem larger, although in order to protect the lustre it is advisable to fix a shelf over the top and mask the sides with trellis and creepers.

Dustbins are a necessary evil but need not be seen. Hide them behind a flower box, stood on the ground and with trellis or netting fastened to posts inserted towards its back. Plant with small conifers, or grow nasturtiums or ivies over the trellis and plant bulbs or annuals in front.

Portable planters stood on concrete can be made to fit existing spaces or designs. They can be fashioned in various shapes – geometrical or oval – of stout one-inch timber (cedar, redwood, oak or teak), glass-fibre or concrete (three parts cement, two parts stones and one part sand) using a mould. Plain sides can be made fancy with cork or cedar shingles if desired. One foot is a convenient depth for these planters.

These are just some of the things you can do to transform dingy, unpromising areas into gardens full of charm and beauty. You will find more ideas in the pages that follow, showing that you do not need a vast garden to practise the art of landscaping.

Tub and pot gardens

All sorts and sizes of plants, from alpines to trees, from dwarf bulbs to shrubs, can be grown in tubs or pots to bring colour and greenery to a patio, balcony or terrace, or to create a roof garden. In this kind of gardening, the containers are almost as important as the plants growing in them. The imaginative use of decorative tubs or pots will ensure that every patio or balcony is unique.

Containers come in a wide variety of shapes and sizes to suit the growth characteristics of almost every plant, and in materials that include wood, metal, concrete, plastic, clay and asbestos-cement. Many traditional models, originally made in stone or wood, are now available in reconstituted stone or glass-fibre; the latter is expensive, but has the advantage of being light and frostproof.

Traditional containers

Many of the more ornate clay containers are decorative versions of the functional flower-pot. (For more information on standard pots and their plastic equivalents, see page 219.) Decorations include piercing, tooling, applied ornament, and horizontal lines or bands. Venetian pots curve slightly inwards at the top, and are ringed with concentric bands. Spanish pots slope outwards and have slightly flared lips. Both are available in a variety of sizes, and provide ideal settings for spreading plants.

Earthenware strawberry pots are shapely versions of the wooden casks, pierced with holes and filled with soil, in which strawberries were traditionally planted. Cups are often added to the holes of the pottery versions, and these pots may be effectively planted with miniature bedding plants, alpines and bulbs (see page 106).

Glazed pots are often successful in hot, sunny regions but they unfortunately tend to look out of place in greyer climes. An added disadvantage is that the glazed finish can be damaged by frost. Tall, bellied jars, with narrow necks, were originally used in the Mediterranean region to store oil or wine. They are ideal containers for low, spreading or trailing plants such as ivy-leaf geraniums (*Pelargonium peltatum*) or trailing *Lobelia*.

You may be lucky enough to find, or buy, a Chinese storage jar. With a flattened base and a wide or narrow mouth, these jars come in a variety of sizes and make unusual containers for plants. They are generally glazed inside and out, and are often decorated with dragon designs; they need drainage holes carefully drilled in the base.

Florentine urns and pedestal vases are ornamental in their own right, and serve best as foils for sculptural plants such as succulents or cacti in summer, or for massed arrangements, for example of geraniums. Wide-mouthed orange and lemon pots were popular in Renaissance Italy. Many modern versions are decorated with ornamental relief work, as well as retaining the traditional bold rim and series of horizontal bands. They are useful for hardier shrubs such as *Rhododendrons* and *Camellias*, as well as orange and lemon trees (*Citrus*).

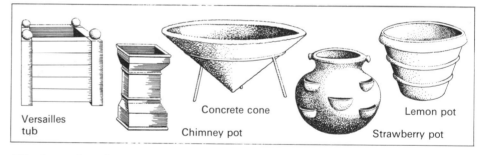

Versailles tub

Chimney pot

Concrete cone

Lemon pot

Strawberry pot

Modern developments

Plain or decorated concrete and asbestos-cement boxes, plant troughs, and pointed cones supported in wrought-iron stands are comparatively recent innovations. Wide, shallow bowls with a soil depth of 9 to 12 inches can be planted with seasonal flowers and bedding plants. Pots with a soil depth of at least 12 inches are useful for growing foliage shrubs to provide background greenery.

Wooden tubs, barrels and boxes provide a natural setting for plants, and standard versions are widely available. Casks with decorative iron hoops may be converted into plant containers, but check that the liquid originally stored in the cask has left no harmful residue. It is sensible to coat the inside with a non-toxic preservative, such as Cuprinol, but do not use creosote. It is usually possible to drill drainage holes in the base. Make sure joints are tight to prevent excessive loss of moisture.

Square boxes are ideal placements for low, bushy plants such as *Azaleas*. Traditional cube-shaped Versailles caskets, which have removable side panels that allow used subsoil to be replaced with fresh compost, are especially suitable for orange trees. *Hydrangeas* blend well with squat tubs, as do bay trees (*Laurus nobilis*).

A variety of unlikely objects can be used for containing plants, provided provision is made for drainage. Logs and tree stumps form attractively natural settings. Baths, sinks, cisterns and even chimney pots can be converted into unusual containers. Their utilitarian origins can be disguised with a coating

Planting and care

Good drainage is essential, so try to drill drainage holes if there are none already, and provide a good layer of crocks or stones. If no holes are possible, extend this layer to as much as a third of the pot's depth. Raising containers on feet or bricks **right** aids drainage and discourages pests entering the soil. Avoid standing containers directly on grass or soil, and if flooring material is likely to stain, provide a drip tray. Use a good potting mixture, such as Mix no. 3, possibly with added peat to retain moisture. Regular watering is essential, and a damp peat mulch will help reduce evaporation in hot weather. Pots and tubs protected by overhangs will need winter watering, too, but do not overdo this. Do not water in freezing weather. Feed plants regularly during the growing season, and pot on or repot when pot-bound (see page 218). If a plant is too big for repotting, replace the top two inches of soil.

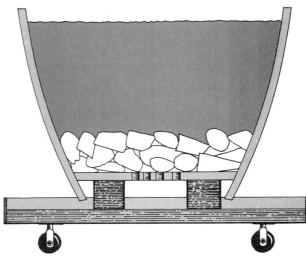

Keeping plants mobile

One of the great advantages of container gardening is that plants can be moved easily. But a soil-filled box only two feet square can weigh hundreds of pounds. To ensure trouble-free transportation, mount all but the smallest containers on castors **above**. Really big, heavy specimens can be raised on trolleys.

The mobility of a container garden means that plants can be rotated, and groupings rearranged, so that the display is always at a peak of perfection. Tender plants should be moved to sheltered sites, or indoors, during winter. If this is impracticable, wrap the container in burlap, or straw and polythene as protection against frost.

of mortar made from two parts peat, one part sand and one part cement. This should be mixed with water to a fairly wet consistency and applied to a thickness of about $\frac{1}{2}$ inch. First coat glazed surfaces with a resin adhesive for grip.

Creating a container garden

To achieve the best possible design effect, a tub or pot garden should consist of comparatively few, well placed containers that blend harmoniously with the architectural surroundings and with other tubs and pots.

In a grouped arrangement, vary the levels by using different sized containers and plants; or stage containers on bricks or pedestals. You can also range pots on stone steps. Combining square or oblong troughs with circular pots will add variety. Or a deliberately uniform grouping of identical plants in identical containers can be effective: a row of junipers (*Juniperus*) on a pebbled stand, for instance, or a line of pots containing ivy (*Hedera*) arranged on a low wall to create a leafy background.

Place tubbed bays or palms on either side of a bench or doorway, or in the centre of a courtyard, to create a focal point. Frame an archway, or brighten a dull corner, with Virginia creeper (*Parthenocissus quinquefolia*) in an oil jar. Raising a container on a pedestal, or a brick or stone plinth, will focus attention on an especially rare or beautiful specimen. It can be offset by smaller containers on a lower level. Pedestal vases and urns are especially effective flanking a stone stairway, or surmounting a gatepost. Used imaginatively such containers can add great style and elegance to the paved area.

Rockeries and raised beds

Rock plants are so compact and dainty that they make ideal subjects for the smallest gardens. Economical of space and extremely varied in habit, they can be grown on walls, in rock garden pockets, in old sinks and similar containers, or between paving stones. Many are of easy culture, but others are difficult enough to provide hobbyist gardeners with a challenge.

There are various ways of utilizing rock plants in paved areas. A small informal rockery between a patio and a path makes a charming boundary and, carefully planted, can provide interest at all seasons. A dry wall holding back a raised bed, with soil instead of concrete between the brick course, provides a home for trailing rock plants (see page 127). And a sink raised to a convenient viewing and tending height can be used as a miniature bed for just one type of plant, or be made into a miniature landscape garden, formal or informal (see pages 188 to 195).

Rock gardens

Most rock plants revel in sun, so choose as open a position as possible for the rock garden, away from the vicinity of shadowing trees and buildings. Avoid waterlogged, damp or airless sites, also such draughty wind funnels as occur between two tall buildings.

When choosing materials, remember that nothing looks as attractive as real rock. But this can be expensive, so always go for local stone (which entails less transport charges) if possible. Westmorland limestone is a beautiful silver-grey, while sandstone is reddish; the former is heavier, however, so you only get half as much rock per ton. Tufa is a very porous, lightweight rock, but it is expensive. There also are some good imitation stones available; these can be weathered to pleasing shades by painting them over with iron sulphate dissolved in water. You can even mould your own rocks using 'concrete' made from one part cement, two parts sand and two parts peat. Brick burrs and flints can also be used.

Stones keep roots cool and make for good drainage – an essential with rock plants. For this same reason, the soil should be well draining. The mixture used will vary according to the plants grown, but those which tolerate lime may be given two parts by bulk of good fibrous loam to one part each of leaf mould or peat and coarse sand, plus half a part each of rotted manure and limestone chippings or mortar rubble. A dusting of bonemeal should also be added. Lime-haters should be given equal parts of loam, sand and peat.

There are, of course, hundreds of kinds of plants that can be grown in rock gardens, particularly alpines and small trailers. You will find many suggestions on pages 160 and 161.

Raised beds

Flower beds and borders raised above the surrounding level are useful to bring visual variety to any paved area or garden. But they are particularly valuable in the small walled courtyard

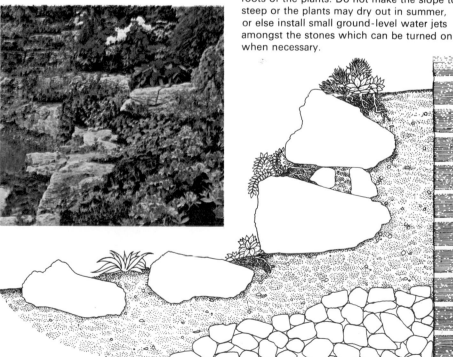

above Raised beds are useful for landscaping a small area or where there are great changes of level, but the effect is generally formal. **below** A rock garden can achieve a similar effect in a less formal way, but needs very careful construction. **opposite left** This unusual rock bank is built from old millstones. **opposite right** An ideal setting for rock plants is a well drained old stone sink raised on stone piers.

Building a rock garden
below Start at the bottom of the rock garden, bedding several large pieces of rock informally with soil. This provides a firm base and resembles a natural outcrop. Fill in behind with rubble to aid drainage. Work some good soil mixture between the stones to make plant pockets, and work your way upwards, letting each rock tilt slightly backwards so that moisture can run to the roots of the plants. Do not make the slope too steep or the plants may dry out in summer, or else install small ground-level water jets amongst the stones which can be turned on when necessary.

or patio garden, where they help break up the boxiness of the area and give a landscaped effect. The height of the bed can be anything from a few inches to about 2½ feet, and the facing wall can be made of almost any walling material – concrete fence panels, paving slabs, bricks or stone.

For the best effect, build a dry wall that can be interplanted with trailers (see page 127). It is much easier, however, to use bricks or paving slabs. The former will need buttresses every four or five feet, or pressure from behind will make it bulge; the occasional space can be left for planting. A particular advantage with brick is that the walling can be curved if you wish.

The easiest but least attractive type is a box-shaped raised bed made with rectangular paving slabs. These need no cementing if they are placed against the straight edge of a concreted or paved terrace, and sunk about 12 inches below ground level. Hardcore piled up behind and rammed well down will keep the slab upright. The hardcore should be about 12 inches deep. Follow this with a layer of smaller stones or rubble, followed by garden topsoil or (preferably) the kind of soil mixture recommended above for rock gardens. You can mask the paving slabs with potted plants or 'window' boxes stood in front.

Almost any plants can be grown in raised beds, depending on their situation – from alpines, hardy perennials and small shrubs to annual bedding plants, bulbs and even vegetables. For the first season, however, it is best to restrict yourself to short-lived plants, since the soil will settle. Then, after it has been topped up, you can introduce permanent subjects such as small shrubs.

Peat-block beds

Preformed peat blocks are very easy to use in making a raised bed, and are particularly suitable if you want to grow lime-hating plants on chalky soil. In such a case, fill the bed with a mixture of one part loam, one part sand and one part peat. A partially shaded position is best, and the only site preparation

Building a raised bed right For ease of construction, use straight-edged paving or concrete to brace paving slabs used to create a raised bed. Dig out the soil in the area of the bed to a depth of 12 inches. Then place a slab in position against the paving, check that it is upright and level, and pile hardcore behind to hold the slab. When all the slabs are positioned in this way, fill in 12 inches of hardcore over the whole of the bed, followed by smaller stones and good soil mixture.

Building a peat bed right A raised bed of peat blocks is probably the easiest of all to make. You need only soak the blocks in water and lay them overlapping, as in a brick wall. Sink the first course half into the soil. Introduce plants and fill in behind with lime-free soil mixture.

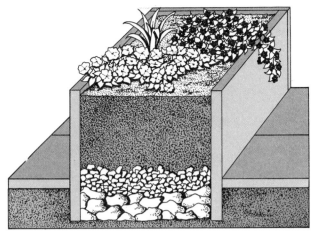

needed is to remove enough soil to half bury the first course of peat blocks.

The blocks, which are generally about 12 inches by 4 inches by 4 inches, should be soaked for 24 hours before use. Simply lay them a course at a time, overlapping them as you would bricks and leaving occasional gaps for plants. Set each course back just a little so that the face of the bed slopes slightly back. It is best to fill in the bed behind the blocks as you go.

Ferns, lilies, small *Azaleas*, heathers (*Erica* and *Calluna*) and gentians (*Gentiana*) are examples of plants that will thrive in such conditions. Others will be found on page 166.

Other ideas

You can make a mock well-head with courses of brick arranged in a circle. Finish off with stone slabs and a sloping roof covered with wood shingles or tiles. Add a bucket and rope, and plant hart's-tongue ferns (*Phyllitis scolopendrium*) in wall crevices inside (if water is present), also thymes (*Thymus serpyllum*), *Aubrieta* and other trailers in the rock crevices around the well outside. Such a false well-head provides a useful method of hiding a manhole cover.

Build a free-standing wall divider between garden features or to finish off a patio. A double thickness of bricks is advisable, secured with concrete or mortar. But leave spaces here and there, also pockets at the top. Fill these with soil and grow rock plants. If you leave a cavity in the middle several inches wide, the wall becomes a narrow raised bed, and can be planted colourfully with the same plants as for window boxes (see page 130). Remember to build in ties to stabilize the two rows of bricks, however.

Vertical gardens

Where space for growing plants is limited – perhaps on a balcony or small patio – the clear answer is to extend your gardening into the third dimension: upwards. Walls clothed with pretty climbing plants are much less of an intrusive eyesore, and form a happy living backdrop to the rest of the garden display. In the same way, pillars and posts can be disguised, and the outline of the whole building can even be softened. Hanging baskets (see page 128) add to the effect.

But it is not essential to have an existing vertical structure in order to create a garden in three dimensions. Plant walls – which can be constructed of such widely differing materials as dry stone blocks and chicken wire backed by peat – can be used to create barriers and define areas as well as to disguise existing features. The more solid kind of wall is, for example, commonly built in place of a steep grassy bank where a garden changes level. But it can equally well form a free-standing structure on one or more sides of a patio or similar area. It can also be used to retain a raised bed (see page 124).

Growing climbers
Some climbing plants cling naturally to a wall, but some kind of support must generally be provided. You can stretch strong wires horizontally across the wall, spaced about a foot apart, between eyes. In some settings traditional wooden trellis is ideal, and is particularly good for extending a low wall upwards; but it will eventually rot and need replace-

ment even if made from such weather-resistant wood as red cedar. (Never use creosote on such trellis, incidentally; treat it with a preservative such as Cuprinol that will not harm the plants.)

In recent years, plastic trellis has been increasingly used. It is very durable, but can be unattractive until well covered by greenery. For such annual plants as sweet peas (*Lathyrus odoratus*), lightweight plastic netting is ideal, as it can be simply cut down with the plant remains at the end of the season. Whatever type of support you use, however, remember to space it an inch or two out from the wall, both to make tying-in easier and to allow self-clinging plants to grow behind.

Where possible, plant climbers directly

left For an effective but delicate screen, climbing plants like this *Clematis* 'Nellie Moser' can be grown either directly in the ground or in a cool, well shaded tub. Where there is a change of level, a dry stone wall **above** or an alpine bank **right** can be constructed and planted with rock plants of trailing or cushion-forming habit. Those **above** include *Aubrieta* and rock *Phlox*.

in the ground, through a gap in patio paving, so that their roots remain cool. It is perfectly possible to plant them in tubs, however, particularly if other potted plants are stood around to shade the tub. Tub-planted perennial climbers will need feeding well, and mulching with leaf-mould or peat to help retain moisture. There is a wide range of varieties you can choose from; some of the best are described on pages 158 and 159, while more suggestions of plants particularly suitable for training up pergolas or verandah supports are given on pages 132 and 133.

Wall gardens
A dry wall can be free-standing (when concrete must be included to give it strength) or used as a retaining wall to hold back soil on a raised bed. The last is very useful in small gardens as it allows flowers to be grown in the top section, with trailing alpines at the sides. Old house bricks, concrete blocks, broken paving or pieces of Portland stone are among the materials that can be used. Where a stronger structure is essential, you can cement the bricks

together, leaving the occasional small gap for plants to be inserted. If necessary, you can use pieces of peat block to wedge the plants in position.

Plants for dry walls should either be of a trailing nature or form compact rosettes which can tolerate a vertical situation. *Sedums* (stonecrops), houseleeks (*Sempervivum*) and *Saxifraga* species come into this latter category. Amongst the trailers that can be used are *Aubrieta*, *Alyssum saxatile*, *Arabis*, *Erinus* (with dainty mauve flowers), some *Dianthus*, *Gypsophila repens*, *Iberis* (candytuft), *Helianthemum*, *Armeria*, various *Campanulas* but especially *Campanula portenschlagiana* (which makes sheets of purple-blue) and *C. poscharskyana* (powder-blue), *Cerastium tomen-*

tosum (snow-in-summer; a rampager under normal conditions, but easily controlled in a dry wall; white-flowered and silver-foliaged) and the yellow-blossomed *Onosmas*. For more details, see pages 160 and 161.

Peat and moss walls

If you want a bed of stunning flowers, but want it covering a wall rather than the ground, then build a peat or moss wall. This kind of structure was pioneered by the Swiss seed firm of Vatter in the mid-1940s, and is very simple in principle. Plants are grown through wire mesh – ordinary two-inch chicken wire – with their roots in peat or sphagnum moss. Regular watering is needed, preferably from a built-in 'leaky hose', and feeding with liquid fertilizer once a week for a moss wall or once every two weeks with peat. The whole system is, in fact, a form of hydroponics,

and it is best to use the kind of fertilizer mix described on page 223.

There is virtually no restriction on the size and shape of a peat or moss wall, and it is easy to make yourself using a simple (but fairly strong) wooden frame. If it is to be placed against an existing wall, it can have a solid back and should be six to eight inches thick. A free-standing version to be planted on both sides should be 10 to 12 inches thick. Large walls need cross-wires to prevent bulging. Treat all wooden parts with a non-poisonous preservative, and install a drip tray. Sphagnum moss – well broken up and thoroughly moistened – is probably the best filling. If you use peat, it is best to have an outer layer of the rough fibrous kind that will not trickle out, backed by finer granular peat, again all thoroughly moistened before use.

The first planting can be made as the wall is filled, in the same way as des-

cribed for the fern column on page 59. Apart from many of the trailing rock plants recommended above for dry wall gardens – especially *Alyssum, Aubrieta* and *Arabis* – many conventional bedding plants will thrive. Among them are *Ageratum, Begonia semperflorens, Calceolarias, Petunias*, pansies (*Viola × wittrockiana*), small *Antirrhinums* and *Zinnias, Calendulas, Impatiens*, dwarf *Salvia* and many others. Spring bulbs also do well, while some people use moss or peat walls to grow herbs, lettuces and strawberries.

The great advantage with these structures is that they are a quick way of hiding ugly features, and they enable you to create sheltered places to sit in privacy even on small balconies or roof gardens. They can also be used to decorate the façades of buildings as well as serving more conventional uses at ground level.

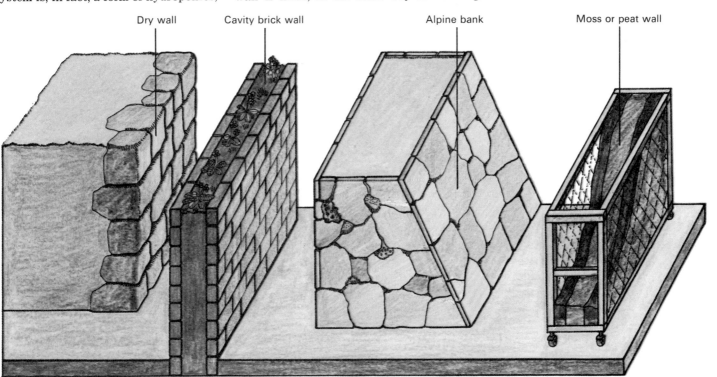

Dry wall   Cavity brick wall   Alpine bank   Moss or peat wall

Building a dry wall

For a retaining wall, set the bottom layer of bricks a little below the path if that is possible; otherwise cement them firmly to its base. They should tip back slightly, but the tops must be level or the whole wall will be out of alignment.
Next spread a layer of soil mixture (equal parts of loam, sand and peat or leaf-mould) over the bricks, firm down and install another course of bricks. Fill in behind with more soil mixture. Occasionally turn one of the bricks endwise so that it bites into the soil behind for extra strength. At intervals, as the wall gains in height, leave spaces between bricks and insert

plants (turned from pots) so that the roots are behind and the growths coming forward. Keep each line level, but with a slight backward tilt to attract moisture. The whole wall should slope back about two inches if it is up to three feet high, or three inches for anything higher. Finish the top with slabs of paving stones or else 9 to 12 inches of soil with more plants.

An alpine bank

A semi-vertical garden can be created by planting alpines and trailers in gaps left between crazy paving slabs set on a slope. Bed in sand, and fill the gaps that are not planted with mortar to stabilize the paving.

A moss or peat wall

Construct a wooden framework with a solid base. For a one-sided display, the back can also be solid and the whole wall six to eight inches thick. For a two-sided display, both sides must be open and the thickness 10 to 12 inches. Treat with non-poisonous wood preservative, and cover with two-inch-mesh chicken wire. Castors can be fitted to the base and a drip tray installed.
Start filling with moistened sphagnum moss or peat – in the latter case using coarse peat on the outside and a finer grade in the middle. As the filling is installed layer by layer, insert plants through the wire. Most small plants,

such as pansies and *Begonia semperflorens*, should be spaced four or five inches apart. Firm the filling down as you go. After planting, thoroughly water and protect from sun and wind for about a week. Never allow the filling to completely dry out; daily watering will be needed in warm weather. But always stop watering as soon as drips run from the bottom, to avoid washing nutrients away. Feed with a balanced liquid feed (see page 223) weekly with a moss filling, or every two weeks if peat is used. A moss wall three feet square and one foot thick may need to be given nearly four gallons of dilute feed per week.

127

Hanging gardens

Using hanging baskets, you can grow attractive plants in the most unlikely places: over doorways or beside windows, swinging from lamp standards or patio rafters, suspended in sun-lounges and conservatories or in basement wells and similar sombre places, in some cases even in porches, halls and living rooms. They allow flowers to be grown at eye level without taking space from a tiny balcony or roof-garden, and they provide softening effects for walls of blank brick.

Various kinds of hanging basket are available, made from wire, plastic, wood or clay. In every case, moisture conservation is vital; wire baskets in particular dry out rapidly in hot or windy weather. Equally, guard against flooding, resulting in the plants rotting off; solid-sided containers must have drainage holes in the bottom.

Points to remember

Be sure to attach all baskets to strong hooks; check that the chains are sound.

Water regularly, either by lowering the baskets into a tub of water until the bubbles cease, or with a small can. Feed occasionally with liquid fertilizer.

Although trailers are ideal, do experiment with plants. Even the most sedate upright growers do surprising things in the air – the branches drooping at first but throwing upright flowering laterals.

Because of their exposed conditions, hanging baskets should not be hung outdoors when there is any risk of frost. If possible, make up in advance and allow them to become established under glass.

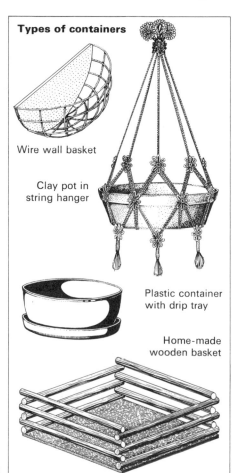

Types of containers

Wire wall basket

Clay pot in string hanger

Plastic container with drip tray

Home-made wooden basket

Planting a hanging basket

Plan a hanging basket for an attractive display with trailers planted near the edge and a bushy centrepiece at the top. With wire or slatted containers, thread some of the plants through the sides. The wall basket **above** was planted like this with ivy-leaved geraniums and a silver-leaved *Helichrysum*.

Line wire baskets with moss, and place a saucer at the bottom (between lining and soil) to retain moisture. Alternatively, the basket can be lined with green plastic sheeting, although this is less attractive. Or use both: first a thin layer of moss, then plastic sheeting. The plastic should always be pierced with a few holes in the side to draw off surplus moisture after heavy rains. Use a peat-based potting mixture for planting; this will hold moisture better than a light sandy type. Use the mixture in a damp but not waterlogged condition, and add a little charcoal to keep it sweet. Stand the basket on a bucket while filling. If threading plants through the wire, do this before filling the basket with potting mixture.

1

2

3

4

5

Planting schemes for baskets

1 Mauve-blue petunias are interplanted with a bright blue lobelia and a variegated ivy. At the top is a shrubby yellow calceolaria.
2 Blue lobelia is also used in this scheme, together with an ivy-leaved geranium – the soft-pink 'Galilee'. The plant at the top with red leaves is a *Dracaena*. **3** A striking yet simple scheme is obtained by interspersing nasturtiums and trailing fuchsias. **4** This 'Symphony in Green' for a shady spot is planted entirely with foliage plants: variegated ivies, *Zebrina pendula quadricolor*, the silvery-blue *Sedum sieboldii variegatum* and, at the top, an *Asparagus sprengeri*.
5 Trailing fuchsias and a variegated ivy are planted with a yellow trailing begonia. At the top is a pink *Begonia semperflorens* variety. A useful alternative to variegated ivies is the silvery-leaved *Helichrysum petiolatum*.

Plants for hanging baskets

For sunny positions

Botanical name	Common name	Colour	Remarks
Campanula isophylla		Flowers blue or white	Propagate by cuttings
Chlorophytum capense variegatum	Spider plant	Green & white leaves	
Chrysanthemum (Cascade types)		Various	Need special training
Columnea × banksii		Scarlet flowers	Best by itself under glass
Ficus radicans; F. pumila	Trailing fig Creeping fig	Green foliage	
Helichrysum petiolatum	Cudweed everlasting	Silver foliage	Pretty with pinks & blues
Lobelia erinus		Blue flowers	Easy from seed
Oplismenus hirtellus variegatus	Basket grass	Green & white leaves	Grassy foliage
Oxalis	Shamrock	Pink or yellow flowers	
Pelargonium (esp. ivy-leaved kinds)	Geranium	White; pink; red; mauve	Many varieties; stand plenty of sun
Petunia		Various	Flower all summer
Plectranthus oertendahlii	Spur flower	Pale mauve flowers	
Saxifraga sarmentosa tricolor	Mother of thousands	Green, red & white leaves	Young plants on runners
Scindapsus aureus	Ivy arum; pothos	Green & cream leaves	Best under glass
Zygocactus truncatus	Christmas cactus	Carmine flowers	Best by itself under glass

For shady positions

Botanical name	Common name	Colour	Remarks
Adiantum; Davallia; Nephrolepis; & other ferns	Maidenhair fern Hare's-foot fern Sword fern	Green foliage	Best grown under glass
Asparagus plumosus; A. sprengeri	Asparagus fern	Green foliage	Divide occasionally
Begonia haageana; B. fuchsioides; B. semperflorens; B. × pendula		Various	Best grown by themselves
Fuchsia (esp. trailing kinds)		Flowers reds & pinks	Rest in winter out of frost
Glechoma (Nepeta) hederacea variegata	Ground ivy	Blue flowers, variegated leaves	
Hedera helix (esp. variegated, small-leaved kinds)	Ivy	Foliage green & gold; silver & green	Very hardy; propagate by cuttings
Hoya carnosa variegata	Wax flower	Flowers white; leaves cream-edged	Avoid draughts
Lysimachia nummularia aurea	Creeping Jenny	Gold flowers & leaves	Very hardy
Sedum sieboldii variegatum		Leaves cream & blue or green	
Tropaeolum majus	Nasturtium	Various flowers	Use trailing & short kinds
Zebrina pendula quadricolor	Wandering Jew	Green, silver & crimson foliage	

For other suggestions of plants to grow in hanging baskets indoors, see pages 52, 84 and 86. For other outdoor plants, see page 160.

Window-box cheer

Where the architectural lines of a house are dull or featureless, or the surrounds leave much to be desired, window boxes filled with bright flowers do so much to soften its façade. They also bring cheer to the rooms behind and impart an air of gaiety to the street beyond. All sorts of plants are suitable for such locations, including climbers and trailers, but one can also grow herbs of various kinds, and even small fruits and vegetables.

Choice of containers

Window boxes can be made of wood, terracotta, aluminium, concrete, resin-bonded glass-fibre and many other materials. In fact, any container that is non-poisonous to plant life and can support a heavy weight of soil and moisture is suitable. Its size will depend on that of the window sill if there is one, but there are no such restrictions if the box is a special feature applied directly to the wall of the house on stout brackets.

For normal windows make the box the width of the sill from front to back plus one inch, and at least nine inches deep. Shallow boxes do not hold enough soil and dry out quickly in summer. It is advisable to set the boxes so that they tip back slightly – easily arranged by fixing wedges under the front edges. Window boxes must be secure to avoid nasty accidents; ornamental guard rails of wrought iron or other materials can be fitted to the front of the sills.

Wooden containers should be constructed of durable timber, such as oak, teak or redwood; soft woods soon rot. The outsides can be painted, but not the insides – although a non-poisonous wood preservative (such as Cuprinol) can be used to protect the interiors. On no account use creosote as this emits harmful fumes and boxes treated with it cannot be planted for a considerable time.

Drainage holes are not essential. Some people use them, others do not. If they are present there is always the risk of drips unless a metal tray is placed beneath the box. The real answer, if you can afford them, is to have purpose-made inner metal liners with drainage holes, or (if they will fit) ready-made plastic containers. These can be moved bodily to give the plants a good soaking away from the window. The ideal is to acquire two containers to each box. Then, as one display passes, it can quickly be exchanged for another box already planted up. Liners are also useful at holiday periods, when they can be removed to a shady place in the garden.

Planting and maintenance

Whether or not there are drainage holes, you must provide a layer of drainage material – broken crocks, clinker or small stones – one to two inches deep, covered with a layer of partly decomposed leaves or moss. Loamless potting mixtures are excellent for window boxes as they are clean and light to handle and, having a peat base, do not readily dry out. For those who prefer to mix their own, an excellent mixture is made from one part each of sharp sand and good leaf-mould or peat, and two parts fibrous loam, with a little well decayed manure or base fertilizer added.

Once the box is full of roots more plant food should be provided, especially for *Cinerarias*, stocks and similar 'hungry' plants. This can take the form of a light dressing of bonemeal, an occasional foliar feed or the insertion of fertilizer 'pills' down near the roots (see page 222). To maintain the quality of cultivation, all the soil should be changed annually. Otherwise the main need is regular and careful watering; wind and sun very rapidly dry out window boxes. Prick over the soil surface from time to time to keep it aerated, and regularly remove dead flowers. Finally, remember not to keep opening the windows; draughts from behind can quickly ruin some plants.

Planting a window box

Provide a good layer of drainage material as well as holes in the bottom. Cover this with peat or similar material, followed by a good, moisture-retaining potting mixture, in which the plants are planted. Renew the potting mixture annually. Alternatively, use potted plants. Sink these in moist peat, and water regularly. Drainage holes are still needed to prevent waterlogging, but plants can easily be replaced as flowers fade.

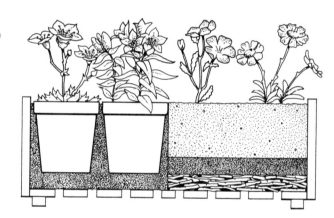

Colour-schemes

Against red brick
Choose white flowers or foliage with soft blues and silvers. **right** For a sunny spot, plant white marguerites with silver *Senecio* (*Cineraria*) *maritima*, blue stocks and blue trailing *Lobelia*. **far right** For spring effect, white tulips are planted with grape hyacinths and variegated ivy. An alternative for partial shade: blue polyanthus and ivy.

Against a grey stone wall
Concentrate on deep blues and purples, reds and pinks. **right** This summer scheme for a sunny place contains *Petunias*, geraniums (*Pelargoniums*) and the blue trailing *Campanula isophylla*. **far right** For partial shade: *Fuchsias* and heliotropes, fronted by trailing *Begonias*. As an alternative, upright-growing tuberous *Begonias* could be planted with silver-leaved edging plants.

Choice of plants

Now comes the most interesting part: planting up the boxes with the most suitable plants for seasonal display. Here, besides the obvious consideration of sun and shade, seclusion or windy aspects, some thought must be given to background. Red flowers will hardly show against red brick, nor white blossoms before a whitewashed façade. Yellow blooms may look terrific in front of a snowy-white building, but they will not always please when the background is pink or red.

Some suggestions to suit particular colour-schemes are given below. As well as these particular colours, full use can be made of silver and green trailers, particularly during the summer months, as foils to the more showy plants. Examples are *Asparagus sprengeri*, periwinkles (*Vinca*) and creeping Jenny (*Lysimachia nummularia*) for shady places, and silver forms of *Helichrysum* and *Senecio* in sun. Remember, too, that the proximity of the house makes scented plants particularly welcome. For more ideas, see pages 152 to 157.

Exposed situations and winter conditions demand special consideration. In windy places go for small evergreens like clipped box (*Buxus*), shrubby veronicas (*Hebe*), certain dwarf cypress (*Chamaecyparis*), *Euonymus* and heathers (*Erica*). These plants are particularly suitable for the corners of the boxes, which take the brunt of the wind. In more exposed situations junipers (*Juniperus*), arbor vitae (*Thuja*), and young trees of dwarf spruce (*Picea*) and pine (*Pinus*) will prove useful. But in very severe climates, where the boxes would freeze solid in winter, it is advisable to empty them late in the season or else store them under cover.

A mixed scheme including *Petunias*, geraniums and *Lysimachia nummularia* (creeping Jenny)

Against white paint
Go for bold colours — scarlet, gold, yellows and greens, **right** For sun, choose *Zinnias*, geraniums (*Pelargoniums*) and marigolds, with trailing *Asparagus* fern or green ivies. Or, for spring, use bulbs and wallflowers.
far right In shade, plant ferns, nasturtiums, Iceland poppies and *Calceolarias*. An alternative for a spring display: *Violas*, polyanthus and hyacinths.

Against dark brickwork
Use pink and white, with a touch of blue; also yellow.
right For a light position in spring, plant *Cinerarias* in a variety of colours. Later, you could use *Phlox drummondii*, *Petunias* and *Antirrhinums*, with *Lobelia erinus* or silver-leaved plants in front. **far right** For partial shade, plant yellow *Begonias*, *Calceolarias* and *Lysimachia nummularia* (creeping Jenny), or (in spring) polyanthus.

131

Balcony and verandah gardens

If you live in a flat or apartment in a tall building, the chances are that your only opportunity of doing any real outdoor gardening may be to cultivate some plants on a narrow balcony. Such a place presents considerable design problems – but considerable opportunities, too. The exact form of the solutions can depend on many things, including whether or not the front of the balcony has railings or a solid barrier up to a convenient height. In some cases, the sides are glassed from top to bottom. The top can be open to the sky (and rain) or roofed by a similar balcony belonging to the next storey.

The equivalent structure for a low-built house is a verandah. This, however, is always roofed, so it is well suited to uncertain climates, for it can be used to give shade in hot sun or shelter from showers. It also presents different design problems, since it generally provides a link between the house and garden; in this sense it resembles a covered terrace (see page 134). In most cases, a verandah – like a balcony – is built at the same time as the house, but where one is being constructed it is best to choose the sunniest side of the house (unless it runs all round the building). Where the roof overshadows windows, reinforced glass is the best material to use.

The wind problem

Undoubtedly wind is one of the gardener's bitterest foes. It dries out soil, breaks tender shoots, blows dust everywhere, scatters (and so starts new colonies of) pests, tears flowers to shreds and murders spring-planted evergreens. For this reason protection at the weather sides of a verandah is almost a must. The same applies with even greater force to a balcony, since this can be extremely exposed; the problems of installing adequate protection can be formidable, however.

Wind protection of verandahs can take various forms. Stone wall boundaries and brick or stone piers supporting a pergola of timber rafters, with clear plastic or corrugated glass-fibre infill, allows opportunities for growing climbing plants and suspending hanging baskets. Alternatively, the ends can be of solid brick or timber, with 'window' boxes attached to their sides. Or lines of deep boxes containing small upright-growing conifers like *Chamaecyparis lawsoniana erecta* or 'Green Pillar' can be stood along the edges to give a measure of protection.

Balcony gardens

Balcony floors can be left as plain concrete, or painted or tiled. Some builders introduce narrow gullies around the edges to drain off surplus water, but since this can create a nuisance to other people underneath, watering should always be undertaken with care.

Because balcony areas are restricted as well as narrow, the emphasis should be on climbing and trailing plants. Boxes of soil along the walls will support climbers, which can either be trained to trellis fixed to the building or grown up canes tied to horizontal wires – the latter

being strung between vine eyes attached to the fabric of the building. Suitable plants for such situations include ivies (*Hedera*) of all kinds, *Hydrangea anomala petiolaris*, *Parthenocissus henryana* (a kind of Virginia creeper that has green leaves with white vein markings), *Vitis vinifera* 'Purpurea' (a variety of grape vine with claret-coloured foliage), true Virginia creeper (*Parthenocissus quinquefolia*) and a honeysuckle such as *Lonicera japonica*.

Deep, narrow boxes placed on the floor near the outer railings can be planted with annual and bedding trailers and climbers in their season. Nasturtiums (*Tropaeolum majus*), for example, will do both, while ivy-leaved geraniums (*Pelargonium peltatum*) and blue *Lobelias* will trail. Canary creeper (*Tropaeolum peregrinum* or *T. canariense*) has pretty yellow, fringed, nasturtium-like flowers, and even the golden hop (*Humulus lupulus* 'Aurea') is useful to mask supports and rails.

The railings of lower-floor balconies are sometimes topped with light, glass-fibre boxes, but these need to be very secure and are not advisable in upper storeys in case they tip over. Wrought iron pot-holders for screwing to walls, or bamboo supports which take several flower-pots are useful to stand in corners, and it is even possible to have small greenhouses on balconies.

There is one type of miniature green-

house that opens up to three half-moon-shaped divisions, with trays at different heights. These hold shingle and water, and so maintain moisture at the roots when pots are stood on top. The sections clip together to make one triangular house, or can be spread open as a long house, or the parts can be used separately. Castors on the feet make for easy movement, and the sides are finished with clear plastic instead of glass. They take up little room and are popular for town balconies.

Gardening on verandahs

Verandahs are usually larger than balconies, so there is more scope for planting and the introduction of garden furniture and features. The floor may be of wood, tiles or concrete, and the supporting posts of timber, brick, cast iron, marble-faced concrete or stone. These should be draped with climbing plants, the roots planted in soil outside the verandah and their stems allowed to twine around the pillars and rails.

The choice of plants for such situations is most important. On no account should they impede light or rampage over the glass roof, nor should they grow so thickly as to impede the view from the house. Thorny shrubs should also be banned, and the best plants for such areas include the vines already mentioned above for use on balconies, together with *Clematis* × *jackmanii*, *C. lanuginosa*, *C. florida* and *C. orientalis* (a yellow-flowered species). By planting a number of these and keeping their roots cool (with stones or other plants), a succession of flowers may be had from late spring until autumn. Honeysuckles (*Lonicera*), passion flowers (*Passiflora*) and *Wisteria* – also, in hot climates or for summer planting, *Ipomoeas* (morning glories) and *Bougainvilleas* – are others which can be tried.

Decorative tubs and pots can be stood near the steps descending to the garden or other vantage points on the floor. Fill these with flowers in season, such as wallflowers (*Cheiranthus*), polyanthus (*Primula* hybrids), daisies (*Bellis*) and bulbs in spring; followed by *Cinerarias* and then, for summer, by stocks (*Matthiola*), *Petunias*, *Calendulas*, *Pelargoniums*, *Begonias* and red-leaved *Dracaenas* or, in light shade, *Fuchsias*, heliotrope (*Heliotropium*) and spotted-leaved crotons (*Codiaeum*).

It is also possible to use more permanent plants in tubs – even tender kinds like *Agapanthus* if these can be protected in winter. The more tolerant *Hydrangeas*, *Rhododendrons* and *Azaleas* are extremely useful, as are lilies (*Lilium*), heathers (*Erica* and *Calluna*), small bay trees (*Laurus nobilis*) and clipped or trained evergreens.

Window boxes can be attached to the house walls for extra drapes (see page 130), and hanging baskets (see page 128) suspended from hooks in the roof. By installing sliding glass panels, a verandah can be protected from cold winds or gales, or even turned into a sun lounge, thus making it possible to cultivate a still wider range of plants in tubs and deep boxes.

Although alike in terms of space – or the lack of it – balconies and verandahs have very different design problems. Balconies must generally be self-contained, whereas verandahs form a link with the garden beyond. **below** Even using little more than window boxes, however, a spectacular display can be created on a balcony and, if repeated on each storey, this makes the whole building a riot of colour. **left** By adding potted plants stood on the balcony floor, including some climbers planted in tubs, a balcony only a few feet wide can be transformed into a small roof garden.

A verandah can offer even more scope. **above** A glass roof gives protection while letting light reach the plants, and hanging baskets can be hung from the roof or from the supporting pillars. Permanent or bedding plants can also be grown in a border immediately in front, framing the whole display.

Beautiful terraces and patios

Patios and terraces represent the nearest this book gets to the garden proper. For many people, they are merely the stepping-off point between house and garden, while to others they form the focus of garden life. In any case, the problems and possibilities they present epitomize many aspects of outdoor gardenless gardening, so they are of interest whether they adjoin grounds of many acres or a mere few square feet of grass.

Of the two, the terrace is the older, originally denoting a flat paved area, sometimes with balustrading, and (usually) on a raised level with sloping or stepped sides of turf, rockery stones or plants. Nowadays the term is also frequently applied to any open paved area (flat or raised) which is near to buildings.

Patios have a southern European context, and originally referred to an enclosed area or outside room, open to the sky but bounded by the four walls of a dwelling. Since shade and water were among the most desirable items in hot climes, these sheltered areas with their playing fountains and bright flowers brought moving shadows, sweet scents and the music of running water to those who dwelt in their vicinity. Today this definition has lost its original meaning and the modern patio consists of a paved area near the house with enclosed back and/or sides, pots of plants and other features. In cool climates it is also more likely to be built by a sun-seeker than one looking for shade.

Setting the scene
Both patios and terraces should have bright, easily cleaned floors. Coloured tiles, stone paving, mixed plain and coloured crazy paving, old bricks or bricks interspersed with large stone cobbles, even marble slabs if funds allow – all these are possibilities. For small patios, however, tiles are probably best; they are easily kept clean and allow the patio to be used as an outdoor room.

Patios in an open position can be enclosed at the back and sides for seclusion or privacy with solid brick walls, strong trellis attached to posts, open-work screen-walling, wattle hurdles, interwoven fencing, a pergola, a yew hedge or a line of closely planted, quick-growing, upright conifers like *Chamaecyparis lawsoniana* 'Green Pillar'. The nature of this background will naturally determine the other features, as will also the space available.

Terrace planting
Where terraces are in open, sunkissed positions the choice is wide. A small tree can be planted to create shade, and sunken or raised beds (see page 124) can be built to hold bright seasonal flowers.

Wide terraces (12 feet or more) can accommodate a small spreading tree like a *Magnolia*, a Judas tree (*Cercis siliquastrum*) with its bunches of cerise, pea-shaped flowers in spring, or an evergreen strawberry tree (*Arbutus unedo*). This last has neat simple leaves and white urn-shaped flowers in winter, often appearing at the same time as the round, edible, strawberry-like fruits. All these trees tolerate careful pruning. A bay

tree (*Laurus nobilis*) is another possibility – but only for areas subjected to no more than light frosts, for hard weather can kill it – and also the weeping silver birch (*Betula pendula* 'Youngii') or the winter-blooming cherry (*Prunus subhirtella* 'Autumnalis'), with light pink blossoms and an ultimate height of around 20 feet.

On smaller terraces, trees grown in tubs – like small Japanese maples (*Acer palmatum* forms), box (*Buxus sempervirens*) or a specimen of the corkscrew hazel (*Corylus avellana* 'Contorta') – create interest at all seasons, while tub-grown *Hydrangeas* and *Rhododendrons* are useful, long-flowering standbys for spring and summer.

Against shady walls *Camellias* can be planted if the soil is lime-free; otherwise, grow in a tub. The rose-pink, single 'Donation' is one of the hardiest and most reliable varieties; it flowers when quite young, even on small bushes. In milder climates, or where shelter under glass can be provided in winter, *Agapanthus*, orange or lemon trees (*Citrus*), sweet-scented pink, red or white, single or double oleanders (*Nerium oleander*), red-flowered pomegranates (*Punica granatum*) and the quaint angel's trum-

pets (*Datura cornigera*), with its huge hanging white or cream, single or double trumpet flowers, can be grown in tubs.

It is also possible to grow plants between the crazy paving stones, particularly low-growing spreaders like rock phlox (*Phlox subulata*), various thymes (*Thymus serpyllum*), *Aubrieta*, *Arabis*, *Helianthemum*, *Androsace*, small *Campanulas* and yellow *Alyssum saxatile*. Even taller plants, like *Aquilegias* and

bluebells (*Scilla non-scripta*) can be tried if the terrace is wide enough, with climbers used to cover corner posts or pillars. Some terraces are roofed with pergolas, of larch tree trunks or trellis, or more extravagantly of bricks with white nylon ropes slung between, to support the plants. When covered with *Wistaria*, roses, honeysuckles (*Lonicera*), *Clematis*, *Actinidias* and other climbers they become most attractive.

In various key situations, such as the top of steps leading down to a path or garden, or framing a house door, twin urns or figures can be sited to make an impressive feature. Large strawberry pots filled with pink, blue and mauve *Petunias* look stunning and last all summer. Other ideas are pink ivy-leaved geraniums (*Pelargonium peltatum*) or sweet-scented *Pelargoniums* with aromatic foliage or, for the spring garden, hyacinths or small double tulips.

Patio planting

The plant drapes for a patio will again depend on background. Climbers can be used to mask trellis, open-work walls or fences; hedges or lines of trees provide their own background; and window boxes can be attached to solid walls (see page 130). Attractive containers of flowers should also be in evidence.

Another idea is to turn the patio into a pool garden. You could install a swimming pool with a lacy stonework screen covered with creepers for privacy, and with flat tiles as flooring. The last will take furniture and plant tubs and pots. Alternatively build an ordinary garden pool. This can be planted up with water-lilies and other aquatics, and have a fountain and fish to bring life to the scene (see pages 170 to 177). If there is a building behind, a wall fountain – which can be in the form of a lion's head, dolphin and so on – can be fitted to spill out into the pool, and a pump installed so that the same water is used over and over again. Illuminations to highlight the fountain, or from ground level to throw up the shape of a tree adds a new dimension on summer evenings.

In general, both patios and terrace gardens need to be light and airy, preferably with strong free-standing trellis or screen walls – both of which let in light and air – as surrounds. Install delicate furniture and have masses of flowers.

Whether a patio forms a screened-off part of a larger garden **above left** or represents the total garden area of the home **top right**, it can greatly enrich the occupier's life by acting as a kind of outdoor room – furnished and usable in all but the worst weather, yet open to the sun and air and decorated with colourful garden plants. An open terrace is more difficult to use in this way, but can still be provided with useful furniture **top** or can simply form an attractive paved area of the garden, perhaps with a pool **above**. Pergolas add to the interest and can create shade as well as supporting climbing plants **left** or hanging baskets **above left**. In some cases, part of the building may provide shade and shelter **right**; if not, you may be able to fit blinds **far right** – or use sun umbrellas **top**.

Shady paved gardens

Shade creates problems wherever it occurs, and can be particularly difficult in small paved areas such as basements and alleys, cobbled courtyards, walled-in city gardens and pedestrian streets. The overall cause of sunlessness in such cases is always other buildings, and the first essential is to try to brighten the surrounds as much as possible. by means of reflected light. Old mirrors fastened to walls do this quite effectively, and colour-washing the boundary buildings with a light-coloured paint cheers the whole area. Even basement wells can be made lighter by such means.

Although expensive, extra lighting from electric light bulbs is another possibility; mercury discharge lamps – the kind often·used for street lighting – are particularly efficient. It is possible to grow plants from seedlings to maturity in artificial light indoors (see page 234), and indeed African violets (*Saintpaulias*), bulbs and even salad crops have been raised commercially in underground chambers by this method. There is no reason why outdoor illumination cannot be boosted in the same way.

It is of course those who live in cold climates who find shade a problem. Dwellers in hot countries seek shade as the northerner does sun, and gardens in such areas are often deliberately enclosed with trees and buildings so as to exclude sunlight. They then become cases of coolness in the heat of the day, with birds in cages singing in the trees, splashing fountains and a wealth of greenery everywhere.

Plants and shade
Green is the colour associated with shade, for many plants will not flower unless they have sufficient energy (derived from sunlight) to make food for blossoms. Some plants – perennials especially – can go for years without flowering if there is insufficient food in store to justify the expenditure, for (unlike leaves) flowers 'spend' food instead of making it.

Plants vary in their light requirements. Some – like the sunflower (*Helianthus annuus*) and African marigold (*Tagetes*) revel in sun. They cannot get too much of it, and make food and grow at a great rate. Clearly there is no point in trying to grow such plants in shady places. Others need shade, sometimes because this slows down water losses from the leaves, but also because of the deleterious effects of sunlight on their green pigment, chlorophyll. Leopard's bane (*Doronicum*), hellebores (*Helleborus*), ferns and primroses (*Primula vulgaris*) are examples, and soon droop if they spend much time in the sun. These are the types to select for shady gardens.

Growing plants in shade
In general, shade-loving plants can be grown in containers in the same way as sun-lovers. However, since many of them are forest-dwellers in nature, they will appreciate more acid conditions than most – particularly those, like *Camellias*, which are calcifuges, or lime-haters. A peat or leaf-mould type of potting mixture is best for these, and the con-

tainers should be top-dressed annually with leaf-mould or well rotted manure.

Exploit what little light there is by reserving well lit situations for flowering plants. In hot countries white blooms are most popular, for they impart an air of coolness and accentuate the greens. They also show up better in twilight than reds and purples, and some plants, like jasmines (*Jasminum*), lilies and the yellow evening primroses (*Oenothera*), smell sweetest in the evening. In cooler countries pastel shades may be preferred for the area farthest from the house, with

Cool shades of green with the occasional splash of colour: this is the basic colour-scheme associated with overshadowed gardens that receive little sun. As these illustrations show, however, such gardens can still be attractive havens of tranquillity among the city's bustle. Exploit silver-leaved and variegated plants to the full, and position shade-loving flowers where their colour will have most impact. It is important to use creatively the hard boundary surfaces: Go for functional but decorative paving materials, and screen-walling that unifies the space without seeming oppressive. If possible, install artificial lighting.

warm reds and oranges in the lightest spots for daytime enjoyment.

If the hard paved area can be broken, it may be possible to plant a tree or trees, and for the rest deep boxes, tubs and other containers must be used. Go for perennials as much as possible, and highlight these in season with smaller flowering subjects.

Garden furniture should be of a light, airy nature – preferably white – and if illuminations can be installed, even the smallest, darkest enclosed garden will become a fairyland at night. Painting the containers white is a good idea.

The woody plants

Among the taller plants likely to succeed in enclosed shady areas are bamboos, which are really huge grasses with an airy, evergreen habit. They whisper and rustle in the slightest breeze and do best in semi-shade. Plant them in spring in deep boxes or soil pockets. Among the most suitable are the broad-leaved *Arundinaria* (now *Pseudosasa*) *japonica*; *Sinarundinaria nitida* and *S. murielae*, both having very fine foliage; and the golden-leaved *Arundinaria viridi-striata*, which needs more light than the others.

Among trees and shrubs, *Arbutus unedo* can be grown (see page 134), as well as birch (*Betula*), small willows (*Salix*) and *Rhododendron ponticum*. But avoid conifers, as these make small enclosed spaces gloomy. *Camellias* are likely to succeed in lime-free soils, but give them a sheltered place and as much light as possible. They do well in deep containers which, if necessary, can be protected or taken under cover in winter.

Others to try are *Ligustrum ovalifolium*, with white, scented privet-like flowers. This does well in shade, but does not retain its foliage so well in winter as when grown in full light. *Mahonias*, ivies (*Hedera*) of all kinds, *Euonymus radicans* in its green and variegated forms, *Vincas* (periwinkles), the golden-flowered, evergreen rose of Sharon (*Hypericum calycinum*), and the white-flowered and fragrant *Sarcococcas* – *Sarcococca humilis* and *S. ruscifolia* – all tolerate shade. Incidentally, ivies can be trained to grow up and cover railings or a lamp standard, and the variegated forms look most attractive like this.

The smaller plants

Among a host of lower-growing plants which can be tried in tubs, boxes and other containers are the *Fuchsias* and tuberous-rooted *Begonias*. These will naturally have to be wintered away from frost. The annual nasturtiums (*Tropaeolum majus*) and forms of *Impatiens* will grow in less light than most annuals, and among the perennials hellebores – especially the lenten roses (*Helleborus orientalis*) and the green-flowered *H. lividus corsicus* – *Primulas* of many kinds, lilies of the valley (*Convallaria majalis*), Solomon's seal (*Polygonatum odoratum*), ferns, foxgloves (*Digitalis purpurea*), the foam flowers (*Tiarella*) and various *Anemones* like *Anemone blanda* and *A. nemerosa*. Details of most of these and some other shade-loving plants can be found on pages 162 and 166. **137**

Exotic patios and courtyards

The 'sub-tropical' patio

As long ago as the eighteenth century, if not long before, the parterres and terraces of the great gardens of France and England were decorated with palms, orange trees and other exotic plants. Every autumn these huge pot-plants were hauled back into the orangeries to overwinter. This practice can still be seen at Versailles in France and at Blenheim Palace in England.

There is no reason why the ordinary gardener should not follow the same practice on a smaller scale. In the summer months a sub-tropical effect can be created on the patio by bringing out tender plants which, while overwintering indoors, have been decorating the house. Furthermore, as there are several

A 'Japanese' courtyard

Centuries ago, Zen Buddhist priests studied the art of garden-making and formulated the principles upon which the modern Japanese garden is based; they strove to create in courtyard or patio a landscape in miniature in which man could feel at ease with his surroundings. It is not easy for Westerners without the Zen cultural and religious background to create a garden in the authentic Japanese manner. But it is well worth attempting, for it can create a sense of spaciousness in the smallest city garden.

Sand and rock

The Zen sand garden is perhaps the best known and most versatile of the traditional Japanese gardens. It can fill a large open courtyard or a small indoor space, or even be confined to a tray, as a bonseki ornament in a living room (see page 187). Like all Japanese gardens, the sand garden is a symbol, a representation of a seascape or a dry and dusty plain in high summer. Hills and undulations are suggested by rocks, laid singly or massed in odd-numbered groups. Flat

land or water is represented by sand, gravel, or small flat stones.

Used imaginatively, stone can express the mood of a garden and lend it an air of age and permanency. Smooth, rounded cobbles beside a pond suggest the marks left on a beach by waves. Statuesque monoliths depict the grandeur of distant mountain peaks. Large, flat rocks set among shrubs, small trees and horizontally spreading plants symbolize a valley or moor, and provide a peaceful view from a large window, or out onto a flat roof.

The hill garden

The hill garden is a more elaborate assemblage of rocks and plants, where the far-off view can be 'borrowed' in the design to create a mountainous landscape in a small place. Careful use of perspective gives the illusion of distance. A small hill set towards the back of a garden will appear quite high; shrubs and tall plants in the foreground and smaller plants farther away will lend perspective. A small pond in the middle or near distance – if space allows – and a winding path complete the picture.

Planning and laying out

The secret of extracting the most from a confined space lies in careful planning on paper, before beginning to lay out the garden. Draw a scaled master plan on graph paper; make sketches and table-top models, or even rough 'on-site' patterns using newspaper and bamboo stakes to represent paths, rocks and plants.

Obtaining suitable rocks and stones may be difficult. It is rarely permissible to take rocks from a public or even a wild place; they may have to be purchased from a supplier. Choosing them takes time and thought, and is one of the early tasks. As a rule, stone of uniform kind and colour should be used in a small garden. Greys and browns are more natural than whites, blacks or bright colours. Rocks should be chosen to balance in proportion with each other, and with the hills, trees and plants.

Walls, fences and gateways of stone, brick, concrete, wood or thick bamboo can add their own charm to patio or terrace, and should be built first. Any necessary earth-works follow – digging a pond, perhaps making a stream bed, constructing hills; and setting rocks plants of tropical appearance that will stand the winters outside in many parts of Britain and places with a similar climate, the basis of the scheme can be permanent. Once planted they will grow rapidly to create a suitable background for the date palm, banana and others brought out in early summer.

With the introduction of brightly coloured bedding plants and geraniums into the scheme, together with the exciting colours and shapes of modern garden furniture and perhaps a bubbling fountain, life on the patio can be as good as a Riviera holiday. It is perfectly possible to relax on a deck chair and look up, not through the leaves of a common tree species, but through the trembling fronds of a windmill palm or the spiky head of an Australian cabbage tree. Or, when the sun gets too strong, you could take to the shade of your banana plant.

The plants

As gardeners are often a little apprehensive about cultivating exotics, it should first be realized that the plants suggested in the table and illustration here are probably easier to grow than many common garden subjects. Naturally, some plants are sensitive to frosts and these must be grown in pots or tubs and taken indoors for the winter, while others may need some wrapping in cold weather. Others, however, will flourish outside in any weather in most regions. *Trachycarpus fortunei*, the windmill palm or Chinese fan palm, for example, has regularly survived temperatures of −18 to −12°C (0 to 10°F) in British Columbia, Canada, and *Yucca filamentosa* will survive even a New York winter.

Exotic plants for temperate regions

Key	Botanical name	Common name	Adult size	Form	Hardiness*	Soil	Remarks
1	*Agapanthus africanus*; *A. 'Headbourne Hybrids'*	African lily	2 to 2½ feet	Strap-shaped leaves; blue flowers	Tender or half-hardy	Well drained	Hybrids hardiest; see page 149
2	*Agave americana*	Century plant	4 feet	Fleshy rosette of leaves	Tender	Mixture no. 2	Variegated form has yellow leaf-margins; see page 69
	Chamaerops humilis	European fan palm	6 to 8 feet	Fan-leaved palm tree	Half-hardy	Mixture no. 3	Spreads by suckers; feed well; see page 43
3	*Citrus* spp	Orange, lemon, etc	8 feet up	Tree; may flower and fruit	Half-hardy or tender	Mixture no. 2	Propagate from cuttings or pips; except for lemon, will stand slight frost; see page 90
4	*Cordyline australis*	Cabbage palm	15 feet up	Spiky leaves on stem	Half-hardy	Poor	Wrap in sacking and plastic for winter when dry; see page 44
	Crinum x powellii		1½ feet	Lily-like; pink or white flowers	Hardy	Rich; well drained	Bulbous; feed well; see page 115
	Cycas revoluta	Sago palm; cycad	3 feet	Stiff fern-like fronds	Tender	Heavy	Very slow-growing and expensive
	Dicksonia antarctica	Tree fern	3 feet up	Giant fern fronds	Tender	Rich; well drained	Needs damp, shady position; see page 56
5	*Fatsia japonica*	False castor-oil plant	6 feet	Glossy, deeply divided leaves	Hardy	Any	See page 38
6	*Musa basjoo*; *M. cavendishii*; *M. ensete*	Japanese banana; dwarf banana; Abyssinian banana	6 to 8 feet	Spectacular, with huge leaves	Tender or half-hardy	Rich	Feed and water well; *M. basjoo* cut down by frost, but produces suckers in spring
	Nerine bowdenii		2 feet	Strap-shaped leaves; pink flowers	Hardy	Any well drained	Bulbous; see page 115
7	*Phoenix canariensis*; *P. roebelinii*	Canary Is date palm; dwarf date palm	8 feet; 4 to 6 feet	Elegant palm fronds	Tender	Mixture no. 3	Feed well; see page 43
8	*Phormium colensoi*; *P. tenax*	New Zealand flax	8 feet	Stiff, sword-like leaves from ground	Hardy	Rich	Likes moisture; variegated and bronze-purple varieties
9	*Trachycarpus fortunei* (*Chamaerops excelsa*)	Chinese fan palm; windmill palm	6 to 20 feet	Fan-shaped leaves; hairy stem when mature	Hardy	Rich, heavy	Feed well; the hardiest palm; see page 43
10	*Yucca filamentosa*; *Y. gloriosa*	Adam's needle	2 feet; 3 to 6 feet	Spiky glaucous leaves from stem or ground; bell-shaped flowers	Hardy or very hardy	Any well drained	Dry, sunny position; *Y. gloriosa* has trunk; *Y. filamentosa* does not and is hardiest

*Key to hardiness Tender: must be kept indoors, out of frost, in winter. Half-hardy: Protect from frost, but can remain outside in sheltered places. Hardy: Can be left outdoors except in the coldest areas. Very hardy: May survive even harsh frost.

(which may need to be stabilized with earth or mortar). A flat garden needs little preparation besides laying gravel or sand and locating stones. The open area should be raked with a garden rake in contours around the rocks and parallel to the edges of the garden, and will require frequent re-raking.

The trees and plants

Existing trees can usually be incorporated successfully into the garden plan, though some ingenuity may be demanded. But make allowance for the size of new trees when fully grown. Dwarf or bonsai trees are suitable for patios, terraces and roofs, where trees planted in containers may be necessary. Small gardens must never be overcrowded; bunch plantings of shrubs, ferns and evergreen plants in one or two places will tend to emphasize size.

Annual flowers are rarely used in Japanese gardens as they tend to distract from the overall composition. Plants and trees are mainly evergreen, with an occasional deciduous tree or shrub. But a single *Chrysanthemum* or flowering cherry can be effective.

A garden in the clouds

A secret garden hidden among rooftops and chimney pots is generally associated with urban living. In fact, almost any building with a flat roof – in towns, suburbs or country – will support a roof garden. Nevertheless, it is to people who have no other outside space on which to grow plants that rooftop gardening appeals most strongly. In size, such a garden can range from a vast penthouse setting to the very modest roof area of a garage or home extension.

Creating a successful roof garden is in some ways more difficult than any other kind of gardening – whether in a real garden or on a paved surface. The aesthetic challenge is somewhat similar to that of creating a patio garden, with the exception that there may be virtually no walls or other nearby buildings to define and contain the space. But, on top of this, a number of stringent practical problems have to be overcome – problems of weight, lack of water and exposure to weather, in particular.

Designing a roof garden

Parapets, sky and a flat surface are the usual starting points in designing a roof garden, and unless the gardener is lucky enough to have a view worth enhancing – or even an unattractive vista or feature that needs to be disguised – he will have to create a focal point from which the total design can be developed. Statuary or a pool with a small recirculating pump forming a fountain could be lined up with the centre of a french window giving access to the house to provide a starting point.

Integrating the garden with the interior (see page 17) will give an added sense of spaciousness. A roof garden is often seen from more than one part of the house, and greenery placed close to the windows will ensure that all views are attractively framed.

On the roof itself, groups of plants can be used to create separate areas. A sitting area surrounded by trees may lead to a dining area which is in turn offset by a series of containers forming the garden proper.

Practical problems

Designing a rooftop garden offers enormous scope to the imagination. But basic problems of weight, accessibility, and protection from sun and wind must be tackled before the pleasurable task of creating a unique garden can be enjoyed.

Plants, screens, furniture, flooring and containers filled with soil (often rain-soaked in winter) all place additional stress on the building structure, and it is essential to ascertain just how much weight a roof will bear. If necessary, ask an expert – an architect or surveyor – to carry out this calculation. Before committing yourself to any major expenditure it is also wise to check plans against local building regulations. Once again, the advice of an expert could be invaluable. And it is worthwhile discussing your ideas with neighbours so that any objections can be ironed out before construction work starts.

Drainage could present another problem, for an accumulation of water on the roof can damage ceilings. If water does

Designs for a roof garden
left On an area only about 12 feet by 15 feet – such as the flat roof of a garage – a kind of rooftop patio can be constructed, ideal for lazy sunbathing days and pleasant evening barbecues. Plants in this case play a somewhat secondary role, providing the background decoration. Heavy plant containers are positioned around the perimeter, where their weight is supported by the structure. The existing house wall is used for attaching a hanging basket. Screen walling and, at the rear, vertical wooden louvres are used as windbreaks.
In complete contrast, the photographs **above** and **right above** show a London rooftop garden whose owner is lucky enough to have an extremely strong concrete base on which to construct. As a result, it is possible to have flower beds, a lawn and a host of roses and other shrubs, forming a real garden among the chimney-tops.
right For most people, however, weight restrictions mean that only potted plants can be grown on the roof.

not flow naturally off, it will be necessary to install drainage facilities. Plant containers should be placed so that they do not obstruct the free flow of water. If necessary they can be elevated over water courses, but these must be regularly cleaned of soil, leaves and other obstructions.

Plants growing on a roof are subject to a high rate of evaporation and may need watering twice a day in very hot weather. Water must be easily obtainable, from a tap on the roof or from a nearby bathroom or kitchen. A hose connection will make watering easier, but in an elaborate garden it may be worthwhile installing an automatic irrigation system, or overhead sprinklers.

Covering the floor
The right flooring for a roof garden provides an attractive setting for plants, and protects the roof surface – usually asphalt – from wear. Ensure that the roof is waterproof and structurally sound before starting work, though, for repairs are much more difficult once the flooring has been laid.

Weight is an important factor to bear in mind when choosing materials. Heavy flooring, such as stone paving, reduces the number of containers that can be used. Asbestos tiles are light and cheap. Other materials include brick paviors and brick paving. Marble, slate, and mosaic and ceramic tiles, both of which must be laid on screed, are among the more expensive materials. Plastic 'turf' can be bought, but must be laid professionally. Straw mats are cheap, but are

only really suitable for a dry climate. Wooden decking is useful if slightly differing roof levels have to be equalized.

Rooftop gardens are usually subject to heavy dirt from pollution, and it is important that flooring materials do not show dirt and can be easily kept clean. Neutral mid-tones are therefore the best colours: shades of brown, green and the darker blues all provide a good background. Strongly coloured or patterned tiles which overpower the plants should be avoided.

Some degree of texture is attractive, however. Quarry tiles, for instance, are subtly shaded as well as physically textured. Ceramic tiles or mosaics should be laid in a range of tones rather than in one colour. The best size for individual paving stones, tiles, and so on is determined by the roof area; small tiles, for instance, will have the effect of visually enlarging a small roof.

Wind and sun protection
A roof garden is very much more exposed to wind than a garden at ground level, and some kind of protection will be necessary. If strong winds are a constant problem, expert advice is called for. But in most parts of the world a screen will provide sufficient protection.

Various types are available. Solid screens made from materials such as armoured glass and acrylic plastic sheet afford complete protection. However, they need strong supports which add to the weight on the roof, and they must be cleaned regularly. In addition it is difficult to train plants over smooth materials, although greenery can be introduced by positioning individual trees, such as bay (*Laurus*) or box (*Buxus*), in front of the screens. Partially open screens in wire mesh, net, and wire netting are lighter and reduce wind efficiently. Trellis-work and louvred boards can also be used, while bamboo canes and reed fencing provide attractively natural backgrounds.

Screens, shrubs and small trees will generally cast as much shade as is needed ·in temperate climates, with sun umbrellas for temporary protection in hot weather. However, in many parts of the world continuous sunshine creates uncomfortably hot conditions on roof gardens, and shade must be provided. A pergola, possibly entwined with vines, is an attractive solution, while slatted screens or bamboo can be positioned to filter the slanting rays of the sun. Adjustable awnings fixed above windows will provide instant solid shade, and can be closed to allow plants their full ration of sunshine. If any kind of permanent overhead shelter is installed, sunlight should be allowed to filter through to the plants; if not, plant only shade-loving varieties in its shadow.

Artificial lighting
Roof gardens, with their instant access to the house, are ideal for summer barbecues and parties. If you want to hold these, install functional lighting. Spotlights can be fixed to walls or pergolas to highlight foliage, flowers and statuary, creating a dramatic effect. In large roof gardens, low-level floodlighting can be used to illuminate the plants. In all cases, it is best to call in an expert, however, as the installation must be weatherproof and meet building regulations.

Housing the plants
Even the best-maintained roof can leak, and repair work could mean destroying the garden if plants are grown in built-in flower beds. Roof gardens are therefore basically container gardens, and it is essential that the containers are movable. More information on tubs, pots, troughs and other suitable containers will be found on pages 122 and 123.

Most of the containers should be as light as possible, although a few heavy stone examples may be used as features – for instance, on each side of a bench. Glass-fibre, plastic and asbestos cement models are all sensible choices. Wooden containers are light, but need regular maintenance, even if they have metal or plastic liners. Mass-manufactured models are usually cheaper than custom-made versions, and using examples from a single manufacturer when grouping plants will create a sense of unity.

On the whole, containers should be plain, blending with flooring material or screens, or both. Use occasional patterned models as features. In positioning the containers, you will probably be governed as much by the roof structure and weight distribution as by your own tastes. This may mean placing most of them around the perimeter, but in planning the arrangement take advantage of any supporting cross-beams.

Choosing the plants
As in any garden, the choice of plants for a roof garden is determined by climatic conditions as well as aesthetic needs. However, the former are emphasized at roof level: the sun is hotter, evaporation is faster, and the wind is stronger. So sturdy, drought-resistant varieties are usually the best. Suggestions for many suitable types will be found in the next part of this book, starting on page 144.

A certain number of good foliage evergreen plants (see pages 144 to 147) are essential if the garden is visible from living rooms throughout the year. Climbing and trailing plants, such as ivies (*Hedera*) and Virginia creeper (*Parthenocissus*), add interest to walls. And trailers cascade attractively from containers to create a natural, tumbling effect. Small trees – bay (*Laurus nobilis*), fig (*Ficus carica*) and small fruit trees, for instance – break the roof space at eye level. Hanging baskets (page 128) and window boxes (page 130) can also be used.

Flowering plants are one of the joys of roof gardening, and many bulbs, perennials, annuals and shrubs can be grown in rooftop conditions. Although these can be planted in the same containers as mainly foliage plants, seasonal varieties will display themselves to better effect in separate containers, in the right kind of soil. A container-bed of roses, for instance, is extremely effective. And, of course, containers can be grouped together to give an array of different flowering plants.

5 Plants for the patio, box and tub

There are countless kinds of plants that you could grow outdoors in even the smallest patio garden. But tiny paved gardens, window boxes and similar places often have far from ideal conditions. They may be exposed, windy or heavily shaded, so that for best results you should choose kinds that will suit the particular situation. The hundreds of plants described on the following pages have been selected with these restrictions in mind; choose from them, and you can be confident of success.

Tub-shrubs and small trees

Trees that have form and character and yet are small enough to be cultivated in tubs or restricted settings add immeasurably to the overall effects of a small patio, terrace or back-yard. They give it distinction and provide a framework for long-distance views from a verandah or house. Additionally, they create pretty and natural surroundings, serve as windbreaks, hide ugly features and generally act as screens wherever needed.

Since containerized trees can be moved about, it is possible to extend the range to doubtfully hardy subjects if these can be overwintered under cover. Many are suitable for loggias and sun-lounges or can be stood about in hallways and passages indoors, if you have room.

Most garden centres stock containerized trees and shrubs, so that they can be transferred to tubs at any season of the year. They should be removed without breaking the soil ball around the roots and planted in good potting mixture (such as Mix no. 3) over a layer of broken crocks. The latter provide drainage. When complete, the soil surface should be two to three inches below the tub rim. This allows ample space for

Camellia japonica 'Magnoliaeflora'

feeding and watering or, in hot situations, to top-dress the soil with moist peat, pebbles or trailing plants to keep the roots cool.

Aftercare consists of watering as necessary, spraying over the foliage in hot weather (particularly important with conifers and evergreens), feeding and pruning to shape. Removing the top few inches of soil and replacing this occasionally with good potting mixture maintains soil fertility. In extreme cold, use straw, sacking and so on to prevent the tub freezing solid.

Almost any slow-growing or dwarf shrub or tree can be grown in a tub, so don't be afraid to experiment.

Evergreen kinds

Bamboos are giant grasses that create elegant, airy effects and even provide music of a kind with the whisper and rustle of their leaves in the slightest breeze. Best for tub culture outdoors are *Phyllostachys aurea*, the golden bamboo, eight to ten feet high in a container; *Sinarundinaria murieliae* (sometimes called *Arundinaria murieliae*), of elegant habit and about the same height; or, for sun rooms, the slightly taller *S. hookeriana*, which has golden canes.

Camellias need shade, especially in summer, and lime-free soil. Mulch with moist peat or rotted leaf-mould, and protect flowers against spring frosts in exposed situations. They have simple glossy leaves and masses of round white, pink or red, single or double flowers in late winter and spring.

Dwarf conifers are useful since they are virtually unchanging and extremely slow growing. They look best when associated with other plants, such as heathers, and are especially valuable in winter. Junipers with narrow needle-like or scaly leaves have fine texture, especially in the prostrate *Juniperus sabina* 'Tamariscifolia' and the upright-growing Chinese juniper, *J. chinensis* 'Pyramidalis' – the bluest of the junipers.

Several *Chamaecyparis* (dwarf cypress, sometimes sold as *Cupressus*) make good tub subjects, especially the widely planted *C. lawsoniana* 'Ellwoodii', of upright habit with deep green leaves, *C. l.* 'Columnaris', which forms a narrow pillar of bluish-grey, and the golden-leaved, three-foot *C. l.* 'Minima Aurea'.

Mixed dwarf conifers and *Hedera* varieties

Juniperus squamata

Acer palmatum 'Atropurpureum'

Skimmia japonica

Rhododendron 'Songbird'

Laurus nobilis

Nerium oleander

Cedars are normally giants, but *Cedrus libani* 'Nana' is a very slow-growing variety of the cedar of Lebanon, eventually reaching 15 to 18 feet, but more commonly only 3 feet tall. It is very compact, with bright green needles.

There are a number of other shrubs and small trees that make good tub subjects. The Chinese fan palm, *Trachycarpus fortunei* (also called *Chamaerops excelsa*) is probably the hardiest palm in cultivation, and adds an exotic appearance to a patio (see page 138). *Buxus* (box), *Laurus nobilis* (bay) and *Taxus* (yew) have a place in formal settings, as by a door or on the floor of a patio, especially when trained and clipped to topiary patterns. This can be undertaken cheaply at home or more expensively by buying established pyramids, balls and other shapes from specialist growers. These must be pruned annually to conserve their form.

Skimmia japonica is a low-growing evergreen with fragrant white flowers which, in tubs, rarely exceeds three feet. Male and female flowers (on separate bushes) must be grown to obtain the scarlet berries, which persist all winter. The same applies to hollies (*Ilex* spp). Many of these can be grown as tub specimens, the variegated kinds being especially attractive. Oleanders (*Nerium oleander*) make showy tub plants, blooming all summer with bunches of single or double red, pink or white fragrant flowers. In cold climates they must be overwintered away from frosts, as must bay trees and some of the other kinds mentioned in this section.

Deciduous kinds
Small Japanese maples (*Acer palmatum*) create year-long interest, with the soft green spring leaves turning yellow or scarlet in autumn. But beware of strong sun, which can 'burn' the leaves. *A. p.* 'Dissectum' and *A. p.* 'Atropurpureum' are good varieties.

Azaleas (strictly speaking, *Rhododendron* spp) require lime-free soil, protection from strong sun and plenty of water in summer. They bear brilliant, variously coloured flowers in spring, with autumn leaf tints in the deciduous kinds. Dwarf true *Rhododendron* hybrids are evergreen and also good for tubs.

Fuchsias are ideal for semi-shaded situations. They can be grown as bushes, or may be trained to various shapes such as pyramids and weeping standards. They need moisture in summer and a rest and protection from frost in winter. There are many varieties with single-coloured or multicoloured flowers in shades of red, pink, white and mauve, but ask for hardier types for outdoors.

Hydrangeas of the Hortensia group (*H. macrophylla* vars), with rounded six- to eight-inch clusters of white, pink, red or blue flowers, remain colourful for months. They grow up to six feet. Pink forms can be kept so by adding lime to the potting mixture, or blue by watering the soil with a blueing compound.

Roses (*Rosa* spp and hybrids) – particularly the Polyantha and Floribunda types, climbers and some Hybrid Tea varieties – can be grown in tubs if they are regularly fed and watered. Keep the roots cool with a top-dressing of pebbles.

145

Smaller shrubs for boxes

Hebe armstrongii

as lavender, rosemary and *Santolina*, are easily increased from half-ripe cuttings taken in midsummer. The best pieces for propagation are side shoots of the current year's growth, pulled from the main stem so that a heel of the old wood is attached. After trimming, these cuttings can be rooted in a box of sandy soil with a sheet of glass over the top. Propagation by seed is also possible, particularly with berried shrubs, and almost any of them can be layered. (See pages 226 to 229.)

Flowering shrubs

Blue spiraeas (*Caryopteris*) grow to about three feet annually and die down in winter. They have small greyish leaves and spikes of bright blue flowers in late summer. *Caryopteris* × *clandonensis* 'Arthur Simmonds' and the American 'Heavenly Blue' are the bluest and best.

Ceratostigma plumbaginoides, the hardy plumbago, is another late bloomer, growing to about two feet. It has indigo blue flowers and small oval leaves which turn red in autumn.

Chaenomeles speciosa and *C. japonica* (cydonia) are spiny shrubs with saucer-shaped red, pink or white flowers on

Chaenomeles sp

Erica carnea

Roof gardens and balconies are often windy, so tall or weak-stemmed shrubs growing in such situations may well be at risk. Additionally, lack of natural shade (as from tall trees), concrete flooring and an open exposure make for cold in winter and excessive heat in summer. Terraces and patios are usually more sheltered, but even these can experience draughts if they are in wind funnels between tall buildings. In the main, shrubs for either situation should be tough and compact in habit, particularly the more exposed outer rows.

Small beds, built up with bricks and filled with potting mixture, large floor boxes or tubs, and window boxes hitched on railings or walls can be employed for growing a variety of such plants, including some mentioned on pages 144 and 145. All these shrubs will require feeding occasionally with either a top-dressing of organic manure or liquid fertilizer and watering in dry weather. And it will be necessary to frequently spray over the foliage in dry or windy weather, to counteract transpiration losses.

Many of the shorter-lived kinds, such

Potentilla fruticosa 'Moonlight'

naked branches in spring. They are followed by large, edible yellow fruits. Bushes spread but can be clipped to shape. Commonly called Japanese quince, they have many varieties.

Daphnes are mostly small, fragrant-flowered shrubs requiring good drainage, rich loam soil, moisture and shelter. *D. mezereum* has red or white winter flowers on the naked branches, followed by scarlet berries. It likes lime and grows to four or five feet. Other good sorts are *D. cneorum* (garland flower), a prostrate grower one foot tall with richly scented pink flowers, but rather difficult to establish, and *D. odora*, a winter bloomer growing up to four feet with cream flowers. The variegated form is hardiest.

Among the heathers, most *Ericas* and *Callunas* are suitable for roof gardens and terraces if grown in acid soil of a sandy nature. They normally dislike lime (although a few are tolerant), so avoid adding lime to Potting Mixture no. 1. But mulches of peat or leaf-mould give conditions they like. They flower best in full sun. After flowering, trim over the bushes with shears to retain their compact growth. Forms of *Erica carnea* can be selected to flower all winter and early spring, and can be followed by *E. cinerea* (bell heather) varieties for summer. Varieties of *Calluna vulgaris* (the common wild heather or ling of Europe) bloom in summer and autumn, with white, pink or crimson single or double flowers. All are around one foot tall.

Hebes are New Zealand shrubs previously included in the genus *Veronica*. They are all evergreen with neat leaves and spikes of white, mauve or purple flowers. They do well in coastal areas but are less successful inland, especially in cold, exposed places. Winter protection helps, and they like well-drained soil and full sun. Their heights vary from

Lavandula sp

six inches to as much as five feet.

Hypericums are shrubby plants with yellow flowers and neat leaves. The one-foot, evergreen *Hypericum calycinum* (rose of Sharon) will grow in shade and dryish soil and is covered in summer with two- to three-inch pincushion flowers. *H.* 'Hidcote' and *H. × moserianum* are others worth growing.

The shrubby potentillas (*Potentilla fruticosa* forms and hybrids) grow three to five feet tall with tiny leaves and masses of small white or yellow flowers all through the summer. They are very hardy but need full sun.

Mediterranean plants

These plants for hot, dry situations may need protection in winter with hessian, burlap or plastic sheeting wraps. Thaw them out slowly if they freeze.

Lavender (*Lavandula*) has blue, white or pink flowers and glaucous foliage. Rosemary (*Rosmarinus officinalis*) has blue flowers and narrow aromatic leaves. *Santolina* has silver foliage and golden ball-like flowers in midsummer. *Cistus* (rock rose or sun rose) has white, pink,

Cistus × purpureus

purple or bicoloured flowers like single roses, and aromatic foliage. All these are evergreen. *Cistus* are the most tender, especially older plants, so renew your stock frequently from cuttings.

Berrying shrubs

Aucuba japonica makes a large, sprawling shrub, but can be trimmed to shape and size. It has large, oval, glossy leaves, sometimes spotted with yellow, and bunches of scarlet berries. Male and female plants must be grown to ensure that the berries appear.

All *Berberis* (barberry) are prickly and have golden or yellow flowers followed by red, blue or black currant-like fruits. There are deciduous and evergreen kinds.

Nandina domestica (heavenly bamboo) is a great American favourite, often planted near front doors as a welcome. It is a slow-growing (to eight feet) bamboo-like evergreen that is grown mainly for its foliage. Its new leaves are pink-tinged and much divided; they develop to green and then crimson in autumn. It has 12-inch clusters of creamy

Aucuba japonica

flowers developing to coral red berries. Semi-deciduous in cold winters, it is hardy to −12°C (10°F).

Foliage shrubs

Artemisia abrotanum is the southernwood, old man or lad's love of medieval England, an aromatic evergreen which forms a sturdy bush around three feet high. The flowers are insignificant. It likes sun, well-drained soil and shelter.

Cordyline australis, the cabbage palm of Australia and New Zealand, makes a small trunk topped by a dense mass of sword-shaped leaves. It is best grown in a tub, and under ideal conditions produces a creamy inflorescence.

Silver-leaved *Eucalyptus*, grown from seed and renewed frequently, make useful 'dot' plants among annuals, and can also be grown in tubs. Prolonged cold kills them and the hardiest are the Tasmanian species, such as *E. gunnii*.

Pinus thunbergii, the Japanese black pine, will only grow four feet in as many years. Another kind, *P. mugo mugo*, can be kept dwarf by continually pinching the young shoots.

Berberis × stenophylla

147

Herbaceous perennials for tubs

Herbaceous perennials die to the ground annually, but the roots persist so that they have an indefinite life expectancy. With some this may be little more than two years, but for others can extend to half a century.

When perennials are grown in containers they experience sharp drainage because surplus water runs out through the drainage holes. This suits some plants, especially those with a Mediterranean background, but others may need frequent watering. On the other hand, the first group will be adversely affected if moisture is retained and prolonged frosts freeze soil and roots. Ground planting provides snugger conditions than raised receptacles, so it may be a good idea to protect the less hardy in winter by keeping the soil fairly dry. This can be achieved by covering the containers with sheets of glass or transparent plastic sheeting, removing these in milder weather to prevent premature growth. In very severe cold, provide protection of sacking or straw, or take the containers into shelter.

Herbaceous perennials of medium height are particularly useful for key positions in patios or to plant at the back of raised beds. A few are suitable for troughs and window boxes, although the need to keep these colourful may limit their usefulness, since most do not bloom continuously.

When perennials are grown and sold in pots they can be planted at any season. But if lifted from the open ground, they

Helleborus orientalis 'Prince Rupert'

should be transplanted in spring or early autumn.

Most perennials like rich, loamy soil, kept fertile by occasional mulches of rotted manure or compost, and plenty of sunshine. The majority are propagated by division in spring or early autumn and this method is essential for named varieties (cultivars). Many perennials can also be grown quite easily from seed. (See pages 226 and 229.)

Perennials for shade

Brunnera macrophylla (*Anchusa myosotidiflora*) is an early bloomer with small forget-me-not flowers and rough, heart-shaped leaves up to six inches across. It likes moist soil and tends to seed itself.

The barrenworts (*Epimedium* spp) make good ground cover, the heart-shaped leaves persisting – although dead – all winter. Cut these back in spring to reveal the dainty flower spikes, white in *E. × youngianum*, bright yellow in *E. pinnatum* and pale yellow with chocolate-blotched leaves in *E. perralderianum*. All grow 12 to 15 inches tall.

Most hellebores (*Helleborus* spp), given moist shade and humus-type soil, drop their seeds and colonize. *Helleborus lividus corsicus* blooms from winter until early summer with trusses of two-inch, cup-shaped, pea-green flowers on two- to three-foot stems. It has dark green, spiny, evergreen leaves. *H. orientalis*, the lenten rose, has green, cream, pink or dark red two-inch flowers on two-foot stems in early spring. *H. niger*, the Christmas rose, has white flowers. It grows one foot tall.

Hostas (plantain lilies or *Funkias*) are primarily foliage plants, although the two-foot spikes of white or mauve tubular flowers are generally showy and in some cases fragrant. They make good ground cover in moist rich soil, but are also useful for troughs and containers in key situations. The leaves are lance- or heart-shaped, green, glaucous or variegated in cream or white. *Hosta*

Hosta sieboldiana

Dicentra spectabilis

crispula, *H. fortunei*, *H. sieboldiana* and their forms are good sorts.

Spring-flowering kinds

Anchusa angustissima (*A. caespitosa*) has sprays of gentian-blue tubular flowers and rough, narrow leaves from spring until autumn. It grows 15 to 18 inches tall. Protect the crowns against winter damp to prevent rotting.

Dicentras are plants with fleshy brittle roots, fern-like leaves and pendant flowers. *Dicentra eximia* (fringed bleeding heart) has grey-green leaves and sprays of rosy-purple flowers. It blooms from spring until late summer in sun or light shade, and grows 18 inches tall. There is a white form called 'Alba'. *D. formosa* 'Bountiful' has deep pink flowers

Achillea filipendulina 'Cloth of Gold'

Primula vulgaris hybrids (Pacific strain polyanthus)

in spring and again in autumn. It is 12 to 18 inches tall.

Polyanthus (in fact, forms of *Primula vulgaris*) are very well known plants that come in a wide colour range and are ideal for window boxes, containers and raised beds. They make good cut flowers. Keep them cool and shaded after flowering and divide the roots if necessary. Seed should be sown as soon as ripe.

Summer-flowering kinds

Achillea is also called sneezewort, because the dried flowers have been used for snuff. *A. filipendulina* varieties have flat heads of many tiny flowers (which can be dried for winter decoration) and deeply cut leaves. They will grow in any soil and like full sun. Good sorts are 'Canary Bird' (bright gold, 18 to 24 inches), *A. millefolium* 'Cerise Queen' (rosy-red, two feet) and *A. ptarmica* 'Boule de Neige' (double white, 12 to 18 inches tall).

Agapanthus 'Headbourne Hybrids' are the hardiest race of these African lilies, two to three feet high. They have umbels of blue, violet or purple flowers six to eight inches across and thick grassy leaves. They are ideal for tubs that can be taken under cover in cold climates.

Various Michaelmas daisies (*Aster* spp) can be grown in containers or raised beds, especially *A. yunnanensis* 'Napsbury', a mildew-resistant sort with mauve daisies on 15-inch stems, and *A. amellus* varieties like 'King George' (with 2½-inch deep lavender flowers) and 'Sonia', which has rosy-pink blooms.

Coreopsis verticillata is a non-stop bloomer with small golden flowers on wiry stems all summer. It grows to about 18 inches.

Cranesbill geraniums – members of the genus *Geranium*, and not to be confused with pelargoniums – thrive almost anywhere in sunny, well drained situations. They bloom all summer with single or double flowers on branching stems, and have deeply cut leaves. *Geranium endressii* 'Wargrave Pink' is rosy pink with aromatic leaves; *G. psilostemon* is brilliant magenta with black basal blotches, and grows two to three feet tall; and *G. pratense* has inch-wide rich blue flowers. The last has forms with white, mauve and pink single and double flowers.

Other good herbaceous perennials for summer flowering are *Erigeron* spp, with mauve daisy-like flowers; *Limonium* (often called sea lavender or *Statice*); *Oenothera missouriensis,* a long-flowering relative of the evening primrose but only six to nine inches high; and *Sedum spectabile,* a late bloomer with flat heads of flower (which attract butterflies) and fleshy leaves.

Agapanthus 'Headbourne Hybrid'

Aster varieties

Erigeron speciosus variety

149

Sturdy patio plants from seed

Sturdy, quick-growing plants that can be raised from seed are the answer for the busy man or woman who wants a brave show but has scant spare time for gardening – and even then only at sporadic intervals. A change of bedding twice annually may be possible, however – particularly if the plants are started by someone else. Most garden centres sell boxes of annuals and biennials, although more dedicated (or impecunious) gardeners will wish to raise their own (see page 226).

Annuals in patios can be used by themselves or mixed with small shrubs and perennials for seasonal patches of colour. It is a good idea to work to a colour scheme. For example, have all the flowers in shades of blue, mauve or purple, or in yellows, golds and oranges. Or use strong contrasts for psychedelic effects. Since the plants die after flowering, frequent changes are possible. The plants should be grouped for maximum impact, with a few taller flower spikes penetrating the shorter kinds to prevent a flat appearance.

All the plants mentioned here are sturdy and reliable, not fussy as to conditions, and long-flowering. None of them require staking. Unless otherwise mentioned they all like plenty of sun and good, well-drained loamy soil.

Early bedding plants

Wallflowers (*Cheiranthus cheiri*) are probably the most widely grown spring flowers, and are esteemed equally for their charming flowers and their delicious fragrance. Although perennial – especially on old walls – they are treated as biennials, the seed being sown in spring in an odd corner and the plants transplanted to their flowering quarters in autumn. The blooms come in many shades from white, cream and yellow to bronze, rose and red. *C. × allionii* (the Siberian wallflower, more properly called *Erysimum*) grows about one foot tall, with brilliant orange flowers.

Dianthus barbatus (sweet William) is another biennial, and produces long and leafy-stemmed clusters of fragrant flowers in vivid combinations of crimson, rose pink, cerise and white.

Hesperis matronalis (sweet rocket or damask violet) grows two to three feet tall with white, mauve or purple, sweetly scented spikes of stock-like flowers. Double-flowered varieties exist, but these must be propagated from cuttings.

Stocks (*Matthiola* species and hybrids) are esteemed for their showy spikes of mauve, purple, pink, red, white or yellow, richly scented double flowers. Ten-week stocks: sow seed under glass in early spring and plant outside 12 inches apart two months later. Brompton or queen stocks: grow as biennials, sowing seed in summer and transplanting to flowering places in early autumn; or, in cold districts, keep in a frame until next spring. Note that when raising seedlings the smaller plants are the most likely to be doubles in most strains.

For summer blooms

Garden snapdragons derive from *Antirrhinum majus*. They are very varied and include tall hybrids (two to three feet) and bedding kinds (18 inches to two feet), intermediates and dwarfs, doubles and penstemon-flowered types in shades of white, yellow, apricot, crimson, pink, lavender and bronze. They are useful for bedding and cutting, with long flower spikes. Rust is sometimes a troublesome disease (see page 233) so rust-resistant kinds are advisable. In sheltered places sow in early autumn outdoors. In colder areas sow at the end of winter under glass and transplant two or three months later. But where summer heat is excessive, sow in early summer.

Callistephus chinensis (China asters) are half-hardy annuals from China and Japan with large single or double 'daisy' heads on rough leafy stems. They are good for cutting, bedding or containers. The flowers are white, yellow, mauve, purple, pink or red. The ostrich-plume doubles and giant singles are the most popular for bedding. Plant them 18 inches to two feet apart.

Impatiens (balsams) are useful because they will take partial shade, and some of the modern mixtures show an incredible variation and brilliance in the flowers. They need moist soil, and make compact plants 15 inches high and as much across, flowering two months from sowing. They are half-hardy.

Other kinds for summer

Acrocliniums (*Helipterums*) have small pink and white stiff-petalled 'daisies' on one-foot stems which can be dried as

Dianthus barbatus varieties

Campanula medium 'Bells of Holland'

Convolvulus minor varieties

everlastings. Dwarf Canterbury bells (*Campanula medium* varieties) are biennial, and since they only grow to 1½ feet are excellent to mix between shorter annuals. *Convolvulus minor* (*C. tricolor*) 'Royal Ensign' has brilliant blue and white flowers with gold centres on sprawling one-foot stems, and likes sun.

Two 'dot' plants grown for their foliage are the two-foot *Hibiscus* 'Red-Leaved' and *Kochia scoparia* 'Childsii' (summer cypress or burning bush), a half-hardy annual producing symmetrical and feathery leafy domes of green which become russet-red in autumn.

Shirley poppies (derived from *Papaver rhoeas*) are gay hardy annuals in delightful pastel shades, which can be sown in spring where they are to flower. They grow to one foot. *Nicotianas* (tobacco plants) tolerate light shade and are at their best at evening because then their rich scent is most apparent. Colours range from white to crimson and there is a green-flowered variety appropriately named 'Lime Green'. They grow about 2½ feet tall.

Nigella damascena (love-in-a-mist) does best on moist soil and grows 1½ feet high, with cornflower-blue flowers set off by cobweb-meshed calyces. Sow where it is to flower.

Continuous bloomers

Calendula officinalis, the pot marigold, is a foolproof annual with large, showy and strongly scented flowers (up to three inches across) on one- to two-

Hibiscus 'Red-Leaved'

Nicotiana 'Sensation'

foot stems. The cultivars are generally double, in shades of cream, yellow, gold and orange, sometimes bicoloured or with quilled centres. They bloom off and on all summer, and the flowers are good for cutting and also have various culinary uses. Seed should be sown outdoors in spring where they are to flower. (See also *Tagetes*, page 157.)

Bedding and collarette *Dahlias* bloom from late summer until the frosts come, with brilliant flowers that are good for cutting. They grow about two feet tall. They should be started under glass and given good but well drained soil in sun.

Petunias are colourful, one-foot-tall half-hardy annuals that should not go outside until the end of frosts. Leggy plants can be cut back and will break and flower again. They like rich soil with plenty of water. (See also page 155.)

The easiest bedding begonias are *Begonia semperflorens*, which are compact, uniform and exceedingly free-flowering. F1 hybrids produce the best results. Raise as half-hardy and give full sun. The flowers are red, pink and white, the foliage green or bronze. They reach a height of 6 to 12 inches. (See page 116.)

Finally, for the fronts of borders with light shade, try long-flowering pansies (*Viola* × *wittrockiana* or *V. tricolor hortensis* varieties). Keep the old blooms removed or they will stop flowering.

Nigella damascena 'Persian Jewels'

Dahlia dwarf hybrid

Papaver rhoeas varieties

Colourful window-box annuals

The importance of window boxes to apartment-dwellers is obvious, but people with small gardens also find them useful, especially in urban areas. Many town gardens are enclosed by buildings and high walls. If these are colour washed to make them appear brighter, and have supports attached to take boxes of pretty annuals, even the smallest plot becomes gayer and seems larger.

The boxes need not be at a uniform height; they look more impressive when staggered at different levels. Naturally, each must be securely fastened with angle brackets. They can be set up as described on page 130 and filled with foliage plants and flowers in season. It is also possible to grow herbs in these elevated boxes – one advantage being their inaccessibility to pets!

Roof-garden boxes, however, should be kept fairly low, to avoid wind damage. If trellis is fixed behind them, brittle-stemmed plants and climbers can be secured to this as a further precaution. Other types of containers, such as tubs, jardinieres, sinks and cisterns, or stone, glass-fibre, terracotta and lead pots can be stood about in key situations to provide gay spots of colour or accent a feature – such as a pool or bird table. Annuals especially may also be grown in small raised beds (see page 124).

The annuals (and a few perennials) described here and on pages 154 to 157 are all of short stature (up to about one foot), so they are ideal for windy or exposed situations. They can be kept distinct, or mixed with others to provide pleasing combinations (see also page 130). They provide quick returns from seed, yet are not expensive or difficult to grow given the basic needs of good but well drained soil and regular watering in dry weather.

Cultivation

Hardy annuals are usually sown where they are to flower, in spring or autumn (the last less reliable in cold soil or exposed situations), and thinned to the recommended distances. These details are normally given on seed packets, but as a rough guide plants ultimately reaching six inches in height will be thinned to three inches and those reaching 12 inches to double this distance.

Half-hardy annuals cannot take frost, so it is usual to raise them under glass in early spring at temperatures of 10 to 15°C (50 to 59°F). They are then potted separately or else pricked out – about two inches apart – in boxes of potting mixture. Later, when there is no more risk of frost, the little plants are planted outside.

Hardy biennials are raised from seed, sown in odd corners or boxes, soon after harvesting. The young plants are then moved to their flowering positions in early autumn. They may need protection in severe cold. Hardy perennials may be similarly treated, or are often started in pots and planted out when big enough. For more details see page 226.

For sheltered spots

The plants grouped here are all tender, and should be raised and kept under glass until it is safe to put them out.

Cineraria cruenta 'Spring Glory'

Myosotis alpestris

Iberis amara varieties

Celosias are striking plants with showy inflorescences of yellow, gold and scarlet. They are all forms of *Celosia argentea*, but may be catalogued under various Latin names such as *C. childsii*, *C. plumosa* and the like. In some, the flowers are packed in stiff plumes – rather like the 'Prince of Wales' feathers – and of these 'Fairy Fountains' and 'Lilliput' are two good dwarf types (10 to 12 inches). Another called 'Cristata' grows to only six inches, and has fantastic crested heads known as cockscombs. Sow *Celosia* seed in spring. (See page 79.)

Cinerarias (generally called *Cineraria cruenta*, though the correct name is *Senecio*) are beautiful spring-flowering plants with branched heads of showy daisy-type flowers in white, blue, purple, pink, red or crimson; there are also bicolours. Average height is 8 to 15 inches; individual blooms are up to three inches across. Sow seed in the summer prior to flowering at 10 to 15°C (50 to 59°F), and keep cool and shaded from sun.

The flame nettles (*Coleus blumei* forms) are grown for their foliage, which is brilliantly patterned in reds, greens, whites, yellows and golds. Sow in spring, summer or autumn and pinch out tops when six inches high to produce bushy growth.

Torenia fournieri is an attractive summer and autumn bloomer with snapdragon-like flowers in 'pansy' shades of light and deep blue. It reaches a height of 12 inches. In cold wet summers the foliage may turn reddish. (See page 79.)

Flowers for spring

Although perennials, cultivars of the English daisy (*Bellis perennis*) are best treated as biennials. The plants need

Coleus blumei 'Rainbow'

Bellis perennis varieties

Viola 'Campanula Blue'

moist soil and make an attractive ground-work for bulbs and spring bedding, or they can be used as pot plants. The round flower heads may have flat or quilled petals, and come in white, pink or red shades. Their height is 9 to 12 inches.

The charming blue forget-me-nots (*Myosotis*) have many uses as they will grow in most soils and situations, either in sun or light shade. They are ideal for mixing with pink tulips or white narcissi, and grow six inches tall.

Annual candytuft (*Iberis amara*) can be sown outside in spring, and after thinning develop rapidly, producing masses of white, pink, red or carmine flower heads on 6- to 12-inch stems. The perennial *I. gibraltarica* flowers in spring with trailing growths of evergreen leaves and showy white blossoms. It reaches one foot in height.

Mossy saxifrages (varieties and hybrids of *Saxifraga moschata*) are perennial and bloom at the tail-end of winter. They form mossy, fine-foliaged hummocks spangled with white, yellow, pink or rose flowers. They reach a maximum height of six inches.

Violas and pansies (all forms of *Viola*) are favourite long-flowering perennials best treated as biennial, although named sorts of violas are usually perpetuated from cuttings. They need moist soil, in sun or light shade, and the old flower heads must be regularly removed or blooming ceases. They are available in a wide range of colours and bicolours. There are also winter-blooming pansies. Use them as carpeters or for edging.

Other spring bloomers described elsewhere include *Cheiranthus* (page 150) and *Limnanthes* (page 156).

153

Summer-blooming annuals

Summer is, of course, the time when window boxes, patio beds and other small planting positions look at their very best. There is such a wide range of compact, easily grown annuals flowering during summer that you can choose virtually any colour scheme you want. For hints on cultivation, see page 152 or, for more details, page 226.

Ageratums, sometimes called floss

Ageratum F1 hybrid 'North Sea'

Eschscholzia californica 'Ballerina'

flowers, are well known half-hardy annuals with fluffy heads of lavender, mauve, purple or white. Ideal for bedding, edging and containers, they are in character all summer, and also make good pot plants for winter flowering under glass. The dwarf forms grow four to six inches in height.

Dwarf snapdragons (*Antirrhinums*) have all the charm and colour range of their taller counterparts. Of easy culture, they appreciate full sun and good soil. Pinching out the tops encourages a bushy habit, and they can be raised from seed sown under glass in early spring for planting outside when conditions permit. F1 hybrids give larger blooms. Certain dwarf types like 'Sweetheart' and 'Floral Cluster' grow to 12 inches, but others are available at eight

Godetia varieties

or nine inches and the 'Little Gem' strain is a mere four to six inches tall.

The shrubby bedding *Calceolarias* derived from *Calceolaria rugosa* (also called *Calceolaria integrifolia*) are invaluable for mixing with other plants in display boxes and hanging baskets. They bloom all summer with showy heads of small, pouched yellow or bronze flowers which are slightly fragrant. The simple leaves are sticky to the touch. They can be raised from seed or cuttings, the latter overwintered away from frost. Their height is 8 to 12 inches.

Dwarf annual larkspurs (sold as *Delphinium ajacis* but more correctly hybrids of *Consolida orientalis*) grow about 12 inches tall, with deeply cut leaves and well-clothed spikes of pink, white, blue and mauve double flowers. Sow the seed outdoors in spring or autumn; they like good soil and sun.

Dorotheanthus bellidiformis (often catalogued as *Mesembryanthemum criniflorum*) are delightful South African plants with fleshy leaves and brilliant little daisy flowers which open only in

Dorotheanthus (*Mesembryanthemum*) varieties

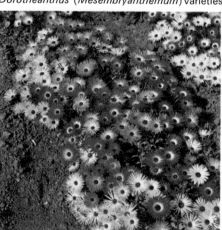

sunshine. Colours range from white, buff, yellow and pink to cerise, crimson and purple. Treat as half-hardy annuals and mix the very fine seed with silver sand to facilitate sowing. They grow to three or four inches tall.

Eschscholzia californica, the Californian poppy, is the state flower of California (it is the origin of the term 'Golden West'), and the American Indians used its leaves as a vegetable and its juices as a painkiller. Its leaves are finely divided, its flowers consisting of four deep orange petals and two sepals which form a pointed hood (like a nightcap) over the buds. There are many cultivars with cream, yellow, gold, pink or crimson flowers. Grow it in well drained soil in sunny situations, sowing the seed in spring or autumn where the plants are to flower. It grows about 12 inches tall.

Gazanias are brilliant South Africans, often known as treasure flowers, with up to three-inch daisies of orange, yellow, pink, red, ruby, light and dark brown, frequently with rings or other colours such as green, white or pink. The long

Gazania hybrids

narrow leaves are green on top and silver underneath, or sometimes all silver. Sun is essential or the flowers fail to open, and well drained soil is needed. Treat as half-hardy annuals or propagate good forms from cuttings and overwinter these away from frost. Their height is about nine inches.

Godetias, long-flowering and easy hardy annuals, are useful for all forms of display. The large, showy, poppy-like flowers (often up to five inches in diameter) appear in quantity on leafy stems and are delicately scented. Sun and moist soil are needed, but do not feed or the plants will run to foliage. Dwarf kinds grow nine to 12 inches tall, in red, crimson, scarlet, pink, white and lilac or a mixture of shades.

Often called toadflax or bunny rabbits, the annual *Linarias* are usually sown in their flowering positions in spring. Small spikes of flowers (individually like a rabbit's mouth) come in a wide colour range, including yellow, pink, light blue, violet and crimson. If untidy, plants can be trimmed over and will then bloom again in late summer. They reach nine inches in height.

Nemesia strumosa is a South African plant which should be grown as a half-hardy annual. The type species produces slender eight-inch stems with terminal clusters of white, yellow or purple flowers, but modern cultivars have extended the range to carmine, cream, scarlet, pink, blue, orange and crimson, including bicolours and tricolours. Sun and well-drained soil are the requirements.

Nierembergia hippomanica (*N. caerulea*) is the cup flower, so called from the shape of its abundant little violet-blue flowers. The habit is bushy, six to nine inches high, and the plants like sun. Treat as half-hardy annuals.

Petunias of all kinds are ideal for window boxes and containers as they flower continuously throughout the summer. The blooms are large and showy, especially among the F1 hybrids, with a wide range of singles and doubles in all shades, many striped or zoned in contrasting colours. They grow 6 to 12 inches tall, but will also trail over the edges of window boxes.

Phlox drummondii is a half-hardy annual which is very suitable for bedding out in pots and boxes, or for edging and small beds. The 12-inch stems terminate in round heads of small white, scarlet, mauve, cream or purple flowers which are extremely gay when grown en masse. They are also good for cutting. A race known as 'Twinkle' has star-shaped flowers on bushy seven-inch plants.

Portulacas are of similar habit to *Dorotheanthus* (see above) but with larger flowers. Double forms are also available. Treat as half-hardy annuals and grow in sun in well drained soil. The brilliant flowers are ideal for hot dry situations. They grow to six inches.

Salvia splendens, the garden sage, is a popular, long-flowering window box and bedding plant. Although perennial, treat it as a half-hardy annual but choose an early-flowering strain to ensure a long season of colour. It has 10- to 12-inch-long spikes of tubular scarlet

Nemesia hybrids

Petunia F1 hybrid 'Sugar Plum'

Portulaca F1 hybrid 'Sunglo'

Salvia 'Red Hussar'

Zinnia 'Persian Carpet'

flowers, and there are also less attractive white and purple forms. The leaves are smooth, oval and lightly toothed.

Window box and bedding verbenas are hybrids derived from several *Verbena* species, none of which themselves appear to be in general cultivation. The crowded flower heads on 6- to 12-inch stems come in intense shades of violet, scarlet, rose, pink, deep yellow, blue and white. The oblong or oval leaves are sharply pointed. Given good soil and a sheltered situation they are reliable plants in either sunny or wet seasons. Grow them as half-hardy annuals.

Zinnias need a hot summer to give of their best, but are then long-lasting and make good cut flowers. Treat as half-hardy annuals but do not sow too early in spring as the seedlings resent checks and cannot go outside until the soil has been warmed up. The brilliant daisy-type flowers come in a wide range of strains and colours, including several dwarf races like 'Persian Carpet' 'Peter Pan' and 'Lilliput' that are only 9 to 12 inches tall.

More annuals for boxes

Fragrant flowers

Easy-to-grow annuals that combine both colourful blooms and sweet fragrance are always doubly welcome, but they are particularly so to city dwellers. By growing plants like dwarf pinks or night-scented stocks in window boxes, a double attack can be made on the world of brick, concrete and diesel fumes. The evening air wafting through an open window brings a happy reminder of the countryside, while the outlook is colourfully softened by foliage and flowers.

Alyssum desertorum is a Mediterranean plant with silvery-grey leaves and masses of pale yellow flowers all through summer. Being dwarf (about four inches) and compact, it makes an

drained soil. They appreciate lime, although this is not essential. Seedlings should be raised in early spring under glass and put outside when there is no more danger from frost.

Exacum affine, a charming member of the gentian family, is often grown as a pot-plant for its richly scented, deep-blue flowers (see page 79). One plant can perfume a room. It has smooth, oval leaves and reddish branching stems, and flowers from midsummer to late autumn. It needs plenty of moisture in summer and shade from hot sun. Treat as a half-hardy annual, sowing seed under glass in early spring and grouping two or three plants in each six-inch pot. It reaches a height of about nine inches.

with green fern-like foliage and a profusion of sweetly scented yellow flowers, edged with white. These are much visited by bees.

Matthiola longipetala (*M. bicornis*) is the night-scented stock, so called because its six- to nine-inch spikes of purplish-lilac, richly scented flowers open towards evening. Since these are rather drab in the day, mix the seed with that of the similar (but scentless) day-blooming Virginia stock (*Malcolmia maritima*).

Oenothera acaulis, a trailing relative of the evening primrose, has large, fragrant, showy white flowers which become rose with age. Treat it as a half-hardy annual and give it full sun.

Reseda odorata, the mignonette, is a

Dianthus heddewigii 'Magic Charms'

Tropaeolum majus 'Jewel'

Dahlia 'Coltness Hybrids'

excellent edging for window boxes and similar containers, or can be used between crazy paving. The white and honey-scented *A. (Lobularia) maritimum* is another good half-hardy annual (see page 160).

Asperula orientalis is a slender hardy annual from Asia Minor with 12-inch branching sprays of small, fragrant, lavender-blue flowers. These should be massed for maximum effect.

Pinks and carnations (*Dianthus* species and hybrids) are notoriously sweet-smelling, and in olden days were tossed into ale and wine to give a scented flavour. There are many perennial pinks including the well-known double white 'Mrs Sinkins', the similar but pink 'Mrs Pilkington' and the harlequin 'Patchwork', which has white and maroon patterning.

Dianthus to raise from seed include the fragrant Indian pinks (*D. chinensis*) with one-foot, loose-petalled but showy single and double flowers of various shades, and Japanese pinks (*D. heddewigii*), which are in character from midsummer onwards with deep crimson, rose or white flowers – often with contrasting zones. There are also fragrant rock pinks (*D. alpinus*) with a good colour range. These grow about eight inches high. Dwarf sweet Williams (*D. barbatus*) also make good window box plants (see page 150).

156   All *Dianthus* need sun and well-

Heliotropium arborescens (heliotrope or cherry pie), although perennial, is often treated as half-hardy for bedding purposes. The large and fragrant flower trusses range from pale mauve to deep violet. Especially good forms can be perpetuated from cuttings. The usual height is 12 to 18 inches, but most seed houses offer smaller and more compact forms. (See also page 81.)

Limnanthes douglasii (meadow foam or poached egg flower) is one of the easiest of hardy annuals, ideal for containers or edging purposes in sunny spots. It grows about six inches tall,

Reseda odorata

north African annual reputed to have been introduced into Europe by Napoleon. At one time it was more widely grown than now, primarily for its unique fragrance. It is ideal for pots in the house, garden or greenhouse, and is easy to grow provided the seed is left uncovered when sown. Thin out the seedlings early and plant four to five in a six-inch pot of rich potting mixture. Feed when the pot is full of roots. It reaches a height of about 12 inches.

Tropaeolum majus (nasturtiums) have a curious 'tangy' scent. Both leaves and flowers can be eaten in salads and the seeds are a substitute for capers. There are many single and double dwarf hybrids around six to nine inches tall, but the brilliant 'Golden Gleam' and 'Scarlet Gleam' doubles have the best scent. They are hardy annuals suitable for poor soil, and flower for long periods in boxes, containers and hanging baskets.

Viola cornuta, the horned violet, has a light fragrance and will tolerate light shade. It is a pretty little plant with long-stemmed violet or white flowers and wavy-margined leaves. It may reach a height of four to ten inches. Most pansies and violas (see page 153) are also slightly scented.

For autumn decoration

Ornamental peppers (*Capsicum frutescens*) are grown for their vivid, cone-like fruits, about two inches in length,

Dimorphotheca aurantiaca hybrids

Tagetes tenuifolia (often called simply tagetes) bloom for months until finally cut by frost. They make compact, bushy plants seven inches tall, with strong-smelling, deeply cut leaves and masses of stubby daisy-like flowers of lemon, gold, bronze or crimson. Treat them as half-hardy annuals.

Dwarf double strains of French marigolds (*Tagetes patula*) can be treated in the same way or can be sown outside in late spring. The showy flowers come in yellow, bronze or gold, frequently splashed or zoned with other shades. The 'Brocade' strain is particularly good. Full sun and good soil are essential for all *Tagetes*, and the old flowers should be regularly removed.

Other plants for boxes

Among the many other useful small annuals you can easily grow in boxes and small raised beds are the following: *Lobelia erinus* varieties, with white, crimson, violet or blue flowers on compact four- to five-inch plants; dwarf China asters (*Callistephus*), with single or double flowers and a mere 8 to 12 inches high; 'Tom Thumb' balsams (*Impatiens*), which are ideal for window boxes and only eight inches tall; also dwarf cornflowers (*Centaurea cyanus*) in white, pink, blue and purple, which grow to a height of 12 inches.

Dimorphothecas, or stars of the veldt, are sun-lovers with brilliant daisy flowers in character all summer. They are

Matricaria eximia 'Snow Dwarf'

good for cutting, on 7- to 12-inch stems. The large blooms can be white (with blue reverses to the outer ring of petals), purple, orange, yellow or brown.

Matricaria eximia (also known as *Chrysanthemum parthenium*) produces round, double, button-like white or golden flowers on eight- to nine-inch stems. It is strong-smelling, both in leaf and flower, but long-flowering. Treat it as a half-hardy annual.

Senecio (*Cineraria*) *maritima* makes an ideal contrast plant, having feathery, somewhat fern-like leaves that are covered in woolly white hairs. Some varieties are an intense silver colour; others have more green to them. It will overwinter in mild areas, but is usually treated as a half-hardy annual. Choose dwarf varieties for edging boxes.

Callistephus chinensis 'Heavenly Comets'

which go from green to cream, through orange to bright red. These are held well above the neat oval leaves, and the whole plant grows to a height of nine inches. Winter cherry (*Solanum capsicastrum*) is similar but with round red fruits. It grows 9 to 15 inches tall. Treat both as half-hardy annuals. (See also page 83.)

Dwarf *Chrysanthemums* are useful late-season plants, especially for window boxes. The small button-flowered 'pompons' (12 to 15 inches tall) are the most suitable.

Dwarf *Dahlias* of the 'Coltness' type can be treated as half-hardy and raised from seed to provide single, double and semi-double flowers in many attractive shades. They grow about one foot tall.

Senecio (*Cineraria*) *maritima* 'Silver Dust'

Tagetes tenuifolia 'Paprika'

157

Space-saving climbers

A group of plants that make only modest demands on space are the upright-growing vines or climbers. These are great stand-bys in small garden areas and patios for masking walls, draping trellis or verandah supports, and affording shade and privacy. Modern wall screens are often austere, although sometimes lacy concrete blocks are used, but climbing plants are useful in both situations to provide handsome living backgrounds of foliage, flowers and (sometimes) fruit.

There is an endless variety of types – annual and perennial, shrubby and soft-stemmed, evergreen and deciduous, showy-flowered or purely of foliage interest. They may climb by means of twining stems or tendrils that attach themselves to any convenient object, or be so weak-stemmed that ties and artificial support are necessary to prevent wind damage. Some climbers grow rapidly but others take years to fill their allotted space, and while the majority like sun a few are happiest in shade.

Essential to the cultivation of them all, however, is good soil, either in containers at least 18 inches deep or in patio beds, stout supports that will not buckle under their weight, and water in summer. They will also need regular pruning and tying-in, for it is important to retain a light effect, especially on verandah rafters, patio pillars and trellis. Normally pruning is undertaken in early spring or when the blooms are finished.

All the climbers indicated are propagated from seed, cuttings or layers.

Rapid and robust growers

Polygonum baldschuanicum is an extremely vigorous climber that grows 15 feet or more in a season and is capable of twining up to 40 or 50 feet. So site it with care. In late summer it produces clusters of frothy pinkish-white flowers. It needs a sunny situation.

Honeysuckles (*Lonicera* spp) like good loamy soil with plenty of moisture, so plant the roots in shade if possible. Many have fragrant flowers, especially *L. caprifolium*, *L. japonica* (an evergreen) and its gold variegated-leaved form 'Aureoreticulata' (which tolerates shade), and *L. periclymenum*. The evergreen, less-hardy *L. sempervirens* (trumpet honeysuckle) with orange-scarlet

Wisteria sp

flowers is scentless, as is the deciduous *L. tragophylla*, the best yellow species.

The vigorous wisterias (*Wisteria* or *Wistaria* spp) are grown for their large and showy trusses of purple, mauve or white spring flowers. The new shoots must be pruned back to spur growths or they may damage tiles and gutters.

Most vines are vigorous but *Vitis coignetiae*, the glory vine, is positively robust, with large 8- to 12-inch-wide leaves which turn scarlet and crimson at leaf fall. It can climb up to 90 feet.

Shade-tolerant types

All the ivies (*Hedera* spp) are shade-tolerant and self-clinging, the smaller-leaved sorts being hardier than the large. Many have gold or cream leaf margins or variegations (see page 51).

Polygonum baldschuanicum

Lonicera sp

Clematis montana

Hydrangea anomala petiolaris (scandens), another self-clinger, is deciduous with showy and symmetrical heads of white flowers in summer. It is one of the best climbers for shade.

Schizophragma hydrangeoides is allied to this *Hydrangea*, but with one very large white bract to each flower instead of five small, uniform sepals. It blooms in summer and is very vigorous.

For sunny or sheltered sites
Clematis need cool feet and a hot head, so plant them in shade where they can climb into the sun, or cover the roots with rocks or other plants. Some sorts require little pruning, but the large-flowered *C. × jackmanii* group should be cut hard back each spring to maintain their health and quality. There are spring-, summer- and autumn-blooming clematis, with white, pink, red, purple, mauve or yellow flowers, and most are deciduous. Some kinds have double blooms, and *C. armandii* is evergreen and flowers in spring.

Two useful hardy shrubs for walls are two species of jasmine: *Jasminum nudiflorum*, winter-flowering with yellow blooms on the naked green stems, and the fragrant white *J. officinale*, which blooms in midsummer. Both need tying and should be pruned after flowering.

Rambler and climbing roses (*Rosa* varieties and hybrids) need strong supports. The latter can be planted with *Clematis × jackmanii*, so that this climbs through the branches of the rose and flowers when the roses are over. Pink, white, red and yellow, single and double roses are available. Mulch the roots annually with organic manure, prune away old wood periodically and tie in frequently to wires or trellis.

Passiflora caerulea (passion flower),

Tropaeolum peregrinum

Pyracantha sp

Cotoneaster horizontalis

being Brazilian, is sometimes killed in hard winters. Covering the roots in cold weather helps or, as a precaution, root some cuttings in small pots and keep these under cover. The remarkable three- to four-inch-wide flowers are purple, white and green (see page 85).

Other attractive and exotic climbers for favoured situations are *Mutisia decurrens*, with large vermilion daisy heads and pinnate evergreen leaves, *Solanum crispum*, the vigorous mauve- or white-flowered potato vine, and *Campsis (Tecoma) radicans*, the trumpet vine, which has huge terminal clusters of orange-scarlet flowers.

Annual climbers
All this group should be raised under glass in spring from fresh seed. Grow the seedlings on in small pots and plant outside when there is no risk of frost.

Rosa 'Climbing Iceberg'

Gourds (*Cucurbita* spp) are grown for their quaint and variously-coloured and shaped fruits, and sweet peas (*Lathyrus odoratus* cultivars) for their exquisite flowers and sweet fragrance. These latter must be picked regularly or they go to seed and stop blooming. Morning glories (*Ipomoea purpurea*, *I. violacea* and forms), with white, blue, purple, pink and red flowers, need full sun and shelter. The flowers close early, so plant them where they can be seen in the mornings.

The brilliant nasturtiums (*Tropaeolum majus*) come in both dwarf and climbing forms, and are tolerant of shade, but watch out for aphids (see page 232). *T. peregrinum*, the canary creeper, climbs readily and has small yellow, fringed flowers and finely cut leaves. *Quamoclit (Mina) lobata* and *Q. pennata* are two tender twiners for sheltered spots, the former with crimson and yellow flowers and the latter with scarlet tubular flowers and finely cut leaves. They are sometimes listed as *Ipomoea*.

In addition to all these true climbers, there are many wall shrubs that can be used to cover boundary walls and buildings. Examples include the green-catkined *Garrya elliptica*, firethorns (*Pyracantha* spp) and the white-flowered, red-berried *Cotoneaster horizontalis*.

Trailers and rock plants

Saponaria ocymoides (left), Sempervivum tectorum (right) and other rock plants

Alyssum maritimum 'Carpet of Snow'

Arabis albida varieties

Aubrieta deltoidea

Gypsophila sp

Trailing plants have a peculiar grace when spilling over the sides of window boxes, jardinieres, sun-lounge shelves or hanging baskets. Many of the best smaller sorts are alpines or rock plants – the two are not always synonymous – and these plants in miniature hold a great fascination for many people.

The easiest subjects are often adaptable. Apart from the uses already mentioned, they will grow in rock pockets, trail over the sides of sinks or raised beds, succeed between the crevices of dry walls, in niches in old mortar walls, or between paving stones. They can also be used as edgings by raising a two-tier course of bricks, with plants (instead of mortar) between those in the top tier.

Most rock plants and trailers appreciate sharp drainage, although there are some alpines that like lots of water in spring (corresponding to the melting of spring snows in their native surroundings). So when they are grown on a flat site the soil should be light. This is less important when growing trailers in hanging baskets, where drainage is naturally free and the difficulty is to conserve moisture rather than lose it.

Propagation of the alpines and rock plants described here is mainly by seed (stratification hastens germination; see page 227) or late summer cuttings (see page 228). If old plants are cut hard back after flowering, the newly emergent shoots are ideal for cuttings. Trailing plants are best established from small pots so that they can forge ahead.

Among the important trailers not covered here are the trailing *Fuchsias* and ivy-leaf geraniums. Neither are hardy but both give brilliant summer displays. For these and other trailers, see pages 103, 104 and 129.

Sun-loving trailers

Alyssum are annuals and perennials requiring sun and good drainage. The annual *Alyssum maritimum* (now officially *Lobularia maritima*) is white-flowered, compact and honey-scented. It is useful for edgings and between paving. *A. saxatile* is perennial and has sprawling stems with silvery leaves and loose bunches of yellow flowers. It is suitable for dry walls and rock and sink gardens.

The rock cresses (*Arabis*) are ever green trailing perennials with silvery hairy leaves and single or double stock-like flowers. Plant in ordinary soil in rock pockets, dry walls, sinks and containers, or use as a carpeter for spring bulbs. Propagate by cuttings taken in summer from young shoots produced after old growth has been cut hard back. *Arabis albida* is white; 'Flore Pleno' is a double white and 'Rosabelle' pale pink.

Aubrieta deltoidea (purple rock cress) is a favourite rock garden subject. It has small evergreen leaves and is smothered in spring with starry, four-petalled mauve, purple, blue or rosy flowers. Some are double or have variegated foliage. They are good for rock pockets, dry walls, sink gardens or as ground cover beneath other plants. Cut back after flowering to restrict seeding. Cuttings root in frames in midsummer.

Gypsophilas (chalk plants) like dryish soil, sun and some lime (preferably in the form of mortar rubble). *G. repens* is a prostrate perennial with glaucous, smooth leaves and white or rose flowers.

Sun- or rock-roses (*Helianthemum*) are hardy, low-growing, small-leaved shrubs for dry walls, crazy paving, rock gardens or sinks with well-drained soil. They may be cut back in very hard winters but mostly remain evergreen. *H. nummularium*, with small yellow flowers, has cultivars with single and double blooms of white, rose, crimson, red, orange, yellow and copper. Trim back after flowering and use the new shoots for cuttings.

Helichrysum petiolatum has long trails of heart-shaped leaves covered with short silvery down; the flowers are insignificant. Its real value is for muting strong colours in hanging baskets, win-

Cerastium tomentosum (snow in summer) is a rampageous plant that needs careful siting. It has silver leaves and white single flowers in early summer. It can be propagated by division or cuttings.

Ivies (*Hedera*), when deprived of the means to climb, droop downwards, so they can be used as the edges of window boxes or hanging baskets. Small-leaved forms of *H. helix* (English ivy) are the best for this purpose. There are many varieties, with all-green or variegated leaves.

Lysimachia nummularia (creeping Jenny) is a useful deciduous plant with long trails of soft leaves and golden flowers. 'Aurea', with yellow leaves, is the most ornamental variety. It can be used to drape fountains and the sides of pools (the roots in water) in sun, or in window

occasionally white – and are scentless.

Hypericums have large goblet flowers filled with golden stamens. *Hypericum olympicum*, which grows eight to ten inches tall, and *H. reptans*, a prostrate form with bright red buds, both have golden blooms two inches across. Both of these are again summer-blooming.

Iberis sempervirens is the evergreen candytuft, and has dark green, glossy leaves. The flat heads of white flowers make a wonderful display, particularly in the pure white variety 'Snowflake'.

For pavements and ash beds
Although many of the plants previously mentioned would also be suitable for small pockets between paving, there are a number of compact, cushion-forming

Lobelia erinus 'Mrs Clibran'

Saponaria ocymoides

Lysimachia nummularia

dow boxes and the like, but it can also be used as ground cover. It is not hardy, so overwinter under cover.

Lithospermum diffusum (now called *Lithodora diffusa*) forms clumps of small evergreen leaves with masses of bright blue flowers. 'Heavenly Blue' and 'Grace Ward' are the best forms. They bloom all summer but dislike lime.

Lobelia tenuior trails long stems of small leaves and rich blue flowers. It makes a good hanging basket subject. The more compact *L. erinus*, also blue but with white, mauve and wine-red varieties, can be used in crazy paving and flat areas. Both plants are annuals.

The alpine *Phlox subulata* is ideal for producing patches of colour in rockeries, sinks, containers and between crazy paving. The flowers are pink, red, mauve or white; they appear in spring. They require deep, rich, but well-drained soil.

Saponaria ocymoides is useful to trail over rocks or sinks, or to cover a dry bank. It has flowers about ½ inch across in pink, white or deep rose.

Thymus is a large genus, mostly evergreen with aromatic foliage. *T.* × *citrodorus* has lemon-scented leaves with silver variegations, and *T. serpyllum* forms flat mats which scent the air when walked on. They are useful for crazy paving pockets or can be made into small paths. The flowers are pink, white or red.

Shade-tolerant types
Acaenas are creeping, mat-forming evergreens with attractive foliage – silvery in *A. buchananii*, with red burred fruits, and grey to bronze in *A. microphylla*.

boxes and hanging baskets in shade.

Parochetus communis, the shamrock pea, is a delightful scrambling, shamrock-like plant with deep blue, pea-shaped flowers on three-inch stems. Moist soil is essential, and cover in winter.

Saxifraga stolonifera (*S. sarmentosa*) is called 'mother of thousands' because of its long thread-like, trailing stolons, which carry series of baby plants. The rounded leaves are hairy – green, red and white in the variety 'Tricolor' – and it has white flowers on 9- to 12-inch spikes. It is ideal for vases and hanging baskets, but is not hardy. (See also page 47.)

For masses of colour
Campanulas (bellflowers) follow aubrietas and other bright spring rock plants, and so provide continuity. The small, dumpy flowers are usually blue. For long blooming try *Campanula portenschlagiana* (*C. muralis*), with four-inch flower stems, *C. garganica* (five to six inches) and *C. cochlearifolia* (fairies' thimbles; two to three inches) and their forms – most of them blue, but occasionally white. The most important trailing type is *C. isophylla*, with its rich blue, inch-wide flowers and its white- and variegated-leaved forms. It is popular for hanging baskets, window boxes and the like. But it is not hardy.

Among the alpine pinks, *Dianthus caesius* (six inches), *D. deltoides* (maiden pink; six to nine inches) and their hybrids all flower throughout the summer. They like lime. They vary in colouring when grown from seed but the flowers are usually pink to crimson –

plants which bear their flowers on raised hummocks of needle-fine foliage. These are particularly valuable for planting between paving stones to add interest and colour to a flat surface.

They include the alpine *Drabas*, with their white or yellow flowers, the hardiest of which is *Draba aizoides*; *Armeria maritima*, the British thrift, and *A. caespitosa*, both with round heads of pink or white flowers; dwarf campanulas like *Campanula arvatica*, *C. tridentata* and *C. bellidifolia*, all of them blue-flowered; *Silene acaulis*, the moss campion, which has bright pink, five-petalled, almost stalkless blossoms on cushions of narrow, pointed leaves; and *Morisea monantha* (*M. hypogaea*), which has four-petalled yellow flowers and likes to be dry in winter.

Campanula 'Norman Grove'

161

Perennials for town conditions

Town gardens and courtyards have special problems, largely because of the lack of light and air in enclosed spaces and the worn-out, sour or impoverished soil. Additionally, vehicle fumes and smog may adversely affect leaves, particularly those of a hairy nature, which can trap soot particles. These can cause burns or leaf drop, so those with a smooth, tough exterior usually fare best in built-up industrial areas.

Patios and terraces in open situations present fewer problems, and there is a much wider choice of plants from which to choose. Windy situations demand sturdy plants, but they must not be tall; otherwise staking may be necessary.

Since herbaceous perennials remain *in situ* for a number of years, they should be planted in good soil in the first place and also receive the occasional mulch of well-rotted compost or manure to keep up the nutrient content of the soil.

The plants described here – all of them approximately one foot or shorter unless specifically mentioned – are selected to provide interest at different seasons or under various conditions. They should be grouped in batches of three, five or seven plants of the same kind (according to habit and the space available), for this makes a much stronger impact on the viewer. Other perennials that include many suitable for town conditions are described on pages 148, 164 and 166.

For light shade
Most of the bellflowers (*Campanulas*) like sun, but *Campanula poscharskyana*

Doronicum sp

is tolerant of shade. A strong grower of trailing habit, it either spreads into flat clumps or will prop itself against a wall or tree trunk and assume an upright habit. The lavender-blue, bell-shaped flowers persist for weeks, starting in early summer. Propagate by division.

Convallarias, or lilies of the valley, are well-loved flowers with sweet-scented sprays of white, bell-shaped flowers that appear in spring. They do best in leafy loam in light shade. Plant the crowns in early autumn when the foliage dies down. Besides the common *Convallaria majalis*, there are varieties with pink flowers, double blooms and gold-striped leaves. 'Fortin's Giant' is a particularly robust form that can be forced into early bloom indoors or in a greenhouse just like many bulbs (see page 107).

Convallaria majalis

Doronicums have large golden, daisy flowers and rough heart-shaped leaves. They bloom with the daffodils in early spring and need moist soil. *Doronicum orientale* (*D. caucasicum*) and *D. clusii* both grow around one foot tall, but the slightly taller *D. plantagineum* (leopard's bane) and its varieties are the most showy kinds.

Iris foetidissima is commonly called the stinking gladwin because of its unique smell. When the plant is untouched this is not unpleasant, reminiscent of roast meat, but if the leaves are bruised the smell becomes most unpleasant. The plant has strap-shaped leaves and bluish-lilac flowers that appear in early summer. These are followed by seed pods that split to reveal rows of brilliant orange-red seeds. These can be used in dried arrangements if the tall stems are hung upside-down to dry. There is also a variegated-leaved form.

Most nettles are weedy, but *Lamium maculatum* makes good ground cover for lightly shaded positions. It has small, white-striped leaves and heads of purple or (in the variety known as 'Roseum') pink flowers that appear in late spring.

The golden-leaved variety 'Aureum' makes a useful edging plant.

Lithospermum purpurea-caeruleum (now more correctly called *Buglossoides*) is the gromwell, a rare British native with narrow alternate leaves and short, two-flowered terminal sprays of nodding flowers which open red and then turn deep blue. They appear in early summer. The bright, glossy seeds which follow are very striking in winter, as they are difficult to break and shine like pearls among the dead stems.

The lungworts (*Pulmonaria*) bloom very early, some having plain, others spotted foliage. The cowslip-like flowers are red in *Pulmonaria rubra*, pink changing to bright blue in *P. angustifolia*, and deep blue in the variety of the latter known as 'Munstead Blue'.

All the buttercups (*Ranunculus*) are moisture-loving, and given moist conditions and light shade *Ranunculus aconitifolius* 'Flore Pleno' (fair maids of France) is a treasure for early summer. It has deeply cut, shining leaves and sprays of double white flowers up to two feet tall at the start of the summer.

Other useful perennials for light shade

Iris foetidissima

Ranunculus aconitifolius

Lupinus Russell varieties

include *Brunnera macrophylla*, hellebores and *Hostas* (see page 148).

For industrial areas

Aquilegias (columbines) are old favourites that associate pleasingly with lupins, irises and day lilies. The flowers may have short nectary tubes or spurs behind ('granny's bonnets') or these may

Aquilegia hybrids

protrude as long as the flowers themselves. There is a wide range of colours, and the flowering season extends intermittently throughout the summer. They like full sun or light shade, and moist but well drained soil suits them best. They are propagated by seed sown in spring; in late seasons, self-set seedlings form natural colonies.

Hemerocallis (day lilies) have showy, trumpet-shaped flowers – often fragrant – of gold, yellow, pink, red and maroon. They grow up to three feet in height. The leaves are grassy. Individual blooms last but a day, but blooming persists over several weeks in summer. Any soil or situation seems to suit them. In cold climates, tie the evergreen leaves together in winter to protect the hearts of the plants from wet and frost.

Many perennial flaxes (*Linum*) are very beautiful summer-bloomers, with wide chalice-shaped flowers of brilliant blue or yellow. They require sun and well drained soil, and can be increased from seed, summer cuttings or careful spring division. *Linum narbonense*, whose flowers are normally a rich blue, also has varieties in deeper and paler shades. Both *L. arboreum* and *L. flavum* have yellow flowers, but the former is not very hardy. It is also the smallest.

Lupins (*Lupinus*) do well in northern Europe, but less satisfactorily in many parts of the United States, where they suffer in hot, dry summers. They bloom within 12 months from seed, the showy flower spikes having various colours.

Kniphofia hybrids

These should be removed regularly, as indiscriminate seeding weakens the plants. They grow three to five feet tall.

Tough plants for town

In addition to the plants described above, tough-foliaged plants likely to succeed in towns include dwarf bearded irises (*Iris chamaeiris* and *I. pumila*),

Bergenia sp

both of which have white, purple, or yellow flowers; *Bergenias*, with white, pink or red flowers and thick round leaves; *Kniphofias* (red hot pokers); *Tradescantia virginiana*, grassy-leaved and two feet tall, with blue, purple or white flowers; and *Ajuga reptans*, which makes good ground cover and has spikes of blue flowers and neat, oval leaves – normally green, but purple in the variety 'Atropurpurea' and bronze, cream and green in 'Rainbow'.

Long-flowering kinds

Long-flowering perennials of short stature include *Dianthus* (see page 161), *Geranium* (see page 149), and the *Campanula poscharskyana*, *Tradescantia* and *Kniphofia* described above.

163

Special-purpose perennials

Oenothera fruticosa 'Yellow River'

All gardens have problem situations, and these may be accentuated in small patios, terraces or courtyards. A hot, dry site presents some of the worst problems, and a sunny patio with light-coloured walls to reflect heat and light can get like an oven in hot weather.

Try your hardest to increase moisture retention; in the first instance by working in plenty of well rotted organic material (moist peat, compost, animal manure and the like) and in subsequent seasons by mulching the ground annually with similar material. Small sprinklers, sunk into the ground and operated by a switch, or a 'leaky' hose, perforated at intervals and laid along the back of a border, also help to keep soil damp. On the small patio or terrace, shade can be provided with rafters – most elaborately with adjustable sun-shading. But the best solution is to go for plants that are naturally at home in hot, dry situations.

There are other perennial plants valuable for particular uses. Taller plants of graceful habit are occasionally planted between short kinds to break hard outlines and provide more pleasing effects. These are known as 'dot' plants, but to be effective they should be of light – even feathery – habit and not require staking. To finish small beds, on the other hand, low edgers of perennial habit are easy to tend and manage. Preferably they should have attractive flowers or foliage – both if possible – and remain in character for most of the summer.

Drought-resisting plants

Achilleas are commonly known as yarrow. *Achillea taygetea* is splendid for hot, dry, sunny places and has silvery pinnate leaves and in summer bears flat, two- to four-inch heads of pale yellow flowers. It grows up to 18 inches tall.

Anthemis are handsome perennials that have elegantly cut foliage and white

Gaillardia aristata

Centranthus ruber

or yellow 'daisy' flowers. Most are good for cutting. *Anthemis nobilis*, the aromatic chamomile of Elizabethan days, belongs here; Drake is supposed to have played his famous pre-Armada game of bowls on a chamomile lawn, and the double-flowered form with masses of white rosettes is particularly attractive. It spreads to form a mat of foliage, and grows only about six inches tall. Use it for paths (it yields its scent only when trodden on), in lawns or between crazy paving. *A. sancti-johannis* has golden summer flowers up to two inches across on 12- to 15-inch stems.

Centranthus (or *Kentranthus*) *ruber*, the spur valerian, thrives on neglect and good drainage. It is a common plant of English railway banks, and has clusters of white, pink or red flowers in summer, and smooth, pointed leaves. The plant's height is 1½ to 2 feet.

Gaillardias are available in both annual and perennial species, but all require sunshine and well drained soil. They bloom from summer into autumn. Cold, wet conditions induce winter mortality, although they are sometimes successful in raised beds where surplus moisture drains away. The perennial *G. aristata* and its cultivars show a wide range of large daisy-type flowers in self colours of orange, yellow or red, but more often they have different-coloured centres. Their height is one to two feet. *G. pulchella*, an annual, is smaller.

Incarvilleas (Chinese trumpet-flowers) need protection in areas with bad winters. This can be done either by covering the crowns first with dried leaves or bracken and then polythene or glass, or by growing them in pots that are sunk outside in summer and brought under cover in winter. They are showy plants, with large, rosy-red, trumpet flowers in early summer and radical, pinnate leaves. *Incarvillea delavayi* and *I. mairei grandiflora* grow 12 to 18 inches high.

Oenotheras have faintly scented, wide funnel-shaped flowers. These are generally yellow and open in the evening – hence the common name evening primrose. *Oenothera missouriensis* blooms throughout the summer with two- to three-inch, bright sulphur-yellow flowers on six- to nine-inch stems. *O. fruticosa* (sundrops) is taller – up to 18 inches – with branching stems carrying a succession of scented, lemon-yellow flowers. Both need a hot, dry position.

Phlomis fruticosa is the Jerusalem sage. It has woody stems, woolly, hairy, wedge-shaped leaves and large, pungent, yellow, nettle-like flowers. It can tolerate a good deal of dryness and is propagated by seed or cuttings. It grows to a height of two feet. *P. cashmeriana* is similar but with purplish-flowers, and also grows to two feet.

The houseleeks (*Sempervivums*) have rosettes of fleshy leaves that are often tipped or flushed with red or purple. They are useful to tuck in crevices in dry walls, where they soon multiply and make large clusters of rosettes. These vary in size, shape and colour according to species, but being evergreen are attractive at all seasons. The variously coloured flowers are borne on thick leafy stems. Good sorts include *Semper-vivum arachnoideum* (cobweb houseleek), *S. tectorum* (common houseleek) and *S. × calcaratum*, with well marked foliage.

Few plants thrive in dust-dry situations as well as *Zauschneria californica*. Of branching habit, the grey-leaved stems terminate in loose spikes of scarlet, tubular flowers. It grows about one foot tall. *Z. cana*, the Californian fuchsia, is similar but with needle-fine silver foliage. Both bloom from midsummer well into the autumn.

Other plants resistant to drought include *Catananche caerulea* 'Major' (cupid's love dart; 12 to 18 inches tall), whose cornflower blooms of deep lavender are set off by papery, silvery sepals, and *Centaurea ragusina* (also known as *C. candidissima*; two feet tall), with silver leaves and stems. Both plants dislike wet cold, so they may have to be overwintered – as plants or cuttings – under cover. *Corydalis lutea* is hardier and long-flowering, with fern-like foliage and clusters of bright yellow flowers. It grows six to ten inches tall.

For edging purposes
Alchemilla mollis is the lady's mantle, so called from the shape of its round, silvery-green leaves. The tiny summer flowers come in a delightful froth of greenish-yellow on 12-inch stems. Self-set seedlings are common. It is excellent for edging beds, reflecting into pools or planting around tree trunks.

Nepeta × faassenii (often listed as *N. mussinii*) is the catmint, a plant of garden origin with silvery leaves and spikes of soft mauve flowers throughout summer. Excessive cold or wet can kill, but cuttings root easily and may be overwintered in pots. It makes a useful, one-foot, long-flowering edging plant.

Saxifraga umbrosa (London pride) is a tough plant with rounded leaves. Delicate sprays of pinkish flowers, spotted with red, appear in late spring. It

Sempervivum tectorum

Alchemilla mollis

will grow almost anywhere, but prefers a sunny position.

Stachys lanata is called lamb's ears because of the shape and feel of its silvery plush-like leaves. The blooms are unexciting and tend to spoil the compact habit, so a flowerless form of three to four inches called 'Silver Carpet' is preferable. Try using this plant also as ground cover beneath red roses.

Veronica incana 'Argentea', silver-leaved with deep blue flowers in spikes, is also good for edging purposes, as are *Epimediums*, *Alyssum*, *Hostas*, *Dianthus* and *Bergenias* (mentioned elsewhere).

Dot plants
Eremurus (foxtail lilies) make flat rosettes of strap-shaped leaves surrounding long smooth spikes of white, yellow, rose or golden flowers. They are good as cut flowers, and generally appear in late spring or early summer. The octopus-like roots need planting six to eight inches deep, resting on sand, and should receive protection from wet in winter. *Eremurus olgae* grows to four feet; *E. bungei* to two to three feet and 'Shelford Hybrids' to four to six feet.

Physostegia virginiana 'Vivid', with bright rose-pink flowers on two-foot stems, is known as the obedient plant because the snapdragon-like blooms can be moved around on the spike and remain where they are pushed. 'Summer Snow' is a white-flowered variety with narrow, toothed leaves. These plants are suitable for heavy soil in sun or partial shade, and flower in midsummer.

Other 'dot' plants can be found among *Delphiniums* (larkspurs), with their tall stately spikes of flowers in many shades of blue, purple and white; the exquisite lilies (see page 114); and the plume poppy (*Macleaya cordata*), which bears three-foot plumes of small white flowers during the summer.

Catananche caerulea 'Major'

Delphinium hybrids

Plants for particular places

Plants are tremendously influenced by soil, aspect and climate. The absence or presence of some mineral, such as lime, in the soil may even dictate what can be grown. Salt-laden winds and atmospheric pollution might be tolerated by some, but are anathema to many. Shade and sun both bring their problems. To succeed in growing many of the more fussy kinds of plants it is necessary to study the soil and the climate, and also to take individual growing conditions into account.

Lime-hating plants

Known as calcifuges, lime-haters become starved of iron in limy, alkaline soils. The leaves show pale green, yellow or white patches – a condition called chlorosis – and in bad cases the plants fail and die. The effects of lime can be avoided by planting in containers in the appropriate soil mixture without lime, or one based on peat or leaf-mould that is recommended for lime-hating plants (see page 218) – and watering with soft water. Or the effects can be neutralized by regularly watering the soil with an iron chelate compound (also known as sequestered iron). The following plants are not recommended for alkaline conditions, but are ideal for acid soils.

Cassiope selaginoides

Andromeda polifolia, the bog rosemary, is a charming hardy shrublet with small white or pink urn-shaped flowers. It has glossy oval leaves.

Androsace carnea, an early bloomer from the Pyrenees, grows only three inches tall. It has narrow leaves and, in early summer, umbels of pink flowers $\frac{1}{4}$ inch across. It dislikes winter damp but tolerates extreme cold, so protect it from rain if possible.

Cassiopes belong to the heather family and form tufts of moss-like leaves studded with hair-fine stems, each of which terminates in a nodding, bell-shaped white flower. *Cassiope hypnoides* and *C. lycopodioides*, both about two inches tall, bloom in spring. They like semi-shade. Others in the heather family that dislike lime include many *Ericas* (see page 147), and the *Gaultherias*, prostrate or dwarf shrubs with white, urn-shaped flowers and striking berries – scarlet in *Gaultheria depressa*, blue-black in *G. nummularioides*.

Gentiana sino-ornata

One of the most popular and beautiful gentians, *Gentiana sino-ornata*, is a lime-hater, but give it cool leafy soil and it rewards with masses of deep, bright blue, trumpet flowers in autumn. It dies back after flowering, forming rosettes that can be separated for propagation.

Lewisias need a well drained site in lime-free soil, also partial shade in hot, dry areas. The flowers are very showy in umbels of pink, white, red and scarlet, usually veined with deeper colouring. The spoon-shaped leaves grow in rosettes. Unfortunately, these plants are not long-lived and dislike winter wet, so are best protected from rain when dormant. When happy they perpetuate themselves by self-grown seedlings. They are not very hardy, so protect from extreme cold.

Most *Pulsatillas* like lime, but *Pulsatilla alpina sulphurea* does not. A European mountain plant, it is considered by many to be the finest of all the anemones. It flowers in spring with clear yellow flowers on 12- to 18-inch stems, and likes sun.

Other plants to avoid in alkaline soils are dwarf rhododendrons, azaleas and *Camellias* (see page 144); *Lithospermums* (see page 161); and the colourful *Rhodohypoxis*, with its pink, white and red flowers on two-inch stems.

Seaside plants

Many plants will not tolerate the salty winds and soil that come with living beside the sea. The following plants are

Rhodohypoxis baurii varieties

suitable for these conditions, however. *Anaphalis margaritacea*, a plant of the daisy family, has heads of white flowers and pearly white bracts. These can be dried as everlastings. The plant grows one to two feet tall.

Aster linosyris (commonly known as goldilocks) is a Michaelmas-daisy-type plant with slender but tough 20-inch stems. The clusters of rich yellow flowers are three to five inches across, and appear in late summer.

Eryngium maritimum (sea holly) is a tough European often found in salt marshes. It has pale blue flowers in conical heads throughout the summer, and stem-clasping, spiny, leathery leaves. It grows 12 to 18 inches tall.

Sedums of all kinds seem to withstand drought and salt winds. *Sedum acre* is small and yellow-flowered, but the taller *S. spectabile* is more showy.

Santolina incana 'Weston' is the smallest of its family. It has woolly white leaves and lemon-yellow flowers in mid-summer. It will stand full exposure to maritime conditions.

Veronica prostrata is a mat-forming plant that grows from three to eight inches, though the variety 'Pygmaea' is only two inches tall. It has small, dense spikes of blue flowers from early summer.

Thymus × citrodorus 'Golden King'

Other kinds of plants to try beside the sea are two varieties of old English lavender, *Lavandula atropurpurea* 'Nana' and 'Munstead Dwarf' (see page 147); *Aubrieta* (see page 160); and *Armerias* and thymes (*Thymus*; see page 161).

Rock plants for semi-shade

Calceolaria darwinii has quaint mocassin-like shaped flowers – deep yellow and white, spotted with maroon – on four-inch stems. It forms a spreading mat and likes rich leafy soil – no lime – but is not always easy to establish.

Anemone nemorosa, the white anemone, has deeply cut leaves, and is a British native. Among its interesting forms are a fine double-flowered variety and another with lavender-blue flowers called 'Allenii'.

Another anemone, *A. apennina*, will naturalize in moist semi-shaded situations. The type has clear blue flowers, but there are forms with mauve, pink or white blooms, and also some semi-

Sedum acre

Hepatica transsylvanica

doubles. Very like these, but earlier flowering, are the *Hepaticas*, with heart-shaped leaves and blue, red, pink or white double and single flowers.

Small cyclamen, like the autumn-flowering *Cyclamen neapolitanum*, grow well beneath trees, forming broad colonies of pink or white tiny blossoms. Top dress the corms occasionally with leafy soil. (See also page 111.)

All *Primulas* like to be protected from the mid-day sun. They can be propagated from seed sown immediately after harvesting, or by division.

For partial shade in normal soils try *Primula juliae*, which has wine-purple flowers, and its forms like 'Wanda' and 'Gloria', in more vivid shades. The blooms are very short-stemmed (about one inch) and often in character with the snowdrops and early daffodils. *P. marginata* and its forms, all about three inches tall, come in shades of blue and lavender; *P. forrestii* (six inches) is

yellow; and *P. sieboldii* has large and fragrant umbels of white and pink to deep lavender flowers on six-inch stems. This one will need protecting in cold areas as it is not very hardy.

In moister soil it is possible to grow *P. denticulata* with its round heads of white to mauve and reddish-purple flower heads the size of golf balls. They grow on 12-inch stems. This species can be propagated from root cuttings (see page 228). Other *Primulas* for semi-shade, and all spring-flowering, include *P. frondosa*, lilac and four inches high; *P. involucrata*, six inches and white; and *P. yargongensis*, six inches and lilac.

For deeper shade

Tolerant of deeper shade than the preceding are the *Trilliums* (trinity flowers), which have all parts of the plant – leaflets, petals, sepals and stamens – in groups of three, and white, pink or red flowers. Other deep-shade plants include *Tiarella*

cordifolia and *T. wherryi* (the foam flowers), which have dainty four-inch spikes of cream flowers and heart-shaped, often mottled foliage that remains evergreen in mild winters.

Ramonda myconi (also known as *R. pyrenaica*) has rosettes of crinkly leaves, and the deep blue, white or pink flowers appear in spring. These are reminiscent of African violets, to which the plant is in fact related (see page 76). It should be planted vertically in rock crevices as it dislikes wet on the foliage. Also belonging to the same family – the gesneriads – *Haberlea ferdinandi-coburgii* requires similar conditions, and has pale to deep violet-blue flowers on four-inch stems. Neither are hardy in extreme cold.

Omphalodes cappadocica needs full shade and moist soil. Given these conditions, it will produce masses of exquisite, pure blue flowers like those of forget-me-nots. They grow on four- to six-inch stems and appear in spring.

Anemone apennina

Primula yargongensis

Ramonda myconi

167

6 Creating something special

Do you want a focal feature to form the centrepiece of your patio or terrace garden? Or are you keen to develop a skill in a particular specialist field of gardening? Three special ways of growing plants are described in this part of The Complete Indoor Gardener. They are water gardening, the ancient Japanese art of bonsai, and the creation of miniature gardens and landscapes in troughs.

They are all fundamentally outdoor techniques ideal even for the smallest area, but indoor versions are possible.

Gardening with water

Water features are not only pleasing in their own right, but add a new dimension to gardening. They are lively and changeable; they attract birds and support a unique range of plants and fish.

Even still water has many moods. It sparkles like diamonds in bright sunshine, but turns darkly mysterious when thunder-clouds form. Wind whips its surface into racing eddies, raindrops dance erratically and even a fish breaking the surface on a still day causes a series of ever-widening circles. There is also music in a water garden. The noisy fandango of a straight waterfall, the gurgling murmur of a stream or the gentle splash of a fountain all have their different notes. Add to these the whispering rustle of reeds and bamboos, the hum of bees and bird song, and there is a veritable orchestra of sounds.

A pool is possible in any garden, from the spacious grounds of a mansion to the tiniest city patio, provided it receives plenty of sunshine. Shady ponds disappoint, for plants fail to flower and the water becomes brackish. You can – with due consideration to the practical problems – even bring water to the balcony or roof garden. Indoor water gardens are also possible, particularly in a garden room or conservatory; details of these are given on page 177.

Water-garden styles

As for shape, design and construction, consideration of these must be linked with suitability to the setting. An irregular outline, whilst well suited to a rock garden or similar 'natural' feature, would look out of place in a very formal setting. Informal pools, moreover, must have their nature and outline disguised – most easily and effectively by sinking them into the ground and masking their edges with turf, plants or rocks. The surrounds of informal pools must never be obvious.

Balanced flower beds, on the other hand, with symmetrical paths, lawns or paving – such as on a terrace of formal design – demand a more austere shape, particularly when fountains are introduced. It is permissible for formal pools to look artificial, so give them broad surrounds, either with ground-level paving or raised stone curbs. They should

There is room to introduce the beauty of water into any garden, however big or small. Where the surroundings are thickly planted and informal, it is generally best for the pool, too, to be of informal shape **above** with the edges hidden by rocks and overgrowing plants. In the more formal setting of an open terrace, however, the pool can look completely artificial **above right** with a broad paved surround. Whether you decide to create a pool like these or one of the others illustrated here, running water adds an extra dimension. If you use a small electric pump to recirculate the water, there is very little wastage of water, and little power is consumed. Such a pump can operate a small fountain, as in the pool **above**, or a waterfall **far right top**. For many, the main appeal of water gardens is the water-lilies. The one shown **far right above** is *Nymphaea* 'James Brydon', a beautiful and adaptable kind that will grow in water from six inches to three feet deep. Apart from the lilies, however, water gardens allow you to grow a unique range of plants.

also be to some extent isolated from fussy flower beds, and have plenty of space around to give them prominence and allow for easy access. Raised curbs are attractive to look at and can be used as seats, but they need to be made of concrete (or bricks, faced with concrete) for strength, so such pools are more expensive than those made with some other materials. For details of how to plan and construct a water garden, see pages 172 and 173.

Roofs and balconies

A gallon of water weighs ten pounds, so naturally weight is important in some situations. Before building a pool on a roof it is essential to check on its strength, whether there is a drain or gully to run off surplus water and the availability of a tap (guarded from frost) for filling up. Water plants like warmth and sunshine, so rooftop exposure suits them in summer – especially since wind is not likely to be a problem with low-growing aquatics and floaters. Cold in winter can, however, create problems, and where there is a risk of the pool freezing solid (always possible if the water depth is less than two feet in Britain or three feet in many other areas) either plants and fish must be taken out and wintered elsewhere, or the pool must be protected and have a thermostatic water heater installed.

Balconies also can be frail and cold, so the same principles apply here. Small, lightweight, resin-bonded glass-fibre pools may be more suitable than concrete or heavy containers for roof gardens and balconies. Or you can use sawn-down wine or beer casks, well scrubbed inside and painted outside. Tubs which have held oily or fatty substances are less suitable as they are difficult to clean, although this can be achieved by filling them with straw, setting this alight and then turning them over (when the sides are just charred) to extinguish the flames. (See page 176.)

Terraces and patios

Terraces and patios offer more scope as they can take greater weight, although on made-up ground there could be subsidence problems. Check this with the builder in the case of new properties; with older houses the ground should have settled and a few test holes (to ascertain the nature of the subsoil) will confirm this point. If the subsoil is pure clay, a butyl sheeting pool or prefabricated plastic liner is safest on terraces – it is less important on patios – as clay contracts in dry weather and concrete may crack as a result.

Of course, any watertight container can be looked upon as a potential water garden, so even an old bath can be sunk into a patio. Or a deep butler's sink, with disguising wood framework outside, can be stood on a terrace or find a place in small gardens. An important aspect always to remember, however, is the nuisance of mosquitoes when pools are adjacent to homes. For this reason it is absolutely imperative to keep fish in all ornamental pools.

Running water

Running water can be provided by means of fountains or waterfalls. These are activated by submersible pumps which work silently to produce the effect of a mountain tarn, straight cascade or rushing torrent – the same water being used over and over again. They operate from a mains electric supply, but before frost occurs should be dismounted, carefully cleaned and stored under cover until the following season. Most pumps come with a sufficient length of sealed electric cable to reach out of the pool to a nearby point. Additional weatherproof cable can then be attached (with special connectors) to reach back to the mains supply in the house.

Waterfalls can be linked to streams and pools by concrete gullies and pockets (masked with rocks and plants), or shaped fibreglass units are obtainable from dealers in aquatic supplies to fit into rock and water-garden features. Fountains for more formal pools are very varied. Some have cone fittings for a jet effect; others are punctured with few or many small holes to provide sprays. For walls there are various devices such as lions' heads, satyrs, sea lions and the like emitting water through their mouths.

There are even fountain and waterfall kits which can be used in sea water. The motors are robust, oil-sealed for safety and with steel drive shafts operating in sintered bearings. So no water garden need be without the music of falling water on a quiet summer evening.

Creating a water garden

It is not difficult to bring the beauty and music of water to your garden, patio or terrace – or even to a roof garden or balcony. There are several methods of construction, and it would be wise to plan very carefully before starting work. You will probably need to go to a specialist water garden centre for materials, plants, fish and other supplies, and such places are generally happy to give free advice to customers. So take advantage of this before you start digging!

Planning the pool

Notwithstanding the fact that an open position is essential for garden pools, some form of shelter – as from trees or buildings – is also advantageous. These break the force of strong winds (bringing dividends in the form of early flowers) and protect the site in winter. But never site the pool directly under a tree, or you will have problems with leaves in autumn unless you cover the pool with a net.

After deciding on its shape and type – formal or informal (see page 170) – peg out the pool outline with sticks and/or white tape. This gives a rough guide as to its ultimate size and effect. You should then decide on the depth. This depends to a great extent upon the climate. Ideally pools should be shallow enough for the water to warm up quickly in spring, thus encouraging flowering (especially of the water-lilies), yet deep enough to give fish protection in hot weather and to prevent a complete freeze-up in winter. Over most of the British Isles two feet of water above the roots of lilies is normally safe from complete freezing, but in some latitudes $2\frac{1}{2}$ feet may be a more realistic depth.

With severe climates, it might even be advisable to drain the pond in winter. The fish and tenderest aquatics can then be stored somewhere else, and the pool surface covered with polythene sheeting or boards and branches to protect the remaining plants. Naturally, if plants are underneath, the covering must be removed as conditions improve, but it is surprising how well water-lilies and other aquatics temporarily exist without water in cold weather.

Materials for pool-making

Artificial pools are usually constructed by one of three methods: with concrete, with butyl (heavy-gauge plastic) sheeting, or with a prefabricated container sunk in the soil to its rim (or just below).

Resin-bonded glass-fibre shells are obtainable in many shapes and sizes, some having sections of different depths (the deepest designed for water-lilies and fish) in the same model. These are the easiest to install, but they are expensive, they bear a certain similarity to countless others and frequently they are too shallow, which precludes their use in cold climates. A variation, particularly suitable for creating a small formal pool on a roof garden, is to build up the pool's shape with waterproof (marine-grade) plywood, and then have this lined with resin-bonded glass-fibre *in situ*.

Concrete pools are durable, and can be fashioned to any shape, size and depth. They are also essential in situa-

Using a glass-fibre shell

This is the simplest way of building a pool. Excavate a hole the correct shape, but a few inches bigger than the shell. Rest the base of the shell on a one-inch layer of sand, making sure that the top edge is level. Then fill the space between pool and excavation, packing the sand firmly and ensuring adequate support for any shelves. Finally, hide the edge of the shell.

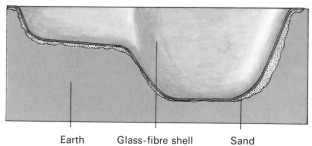

Earth   Glass-fibre shell   Sand

Using a butyl pool-liner

After marking out the area of the pool, excavate to the shape and depth required, allowing a shallow edge shelf for marginals. The sides should slope at about 60°. Remove any sharp stones and work in an inch-thick lining of sand to give smooth sides and bottom. Then drape the liner evenly over the excavated hole, and weigh down the edges. Now start filling the pool, easing off the edge weights as the butyl sheeting stretches and sinks, taking the pool's contours. Finally, cut off all surplus liner material with a pair of scissors, except for about six inches all round the edges. Tuck this spare into the soil and cover it with earth, rocks, turf or paving stones.

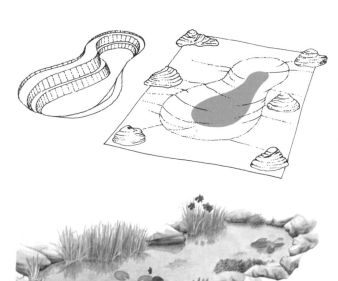

tions where raised stone curbs are required. Although not cheap and rather laborious to construct, even amateurs can make them, and 'ready-mixed' concrete lessens the labour. It is however essential to use clean sand and aggregate and good quality cement, otherwise they may leak. There are proprietary sealing compounds for waterproofing concrete pools; they are painted on the inside. But repairing leaky pools is both difficult and messy! If in doubt consult your local builder. A raised pool on a patio can also be built of brick, with a concrete lining, but it is best to get professional advice on strength and construction, since deep water exerts considerable sideways pressure.

New concrete pools must be 'matured' before plants and fish are installed, for free lime is released to the water in the early stages after construction, and this can kill fish and damage aquatics. If the pond is made in the autumn and kept full of water until spring, and then it is emptied and rinsed, this is usually sufficient. Alternatively, newly made pools should be filled and enough permanganate of potash crystals added to turn the water wine-red. If this is left for three days, then emptied, scrubbed and rinsed again, it should be safe for filling and planting.

Plastic liners represent the cheapest method of pool-making, and are almost as easy as using preformed glass-fibre

shells. Water-garden centres supply the special heavy-duty plastic, and will advise on the size needed. As a rough rule of thumb, though, add twice the pool's overall depth to both the length and width. Plastic pools of this nature should always be kept full of water to prevent sun rotting the fabric. They should also always have their edges hidden. They last for years, and when no longer required can be lifted and packed away.

Introducing the plants

Water plants should be established in spring or early summer, and this is also the best time to lift and divide them. There are five main groups, and detailed descriptions of popular varieties will be found on pages 174 and 175.

Water-lilies and other deep-water aquatics require fibre-free soil. Anything organic – such as peat, leaves and fibrous loam – should be avoided since the decomposition of the organic matter will release salts into the water. These salts encourage algae, which turn the water green or murky. Plain heavy loam with a little decayed cow manure (one sixth of its bulk) or coarse bonemeal (a handful to a bucketful of loam) is good for water-lilies.

It is best not to have a permanent layer of soil at the bottom of small pools; instead, the water-lilies should be planted in aquatic baskets. These have holes all round their sides. Tubers of the

rhizomatous lilies should be laid horizontally and just covered with soil, but all the others can be planted in an upright position. In each case leave the crowns exposed, and plant very firmly. Next spread half an inch of clean pea-sized shingle over the soil, to prevent fish rooting into and stirring up mud, and lower the basket into the water. Prop it on bricks at first, so that the crown is only just covered, and lower it gradually as growth proceeds. In cool weather it may take six to eight weeks before reaching its ultimate depth.

Shallow-water aquatics (sometimes known as marginals) need no fertilizer – just plain loam. Plant these in shallow water, in pockets, pots or boxes. Submerged oxygenators are usually anchored with narrow strips of lead. These are lightly pressed around several plant stems – such plants have few if any roots – and thrown into the water. The lead prevents them floating up to the surface, but as growth goes forward they adjust to the water and keep their place.

Floating plants are simply placed on the water surface, but bog plants, being above the water level, are treated more like land plants. They require soil constantly damp but never waterlogged, and appreciate richer conditions. Accordingly, rotted manure or compost can be dug into the soil before planting and the ground mulched from time to time with moist peat, leaf-mould or compost.

Making a concrete pool

For a concrete pool, the excavation should reach down to consolidated subsoil, to avoid subsidence and consequent cracking. After a good layer of hardcore or broken brick is rammed down, concrete should be laid to a thickness of six inches for both sides and bottom. Large pools need reinforcement, but not small ones. Alternatively, plaster several thin layers of concrete over the hardcore. To make a fountain or waterfall, install a waterproof pump and hidden pipe leading to the upper part of the pool, to recirculate water.

The completed pool

The deepest part of the pool should be at least two feet deep – more in very cold climates. The side shelf for marginals should be about nine inches deep and nine inches wide. Both marginals and deep-water aquatics are best planted in baskets or boxes. The soil should be covered with a layer of gravel, and the container supported on bricks at first, until the plants start to grow Underwater oxygenators are weighted down with thin lead strips, while floating plants are of course simply placed on the surface.

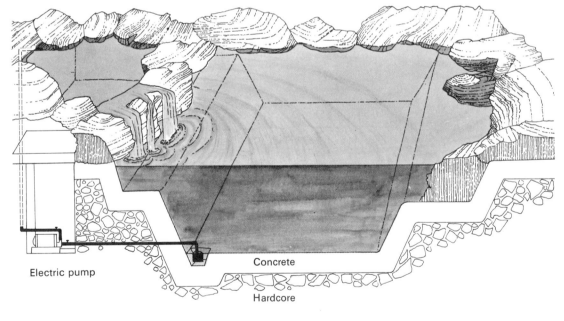

Electric pump

Concrete

Hardcore

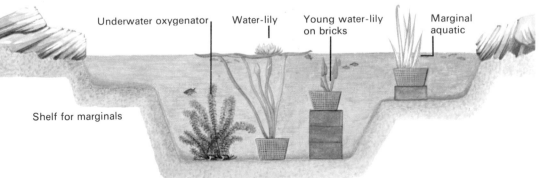

Underwater oxygenator Water-lily Young water-lily on bricks Marginal aquatic

Shelf for marginals

Water-garden plants

There are five groups of plants for water gardens, all with different functions. The first, the deep-water aquatics, such as water-lilies and water hawthorns, have their roots in mud and floating leaves and flowers. These are purely ornamental, although they provide shade and shelter for fish and also inhibit algal growth. They need a water depth of one to three feet.

The next group, the marginal aquatics, like wet feet, but everything else – stems, leaves and flowers – grows up into the air. Between one and three inches of water is normally sufficient for these, so they can be planted on shelves at the edges of pools, or supported on brick piers. The third group, the underwater oxygenators, help maintain water clarity and are essential for a well balanced community. These are simply weighted down on the bottom with small lead strips. The fourth, the floaters, cast shade and shelter for small creatures, and the fifth group, the bog plants, form a bridge between land and water. These last like soil which never dries out but on the other hand is never waterlogged.

Deep-water plants
The most important of these are the water-lilies (*Nymphaea*), the hardy varieties of which have floating flowers in white, cream, yellow, flesh, rose, red, carmine, and various in-between shades. The blooms can be as large as a dinner plate or small enough to slip through a wedding ring. Some are scentless, others fragrant. A few are miniatures and only suitable for tiny containers and very shallow water; there are many in the one- to two-foot depth range and several for three feet.

For small pools, medium-sized varieties should be sought, and the best of these are listed below in their various colour ranges. Among the white-flowered kinds are *Nymphaea candida*, *N.* 'Gonnêre' (a semi-double), *N.* 'Albatross', and also *N. tetragona*, a miniature for two to six inches of water. The best yellow varieties are *N.* 'Sunrise', *N.* 'Marliacea Chromatella' and, for very small containers, *N.* 'Pygmaea Helvola'. Pinks include *N.* 'Pink Opal', *N.* 'Laydekeri Lilacea', *N.* 'Caroliniana' and *N.* 'Rose Nymphe'. Four beautiful red-

Aponogeton distachyos

flowered kinds are *N.* 'James Brydon', *N.* 'Laydekeri Purpurata', *N.* 'Froebelii' and *N.* 'Wm. Falconer'.

Other deep-water aquatics include *Aponogeton distachyos*, the water hawthorn, with strap-shaped leaves and forked spikes of black and white fragrant flowers; and *Nymphoides peltata*, the water fringe, which has three-petalled bright yellow, fringed flowers and round, crinkly-edged, floating leaves.

Marginal aquatics
For spring flowering the *Calthas* (kingcups or marsh marigolds) are unexcelled. *Caltha palustris* has round, smooth leaves and bunches of large golden, buttercup-like flowers. The variety 'Plena' is double and 'Alba' white. All of them grow 9 to 12 inches high. The nine-inch blue water forget-me-nots (*Myosotis palustris*) are other early bloomers, as is *Lysichitum americanum*, a giant aroid with 12- to 15-inch-high brilliant yellow flowers which appear before the leaves. The latter are large, so this is a plant for pools of medium or large size.

Two aquatics of creeping habit, equally at home in wet mud or shallow water, are the bog bean (*Menyanthea trifoliata*), with bunches of pink and white fringed flowers and bean-shaped leaves, and the bog arum (*Calla palustris*), which has small white 'arum' flowers followed by red berries and shining heart-shaped

leaves. Both grow to a height of about eight inches.

Later in the season come the aquatic *Irises*, particularly *Iris pseudacorus* 'Variegata', with yellow flowers and leaves splashed in cream and green, and *I. laevigata*, which is deep blue – or white, pink and bicoloured in its forms – all of which grow around two feet tall. The flowering rush (*Butomus umbellatus*) grows to two feet, with umbels of pink blossoms and long narrow leaves. The pickerel weed (*Pontederia cordata*), also two feet tall, has spikes of soft blue florets throughout the summer, and shiny, heart-shaped leaves on long stems.

For contrast, there are ornamental sedges and rushes like the porcupine quill or zebra rush (*Scirpus tabernaemontani* 'Zebrinus'), with fat, rush-like stems alternately barred in white and green, or *S. albescens*, which is longitudinally striped. Both are four to five feet tall. *Juncus effusus* 'Spiralis' grows like a corkscrew, and *Acorus calamus* 'Variegatus', a striking member of the arum family, looks like a variegated *Iris*, but with brown horn-like spikes of flowers and aromatic leaves and roots.

Underwater oxygenators
These are largely unseen in ponds, except for a few which come to the surface to flower. Most have tiny or finely divided leaves, but few roots. Since they are largely present to maintain balanced conditions it is important to select those that are best for oxygenating purposes.

These include the water crowfoot (*Ranunculus aquatilis*) with white flowers which, in a thriving community, spangle the surface in early spring; the water violet (*Hottonia palustris*), with spikes of pale mauve florets in whorls on three-inch stems; Canadian pondweed (*Elodea canadensis*); water thyme (*Lagarosiphon major*); various pondweeds like *Potamogeton natans* and *P. crispus* (frog's lettuce); and the starworts: *Callitriche palustris* (*C. verna*) for spring and *C. hermaphroditica* (*C. autumnalis*) which persists throughout the autumn.

Floating plants
Since the most decorative floaters are tropical, they are unsuitable for outdoor

Nymphaea 'Pink Opal'

Nymphaea 'Marliacea Chromatella'

Pontederia cordata

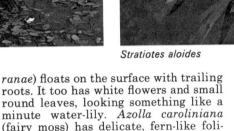
Stratiotes aloides

pools in cold or cool climates. But they can be grown in indoor water gardens (see page 177) and be put outside for the summer. Among the hardiest are the water soldiers (*Stratiotes aloides*), which have spiky leaves resembling pineapple tops. These remain under the surface but come up to flower; the three-petalled, white flowers are similar in the sexes but these are on separate plants. In autumn, winter buds are formed and sink to the bottom, where they remain until life begins again in spring.

The frogbit (*Hydrocharis morsus-ranae*) floats on the surface with trailing roots. It too has white flowers and small round leaves, looking something like a minute water-lily. *Azolla caroliniana* (fairy moss) has delicate, fern-like foliage that turns red in autumn.

Bog plants

Many bog plants can be grown without a pool of any kind, but the bog is their true home and in soil which never dries out there is a marked difference between these and border specimens. To keep up the moisture content, mix the existing soil with liberal quantities of leaf-mould or peat, rotted manure and coarse sand. In very porous ground it may be advisable to take out 12 inches of soil and line the excavation with plastic sheeting, punctured in places around the sides. Or install a thin shell of concrete (so that this slowly leaks). Put two or three inches of stones over the bottom and return the soil.

Suitable for boggy areas are most of the monkshoods (*Aconitum napellus* and its varieties), mostly blue and bicoloured, and summer-flowering; the feathery *Astilbes*, in pink, white, red or dark crimson and around two feet tall; and all the trumpet-flowered and sweetly scented day lilies (*Hemerocallis* hybrids) in gold, pink, crimson and yellow. These look well even when out of bloom.

Moisture-loving *Irises*, like the grassy-leaved and mostly blue-flowered *Iris sibirica*, come in early summer, followed by the flat heads of *I. kaempferi*, in self-colours or marbled, splashed and striated with several shades. The last need dryer conditions in winter but are worth trying for they are so striking. All are around two feet tall.

The globe flowers (*Trollius europaeus* and other species and their hybrids) look like giant round-headed buttercups. There are also hosts of waterside *Primulas*, of which the candelabra types like *Primula japonica*, *P. pulverulenta*, *P. beesiana* and *P. sikkimensis* are gayest.

Ranunculus aquatilis

Iris laevigata 'Oxford Blue'

Lysichitum americanum

Primula japonica

175

Water-garden health

A balanced pool is the key to clear water and healthy conditions in waterside features. Within its confines is represented a complete world in miniature, with plants and fish living in partnership, each utilizing the others' wastes.

Perhaps the most important single item in ensuring clear water is plenty of submerged vegetation. When pools become green or discoloured it is because there is too much organic matter present and insufficient plants. As a consequence, airborne spores of algae arrive, feed on the mineral salts released by the rotting organic material, and multiply at a rapid rate. It is these minute algae that make the water a murky green.

To check their growth there must be competition for food and a curtailment of light – another essential for algae. Underwater plants absorb the salts; water-lily leaves and other aquatics shade the pool surface. Additionally, the first are oxygenators and take up carbon dioxide (emitted by fish and other creatures) in order to make food. In so doing they have their own waste product – oxygen – and this is released to the water for the fish to breathe. Thus there is a continuing cycle. Submerged plants also provide nurseries for fish eggs, and their tangled masses shelter the young fry from enemies – including their own cannabalistic parents.

To ensure clear water, then, never use organic material in plant containers (see page 173), plant plenty of underwater plants, prevent organic seepage draining into the pool and don't introduce the wrong fish. No pool is balanced without its quota of fish, but do choose varieties which keep near the surface – like goldfish, golden orfe, comets and shubunkins – rather than bottom-dwellers like tench which constantly stir up mud.

Balanced quotas

Contrary to popular belief, there cannot be too many oxygenators in the early stages. Once the pool settles (usually after 12 or 18 months) any surplus can be pulled out as required. When deciding on the number of fish, allowance must be made for growth.

Snails are *not* essential. Some scavenge waste material, but fish manure helps to fertilize plants, and certain snails attack plants. If you must have them go for ramshorns (*Planorbis corneus*) or freshwater winkles (*Paludina vivipara*) – never the freshwater whelk (*Limnaea stagnalis*).

As a very rough guide to quotas, a pool six feet square (or seven feet in diameter) can accommodate 1 water-lily, 18 oxygenators, about 8 ornamental aquatics and 6 fish. One 9 by 12 feet (or 12 feet in diameter) can take 2 lilies, 24

Two species of *Cyperus* in a conservatory pool

oxygenators, 12 ornamentals and 18 fish. A tub, approximately 20 inches high, will hold one water-lily, six underwater oxygenators, three or four ornamental aquatics and about four small fish.

Water-garden troubles

Floating scum
Green or brown floating scum, sometimes accompanied by an oily film, often occurs in brand-new pools. This is easily removed by drawing a sheet of newspaper across the surface, or flooding over the water so that it is carried away on to the surrounding ground.

Blanket weed
This is the name given to filamentous types of algae which form long tresses and twine round the stems of plants. These are best removed by hand or with a butterfly net. Twirling a notched stick in the centre of the patches also brings it out.

Winter protection
With some pools and in some areas, you may need to provide winter protection. Float a ball or block of wood in the pool in autumn, and in prolonged frosts let an inch of ice form. Then remove the ball by pouring boiling water over it, and bale out about an inch of water from below the ice. Cover the hole. The ice acts like the glass of a greenhouse; the layer of air between it and the water minimizes the effect of further freezing weather. Naturally, the water must be topped up again after each thaw. Alternatively, with very small containers, a pool heater, with thermostatic control, can be installed.

Aphids
To remove aphids on water-lily leaves, hose them into the water for the fish to devour. In bad cases submerge the leaves for a few hours (by laying a hoop over the crowns) and let the pests drown. Never use pesticides, or you may poison the fish.

Problems with fish
Sudden death of a fish can be due to cats, rough handling, or weedkillers or pesticide sprays seeping or drifting into the water. There are also various diseases and parasites that may afflict fish; you should consult a specialist book or supplier for advice.

A water-lily tub

If you have no room to construct a proper pool, you can still grow water plants and keep a few fish in a tub; a half-barrel about two feet in diameter and 12 to 18 inches deep is suitable. Choose a water-lily to suit the depth of water, and plant it and a few ornamental aquatics in small baskets. Be sure to include some underwater oxygenators. You can have about four small fish.

In the depths of winter such a tub can be moved to a sheltered place and protected with straw packed around the outside, tied with string or sacking. Cover the top with glass, but allow air to get in.

Indoor water gardens

With increasing interest in sun-lounges, lean-to greenhouses or conservatories and garden rooms, indoor pools are becoming popular. These provide an extremely attractive focal point in such a setting. They also provide a home for colourful fish – tropical or hardy.

Indoor pools should be constructed of concrete with a waterproof finish (even if they are to be faced with tiles). They can have raised sides – being built on to the floor – or be partially sunk, but in any case must have a curb of some kind. This is essential to prevent accidents and stop things rolling into the water,

Nymphaea stellata

and it also provides a seat or shelf for pot-plants. Indoor pools should also be connected to a drain and have a plug for emptying. If the plants are grown in pots, it is a simple matter to remove these for cleaning purposes. Heating (if required) can be provided with water-proof pool-heater units, which are obtainable from aquatic dealers.

It is also possible to use free-standing tubs or large glass-fibre containers as indoor pools. Or, for a very simple, shallow pool in a conservatory – really suitable only for growing a few potted marginals – use a butyl pool-liner inside walls formed from stacked (but not cemented) bricks. The scope for indoor pools is wide and not yet commercially exploited, but fountains and running water effects are possible, using a pump.

Indoor aquatics

In general, the planting methods and soil used for indoor water-garden plants are similar to those recommended for outdoor pools (see page 173) and many of the same species can be installed (page 174). Among a number of exotic and interesting aquatics that can only be grown indoors in cool climates are tropical water-lilies derived from *Nymphaea capensis*, *N. stellata* and *N. lotus* (the last night-blooming). The flowers of these stand well above the water, and there are blue and purple sorts as well as white, yellow, pink and red. The tubers are started into growth in early spring – they need warmth at this stage, so a heater is helpful – and at the end of summer die down and disappear. The exciting lotus (*Nelumbo nucifera*), with long-stalked round leaves poised like tea trays, and large pink, rose or white blooms, is another possibility.

Some easily grown marginals include the Egyptian paper rush (*Cyperus papyrus*), a splendid plant with huge 'mop' heads of grassy inflorescences on six-to eight-foot stems, as well as a number of smaller species of *Cyperus* (see page 54). You can also grow the taro (*Colocasia esculenta antiquorum*), with large green or purplish leaves shaped like elephant's ears, and yellow arum-like flowers on 18-inch stems. *Xanthosoma nigrum* (*X. violaceum*), the spoon flower, is also bright yellow and arum-like, but has arrow-shaped, purplish, smooth leaves on three- to five-foot purple stems.

Rice (*Oryza sativa*) and sugar cane (*Saccharum officinarum*) can also be grown in indoor pools, together with the lovely floating water hyacinth (*Eichhornia crassipes*), scourge of the tropics but harmless in cool climates. This forms a rosette of leaves, with swollen sausage-shaped leaf-stalks which make them buoyant, and has spikes of showy mauve-blue and gold flowers.

Indoor fish

In unheated indoor pools the best fish to keep are shubunkins, comets, veiltails and moors – all colourful goldfish varieties but too delicate to leave outside. Heated pools will provide a haven for all sorts of tropical fish, such as guppies, sword-tails and gouramis.

An indoor water garden like that **below** (in the Berlin botanical gardens) brings an extremely exotic effect to a conservatory. **above** Pools are also possible in the home, but must be well lit for plants to thrive. Less opulent versions are quite easy to build.

177

Bonsai, the ancient art

The Chinese first began transplanting naturally dwarfed trees from mountainsides and cliff-tops into ornamental containers, and it was they who first began to appreciate the weird, twisted beauty of these trees in their own homes and gardens. The Japanese, however, have since been responsible for perfecting the art of cultivating bonsai trees. The word *bonsai* simply means 'a plant in a tray'. Authentic records of bonsai trees date from the early 14th century, and it is quite possible that their culture originated over a thousand years ago. Recently the interest in bonsai culture has spread to the West, and today bonsai clubs can be found in most countries.

Although perennial herbs and even common weeds are sometimes grown as summer bonsai, it is generally accepted that most bonsai are trees or shrubs. These can be gathered in the wild – with the landowner's permission when necessary! – naturally dwarfed because of the soil and climate conditions in which they have grown. Or they can be cultivated from seed, cuttings, layering or grafting (see page 228). Although a number of bonsai trees produce seed, when planted their seed will not automatically produce a dwarfed tree. Grown unchecked, seeds and cuttings too will naturally assume the height and form of their species. Special training methods, as explained on page 184, are essential.

When one first sees a 25-year-old maple that mirrors its counterpart in a garden or meadow – except that it is only 12 inches high – it is excusable to regard it with a certain disbelief. How is it possible to keep a tree so small? Surely it must take considerable skill and expertise? In fact this miniaturization of a tree or shrub is not at all difficult, although it demands time and patience.

The everyday needs of a bonsai tree are exactly the same as those of any other tree. It must never be allowed to dry out; it needs nourishment and a good growing mixture for the roots to develop. And it needs air and light; no bonsai should ever be kept permanently indoors. Initially, by confining any wide-rooting plant in a container, it will tend to grow more slowly than when planted in the open, but the plant will still grow, and it is essential that a natural balance be maintained between the size of the root ball and the spread of the top growth. So top-pruning is necessary to keep the tree healthy, to maintain its size and to shape it.

Bonsai culture is not cruel, any more than is the practice of keeping houseplants in pots, or of pruning fruit trees or hedges. Bonsai trees live for hundreds of years. They flower and produce fruit in season, and if properly cared for will long outlive their relations in fields and woods. Occasionally one will come across a bonsai tree hundreds of years old. Such trees are highly prized in the bonsai world and the wealthy enthusiast will pay highly for these rare and beautiful specimens. But beginners in bonsai culture, like amateur artists, may find consolation in the thought that their own efforts can be just as satisfying as someone else's masterpiece.

A Western-style display of bonsai trees against a terrace wall

A ten-inch-tall needle juniper (*Juniperus rigida*) 90 years old, in split-trunk style

Trees for bonsai culture

Since the aim of bonsai is to mirror in miniature the whole form of a mature wild tree, care is needed when choosing varieties for bonsai culture, for the parts of the tree should always remain reasonably in scale. Generally speaking, kinds with small needles or leaves are best, since, although the leaves of deciduous trees can be reduced in size to a certain extent, this is much more difficult with conifers.

Japanese hornbeam (*Carpinus japonica*) group

A guide to bonsai leaves

A wide range of trees and shrubs can be grown as bonsai, and **above** are the leaves of a number of common subjects — approximately life-size — that you may find in a bonsai nursery: **1** Japanese black pine (*Pinus thunbergii*), **2** a short-needled variety of spruce (*Picea*), **3** the yew (*Taxus bacata*), **4** Japanese cedar (*Cryptomeria japonica*) and **5** Chinese juniper (*Juniperus chinensis*) — all evergreens — and the following deciduous trees: **6** trident maple (*Acer trifidum*), **7** beech (*Fagus* sp), **8** birch (*Betula* sp), **9** Chinese elm (*Ulmus parvifolia*) and **10** hornbeam (*Carpinus* sp). The others also bear flowers: **11** crab apple (*Malus floribunda*), **12** various species of *Prunus*, including flowering cherries, peaches and apricots, **13** *Wisteria*, **14** rock cotoneaster (*Cotoneaster horizontalis*) and **15** small-leaved species of *Azalea*.

A young double-grafted bonsai peach (*Prunus persica*)

The most popular evergreen trees for bonsai are pines (*Pinus*), junipers (*Juniperus*) and spruces (*Picea*). The two latter generally have very short needle-like leaves. Among the pines, short-needled varieties are preferable, although the Japanese black pine (*Pinus thunbergii*) can have its rather long needles reduced in size by removing all new growth every second year. Other popular evergreens include *Cryptomeria* (Japanese cedar) and yew (*Taxus*).

Most deciduous trees can have their leaves dramatically reduced in size by not re-potting too often and by leaf cutting (see page 184). Again, varieties with fairly small leaves are generally preferred to begin with, and these include various maples (*Acer*), elms (*Ulmus* and *Zelkova*), hornbeams (*Carpinus*), beeches (*Fagus*) and birches (*Betula*).

When choosing flowering and fruiting trees, bear in mind the size both of leaves and of flowers and fruit, so that the tree will look in scale at all times of the year. For instance, a normal apple tree will look very odd when it fruits, but crab apples (*Malus*) will look perfectly in scale, the fruit being about the size of a large cherry. Many shrubs with small flowers and fruit – such as *Cotoneaster* – make excellent bonsai.

179

The beauty of bonsai

A bonsai tree growing for years in a simple container is not a contradiction of nature: it is an attempt, however modest, to portray nature in miniature. The purpose of a bonsai tree is not, however, simply to emulate nature, but rather to capture the essence, the spirit of its wild brother, so that by gazing upon it one should be able to envisage where the tree might be growing. Rugged and twisted junipers and pines suggest the weight of snow on their lowered branches and their brave struggle for survival through years of fighting the elements. A group of slender-trunked maples imply gentle country meadows and the warmth of the summer sun.

The grandeur of the wild tree is maintained by training in the bonsai. Like a wild tree, the bonsai is unique, but unlike the natural tree, every moment in the life of a bonsai can be shared. In the spring, one is struck by the beauty of the first orchard of the year in full bloom, and the millions of flowers will be remembered; but because of their sheer number it becomes impossible to fully appreciate each one. A bonsai crab apple each year brings forth a multitude of delicate flowers and one is able to observe the perfection in the silent opening of a single flower. With a small collection of bonsai trees one no longer misses the small wonders of nature that were lost before. After noticing the reddening of the autumn leaves or the stark elegance of a bonsai tree in winter, one will regard the greater expanse of nature with newly opened eyes.

The pot and stand

In the bonsai composition, the pot has a purpose similar to that of a picture-frame. It must complement the tree and not detract from it by being too showy or highly coloured. As the container must last for two or three years – sometimes more with older trees – it should be chosen with considerable care.

Container sizes range from less than an inch to more than 18 inches high. The very shallow ones are often used for groups of trees or miniature landscapes; tall containers, usually round or square, are designed for cascade trees. The pot should be roughly one-half to one-third the capacity of the upper part of the tree.

Colours are usually restrained. Shades of brown, dark blue, green or off-white are common. Brighter colours are occasionally used with flowering trees, but to avoid mistakes it is always safer to stick to more subdued shades. The pot may be glazed outside, but never inside. Plainer shapes – rectangular, oval, round or hexagonal – are usually better than more fancy designs, especially for evergreens and the more formally trained trees.

Bonsai pots should have sufficient drainage holes to allow stale water to seep away and to allow good air circulation around the roots. As the tree will spend most of the year outside, both winter and summer, the pot should be frost-proof, so that it does not shatter in freezing conditions. Bonsai suppliers generally stock a range of home-produced and Japanese bonsai pots.

A simple stand – a slab of wood or a

A 40-year-old trident maple (*Acer trifidum*) trained in the informal upright style

Bonsai pots and trays

Containers for bonsai trees vary in form, but shapes are generally simple and colours restrained. The tall pots are used only for cascade trees, while the shallow pans are for groups and landscapes. Ornaments, such as the Japanese lantern shown, are often used in landscapes or to set off a bonsai display.

split bamboo mat, for example – can enhance the bonsai display in the home. Taller trees and cascade trees need a higher and wider stand. A small ornament, a bronze figurine or even a stone can complement the composition.

Bonsai styles

Bonsai trees and plants vary greatly in size and style. Miniature specimens, up to six inches high, are usually naturally dwarf plants trained even smaller than normal, or plants with very small leaves and flowers. Small bonsai are grown up to 12 inches, and medium trees from 1 to 2½ feet high. Bonsai do not have to be small, and large bonsai trees over three feet high are grown; some magnificent specimens at the Imperial Palace in Tokyo are more than six feet tall and hundreds of years old.

The most important classification of style refers to the angle at which the trunk stands in the container. The formal upright tree is planted vertically, with the branches forming a triangular silhouette. A classical style, it is particularly suited to needle evergreens. An informal upright tree leans slightly to one side, and has a more relaxed feeling. In the leaning style, the trunk is trained at approximately 45° and gives the impression of a tree growing against sea winds. Except for naturally upright trees, most varieties are suitable for this style.

The semi-cascade tree grows almost horizontally, giving the feeling of a barren mountain-side and a fight to stay alive. The full cascade, in which the tree is trained downwards, evokes the image of a wild tree growing on a steep cliff, turbulent with frequent falls of rock and a battering wind, forced to bend against the elements. Only trees which grow naturally in such locations – pines, junipers and *Cotoneasters* – are suitable.

Groups and landscapes should always be planned in uneven numbers of trees to avoid symmetry. Most trees can be grown in the double or triple trunk style, but a fairly easy way to produce a group is to lay a tree down in the pot, burying the trunk. The branches are then trained upwards to form the 'trees'. More elaborate trees and groups are trained so that the roots grow over a stone. Most trees can be cultivated in this way, but maples are most favoured in Japan.

A bonsai *Ginkgo* 80 years old

Styles of bonsai trees

Bonsai styles are classified according to the angle at which the trunk stands in the pot, and range from the formal upright style, in which the trunk grows straight and vertical, to the full cascade, in which it is trained so that the upper growth sweeps down below the pot. The most popular bonsai styles today are the simple but relaxed forms, such as the informal upright and leaning styles, together with small groups.

Semi-cascade

Leaning

Cascade

Formal upright

Informal upright

Roots-over-rock

Double trunk

Raft

Windswept

Group

181

Acquiring and caring for bonsai

Most bonsai trees sold at garden centres and shops, and at specialist nurseries, are of excellent quality, but there are a few points to bear in mind when buying. Besides the age and shape of the tree, its general health is of the utmost importance. The soil should be damp but not sodden unless it has just been watered; it should certainly not be rock-hard and dry. The leaves should look bright and healthy, not burnt around the edges or spotted. If buying a deciduous tree in winter, the last year's growth should be smooth and plump, with no sign of the bark wrinkling.

The tree should be steady in its container – which ought to have at least one drainage hole. Moss growing on the surface could mean that the tree has been in its pot for months or years – or that the dealer has taken trouble in potting it. A white fungus in and around the drainage hole is natural and harmless.

General care

When buying a tree from a shop during the summer, be sure to give it at least two weeks outside, avoiding heavy rain and high winds, before displaying it indoors. However, if a tree is bought from an indoor centre in winter, do not allow it to be exposed to frost for the rest of the season as it will probably have begun to shoot. This is most important with deciduous trees, and while varieties of junipers are very hardy, it is as well not to take any chances. They will, of course, benefit from fresh air during milder weather, or can be kept in a cool greenhouse or conservatory.

Bonsai trees are *not* permanent houseplants; even semi-tropical trees should be stood outside when the weather permits. Most bonsai are hardy trees and shrubs whose natural habitat is the open air. Even with the most exacting care it is wrong to assume that they can be made to live indoors for more than a few days at a time; extending this can only damage the tree. During the summer the plant must be able to carry out the process of photosynthesis, and during the winter it is resting and building up its strength for the coming spring. Too long in a warm room will persuade it that spring has arrived early and it will start budding. If this happens more than once, the tree will simply die of exhaustion.

When trees are occasionally brought indoors, their position should be chosen with care. The ideal spot is light, but away from sources of high temperature such as a fire, radiator or even the top of a television. The whole tree should be sprayed once or twice a day, more often in centrally heated houses. Check the tree daily for dryness, and water when necessary. Trees in shallow pots will need spraying and watering more often than those in deep pots. Do not leave the trees standing in a bowl of water as this may rot the roots. In winter it is a good idea to put the tree in a cold room overnight. When replacing the tree outdoors be sure not to allow it to freeze for at least two weeks.

Regular and continuous care – a few minutes of attention each day – will keep a collection of bonsai trees alive and well.

A good specimen of Chinese juniper (*Juniperus chinensis*) 45 years old, in coiled style

Bonsai care

Watering
In summer, trees may need watering twice a day; in winter, perhaps only once every few weeks. The amount of watering needed depends on the dryness of the soil. Rainwater is best, but tap water that has stood for a few hours is adequate. Use a watering can with a fine rose. In summer, trees should be watered in the early morning or late afternoon to avoid the midday heat. In winter, water early to permit any excess to drain before the night frost. Plunging the pot into a bowl to soak is ideal for recently potted trees, small collections and for trees that have dried out.

Feeding
Trees should be fed with a weak liquid organic fertilizer at intervals of 10 to 12 days during spring and summer. Solid organic fertilizers can be used, but they sometimes form moulds or produce smells. During wet weather cut down on the feeding or weak, sappy growth will result.

Mildew
If air circulation is good, spraying the leaves with cold water will help inhibit mildew. But if necessary treat with a proprietary brand of fungicide.

Pests
Any insect pest likely to attack a tree growing wild will also attack a bonsai specimen. Aphids are particularly troublesome, but a heavily diluted insecticide will control insect pests. Ants and worms disturb the soil surface, and the former encourage their 'herds' of aphids. Both can be removed by plunging the whole tree into water for 24 hours. Wood lice hide under pots, so lift them regularly for inspection. Regular spraying with cold water will discourage insect attack.

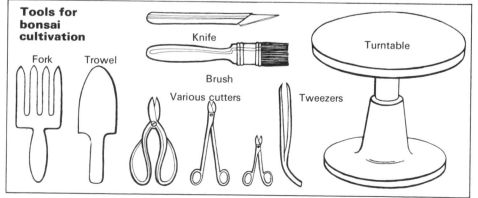

Tools for bonsai cultivation

Fork • Trowel • Knife • Brush • Various cutters • Tweezers • Turntable

The natural tree

In Japan, the most admired bonsai trees are those that nature has trained herself. Wherever growing conditions are a struggle, the tiny tree that has fought for decades to survive storms and droughts might be found – high in the mountains clinging to a cliff, or even on a grassy moorland constantly being pruned back by wild deer.

When collecting from nature there are three essential rules: First find a suitable tree; second, always secure the owner's permission before removing it; and, third, be sure that it can be looked after: Wild trees, unless little more than seedlings, need almost constant care for the first few months, as the shock of transplanting is considerable.

The best season to lift a wild tree is the early spring. The necessary tools are a small spade or strong trowel, secateurs, a saw, a strong knife, plastic bags or polythene sheeting, sphagnum moss, scissors and string.

The first step is to dig a trench around the tree at the farthest extent of its branches. The roots of normal trees extend this far; the roots of dwarfed trees have often been forced to seek nourishment much farther from the main trunk. Avoid cutting roots over half an inch in diameter until the trench is complete.

Once the trench is dug, cut all the roots over half an inch in diameter. All roots should be cut so that the cut slants in at the bottom, helping to prevent moisture lying on the wound. If the soil is firm, and there are plenty of small roots near the

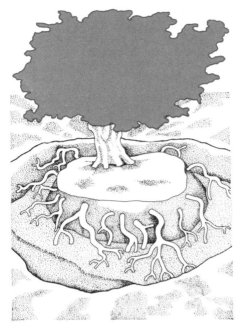

Lifting a wild bonsai tree
To minimize shock to the tree, raise it in one session only if there is plenty of fine root growth near the trunk. Otherwise, cut a few roots at a time over months or years.

trunk, grasp the root-ball in both hands and gently rock it to and fro. If there is no tap root the tree can be lifted almost straight out; otherwise the tap root should be cut as low down as possible. The

tree should then be studied carefully and all unnecessary foliage and branches be trimmed out. This gives the roots a chance to recover and reduces the surface area that can lose moisture.

If the tree has only a few hair roots close to the trunk and the main roots are thick and long, it will be at least a year before the tree can be lifted with safety. Cut only half the roots on the first visit, leaving the others undisturbed; fill the trench with peat moss. After a year – and providing that the fine ciliary roots have grown sufficiently – the remaining roots may be cut and the tree lifted. Some specimens, especially the older pines, may have to be left longer, the roots being cut over a number of years.

Once the tree has been lifted, large wounds on the roots should be sealed with proprietary sealant, as used in tree surgery. Pack damp sphagnum moss around the root-ball and keep it in place with a plastic bag. Another large plastic bag put over the top of the tree slows down evaporation during the journey home.

The tree can be planted straight into a training pot if the root-ball is small enough; otherwise it should be planted in the open ground for a year to allow the ciliary roots a greater chance to develop. Pruning should be carried out whenever necessary, but do not attempt any training with wire during the first year. After replanting, the tree should be protected from strong wind, heavy rain and harsh sunlight, and sprayed with cold water at least twice a day for three months.

Shelter and display

Although most bonsai trees are hardy, prolonged frosts can occasionally cause damage to the more delicate varieties, and winter protection should be given to them. This need be little more than bringing the tree into a cold garage or even turning a small cardboard carton over the top of the tree. However, to help both the outdoor display of the trees and their seasonal protection, it is well worth constructing a more lasting display bench in a quiet corner, preferably against a western hedge or fence.

The number of trees in the collection will determine the size of the stand. When calculating the dimensions, be sure to allow each tree plenty of space. To allow for easier working the stand should be made a little higher than an indoor table. It should be made of good quality wood, treated with a preservative, or it could have a metal frame with a wooden top. The trees can be placed on a gravel bed as this cuts down on the need to water; but in this case they should be lifted every now and then to make sure the roots are not growing into the gravel.

Above the stand, around the sides and at the back a weather-shade of thin timber laths or canes should be made. Each strip should be secured an inch apart. This will help protect the trees from all extremes: hot sunlight, heavy rain, high winds and even a certain amount of frost. For harder winter conditions the bottom of the stand can be enclosed and the trees placed inside. A tool drawer or rack can be incorporated under one end.

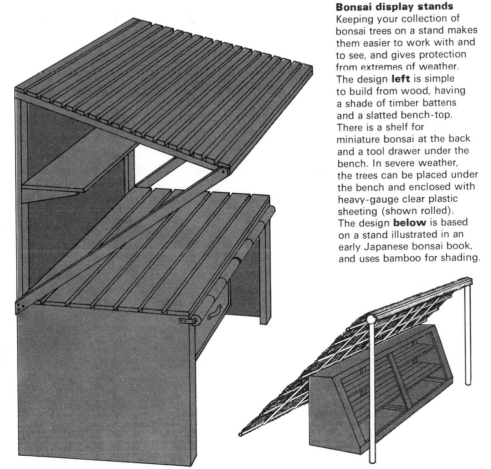

Bonsai display stands
Keeping your collection of bonsai trees on a stand makes them easier to work with and to see, and gives protection from extremes of weather. The design **left** is simple to build from wood, having a shade of timber battens and a slatted bench-top. There is a shelf for miniature bonsai at the back and a tool drawer under the bench. In severe weather, the trees can be placed under the bench and enclosed with heavy-gauge clear plastic sheeting (shown rolled). The design **below** is based on a stand illustrated in an early Japanese bonsai book, and uses bamboo for shading.

Training bonsai trees

Bonsai trees need training throughout their life. This has two main purposes: first, to maintain the small size of a naturally large tree and, second, to give it an appearance of age and maturity. Pruning and wiring are the two principal methods used, and pruning is by far the most important. It is carried out throughout the life of a tree, whereas wiring is only used to change the shape of the tree fairly radically or quickly – generally when it is young. Most pruning is very slight, but is carried out frequently. And even when the position of just one branch requires adjustment the rest of the tree still has to be pruned.

Also important for maintaining a good tree are repotting and root pruning, but root pruning alone has relatively little

The same seedling juniper after potting, wiring and initial pruning

A seedling juniper (*Juniperus communis*)

effect on the overall growth of the tree. For a few weeks growth will be retarded, but as the fine ciliary roots grow closer to the trunk the tree tends to grow more vigorously than before.

How to prune

Branch, twig and leaf pruning are among the most important processes in the life of a bonsai tree. They maintain the health of the tree by removing dead or diseased wood and maintaining a balance between the size of the root ball and the extent of the top growth. Pruning creates and preserves the desired shape of the tree; it also helps to keep the leaves small and encourages the production of flower buds.

Pruning instruments should always be sharp and clean. Blunt tools leave a ragged stump, a doorway for disease and insect pests, and clean tools prevent the spread of disease from one tree to another. Heavy pruning cuts should be whittled down to a slight hollow in the trunk or branch, to encourage the formation of a callous. Large cuts can be painted with protective paint. When pruning a branch try to make the cut just above a bud that is pointing in the direction you want the branch to grow. If the cut slopes downwards, then water will run off and the chances of rot will be considerably lessened.

Branch and twig pruning

When carrying out basic pruning in order to create a tree's style, begin by deciding which is the front of the tree.

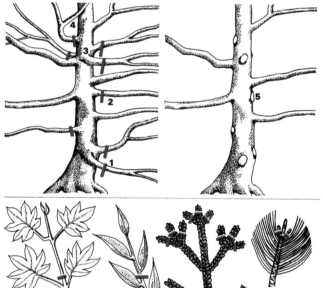

Main branch pruning

Heavy pruning should be carried out in autumn, winter or early spring, and is the major way of shaping a bonsai tree. The main priorities are to remove any branch that is too low at the front **1**, any branch directly opposite another **2**, any that creates a so-called cartwheel effect **3** and any that crosses the front or back to the other side of the tree **4**. Hollow out all stumps with a sharp knife **5**.

General pruning

Throughout the growing season, cut back shoots of maples **1**, zelkovas **2** and other broad-leaves to the first or second pair of leaves. Pinch out the tips of juniper shoots **3**. With pines **4**, remove the centre 'candles' and pinch back the others.

Leaf cutting

Do this in early summer on deciduous trees that do not flower or fruit. Use sharp scissors to remove half of each leaf **1** on weak branches or trees, but all but the stalk **2** on strong wood. In a few weeks the stalk will drop and new small foliage and shoots will grow.

Studying it at eye level, the front is the angle at which the tree looks best and most natural. There should be few branches at the front, but ample around the sides and at the back; most bonsai trees in the upright styles also lean slightly towards the front.

First remove all dead or diseased wood, together with any branches growing directly to the front if they come from the lower half of the trunk. You should generally remove any branch growing opposite to one that you want to keep, and also any branch growing from one side to the other, around the front or back. Finally, where four or five branches grow at the same level – the 'cartwheel' effect common in pines in particular – they should be thinned to one branch only.

Any remaining branches can now be thinned so that they form a spiral which becomes thicker near the top of the tree: a branch to the left, one to the right and a smaller one at the back of the tree, so progressing up the length of the trunk. Much the same rules apply when pruning twigs, except that they do not need to be grown in a spiral. All branchlets and twigs should be shortened so that the 'top to bottom' balance is preserved.

Prune the main branches of most trees at the end of the winter. Flowering trees, however, should be cut back hard after flowering, and pruned as little as possible during the growing season. General pruning is nevertheless necessary all through the growing season on both deciduous and evergreen trees. Where possible, use your finger tips. This is particularly important on junipers and other evergreens; cutting their leaves will make the remaining tips turn brown, and it will be a full season before they recover. On deciduous trees, you can avoid too much cutting by rubbing off unwanted buds. Then allow those remaining to develop into branches with four or five sets of leaves before pruning back to the first or second leaf.

Leaf cutting
In early summer, provided that the tree is healthy and not too old, and has been well fertilized, leaf cutting can be carried out on deciduous trees that do not produce flowers or fruit. This is one of the 'secrets' of bonsai training, and its effect is to produce fine, bushy growth, smaller leaves and better autumn colouring. It consists simply of snipping off some or all of the leaves. The tree then has a false autumn, the petioles (leaf-stalks) drop, and new, finer growth soon sprouts from the leaf buds.

Wiring
Often considered the most difficult training technique, wiring is used to bend the trunk and branches of a tree to the required shape. Beginners can learn to judge tension in different sized branches, and the various ways of securing wire, by first practising on a small branch from an ordinary tree or shrub. Never rush. It is important to consider the tree from all angles, deciding upon the style to be achieved and the position in which each branch is to be trained, first.

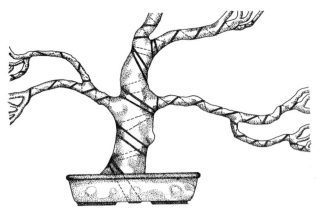

Copper wire, though expensive, is most suitable since it remains soft after being annealed in a slow fire. Galvanized iron or plastic-coated wire can be used, though they are less easy to work with and look ugly on the tree. Suitable wire sizes range from 8, the largest, to 24. Gentle bending of a branch before wiring will increase its flexibility and indicate the correct wire to be used – the one with slightly more tension than the branch. Tender-barked trees, such as maples, should be wired with paper-wrapped wire to protect the bark.

Deciduous trees should be wired after their leaves have matured, in early summer, and the wires removed in autumn to avoid wounding the bark. Coniferous trees should be wired during the winter months; since they take considerably longer to become fixed in

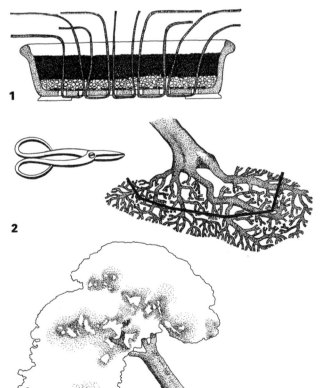

1

2

3

Wiring a tree
Begin wiring from the base of the trunk, anchoring the wire in the soil. You may need two wires to hold the trunk in position. Then proceed to the main and the smaller branches, ending with the highest twigs. Wires should be wound at about 45° to the line of the branch; at a much greater or lesser angle it will not hold the branch. Gauge the tension carefully. Tight wiring cuts into the bark, but loose wiring will slip.

position, the wires should be left for 12 to 18 months. All trees should be protected from hot sun and heavy rain for a month after wiring.

Repotting and root pruning
Bonsai trees should be repotted every two to three years, preferably in early spring, though winter jasmine and certain other trees can be repotted at almost any time of the year. A pot of the same size, or slightly larger, should be used. At the same time, the root ball should be pruned and any dead growth removed.

The soil mixture consists of seven parts of sterilized loam to which is added three parts of sharp sand for evergreens, two parts of sharp sand and one part of peat for deciduous trees, or one part of sharp sand and two parts of peat for flowering and fruiting trees.

Repotting and root pruning
Remove the tree from its pot by running a knife around the sides and knocking the outside with the heel of the hand. **1** Clean the pot and cover the drainage holes with small pieces of plastic netting. Insert holding wires – garden wire used to hold the tree in position – through the drainage holes. Sprinkle sterilized gravel or flint chippings on the bottom for good drainage, and cover with a layer of suitable potting mixture. **2** After teasing the roots out, remove dead growth and cut back the remaining root ball by one to two thirds, according to the age of the tree. **3** Position the tree and tie it in with the wire, taking care not to damage the roots. Fill with more soil to within a quarter-inch of the rim, firmly working it into every crevice. Finish with a layer of finer soil. Thoroughly water the tree by immersing it to the rim in rainwater. Protect it from harsh sunlight and heavy rain for at least two weeks, watering only when needed. Do not fertilize the tree for a month.

Special bonsai plantings

The exquisite beauty of a bonsai tree well trained in a simple style, and growing in a pot of suitable size and shape, can be the focus of many hours of happy contemplation. For many people, such simplicity is all that is necessary for their enjoyment of bonsai. But others may prefer the more complex drama of a tree trained to cling to a rock, or the greater scale of a bonsai group planting. Such schemes are more complicated to create, but the basic rule of all bonsai still applies: the finished planting should evoke a natural scene.

Rock plantings

The idea for planting trees on or over rocks has sprung from nature herself – from the sight of a gnarled pine clinging to the protection of an outcrop of rock, or of small, twisted trees growing on a cliff face. In rock plantings the tree can either be planted in or on the rock itself, or it can be trained over the rock, the roots buried in soil in the container.

Rocks used for such plantings should be fairly hard, since soft rocks tend to rot after prolonged exposure to rain and frost. They should not be too smooth and should be pitted with plenty of crevices and small pockets where the roots can get a grip. Rocks with a saddle-shaped depression or a large, deep pocket are ideal for planting directly onto the rock.

A relatively small tree with small leaves – a *Cotoneaster* or a trident maple with its ample, vigorous root growth, for example – are ideal for planting on rock. A suitable 'potting' mixture can be made from five parts of sterilized loam,

A rock planting of a 50-year-old Japanese or mountain maple (*Acer palmatum*)

Planting a bonsai tree on rock
Choose a hard, rugged rock with plenty of crevices. If the tree's roots are to straddle the rock, choose also a suitable pot.

Fix copper rings to the rock with epoxy resin glue. When the glue is dry, smear a muddy potting mixture over the rock and into all cracks. Carefully wash the tree's roots.

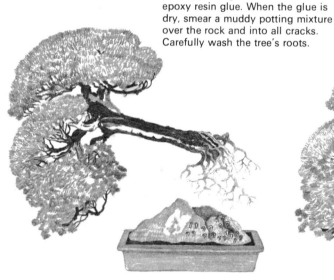

Position the tree with the roots leading down into the pot. Protect the roots with rubber and tie the tree with copper wire. Cover the roots with mud and plant moss.

four parts of wet peat and one part of coarse sand. These should be mixed with water to form a sticky mud and smeared on the dampened rock where the roots are to be secured, in crevices and small pockets. If the tree is to be stood in a large hole in the rock, the mixture should be drier – similar to that used for normal bonsai (see page 185).

The tree can be secured in position by means of small copper rings cemented onto the rock, through which wires are threaded. If the rock has plenty of cracks, a lead fishing weight can be strung onto

each length of wire, and the weight can be hammered firmly onto a crack. If the wires are to be removed eventually they can be twisted right around the rock.

Having prepared the rock, the roots of the tree should be washed, and then the tree positioned over the wet mixture and secured with the wire. Thin strips of rubber placed over the roots will protect them where the wires hold them. Smear further layers of soil mixture over to cover them. Finally, plant fine moss, secured with V-shaped pieces of copper wire; this will prevent erosion of the soil

and cut down evaporation of moisture.

Trees intended to straddle the rock should be planted in exactly the same way, except that the roots are led down into the pot. The potting mixture used is the same as normal for the type of tree. If a tree is planted directly into the rock, this can be stood in a shallow pot without drainage holes which is then half filled with coarse sand and water, to give the impression of a rocky island.

All rock plantings should be protected for a month after planting. They should be sprayed with cold water every day.

Group plantings

Whether planting a small copse of three trees, or a more ambitious miniature forest, the composition should first be planned out on paper. A shallow but wide container should be used; it can be rectangular or oval, but the latter is easier to plant. The trees selected should be of the same variety, but of various heights. They should always be planted in odd numbers – not only because the Japanese abhor even numbers (particularly four), but because it will be found in practice that a balanced composition is easier to create with odd numbers of trees (see the photograph on page 179).

The soil mixture is that used normally for the type of tree. Always start by planting the largest tree. The focal point of the composition, this main tree should be set to left or right of the centre line of the pot as seen from the front. The second tallest tree is then planted to complement the first, and so on with the remaining trees. Do not tie down the trees until the exact position for each tree has been determined.

Taller trees are usually planted to the front and smaller trees at the back and sides. This gives perspective and makes the group appear larger than it really is. Trees planted on the same line from the front to the back or from side to side would look unnatural. After planting, thin out inward-growing branches and twigs but leave them around the outer edges, except at the front.

In place of a container, groups can be planted on slabs of rock. Holes should first be drilled in the rock and securing wires threaded through them. The soil mixture used should have an extra part of peat added to conserve moisture, and when the planting is finished the soil should be covered with moss to stop the rain washing it away.

Saikei, bonseki and bonkei

Group and rock planting can be taken a stage further by adding small underplantings of alpine plants and little shrubs. Rocks can be embedded into the soil and small streams suggested by white sand. Such a planting is generally termed *saikei*. Sometimes small figures, bridges and perhaps a model hut is used to create reality. It is not necessary to use bonsai trees for saikei plantings, and relatively inexpensive landscapes can be made by using ordinary small trees and plants from a nursery. These may have to be pruned quite frequently to prevent the more vigorous plants from overrunning the others.

With a shallow tray of almost any material you can try to construct a *bonseki* composition. This generally consists of a group of rocks and stones placed in raked sand, giving the effect of small islands in the sea. Bonseki requires very little care, of course, and can be kept indoors indefinitely since there are no plants that can suffer. A larger-scale scheme can be built at floor level, making a major focal point for the room.

Bonkei is another type of tray landscape which attempts to copy exactly natural or imaginary scenes, using every available material. You can use either model or real plants, including bonsai trees, with figures, false rocks and even paint to achieve the finished effect. Bonkei is sometimes made as a picture in relief, to be framed and hung on the wall.

Bonsai group plantings
left Planted on a marble slab some three feet wide is a landscape containing, in the foreground, a number of deciduous Chinese elm (*Ulmus parvifolia*) and, behind these, evergreen spruce (*Picea*). The trees vary in age from 8 to 18 years, and are underplanted with small evergreen shrubs and moss. Rocks and gravel (to suggest a path) give a sense of perspective to the composition.
bottom An even more realistic saikei landscape here includes a bonsai rock planting, water and sand, and a model boat.
below left A bonseki tray composition uses only rocks and raked gravel.

Gardens in miniature

The charm of miniature trees and plants fascinates people of all ages and all walks of life. Many who appreciate beauty on a small scale find these enchanting little plants quite irresistible. Reginald Farrer once wrote, 'But a little garden, the littler the better, is your richest chance of success and happiness.'

Miniature gardens have a particular appeal to people who, because of lack of space or time, are deprived of full-scale gardening. For disabled or elderly people who can do no very active work, a miniature landscape creates a new world of pleasure and an enthralling hobby.

There is a wide selection of natural miniature conifers, roses, *Primulas*, daffodils, *Dianthus* and scores of other charming plants that are tiny replicas of familiar garden plants. To many people who see them for the first time they seem quite unreal. The general reaction is to marvel that these plants – so minute, so exquisitely proportioned, so delicate in appearance – are really quite hardy and not difficult to grow.

These miniatures can be planted in a window-garden or a trough, in a cavity wall or on a flat roof. The staging in a greenhouse or conservatory can be devoted to creating one complete landscape. A trough garden on a pedestal 18 to 24 inches high, or placed on a window ledge or balcony, enables one to see in full detail the beauty of the trees and plants, which might not be observed at ground level. A number of styles of miniature gardens, together with details of plants to grow in them, will be found on the following pages.

Miniature landscapes right Raised on a pedestal, a miniature trough garden is easy for an elderly or disabled person to care for. **above** In a trough 16 by 9 inches – shown about half size – are planted ten different miniature plants. At the back, from left to right, are *Rosa* 'Maid Marion', *Erinus alpinus* 'Carmineus', *Sempervivum octopodes* 'Petalum', *Zelkova nivea* (the tall shrub) and *Mesembryanthemum ornatulum*. At the front are *Hypericum anagalloides*, *Rosa roulettii*, *Centaurium portense*, *Selaginella apus* (between the rocks) and *Sedum humifusum*.

Miniature garden care

Some people think that because alpines are miniature they do not grow, and they expect them to stay the same height and spread as when first planted, remaining static without any attention. In fact, weeding, watering, cutting back, lifting and dividing are as necessary in trough gardens as in a full-scale garden.

Watering is very important because the plants' roots cannot go down in search of moisture, as they would in the open ground. Even in winter this might be necessary (but should only be done on a mild day), because excessive dryness causes the potting mixture to shrink, leaving cracks or a gap just inside the walls of the container. Then, the water runs through without any benefit to the plants. Compensate for the shrinkage by gently pricking over the surface. Water thoroughly as and when necessary, rather than giving a little and often, when the moisture might evaporate before reaching the roots.

It is best not to use fertilizers if the trees and plants are healthy, because applied unnecessarily they cause lush growth, so that the plants lose their compact habit and produce few flowers. However, if the foliage is of poor colour and lacking in vigour, a fertilizer can be given, but only in small amounts. It is essential to find out first whether the trouble is caused by an insect pest rather than lack of nutrient.

Creating a miniature garden

Containers for miniature gardens can be any size or shape, but should preferably be shallow to make a frame in proportion with the miniature trees and plants. Most people prefer square or oblong troughs, but round, oval or irregular ones can be used. A porous material is best, but one or more drainage holes are essential in any case.

Genuine old stone sinks are excellent, but are scarce and extremely heavy. A good substitute is concrete, which can be made to any size, and (if reinforced) very thin to reduce weight. But concrete must be weathered before planting. There are containers of asbestos cement, which is both light and strong. Plastic containers are satisfactory, but because of the lack of porosity they need extra drainage holes. The bright harsh colours detract from the beauty of the plants; black or grey make a neutral setting. Glass-fibre, which is very strong and light, can be made to any size or shape.

Apart from such containers, miniature gardens can be planted in cavity walls made of stone or old bricks. On flat roofs (where weight is an important consideration) miniature trees and plants will grow in a shallow enclosure of walling stone, or just one course of brick. This would give a soil depth of three inches, which is quite sufficient.

When to plant

A newly planted garden needs more care than one that has been through a whole year's cycle of seasonal changes, so that the time for planting needs careful thought. As most miniature trees and alpines are sold in pots, they can be transplanted at any time of the year without disturbing the roots. In a reasonably mild climate the autumn is the best planting season, because the plants will then be established by the spring, when many alpines come into flower.

Even where there is a prolonged snowy season this should be satisfactory, as such conditions are normal for alpines in their native habitat. But where heavy rains are followed by severe frost, it is better to postpone planting until the early spring. It must be emphasized that, although the plants will withstand frost, they will not tolerate being waterlogged. Plants purchased in the spring will be growing and probably in bud, so disturb them as little as possible.

Aspect

The selection of trees and plants should be governed by the position in which the garden is to be placed. It is quite impossible to give any definite rules, because there are so many factors to be considered. For instance, some plants classified as sun-loving may seed themselves prolifically in the shade of a fair-sized conifer; so by all means experiment in special conditions. However, although some sun-loving plants will flourish in the shade, it is not advisable to put plants which do need shade somewhere that has none. However, additional peat to hold moisture will sometimes compensate for a dry, sunny position.

Planting a trough

First cover each drainage hole with a curved piece of broken flower-pot. This will allow any excess moisture to drain away, but prevent the potting mixture seeping through. Then cover the base with a layer of small, clean crocks. Over these spread a layer of peat. This absorbs and holds some of the moisture, and also forms a blanket, dividing the planting medium from the drainage material. Next, water the peat thoroughly and allow to settle; check that any excess water does seep through. The next stage is to one-third fill the container with good damp potting mixture. Mixture no. 2 is satisfactory for general collections, but add some extra peat around the roots of conifers or any ericaceous (lime-hating) plants. Then position the rocks so that they will appear partly buried when the garden is complete.

Trees and shrubs can then be placed in relation to the rocks. Next, put in any cushion plants to nestle between the rocks; lastly, the trailing plants that will overhang the sides of the trough. Fill all gaps with potting mixture. When the plants are all firmly positioned the surface and the collar of the plants should be just below the top of the container. It can then be covered with a dressing of limestone chippings for lime-loving plants or granite chippings for lime-hating and neutral plants. Water thoroughly and fill any subsidence a few days later.

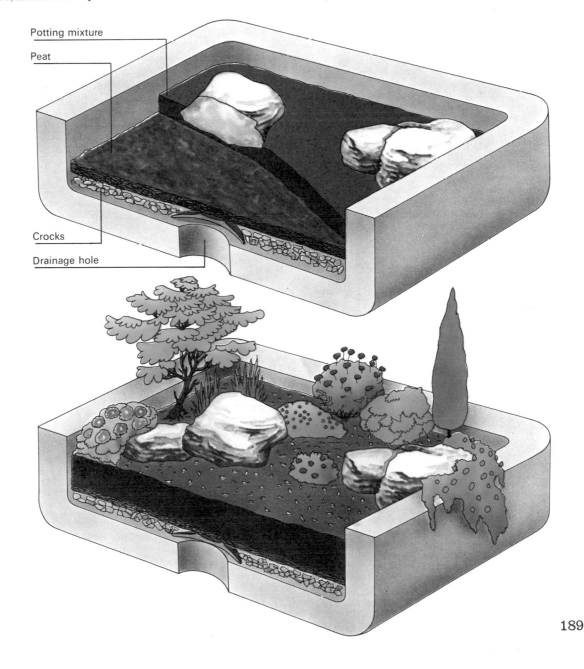

Potting mixture

Peat

Crocks

Drainage hole

189

Plants for miniature gardens

A well designed miniature garden needs a selection of kinds of plants to give it scale and proportion – but undoubtedly it is the miniature flowers that have the most immediate appeal. Although the spring and early summer are the best times for a wide range of flowers, the tiniest daffodils commence to bloom in winter and there is usually some plant in flower through to the next winter.

With the exception of the roses, most of the miniature flowering plants were originally natives of mountain ranges in various regions, and are usually referred to as alpines. The exposed conditions and intense light at high altitudes are two of the main factors which cause these plants to develop the compact habit of growth which is so endearing. They are not 'dwarf' in the sense of being just short, but are perfectly proportioned in leaf, bud and flower.

Happily for those who wish to cultivate these plants, many of them will, if given the right conditions – an open position, good drainage and a porous growing mixture – retain their miniature habit of growth. There are, of course, some plants that grow at high altitudes in sheltered positions that are also classed as alpines, but are not miniature.

Miniature plants can be divided into five types. First, there are those with minute stemless leaves densely crowded to form a dome, with flowers radiating from the dome. These are known as cushion plants, and include *Drabas* and Kabschia *Saxifragas*. Second, there are flowers like *Primulas* that have a rosette of foliage with flower stems rising from the centre. Then there are those that wind their way between rocks and other plants, flowering at irregular intervals; *Campanulas* are an example. Mat-forming plants, such as the smallest thyme and the *Raoulias*, root as they spread. Finally, there are plants of trailing habit – such as *Gypsophila*, *Veronica* and *Helianthemum* – which are excellent for overhanging the edge of the trough.

Miniature roses

Of all the miniature plants, the roses seem the most remarkable. They look delicate, but are quite hardy – that is, so long as they have been raised to be grown outdoors. They need regular pruning, cutting back any coarse basal shoots and branchlets to keep the bush shapely. Remove any dead flowers, and always watch for aphids, red spider mite and mildew (see pages 232 and 233).

Miniature roses can be grown as individual pot-plants, and one or more can be introduced into any design or size of miniature garden. Planning and creating a garden devoted entirely to roses and watching it develop is a fascinating project. Such a garden can be almost any size; in one 36 by 24 inches or larger it is possible to embody some features of a full-scale rose garden. It is best to keep the design fairly simple and to be sparing with ornaments, bearing in mind that the roses are the main feature. A trellis background with a central arch and tiny paths dividing the beds, each planted with a different variety of rose, can be really charming.

above In a concrete trough are planted more than 25 different kinds of plants. Among those in flower are *Linaria alpina* (on the far left); *Silene acaulis* (with pink flowers) and *Erinus alpinus* 'Albus' (white), both immediately in front of the tree; *Saxifraga cymbalaria* (with yellow flowers, edging the path); *Gentiana verna* (blue, in front of the *Saxifraga*); and several miniature roses (on the far side of the path). To the right of the bridge is the pink variety of *Erinus alpinus*, while farther right are the yellow flowers of *Primula* 'Blairside Yellow' and (in the corner) the pink *Dianthus* 'Prince Charming'. The pink flowers in the right-hand back corner are of *Rhodohypoxis baurii*, while in the centre at the back, a paler pink, is *Alyssum spinosum* 'Roseum' and (with white flowers) *Ionopsideum acaule*. In the far left-hand corner is the tiny *Saxifraga primuloides*.

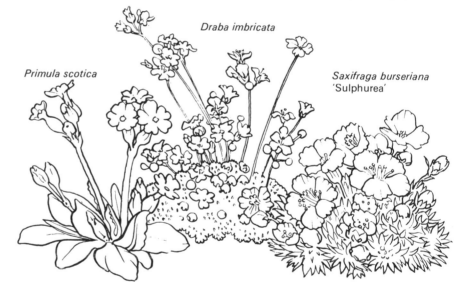

Primula scotica

Draba imbricata

Saxifraga burseriana 'Sulphurea'

Cushion plants

Dianthus musalae is a hummock of grey-green foliage, with flowers of rich pink in summer. *D.* 'Prince Charming' is slightly larger, with pale pink flowers. *Douglasia vitaliana* has grey-green foliage and stemless yellow flowers in spring. *Draba aizoides* has dark green rosettes and yellow spring flowers. *D. imbricata* is smaller, with yellow flowers.

The neatest and most compact saxifrages are of the Kabschia group, having grey-green foliage and beautiful five-petalled flowers borne singly in spring. *Saxifraga burseriana* 'Gloria' has pure white flowers, *S.* 'Cranbourne' is deep rose-pink, *S.* 'Faldonside' has clear yellow flowers, and *S. irvingii* is pale pink.

Rosette-forming plants

Astilbe glaberrima 'Saxosa' has fern-like leaves with spikes of tiny pink summer flowers. *Erinus alpinus* has tufts of dark green leaves with racemes of pink, purple or white flowers in early summer. *Limonium minutum*, a miniature statice or sea lavender, has dark green leaves and spikes of lavender-blue flowers in summer.

Primula frondosa has pale green leaves with a film of white powder on the under-surface and umbels of rosy-lilac early summer flowers. *P. scotica* is a minute replica of the above; the flowers, a rich purple with a white centre, appear in spring.

'Winding' plants

These trail between rocks, flowering at irregular intervals. *Campanula cochlearifolia* has bright green leaves and two to six nodding bell flowers – purple in the type, but white in 'Alba'. *C. pulla* is similar, but the flowers are a richer purple and it does not spread so quickly. *Hypsella longiflora* grows low on the ground, with oval, stemless leaves and quaint white flowers, with crimson markings, in summer. *Veronica telephiifolia* has small round leaves of pale green and clusters of tiny summer flowers of milky-blue. *Viola hederacea* (Australian violet) has creeping stems, ivy-shaped leaves of pale green, and white flowers with a purple centre.

Mat-forming plants
Anagallis tenella (bog pimpernel) has trailing stems with minute round leaves and upturned flowers of palest pink, borne singly in summer. *Arenaria balearica* grows in a flat carpet of bright green, and in late spring bears small, single flowers of clear white on slender stems. *Lobelia linnaeoides* has small dark green leaves, with myriads of single flowers on hair-like stems. They are white, flushed with pink, and appear in summer.

Erinus alpinus varieties

Raoulia australis has small stemless leaves of metallic silver. It is grown for the foliage rather than the flowers, which are inconspicuous. *R. glabra* is similar, but the foliage is dark green. *R. lutescens* is even smaller. Its foliage makes a mere film of grey-green, with microscopic flowers of a dull yellow. *Sibthorpia europaea variegata* (Cornish moneywort) has tiny leaves of pale green with creamy margins and is also grown for the foliage, as the flowers are insignificant. It needs a sheltered position.

Trailing plants
Dianthus myrtinervis has dark green foliage and terminal sprays of vivid pink flowers in summer. *Frankenia laevis* (sea heath) has fine heather-like foliage, which turns bronze in autumn, bearing numerous tiny stemless flowers of clear pink all the summer. *Helianthemum alpestre*, a miniature sun rose, has grey-green leaves and a profusion of bright yellow flowers all the summer. *Hypericum anagalloides* (St John's wort) has pale green leaves and bright yellow flowers all summer. *Linaria alpina* (alpine toadflax) has grey-green foliage and summer flowers of bright purple with orange markings. *Linnaea borealis* (twin-flower) has prostrate rounded leaves and slender flowers of pale pink. These swing gracefully in pairs. *Phlox douglasii* 'Eva' is available in pink, white and pale mauve varieties. It flowers in early summer. *Pimelia coarctata* (rice plant) has grey-green foliage and minute white flowers in late spring, followed by gleaming white berries.

Other miniature plants
Asperula suberosa grows in tufts of pale grey-green foliage, with terminal clusters of delicate pink tubular flowers. It flowers from spring to mid-summer. *Centaurium portense* (*Erythraea chloodes*) is a neat little plant of the gentian family, with vivid pink flowers in summer. *Erodium chamaedryoides roseum* has flat rosettes of dark green leaves and numerous single, pink upturned flowers, also in summer. *Gentiana verna*, the spring-flowering gentian, is a glorious royal-blue. *Myosotis rupicola*, a diminutive forget-me-not, bears clusters of sky-blue flowers in early summer. *Potentilla verna pygmaea* has dark green foliage and golden-yellow flowers; although labelled 'verna' it usually flowers throughout the summer. *Soldanella alpina* is one of the loveliest of all alpines. It has rounded leaves and nodding, fringed bells of pale mauve in spring. A few small *Sedums* are grown mainly for their foliage. *Sedum dasyphyllum* has small fleshy leaves which vary from glaucous green to rosy-pink. The flowers are

Miniature rose varieties
The smallest of miniature roses, *Rosa roulettii*, has minute semi-double pink flowers. It was found about fifty years ago in a Swiss village, where it had been grown for generations as an indoor pot-plant, although it is known to be hardy. Its origin is still unknown. Most of the other miniature roses are hybrids. A few of the best kinds are *Rosa* 'Cinderella', with double flowers in clusters of three or four, pearly-white flushed with pink; 'Elf', a beautiful rich dark red, semi-double, of velvety texture; 'Peon', bright crimson with a white centre; 'Simple Simon' **right**, a brilliant pink, paler on the reverse of the petals; 'Sweet Fairy', with fully double petals of the palest pink and a strong rose perfume; and 'Yellow Bantam', which has buds of bright yellow, opening out to a paler colour.

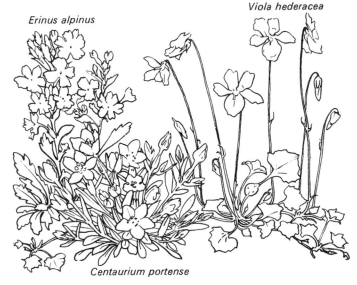

Erinus alpinus

Viola hederacea

Centaurium portense

white. The foliage of *S. farinosum* varies from silvery-grey to rose-pink, and is covered with a fine white powder. Its flowers are also white. *S. humifusum* is a little gem, with minute stemless leaves of palest green, and yellow flowers. The *Sempervivums* (houseleeks) have fleshy rosettes of leaves, and make a fascinating contrast to the other plants. *Sempervivum arenarium* grows in small stemless rosettes which turn crimson, while *S. arachnoideum* is covered with fine white 'cobwebs'. Both have small flowers in summer.

Sempervivum arachnoideum

Miniature trees and shrubs

The most important feature of any miniature garden is the tree or group of trees, for this gives the whole landscape scale and impact. Many of the miniature trees are evergreen conifers. The broad-leaved, deciduous trees are described on the opposite page with shrubs.

Natural miniature conifers are as beautiful and as varied as their full-scale counterparts. They should not be confused with the trained Japanese trees known as bonsai, because those described here have a naturally slow rate of growth. The beauty of their form and colour is remarkable; some are of dense, spreading habit, some slender, symmetrical and erect, and others are pendulous or even prostrate. Although referred to as evergreen, these conifers

Picea mariana 'Nana'

are not monotonously so. Their colours range from the palest to the darkest green, from gold to bronze, and from grey-green to silvery-blue. Some change colour in the winter, whilst the delicate green of the emerging spring foliage at the tips of the *Piceas* is quite spectacular.

These conifers are hardy, and do well in a peat-based mixture. They must never be allowed to become waterlogged,

Miniature conifers
The best known miniature conifers are forms of dwarf cypress (*Chamaecyparis*) and juniper (*Juniperus*), but there are also miniature varieties of spruce (*Picea*), Japanese cedar (*Cryptomeria*) and arbor-vitae (*Thuja*). All the slowest-growers are cypress and junipers, however.

Slowest-growing kinds
Chamaecyparis obtusa 'Nana Caespitosa' grows in a compact dome of rich dark green, concealing the trunk. *C. obtusa* 'Nana Flabelliformis' is very handsome, with a sturdy trunk and crowded, fan-shaped branchlets which turn upwards. *C. obtusa* 'Nana Juniperoides' is similar to the above, but more dome-shaped. *C. pisifera* 'Plumosa Aurea Compacta' is bush-like in habit, with very close golden-green foliage if grown in full sun, but almost glaucous if grown in shade. *Juniperus communis* 'Echinoformis' (hedgehog juniper) forms a compact, almost spherical tree with stiff, sharply-pointed leaves. *J. scopulorum* 'Repens' is an exceptionally attractive

but being too dry in hot weather is even more disastrous. They vary in their rate of growth, and there are three main groups. Those that are extremely slow-growing can remain in a trough garden indefinitely. For example, *Chamaecyparis obtusa* 'Nana Flabelliformis' may reach a height of only 14 inches in forty years. Others that are not quite so slow-growing can remain in the trough

Chamaecyparis thyoides 'Andelyensis'

Chamaecyparis pisifera 'Squarrosa Dumosa'

prostrate conifer with glaucous-green foliage and numerous minute cones.

Medium-speed growers
Chamaecyparis obtusa 'Nana' is among the most popular in this group, but is very variable in form; it can be compact or loose and open. It is generally grafted onto a sturdy trunk, and has spreading branches of rich, dark green. *C. obtusa* 'Nana Kosterii' is similar, but the branches are horizontal and the fan-shaped branchlets curve gracefully downwards. *C. obtusa* 'Tetragona Aurea' has an erect trunk and spreading branches, with irregular, crowded branchlets of bright golden foliage. *C. pisifera* 'Boulevard', pyramidal in form, with feathery foliage of a beautiful silvery-blue, is a good tree for a shady position. *C. thyoides* 'Andelyensis' is symmetrical and conical in shape, with fine heather-like foliage; in winter or early spring the tips of the branchlets have microscopic flowers which look like crimson beads. *Juniperus communis* 'Compressa' is always attractive. Forming an erect,

up to twelve years, but might then need to be transplanted elsewhere. Finally, the quickest-growing types are excellent for beginners, or those who want immediate results, but would outgrow the garden in four to six years. Remember, though, that the above is only a rough guide, as much depends on the age of the tree when it is planted and on the size of the container.

Chamaecyparis lawsoniana 'Minima Aurea'

Juniperus squamata 'Glassell'; *Thuja orientalis* 'Rosedalis'; *Juniperus communis* 'Compressa'

slender spire of glaucous-green, it is an elegant tree especially suitable for planting in pairs in a formal garden. *Microcachrys tetragona* is most unusual, having long trailing stems with tapering branchlets, minute leaves which form whipcord-like shoots, and numerous tiny cones. *Picea mariana* 'Nana' is a dense, rounded tree of glaucous-green. The new spring growth appears tipped with crimson, which gradually turns to a delicate apple-green and then to the darker mature foliage colour. *Thuja orientalis* 'Rosedalis' is bushy in habit, rounded at the top and tapering at the base. The tiny needle leaves change colour from bronze in winter to pale golden-green in spring, then glaucous-green in summer.

Quicker-growing types

Chamaecyparis lawsoniana 'Elwoodii' forms an erect column of glaucous-green when grown in semi-shade, but in full sun it tends to become rather dingy. *C. lawsoniana* 'Minima Aurea' is an erect pyramid with flattish branchlets of brilliant gold; it bears

Picea excelsa 'Compacta'

Chamaecyparis obtusa 'Nana'

numerous cones of a most unusual dark greenish-blue. *C. pisifera* 'Nana' is generally bushy in habit. The foliage is slightly pendulous at the ends of the branches, and is dark green above and silvery on the under-surface. There is a variegated form with branchlets flecked with creamy-yellow. *C. pisifera* 'Squarrosa Intermedia' is one of the few miniature conifers that can be pruned if it produces any shoots which spoil its appearance. It usually grows with several stems, rather than one trunk, and has foliage of a silvery-

grey colour.
Cryptomeria japonica 'Vilmoriniana' is an erect, irregular-shaped conifer, densely covered with sharp-pointed leaves, which turn russet brown in winter and grass-green in summer.
Juniperus procumbens 'Nana' is one of the few really prostrate miniature conifers. It is quite decorative against a rock, or beside a pool, giving a windswept effect. The foliage is stiff, dark green. *J. squamata* 'Wilsonii' grows erect, but the branchlets, crowded with stiff, sharply-pointed little leaves of grey-green, are semi-pendulous. It sometimes bears minute flowers, which are followed by glossy black berries.
Picea albertiana 'Conica' is very popular because of its brilliant green foliage and delightful pine fragrance, but is susceptible to attack by red spider mite. *P. abies* 'Clanbrassiliana' (a miniature variety of Norway spruce) is an irregular-shaped tree with stiff little branchlets and sharply pointed leaves. The new spring growth is a brilliant fresh green, in striking contrast to last year's foliage.

Miniature shrubs

There is not such a great variety of miniature shrubs and deciduous trees as the conifers, but a number of interesting and attractive kinds are available. *Cassiope lycopodioides* has semi-prostrate branchlets, densely covered with minute stemless leaves and single pure white bell flowers which swing from erect, reddish stems. *C. tetragona* is similar in foliage and flower, but erect and pyramidal in habit. They are both handsome plants that do well in semi-shade. *Corokia cotoneaster* is a quaint shrub with slender branches, all twisted and interlaced. The small, widely spaced leaves are dark green above, silver below; the yellow flowers are delicately fragrant.
Erica vulgaris foxii nana, a true miniature heather, has rosy-lilac flowers. *Grevillea alpina* is very attractive, with slender grey-green leaves and decorative flowers of bright pink. *Helichrysum selago minor* has minute grey-green stemless leaves overlapping each other, in a whipcord effect, the branches terminating in small

white 'everlasting' flowers. *Jasminum parkeri* is a true miniature jasmine with stiff branchlets, dark green leaves and scented yellow flowers, followed by black shining seed-heads. *Leiophyllum buxifolium* is an evergreen bush with small glossy leaves and clusters of minute flowers, deep pink in the bud, opening out to white. *Leptospermum scoparium prostratum* is a beautiful shrub with tiny leaves and flowers of rich pink.
There are several miniature *Salix* (willows) and one of the best is *Salix boydii*, extremely slow-growing with erect branchlets and unusual leaves of silvery-grey which are rounded and crinkled. *S. herbacea* (the least willow) creeps close to the ground, with bright green leaves and microscopic yellow catkins. *S. retusa pyrenaica* is semi-prostrate with oval leaves and erect crimson catkins which turn yellow as the stamens develop. *S. serpyllifolia* is prostrate, the branches hugging the ground; the leaves are small and the yellow catkins minute.
Ulmus parvifolia 'Chessins'

is a true miniature elm which is deciduous; it has spreading, sometimes pendulous branches and tiny dark glossy leaves. *Zelkova nivea*, a Japanese elm species, is similar in habit, but the leaves are larger, pale green with a creamy margin. Both the *Ulmus* and *Zelkova* are most desirable shrubs, but they may require pruning to keep them shapely.

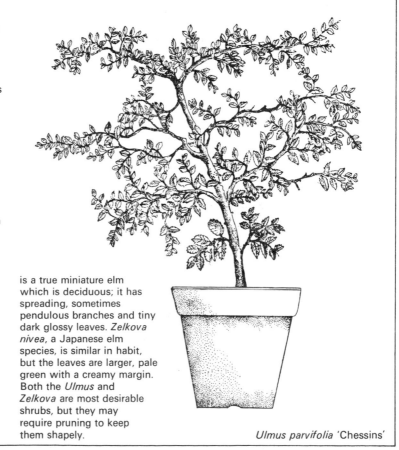

Ulmus parvifolia 'Chessins'

Water in miniature gardens

Pools for miniature gardens can be any size or shape to suit the type of garden: preferably symmetrical for a formal design, but for a rock garden irregular in contour. Some pools of the latter type, made of transparent plastic, can be bought at pet shops, but generally the former have to be made especially to suit the design of the garden. Pools can be of glass-fibre, or any other material that holds water. This is vital, as leakage would leave the aquatics high and dry,

and saturation would also be harmful to the plants beside the pool. The water should be at least two inches deep.

When positioned, the pool should be evenly supported. It should have a thin layer of fine gravel mixed with a little charcoal at the base and then about a $\frac{1}{2}$-inch layer of soil. The pool can then be filled carefully with water and the contents allowed to settle before putting in the aquatic plants, which will float on the surface. A small figurine – such as a boy on a dolphin, to represent a fountain in the centre of the pool – adds to the charm. If the pool is in a rock garden and its size permits, an island of moss-covered rock could be added.

One of the best plants for small pools is *Azolla caroliniana* (fairy moss), which is like a bluish-green microscopic fern. It increases rapidly, turns bronze and dies down in the winter, and reappears in the late spring. Equally useful is *Hydrocharis morsus-ranae* (frog-bit), which has kidney-shaped leaves that rest on the surface of the water like a water-lily's and three-petalled white flowers that rise above it. This also dies down in winter and new growth reappears in the early summer.

These plants use up a certain amount of water, and some evaporation will also take place, so replenish the pool occasionally. Before doing this it is best to see if there is a film of dust on the surface which should be skimmed off before adding fresh water. Gently break any ice that forms, but it is best to protect the pool in severe frost.

Soil

Azolla caroliniana

Gravel and charcoal

Hydrocharis morsus-ranae

Miniature pools
A pool gives any miniature garden a delightful focal point, and is quite easy to install. An irregular shape suits an informal garden **top**, and in a rock garden **above** small rocks can mask the sides. A more regular shape is best in a formal setting **right**. You can add a miniature statue or a bridge, and grow miniature aquatics. The red-leaved plant is *Azolla caroliniana*.

Indoor miniature gardens

All the miniature gardens and plants described in the past few pages have been essentially outdoor subjects, but it is possible to construct an indoor version. An indoor landscape needs to be very carefully planned, however, as it is constantly seen at close quarters and also because it usually has to contend with the adverse conditions of a hot, dry atmosphere and reduced light. Although most alpine plants need direct light above them, there are a few that will do well in semi-shade, and these can be grown indoors. But it is essential that they should be given the maximum light available in the living-room, so the best position is on a window sill where the light is not reduced by curtains.

Indoor gardens also require more attention than those in the open, because they are deprived of the evening dew, which is so beneficial. To compensate for the lack of humidity it is important to dampen the foliage daily with tepid water in a fine syringe; this is just as important as watering the roots when necessary. If the garden is portable,

Mesembryanthemum ornatulum

A sunny window sill is the best position for an indoor miniature garden, but not above a radiator, as hot, dry air harms alpines.

and you can put it out in the open for an airing and some direct light occasionally, the plants will benefit. This will enable you to have a wider range of flowering alpines, but do not make the sudden change from a warm room to the open on a very cold day.

For anyone who has a cool greenhouse, or a cold frame, it is a good plan to have two gardens and change them over when the one indoors shows signs of needing more light. (A clear indication of this is if the leaves become pallid and stretch towards the light.) This plan

Plants for indoor gardens
At least one tree, or tree-like shrub, is essential in an indoor miniature garden, as well as one or more of the miniature roses. Two of the best trees for indoor cultivation are *Chamaecyparis pisifera* 'Boulevard', which has beautiful blue-grey foliage, and *Crassula sarcocaulis*, which is in fact a decorative flowering tree-like shrub with gnarled branches and clusters of tiny pink flowers. All varieties of miniature roses do well indoors, provided they are given reasonable protection from insect pests and mildew, both of which increase more rapidly in a warm atmosphere.
Other plants which have been found suitable for indoor culture include the following: *Acorus gramineus pusillus*, a slender rush two inches high, is especially attractive beside

Selaginella apus (in front); *Acorus gramineus pusillus*

a pool. *Crassula bolusii* forms a hummock of small fleshy leaves with clusters of tiny pink flowers in the late summer or autumn. *Soleirolia soleirolii* 'Golden Queen' is a bright yellow form of mind-your-own-business (baby's tears), but is not so invasive. The variety 'Silver Queen' has leaves of silvery-green

would be of great value to invalids who would not only have the advantage of two different landscapes, but would also have the pleasure of seeing the marked development and improvement the trees and plants would show as a result of the time spent in direct light.

The design of an indoor miniature garden can vary according to individual taste from a simple group of plants, with or without rocks, to a formal garden. If a small pool can be introduced this will not only add to the attraction with tiny aquatic plants, but will be beneficial to the garden by creating some humidity (see the opposite page). The water will need to be replenished if it evaporates in the warm atmosphere.

with a creamy margin. These are both invaluable for indoor culture.
Selaginella apus grows in a minute cluster of fan-shaped, lacy fronds; it is a plant of delicate beauty. *S. krausiana* is of trailing habit with fern-like foliage of a brilliant green; it grows more quickly than the above. *S. krausiana aurea* is similar in habit and the foliage is a bright gold.
Other plants which do well indoors include the following, which are fully described on pages 190 and 191: *Anagallis tenella, Arenaria balearica, Asplenium ruta-muraria, Asplenium trichomanes, Centaurium portense, Erodium chamaedryoides roseum, Hypericum anagalloides, Laurentia tenella, Mentha requienii, Rhodohypoxis baurii, Sedum humifusum* and *Viola hederacea.*

195

7 Fun plants and food-growing

You can grow plants for all kinds of reasons – and they need not be serious ones. Children, in particular, often enjoy growing things for the sheer fun of it, perhaps because the plants are particularly flamboyant or because they move, catch flies or do other strange things.

Some children also enjoy creating their own private miniature gardens, or growing plants from fruit stones and scraps.

You will find ideas for all these in this part, together with something just a little more serious: how to grow fruit, vegetables and herbs even if you have no garden.

Free plants from fruit pips

Whenever you eat fruit, the chances are that you swallow or throw away the makings of a flourishing indoor or balcony garden. Why scrap the stone of a peach, date or plum – or an avocado stone or an orange pip – when, with a little attention and some luck, they could be grown into attractive plants?

For fruit stones – and pips, too – are all seeds, and can be germinated in the right conditions. Generally, putting them in a pot of damp potting mixture in a warm, dark place will do the trick, but some respond better to other treatment. For example, the hard seeds of trees and shrubs that grow in cold areas may need a period of alternate freezing and thawing to break their dormancy. This is called *stratification* (see page 227).

The main requirement when growing plants from pips and stones is patience. It may be three months or even longer before some kinds sprout – and some stones never do. Of course, cooking or canning will kill them anyway, so always use pips and stones from fresh fruit. But once they do germinate, they will quite quickly grow, so long as they are kept in a light, airy but warm place – or outdoors in some cases.

The list of fruit that can be given this kind of treatment is almost endless. Apricots, nectarines, lychees, mangoes and cherries all have stones that you can grow. Or you can try pips from apples, lemons or pomegranates, or seeds from melons, tomatoes, or marrows. It is possible to grow seedling trees from nuts, too – from peanuts to acorns.

Date

A date palm (*Phoenix dactylifera*) makes a handsome houseplant. Germinate a date stone – from a fresh date – in water, or plant it ½ inch deep in damp potting mixture.
right Keep it warm – at least 21 °C (70 °F) is needed – dark and damp, and the first leaf should emerge in a month or two. It is thick, coarse and grass-like. Now put the pot in good light.
below With occasional feeding and annual potting on, you should have a large palm tree in some years.

Date palm

Avocado; lychee; mango

One of the most handsome and popular do-it-yourself houseplants (see the photograph **above**) can be grown from an avocado stone. One from the smaller variety of avocado 'pear' usually seems to grow best. Wash it in warm water, removing any loose skin.
right Germinate your avocado in a glass of water. Use pins, toothpicks or a cardboard collar to suspend the stone so that the bottom just touches the water. Put it in a warm, dimly lit place and keep the water level topped up. In three to eight weeks the stone should split and a root and shoot emerge. Then move it into stronger light. Once there are several strong roots, carefully transfer it to good, sandy potting mixture in a six-inch pot. Leave a little of the stone sticking out of the soil; be careful not to damage the roots.
It will grow rapidly in a warm, sunny spot, developing lush green, pointed leaves and, in time, a woody trunk. If you want your tree to bush out, pinch out the top inch or so of soft growth; then side-

branches will form. Keep the plant out of draughts and water it whenever the potting mixture gets dry. In summer, feed it every three weeks or so. Spray the foliage occasionally.
The stone of a lychee or mango can be grown in just the same way, though both may take longer to germinate. Also, they like a warm, moist atmosphere even more than avocado trees do. Whole peanuts can also be grown into attractive vine-like plants in warm conditions. Germinate in damp potting mixture.

Avocado

Lychee

Mango

Acorn; chestnut; pine-nut
These can all be grown into attractive small trees in cool conditions – preferably outdoors. Collect the seeds from woods in spring if possible; you may then find some that are already sprouting. Plant the seedling or seed about an inch deep in firm potting mixture in a four-inch pot, and leave it on a window ledge or patio outdoors. Keep it well watered and pot on each year as it grows.
right The oak seedling will grow more slowly from its acorn than the pine, but both make attractive pot plants if the growing tips are removed to make them bush out. The horse chestnut is particularly attractive as a small tree in sunny but cool indoor positions. Exactly the same treatment can be given to walnuts, pecans, hazel-nuts, beech-nuts and the seeds of other woodland trees. Deciduous kinds lose their leaves in winter, of course, but the fresh green spring foliage is attractive. Many trees of this kind, if pruned and trained correctly, can be made into miniature, or bonsai, trees (see pages 180 to 187).

Pine   Oak

Horse   Walnut
chestnut

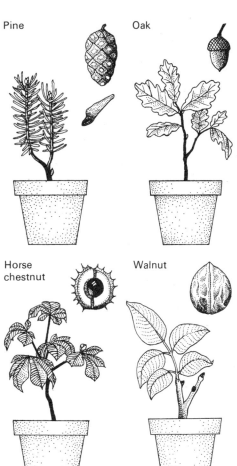

Cherry; peach; plum
Almonds, apricots, cherries, nectarines, peaches and plums are all closely related. They can all be grown from their fruit's stones, and will eventually form handsome trees. Most are fairly hardy, though apricots, nectarines and peaches do best under glass or against a sunny wall in cold areas. They can be trained into a fan or espalier shape by careful pruning.
right above They will produce beautiful flowers – generally white or pink – in winter or spring when only bushes. Given good weather, they may fruit. The stones do not need such high temperatures for germination as orange and lemon pips, and the hardier kinds (such as plums, cherries and almonds) germinate best after a winter outdoors with alternate cold and mild spells. Also, try very gently cracking the hard shells of apricot, peach and almond stones with nut crackers before planting. Be careful not to damage the kernel, however; this is the living seed. Plant one stone an inch deep in a four-inch pot. **right below** Pot on the resulting 'tree' each spring.

Peach

Lemon; grapefruit
These and similar fruits, such as oranges, limes and mandarins, are all closely related. The trees are very attractive, with dark green foliage. **left** When they reach a height of about six feet they may bear fragrant flowers and fruit of their own. They can be kept smaller by pruning, however. They are not really hardy, so they need winter shelter in cold areas, at an average temperature of 8 to 10°C (46 to 59°F). In summer they like plenty of sunshine, air and water.
right Grow the pips (lemons and grapefruit are best) in damp potting mixture, planting three or four pips ½ inch deep in a four-inch pot. Keep the pot warm and dark until the pips germinate and shoots appear. Transplant into individual pots when the seedlings are about four inches tall, and pot on each year in Mixture no. 3.
right Pips of the miniature *Citrus mitis* (calamondin orange) sold as a houseplant can be treated in the same way, but the tree will not, of course, grow so big as a true orange. It should flower and fruit when little more than a foot tall.

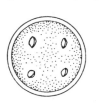

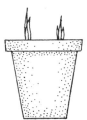

Calamondin
orange

Pomegranate
below The pomegranate (*Punica granatum*) forms a very attractive bush for the sun-lounge or sheltered patio. It has light green leaves and, in summer, scarlet flowers up to two inches long. In good sunshine the orange fruits may ripen enough to eat. The fruit is full of seeds, and these can easily be grown into plants. Sow the dried seeds in spring at a temperature of about 16°C (61°F). Put the seedlings in individual four-inch pots and pot on each spring. Water well in summer. Protect from frost in winter.

Pomegranate

199

Pot-plants from kitchen scraps

Every day, the kitchen waste-bin contains food scraps that can be grown into attractive plants. For example, the sprouting tops of fresh carrots, beetroots, parsnips and other root vegetables can form eye-catching foliage. A pineapple top grown in the same way forms an exotic houseplant, and it might one day flower and produce fruit of its own. An easier plant to grow is an onion – so long as you don't mind the smell!

And there are plenty of other things to experiment with: fresh beans, peas and lentils, potatoes and sweet potatoes, a ginger root, a sprig of fresh mint or rosemary . . . just look around the kitchen and use your imagination. There are many things that will flourish on the window sill if given a chance.

Carrot; beetroot; turnip

It is very easy to grow a delightfully ferny foliage plant from a carrot top. Cut the top inch from a large, fresh carrot. Stand it, cut end down, in a saucer of water, and keep it in full light. Keep the water level topped up, and the carrot will soon sprout.

You can make an attractive single-plant hanging display from a carrot. You will need about a two-inch section. Hollow this out to form a water reservoir, and use a skewer and string to hang it. **below** Keep the reservoir topped up, and the foliage will grow upwards around the carrot top.

Exactly the same treatment can be given to the top of a beetroot, turnip or parsnip. Beetroot leaves are particularly attractive: a glossy rich green with prominent red veins.

Parsnip

Beetroot

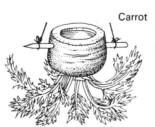

Carrot

Potatoes; sweet potatoes

Both potatoes and sweet potatoes can be grown if they are placed whole on a jar of water so that the bottom just touches the water. Choose an untreated 'seed' potato if possible, and one with plenty of 'eyes'. If necessary, use a cardboard collar to support it in the jar with the eyes at the top. With a sweet potato, put it narrow-end down.

Potatoes need cool, dark conditions to sprout; sweet potatoes prefer light and warmth. Roots will first grow, then shoots. Cut off all but one or two shoots if you want a lot of decorative top growth. This can grow to a length of several feet, and (like bean shoots) can be trained around a window frame. If you want to grow potatoes to eat, you should plant them in a large pot.

Potato

Pineapple

A pineapple plant is very handsome, with long, fleshy leaves arching out from the centre. It is quite easy to grow from the sprouting top of a fresh pineapple fruit, though some refuse to take root.

Slice the top off the fruit, leaving about an inch of fruit attached. Trim away the flesh to the hard, stringy part in the centre. Leave it to dry for two or three days; this helps to prevent rotting. Remove the bottom leaves, and plant the pineapple in a damp, sandy potting mix in a five-inch pot. If necessary support it with sticks, and keep it in a light, warm place – at least 18 °C (64 °F) at night. Do not keep the potting mixture too wet, but spray with water regularly. If you are lucky, it will develop roots and can then be treated like any other houseplant. Water and feed it regularly. After some years' growth, it may produce fruit of its own – though this is not very likely indoors (see page 72).

Tomato; capsicum

You can grow tomato plants from your own seed if you scoop these from a ripe tomato. Sow in spring ¾ inch apart in seed mixture. Cover with glass, and germinate at about 16°C (61°F). Plant out the seedlings into individual pots when they are big enough to handle. After this, grow as described on page 213, either outdoors on a warm sunny terrace or in a sun-room or conservatory. You can grow capsicums (sweet peppers) in exactly the same way.

Capsicum   Tomato

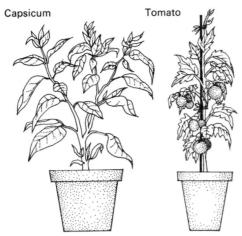

Onion; garlic

Onions and garlic cloves are both bulbs, and can very simply be grown in exactly the same way as other bulbs (see page 106). Both have round heads of flowers that are particularly spectacular in onions. The onion flowers are mauve, the garlic white with a red tinge. The main problem is, of course, the smell. But if you do not mind this, plant good-sized bulbs of either in the same way as other bulbs. Both can be planted outdoors at the end of winter in a sunny place.

Onion

Mint; rosemary; etc

Many herbs — as well as hosts of other plants — can be propagated from cuttings. So you can easily start your own herb garden — in a window box, perhaps — from fresh herbs bought in the shops. Mint, rosemary, bay, tarragon, thyme and marjoram are good ones to try.

Choose really fresh shoots about three to four inches long, and plant them in pots containing equal parts of moist peat and sand. Put the pots in the open, with a clear plastic bag inverted over the top of each to retain moisture. Keep the peat/sand mixture moist. Once rooted, transplant into normal potting mixture. Woody herbs such as rosemary may root in water.

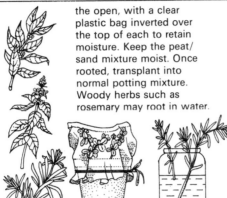

HERB GARDEN

Beans; lentils; peas

Beans are ideal for showing children how seeds sprout and grow. **below** The best way is to put a few beans between a roll of blotting paper and the glass of a jar or tumbler. Position the beans about half-way up the glass, and put a little water in the jar so that the blotting paper is wet. Keep it in a warm place; soon the roots and shoots will grow, and before long the bean plants will have several leaves.

right If you want to grow a proper bean plant, it is better to plant the seed in potting mixture in a pot. One of the best kinds for a child is a climbing green bean, which can be trained up a cane or around a window frame. If you use a bean seed from a fresh bean, make sure that it is fully ripe, and dry the seed in the sun first. Whole lentils can also be planted in a shallow dish of moist potting mixture, and form attractive green foliage.

Ginger; coffee

If you can find a fresh ginger root in a food shop, you can grow it into an extremely handsome indoor foliage plant, with glossy dark green leaves. **below** Simply suspend the root in water until it sprouts, and then plant in a pot of good potting mixture. Keep it warm and light.

You can also grow a plant from a fresh unroasted coffee bean. It needs warm, damp potting mixture to germinate, but once you have a coffee plant it likes only moderately warm conditions — a minimum of 10°C (50°F) — and prefers shade and plenty of air. The leaves are a coppery colour when they first emerge, and turn a dark, glossy green. The small white flowers smell sweet, and are followed by red berries that contain coffee beans. Once mature, prune the bush to keep it neat for the house.

Ginger

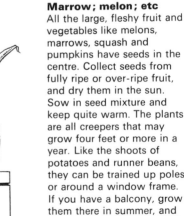

Coffee

Marrow; melon; etc

All the large, fleshy fruit and vegetables like melons, marrows, squash and pumpkins have seeds in the centre. Collect seeds from fully ripe or over-ripe fruit, and dry them in the sun. Sow in seed mixture and keep quite warm. The plants are all creepers that may grow four feet or more in a year. Like the shoots of potatoes and runner beans, they can be trained up poles or around a window frame. If you have a balcony, grow them there in summer, and you may get flowers and fruit.

Marrow

Gardening for fun

There are children, of course, who hate anything to do with gardening. The interest of others will be captured by something quick and colourful, but soon boredom will set in. The best plants for them are the free-flowering hardy annuals, as described on page 206. There are also a number of individual plants that can amuse and intrigue, as described on page 204. When a child has a little more patience, however – or where a parent is willing to take over between the child's bursts of enthusiasm – some more elaborate gardening projects can be undertaken, indoors or on an outdoor balcony or terrace. Most of those described here need only intermittent attention once established, although with younger children most of the work will no doubt end up being done by the parents!

Planting a brick

If you can find a brick of the kind **right** that has rows of holes running through, this can be made into an unusual plant 'pot'. Stand the brick on a tile, and fill the holes with good potting mixture to within two inches of the top. Plant it in the autumn, putting a crocus corm in each hole and covering with more potting mixture. Keep it in a cool place until the flower buds appear, then bring it indoors. Apart from other baby bulbs, another good plant to grow outdoors is the houseleek (*Sempervivum*; see page 165).

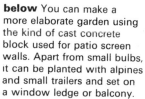

below You can make a more elaborate garden using the kind of cast concrete block used for patio screen walls. Apart from small bulbs, it can be planted with alpines and small trailers and set on a window ledge or balcony.

Desert in a dish

Cacti and succulents, with their reminders of cowboy films, have a natural fascination for very many children. **above** A simple cactus and succulent garden can be planted in a dish only a few inches across. A drainage hole is needed, plus an inch-thick layer of gravel or crocks. Grow the plants in a ready-made cactus potting mixture, or use the mix given on page 61. Do not crowd the plants. Use pieces of rugged rock to fill any gaps; these can be removed as the plants grow. The rocks and a layer of gravel on top of the soil add to the desert appearance.

Choose plants of varied shape, making sure that you have slow-growing succulents if you mix these with true cacti. Among the most fascinating succulents are the living stones (*Lithops*); a small dish planted with these makes a good fun group for a child's window sill (see page 70).
Be sure never to over-water cacti and succulents, particularly in winter, when true cacti need virtually no water at all. Give the plants plenty of light and warmth in summer, but keep them (especially cacti) quite cool in winter. In summer, let them dry out before watering thoroughly.

A miniature rose garden

For a child interested by small things, a miniature garden is ideal. Most truly miniature plants used for the kind of trough gardens described on pages 188 to 195 are alpines that only thrive outdoors, in bright light and fresh air. But some kinds will grow happily on an indoor window sill, particularly if they are put outdoors for an occasional 'rest' in warm weather. Miniature roses of many colours can be grown in this way in a small trough or pan.
below They can be laid out to form a complete rose garden. For 'grass' use *Soleirolia soleirolii*. You can make paths of gravel and, by sinking a small jar so that its rim is level with the surface, introduce a miniature pool. *Azolla caroliniana* (fairy moss) is a minute floating plant ideal for the pool.

Plant on a log

A number of houseplants live naturally on the branch of a tree, and **below** you can grow these on a log on a window sill. Probably the best kind to try is one of the bromeliads (see page 72). Remove the plant from its pot and wrap the root-ball in moist sphagnum moss. Then use wire to fix the plant to the log. Spray the plant and the moss regularly, and keep the 'urn' in the centre of the rosette of leaves topped up with water.

Water garden in a bowl

Most children love water and water gardens. If you cannot build a permanent pool, a water-lily tub can be planted and placed on a patio or balcony (see page 176). Even more simply, a bowl six to nine inches deep can be planted with miniature water-lilies. A decorative bowl is best, but a simple washing-up bowl will do. Or you can use an old sink. The smallest cultivated water-lilies are the white *Nymphaea pygmaea alba* and the yellow *N. pygmaea helvola*, whose flowers are only about an inch across. Another very small white

variety is *N. candida*, while *N. x laydekeri purpurata* is wine-red. All these should be planted in late spring or early summer in a three-inch layer of ordinary soil, covered if you wish with a thin layer of gravel or pebbles. Cover the plants only shallowly with water at first, increasing the depth as they grow.

Another attractive aquatic is the floating water hyacinth, *Eichhornia crassipes* (*E. speciosa*) — which is also cheaper than water-lilies. The whole plant floats, supported by the spongy petioles (leaf-stems), but a layer of soil is still needed to

provide nutrients in the water. The plant has three-inch spikes of beautiful blue flowers on nine-inch stems. It is tender, however, and must be wintered indoors in wet soil.

Other attractive floating miniature aquatics that can be added to your water garden bowl include *Azolla caroliniana* (fairy moss), a small fern-like plant that turns red late in the season, and *Hydrocharis morsus-ranae* (frogbit), which is rather like a minute water-lily with white flowers. These can be grown in a goldfish bowl on a window ledge.

A woodland terrarium

A terrarium is just another name for a garden in a glass case, bottle or jar. With a glass lid to keep in moisture, many plants will thrive with very rare watering — or none at all, after first planting, if the lid is close-fitting. Many kinds of houseplants can be grown successfully in terrariums, as is explained on page 30. But it is often more fun to collect your own plants to make a miniature woodland landscape. One word of warning, however: Only take common plants. A terrarium with a wide top is much easier to plant and look after than a narrow-necked bottle garden. An aquarium tank is ideal. Cover the bottom with a layer of gravel mixed with lumps of charcoal, heaping it up at the back or at one end. A piece of lichen-covered rock or bark adds interest. Then

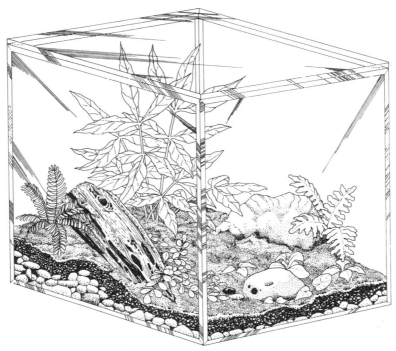

spread a one- or two-inch layer of moist potting mixture over the gravel. The best time to collect woodland plants is in the autumn. Use plastic bags to carry plants home. For 'ground cover', there are many kinds of moss. Small ferns are ideal subjects. A few seedling trees four or five inches high make points of focal interest; evergreens such as pine, fir, juniper or cedar are best.

Once planted, make sure that the soil is nicely damp and then put on the lid. Stand the terrarium in a light, fairly cool place. Some sun is welcome in winter, but do not leave it in the hot summer sun. If watering is necessary, use a fine spray. Trim back any plants that grow too fast, and remove dead flowers and any plants that develop brown patches, indicating a fungal infection.

Indoor 'topiary'

A project that needs a good deal of patience is the creation of animal and other shapes with climbing or trailing houseplants. Well done, this can look as attractive as genuine topiary created by clipping hedge plants. There are two main ways — by growing creeping plants over wire-mesh shapes stuffed with sphagnum moss, and by training pot-grown plants over metal frames. Ready-made mesh forms can be bought in some countries — in shapes such as dogs, owls, squirrels or simple geometrical shapes. Otherwise, use chicken wire and rustproof wire (such as the plastic-coated type) to make your own shape. Then stuff this with moist

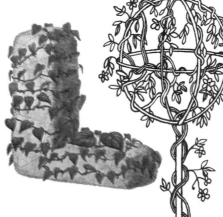

sphagnum moss, using a thin rod to poke it through the holes. Cover the outside with a layer of damp moss, held in place with rust-proof wire. Finally, plant rooted cuttings

of a very small-leaved ivy (such as *Hedera* 'Mini-Green', 'Glacier' or 'Needlepoint') in the moss, holding them in position with hairpin-shaped pieces of rustproof wire. Mist the

ivy daily with a syringe, and feed with a spray of liquid fertilizer every two to three weeks. Pin down ivy shoots to cover the shape, and trim off any obstinate bits that cannot be trained.

Using metal frames for training, other climbing houseplants can be used, including *Ficus pumila* (creeping fig), *Cissus antarctica* (kangaroo vine) and *Rhoicissus rhomboidea* (Natal vine, or grape ivy), as well as ivies (*Hedera*). Stiff wire supports, with weighted bases, can be bought or made in various shapes, including circles, hearts, candelabras, lollipops or fans. The base of the shape should be placed in the pot before planting. Use wire ties to train the plant over the form.

Fun plants for children

Plants are mainly grown indoors for their decorative qualities, but some are interesting in very special ways. Some can grow without soil, others move in various ways, a few eat insects, and some will multiply alarmingly. These fun plants made good presents to people of all ages. They will capture the imagination of children and stimulate an interest in gardening and botany. They will fascinate adults who normally find the hobby rather dull. Much amusement and entertainment can be obtained by growing them, and a basic knowledge of plants gained by watching them, and finding out why they behave so oddly.

Plants that need no soil

No plant needs soil in the very first stage of its life. The seed, bulb, corm, tuber or rhizome from which it grows contains all the food the young plant will need. It needs only warmth and water to start it growing. But, sooner or later, the shoot will use up this food and require nutrients. Normally soil is required to provide the nutrients, and unless the shoot is planted in soil, it will die.

Some plants, however, are parasites and get their nutrients by growing on other plants. Plants can also continue to grow without soil by feeding them with artificial nutrients and water; this is the basis of hydroponics, the soil-less culture of plants (see page 223). However, some plants can be raised to a useful or decorative stage without soil and without resorting to hydroponics.

Almost every child, at least in temperate climates, has at some time grown mustard and cress on wet blotting paper. The seeds sprout easily and the shoots can be used to flavour sandwiches. Mung beans are another good choice, for they grow quickly and the shoots can be used in cooking. Ways of growing these vegetables indoors are described more fully in the section on vegetables (see page 212).

Some flowers can be grown without soil, too. Crocuses will flower simply by placing some corms on a layer of clean pebbles an inch deep in a small bowl, and keeping an inch of water in the bowl. The bowl should be placed in a light and warm position. Hyacinths can also be made to bloom without soil in a

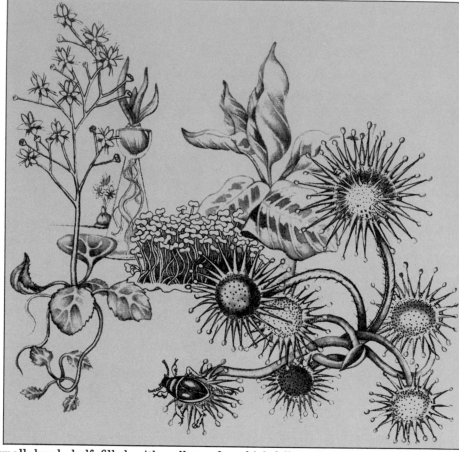

small bowl, half filled with pellets of newspaper that have been soaked in water and then squeezed into a pulp. Alternatively, a hyacinth bulb can be placed in a bulb glass so that its roots grow down into some water. For more details of growing bulbs in this way, see page 107.

Some plants will flower not only without soil, but even without water! The monarch of the east (*Sauromatum venosum*) will produce flowers and leaves from its tuber if you simply place it in a warm, dry spot out of the sun. The flowering period is early spring, and the flower is surrounded by an olive-green spathe that has purplish-brown markings. The snag is that the flower has a foul smell of rotten meat. The leaves,

which follow the flower, are very decorative, however. After flowering it is best to pot the plant in potting mixture until the top withers away in autumn. Then store the tuber in a dry place until growth starts again.

Easier to buy than *Sauromatum*, corms of some meadow saffrons (*Colchicum*) will flower if placed on a sunny window sill in late summer. The best kinds to try are *Colchicum autumnale*, which has pink or white flowers, *C. byzantinum*, with bright mauve flowers, or the various hybrids. *C. speciosum* will also flower without soil, but all the corms should be planted outdoors immediately after flowering. Then leaves will appear in spring and a new display of flowers the following autumn.

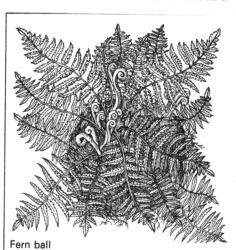

Fern ball

A fern ball

An attractive and novel feature is a fern ball. It consists of a compact mass of fern roots – usually *Davallia bullata* (squirrel's-foot fern), *D. mariesii*, *Polypodium polypodioides* or *Selaginella lepidophylla* (resurrection club-moss) – sold in a dry, dormant state. If soaked in a bucket of water and hung up in a warm, moist but shady place, the roots will begin to grow fresh green fronds. Once growth starts the ball should never be allowed to become dry.

Spider plant

Plants that eat insects

The Venus fly-trap (*Dionaea*) is the best known insect-eater. It has jaw-like traps at the ends of its leaves. When an insect touches the feelers on a trap, it springs shut and catches its victim. The plant then slowly digests the insect with its digestive juices. A Venus fly-trap will eat small pieces of meat, egg-white or cheese in addition to any insects it happens to catch. But it cannot be fooled by feeding it something it cannot eat, for the traps soon open again and reject the indigestible object.

Venus fly-traps are bought as root crowns, often potted in a mixture of sphagnum moss, peat and sand. The plants come from marshy ground, so the pot should be placed in a pan or saucer of water to keep it moist all the time. The pot should be put in a sunny position, and kept warm in winter at a minimum temperature of 10°C (50°F). A glass or plastic cover should be placed over the pot to keep the air around the fly-trap warm and humid.

Sundews (*Drosera*) are related to Venus fly-traps, and can be raised in the same way. The leaves do not have jaw-like traps but bear hairs that produce a sticky fluid. The fluid attracts insects, and holds and digests them.

Pitcher plants (*Sarracenia* and *Darlingtonia*) have funnel-shaped leaves containing a fluid. Insects are attracted to the leaves, but fall into the fluid and drown. The fluid then slowly dissolves the insect as the plant digests it.

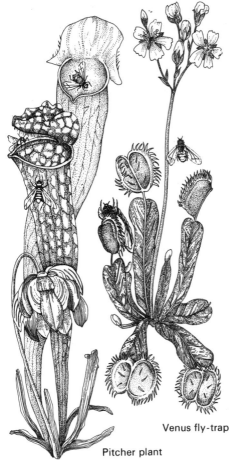

Venus fly-trap

Pitcher plant

Plants that move

Several plants will perform actions in response to certain situations. One of the best known is the sensitive plant (*Mimosa pudica*). Its small, feathery leaflets fold up tightly if they are touched, or if the plant is shaken, or even if you hold a lighted cigarette near it. The leaf stalks droop towards the stem, as if the plant is shrinking away from its attacker. When left alone, the leaves slowly open again and the plant straightens up. The sensitive plant is not hardy and is usually grown from seed in a pot as an annual. It grows to a height of about two feet.

The telegraph plant (*Desmodium gyrans*) is related to the sensitive plant, but behaves rather differently. They both fold their foliage at night, but the telegraph plant has a pair of small leaves that move round in a jerky manner when it is warm. This circular motion resembles the movement of an old telegraph or train signal, hence the name.

Several plants close their leaves or flowers at night as if they are going to sleep. The movement is slow, but can sometimes be seen. Wood sorrel (*Oxalis acetosella*) is an outdoor plant whose flowers go to sleep at dusk. Crocuses close their flowers when the temperature drops. Among houseplants, the prayer plant (*Maranta leuconeura kerchoveana*) folds its leaves like hands clasped in prayer as night falls. The prayer plant is among the easiest of indoor plants to grow (see page 49).

Sensitive plant

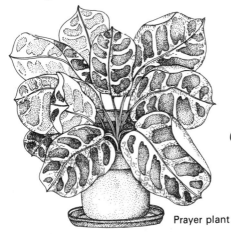

Prayer plant

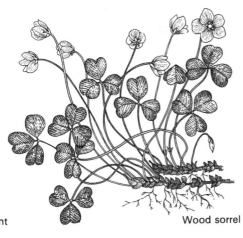

Wood sorrel

Plants that multiply

Some plants reproduce by putting out runners from which new plants grow. Indoors they can be placed in hanging baskets or in pots in open positions. The runners will hang down or spread out, surrounding the plant with a host of new little plants. The new plants can be grown in pots and they will take root and send out their own runners. In the end, you may have a whole string of plants linked to each other.

The best-named multiplier is mother-of-thousands (*Saxifraga stolonifera* or *S. sarmentosa*). It has leaves gathered into rosettes, and new little rosettes grow from the long red runners. The leaves are red below, and so mother-of-thousands is best grown in hanging

baskets or placed in a high position so that the undersides can be seen. It should be kept near a window (see page 47).

The spider plant (*Chlorophytum comosum variegatum* or *C. elatum* or *C. capense*) has narrow grass-like leaves with a broad central white line. Tufts of new leaves grow at the ends of the runners (see page 54).

The pick-a-back plant (*Tolmiea menziesii*) has downy leaves at the base of which new plantlets form. The leaves can therefore be removed and placed in water or planted in damp sand, and the plantlets will develop roots and grow. The plant also produces runners with plantlets that root. It is very easy to grow, though it must not be allowed to dry out (see page 55).

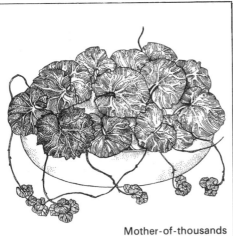

Mother-of-thousands

205

Quick colour from seeds

Children tend to be impatient gardeners. A plant has to yield quick results if it is to capture their interest and attention. For this reason those suggested here are all hardy annuals. These have the advantage that the seed is usually easy to handle and germinates quickly. Propagators and high temperatures are unnecessary and undesirable. The plants can be grown in pots indoors or outside exposed to the weather.

If possible, obtain pelleted seed. This is much easier for small fingers to manipulate. Should F1 hybrids be offered, these usually grow more vigorously. In any case always get good varieties of the flowers and buy from reputable firms – just as you would if you were obtaining the seed for yourself, and for the show garden. Seed tapes are easy to use for window boxes and troughs.

All the hardy annuals can be grown in pots of potting mixture to give results frequently far better than when grown

Cornflower

in the ordinary garden. Indeed, the flowers may grow so superbly that you may not recognize them as the humble hardies of outdoors. This of course is mainly due to the use of properly balanced potting mixture (see page 218). However, it is essential to impress on the children that the plants are *hardy*. The conditions under which they grow should be cool, very light, and airy. A very bright window sill indoors or outdoors, or a bright place on a patio, must be chosen. A window box is also suitable – preferably one with a sunny aspect.

Persuade the children to sow the seed thinly, just covering it with potting mixture. It is usually easier for them to thin the seedlings if necessary by pulling out the surplus to avoid overcrowding. It is also probably better for them to sow directly in the pots the plants are to grow in rather than to prick out from trays or pans. All sowing is best carried out in early spring.

Calendula, or pot marigold
The bright yellow and orange flowers of calendulas, or pot marigolds (*Calendula officinalis*), delight children. They are extremely easy and will grow well even with neglect and in poor soil. Modern varieties are far different from the old, rather weedy garden kinds. Choose the more dwarf forms such as 'Baby Gold' and 'Baby Orange', which in good light grow about 15 inches tall. These have lots of small double flowers. A variety with huge blooms is 'Golden King'.

Sunflower

Clarkia

Cornflower
Although cornflowers (*Centaurea cyanus*) are noted for their beautiful blue colour, fine modern varieties in rich pink are available, and also in white. Again the dwarf types should be selected. Two excellent varieties are 'Snowball', which is white and very compact, and 'Polka Dot', notable for a wide range of colours.

Clarkia
All varieties of *Clarkia elegans* tend to grow rather tall and are best avoided for window boxes. In pots they give a fine display but need the support of a few fine sticks or canes. The double varieties in shades of red and purple are recommended.

Convolvulus
Modern varieties of *Convolvulus minor* have gay flowers in many colours, often with contrasting centres. They are ideal for window boxes and will thrive in poor soil and dry conditions.

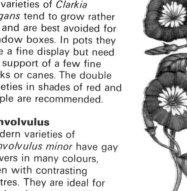
Convolvulus

Sunflower
The giant sunflower, *Helianthus annuus*, is great fun to grow, and the size of the enormous flowers fascinate children. Then, when the flowers fade, they can eat the seeds. It is of course only suitable for a patio or terrace where it can be grown in a large pot or small tub. It is best grown against a sunny wall where it is sheltered from wind. The plant can be supported if necessary by securing the stem to trellis fastened to the wall, and adults will have to help small children with this, as some varieties reach a height of six feet. Several low-growing forms will also be found listed in seed catalogues; 'Dwarf Sungold' is a variety that grows only about two feet tall.

Candytuft
Good dwarf varieties of this quick-flowering annual (*Iberis amara*) are available. 'Fairy Mixture' is very compact, with a wide range of colours. One of the brightest is 'Red Flash', whose flowers are a dazzling crimson. The heights of these should not exceed 12 inches.

Toadflax, or bunny rabbits
This delightful annual (*Linaria maroccana*) is bound to delight children. The flowers are dainty and very freely borne in many beautiful colours. They are rather like miniature snapdragons in shape. The variety 'Fairy Bouquet' is especially recommended. This is compact, and the flowers brilliantly coloured. It is good for pots or window boxes.

Candytuft

Nigella

Shirley poppy

Virginian stock
This dainty-flowered plant (*Malcolmia maritima*) has long been recommended for even young children to grow, although the colours have in the past been unexciting. However, in good modern seed strains the flowers are brighter and more vivid in hue. 'Crimson King', for example, is a rich rosy-crimson. Virginian stock often does well in fairly shady places, and is easy in window boxes or pots, although the flowers are not long-lasting

Nigella, or love-in-a-mist
This annual (*Nigella damascena*) has delicate feathery foliage and, generally, dark blue flowers. In the form 'Persian Jewels', however, there are also various shades of pink and white. It is usually available as pelleted seed, but can get untidy in window boxes exposed to wind.

Poppies
Both the handsome, showy flowers and the quaint seed capsules of poppies (*Papaver* species and varieties) attract the attention of children. Poppies flourish in the poorest soil and with the minimum of attention. The old-fashioned 'Shirley' double poppies have many colours and large flowers. Children often like to use the petals as 'confetti'. The carnation-flowered varieties are also suitable. Very eye-catching are the varieties derived from the opium poppy, *Papaver somniferum*, which have vivid red petals with a jet black spot at the base of each.

Double dwarf nasturtiums

French marigold

Butterfly flower
Schizanthus hybrids are described on page 78 as greenhouse or conservatory plants, but they are so easy that the dwarf forms can be managed by children without problems. The variety 'Hit Parade' is especially recommended. They look extremely exotic, and are sometimes known as the 'poor man's orchid'.

African marigold
African marigolds (*Tagetes erecta* hybrids), although impressive flowers for the garden, are so easy that children will have no trouble with them. There are a host of varieties, often **F1** hybrids, offered by seedsmen. The flowers are outstanding for show and long-lasting qualities. Varieties will be found suitable for small containers and pots, and there are giant forms for larger containers on the patio. The plants are regarded as half-hardy, but flowering takes place very quickly and children can grow them from seed sown in spring.

French marigold
These (*Tagetes patula* hybrids) can be cultivated in a similar manner to African marigolds. They are all much more compact, and are ideal for window boxes. There are many varieties with single and double flowers, and they have also been hybridized with African marigolds to give 'Afro-French marigolds'. As would be expected, these are intermediate in size between the two, but the flowers are often very large.

Butterfly flower

African marigold

Climbing nasturtiums

Nasturtium
Old varieties of nasturtium (*Tropaeolum majus*) tended to be very leafy, the foliage often obscuring the showy flowers. Splendid new varieties can be had in a bright colour range, and the dwarf types are particularly suited for children to grow. The seeds are easy to handle, quick to germinate, and easily grown in the most adverse conditions. 'Dwarf Jewel' has all the usual bright colours as well as some unusual shades, and it produces large double blooms well above the foliage. Of special interest is the new variety 'Alaska', which is notable for its unusual foliage, variegated in green and cream. Its flowers are all the shades you expect to get from mixing bright red and yellow.

Ornamental grasses

Children should also have little difficulty in training the tall climbing varieties up bamboo canes.

Ornamental grasses
Several ornamental grasses are fun for children to grow. Their favourite is undoubtedly hare's-tail grass, *Lagurus ovatus*, with its delightful soft, fluffy heads.
Also liked is squirrel-tail grass, *Hordeum jubatum*, which is barley-like in appearance. Quite different is quaking grass, *Briza maxima*. This has heads bearing several nodding spikelets and is so named because these produce a rustling sound when brushed together by the wind. All of them grow quickly from seed, and many seedsmen offer mixed packets of various ornamental grasses.

207

Fruit without an orchard

Even those with no space outside to use as a garden can still enjoy eating their own home-grown fruit. There is a miniature variety of eating apple that can be grown indoors in a pot placed in a sunny window. It is supplied as a little tree only three feet high, and will bear about five pounds of fruit in the first year. The yield will go on increasing every year until it is producing more than 20 pounds when it is five years old. Yet the tree never grows higher than 4½ feet! It will last as long as 15 years, and needs little attention except watering and feeding.

Mini-apples are, however, an exception to the general rule that fruit-growing is best left to those who have space outside, for most fruit trees and bushes are too large to grow indoors, and need plenty of sunshine to ripen. Those lucky enough to have a large conservatory or garden room with a glass roof have far greater opportunities, however. Grapes and passion-fruit, oranges and lemons, even bananas – all these will flourish under glass if you can give them enough room.

With a patio or roof garden, too, a wide range of the hardier fruits can be grown. Soft fruits such as blackcurrants and raspberries can be raised in tubs, and strawberries can be grown in a variety of ways. Most fruit trees, especially apples, pears and figs, do well in large tubs, though plums and cherries grow too big to be worth trying. Several trees can be trained back against a wall with their branches spread in a fan. Vines can be grown to climb over a fence, trellis or overhead frame. A few kinds of nut trees can also be grown.

Fruit trees and bushes are a very long-lasting feature of any garden. They tend to dominate because of their size, and few will be required on a small patio. A good idea is to train a fruit tree or two over a wall as a backdrop to the rest of the garden. However, the wall must receive a lot of sun for the trees to bear

fruit. Apples and pears are perhaps the most popular pot fruit trees. In addition to the fruits of summer and autumn, their delicate blossom is a delight in spring.

When choosing fruit trees and bushes, bear in mind the problem of pollination. Some trees are self-fertile and produce fruit alone. But others are self-sterile, and must be pollinated by another tree if fruit is to form. If the patio or roof garden is to have a single fruit tree or bush, then it must be a self-fertile one. If self-sterile trees or bushes are wanted, the nurseryman will advise on the best combinations of varieties to purchase.

While fruit trees and bushes can be raised from seed or seedlings, it takes

a long time before any fruit is obtained. It is both easier and quicker to buy established young trees or bushes. In general, they must have a sunny position and should be grown in well-drained soil. They require an annual feeding with fertilizers, usually sulphate of ammonia and sulphate of potash, and they must be sprayed to kill pests and blight.

Pruning is also necessary every year. Most trees or bushes can be pruned and trained into cordons, in which the fruits grow close to the stem or trunk, making a thin, space-saving tree or bush. They can also be made into fans or into espaliers, in which the branches grow in horizontal tiers in one plane, to grow against walls.

Soft fruits

Blackcurrants may yield as much as ten pounds of fruit per bush. They are hardy plants, but should be kept in the sun or in partial shade. The fruits grow on young wood, so the old shoots should be pruned away close to the soil after fruiting or in winter. New bushes can be grown by planting cuttings in autumn. Red currants and white currants can be grown as bushes, or as fans trained against a wall or fence. They need a sunny, sheltered position. Unlike black-currants, the fruit grows on old wood, and the only pruning needed is to cut away about half the main new growth, pruning other new shoots more drastically. Propagation is by cuttings in the autumn.
Gooseberries grow well on a well drained, medium loam soil. They can be grown as

bushes or single-stem cordons. Pruning is like that of red currants, except that it need not be so severe as the young wood does produce fruits. Birds are likely to damage the plants in winter, so tie cotton thread around the bushes to discourage them.
Propagation is by cuttings taken in the autumn.
Raspberries grow as single canes that shoot from the base of the plant each year. They take up little room and and are therefore an ideal choice of fruit for the patio. Raspberries are grown from healthy canes bought from a nursery or garden centre. Plant them in winter in a sunny position, and cut down to 12 inches in spring to encourage growth. The canes will need supports when grown. Those canes that bear fruits must be cut back to soil level in the autumn, and the others

(which will bear next year's crop) should have their tips removed in early spring.
Blackberries and loganberries can be trained in fans on wires supported above the pots or tubs, and do well against a fence or wall. Fix wires at three, five and six feet above soil level, and tie the stems to these.
Treatment is like that for raspberries. Thornless varieties can be bought.

Strawberries

Strawberries can be grown in barrels, in special strawberry pots, on movable strawberry walls, and in hanging baskets. So they can be moved around easily. Strawberries need good drainage and a soil with plenty of humus. You can grow them from healthy plants bought from nurseries or garden centres, or the plantlets that form on the varieties with long

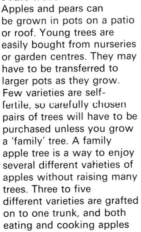

runners can be pegged down to form new plants that are planted out in the summer. Strawberries must be protected against frost when flowering and fruiting. They should not be kept for more than three years as virus diseases are likely to occur. The old plants should be burned and new planted. You can make a strawberry barrel by taking one end out of an old barrel, drilling drainage holes in the other end and making two-inch holes in two or three rows around the sides. The first row should not be less than two feet from the base of the barrel, and the positions of the holes should alternate so that the holes in adjacent rows are not directly above or beneath each other. Place a two-inch perforated zinc tube in the centre of the barrel as low as the first row of holes, for watering, and fill around it with Potting Mixture no. 3. Place a strawberry plant in each hole and some more in the top of the barrel. Place the barrel in a sunny position. Keep it well watered once growth starts, and add manure or fertilizer in mid-spring. The strawberries will grow and run all over the barrel. It can later be used for flowers such as aubrieta instead of strawberries if a change is desired. A strawberry pot is just like a small version of a strawberry barrel, but made of clay. It is so used in just the same way, but needs more frequent watering as it dries out quickly.

A strawberry wall is made of a framework of wire mesh (see page 127). Strawberries are planted at the bottom and trained to climb up and over the wall. Like the strawberry barrel, it can be moved to

keep it sheltered from frost early in the year and to take it out of the sun later on. Another good way of growing strawberries is to use hanging baskets, as the runners will hang down. Alpine strawberries, which are small and sweet, are the best to use. They should be raised from seed. Perpetual-fruiting alpines continue fruiting well into the autumn. They prefer a partially shaded position.

Fruit trees

Apples and pears can be grown in pots on a patio or roof. Young trees are easily bought from nurseries or garden centres. They may have to be transferred to larger pots as they grow. Few varieties are self-fertile, so carefully chosen pairs of trees will have to be purchased unless you grow a 'family' tree. A family apple tree is a way to enjoy several different varieties of apples without raising many trees. Three to five different varieties are grafted on to one trunk, and both eating and cooking apples

can be harvested from the tree. Family apple trees do not always last very long, as the strongest varieties tend to take over the tree. The chosen varieties will usually fertilize each other. Container-grown apples and pears need a little trouble. Fresh soil must be packed around the roots every year, and they must be protected from frost. Dwarf varieties are best, and they can be trained into pyramid shapes, or into cordons or espaliers. Prune in winter to maintain the shape of the tree, and again in summer to cut back new growth so that light can get to the fruit. The trees also need spraying in summer and winter to kill pests and blight.

Figs are a good choice for pot growing, if you have a sunny site for them, because restricting their roots keeps them under control and aids fruiting. Buy a growing tree already in a pot. The fruits will only ripen in cooler climates if they are well sheltered and get a lot of sunshine. The best way to raise them is to train the tree in a fan against a sheltered wall that faces the midday sun. The fruits form on shoots produced during the previous summer, and these shoots need protection from frost by covering them with sacking. Pruning should be carried out in spring to remove old growth and overcrowded shoots.

Peaches and nectarines can be trained in fans against a sunny wall, and in fact you can buy ready-trained trees. The site must be frost-free, because the trees flower early. They must be watered well in dry summers. Prune in early summer, cutting away all side growth along

the branches except at the base and tip. Spray with pesticide in late winter. Apricots are raised in much the same way as peaches. Buy a dwarf fan-shape tree and train it against a sunny, sheltered wall. It will grow to about 10 feet, which may be too large for many patios.

Grapes

Delicious grapes can be grown under glass, and there are many varieties for warm climates. Hardy varieties of grape vines can be raised outside in cool climates, though sun and warmth are needed to ripen the fruit. The vine can be grown from a young plant placed in a large tub. A compact plant can be developed by allowing the strongest shoot to grow and cutting the others back in winter to one bud. Fruit will form from this main shoot, but the bunches may have to be sheltered if they are to ripen. A new main shoot is chosen every winter, and the old one cut away. Alternatively, the vine may be allowed to climb over a trellis, pergola or fence if it is required more for decoration than for fruit.

Nuts

Cobnuts or filberts, which are varieties of hazelnuts, can be grown as bushes in tubs. They flower early and therefore need protection from frost in cool regions. The male catkins must shed their pollen before pruning. Leave last year's growth, but cut back old wood to one catkin. Another pruning is done in midsummer, cutting back side shoots to half their length or breaking them and leaving the ends hanging. The nuts can be harvested in autumn and

stored for winter use. Chinese peanuts are an interesting variety of peanuts that can be grown from seeds. Grow them in pots indoors in a sunny position. After flowering, the young fruits bore themselves into the soil. Dig up the nuts when the plant has turned yellow; they taste good.

Herbs in pots and boxes

Marjoram, wrote Nicholas Culpeper, an astrologer-physician of the 1600s, in his *Complete Herbal*, 'strengthens the stomach and head much; there is scarcely a better herb growing for relieving a sour stomach, loss of appetite, cough, consumption of the lungs; it cleanses the body of choler, expels poison, remedies the infirmities of the spleen, and helps the bites of venomous beasts. It provokes urine and the terms in women, helps the dropsy, scurvy, scabs, itch, and yellow jaundice.' Basil, on the other hand, was looked on with suspicion: 'Hilarius, a French physician, affirms upon his own knowledge, that an acquaintance of his, by common smelling to it, had a scorpion bred in his brain.'

We no longer ascribe quite such miraculous powers to herbs, but they are rightly valued for their fragrance and taste. Many meat and fish dishes, soups, salads and sauces are improved enormously in flavour by adding herbs, and bunches of herbs sweeten the air throughout the home. You can keep cupboards and drawers sweet-smelling by leaving small sachets of mixed herbs in them.

You can, of course, always buy your herbs – dried or fresh – but the flavour is never so good as in home-grown, freshly harvested herbs, and the more unusual kinds are generally unobtainable. There is no difficulty in growing them indoors in pots on window sills, or on window ledges outdoors. Larger pots or tubs of herbs can be placed on a patio or balcony, or in a porch. As friends enter and leave, the herbs may release their fragrance as the visitors brush against them.

Cultivating herbs
Herbs generally need sunshine and a light, fertile and well drained soil to grow well. Improve the drainage of clay or plastic pots with a layer of broken crocks. Suitable potting mixtures are no. 1 or no. 2, or equal parts of soil, sand and leaf-mould. The plants should be kept just moist as they grow. Most herbs can be grown from seeds, which should be planted $\frac{1}{4}$ to $\frac{1}{2}$ inch deep. Alternatively, small pots of growing herbs can be bought at nurseries and garden centres, and replanted in larger pots. Some kinds can be grown from cuttings (see page 228).

An easy way of raising herbs is to buy special packs of seeds and soil designed to aid germination. The packs are made up of sets of small peat pots, each containing seeds of one species of herb and a suitable soil. The pots are covered by transparent plastic domes. To grow the herbs, simply moisten the pots and place them on a sunny window sill. The plastic cover acts like a miniature greenhouse, and the plants soon start to shoot. Thin out the shoots as they grow, and then transfer the whole pot to a clay pot filled with soil. The clay pots can then be placed wherever wanted, and the herbs will grow to full size. Their roots will grow through the peat pots into the soil.

Indoors, herbs can be grown in pots on sunny window sills at any time of year, provided they get enough warmth, light and moisture. It is best to grow each kind in a separate pot, rather than try to grow a complete indoor herb garden in one long box. Individual herbs can then be moved about and used without disturbing the others. Herbs may also be grown in small bottle gardens (see page 33).

Outdoors, most herb seeds should be planted in the spring when there is no longer any danger of frost. Small pots can be placed together in window boxes and boxes for balconies. There is also scope for growing several herbs together in the same tub, although all of them should require the same amount of water if they are to do well. Flowers may be included to add colour; geraniums are a good choice, or plant *Scilla* bulbs in a tub of parsley. The herbs themselves generally bear small flowers – usually

Parsley and spring bulbs

white, pink or purple – but they should be pinched out to promote leaf growth.

Many herbs are annuals, and so the question of tending these through the winter does not arise. Less hardy perennials, such as rosemary and bay, should be brought indoors in extreme cold.

Using herbs
One advantage of growing herbs indoors is, of course, that fresh herbs can be available for cooking at any time. When picking them, pinch out the uppermost growing tips. This will help to keep the plant bushy. Dried or frozen herbs may be used instead of fresh herbs. To dry them, gather the leaves carefully, preferably before the plants are in full flower, and place them in a warm, dry, airy place out of the sun. An airing cupboard is a good place, and the sheets will gain a slight fragrance. The leaves should be turned every day, and will dry in about a week. Alternatively, sprigs of leaves can be hung up in a warm, dry place. When they have become brittle, store the leaves in tightly sealed jars. Take care not to crumble them.

For freezing, wash the leaves and then blanch them by placing them in boiling water for a minute. As soon as they are cold, the leaves should be placed in the deep freeze. Frozen herbs can be cut and placed straight in the cooking pot without thawing.

Herbs need not only be used for cooking. Sprigs of dried herbs, especially rosemary, thyme and marjoram, produce a delicate fragrance that sweetens the air. Dried lavender flowers are tied up in sachets and used to perfume linen. Potpourris are made by mixing dried herbs, flower petals and spices, and placing the mixture in bowls to scent the air in a room or cupboard.

Balm
A hardy perennial, balm grows to a height of about two feet. Seeds should be planted outdoors in spring, or old plants can be divided and repotted. The leaves have a strong lemony scent, and can be used to make tea and to add a refreshing taste to ice drinks. Fresh chopped balm leaves can be incorporated in salads, sauces for fish dishes, and omelettes.

Balm

Basil
Basil is a half-hardy annual, growing to about one foot. Seeds should be planted outdoors in late spring or early summer. The leaves have a strong spicy scent. They can be used to flavour soups and stews, and go very well with tomato salads and other tomato dishes.

Basil

Bay
Sweet bay makes a splendid tub plant, growing ten or more feet tall if unchecked, and needing pruning twice a year to keep it an attractive shape. Equally, small specimens can be grown in pots and boxes. It is a fairly hardy evergreen shrub best bought as a pot-plant or grown from cuttings taken in summer. The leaves have a sweet, spicy aroma, and are used to flavour a wide range of dishes, from fish and meat stews to milk puddings.

Bay

Chervil
Usually grown as an annual, chervil reaches about $1\frac{1}{2}$ feet in height. Outdoors, the seeds may be sown from early spring to midsummer. The leaves are ready to use six weeks after planting, and a continuous supply can be assured by planting at six-week intervals. They have an aroma rather like parsley and are used in sauces and soups.

Chervil

Chives
Chives are easy-to-grow hardy perennials, reaching a height of nine inches. Plant the seeds outdoors from spring to midsummer, or propagate by dividing a clump. The grass-like leaves have a sharp, oniony flavour, and are added freshly chopped to salads and egg and cheese dishes. Bacon sandwiches containing chives are delicious. Chives will remain evergreen throughout the winter if brought indoors.

Chives

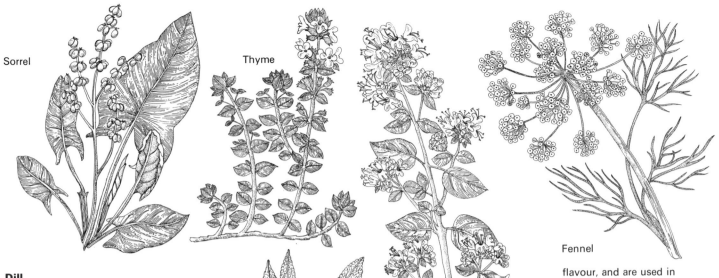

Sorrel

Thyme

Sage

Savory

Marjoram

Fennel

Dill

Dill is an annual, growing two to three feet high. Seeds should be sown outdoors when frost is no longer likely, up to midsummer. The leaves and dried seeds are used to flavour pickles and vinegar. In cooking, dill leaves add an aniseed-like taste to salads, sauces and fish dishes.

Fennel

A hardy perennial, growing from two to five feet in height, fennel can be kept compact by pinching out the growing points. Plant the seeds outdoors from spring to midsummer. The leaves have a flavour rather like that of aniseed and can be used fresh or dried for making tea and sauces. Fennel goes well with fish, pork and veal, and the fresh leaves make a good soup.

Marjoram

Sweet marjoram is best grown as a half-hardy annual in cool climates, but is perennial in warmer regions. It grows to a height of about 1½ feet. Seeds should be planted outdoors in late spring or early summer. Marjoram has an aromatic scent rather like thyme. It is used fresh or dried, to flavour meat, poultry, soups, stews, omelettes and stuffing.

Mint

Common mint, or spearmint, is a hardy perennial growing about two feet high. Seeds can be planted at any time from autumn to spring, but it is easier to plant stem cuttings or pieces of root. The strongly scented leaves are used to make refreshing cold drinks and to brew tea. They are

also added when cooking vegetables, especially peas and potatoes. Finely-chopped fresh leaves are used to make mint sauce and jelly, the traditional accompaniment to roast lamb in Britain.

Parsley

A hardy perennial usually grown as an annual or biennial, parsley reaches a height of one to two feet. Outdoors, seeds are planted in early spring for a summer and autumn crop, and in midsummer for a winter and spring crop. It can be grown decoratively in a pot like a strawberry pot. Fresh-chopped parsley leaves are a common ingredient of sauces, especially for fish. Butter containing parsley and garlic is ideal for cooking snails and shrimps. Sprigs of fresh parsley are often used as a garnish.

Rosemary

A perennial hardy in many areas, rosemary may have to be taken indoors in severe

winters. It grows to a height of two to five feet, but pinching out the growing points keeps the plant compact. It is best grown from six-inch cuttings planted in spring or autumn. The leaves have a spicy aroma, and add to the flavour of all kinds of roast meat, especially lamb, and grilled fish. Fresh sprigs or dried leaves may be used.

Sage

Sage is a hardy evergreen shrub reaching a height of 1½ feet. Sow seeds outdoors from late spring to midsummer, or grow from cuttings taken in summer. The fresh leaves may be used to make tea, but sage is mainly used as an ingredient of stuffings for poultry. It has a heavy, aromatic flavour.

Savory

Summer savory is a hardy annual, growing up to one foot in height. Plant seeds outdoors in spring. The leaves have a sharp, spicy

flavour, and are used in salads, soups, fish and egg dishes. Dried summer savory may be used in making stuffings and flavouring sausages. Winter savory, although used in the same way, is a hardy perennial, growing to two feet. It has a slightly more bitter flavour than summer savory.

Sorrel

A hardy perennial, sorrel grows about one foot high. Outdoors, the seeds can be planted at any time from autumn to spring. The plant likes moist soil. The large leaves have a bitter flavour, and can be eaten raw in salads or cooked with butter to make a purée to be eaten with pork, veal, fish and eggs. Sorrel soup is a good start to a meal.

Tarragon

An almost hardy perennial, tarragon reaches a height of 1½ feet. The seeds should be sown outdoors from autumn to spring. The leaves have a strong aniseed flavour. They are used to make tarragon vinegar and, freshly chopped, to flavour soups and sauces. Tarragon goes very well with chicken. The leaves lose their flavour when dried.

Thyme

Thyme is a small hardy shrub, growing about nine inches high. Grow from cuttings taken in early summer. The strong, aromatic flavour of the leaves make thyme one of the most popular herbs. They are used, fresh or dried, in cooking soups, fish, savory meat dishes and vegetables, and in making stuffings for poultry.

Vegetables without a garden

The delights of fresh vegetables within arm's reach of the kitchen are as easily available to the gardenless city dweller as to those who have a vegetable patch handy. Salad vegetables – particularly lettuce, spring onions and radishes – can easily be raised in a box placed on a sunny window sill.

Some kinds are, admittedly, best avoided. Horse-radish, for example, should not be grown in the salad window box, as it will soon take over. Neither should carrots or beetroot, unless the box is deep enough to take them. But another valuable vegetable that can easily be raised indoors is the tomato. It needs more special treatment than the other salad vegetables, and so should be grown separately in pots and not alongside the others in the salad box. But the taste of freshly picked tomatoes is well worth the trouble. Other indoor vegetables include mustard and cress, mung beans and mushrooms.

If you have a terrace or balcony, you have much more scope for growing vegetables. Indeed, you can raise whatever vegetables you wish, although there is little point in growing cabbages, cauliflowers or Brussels sprouts, as they take up so much room and are readily available in shops. But most other kinds of vegetables are worth growing. It is a good idea to raise potato plants in separate pots. They can be pulled up in early summer before they get too large, and you will then have delicious new potatoes to eat at a time when they are still expensive in the shops.

A vegetable garden on a patio or balcony can be both useful and decorative. You can use a variety of pots, tubs, window boxes, large floor containers and hanging baskets (in which some varieties of tomato can be grown). Herbs should be added here and there (see page 210), and flowers will improve the appearance. For example, dwarf marigolds can be grown among the lettuces of a salad box.

Some decorative vegetables should be included to vary the appearance of the garden. Variegated kale, with its curly leaves of purple, pink and white, is a good choice. Trellises and stakes should be provided for some of the climbing vegetables, such as cucumbers, peas and beans, which may form a green backdrop to the patio or balcony. A vegetable garden makes a good place to entertain guests in the summer. What more pleasant way is there to begin an evening than to sip a beer, aperitif or cocktail, and munch some tiny fresh tomatoes dipped in fresh chopped basil and salt and a little olive oil?

Cultivation

In general, vegetables need plenty of sun and good drainage. The containers should have holes in the bottom to let excess water escape, and a layer of gravel or small stones below the soil. Almost all vegetables are annuals, and so the composition of a vegetable garden can be changed from year to year. Where vegetables are raised outside, they should be thoroughly washed before use. Pollution from city streets may help them to grow by killing blight and pests, but it will not do you any good!

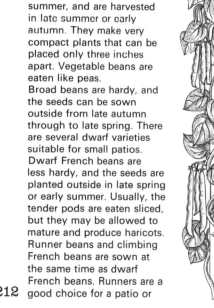

Aubergines
Like tomatoes, to which they are related, aubergines or egg plants are tender, and cannot be raised outside in cool climates. However, you can grow them from seed indoors in much the same way as tomatoes (see below). The large purple fruit has a spicy flavour and is striking to look at. It is essential for many Mediterranean dishes.

Beans
So-called vegetable beans, which are varieties of soya beans, are the most nutritious of vegetables because they contain large amounts of protein. Hardy varieties will thrive in cool climates, unlike the tropical soya bean. They are grown outside from seeds planted from mid-spring to early summer, and are harvested in late summer or early autumn. They make very compact plants that can be placed only three inches apart. Vegetable beans are eaten like peas.
Broad beans are hardy, and the seeds can be sown outside from late autumn through to late spring. There are several dwarf varieties suitable for small patios. Dwarf French beans are less hardy, and the seeds are planted outside in late spring or early summer. Usually, the tender pods are eaten sliced, but they may be allowed to mature and produce haricots. Runner beans and climbing French beans are sown at the same time as dwarf French beans. Runners are a good choice for a patio or balcony garden, for they are decorative, with bright orange or scarlet flowers. Sow them outside in early summer. Lengths of string should be tied between the container and the wall or fence so that the beans can climb easily. Alternatively poles or a trellis may be used. Mung beans provide the succulent bean shoots used in Chinese cooking. Grow them indoors in a warm place. The beans are placed on a layer of wet cotton wool or flannel after soaking them overnight in cold water. You should then place the bowl containing the beans in a plastic bag and cover it with paper to keep out the light. After a week or so, the beans will have sprouted and the shoots can be gathered.

Beetroot
Beetroot has decorative leaves as well as a tasty root. Plant the seeds outside from spring to midsummer. Beetroot is normally red, but golden and white varieties exist. Apart from their interesting colours, the leaves of these varieties have a flavour rather like spinach.

Carrots
Like beetroots, carrots go well with salads. The seeds should be planted outdoors from spring to midsummer. There are several stump-rooted varieties that should be chosen for shallow boxes.

Celery
Self-blanching varieties should be used. Sow the seed in a box in early spring but keep it at a minimum temperature of 13°C (55°F). Then plant out the shoots in a rich soil in early summer. The celery will be ready to eat in autumn.

Chicory
Chicory is a winter vegetable, used in salads or braised with butter. Sow the seeds in early summer. The roots need plenty of room. In late autumn, lift the plants, cut off the roots and place them in boxes under light soil. For use early in winter, store one box in a warm dark place. Leave the other boxes in a cool dark place for later eating. The variety 'Crystal Head' produces heads (chicons) even in daylight.

Courgettes (zucchini)
These are young marrows (squashes), usually cooked in butter. The seeds can be sown outside in early summer. The courgettes are harvested when they are about four inches long.

Cucumbers
Cucumbers have a very low calorie content, and so are good for a slimmer's diet. Hardy varieties can be grown in cool climates from seed sown outside in a large pot in late spring or early summer. The cucumber vines can then be trained to grow up trellis above the pot. Special small varieties for use in patio or balcony gardens have been produced. Others do well under glass. Apart from frequent watering, cucumbers need little attention. Male flowers should be removed, as pollinated cucumbers have large seeds and are bitter.

Garlic
Garlic is essential to flavour many dishes, but it is expensive to buy in cool climates. However, it can easily be grown. The cloves are separated from the bulbs and planted an inch deep in spring. Harvest at the end of summer. Bulbs of garlic keep well hung up in bunches.

Kale
Kale is a handsome plant, with its tightly curled leaves. Most varieties are green, but variegated kale is purple, pink and white. Sow kale in late spring and then transplant in midsummer. Kale is well worth growing; apart from its decorative qualities it is very hardy and continues to grow throughout winter when fresh vegetables are scarce. The outside leaves are cooked like cabbage.

Leeks
Like kale, leeks are hardy winter vegetables. The seeds are sown in spring and the young leeks transplanted in midsummer. They should be earthed up to blanch the stems. There are quick-growing varieties for autumn use.

Lettuce
Lettuce is a must for the indoor gardener. There are many different varieties, including dwarf kinds ideal for salad boxes. Seeds or seedlings can be sown or planted at almost any time

and the lettuce can be harvested all the year round. There are hardy varieties for outdoor use at all times. Lettuce grows well on a rich, moisture-retaining soil. The plants should be well watered to keep bright green.

Mushrooms
Mushrooms are the most indoor of all vegetables, for they can be grown in the dark at any time of year. In fact, darkness is not essential but sunlight must be avoided. A temperature of 10 to 15°C (50 to 59°F) is required. The best way to grow mushrooms is to purchase special sterilized compost and mushroom spawn. If the instructions are followed correctly, the mushrooms should be harvested six to eight weeks after planting the spawn in the compost.

Mustard and cress
Mustard and cress grow in exactly the same way, and are often grown together. Simply scatter the seeds on the surface of some soil or bulb fibre in a pot or tray, or you can even grow them on wet blotting paper. To be ready at the same time, cress seeds should be sown first and mustard seeds added four days later. The pot or tray should be well watered and then covered with paper or put in the dark until the seeds germinate. The shoots will be ready to eat within three weeks. Indoors, mustard and cress can be grown at any time. Outside, the seeds should be sown during the spring and summer.

Okra
Okra, or ladies' fingers, are slender green vegetables with

a delicate taste. They are used in soups and sauces, and also in Indian and Mediterranean cookery. They are tender plants, but seeds can be successfully sown outside in cool regions in a sheltered position in summer.

Onions
No salad is complete without spring onions. The seeds can be sown in indoor salad boxes and pots from spring to early autumn, and several crops can be obtained. Hardy varieties can be planted later for an early crop the following spring. Bulb onions are a vital ingredient of many dishes, but grow slowly from seed — taking a year from sowing to harvesting. Onion sets — small bulbs — are quicker and easy to use. Plant them in mid-spring with the tip of the bulb just showing, and the onions will be ready by early autumn.

Peas
Peas are among the most popular vegetables. Ordinary varieties will need a cane or trellis to climb along, but there are dwarf varieties that can support themselves. They have pretty flowers that add to the appearance of the vegetable garden, and one variety even has purple pods! Different varieties can be sown outdoors from early winter through to summer to produce crops throughout the season, from spring to autumn.

Peppers
Peppers (capsicums) are often used in Mediterranean and Eastern cooking. They are tender plants, and in cool areas must be sown indoors in spring at a temperature of 18°C (64°F). The seedlings

can be planted outside in a sunny, warm position when summer comes.

Potatoes
Grow potatoes from tubers ('seed potatoes') that are kept indoors in winter until they begin to sprout in early spring. Reduce the number of sprouts on a tuber to three before planting outside in a large pot. Early growth must be protected from frost by covering with straw or soil. The potato plant should be earthed up in late spring and early summer, and new potatoes will be ready in midsummer.

Radishes
Radishes can be grown very easily in salad boxes by sowing seed from spring to late summer outdoors. The plants are ready about a month after sowing, so several crops can be obtained by successive sowing. Alternatively, you can use a special mixture of seeds that can be sown together but will harvest at different dates.

Spinach
Spinach is delicious cooked in butter. There are both summer and winter varieties, so that a constant supply of spinach can be had by sowing both kinds in succession.

Sweet corn
Although sweet corn normally grows very high, compact varieties have been developed. Seeds can be sown outdoors in early summer in a sunny position.

Tomatoes
Tomatoes are favourite vegetables for salads or cooking, and nothing compares with the flavour of your own freshly picked crop. There are many different

varieties of tomatoes, but the smaller ones are probably best for those without gardens. Some, such as 'Small Fry', can even be grown in window boxes. Tomatoes are tender plants and can be grown outdoors in cool areas only by planting out seedlings in early summer. The seedlings are raised from seeds sown in spring and kept at a temperature of at least 15°C (59°F). They need rich soil. A sheltered, sunny position is needed if the tomatoes are to ripen. The fruits may have to be brought indoors to ripen if the summer is cool. Even if they do not ripen, the green tomatoes can be used to make chutney. Indoors, sow tomato seeds in late winter. The pot or tray should have a glass cover to keep in the moisture. Potting Mixture no. 3 should be used, and kept moist. The seedlings should be transferred to small peat pots, and transferred complete to larger clay pots when the young plants are six inches high. Keep them in a sunny, airy place. When the fruits begin to grow, the pots should be stood on a tray of wet pebbles to provide a moist atmosphere. The plants will need to be staked as they grow, and the trusses of fruit should be tied up to support them. Pick the fruit as it ripens, for this helps the other tomatoes to grow. A so-called Cherry tomato can be grown overhead in a hanging pot. The branches grow out horizontally at first, and then cascade down as the fruits grow. One established plant should be planted in the pot, and the soil pushed well down beneath the rim so that a lot of water can be given.

8 Techniques and technicalities

Some green-fingered people can do no wrong with their plants; to others the techniques of gardening are a complete mystery. In fact, there is no great difficulty in achieving success with plants, as the articles in this part show. It covers such topics as feeding and watering, plant health, growing plants from seeds and cuttings, tools, pots and potting, and a special section devoted to the difficulties of the elderly or disabled gardener.

Following this reference section are useful charts to help you choose the best plants for your needs, plus extensive indexes, a book list, and useful addresses.

Understanding your plant

Plants, like all living things, make certain demands on their surroundings in order to carry on the activities they need for continued healthy growth. Although many plants can manage very nicely without assistance, most plants – particularly indoor ones – are sufficiently sensitive to their care and surroundings for these to make the difference between an indifferent – hopefully not yet dead – plant, and something of remarkable beauty. You can avoid much of the trial and error of gardening if you understand a little about the workings of the plant itself. The mysteries of pruning, for example, are banished when you know what actually happens when you cut a shoot in one place rather than another.

The essential activities of a plant are similar to our own, but they may not be so easily recognizable. Most gardeners are aware of their plants feeding, growing and reproducing, but respiration, excretion, sensitivity and movement are less apparent – though just as vital. And in order to perform these activities plants have needs very similar to our own: food, water, light, warmth and air.

How plants feed

A plant clearly cannot search out food in the way that animals do, so it is restricted to absorbing the necessary chemical substances from its immediate surroundings – the atmosphere and soil. A green plant builds up its own food from the carbon dioxide and water it absorbs. With the help of energy from sunlight, it manufactures sugar, its food, in the leaves. This process is called photosynthesis. The sugar is then carried to active regions to be used, or to storage organs to be stored as starch. Some starch is also stored in the leaves.

If the sugar is to be used immediately for activity, oxygen from the atmosphere is used to release energy from it during respiration, just as we use oxygen to release energy from the food we have eaten. Fortunately for us, the oxygen in the air is constantly replenished by plants during photosynthesis.

Why plants drink

Another vital plant activity influenced by the gardener is the plant's ability to give off water to the atmosphere from the leaves by transpiration, in much the same way that animals sweat. This has a cooling effect, as it does on our skin, and also controls the uptake of water and mineral salts by the roots. High temperatures, a dry atmosphere or a draught will increase the rate of transpiration, so adequate water at the roots is essential to replace that lost from the leaves. Excessive humidity or cold will slow down transpiration, however, so give less water in cold weather.

Greenhouses and conservatories should be kept humid in hot weather by 'damping down', or the plants will dry out. Young seedlings have only tiny roots, and may wilt through excessive transpiration if planted out in hot weather. Cuttings have no roots at all at first; this is why a propagating box with a glass or plastic cover to trap humidity helps them become established.

Teamwork of the green plant

CO₂ 1 O₂ 2

O₂ CO₂

The leaf: food-maker above The broad, flat shape of a plant's leaves provides a large surface area for gases to diffuse in and out through the many tiny pores (stomata) – mostly on the under surface – and for sunlight to be absorbed. During food manufacture **1**, carbon dioxide (CO_2) is absorbed by the leaf from the air and joins chemically with water brought to the leaf by way of the roots and stem. With the help of sunlight trapped by the green pigment chlorophyll, the plant's food, sugar, is manufactured. Oxygen (O_2) is given off. During respiration **2**, oxygen is also absorbed by the leaf and used to release energy from the sugar. Carbon dioxide is given off. Water passes out of the leaf by transpiration, mainly through the leaf pores. As the water is evaporated away, this creates a 'pull' throughout the whole plant right down to the roots, which exert a pull on the water in the soil.

The stem: the vital link right The stem, whether woody or relatively soft, supports the leaves and flowers. More important, it contains the vessels that carry water up from the roots and food from the leaves to active regions or for storage.

The roots: supply centre right The whole plant depends on the roots to supply sufficient water. Like all parts of the plant, the roots need to 'breathe'. If you over-water a pot-plant, so that the potting mixture becomes waterlogged, with no air pores, the roots will 'drown' and can no longer function. The reverse happens if water is given off by the leaves quicker than the roots can replace it; in this

case the plant wilts.
above left Normal, turgid plant cells are full of water.
above right When cells lose water, becoming flaccid, the plant wilts.

Leaf and root care

The leaf, whether decorative or not, must be protected from damage, from overcrowding which restricts access to light or air, and from dust which might block the pores. The roots, too, must always be able to absorb water, and the tiny root hairs near their tip must not be damaged when re-potting or transplanting.

Storage of food

Just as food is stored in the form of fat in our own bodies, so plants store starch until it is needed for rapid growth. Plants that over-winter in a dormant state have various devices for storing food for next season's growth. Special storage organs include bulbs, corms, rhizomes and tubers; some plants simply store food in their roots.

You should encourage maximum food storage in order to have the best possible growth in the next season. You can prevent wastage of food to parts no longer productive by removing dead blooms and, in the case of herbaceous perennials, by cutting down spent shoots.

below A daffodil bulb consists of fleshy leaf bases, swollen with food, surrounding a bud which will be the next year's flower. After flowering, the green leaves should not be cut back, for they continue to manufacture food which passes back into the bulb for storage until the next season.

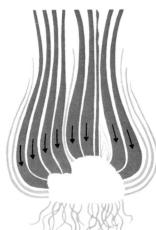

How a plant grows

A plant does not grow equally in all parts, but only at or near its extremities. These parts can be stimulated into activity to produce whole new organs, so the plant can recover from the loss of whole parts.

Growth in the dark

Although light is usually essential for plants, growth can continue in complete darkness as long as food reserves are present. In fact, growth is faster, because light produces a chemical substance in the plant that slows growth. However, the leaves will be yellow rather than green, because chlorophyll will not be built up without light. In effect, this is what happens when celery, leeks

or rhubarb are forced. The shoots stretch up tall to reach for the light, and the parts in darkness will be pale, or blanched — fine for celery or leeks but not for a healthy display of hyacinths.

How pruning works

Correct pruning can stimulate a plant to grow in the way you want. The terminal (end) bud of a branch or stem puts a brake on the development of the lateral buds. **below left** As a result, a foliage pot-plant may grow lanky. **below centre** If you remove the terminal bud, the lateral buds, otherwise dormant, will develop. **below right** As a result, the plant grows more bushy. 'Stopping' *Chrysanthemums* works in the same way (see page 225).

How plants multiply

Although the gardener's main preoccupation may be to produce plants with prolific blooms in order to have a colourful show to admire, he seldom stops to think why the flowers are there at all.

above The flower is in fact the sexual reproductive part of the plant, and the brightly coloured and often scented petals are there to attract insects. In seeking nectar and pollen, these conveniently pollinate the flower. Inconspicuous, unscented flowers are more typical of plants pollinated by some other means, such as wind.

Pollination and after

Pollination is the depositing of the male pollen grains from the stamens onto the stigma of the female carpels in the centre. Fertilization can then take place, and the formation of fruits and seeds follows. The fruit is simply the swollen ovary around the seeds, and is there to protect the seeds and help their dispersal. The petals and other flower parts, having served their purpose, then wither away.

Fruit plants grown indoors are less likely to be visited by insects. They may need help to ensure pollination, otherwise no fruits will be formed. By means of a fine paint brush, pollen may be dusted gently from the stamens of one flower onto the stigmas of another. On the other hand, cucumber plants produce bitter fruit (the 'cucumber') after fertilization, and male flowers should be removed. Although many plants carry both male and female blossoms, and individual

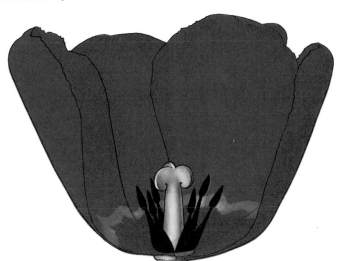

flowers both male and female parts, they are usually arranged so that self-pollination is impossible.

Plants' life cycles

For all plants there is at some stage the familiar life cycle of a seed, which germinates to grow into a mature plant, which in turn produces more seeds. Some plants — annuals, such as *Petunias* — complete this cycle within a year, or even in a few weeks, after which the parent plant dies off, surviving as seeds only. Biennials flourish for two years, though they do not normally flower until their second year, when they produce seeds and die off. Foxgloves (*Digitalis*) do this. They manage to survive the one winter by storing food in their roots.

Perennials can persist and flower continuously for many years. Herbaceous perennials die back in winter, storing food for the next year's growth below ground either in the roots or in a swollen corm, bulb, rhizome or tuber. The stems of woody perennials — trees or shrubs — persist during winter, either shedding all their leaves in the autumn (in deciduous kinds) or shedding them unnoticed throughout the year (in evergreens).

Propagation from bulbs

Many underground storage organs are in fact modified stems, and like all stems have lateral buds which can develop into new shoots. Many can develop into whole new plants from this parent stem. This is what happens when bulbs naturalize and multiply, or *Dahlia* tubers are divided.

217

Pots and potting

Almost any plant can be grown in a pot or container filled with a suitable potting mixture (often known as potting compost, although the term 'compost' is also used for rotted plant remains). A successful potting mixture should have the right texture for pots. It will hold moisture without becoming waterlogged, and will allow free drainage. It also has the right balance of plant nutrients for plants grown in pots. Especially important is the fact that it is free from soil pests, weed seeds, and plant diseases. To have these ideal conditions it is best to use as your base a commercially prepared pasteurized soil. If such materials are not available, start with a garden soil that is somewhat crumbly and moderately fertile.

In order to allow you to stock and mix as few ingredients as possible and still be able to accommodate the needs of most plants, we have developed four mixtures. We might be guilty of some oversimplification but these formulas will work nevertheless. The mixtures differ only in the amounts of lime and fertilizer they contain. Potting Mixture no. 1 is for slow-

The pot-bound plant

above Learn to recognize a pot-bound plant. Growth is slow, even in good light and warmth, and with regular watering and feeding. Roots may grow from the drainage hole **left** but this is not an infallible guide. To make sure, carefully remove the plant from its pot. In a pot-bound plant **right** the roots are thickly matted and twine around the pot.

Soilless, or peat-based, potting mixtures avoid the use of loam, and tend to be cheaper and more easily available. Many versions are based on peat entirely, others have sand or grit added. The latter give more weight to a flower-pot and there is less tendency for a large plant to topple over. Drainage is also improved. Packs of ready-mixed chemicals are also sold for incorporating with your own peat or peat/grit mixture. Again, omit lime for acid-loving plants.

The peat used in making potting mixtures should always be thoroughly moist; but the sand should be dry when mixing, and so should the sterilized loam if used. The made-up mixture should be moist but not sodden. Mixtures consisting mostly of peat should never be allowed to dry out or they will become difficult to re-wet. Plants growing in them should never become absolutely dry at their roots.

Some plants are not suited by any of the general-purpose potting mixtures – for example, orchids and cacti. Details of special mixtures for these are given with the individual plant descriptions.

Potting on

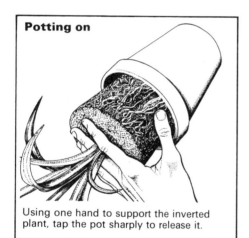

Using one hand to support the inverted plant, tap the pot sharply to release it.

Prepare a slightly larger pot with crocks and potting mixture. Tease out the roots.

Position the plant and fill in at the sides with potting mixture. Water well.

growing plants, no. 2 serves as a general-purpose formula for most houseplants, while no. 3 is particularly well suited to fast-growing subjects. Potting Mixture no. 4 is also highly charged with nutrients for quick growth.

Soilless potting mixtures are those formulated with inert ingredients as a base. Perlite, vermiculite, sand or peat moss are used to overcome insects or weeds so often present in garden soil. These mixtures are most often used for sowing seeds, and while they will do equally well as conventional soil mixtures for the continued growth of mature plants, they do require the periodic addition of fertilizers and, too, they do not support large top-heavy plants very well because of their extreme lightness.

For calcifuges or lime haters – plants that like acid soil (as indicated in the individual descriptions) – a special lime-free mix is necessary. Heathers, camellias and azaleas are among the plants that need a mix of this type.

Unlike plants growing outdoors, those confined to containers use up a more limited supply of nutrients because these are leached from the soil to some degree with each watering. Also, with time

there is a change in the soil's texture. So the plant must be placed in a proper growing medium at the outset, and it must also be renourished and repotted periodically. However, the initial potting is crucial for getting the plant off to a good start with vigorous root development. Although it might be difficult to locate a small supply of lime or a particular fertilizer for ready use, the plants' superior color, texture and flowering will make the effort worthwhile.

Potting mixtures
Prepare a basic mixture of seven parts loam (pasteurized if possible), three parts peat moss and two parts coarse builder's sand. To make Potting Mixture no. 1, add to one bushel of above basic mixture ¼ lb of complete fertilizer and 1 oz of ground limestone, omitting the latter for lime-hating plants. To make Potting Mixture no. 2, double the amount of fertilizer and ground limestone added to one bushel of the basic mixture.

For Mixture no. 3 treble the amount of added ingredients and quadruple the amounts for Mixture no. 4.

Peat-based mixtures
There are a whole series of University of California formulations; the general purpose type is made by mixing thoroughly equal weights of peat and washed sand or grit. Add to each bushel 1 teaspoon potassium sulphate, 7 tablespoons dolomitic limestone, 2½ tablespoons agricultural

limestone, 2½ tablespoons superphosphate – 20% powdered and ½ teaspoon chelated iron. Omit limestone for lime haters.

The equally successful Cornell Mix is prepared as follows (for one bushel). Mix ½ bushel sphagnum peat moss with ½ bushel horticultural grade vermiculite; or mix ½ bushel perlite, 5 tablespoons ground limestone, 2½ tablespoons superphosphate – 20% powdered, and 7½ teaspoons 5-10-5 fertilizer.

Flower-pots
Special tubs and decorative pots may be used for specimen plants, but ordinary flower-pots are a basic need of the gardener without a garden. You can generally buy either plastic or clay (earthenware) pots, although the latter may be difficult to find nowadays. Plastic pots are, in any case, preferred by many gardeners. They are lightweight, less easy to break and very easy to clean. But plants growing in them need water-

ing less frequently than those in clay pots. It is vital to remember this, since overwatering is a major enemy of pot-plants. However, drainage is helped by plastic pots having many holes in the bottom rather than just one.

Potting on
When growing plants in pots, never use an unnecessarily large pot. Growing plants should be started off in the smallest possible pot and moved to larger sizes as their roots fill the pot. This is called potting on, and ensures that there is always fresh compost, and consequently plant foods, for the plants' roots to penetrate. Repotting, as explained below, is a different process by which a well established plant is put in a new pot of the same size, with some new potting mix to replace some of the old.

Generally, pot a plant on only when it is pot-bound. (Though some plants flourish best when pot-bound, as is explained in individual cases.) The roots of a pot-bound plant may be growing out through the drainage holes, but to be sure you must inspect the root ball.

Top-dressing
If a plant is too big to take out of its container, remove the top two inches of soil in spring and replace with fresh potting mix.

containers must be thoroughly clean before use. Clay pots must be soaked overnight in clean water. Cover the drainage holes with some broken pot or stones (called crocking) before filling with potting mixture. This is not so essential with plastic pots that have

mixture an inch or so below the top of the pot. This is to give space for watering, and helps you to judge the amount of water given. The potting mix should completely cover the roots but not encroach on to the green stem or lower foliage. Modern potting mixtures should be pressed down only with sufficient pressure to hold the roots and the plant securely. Excessive force is undesirable as it may hinder drainage. (Again, there are a few plants, as noted individually, that prefer firm potting.)

Repotting
For most popular pot-plants, 2½- to 5-inch pots will be found most useful. Perennial plants cannot be potted on indefinitely, although large specimens for conservatories may end up in small tubs or pots of similar size. It may be necessary to repot these each year or less frequently depending on their vigour or type. Repotting entails removing the plant from its pot, reducing the size of the root ball by carefully pulling away some of the old potting mixture and cutting away old useless roots, and

Repotting

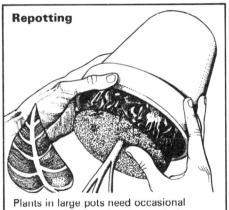

Plants in large pots need occasional repotting. Remove the plant as before.

Carefully cut away excess roots and remove up to a third of the old potting mix.

Replace the plant in a clean pot of the same size, using fresh potting mixture.

Invert the plant and its pot, passing the stem between the fingers of one hand. Tap the rim of the pot sharply on the edge of your bench or table, and the pot will be released, allowing it to be slid off the root ball with the other hand. If the plant is pot-bound, the roots will be matted and will coil around, almost obscuring the potting mixture from view.

When potting on, choose a new pot that will allow about 1½ inches of extra space for the roots. All pots or other

many holes in the bottom, but is always a good idea to ensure good drainage. Also, do not crock the drainage holes if the pot is to be stood on any form of capillary sand tray or automatic watering bench (see page 236).

Then place some moist potting mixture on top of the crocks, and hold the plant in position with one hand while running more potting mixture in around the roots. The final position of the plant should be central and the surface of the

potting in a pot of exactly the same size as the one it was removed from, using fresh potting mixture. The procedure is best done when a plant is at rest and just before it is due to begin growth again.

After all potting, potting on, or repotting, the plants should be watered sufficiently to see that the compost is nicely moist. It should not be too wet, however, since this is likely to encourage rotting of any roots that may have become damaged.

Kinds of pots
Clay pots **left** are heavier and easier to break than plastic pots **right**. In spite of the extra drainage holes, it is easier to overwater a plant growing in a plastic pot.

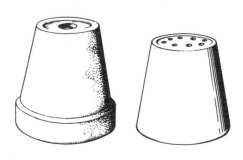

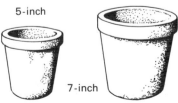

Orchid pot
3½-inch
2½-inch
5-inch
7-inch
Half-pot
Seed pan

Sizes of pots
Flower-pots are measured across the top, inside the rim, either in inches or centimetres. The cast number (representing the number of pots of that size made from a standard batch of clay) may

also sometimes be used. The most useful sizes are generally 2½-inch (6.5-cm, or number 72), 3½-inch (9-cm, or no 60), 5-inch (13-cm, or no 48) and 7-inch (18-cm, or no 28). You may need a few even larger

pots for mature plants, and half-pots (which are half the normal depth) are useful for some shallow-rooted types. Seed pans are even shallower, while special perforated pots for orchids have holes in the side.

219

Plants' basic needs

Water

More indoor plants are killed by kindness than neglect, for people tend to give them too much water. There are certain times of year when plants need little water and other times when they need a lot. Giving the same amount all the year round does plants no good at all. Plants need most water when they are actively growing – that is, when the light is bright and the temperature high. Seedlings use a lot of water, and plants on a sunny, warm window sill may need watering several times a day in summer. But you may well find that in winter you need to use the watering can only once or twice a month.

It is dangerous to set any general rules for watering pot-plants, but you will usually find that plants in clay pots need more frequent watering than those in plastic pots. Also, small pots dry out more quickly than large, so they need more frequent attention.

Never leave watering so long that the plant's leaves begin to droop. On the other hand no plant, with the exception of semi-aquatic kinds, such as *Cyperus*, will survive if its roots are perpetually waterlogged. You should try to learn to judge the difference between potting mixture which is wet and that which is nicely moist, but if you want to be safe, invest in a moisture meter (see page 236). For most plants, aim to keep the potting mixture slightly moist, but some kinds (as detailed with their descriptions) should be allowed to almost dry out between waterings. Never let peat-based potting mixtures dry out completely, however, or they will become very difficult to re-moisten.

When you do water your plants, do so thoroughly, so that the water reaches all parts of the pot. But do not give so much water every time that some always drains from the bottom of the pot, or valuable nutrients will be washed away. If water does drain away, make sure that the pot is not left standing in a saucer of water, for this encourages the roots to rot. Some plants, such as *Cyclamen*, gloxinias (*Sinningia*), miniature orange and lemon trees (*Citrus*) and African violets (*Saintpaulia*), should be watered from below. Stand the pots in water so that the water is at the same level as the potting mixture. Leave them to soak until the water begins to wet the surface of the soil, and then allow to drain.

Just as indoor plants are often overwatered, outdoor plants frequently receive too little water. It is not enough just to moisten the soil with a trickle from a watering can or a hose. Make sure enough water is given to reach down to the roots. Evening or early morning is the best time to water outdoor plants; never splash water on the leaves of plants in direct hot sunshine.

In general, use tap water for watering plants. However, if your tap water is hard, the limy salts dissolved in it may harm plants that prefer acid soils. These plants – known as calcifuges or lime-haters – include many heathers (*Erica*), *Grevillias*, orchids, many *Primulas*, and many species from woodlands, such as *Rhododendrons* and *Azaleas*. If possible, water them with rainwater collected in clean bowls and stored in clean, closed bottles. Do not use rainwater from butts or drain-pipes because it will introduce pests, diseases and weeds to your plants. Soft water can also be obtained as frost melts when the refrigerator is defrosted, but allow it to warm up to room temperature before use.

Heat

The heat requirements of plants vary greatly from one species to another. Buy houseplants to suit the conditions in your home; plants that like cool surroundings will not survive if you like living in a hot-house atmosphere, and tropical plants will fail if your home life is spartan.

Plants are often described as 'hardy', 'half-hardy' or 'tender'. Hardy plants are suited to cool conditions, although some hardy annuals can be grown indoors in a light, airy position. They can withstand frost, although the actual degree of frost they can survive varies. For example, many varieties that are considered hardy in England cannot live through the winter outdoors in north-eastern Scotland or the north-eastern United States.

Half-hardy plants need protection from frost, but they may do well if planted against walls that receive the midday sun or if kept in a sheltered position on a patio. Temporary protection over winter with plastic sheeting or glass frames may be enough, but they cannot hope to survive outdoors in, say, a New York winter. Tender plants are suitable only for indoor conditions in temperate regions, although some of the tougher kinds will enjoy a spell outdoors in the warm weather of summer. The extra light will help them, but they must return to the shelter of the home or conservatory before autumn.

In general, a constant room temperature of 18 to 21°C (64 to 70°F) should satisfy most houseplants, but always inquire about a particular plant's preferences when buying. Those preferring cool surroundings can generally find a home in bedrooms, hallways or corridors. Do not keep houseplants at a temperature above 24°C (75°F); at such high temperatures, plants need more light than they can get indoors.

Light

All plants must have light in order to manufacture food and grow. If the light is insufficient, they will grow long, weak stems and pale leaves. They may not flower and they will eventually die.

As with other requirements, however, plants' light needs vary, so always take this into account when making a choice. Few houseplants, for example, need so much light that they can withstand direct sunlight all the time. Desert cacti and succulents should be given full sun in summer, but most houseplants are suited to indirect light or only a few hours of sunshine a day. Even sun-lovers may need some shading to prevent scorching in strong, hot sunlight coming through glass (see page 23). On the other hand, you do not need daylight at all to grow houseplants, as they can thrive under artificial light (see page 234).

Quite apart from the strength of light, the actual period of illumination has a profound effect on some plants. Some, for example, are so-called 'long-day' plants, and will only come into flower when the period of daylight exceeds a certain length. *Fuchsias* are an example. 'Short-day' plants, on the other hand, flower naturally only with the lengthening nights of autumn. *Chrysanthemums* are the best-known example, but the poinsettia (*Euphorbia pulcherrima*) and Christmas cactus (*Zygocactus truncatus*) behave similarly. By artificially lengthening their daily period of darkness to at least 12 hours, they can be induced to flower at any season.

Air

During the day, plants consume carbon dioxide from the air and produce oxygen as a by-product of photosynthesis. At night, when photosynthesis stops, plants respire, taking up oxygen and producing carbon dioxide. Plants therefore need air, but they can maintain the necessary balance of gases in the air by their own

Watering problems
If, when you water a plant, the water runs straight out of the pot **left**, the potting mixture is too dry and has shrunk. If the water will not soak in at all **centre**, the mixture is caked. In either case, soak the pot **right** after carefully pricking over the surface of the potting mixture.

220

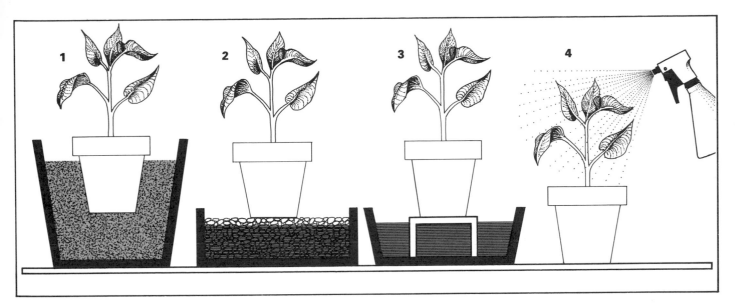

processes of life. For this reason, plants can live in sealed bottles (see page 32).

Although a change of air is not necessary to keep a plant alive, in certain circumstances movements of air are most desirable. Ventilation can help to keep down the temperature in summer. This does not mean that the plants should be subjected to cold draughts. Most houseplants will wilt and shed their leaves if they are exposed to chilly currents of air. But gentle air movement helps to reduce fungus diseases. Use a small fan to circulate the air rather than let in cold air from outside, at least during the winter.

Outside, winds can damage even strong plants. If you live in a windy place, choose sturdy dwarf varieties for your window boxes and patio tubs, and secure tall plants with canes or other supports. Winds are a particular problem on high roof gardens and balconies.

Many houseplants are sensitive to the fumes that come from gas fires, coke and anthracite stoves, and dirty oil heaters. If you want to raise plants in rooms heated in these ways, choose varieties with thick and leathery leaves.

Humidity

Although desert cacti and succulents can thrive in dry air, most foliage house-plants prefer air that is moist. Many fail because central heating dries the air. Air-conditioning that includes humidification is much better, but the air in a room can also be made more moist by hanging humidifiers on radiators or installing electric humidifying devices.

If you do not want to treat the whole room, you can create a moist 'micro-climate' around your plants. Stand the pots on trays of wet gravel, or place them in large ornamental bowls containing water, using supports to raise the pots just above the water level. It is also a good idea to group several pots together in one ornamental container, and then pack moist peat around the pots.

Many plants enjoy being sprayed with a fine mist of water from time to time. This freshens the foliage and increases humidity. Do not spray plants that are standing in strong direct sunlight, however, nor in cold conditions. It is best to use soft water for spraying, to avoid leaving white marks on the leaves.

High humidity is a disadvantage in

Increasing humidity
There are various ways of increasing the humidity around your plants: **1** Plunge the pots in damp peat, **2** stand them on wet gravel or **3** stand them above a dish of water. **4** An occasional fine spray of water is beneficial.

cold conditions, as it encourages fungus diseases in the plants. So try to reduce air moisture in conservatories and porches in winter. In summer, however, humidity should be kept high by sprinkling water on the floor (see page 26).

Keeping leaves clean
Plants absorb light through their leaves, so cleaning the foliage not only improves their appearance, but also helps the plants to live. Spraying, as described above, is helpful and refreshing, and special leaf-cleaning products can be bought from garden shops and centres. They are intended for houseplants with smooth, glossy leaves, and should not be used on hairy-leaved varieties.

Plants at holiday time
The main problem your plants will face when you are away on holiday is lack of water. If a friend or neighbour cannot call to help, then automatic watering devices can be purchased (see page 236). They will keep plants moist for many weeks if need be. Before leaving, take all houseplants away from window sills, and shade conservatory windows.

Automatic waterers are not essential. In winter, surround plant pots with damp peat. In summer, a simple way to keep plants fresh is to water well and then enclose the whole plant – including the pot – with a polythene bag. First remove any flowers or buds that are about to open, and cut away any foliage that is in poor condition.

Outdoors, plants should be well watered before departure, and those in shady places should be covered with polythene bags. Plants growing in soil can be mulched with peat after watering well, or a few flat stones or tiles may be placed around the roots to stop water evaporating too quickly. Move tubs and other portable containers into the shade.

Lighting problems below Plants lit only from one side grow towards the light, so give their pots a one-third turn every few days. **right** 'Short-day'

plants like *Chrysanthemums* will only flower if they have more than about 12 hours of darkness each day.

221

Feeding your plants

Air, water and light are, as explained on pages 220 and 221, basic needs that a plant must have in order to live and grow. But they are not enough on their own. Plants also need various chemical substances generally known as plant foods or nutrients. The most important of these are substances containing the chemical elements nitrogen, phosphorus and potassium. Nitrogen is the most important of all; it is needed for general growth and, in particular, leaf development. Phosphorus promotes root development and the production of seeds and fruit, while potassium is essential to flower and fruit formation and also keeps a plant healthy and disease-resistant.

These elements are of no use on their own. There is plenty of nitrogen in the air, but plants cannot use it directly. They need 'fixed' nitrogen in the form of substances called nitrates. Similarly, pure phosphorus and potassium cannot be used, and plants must take up compounds such as phosphates and potash to get them. Other elements are also needed – among them iron and magnesium, which is necessary for making the green pigment chlorophyll. Some nutrients are needed only in very small amounts; these are termed trace elements.

All these chemicals take part in the intricate web of chemical reactions that keep a plant alive. Normally the soil contains the necessary nutrients, which are absorbed by the plant through its roots, dissolved in water. If plants have grown in the soil for a long time, however, its nutrient content may be exhausted. Or the plant foods may be washed from the soil by rain or watering. The problem becomes critical with pot-plants, for the small amount of potting mixture in a pot may contain enough food to supply the plant for only a few months. It must be replaced, and this is done with fertilizers and manures.

Kinds of fertilizers

Fertilizers can range from synthetic chemicals to the rotted remains of dead plants and animal wastes. 'Natural' (or organic) fertilizers are not inherently better than synthetic ones, though they differ in the way they make plant foods available to the plants. Synthetic chemicals are quick-acting, because they can be absorbed more or less directly by the plants' roots. Organic fertilizers, on the other hand, contain extremely complex chemical substances that have to be broken down by soil bacteria before plants can use them; they are therefore slow-acting but longer-lasting.

Among the best known organic fertilizers are dried blood, which is expensive but supplies a lot of nitrogen quite quickly, and bonemeal and fish-meal, which give phosphate and a little nitrogen and potash. Manure provides a wide range of plant foods, but often in low quantity; it is best to obtain the well rotted, sterilized kind. Wood ash is a good source of potassium, and seaweed is especially high in trace elements. A good general fertilizer is made by rotting down plant waste from the garden to make compost; this should always be done if you have room for a compost heap.

Methods of feeding plants

Watering with dilute liquid fertilizer is the most convenient way of feeding indoor plants.

Solid fertilizers mixed into the top layer of potting mixture are slower- and longer-acting.

Special foliar feeds and some soluble general fertilizers can be sprayed on plants' leaves.

Slow-dissolving fertilizer pills can be buried in the potting mixture among the roots.

'Straight' fertilizers are simple chemical substances that provide one or sometimes two of the essential plant foods. For example, nitrates, ammonium compounds and urea provide nitrogen, while superphosphates are rich in phosphorus, and various potassium compounds provide potash.

The most widely used general fertilizers are so-called balanced or compound fertilizers. They are mixtures, sometimes containing both organic and synthetic material, designed to provide a balanced range of plant foods. For satisfactory growth, the proportions of nitrogen (whose chemical symbol is N), phosphorous (P) and potassium (K) must suit the plant. Too much nitrogen in comparison with the other elements, for example, will make it too leafy at the expense of flowering and general strength. This is fine for grass, but not, say, for geraniums.

The labels of most proprietary compound fertilizers have a series of three numbers which give the percentage – and thus the relative proportions – of the three main foods, always in the order N:P:K. For example, 8:6:12 means that a fertilizer contains 8 per cent nitrogen, 6 per cent phosphate (P_2O_5) and 12 per cent potash (K_2O). The high proportion of potash makes this a good fertilizer for flowering plants. Roses prefer a balance of 5:9:6, and vegetables do well with an evenly balanced fertilizer, such as one with an analysis of 7:7:7. Most foliage houseplants with confined roots need a high-nitrogen feed of say 15:5:5.

Giving plant foods

The above technicalities do not, however, need to concern the average amateur indoor gardener very much. There are many general-purpose compound fertilizers available, often containing trace elements such as magnesium, iron and manganese as well as the basic essentials. If in doubt, you should rely on the advice of a good garden centre or shop, or write to fertilizer manufacturers.

Avoid all crude animal manures for indoor, window-box or patio gardening. Since plants 'drink' their food, liquid compound fertilizers or soluble plant foods, which are dissolved in water before use, are more convenient and are particularly good for indoor plants. Solid fertilizers are slower- and longer-acting, and do not need to be given so often. There are also branded tablet plant foods that give a balanced supply over a long period. One basic rule is to always follow the instructions on the label. For safety, wear rubber gloves when handling organic fertilizers such as bonemeal.

Do not feed plants any more than is necessary. Too much fertilizer can do considerable harm as salts build up around the roots, causing root damage. Give a little dilute fertilizer rather than an occasional dose at high concentration. Plants potted in various loam-based potting mixtures (see page 218) will need no feeding at all until they are well advanced and the pots are full of roots. Plants growing in peat-based mixtures, however, generally need feeding after about three to four months of active growth following repotting or potting on. The frequency of feeding varies with a plant's vigour, but manufacturers of proprietary fertilizers usually give general guidance on packets.

In all cases, feed plants only when they are actively growing; forcing growth by feeding during dormant periods will cost them strength. Also, do not feed a plant if it is sick or if its roots are dry. Plants growing in pots and other containers outdoors will need more frequent feeding than indoor plants, because rain washes nutrients from the potting mixture. Flowering climbers should be fed cautiously; if overfed, they may become rampant, forming much stem and leaf at the expense of flowers.

Old, well established plants in large pots may be top-dressed at the beginning of the growing season. Simply mix a sprinkling of dry compound fertilizer in the top of the potting mixture. Alternatively, remove the top inch or so of mixture and replace it with fresh, with a little fertilizer added.

Foliar feeding
As a general rule, fertilizers should be kept off leaves, as they may harm them. However, special formulations called foliar feeds can be sprayed over the leaves. The plant foods are then absorbed through the leaves without causing damage. They are rapidly taken up by the plant. If a plant is languishing badly, foliar feeding may aid recovery. The feeds often contain certain vitamins that have a remarkable growth-promoting effect, and also trace elements in a form the plant can easily absorb.

Sequestered elements
Plants growing in chalky or limy soils may have difficulty in absorbing essential trace elements – particularly iron, magnesium and, especially in the case of *Hydrangeas*, aluminium. The problem usually arises when growing plants – lime-haters such as *Rhododendrons* in particular – in alkaline soil outdoors or in a potting mixture that contains chalk. The result is pale, yellowish leaves – known as chlorosis – poor growth and flowers that are of poor colour. *Hydrangea* flowers of varieties that should be a clear, bright blue, for example, appear a dingy pink.

In such cases, foliar feeding (see above) can work wonders, but there are also proprietary formulations of 'sequestered' trace elements that can be watered into the soil or potting mixture. The elements in these mixtures are in a form that can be absorbed even in alkaline conditions. For *Hydrangeas* there are branded 'blueing' compounds, or simply watering in a solution of aluminium sulphate may be enough to restore the plants' colour.

Growing without soil
So long as a plant is supported in some way and receives nutrients, water, light and air – the last to its roots as well as its leaves – soil is not essential. In fact, plants are easy to grow without any soil or potting mixture at all by the technique of hydroponics, or hydro-culture (which literally means *growing*

Hydroponic pot-plants
It is perfectly feasible to grow plants without normal soil or potting mixture of any kind, using hydroponic methods. **below** Grow the plants in clean coarse sand or vermiculite in a well crocked flower-pot. Keep this growing medium moist – but never waterlogged – with a solution of balanced plant foods. Keep the pot raised above the liquid level in the drip saucer to make sure that air reaches the roots, and rinse through with clean water every ten days or so.

Foliage houseplants are sold growing in light expanded clay aggregate in special pots **below right**, but it is quite possible to set up your own installation. The inner pot containing the plant's roots must have ventilation holes or slots in the side. The water level indicator is a simple float device that shows 'empty' when the water level is at the

bottom of the inner pot and 'full' when it reaches about one-quarter to one-third the way up. Top up with tap water only when it has shown 'empty' for several days. Every six months, sprinkle a 25cc tube of Lewatit HD5 ion-exchange fertilizer on the surface of a 7-inch (18-cm) pot, or more for a larger size, and water it in.

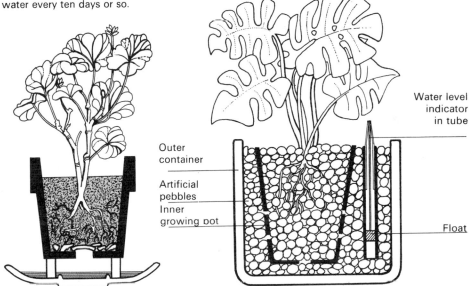

Water level indicator in tube

Outer container

Artificial pebbles

Inner growing pot

Float

in water). They are planted in an inert medium such as vermiculite chips, coarse sand or lightweight artificial pebbles. They may be watered with nutrient solutions that supply both water and plant foods, or fed with special fertilizer that slowly releases nutrients into the water.

The latter is used in some commercial hydroponics systems for houseplants. These are sold ready planted in pebbles made from expanded clay that were first developed for making lightweight concrete; they have a honeycomb structure, and water clings to them by capillary action, keeping the roots moist. The roots must not chill below 16°C (61°F), but otherwise there are no special requirements. You only need to add tap water (see below) and feed with the special fertilizer about every six months.

The fertilizer is known as an ion-exchange type, in which nutrient particles are chemically bonded to resin granules looking like coarse brown sugar. The best-known brand for houseplants has the trade name Lewatit HD5. Minerals dissolved in tap water cause gradual release of the nutrients. This ion-exchange process does not work with rainwater or soft tap water, so if your water is soft add two drops of concentrated liquid fertilizer to get it started.

For an ordinary sand or vermiculite growing medium, you can buy hydroponic nutrient mixtures or complete liquid fertilizers; manufacturers will advise on quantities to use. Or make up

your own feed by combining 10 oz ammonium sulphate, 3½ oz potassium sulphate, 5 oz calcium superphosphate, 3 oz magnesium sulphate and a small pinch of iron sulphate. Use commercial-grade, not pure, chemicals to provide valuable trace elements. For use, dissolve ½ oz in a gallon of rainwater.

For success with hydroponics, air has to reach the plants' roots. With commercial systems using lightweight pebbles, be sure to let the water level drop to the minimum mark – corresponding to the bottom of the inner pot – for four to six days before topping up. Elaborate electrically aerated troughs are available for use with vermiculite, but ordinary pots are suitable for the amateur so long as they are very well drained. The growing medium should be kept just moist with the nutrient solution and stale nutrients rinsed away with clean water every ten days or so.

You can grow almost any plant hydroponically, from herbs and vegetables to houseplants and flowering pot-plants. (*Begonia rex* is a notable exception.) For best results, grow plants from seed sown in vermiculite or cuttings rooted in plain water or moist sand (see page 229). With care, healthy plants can be 'converted' from growing in potting mixture so long as you wash every scrap of the mixture from their roots first. Keep them warm – at least 21°C (70°F) – and frequently spray the foliage with water while new 'water' roots grow.

Keeping your plants tidy

Most plants need attention at some time or other to keep them neat and tidy. Some may have to be pruned in order to train them to grow in a particular shape, such as a bush, standard, fan or pyramid. Pruning may also serve to direct a plant's resources to the production of flowers or fruit. To keep their shape, tall plants may need supporting, and stems may have to be tied to canes or wires to guide them in the right direction.

Pruning trees and shrubs

Shrubs and small trees growing in confined spaces – perhaps in tubs – may need more frequent attention than if they are given plenty of room in an ordinary garden. However, do not prune unless you think it is really necessary. Most shrubs and trees – particularly deciduous kinds – do not demand yearly pruning as a routine. Young plants should be only lightly pruned, if at all. Any initial pruning has usually been done by the supplier. Evergreen shrubs and trees also generally require little pruning, except for hedges, which you must clip regularly. But do not leave faded flowers on evergreens.

Before pruning, find out whether the particular plant is one that produces flowers on the previous season's growth, or on stems formed during the same season. In the first case, do not prune until flowering is over. Then remove all weak or untidy growth, and cut the plant to the desired shape. If necessary, thin it by removing shoots from just above soil level. In the second case, prune early in the year, before new growth commences. In general do not be afraid to prune this second group of plants severely; it is often best to cut them back almost to ground level.

Pruning climbing plants

These can be pruned in a similar way to shrubs. Some rampant climbers like the passion flower (*Passiflora*) and Chinese

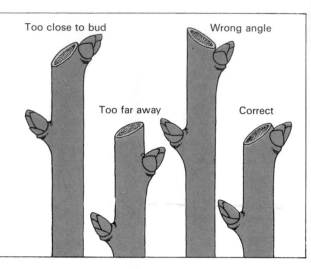

How to prune
When cutting stems, always make the cut just above a bud where a new shoot is expected to form. Do not trim too close or too far away, sloping the cut downwards away from the bud. Always use a very sharp knife or pair of secateurs so that the stem is not bruised. When dealing with small trees or large shrubs, a pruning saw may be needed. Coat cuts made in branches or large woody stems with a proprietary sealant to keep out disease organisms and prevent any rotting.

Too close to bud   Wrong angle
Too far away   Correct

jasmine (*Jasminum polyanthum*) may need quite drastic pruning to avoid tangled, untidy growth. Examine climbers with variegated ornamental foliage for any loss of variegation. Cut out completely any shoots bearing plain leaves. Prune evergreen climbers in early spring and deciduous types in winter.

Pruning roses

The basic principles of pruning already outlined also apply to roses. However, with roses you particularly need to discourage criss-crossing stems and stop dense central growth. Prune always to an outward-pointing bud, to keep the centre of the plant open. Unless pre-pruned by the supplier, newly planted roses can be severely pruned, retaining only strong wood for supporting subsequent growth. A new rambler or climber may be cut back to about 12 inches above soil level to induce new growth from the base.

Well established roses vary in their pruning requirements, but nearly all need yearly attention in early spring.

Prune Hybrid Tea roses by cutting back the shoots to within two to six buds of the base, leaving the most buds on the strongest stems. The more vigorous roses, such as Polyanthas, Floribundas, and Polyantha hybrids, should be treated less drastically. Shorten these back to about six buds from the base. Generally, prune severely if you want a few high-quality blooms and less severely if your aim is plenty of colour.

Prune climbing roses by cutting back lateral short shoots on the main branches to about three buds. New vigorous shoots that will not flower the first year can be retained, eventually to replace old growth and extend the plant. Prune ramblers as soon as flowering is over by cutting back completely the stems that have flowered. If there are insufficient new shoots, however, keep some of the old stems for a second season. Weeping standards should be pruned in a similar way.

Pruning fruit trees

It is impossible to give detailed instructions on the many methods and ways of pruning the wide range of fruit trees and bushes that can be grown. Most fruit suitable for pots or for growing on patios or in confined spaces will have been trained to some extent by the nursery supplier before planting. Ask the nursery for advice regarding further training and pruning, or consult a specialist book.

Pruning indoor plants

Most indoor perennials can be pruned drastically to great advantage. This is particularly true of plants that make annual vigorous growth, such as *Pelargoniums* (geraniums) and *Fuchsias*. Prune these by cutting back severely just as growth is about to commence; otherwise straggly, untidy plants will eventually result. Care is of course needed if *Fuchsias* are being trained to a particular shape.

Indoor plants are on the whole pruned along the same lines as outdoor plants, but many pot-plants have to be 'stopped' from time to time to encourage bushy growth, which in turn results in more flowers. Stopping merely means removal of the growing tip of the stem or shoot. It is also used to develop a particular shape to a plant. Stopping should be

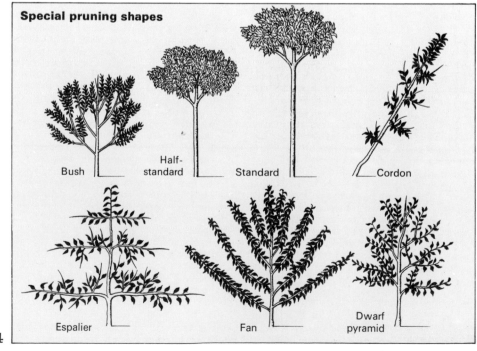

Special pruning shapes

Bush   Half-standard   Standard   Cordon
Espalier   Fan   Dwarf pyramid

carried out only when the plant is actively growing. As it temporarily checks growth, feed and water the plant carefully after stopping until new growth becomes visible.

Tidying herbaceous plants

Herbaceous plants (those that die down in winter) must not be allowed to accumulate decaying remains, whether indoors or out. At the end of the growing season, remove all dead top growth and if possible burn it to destroy any disease organisms or pests. This is especially important where a proper compost heap cannot be constructed. Do not prune plants that grow from crowns, such as African violets (*Saintpaulia*). When plants get too large, remember that taking cuttings (see page 228) will reduce their size and produce new plants.

Creating topiary

right Clipping hedges or trees to form figures or geometrical shapes needs patience, but such topiary is ideal for a terrace of formal design. Beginners should attempt simple shapes like pyramids, cones, spheres, or perhaps corkscrews. Suitable evergreens include box (*Buxus*) and yew (*Taxus*). Ordinary garden shears or electric clippers can be used, but you may need to train branches into desired positions for some years to get the basic shape for clipping. The best time to carry out clipping is at the end of the summer.

Growing standards

right Many shrubby or sub-shrubby plants can be trained to form standards, with bushy foliage on top of a long stem. *Pelargoniums* (geraniums) and *Fuchsias* are particularly suitable. The general rule for any plant is to grow on from a rooted cutting, removing all side-shoots that form but not the foliage on the main stem. When the desired height is reached, snip off the top and allow side-shoots to form there. Bushiness will be encouraged by pinching out the growing tips of the shoots. Only when the head of the plant has been formed to your liking should the foliage on the supporting stem be removed. You will have to keep the plant growing slightly in winter while the stem is developing.

Producing a standard geranium (*Pelargonium*)

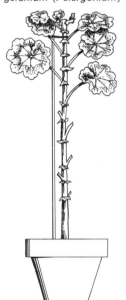

Stopping pot-plants

Pinching out the growing tip of any stem or shoot will encourage side-shoots to develop. This is called stopping, and is useful for encouraging bushy growth in many foliage houseplants. It is vital with such flowering pot-plants as carnations (*Dianthus*) and *Chrysanthemums*. With proper stopping **below** and **right**, many sprays of blooms can be obtained from a single plant (see page 80).

Second stopping of *Chrysanthemum*

First stopping of *Chrysanthemum*

Supporting plants

Tall outdoor plants exposed to wind must be tied to suitable supports, such as bamboo canes or stakes. To train thin-stemmed climbers against a brick wall, use a plastic net rather than a wooden trellis. Stems can be tied to the mesh at any place. When stems are few, as for example in the training of fan fruits, use wires. Special strong wire and wall fastenings can be obtained for the purpose. Decorative patio arches made of plastic-covered thick wire or wrought iron can be bought to support climbers.

Small plastic trellises can be used to support indoor climbers. Alternatively, you can make an attractive framework of split canes, as illustrated, or use decorative chain hanging from the ceiling. For the taller pot-plants there are proprietary wire-ring supports, while tall houseplants will have to be tied to stakes as for outdoor plants. Always try to avoid causing root damage when using such stakes. Moss-covered poles are excellent for supporting houseplants that send out aerial roots, such as many *Philodendrons* and related plants. Epiphytes can be grown on mossy branches (see page 73).

A moss pole

left To make a moss pole for supporting plants with aerial roots, simply wrap wet sphagnum moss thickly around a wooden stake and secure it with green plastic-covered wire. Spray regularly with water to keep the moss damp. Use green string or plant ties to secure the plant at first, but once its aerial roots penetrate the moss it should become self-supporting. An alternative method is to use chicken wire, as for the fern column described on page 59.

Houseplant trellis

right You can make your own trellis for supporting climbing houseplants, such as ivies (*Hedera*) and *Cissus antarctica* (kangaroo vine). Use bamboo or split cane, tied firmly to cross-pieces.

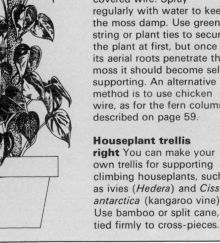

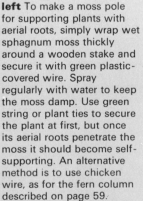

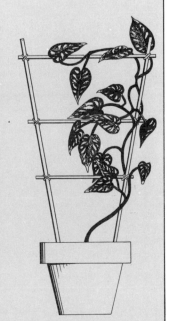

Growing plants from seed

The easy way to build up your stock of plants is of course to buy potted house-plants – or, for stocking a balcony, window box and so on, bedding plants or seedlings – from a nurseryman or garden centre. You can see exactly what you are getting, and there is little fuss or trouble. But you have to pay for the privilege.

It is much cheaper to grow your own plants from seed, and this is often the only way of acquiring the more off-beat kinds of plants. (Botanical seedsmen stock a far wider range than even the biggest exotic plant nursery.) It is, of course, much more trouble and space-consuming, but you will gain the extra satisfaction of producing a plant collection that is entirely *yours*. And while some plants are admittedly slow and tedious to raise from seed, very many – particularly annuals, biennials and free-flowering perennials – give quick and flamboyant results.

Apart from widening your plant collection with seed-grown specimens, it is usually easy to multiply your existing woody and herbaceous perennial plants by division, cuttings and similar methods. For these methods, see page 228.

Growing from seed

It is possible to raise new plants by saving the seeds produced by your existing collection, but without controlled pollination the plants may not breed true – that is, the offspring may be different, and often inferior, to their parents. Buying seed from reputable seedsmen means that you can obtain choice varieties. More and more plant seeds are now being offered as F1 hybrids. These are the first generation offspring of two pure-bred strains. To obtain them hand pollination is necessary – hence the seeds are more expensive – but they produce vigorous, free-flowering plants, often with extra-large blooms.

Always try to ensure that the seed you buy is fresh, and sow it as soon as possible (though following the instructions as to season). The more popular varieties are often available as pelleted seed, coated with an inert substance to increase its size for easy handling. As a result, you can sow thinly so that there is less wastage from thinning out seedlings. Also, the coating may contain a fungicide that protects the seed before and during germination.

Large seeds and those of many hardy annuals can usually be sown directly in the pots, boxes or beds where the plants are to be grown. In this case use a potting mixture such as John Innes 1 (see page 218). But fine seed must first be germinated in a tray or pan of special seed growing mixture (see right), and the seedlings transferred to other containers when large enough to handle. Warmth and moisture are always needed for germination, but the temperature needs differ, and you should follow the seedsman's instructions. The seeds of many houseplants of tropical or sub-tropical origin need temperatures as high as 24°C (75°F). This is best attained in a heated propagating box (see opposite), but you may be able to find a warm enough place in the home.

Sowing and growing from seed

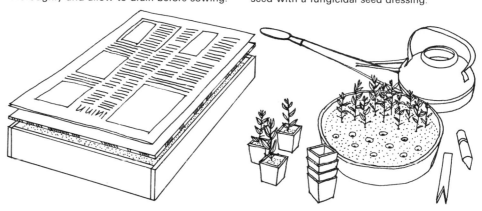

Cover the bottom of the seed tray or pan with broken crocks and fill to within ½ inch of the rim with seed mixture. Level it off. Gently firm down loam-based mixtures, but not the peaty kind. Water the mixture thoroughly and allow to drain before sowing.

Sow the seed thinly and evenly. With extremely fine seed, mix first with a little dry silver sand. Cover the seed with about its own depth of seed mixture, but do not cover very fine seed at all. Treat slow-germinating seed with a fungicidal seed dressing.

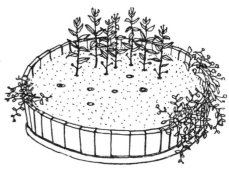

Cover the seed tray with a sheet of glass to retain moisture. Wipe the condensation from the under-surface daily and water the seeds when necessary with a fine spray. Keep out of sunlight or cover with newspaper until the seedlings appear. Then give full light (but not direct sunlight).

Remove the glass a few days after germination. When big enough to handle without damage, prick out the seedlings into trays, pans or small peat pots. Use tweezers or a V-notched stick to uproot the seedlings, and plant them in holes made with a dibber (blunt-ended stick). Water well.

The seedlings should not be crowded; plant them at least 1½ inches apart. Grow them on in warmth and good light until they are sturdy young plants. Then transfer to 2½-inch pots or permanent positions. If peat pots are used, the seedlings' roots penetrate the peat. Transplant pot and all.

Seed-growing mixtures

Seeds are best sown in special soil mixtures. If you want to make up your own, the formula for John Innes seed mixture is as follows: Thoroughly mix two parts (by volume) sterilized loam, one part washed sand and one part peat. To each bushel of the mixture add 1½ ounces superphosphate and ¾ ounce powdered chalk.

To make the University of California peat-based mixture, mix equal parts by volume of peat and washed sand, and add to each bushel ½ ounce ammonium sulphate, 1 ounce superphosphate, ¾ ounce potassium sulphate and 4 ounces powdered chalk.

Problem seeds

If a seed has a thick or fleshy coat, germination may take a long time. To improve water uptake, and so hasten germination, they must receive special treatment. Fleshy seeds such as those of peas and beans should be soaked in water overnight before planting. Hard-coated seeds should be scarified (chipped or scratched with a knife or nail-file), but avoid damaging the 'eye' of the seed or the interior. Large nuts and kernels can be gently cracked with nutcrackers.

Stratification is needed for the seeds of alpines and for some hardy shrubs and herbaceous plants. This breaks their dormancy by mimicking their natural winter treatment in the wild. Mix the seeds with some moist sand in a shallow tray, and expose them to winter conditions for two to four months – ideally with alternate freezing and thawing – before sowing. Alternatively, put them in a refrigerator.

Growing on the seedlings

Seedlings can be grown on to the planting-out stage either in boxes or trays or in individual peat pots. They continue to need warmth and moisture to develop their roots, and it is wise to use Cheshunt Compound or another fungicide to prevent damping off. (In this, a fungus attacks the base of the seedling's stem, causing it to topple over.)

Generally, plant out the seedlings when a few inches high (although this of course depends on the mature size of the plant). Outdoor plants should not be planted out if frost is still expected. In any case, harden off the seedlings first: gradually lower the temperature and then put them outdoors for a few hours each day, increasing this until they are left out all night for a few days before planting. Try to cause as little root disturbance as possible when transplanting, and water well. Seedlings in peat pots are planted complete with the pot.

Propagators

Most forms of propagation – from seeds or from cuttings – need warmth and a moist atmosphere. These conditions are best achieved with a propagator. Many kinds are available. At their simplest, they consist of merely a plastic dome to cover a single pot or seed tray – or you can improvise these with clear plastic sheeting or even a glass jar. Inexpensive electric models simply warm a single seed tray which you cover with glass. More elaborate kinds consist of a large electrically heated chamber controlled by a thermostat. In a greenhouse or conservatory you can install a mist propagator, which produces a fine mist of water over the propagating bench and is ideal for raising sensitive cuttings.

If you buy a propagator, an electrically-heated model is best – preferably thermostatically controlled in a range of 15 to 27°C (59 to 81°F). With such a propagator, you can easily germinate seeds of annuals and root hardy cuttings at the lower end of the temperature range and, at higher temperatures, grow tropical and sub-tropical plants from cuttings and seeds.

Making a propagator

Basically, a propagator consists of a box that can be heated in some way, some moist sand at the bottom to maintain humidity, and a glass or plastic cover to keep in the moisture. A wooden box should have a waterproof lining. Pots or seed trays are placed in the box, which can be placed above an oil heater or radiator. A thermometer is essential to check temperature. Electric heating is more versatile. The photograph **above** shows the construction of a propagator with cables for heating both the sand at the bottom and the air — both with controlling thermostats. The air-warming cables are useful if you want to overwinter tender plants in the propagator, but are otherwise not essential. In both cases, special cable supplied by the makers of greenhouse equipment should be used.

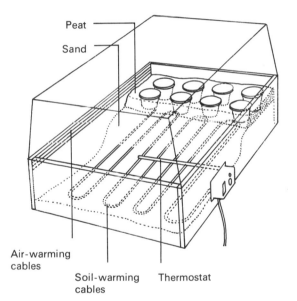

Peat

Sand

Air-warming cables

Soil-warming cables

Thermostat

Simple propagators

above A clear plastic dome or plastic bag covering an ordinary flower-pot makes the simplest propagator. Low-cost electrical units **right** accommodate pots or seed trays on a waterproof tray covered with a plastic dome or lid.

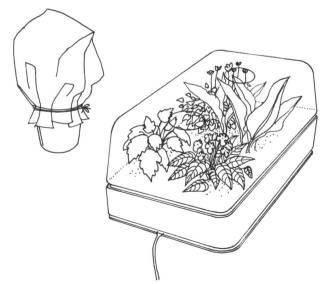

Growing plants from cuttings

When a plant gets too large or straggly, or when you simply want some more plants of the same kind, then the answer often is to propagate new plants from cuttings. At its simplest, you cut off a young part of the plant, stick it in some suitable soil and wait for it to grow new roots and develop into a whole new plant. Pieces of stem or roots, single leaves or even pieces of leaves can be used. Some plants send out runners that grow new plants at the end. Others form clumps that can be divided, or have bulbs that produce baby bulbils.

All these methods are technically forms of vegetative propagation. They form by far the best way of multiplying plants that are difficult to grow from seed. Hybrids and 'sports' may not breed true from seed, so propagation by cuttings is needed to preserve their characteristics. And, of course, it is the ideal way to increase your plant collection.

How to grow cuttings

Just like a seed, a cutting needs warmth (especially from below) and moisture in order to grow. As it has no roots, water uptake is very inefficient, so a moist atmosphere is essential to reduce transpiration water loss and prevent wilting. The best way is to use a propagator or put a clear plastic dome over the pot containing the cuttings (see page 227).

A well drained yet moist growing medium is essential. Generally use a mixture of equal parts of peat and washed grit or sand, without any fertilizer added. Sometimes plain grit, vermiculite or a similar inert substance that retains moisture can be used. In a few cases – such as *Fuchsias*, African violets (*Saintpaulia*), busy Lizzies (*Impatiens*) and *Nerium oleander* – cuttings will develop roots simply standing in a glass of water; the roots will be soft, however, and the new plants will have to be potted very carefully. Where cuttings are reluctant to root, try dipping the cut end in a hormone rooting powder.

Cuttings can be rooted in pots or trays. In trays, space them out evenly, but rooting is aided in pots if you insert the cuttings at the edge. One pot will generally take several cuttings. If a propagator is not available, a warm, well lit place – such as on a window sill above a radiator – is an ideal place to grow them. Spraying them occasionally with a fine mist of water will help, and a mist propagator unit in a greenhouse is the ideal, if expensive, arrangement.

Once the cuttings have formed roots and are growing well, transplant them into small pots of proper potting mixture. Peat pots can be used. Then grow them on as for seedlings.

When to propagate

The best time to take cuttings is generally the spring, when strong growth is just starting and the new plant will have a whole season to become established. However, for leaf cuttings you must wait until the leaves are well formed. Such plants as *Fuchsias* and *Pelargoniums* (geraniums) can be propagated in autumn if you can provide enough warmth and light over winter.

Stem cuttings

By far the most popular and common method of propagating plants is to take softwood cuttings. These consist of non-woody shoots, and they can be taken successfully from a wide range of soft-stemmed houseplants as well as *Fuchsias*, *Pelargoniums* (geraniums), *Chrysanthemums* and the like.

With a sharp knife, cut off young shoots that are no more than two inches long; they should have four or five nodes (leaf joints), and the leaves must be healthy and in good condition. Trim the stem back to just beneath a node and then gently pull off the leaves at this node. Any flower buds should also be removed. Insert the cutting in the cutting mixture so that the leaves left on the stem are just above the surface.

Hardwood cuttings, taken from shrubs, are treated in a similar way except that they are longer and more of the lower leaves are stripped away. Plant them in a V-shaped hole in open soil with a little sand at the bottom. Fill the hole firmly.

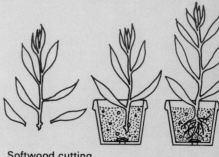

Softwood cutting

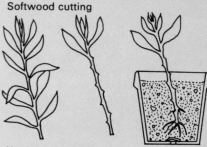

Hardwood cutting

Leaf cuttings

Plants can be propagated from leaves in several ways, depending on the kind of plant. Plants with long leaves, such as *Sanseveiria* (mother-in-law's tongue, or snake plant) and *Streptocarpus* can often be rooted by cutting the leaves into sections and inserting each piece in cutting mixture. (The yellow stripe of *Sansevieria trifasciata laurentii* (see page 68) is not retained with leaf cuttings, however, but only with root division.) The best method for African violets (*Saintpaulia*) is to remove a leaf with a stem attached and insert the stem in some cutting mixture. A new plant usually arises from where the stem joins the old leaf. *Saintpaulia* leaf cuttings may also root simply by placing the stems in water. With decorative-leaved *Begonias* (which have prominent leaf-veins), you can cut a leaf into small triangular pieces. Make sure that a vein ends at a point of each triangle. Gently push the pieces of leaf into some cutting mixture, vein-point first. Cover and keep warm, and each piece should root and form a new plant.

Saintpaulia leaf cutting

Sansevieria leaf cutting

Begonia leaf cutting

Root division

Perennials that form clumps – including *Streptocarpus*, African violets (*Saintpaulia*), *Primulas*, polyanthus, most alpine plants, and many herbaceous plants that can be grown on patios – can be propagated by dividing the roots into several smaller clumps. The best time is just as the plants are about to start a new growing season. The roots in a clump should be carefully teased apart so that some top growth remains attached to each piece. If the roots are matted and thick, cut through the clump with a sharp knife. Each separate piece should then be potted and watered very carefully at first, until new growth is seen.

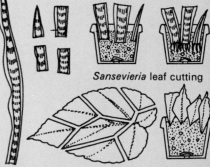

Root division

Root cuttings

Herbaceous perennials and shrubs with fleshy roots can be propagated by cutting up the roots and potting the pieces. Plants which produce underground rhizomes, such as lily of the valley (*Convallaria*), can also be grown from similar cuttings.

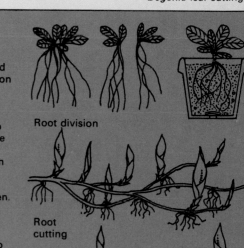

Root cutting

Leaf-vein cuttings

Another method of propagating *Begonias* with prominent leaf-veins is as follows: Remove a healthy leaf, cut nicks in the veins that stand out on the underside, and rest the leaf underside-down on some cutting mixture. Weight the leaf with a few small clean pebbles. Cover the container with a sheet of glass or place it in a closed propagator. Roots should form where the cuts were made and tiny new plants will grow at each cut. When they are large enough to be handled easily, pot them individually. This method works well with many gesneriads, such as gloxinias (*Sinningia*) and *Smithianthas* (temple bells).

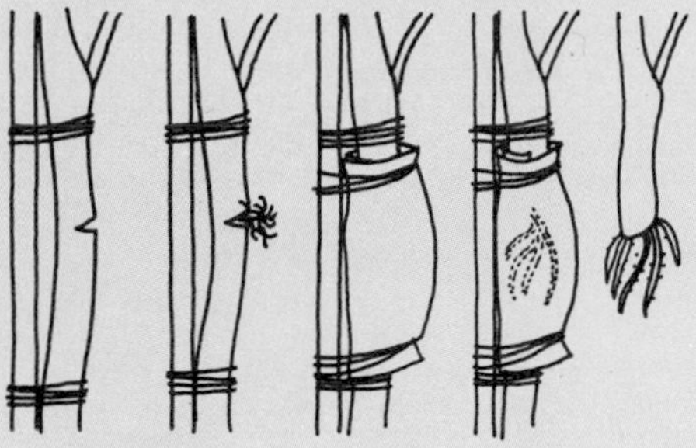

Begonia leaf-vein cutting

Air layering

Air layering is a good way of propagating tall woody houseplants that have become 'leggy' or lost their lower leaves. Supporting the stem with a stake, cut a slit in it just below the foliage. Dust the slit with hormone rooting powder and carefully push some moist moss into the slit. Then wrap some more moss around the wound and hold it in place by tying a piece of transparent plastic sheet around the moss, securing it above and below the slit. Roots should eventually form; they will be visible through the plastic. Then cut through the stem just below the roots and pot the new plant.

Air layering

Soil layering

Climbers and trailers can be propagated by soil layering. This method is particularly suitable for plants with aerial roots, such as *Philodendrons* and ivy (*Hedera*). Lead a stem down across the small pot of cutting mixture, and place it in contact with the mixture after making a slit or removing a tiny piece of the outer skin or bark. Weight the stem down with a small pebble. Roots should form, and the new plant can then be cut away from its parent, and potted in potting mixture in the usual way. The same method can be used with many outdoor shrubs, and also with pinks and carnations (*Dianthus*). Plants such as the spider plant (*Chlorophytum comosum*) which produce plantlets on runners can very easily be propagated in much the same way.

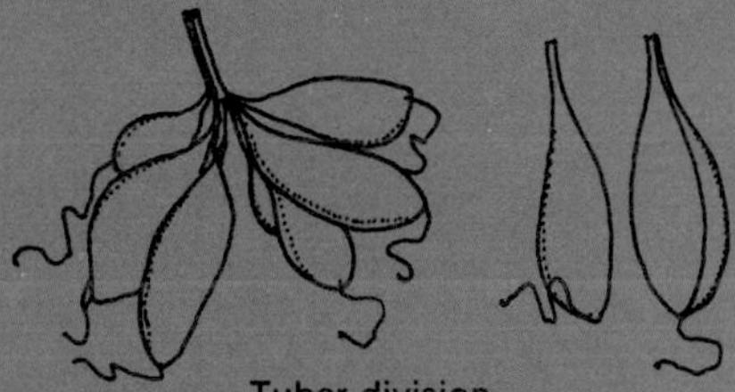

Hedera soil layering

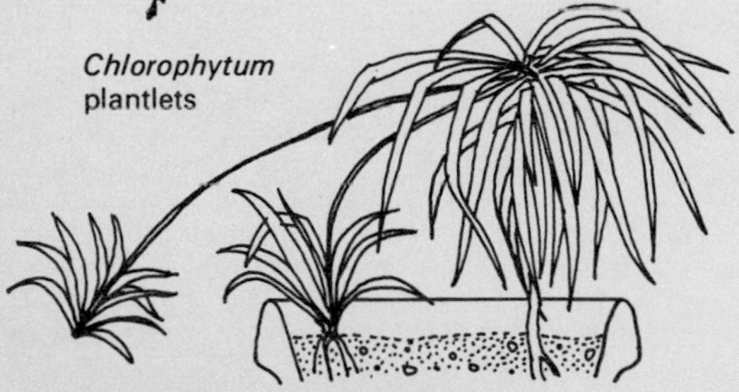

Chlorophytum plantlets

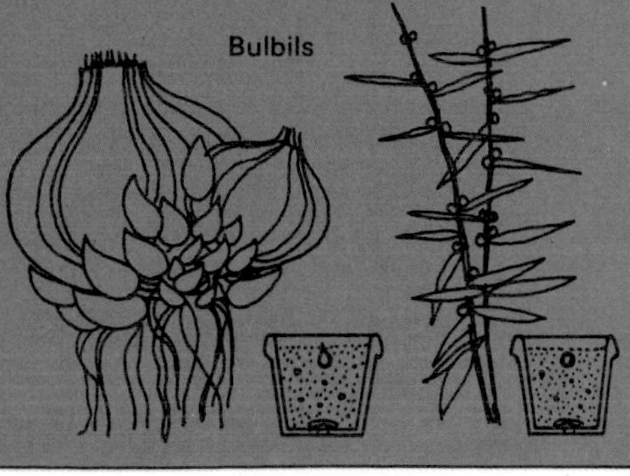

Tuber and bulb division

Some tubers and corms can be divided when they have started to shoot. Pieces should be cut so that there is a shoot on each piece. The cut surface should be dusted with a fungicide powder as a precaution against the root rotting. Tuberous *Begonias* can be propagated in this way. *Dahlia* tubers are cut so that each piece retains a section of the stem, as the tubers have no buds. Some bulbs and corms form offsets — tiny bulbils (bulblets) or cormlets that grow around the parent bulb. These can be separated and potted. For a year or two they will produce only foliage as the new bulb or corm grows and stores food, but they will eventually flower. In some cases, bulbils form on the aerial parts of plants, for example on the stems of some lilies. These bulbils can be detached and planted to form new plants. However, it takes a long time before the new plant flowers. Some ferns can be propagated in the same way (see page 56).

Tuber division

Bulbils

The healthy plant

The quality and health of your plant collection not only advertises your prowess in horticulture, but also makes all the difference between a straggly, messy collection of indifferent greenery and something of real beauty that will enhance your home. And to ensure that your plants look beautiful, concern for their health should start when you first buy them and continue throughout their life.

Choosing quality plants

Always buy from reputable shops, nurseries, garden centres, seedsmen and plantsmen. Well-established firms have the necessary experience to ensure a reliable product, and they will usually provide expert advice should you need it. Unless it bears a grower's label, you cannot be sure of the quality of a plant bought from a general supermarket or fruit and vegetable shop.

Take special care when buying seeds. Some firms sell hermetically-sealed packets of seeds that have been stored in conditions of controlled humidity. Seed stored and packaged in this way is more likely to germinate successfully. Buy fresh seed if possible, and always sow as soon as you can after receipt. If you have to keep seeds, do not store paper packets of seed in damp places or where the temperature varies a lot, for the seed may rot or decompose. Whenever possible, buy F1 hybrid seeds, which are more vigorous and resistant to disease than ordinary varieties. Pelleted seeds treated with fungicide reduce the risk of non-germination or damping off of seedlings.

Carefully inspect bulbs, corms and tubers if you are buying in person and not by mail-order. Reject any that are soft or spongy, show signs of rot, are bored with holes, are in an advanced stage of sprouting, or are affected with mould or mildew. Look under the scales of bulbs like lilies, or under the skin of bulbs such as tulips or narcissi, for mould and mildew.

Although large, specimen houseplants make an immediate impact, younger plants will often grow better in your home so long as you are careful to introduce them gradually to any radical change in conditions. Furthermore, older plants are more expensive – so do not assume that dearest means best. Avoid any plants that are standing outside in cold weather, for wide temperature fluctuations spell death to many plants. Select strong, sturdy plants that are of good colour. Professional nurserymen admire what they call 'well-furnished' plants – ones of full, bushy appearance with leaves all the way down the stem. You should certainly shun any that are yellowed, mottled, spindly, wilted, damaged or appear unsatisfactory in any way. Inspect the plants closely for pests, paying special attention to the undersides of leaves. A hand lens will help.

Check with the nurseryman that any outdoor bedding plants you wish to purchase have been properly hardened off (see page 227). Check also that any trees, shrubs, vines or climbers have been pruned or trained as necessary. Buy potted or container-grown perennials when possible, as these will suffer less of a setback when planted out.

Choosing the best varieties

In many cases, you will be faced with a choice of several different varieties of a particular plant. Each variety may have certain advantages over the others, such as a certain size, colour or degree of hardiness. It may be more free-flowering, or may bloom particularly early or late in the season. Its flowers may be extra-large or double.

It is best to acquaint yourself with the possible varieties before buying, so that you can make the best choice for your requirements and conditions. However, if you are faced with a puzzling array of different varieties, the nurseryman or seedsman will usually be pleased to advise you. Always go to specialist growers when buying such plants as orchids, with thousands of varieties.

The plants' environment

It is much, much better to select plants to suit the conditions that your home offers than to choose a difficult plant that you happen to fancy and then try to alter your home environment to suit it. Get to know what plants expect. You are courting disaster if you buy cacti and other succulents and then place them in shade, or put tropical plants in draughty or cool rooms, alpines in hot stuffy rooms, ferns in bright windows or many foliage houseplants in a dry atmosphere.

To avoid failure, check up on the natural habitat of the plants you fancy and place them accordingly, particularly with regard to temperature, light and moisture. Find out also the size and height to which the plant will grow, so that you can give it enough room, and find out whether any pruning or training will be needed.

When to buy

Buy outdoor plants only during the recommended season, and plant them as soon as the weather is favourable. Generally, plant shrubs, roses and herbaceous perennials in autumn, though some kinds may be planted in spring. (If in doubt, ask your supplier.) However, plants raised and sold in pots or other containers can be planted at any season – unless the weather is very hot or cold – since there is no risk of root disturbance during planting. Seedling annuals and biennials are normally sold only during the correct planting season – generally spring or autumn. Spring-flowering bulbs should be planted in autumn; summer- and autumn-flowering kinds in spring.

Buy indoor plants, if possible, during warm weather. They are then less likely to suffer from the cold during travelling. Otherwise, wrap the plants well in polythene bags to protect them during the journey home. It is best to buy flowering houseplants and pot-plants in the early stages of budding.

Keeping plants healthy

Plants will thrive only in the correct conditions of light, temperature, moisture (both at the leaves and at the roots) and soil, and they need feeding with the proper nutrients. Too much or too little of any of these things may spell disaster. Information on providing the correct amounts of moisture, light and heat, and on cleaning plants, which may also be essential to health, appears on page 220. Information on fertilizers and feeding appears on page 222. Plant health also depends on the kind of soil or potting mixture in which the plant grows. Details of the best mixtures for pot-plants are given on page 218.

Common troubles

If, in spite of the advice given in this book, your plants still do not thrive, try to diagnose the trouble from the information on the opposite page. Where specific pests and diseases are concerned, details of treatment are given on pages 232 and 233. But always remember one over-riding truth: The majority of common plants thrive on neglect; they are more often killed by over-enthusiasm.

Acquiring healthy stock

If you want the best possible display, you must take great care in choosing your plants, seeds, bulbs and so on. Never be afraid to inspect them thoroughly before purchase; no reputable plant supplier will object so long as you do no damage. A small hand lens is a useful aid when looking for pests or signs of disease.
Choose plants that look sturdy, clean, well potted, shapely and well clothed with leaves. They should be properly labelled, with the name of the variety where appropriate and, for preference, with cultural instructions and the name of the grower. Check the date stamped on seed packets, and watch for any signs of mildew or rotting with bulbs, corms and tubers.

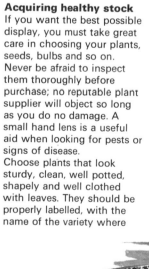

Diagnosing plant troubles

Poor growth
Don't worry if it is winter. This season is a period of dormancy for most plants, so do not force the plant to grow. However, if growth is poor or slow in summer, then something is wrong. Over-watering or under-feeding is the most probable cause. Otherwise the plant may need potting on (see page 218). If the leaves are pale and the plant spindly, then it may be getting too much warmth and moisture during the winter and early spring, thus forcing growth at a time when there is insufficient light. Pale leaves and spindly growth during the growing season are produced by under-feeding and insufficient light.

Mottled leaves
Mottling **1** is serious, as it is a frequent symptom of virus disease. These diseases usually also cause distortion and striping of flowers, and may produce stunting of the plant. Mottling may also be caused by red spider mites and other pests — so inspect the undersides of the leaves for them. Moulds and other fungi may also attack the undersides of leaves and produce mottling that shows on the upper surface.

Leaf spots
Thrips can cause white dots **2** and streaks to appear on leaves, and many fungus diseases form spots in the early stages. Spots may also be caused by droplets of water falling on the leaves in sunshine; they act as tiny lenses and concentrate the sun's rays sufficiently to scorch the leaf surface. Leaf spots may also be produced by spraying with incorrect or over-concentrated pesticides.

Yellowing leaves
Do not be alarmed if the odd lower leaf turns yellow **3**, but if several leaves follow suit then your plant is in trouble. Over-watering or exposure to chill or draughts is most likely the cause, especially if the leaves fall. Dry air may also be to blame. If the yellow leaves do not fall, then you may be growing lime-hating plants (calcifuges) in an alkaline potting mixture or soil, or giving them hard water. Correct these faults, and water with sequestered trace elements (see page 223). Lack of nutrients, particularly nitrogen, results in small yellow leaves. Yellowing between the veins may indicate a magnesium deficiency.

Dropping leaves, etc
A sudden change in the plant's environment, causing a shock to the plant, is the most frequent cause of leaves, buds or flowers dropping **4**. A sudden large fall or rise in temperature or change in light is usually to blame, but overwatering may be the cause (though so too may dryness at the roots). Overfeeding is another possibility, and so is the lack of balanced feeding.

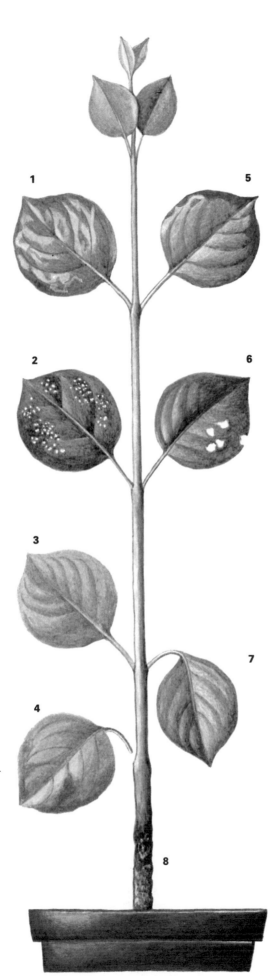

Failure to flower
There are many possible causes, but first check that the fertilizer balance is right for the plant. If there is excessive foliage, overfeeding may be to blame. Repotting in a smaller pot may be the answer, and correct pruning or stopping may also make the plant flower. Some plants have to reach a certain stage of maturity before they flower, and in such a case you simply have to wait. Too much or too little warmth could also be the reason for flower failure, while some plants (such as African violets) flower best if their potting mixture is kept a little drier than normal. Others flower only if kept in the dark for a sufficient period of each 24 hours.

Brown leaf patches
Browning of leaves **5**, which indicates dead tissue, is commonly caused by extreme and sudden chill or by frost. In summer, extreme heat and intense sunlight could well be the cause. A lack of potash in the soil may also be the culprit, but so may overfeeding. Browning is the final stage of some fungoid diseases. Splashing the leaves with strong or unsuitable liquid fertilizers or pesticides, exposing the plant to fumes of oil heaters or wood preservatives (especially creosote), and contamination with weed killer are other possible causes of browning.

Holes in leaves
The cause of leaf holes **6** usually lies with leaf-eating insects such as caterpillars and earwigs. These insects may also eat flowers. Outdoor plants are more likely to suffer than indoor plants. Remember, though, that some indoor plants — particularly *Monsteras* — naturally develop leaf slits and holes.

Wilting
If a plant wilts **7** it may be in need of water or may be receiving too much heat or light. Water the plant and also spray its leaves to revive it. If these causes are not to blame, then something is wrong at the roots. Wilting happens when plants are demanding more water than the roots can take up from the soil. The reason may be root damage produced by rotting — due to overwatering in most cases — or by pests. Overfeeding is another cause, as the fertilizer salts build up around the roots and cause damage. If watering is adequate and none of these causes seems to be to blame, then the plant probably needs cooler and more shady conditions. Do not give it more water.

Rotting
Overwatering, particularly in cold weather, is almost always the cause of rotting **8**. Damp cold conditions encourage fungi that produce rotting. Seedlings may suffer from damping-off — an attack by fungi — and topple over. The risk is reduced by using sterilized potting and seed-growing mixtures.

Plant pests and diseases

The U.S. Department of Agriculture is constantly evaluating materials used for the control of insects and plant diseases. A material touted as the panacea one year is apt to be blacklisted the next, so reappraise your spray materials annually. Check with your County Extension Service (usually located in the county seat) for its latest published recommendations.

Plants can be plagued with a great variety of pests and diseases, and if you want your collection to look its best you should always be on the lookout for trouble. Inspect your plants regularly, and take prompt action against any pests and diseases as soon as any are discovered. During inspections, pay close attention to the undersides of leaves, for this is where pests often congregate and fungi attack. Examine young plants frequently and carefully, for they are particularly at risk. Well grown plants are less prone to attack and respond better to treatment.

To reduce the risk of pests and diseases, take trouble to uproot all weeds outdoors, for they harbour pests. Indoors, poor ventilation encourages fungus diseases, especially where the temperature is low. In all cases, remove dead vegetation, such as faded flowers and fallen leaves, as soon as you notice them. A dirty environment places plants at risk, so cleanliness is vital – especially in glass enclosures, whether terrariums or conservatories. Keep pots, glass, shelves and all surroundings clean. Always use sterilized soil mixtures when potting plants, sowing seeds and planting seedlings, otherwise root pests and fungus diseases are bound to cause trouble. If any plants appear sickly, take them away from their healthy neighbours, for trouble can quickly spread.

The pests and diseases that are most likely to cause trouble are detailed. The pesticides mentioned will work well, but may be superseded by new products in some cases. Information on the latest pesticides can be obtained from garden shops and centres, or manufacturers.

Applying pesticides
Always check the label of a pesticide to make sure that it is suitable for the plants to be treated. Some pesticides damage certain plants (see opposite). In general, pesticide dusts are less effective than sprays or fumigants. However, dusts may be best for open blooms as they are less likely to cause damage.

When using pesticides, always follow the maker's instructions exactly. Treat plants thoroughly, paying special attention to the undersides of leaves. If spraying is necessary, use a fine mist.

Be sure never to use a pesticide indoors if the label states that it is only for outdoor use. Take great care not to inhale pesticides, and wear rubber gloves so that none can get on the skin. In any case, wash after using them. Make sure all containers are thoroughly fastened, and place them well out of the reach of children. Never use unlabelled or wrongly-labelled containers.

When fumigating a conservatory, block cracks in door and window frames with wet sacking or a similar material. The fumes must not be allowed to escape into the house. Do not fumigate when the weather is hot and sunny. The evening is the best time, for the fumes can be left to work overnight. Ventilate well the next morning. Calculate the volume of the conservatory first, so that you will know how much fumigant to purchase.

Common plant pests

Ants
Ants often cause trouble in warm sandy soil outdoors, and they may enter the home and affect indoor plants. Although ants are not in themselves harmful, they tunnel through the soil, loosening it and disturbing plant roots. They also carry aphids about, transporting these pests from one plant to another. Ants should be treated with proprietary ant-baits and ant-killers.

Scale insects
Scale insects infest stems and leaves. They are usually pale brown in colour and suck sap. They produce honeydew like aphids, and weaken the plant. Wipe the insects off the plant with a cotton-wool swab soaked in denatured alcohol.

Mealy bugs
These are small, grey-white insects with woolly coats. Their eggs form in woolly masses. Destroy them by swabbing with cotton wool soaked in denatured alcohol.

Aphids
Also known as greenfly, plant lice and aphis (their scientific name), aphids are one of the most common plant pests. Some plants seem to attract them, and few are immune. They are small insects, coloured green, brown, black or grey, that suck the plant's sap and cause yellowing, distorted leaves and poor growth. Aphids secrete a sticky, sugary substance called honeydew upon which a black mould often grows. The mould not only looks very unsightly, but interferes with the leaves as well. Malathion sprays work well against aphids.

Caterpillars
Caterpillars are the larvae of butterflies and moths. They cause considerable damage very quickly by eating leaves. Pick off the caterpillars by hand and destroy them. If you do not wish to handle them, liquid derris sprays will deal with caterpillars without, in most cases, affecting the plants. Rotenone is poisonous to fish, however, so cover fish tanks before spraying.

Earwigs
Earwigs sometimes eat holes in petals and leaves. They are rarely spotted because they hide away by day and fly to the plants at night. Indoor and outdoor plants are liable to attack. Malathion can be used on flowers. Put down ant-bait in cracks or holes that may hide earwigs.

Red spider mites
These minute reddish mites – almost too small to see with the naked eye – cause yellowish mottling of the leaves, and the leaves may eventually become brown and shrivel. A fine white web spun on the underside of leaves is another sign. Attack occurs only in hot, dry conditions, as in sunny rooms and conservatories. Liquid rotenone (not rotenone dust) is an effective control, but it is better, if possible, to fumigate with azobenzene.

Worms
Worms sometimes get into pots when they are stood outside during the summer. They disturb plant roots. Placing pots and containers on a layer of coarse shingle will prevent worms reaching them. If worms are thought to be in pots, water with a solution of potassium permanganate to bring them to the surface.

Cyclamen mites
These mites are a common pest of indoor plants, like *Saintpaulias* (African violets), and are particularly troublesome in parts of America. The insects are difficult to spot but their effects are not, for they cause stunting of leaves and flowers, and often distortion and curling of leaf edges. Cyclamen mites are difficult to control with safe insecticides, and it is best to destroy infected plants.

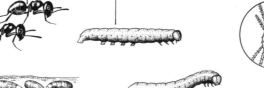

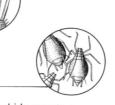

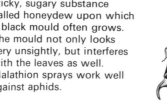

Pesticide precautions

Virtually all pesticides are poisonous to some forms of life apart from the pests they are designed to attack, so always take great care in storing and using them. Above all, they must be kept out of the reach of children, so store them under lock and key if possible. Never keep liquids in any but the original bottles; soft drink bottles are particularly dangerous if children can reach them. If possible, move plants to an outbuilding for treatment. Wear gloves when using sprays, and always protect household pets, fish-tanks and ponds.

Bad pesticide-plant combinations

Some pesticides are harmful to certain plants, and these are usually listed on the package. Houseplants are not usually covered, however, and you should also avoid the following plant-pesticide combinations:

Azobenzene: ferns; *Pileas*; *Schizanthus*; *Stephanotis*; young plants; plants in flower
BHC: *Hydrangeas*; *Kalanchoë*
Demeton-S-methyl: Some *Chrysanthemums*; *Primulas*
Diazinon: *Adiantum*
Dichlorvos: Some *Chrysanthemums*; *Tradescantias*
Dimethoate: *Calceolarias*; *Chrysanthemums*; *Cinerarias*; *Fuchsias*; *Hydrangeas*; *Primulas*
Ethoate-methyl: *Chrysanthemums*
Formothion: *Chrysanthemums*
Malathion: ferns; *Petunias*; *Pileas*
Nicotine: Some *Chrysanthemums*
Parathion: *Cyclamen*
Petroleum oil: *Asparagus*; *Fuchsias*
Phosphamidon: *Cinerarias*

Thrips

Thrips are tiny, black-winged insects. They cause whitish patches, usually surrounded by small black specks, on leaves. If an affected plant is shaken over some white paper, the insects will fall out and be seen. Rotenone or Malathion will provide effective control.

White flies

White flies are tiny and triangular in shape. The larvae suck sap and exude honeydew, causing yellowed foliage. Disposal of this pest is often difficult, but try malathion aerosols and repeated liquid rotenone sprays.

Slugs; snails; woodlice

These common outdoor pests may also get indoors, especially in conservatories. They eat holes in leaves, and woodlice may damage roots. Proprietary slug and snail baits are effective, and strange as it may sound, a shallow dish of beer will lure and kill slugs with equal dispatch.

Sciarid-fly maggots

These maggots, which are also known as fungus gnats, look like tiny black-headed worms. They infest soil in pots and eat plant roots. Damp and humid conditions encourage them. The flies or gnats that emerge from the maggots are harmless, but killing them with a general fly-killer may prevent them laying eggs. Kill the maggots by watering the potting mixture with malathion.

Common plant diseases

Botrytis

Grey mould is one of the many common names for *Botrytis cinerea*, a fungus that looks like a grey-brown furry mould. Botrytis mostly attacks indoor and conservatory plants. When an affected plant is disturbed, clouds of fine dust rise from it. The dust consists of the spores of the fungus, and spores are always present in the air. In the right conditions, they will grow to produce the mould.

Cool, moist and still air provides the conditions for botrytis to attack healthy plants. Stems, leaves, buds, flowers and fruits may be affected. To remove the mould, improve ventilation and lower the humidity of the air around the affected plant. In conservatories fumigate with Benlate.

Mildew

A great variety of mildews affect indoor and outdoor plants. The symptom is a greyish-white powdery mould on stems, leaves and buds. Roses, *Chrysanthemums* and *Asters* are especially prone, as are fruit trees and bushes. Over-crowding and over-watering are common causes, and affected indoor plants may need better ventilation. Benlate is excellent for preventing and controlling mildew.

Damping off

Damping off is the common name for attack by fungi on seedlings. The fungi weaken the bases of the seedlings' stems, causing them to topple over. Damping off

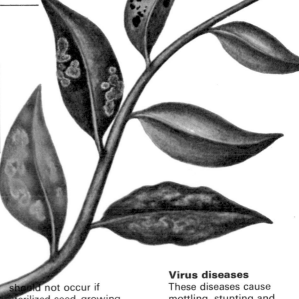

should not occur if sterilized seed-growing mixtures are used. However, as a preventive measure, water the sowing medium with a proprietary chemical such as Damp Off 24 hours before sowing seeds, or water seedlings with Cheshunt Compound after pricking out (see page 244).

Rusts

Rusts are fungi that produce red-brown spots and patches on leaves. There are many kinds, but *Pelargoniums*, carnations (*Dianthus*) and *Antirrhinums* are commonly affected. Use a dithane spray as soon as any rust spots are seen on plants.

Virus diseases

These diseases cause mottling, stunting and distortion of leaves, and malformation and striping of flowers. Virus diseases are easily spread by handling infected plants. If virus disease is suspected, burn the affected plants immediately to prevent it spreading to others.

Artificial-light gardening

Instant 'sunlight' at the flick of a switch – with the help of artificial lighting you can grow plants in the gloomiest of situations. A shelf too dimly lit to accommodate anything other than ferns can be enlivened with the brilliant flowers of African violets, gloxinias or small *Begonias*. You can create a flourishing indoor garden under the stairs or in a dim corner of a room. Even a basement 'greenhouse' without a single window is a possibility – allowing the gardener with no room for a proper greenhouse to grow orchids and other exotic and not so exotic flowers all the year round.

The range of plants you can grow successfully under artificial light is wide. Many foliage houseplants do not, in any case, need very bright light, so it is easy to give them a slight boost so that they can grow happily in a dark corner. A spotlight or two – or even bright room lighting – may be enough for them. *Philodendrons* and their relatives, palms and the *Aspidistra* are among the plants that come into this category.

Where better illumination is essential, you must restrict yourself to plants of limited height. This is because normal artificial lighting cannot give a light intensity even remotely matching that of daylight unless it is very close to the plants. Most of the popular small foliage plants like *Marantas*, *Peperomias*, bromeliads, foliage *Begonias*, and a host of others are ideal. But you can take special advantage in growing flowering pot-plants like gloxinias (*Sinningia*), *Streptocarpus*, flowering *Begonias*, orchids, *Calceolarias*, *Cinerarias*, *Campanula isophylla*, *Achimenes* and particularly *Saintpaulias* (African violets). The last mentioned react very well to artificial light, and indoor units have been specially designed for them.

The seedlings of many flowers and vegetables – to be subsequently planted in the open or under glass – also benefit from a period under artificial light, generally to supplement normal daylight. They usually become more sturdy, and flower or fruit earlier. Tomatoes, cucumbers and lettuce all do well.

Sources of light

Ordinary floodlights and spotlights can be used from a distance to make a display of plants more attractive, and to illuminate rather than irradiate them. In this case, although the lamps may not give a great light intensity, it is usually sufficient to improve growth. A portable lamp, or a battery of lamps on a stand, can also be brought into action to extend 'day length' or give extra light to improve plants that have to be sited in unfavourable, normally poorly lit places. An extra hour or so in the morning or evening may make a considerable difference to plant health in such cases.

Probably the most convenient source of artificial light for growing plants in the home is the fluorescent tube. It does not give out enough heat to damage plants, but its slight warmth can prove useful. As well as straight tubes of various lengths there are square panels and rings that are especially useful for illuminating plant groups and plants in bowls

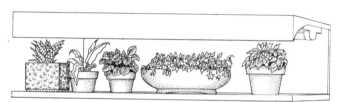

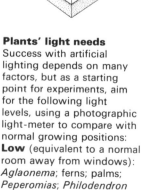

Plants' light needs
Success with artificial lighting depends on many factors, but as a starting point for experiments, aim for the following light levels, using a photographic light-meter to compare with normal growing positions:
Low (equivalent to a normal room away from windows): *Aglaonema*; ferns; palms; *Peperomias*; *Philodendron scandens*

Medium (equivalent to a normal room near a window): *Asparagus* ferns; *Begonias* (foliage types); bromeliads; *Chlorophytum*; most *Dracaenas*; *Episcia*; *Fatsia japonica*; *Ficus pumila*; *Ficus radicans*; *Fittonia*; *Hedera* (ivies); *Soleirolia*; *Hoya*; *Maranta*; *Pileas*; *Scindapsus aureus*; *Tradescantia*; *Zygocactus* (Christmas cactus; must have short 'days' to flower)

High (equivalent to a well lit window sill): *Begonias* (flowering types); *Citrus*; *Euphorbia* (poinsettia; needs short 'days' to flower); *Gynura*; most orchids; *Saintpaulia*
Very high (equivalent to a sunny window sill): *Calceolaria*; *Cineraria*; *Codiaeum* (croton); *Coleus blumei*; *Impatiens*; *Kalanchoe*; *Pelargonium* (geranium); *Sinningia speciosa* (gloxinia)

Artificial-light fittings
For closest environmental control, a heated and lit terrarium **left** and **right** is the ideal, particularly for plants like African violets. Simple shelf units and adjustable stands **below left** are suitable for small plants, while attractive floor fitments **far right** and **below far left** make display features. For the serious grower, there are multi-tier carts **below**, while a cellar can be fitted with benches and strip lamps **below right**.

or tubs. Fluorescent tubes can be used singly or in multiple banks or lengths. In all cases, one long tube is better than two short, however, as it is the middle section that gives out most light. Tubes specially made for indoor gardening are obtainable, such as the Gro-Lux. These give out most of their light in the red and blue wavelengths that plants particularly need. If using ordinary tubes, choose the types generally described as 'daylight', or combine one 'daylight' with one 'cool white' tube.

Ordinary tungsten filament lamps can be useful for limited purposes – mainly for controlling flowering – but many artificial light gardeners combine them with fluorescent tubes in order to boost the red wavelengths. The snag is that they emit considerable heat, and may damage plants if not used cautiously. For large-scale work, mercury fluorescent lamps like those used for street lighting can be employed. These combine a tungsten filament with a mercury arc and fluorescent coating. They are usually rated at about 160 watts and give a good percentage of red wavelengths.

In all cases reflectors greatly improve efficiency. As a rough guide, tubes or lamps should be arranged so that each square foot of growing space receives about 15 to 20 watts of light, the source of illumination being about 12 to 18 inches above the tops of the plants. You may have to make considerable adjustments, however, in order to suit your particular conditions and plants. Only by experiment can you decide on the optimum distances. Where plants of different heights are being grown, it may be necessary to raise some of the pots on supports to bring them nearer the lights. Generally, plants that are not receiving enough light will tend to grow tall, weak, pale green stems. Too much light, on the other hand, has a bleaching effect: Plants lose contrast in colours, variegation and markings. A great excess may cause leaf browning or shrivelling.

Artificial-light fittings
Commercial fittings are available, and these vary very widely in design, size and price. Where these are not obtainable, or are too expensive or unsuitable, it is not very difficult for the home handyman to construct his own unit. Take strict care over electrical safety, however, since damp may penetrate the electrical parts; if in doubt, leave this part of the job to a qualified electrician.

Installations of various kinds are illustrated on these two pages. Simple commercial units consist of a trough with a suitable fluorescent tube mounted above, on legs, generally with a height adjustment. There are also small bowl types with a ring-shaped tube arranged rather like a table lamp. Larger, more elaborate units can consist of a multi-tier plant stand, with light fittings under each shelf shining on the plants below. Units of this kind specially designed for *Saintpaulias* are available. In some countries you can also buy terrariums with built-in fluorescent lighting (see page 30).

If building your own installation, arrange the lights so that all the illumination is directed down onto the plants and not into the faces of viewers. For best results, plunge the plant pots in troughs of moist peat or stand them on trays of wet shingle. Either arrangement increases humidity, as of course does enclosing the plants in a glass terrarium. To help you gauge how much light the plants are receiving, use a photographic light meter, aiming for a reading like that of a well-lit but shady spot outdoors on a sunny day.

Everyday care
When growing under artificial light, the brightness of the illumination is not the only factor that needs to be taken into account. Others include the period of illumination and the temperature.

Continuous exposure to light will not affect some plants, but will upset others. So experiment to find out the best 'day length' to suit your plants. As a rough guide, switch on the lights for 12 hours each day. For some plants, up to 16 hours has been found better, but too long can inhibit flowering in certain plants – orchids, *Chrysanthemums* and poinsettias being notable examples. A time-switch makes control automatic.

When light is good, quick and sturdy growth results when the temperature is increased slightly. This may be an advantage with raising seedlings or encouraging the development of slow-growing plants. However, when it is desired to keep ornamentals short and compact there is no advantage in excessive temperature. This is one reason why lamps that evolve much heat are undesirable for most plants.

Apart from such considerations, plants growing under artificial light need just the same care as any other house or conservatory specimens. Water and feed them as necessary, remembering that they will have no dormancy period so long as they are under the lights; so continue to give water and weak fertilizer all the year round. For flowering plants, a high-phosphate compound fertilizer will generally give best results (see page 222). Granted such care, there is no reason why artificially lit plants should not equal or better those grown in greenhouses or conservatories. This has been amply proved by professional growers; slowly their skills are spreading to amateur indoor gardeners.

Tools and technicalities

To start gardening indoors, you need only a few pot-plants and some interest in their well-being. As you become more enthusiastic, however, you will find that a few items of equipment will help in managing your growing plant collection.

The basic need for gardenless gardening is, of course, a collection of pots and containers in which to grow your plants. Ordinary flower-pots of plastic or clay are always needed (see page 218). For window-ledge gardening, you can stand flower-pots in a trough, or you may prefer to plant directly in window boxes (see page 130). If you have a balcony, patio or similar place, a few large pots or tubs will be needed for the bigger plants; they are available in a wide range of functional or decorative styles (see page 122). Hanging containers are useful where space is short (see page 128).

Apart from these, you will need some tools for planting, weeding, repotting, watering, and so on. As with every hobby, sophisticated gadgets are available to tempt the real enthusiast – particularly when growing an extensive collection in a conservatory – but the essentials are simple and inexpensive.

Watering cans; sprayers
A watering can is a vital piece of equipment. For watering pot-plants and window boxes, choose one with a fine nozzle and long spout **right below**.
It is wise to have two sprayers **right** – one for water and the other for pesticides. There are neat hand models suitable for treating plants indoors in confined spaces. The sprayer used for clean water should be clearly marked and used for nothing else. Many plants benefit from an occasional fine overhead spray, especially in the dry atmosphere of the home.

Automatic watering
Special self-watering pots and troughs are available for houseplants. They have a water reservoir that needs to be topped up from time to time. Water is conveyed to the potting mixture by a wick, generally of glass-fibre. You can, in fact, improvise such an arrangement yourself **right**, using a lamp wick and a waterproof pot-holder. Do not crock the flower-pot, and make sure that the water level is always below the bottom of the flower-pot. For more elaborate pot-plant arrangements, you can use a simple adaptation of the greenhouse or conservatory capillary bench (see opposite). Any reliable automatic watering system is useful for holidays, but check its efficiency first.

Simple tools
You will need virtually no gardening tools as such if you simply grow a few pot-plants on a window sill. An old dinner knife and fork will be useful for loosening the surface of the potting mixture in small containers and removing the occasional weed, and a spoon will help with potting on. But with window boxes and more extensive container gardens, small hand trowels and forks **right** are a help. A dibber (basically a short blunt-ended stake) is useful for planting bulbs. For simple pruning and removing dead flowers, use some thin-pointed scissors or secateurs. You may need canes for supporting plants; the green-stained type, used with green twine or ties of plastic or wire, are less conspicuous. Special wire-hoop supports are available for larger plants.

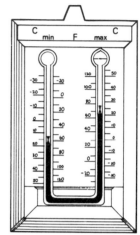

Moisture meters
The number one killer of pot-plants is overwatering, and an instrument that measures soil moisture takes the guesswork out of watering. Such a moisture meter generally has a long soil probe (designed to minimize root disturbance) that is simply pushed well down into the potting mixture. Some types have a direct-reading dial **right**; others have flashing lights to show 'dry', 'moist' or 'wet' conditions. Plants' needs vary, of course, but in general a houseplant's pot should never remain in the 'wet' or 'dry' zone for too long.

Hygrometers
A hygrometer is extremely useful when growing plants indoors. It tells you how much moisture there is in the air — particularly important for houseplants of tropical and sub-tropical origin. The most convenient hygrometer is the direct-reading kind. This has a dial calibrated in percentages of relative humidity **right**. A reading below 50 is usually considered 'dry', 50 to 75 'normal' and 75 to 100 'moist'. For most houseplants it is best to avoid the 'dry' region.

Other meters
Keen indoor or conservatory gardeners may find useful a light intensity meter and a fertilizer concentration meter. The latter helps to avoid over-feeding your plants.

Thermometers
A thermometer is essential if you want to grow any but the very simplest plants. It should preferably be of the maximum-minimum type **below**. This has indicators that show the highest and lowest temperatures over a period.

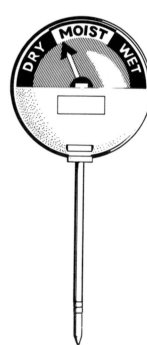

Keeping a conservatory

A conservatory is managed in much the same way as a greenhouse, except that special attention needs to be paid to appearance and personal comfort. Heating, ventilation, watering and humidity can all be controlled by automatic devices, while shading is vital unless the conservatory faces away from the sun. High humidity is particularly important in summer, but it should be kept low in winter in a cool conservatory, so switch off any automatic watering benches.

Cleanliness is vital to the success of all gardening under glass. Grow all your plants in sterilized potting mixtures (see page 218), and take care to keep benches, pots and floors clean. Clean down the glass regularly. In towns, the exterior glass may need frequent cleaning in winter to remove grime. Keep snow off the roof, as it will cut down the light.

Make routine inspections of the plants to check for diseases and pests, paying close attention to the undersides of leaves. Take immediate action if necessary. If the conservatory adjoins a living area, though, take particular care when applying pesticides. Avoid those with unpleasant or persistent odours if possible, and never use poisonous fumigants. Generally, dusts and sprays that can be kept confined to small areas will be found the most convenient. It is wise to throw out sickly plants if they do not respond to simple treatment, otherwise they may infect and ruin the whole collection.

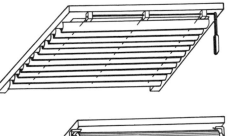

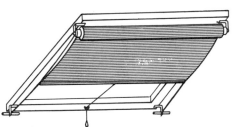

Ventilation
Automatic ventilation is best. Hinged vents or windows can be fitted with temperature-sensitive vent-openers **right**. These are very reliable, and can be adjusted to open at any desired temperature. Electric fan ventilation, thermostatically controlled, is also useful. But exclude draughts in winter.

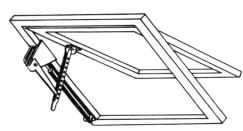

Shading
above Shading is vital if the conservatory receives much sun. Roller slatted blinds fitted above the roof are best. Interior blinds are less effective in keeping down temperatures, but do help to stop plants scorching. Blinds help conserve warmth on frosty nights, but always raise them in the morning.

'Double glazing' with clear plastic sheeting an inch below the glass also helps to retain heat in winter. An electrostatic shading paint (such as Coolglass) is a cheap and simple way of providing summer shading. It can be brushed or sprayed on the outside of the glass. It is not removed by rain, but can be wiped off when dry.

Pest control
There are automatic pest controllers **above** that work by vaporizing suitable pesticides, but these should not be installed without consulting the manufacturers about safety. Extra care is needed if the conservatory is lived in.

Heating
For economy, extend the home central heating system into the conservatory if possible. Alternatively, greenhouse heating equipment can be used. An electric fan heater with a separate thermostat to control both air circulation and heat simultaneously **above** is very efficient but expensive. Electric convection heaters may also be used. Oil heaters with wicks are popular, but need manual control; the blue-flame type is best as it is relatively fume-free. Independent boilers can also be used.

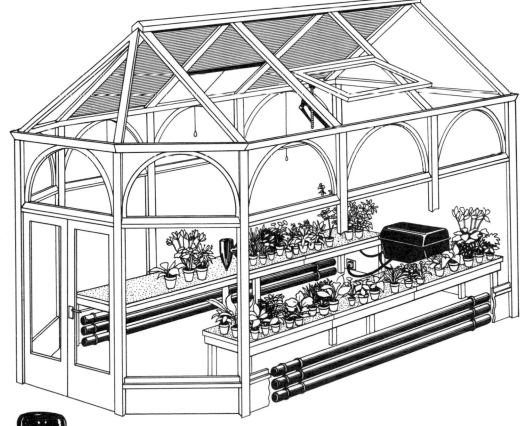

Watering and humidity
Splashing water on the floor ('damping down') is a good way to maintain humidity, but it is often not convenient. Automatic electric humidifiers are available. An automatic capillary bench in place of ordinary staging will aid humidity as well as watering pot-plants without your attention. Sand on the bench is kept damp via an automatic water-feed device **left**. Plant pots are pressed down onto the sand; they are not crocked, so the moisture is drawn up into the potting mixture by capillary action.

The disabled gardener

Indoors or out, gardening is a valuable hobby for anyone who is disabled or infirm. Even a totally bedridden person can gain great pleasure from tending some pot-plants on a wheeled plant stand, while the person who is a little more mobile can easily grow plants indoors or on a patio or terrace. Special adaptations and allowances may have to be made, and the help of a fitter person will be particularly useful in the early stages of constructing a patio garden. But the elderly or disabled person will then find both physical and psychological benefit in growing decorative plants and vegetables.

Growing houseplants

Indoor gardening is, of course, ideal for the person who is housebound, and very many of the plants described earlier in this book can be grown. It is probably best to choose the easier kinds that do not need much attention – plants like the *Chlorophytum* (spider plant), ivies (*Hedera*), geraniums (*Pelargonium*), *Rhoicissus* (grape ivy, or Natal vine), *Sansevieria* (mother-in-law's tongue) and busy Lizzie (*Impatiens*). Cacti and succulents are useful for a sunny window sill, and most kinds will survive considerable neglect. For an indication of more houseplants that are easy to care for, see the chart on page 242.

Terrariums and bottle gardens (see pages 30 to 33) are fun to plant, and once established need very little attention. In a quite different vein an indoor miniature garden on a window sill (see page 195) enables the housebound person to create a complete landscape in a small trough. For the bedridden patient, a small artificially lit plant stand enables houseplants to grow near the bed even in a dark room (see page 234).

Patios and terraces

Most of the outdoor situations described in this book – including patios, terraces, courtyards, balconies and roof gardens – can be adapted for easy management by those who find it difficult to stoop, to bend, or just to get around. Every garden should, after all, be designed to suit the needs and limitations of the gardener.

When planning a garden of this kind for the disabled or elderly, every care must be taken to save the gardener unnecessary effort. Each part should be easy to reach, and beds and borders should be no more than two feet wide to avoid difficulties in weeding, planting and pruning. Resting places – a small bench or a garden chair – should be placed strategically.

Steps can be supplied with a strong handrail for safety, but should be replaced by a ramp – about three feet wide

– for wheelchair gardeners, with a gradient no steeper than 1 foot in 15 if possible. A brick edging on either side of all ramps and paths will prevent a wheelchair from running over the edge.

Slippery and uneven paved areas are a particular hazard for those who are not too nimble. Concrete is the safest surface because the tamped (rippled) surface provides a better grip for walking, for sticks and for wheelchairs. Alternatively, non-slip paving slabs can be laid and set in mortar. Great care must be taken to ensure that the slabs are laid evenly, and the gaps between should be filled in with mortar. It is best to avoid using old York paving slabs, as they can become slippery in winter, and crazy paving is apt to become uneven unless very carefully laid.

Easy-maintenance features

Many simple ideas make gardening easier and safer for disabled and elderly people, and they are also useful spacesavers in the kind of situations covered by this book. Raised flower beds, for example, are attractive features for any small paved garden (see page 124). They also eliminate the need to stoop or bend, and are essential for anyone who must work from a wheelchair. The bed should be about two feet high, and built so that any part of it is within arm's reach of the

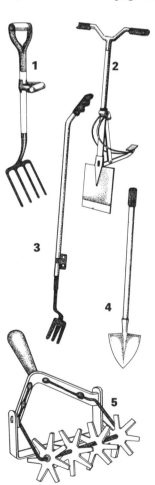

Working from a wheelchair right A design for a patio for a gardener confined to a wheelchair includes many easily tended features. The gardener is working on a raised flower bed formed from paving slabs stood on edge, as described on page 125. On the far right are two sink gardens, one planted

with alpines, the other with bulbs and bedding plants. The pool, too, is raised for safety, and trailing plants and alpines are planted in soil pockets. At the back are fan-trained fruit trees, while the left-hand boundary is formed by a Bouché-Thomas fruit hedge. The path is wide and rough-surfaced.

Useful tools for handicapped gardeners

Digging tools
For digging low beds without stooping, the west-country shovel has an extra-long (4½-foot) shaft **4**. The pointed blade bites easily into the ground. The Wolf Terrex spade **2** has a long, adjustable shaft and a handlebar grip. The gardener uses a foot pedal to push the blade into the ground, and pivots the shovel to throw soil upwards and outwards. There is no need to bend down when using it. A conventional fork or spade can be bought fitted with an extra handle grip **1** on the shaft for better leverage, or this can be bought separately. Other useful tools include the adjustable Wilkinson telescopic fork **3** and a lightweight border

fork, which has a short handle, with a grip for use by a seated gardener.

Planting and weeding
Light soil can be broken up, ready for planting, by the Wolf Soil Miller **5**, which can be used by a standing gardener or towed from a wheelchair. The Baronet weeder **6**, with its 33-inch handle, is useful for both planting and weeding. Its spring jaws, operated by a lever, will either pull out weeds and their roots or hold a plant ready for release into a prepared hole.

Hoes and thinning tools
You can buy hoes in a wide variety of weights, with dual-purpose, adjustable or interchangeable heads, and long or very short handles. Old-fashioned Dutch and draw hoes can be tiring to use, but modern designs **10** work with a push-pull

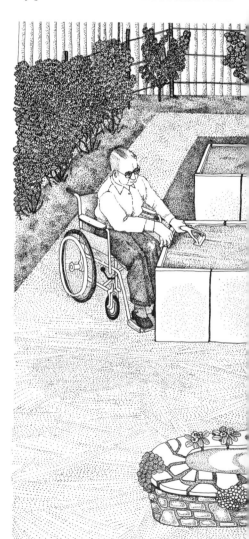

seated gardener – two feet wide, or four feet if it is accessible from both sides. It can be built from bricks, stones, paving slabs, concrete blocks, peat blocks, or even old railway sleepers (ties).

A raised water garden (see page 172) will give unexpected interest to any garden or patio, and is easy to tend. Pedestal trough gardens (see page 188) and raised rock banks are also ideal, and plants can be grown in the cracks and crevices between the stones of a raised bed or a dry stone wall (see page 126). Concrete troughs, barrels and ornamental urns (see page 122) provide an easily accessible home for flowers, shrubs and small trees; they can be raised to the correct height, if necessary, on stone blocks. For those of a certain temperament, great pleasure may be had with little effort in tending a collection of bonsai trees (see pages 178 to 187).

Almost any plant will grow in a raised bed, but the disabled gardener may prefer to choose plants that are easy to care for. Staking can be difficult and dangerous for those whose balance is unsteady, but there are many self-supporting plants – most annual flowers and dwarf perennials, for example. Ground-cover plants, such as plantain lilies (*Hosta*), periwinkles (*Vinca*), stonecrops (*Sedum*) and many others join together in a cluster, choking weeds, and so make

weeding unnecessary. Small shrubs and trees can also be grown, and alpines are useful for shallow troughs, rock gardens and walls. For bright spring colour, bulbs are ideal, and most kinds will naturalize (see pages 106 to 115).

Growing fruit

Fruit-growing is not outside the scope of disabled and elderly gardeners if the right fruit types are chosen. Soft fruit bushes, such as gooseberries and various currants, are ideal. Espalier, fan-trained or cordon apple and pear trees are easy to reach, even from a wheelchair, but need regular pruning. Dwarf pyramid fruit trees are easy to manage and need less pruning. There are, in any case, lightweight pruning tools that can be used, including battery-operated types.

An old idea revived in recent years is the Bouché Thomas fruit hedge. Mature dwarf pyramid apple or pear trees are planted in a row, about five feet apart, but a foot deeper than normal. As a result, the lower branches are covered in soil, and new shoots are sent up from below ground level. Wires are strung along the row from stakes, and branches are tied in to these. Any outward-growing branches should be cut off, and the top trimmed if it grows too tall. The result is a fruit hedge that can be easily tended by a standing or sitting gardener.

Special tools and aids

Strenuous gardening tasks can be made easier if the disabled gardener uses lightweight tools and tools designed specially for his needs. Most of these are only a little more expensive than conventional tools, and many can be used for more than one purpose. A number of kinds available in Britain are illustrated here, and readers in other countries should inquire at large garden centres or department stores about the availability of these or equivalent types. Remember that even if you use conventional tools, you may be able to fit these with rubber or plastic hand-grips to make them easier to handle.

But specialized equipment is not always necessary – a little imagination is usually less expensive. Plastic-covered wire is easier to tie than twine, saving time and effort. Bamboo canes and trimmed pea-sticks can be used with split wire rings for staking plants. Rockery tools are small and light in weight. A trowel attached to a broom handle will make a convenient small spade. Plastic plant-pots are lighter and cheaper than clay pots, and window boxes and ornamental gardens can be made in cheap plastic troughs and urns. All these will make the elderly or disabled gardener's tasks easier, and enable him to get great pleasure from his hobby.

action. The Spearwell Scuffle hoe **8**, with its diamond-shaped head, will remove a single seedling or weed without disturbing those around it.
The Wolf Midget Grubber **7** can be used with a long handle for cultivating a border as well as acting as a rockery or raised-bed cultivator when fitted with a short handle. A similar but larger tool is the Wolf Adjustable Cultivator. The Wolf double hoe **9** has a blade for chopping weeds and, on the other side, two prongs for cultivating; it too can be fitted with long or short handles.

Other basic aids
For those who cannot bend down, but are able to kneel, the Easi-Kneeler stool **11** will make gardening work much easier. Used one way round, it forms an 18-inch-high

stool for sitting, while reversing it gives a low-level kneeling platform with side supports that help the gardener raise and lower himself. Of course, a handyman can easily make himself a similar aid, possibly using a wooden box to provide a container for weeds and so on at the same time.
A two-wheeled wheelbarrow **13** is a more expensive buy, and not really necessary for a small patio garden. But for people with a larger area to tend it is invaluable. With some types, the handle can be hooked over the back of a wheelchair for towing. A pick-up grab **12** is useful for picking up rubbish, leaves, weeds and so on. Ready-made types, such as the Anita, can be bought, but it is not a difficult tool to make for yourself.

Drying flowers and leaves

In summer, your home may abound in the colours and scents of fresh flowers, either picked from the garden or bought from florists. But as soon as winter arrives and you really need cheering up, there are no more flowers to be had, unless you pay high prices for forced and imported blooms. There are, of course, pot-plants that provide colour in winter, as described on pages 82 and 83. However, there is another way to decorate the home in the winter without it costing much. This is to preserve flowers and leaves gathered in the summer and autumn. Many garden plants are suitable – including a number of those recommended earlier in this book for growing on patios, terraces, balconies and roof gardens. Although none will retain their scent, many will keep their colours and brighten the gloomy days of winter.

Natural drying

Many flowers can be preserved simply by hanging them up to dry. Hang bunches of flowers upside-down in a dry, airy place until they feel dry and crisp. 'Everlasting' flowers are a good choice, for the flowers still look as good as new when dried. Good ones include sea holly (*Eryngium*), which has blue teazle-like flowers; straw flowers (members of several genera, including *Helichrysum* and *Helipterum*, which is often called *Acroclinium* or *Rhodanthe*); and sea lavender or statice (*Limonium*), which has heads of small flowers in a wide colour range.

Other good flowers for drying include spikes of *Delphiniums* and lupins, which should be hung up to dry singly and not in bunches. *Gypsophila* has elegant sprays of tiny white flowers that dry well. *Hydrangea* flowers can be dried too, but the stems should be placed in water and left in an airy cupboard until the flowers are crisp. All flowers should be picked as they open when the weather is dry and the dew has evaporated.

Dried seed pods, as well as flowers, make attractive decorations. They should be picked as they ripen and begin to go brown, and dried in the same way as flowers. Good choices are hollyhock, foxglove, poppy, *Delphinium*, sorrel and teazle. The most attractive, long used in dried flower arrangements, is Chinese lantern or cape gooseberry (*Physalis*), which has red lantern-shaped fruits. Another showy choice is honesty (*Lunaria annua*), whose dried seed pods can be rubbed to produce a silvery colour.

Grasses and cereals can also be dried well. A very good choice is pampas grass (*Cortaderia selloana*, or *Gynerium argenteum*), which bears filmy plumes as the flowers emerge. It dries a lovely creamy-white colour. Dried wheat and barley also make good background to a dried flower arrangement, and so do many dried leaves. Most go brown of course, but eucalyptus leaves dry grey-blue.

Artificial preserving

Chemical drying agents extend the range of dried flowers. A mixture of silver sand and borax may be used, or silica gel crystals or powder. (The latter should be regenerated from time to time in a warm oven.) Flower heads or sprays of berries or leaves are placed on a half-inch layer of the drying agent in a box, more is sprinkled over them, and the box is left in a warm place until the plants are crisp and dry. This usually takes only three days or so. Good choices include roses (especially orange and red varieties), geraniums (*Pelargoniums*), gentians, *Fuchsias*, *Delphiniums*, and pansies. The colour will usually be retained.

Sprays of tree leaves are essential to any dried flower arrangement, and they can be preserved by using glycerine. The leaves should be gathered in dry weather when they are fully grown but not yet turning brown. Hammer the ends of the cut stems so that the leaves will take up the glycerine quickly. Then stand the ends in one part glycerine mixed with two parts of warm water.

Good choices include beech, oak, hornbeam, laurel, *Aspidistra*, horse chestnut, sweet chestnut and *Elaeagnus* (a genus of shrubs that have glistening gold and silver leaves). The leaves usually change colour, ending up any shade from white through tan to deep green-bronze. Glycerine treatment will preserve the colours of many flowers, however, and it also helps them to stay open. The flower heads may need florist's-wire supports.

Using dried flowers

Dried and preserved flowers will last through the winter stood indoors in empty containers. The air should be dry, and arrangements keep well in centrally heated rooms. Fresh flowers may be introduced into a dried flower and leaf arrangement, but water may be necessary to keep the fresh flowers alive. In this case, the stems of the dried or preserved plants should be varnished or dipped in molten candle wax to stop them rotting. To dust the plants, simply puff air over them with a bicycle pump.

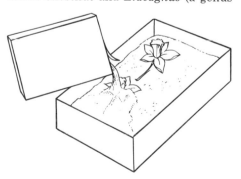

Drying with borax, etc
A wide range of garden flowers can be dried by covering them with silica gel crystals or a mixture of borax and silver sand.

Drying with glycerine
To dry beech and other leaves and also many kinds of flowers, stand the stems (crushed if necessary) in glycerine and water.

A last word

Pressing flowers

Pressing flowers is another simple way of preserving them. Spread the flowers out carefully between sheets of blotting paper, arranging the leaves and petals for the best effect. Press the paper between heavy books, and leave the flowers for about a month. A flower press can be used instead of books; it takes up less room, and is more convenient. You can then carefully stick the flattened preserved flowers on cards or cloth, and mount them in frames, either singly or in arrangements.

An interesting project is to identify and press all the flowers in the locality and then exhibit them on your walls. Most wild flowers press well, though blue flowers such as harebells tend to fade. Remember, though, that several wild flowers are protected by law in some countries. In any case, take any wild flowers only if they are plentiful.

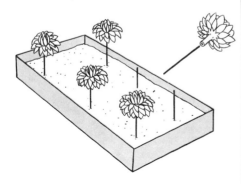

Drying naturally
top Many kinds of flowers can simply be hung up to dry, but stand short-stemmed types upright on lengths of stiff wire **above**.

'O Tiger-lily,' said Alice, addressing herself to one that was waving gracefully about in the wind, 'I wish you could talk!' *'We can talk,' said the Tiger-lily, 'when there's anybody worth talking to.'*

Outside the Looking Glass world a conversation with a plant can be a discouragingly one-sided affair; but amid the *furor hortensis* which in recent years seems to have overrun most of the Western world, amateur horticulturalists and even the odd expert have claimed that chatting to their plants from day to day helps them to grow bushier, taller, more healthy. Now and again a professional gardener will declare that his success has always depended upon it. Plants, they all say, flourish when they know they are loved.

The gardening world has divided itself into two schools of thought on the subject: the believers and the sceptics. The former, naturally gregarious souls at heart, rattle on enthusiastically to their green companions about this and that, reminiscing for hours over past glories; coyly revealing the innermost secrets of their hearts and the occasional shy hope for the future. The latter are mostly scientists. Plants cannot experience the emotions of human beings, they argue, because they have no nervous system. And politely but objectively keeping their heads while all about them are losing theirs, they pooh-pooh the whole idea of plant responsiveness.

And that was that; until 1966 when Cleve Backster, the American CIA interrogation expert of lie-detector fame, first used his polygraph to try to record the stress reactions of plants.

A polygraph, or lie-detector, monitors changes in the emotional state of a human being by recording variations in the electrical reactions of his skin under different stress situations. In February 1966 Backster tried to measure with his polygraph the rate at which a freshly watered plant would absorb moisture, by recording the change in the electrical resistance of its leaves as the water reached them. The experiment failed, and Backster formulated the idea of burning one of the plant's leaves to see if this would produce any results. Before he was able to do this, he was startled to see that at the very instant he had had this thought, the polygraph had recorded a stress reaction from the plant.

In a later experiment, Backster recorded a similar reaction from his plants whenever live shrimps were dropped by a machine into boiling water. The scientific world was mildly staggered, and forced at last to ask itself a leading question: Are plants aware?

More recently, the power of the human mind has been used in France to impede the natural growth of fungi; in Bulgaria, the power of suggestion was successfully employed to encourage it. An ITT engineer used a plant to break an electrical circuit; another scientist claims – and you are by no means obliged to believe this – to have taught a cactus to count!

The doubters, as usual, have refused to go away – but then, so have the phenomena. Scientists mutter grudgingly about changes in electrical fields. Cleve Backster has evolved a theory of primary perception in all living organisms which, he says, have the capacity to receive (and, presumably to react to) signals from other living cells – over great distances, it seems, and even through lead and other shields which cannot be penetrated by the range of radiation known to man. In Czechoslovakia the term 'psychotronics' has been coined to describe the form of energy thought to be an invisible property of all forms of life, and which may be the medium responsible for carrying such unexplained occurrences as clairvoyance, telepathy and precognition.

Back on the plane of everyday experience, however, it appears that plants are able to feel pain, just as we do. Sir Jagadis Chandra Bose, an Indian, claims among other things to have recorded the screams of tomatoes being cut up and the cries of flowers being picked, a spine-chilling experience which must create something of a dilemma for vegetarians and health food addicts. Perhaps they can take some comfort in the thought that, in the great struggle for survival, all flesh is grass. We all, ultimately, depend upon plants for our food.

But most of the findings related above seem to indicate that plants respond with sympathy to human emotions. If this is true, our domestic responsibilities seem to have increased. Not only must we care for our plants in the traditional, time-honoured ways – watering and fertilizing them, making sure they are put in the right sort of spot, not kept too cold and so on – but we must make sure that they are happy. Our own inner happiness may be measured in the number of healthy young shoots, buds and leaves produced each growing season. Perhaps our depressions and internal conflicts stare reproachfully back at us, unignorable, in the form of a yellowed, wilting *Monstera deliciosa*, or a sad little pile of fallen *Azalea* petals.

The problem that faces you is *how* do you keep your plants happy, always assuming that you can first keep yourself happy? Some people advocate peptalks for failing specimens – and praise, of course, for the first sign of a new shoot. Intellectuals read poetry to their greenhouse exotica, and music is generally well-received by most plants. The kind of music is a question of trial and error. In India, Sir Jagadis Chandra Bose has for years been busily broadcasting ragas to fields of rice and Western classical music to wheat crops for half an hour a day. Perhaps only hardy annuals really take to hard rock, while a flowering cherry might be induced to drown its problems in a track or two of biwa music first thing in the morning.

And the whole subject raises new questions, hitherto unbroached: What do plants think of us? ('I don't care about colour,' the Tiger-lily remarked [about Alice]. 'If only her petals curled up a little more, she'd be all right.') The time for a re-evaluation of our attitudes and values is nigh. Do you, for example, address your favourite houseplants respectfully, with their personal names?

Indoor plant selection guide

Which plants will best suit your decorative needs ? Will they grow well in your home conditions ? Information on about 100 of the most popular indoor plants is summarized here, with page references to earlier parts of the book, where more information can be found to help you choose.

Characteristics

A : Annual
B : Biennial
C : Perennial
D : Bulb, corm, tuber, etc
J : Bromeliad
K : Cactus/succulent
L : Palm
M : Fern
Q : Climber
R : Trailer
S : Bushy
T : Tree-like

W : Attractively marked or coloured leaves
X : Deciduous
Y : Flowering and/ or fruiting
Z : Fragrant

A letter in brackets means that the plant *can* be treated this way, or that the feature is temporary or of lesser importance.

Flowering season

1 : Spring
2 : Summer
3 : Autumn
4 : Winter

A number in brackets means that this is not the main flowering season.

How easy to grow

−   A challenge
+   Rather difficult
++   Fairly easy
+++   Easy

Temperature needs

−   Must have cool conditions

+   Survives cool conditions ; minimum 7 to 10°C (45 to 50°F)

++   For intermediate conditions ; minimum 10 to 13°C (50 to 55°F)

+++   Needs warmth ; minimum 16°C (61°F) or more

Light needs

●   Needs maximum possible sun
   Likes some direct sun
   For a bright position out of direct sun
   Tolerates continuous shade

Humidity needs

□   Must have dry air
   Tolerates dryness
   Likes moderate humidity
   Needs high humidity

Botanical name	Page	Mature height	Characteristics	How easy to grow	Flowering season	Temperature needs	Light needs	Humidity needs
Achimenes spp	77	1 ft (30 cm)	C D X Y	++	2 3	+++		
Adiantum spp	57	1 ft (30 cm)	C M	++		+		
Aechmea spp	72	2 ft (60 cm)	C J W Y	+++	2 3	++		
Aglaonema spp	48	6 in (15 cm)+	C W (Y)	+	2	+++		
Aloe variegata	68	1 ft (30 cm)	C K W (Y)	+++	1	+		
Aphelandra squarrosa	74	1½ ft (50 cm)	C W Y	+	2 3	+++		
Araucaria excelsa	36	4 ft (1.2 m)	C T	++		++		
Asparagus spp	57	2 ft (60 cm)	C M (Q/R)	+++		++		
Aspidistra eliator	40	2 ft (60 cm)	C	+++		+		
Asplenium nidus	56	2 ft (60 cm)	C M	++		++		
Azalea indica	82	1½ ft (50 cm)	C S Y	++	1 4	−		
Begonia 'Gloire de Lorraine'	117	1 ft (30 cm)	C X Y	++	4	++		
Begonia masoniana; B. rex	46;48	1 ft (30 cm)	C W	++		++		
Begonia semperflorens	116	9 in (25 cm)	(A) C Y	+++	(1) 2 3 (4)	++		
Begonia x tuberhybrida	116	1½ ft (50 cm)	C D X Y	+	2 3	++		
Beloperone guttata	89	1½ ft (50 cm)	C S Y	++	1 2 3	++		
Billbergia spp	72	1½ ft (50 cm)	C J Y	+++	(1 2 3 4)	++		
Cacti	62-67	3 in (8 cm)	C K (Y Z)	+++	1/2/3	+	●	
Caladium vars	40	1 ft (30 cm)	C D X W	+	1 2	+++		
Calathea spp	48	1 ft (30 cm)	C W	−		+++		
Calceolaria vars	78	1 ft (30 cm)	(A) B Y	++	(1) 2 (4)	−		
Chlorophytum comosum	54	1 ft (30 cm)	C W	+++		+		
Chrysanthemum vars	80	2 ft (60 cm)	C X Y	++	(1 2) 3 4	−		
Cineraria (Senecio) cruenta	78	1½ ft (50 cm)	(B) C X Y	++	1 2 4	−		
Cissus; Rhoicissus spp	50	6 ft (2 m)	C Q S	+++		+		
Citrus spp	90	1½ ft (50 cm)+	C S (T) Y Z	++	2 3	++		
Clivia miniata	80	1½ ft (50 cm)	C Y	++	1 2	+		
Cocos weddeliana	43	1½ ft (50 cm)	C L	++		+++		
Codiaeum variegatum	46	2 ft (60 cm)	C S W	+		+++		
Coleus blumei vars	47	1½ ft (50 cm)	(A) C W	+++		++		
Convallaria majalis	109	6 in (15 cm)	C D Y Z	++	1 4	−		
Cordyline terminalis	44	2 ft (60 cm)	C S (T) W	++		+++		
Crocus spp	110	4 in (10 cm)	C D Y	++	1/3/4	−		
Cryptanthus spp	72	4 in (10 cm)+	C J W	+++		++		
Cuphea ignea	78	1 ft (30 cm)	C S Y	+++	1 2 3 4	+		
Cyclamen persicum	82	6 in (15 cm)	C D Y	++	1 4	−		
Dieffenbachia spp	40	3 ft (1 m) +	C S (T) W	+		+++		
Dizygotheca (Aralia) elegantissima	38	4 ft (1.2 m)	C S (T)	++		+++		
Dracaena godseffiana	49	2 ft (60 cm)	C S W	+++		+++		
Dracaena marginata	44	4 ft (1.2 m)	C S (T) W	+++		++		

242

Botanical name	Page	Mature height	Characteristics	How easy to grow	Flowering season	Temperature needs	Light needs	Humidity needs
Dracaena sanderiana	45	1½ ft (50 cm)	C S W	+++		+++		
Echeveria spp	68	3 in (8 cm)	C K W (Y)	+++	2/3	++		
Epiphyllum vars	67	2 ft (60 cm)	C K Y (Z)	+++	1 2	+		
Euphorbia pulcherrima	82	2 ft (60 cm) +	C S X Y	++	4	+++		
Exacum affine	79	1 ft (30 cm)	A (B) Y Z	++	2 3 4	++		
Fatshedra lizei	39	4 ft (1.2 m)	C (Q) S	+++		+		
Fatsia japonica (Aralia sieboldii)	38	4 ft (1.2 m) +	C S	+++		+		
Ficus benjamina	37	6 ft (2 m)	C T	++		++		
Ficus diversifolia	39	1½ ft (50 cm)	C S Y	+++	1 2 3 4	+++		
Ficus elastica; F. benghalensis	36-37	6 ft (2 m)	C T	+++		++		
Ficus lyrata	37	6 ft (2 m)	C T	+		+++		
Ficus pumila	52		C Q R	+++		+		
Freesia vars	115	1½ ft (50 cm)	C D X Y Z	++	1 2 4	−		
Fuchsia vars	103	2 ft (60 cm)	C S X Y	++	2 3	−		
Grevillea robusta	38	3 ft (1 m)	C S (T)	+++		−		
Gynura spp	50		C Q R W	+++		++		
Hedera spp & vars	50		C Q R W	+++		+		
Helxine soleirolii	52		C Q	+++		+		
Hibiscus rosa-sinensis	88	4 ft (1.2 m)	C S Y	++	2 3	+		
Hippeastrum vars	115	1½ ft (50 cm)	C D X Y	+++	1/2/3/4	+++		
Howeia (Kentia) spp	43	4 ft (1.2 m) +	C L (T)	+++		++		
Hoya carnosa	85		C (W) Y Z	++	1 2 3	++		
Hyacinthus orientalis	108	8 in (20 cm)	C D X Y Z	+++	1	−		
Hydrangea macrophylla	102	3 ft (1 m)	C S Y	++	2	+		
Hypocyrta glabra	85	9 in (25 cm)	C (R Y)	++	1 2	+++		
Impatiens spp	81	2 ft (60 cm)	C Y	+++	1 2 3 4	++		
Jasminum polyanthum	91		C Q Y Z	++	1 4	−		
Kalanchoë spp	69	1 ft (30 cm)	C K Y	+++	1 4	+		
Lilium spp	114	2 ft (60 cm) +	C D Y Z	++	2 3	−		
Lithops spp	70	1 in (2.5 cm)	C K W (Y)	+++	2 3	+		
Lobelia tenuior	78	1 ft (30 cm)	(A) C (R) Y	++	1 2 4	+		
Maranta leuconeura vars	49	8 in (20 cm)	C W	+++		++		
Monstera deliciosa	40	6 ft (2 m) +	C Q	+++		++		
Narcissus vars	108	1¼ ft (40 cm)	C D X Y (Z)	+++	1 4	−		
Neanthe (Chamaedorea) bella	43	1½ ft (50 cm)	C L	+++		++		
Pelargonium vars	104	2 ft (60 cm)	C Y	+++	1 2 3	+		
Peperomia spp	54	8 in (20 cm)	C W	++		++		
Philodendron bipinnatifidum	41	3 ft (1 m)	C S	++		+++		
Philodendron hastatum, etc	41	4 ft (1.2 m)	C Q	++		+++		
Philodendron scandens	51		C Q	+++		++		
Pilea spp	55	1 ft (30 cm)	C W	+++		++		
Platycerium bifurcatum	56	1½ ft (50 cm)	C M	++		++		
Primula spp	83	1 ft (30 cm)	(A) C Y	++	1 4	−		
Pteris spp	57	1 ft (30 cm)	C M	+++		++		
Saintpaulia ionantha	76	4 in (10 cm)	C Y	++	(1) 2 3 (4)	+++		
Salpiglossis vars	78	2 ft (60 cm)	A (B C) Y	++	1 2 3	+		
Sansevieria trifasciata	68	1½ ft (50 cm)	C K W	+++		+		
Saxifraga sarmentosa	47	1 ft (30 cm)	C Q W	+++		+		
Schefflera actinophylla	36	6 ft (2 m)	C T	++		++		
Schizanthus vars	78	1½ ft (50 cm)	A (B) Y	++	1 2 3	+		
Scindapsus aureus	53		C Q R W	+		+++		
Senecio macroglossus	51		C Q W	+++		+		
Sinningia speciosa	77	10 in (25 cm)	C D X Y	+++	1 2	+++		
Syngonium (Nephthytis) podophyllum	41		C Q W	++		+++		
Tradescantia; Zebrina spp	53		C R W	+++		+		
Tulipa vars	108	1 ft (30 cm) +	C D X Y	+++	1	−		
Zygocactus truncatus	67	6 in (15 cm)	C K Y	+++	3 4	++		

Soleirolia soleirolii − see Helxine soleirolii

Glossary

Gardening, just like any other human activity, has its jargon, and although this book has been written with the non-expert in mind, you will no doubt find some terms that you do not understand. This glossary should help you with these and with some of the terms that you will come across if you read further — in gardening magazines and elsewhere. Generally speaking, processes, techniques and items of equipment are not covered here, but their occurrences in the book are listed in the general index.

Adventitious: Describes growth from an unusual place; eg, roots growing from a stem.

Aerial root: A root that grows out from a stem above ground level, as in many *Philodendrons* and their relatives.

Alpine: Strictly, a plant native to mountains, but generally any small-growing plant suitable for a rockery, etc.

Annual: A plant that grows from seed, flowers, produces seed and dies in one season; also, loosely, any plant that can be treated this way.

Aquatic: A plant that lives partly or wholly in water.

Areole: A woolly or hairy tuft found on cacti; see page 60.

Aroid: A member of the Araceae, the family that includes the *Caladium, Monstera, Philodendron*, many other houseplants, and the *Arum* — whence the name.

Axil: The angle between a stem and a petiole. An *axillary bud* often grows there.

Bedding plant: Any plant used for temporary display in a garden.

Bicoloured: Describes a flower having double colouring on the same petals.

Biennial: A plant that grows from seed one year, overwinters, and flowers the next season, then dying; or a plant treated like this.

Bigeneric: Of a hybrid, having parents from two different genera.

Bracts: Modified leaves surrounding a flower, sometimes (as in the poinsettia) much more colourful than the flower itself.

Break: Formation of side-shoots, generally after stopping.

Bromeliad: A member of the pineapple family; see page 72.

Bulb: Swollen underground bud that stores food and enables some plants to overwinter; see page 217.

Bulbil: A small, immature bulb.

Calcifuge: A lime-hating plant — one that will not grow in chalky or alkaline soil.

Cheshunt compound: A mixture of 2 parts copper sulphate and 11 parts ammonium carbonate, used to protect seedlings from fungal attack. For use, dissolve one ounce in two gallons of water and use immediately.

Compost: Either decomposed plant remains, or the mixture of soil and other ingredients used to grow plants in pots, etc. In this book, the term potting mixture is generally used for the latter meaning.

Compound: Describes a leaf made up of two or more distinct parts called leaflets, or a flower composed of many florets.

Container plant: One that is grown and sold by a nurseryman in a pot or other container. Since root disturbance is minimal, such a plant can be planted out at almost any season.

Corm: The swollen base of a plant's stem, serving the same function as a bulb.

Crocks: Pieces of broken pot, stones, etc., used to aid drainage in pots; see page 218.

Cultivar: A *culti*vated *vari*ety, a variety of a plant bred in cultivation. See page 11.

Cutting: A piece of a plant used to grow a whole new plant; see page 228.

Deciduous: Describes plants that shed their leaves in winter.

Dormant: Describes a plant that has temporarily stopped growing, generally (but not always) in winter.

Double: Describes a flower that has more than the normal number of petals, or a variety of a plant having such flowers.

Epiphyte: An 'air-plant': one that lives above ground level, generally on tree branches or rocks, but not a parasite. It obtains food and water from falling debris, rainfall, etc. Examples include many bromeliads and most cultivated orchids.

Epiphytic: Describes an epiphyte.

Evergreen: A plant that retains leaves all the year round.

Everlastings: Plants with dry, straw-like flowers that can be preserved as cut flowers for long periods. Also called *immortelles*.

F1 hybrid: A first-generation hybrid whose parents are different pure-bred strains. Such plants are generally more vigorous than ordinary hybrids, but the seed must be produced by controlled hand-pollination.

Family: One of the major groupings of plants, made up of genera whose members have broad similarities. See page 10.

Flore pleno: An extreme double.

Forcing: The use of heat and/or light to induce abnormally early growth or flowering.

Fungicide: A chemical used to combat fungus diseases.

Fungus: A form of plant life that includes mushrooms and toadstools, and also some of the most important microscopic disease-producing organisms of plants; see page 233.

Genus: A fundamental botanical grouping containing anything from one to hundreds of species. The plural is *genera*. See page 10.

Gesneriad: A member of the African violet family, the Gesneriaceae; see page 76.

Glabrous: Smooth, not hairy (of a stem, etc).

Glaucous: Bluish-grey or bluish-green.

Glochid: A hooked hair found on some cacti; see page 60.

Grafting: Joining a detached stem or branch of one plant on to that of another, so that they unite.

Habit: The general shape or growth form of a plant; eg: trailing, climbing, bushy, etc.

Half-hardy: Describes a plant that cannot spend all the year outdoors, generally being killed by frost.

Leaf forms and arrangements

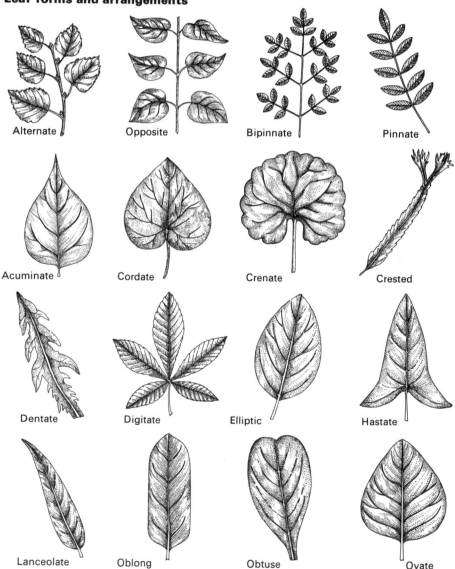

Alternate   Opposite   Bipinnate   Pinnate

Acuminate   Cordate   Crenate   Crested

Dentate   Digitate   Elliptic   Hastate

Lanceolate   Oblong   Obtuse   Ovate

Hardening off: Exposing a young plant grown under glass to gradually reducing temperatures before planting out.

Hardy: Describes a plant that can generally remain outdoors in all seasons, although a plant that is considered hardy in one area may not be so in a place that has very severe winters.

Herbaceous: Describes a plant having a soft – not woody – stem, which generally dies down in the dormant period.

Humus: Decayed organic matter, a vital component of good topsoil.

Hybrid: A plant produced by cross-breeding two plants of different species or genera.

Inflorescence: The arrangement of one or more flowers in a group on a plant; see the illustration below.

Insecticide: A chemical used to combat insect pests.

Internode: The portion of stem between two nodes.

Leaf-mould: Partially decayed leaves, also called leaf-soil.

Leaflet: One of the individual small 'leaves' making up a compound leaf.

Loam: Good, fertile soil that is neither too heavy with clay nor too light with sand, and is rich in humus.

Mulch: A layer of peat, compost or other organic material spread on top of the soil around a plant, serving both as fertilizer and to retain soil moisture.

Node: A joint from which a leaf or side-shoot grows from a stem.

Offset: A small plant that grows from its parent. It can be detached and grown on separately. Bulbils and cormlets are kinds of offsets (see page 217).

Peat: Partially decomposed organic matter – particularly dead mosses or sedges – dug from boggy or fenland areas. Known as peat-moss in the US.

Perennial: A plant that can live for a number of years, in contrast to annuals and biennials.

Petiole: A leaf-stalk.

Pollination: The transfer of pollen from the stamens to the stigma of the same or another flower, the necessary first stage of fertilization and seed production.

Pseudo-bulb: A swollen stem formed by orchids to store water; see page 92.

Quadrigeneric: Describes a hybrid whose ancestry includes four different genera.

Rhizome: A horizontally growing underground stem, serving a similar purpose to bulbs and tubers.

Kinds of inflorescence

Root-ball: The thickly matted roots and soil filling the pot of a flourishing pot-plant.

Runner: A shoot that grows along the ground, rooting to form new plants.

Seed-tray: Known as a flat in the US.

Seedling: A young plant grown from seed.

Self-coloured: Describes a flower having a single pure colour.

Sessile: Describes a leaf that has no stalk, but grows directly from a stem.

Shrub: A woody-stemmed plant with no trunk (unlike a tree).

Single: Describes a flower with the normal number of petals, as opposed to a double flower (see illustration).

Spadix: A fleshy flower spike generally surrounded by a spathe, as found in *Anthurium*, *Spathyphyllum* and *Zantedeschia*.

Spathe: A large, often colourful bract surrounding the spadix of various plants.

Species: A distinct kind of plant that always breeds true. The principal division in the living world, forming a sub-division of a genus. See page 10.

Spore: The equivalent of a seed in lower plants, such as ferns.

Sport: A plant that suddenly develops an unusual characteristic, such as different leaf or flower colouring, that will be passed on to its offspring.

Stamens: The pollen-bearing parts of a flower (see page 217).

Standard: A tree or shrub grown on a single tall trunk – eg, a standard rose. Generally known as tree in the US.

Stigma: The female part of a flower, on which pollen is deposited in pollination.

Stolon: A rooting stem or runner.

Stopping: Pinching out the terminal bud(s) to encourage the formation of side-shoots; see page 225.

Strain: A particularly fine selection from a seed-grown variety.

Strike: The rooting of a cutting.

Sub-shrub: A plant part-way between a shrub and a herbaceous plant, with some woody growth and some soft.

Succulent: A plant with thick, fleshy stems or leaves that store water.

Systemic: Describes an insecticide or fungicide that acts through the plant. It is absorbed by the plant from the soil or through its leaves, and by the disease organism or pest from the plant.

Tender: Describes a plant that must generally be grown indoors or under glass except in the warmest weather. Of course, such plants can grow outdoors at all times in warm climates.

Tendril: A small twining stem that helps a plant climb by clinging to supports.

Terminal: Describes the bud or shoot at the end or top of a stem.

Terrestrial: Growing in soil.

Tessellated: Describes petals or leaves that are patterned in contrasting shades or colours, often with a marbled effect.

Tuber: A swollen root or underground stem acting as a food store, much like a bulb, corm, etc.

Variegated: Describes leaves that are patterned, blotched or spotted with contrasting colours, generally green with cream, white or silver, but sometimes with other colours.

Variety: A sub-division of a species; see page 10.

Whorl: An arrrangement of leaves or flowers like the spokes of a wheel.

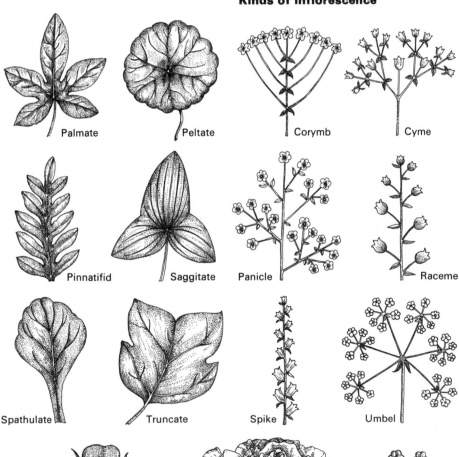

Palmate | Peltate | Corymb | Cyme

Pinnatifid | Saggitate | Panicle | Raceme

Spathulate | Truncate | Spike | Umbel

Single flower | Double flower | Whorl

Bibliography

General reference books

L. H. Bailey, *The Standard Cyclopedia of Horticulture* (Macmillan, 1943)

L. H. and Ethel Zoe Bailey, *Hortus Third* (Macmillan, 1977); a new revised edition of this standard American work

Frances Perry, *Flowers of the World* (Crown, 1972); large format, beautifully illustrated by Leslie Greenwood

Reader's Digest Encyclopedia of Garden Plants and Flowers (Norton, 1978); a well-illustrated single-volume reference book of indoor and outdoor plants

10,000 Garden Questions (American Garden Guild and Doubleday, 1977); edited by Marjorie J. Dietz; original editor, F. F. Rockwell

Royal Horticultural Society, *Dictionary of Gardening* (4 vols., Oxford, 1965, and supplement, 1969); a standard reference work on all aspects of horticulture

Donald Wyman, *Wyman's Gardening Encyclopedia* (Macmillan, 1977); an expanded and revised edition of this standard single-volume reference

Indoor plants

George Abraham, *The Green Thumb Book of Indoor Gardening* (Prentice-Hall, 1967)

Jocelyn Baines and Katherine Key, *The ABC of Indoor Plants* (Knopf, 1973)

Ernesta Drinker Ballard, *Garden in Your House* (Harper & Row, 1971)

Kenneth and Gillian Beckett, *Illustrated Encyclopedia of Indoor Plants* (Doubleday, 1976)

James Underwood Crockett, *Crockett's Indoor Garden* (Little, Brown, 1978)

Thalassa Cruso, *Making Things Grow Indoors* (Knopf, 1971)

Joan Lee Faust, *The New York Times Book of House Plants* (A & W Visual Library, 1975)

Charles Marden Fitch, *The Complete Book of Houseplants* (Hawthorn, 1972)

Alfred B. Graf, *Exotic Plant Manual,* 5th rev. ed. (Roehrs, 1978), with 4,200 photographic illustrations; *Exotic House Plants* (Scribner, 1976), with 1,200 photographic illustrations

Jack Kramer, *1000 Beautiful Houseplants and How to Grow Them* (Morrow, 1969)

Jack Kramer and Andrew R. Addkison, *How to Use Houseplants Indoors for Beauty and Decoration* (Doubleday, 1974)

Dr. Dennis B. McConnell, *The Indoor Gardener's Companion* (Van Nostrand Reinhold, 1978)

Helen Van Pelt Wilson, *African Violet Book* (Hawthorn, 1970), and *Houseplants Are for Pleasure* (Doubleday, 1973)

Outdoor gardening

Illustrated Guide to Gardening, (publ. by Reader's Digest; Norton, 1978)

Rhoda Sprecht Tarantino, *Small Gardens Are More Fun* (Simon & Schuster, 1972)

Michael Wright, ed., *The Complete Book of Gardening* (Lippincott, 1979)

Special topics

African Violets and Gesneriads Virginia F. and George A. Elbert, *The Miracle Houseplants* (Crown, 1976). Montague Free, *All About African Violets* (Doubleday, 1979); revised and expanded by Charles Marden Fitch

Begonias Jack Kramer, *Begonias as House Plants* (Van Nostrand Reinhold, 1976)

Bonsai Robert Lee Behme, *Bonsai, Saikei and Bonkei* (Morrow, 1969). George F. Hull, *Bonsai for Americans* (Doubleday, 1964). John Yoshio Naka, *Bonsai Techniques* (Dennis-Landman, 1976); an excellent practical manual

Bottle Gardens and Terrariums Virginia F. and George A. Elbert, *Fun with Terrarium Gardening* (Crown, 1975). Charles Marden Fitch, *The Complete Book of Terrariums* (Hawthorn, 1974)

Bulbs Ronald Vance, *The Home Gardener's Guide to Bulb Flowers* (Abelard-Schuman, 1967)

Cacti and Succulents Claude Chidamian, *The Book of Cacti and Other Succulents* (Doubleday, 1958). Margaret J. Martin and Peter R. Chapman, *Succulents and Their Cultivation* (Scribner, 1978). Martha Van Ness, *Cacti and Succulents Indoors and Outdoors* (Van Nostrand Reinhold, 1971)

Children Virginia M. Musselman, *Learning About Nature Through Indoor Gardening* (Stackpole, 1972). Aileen Paul, *Kids Gardening* (Doubleday, 1973)

Container Gardening Elvin McDonald, *Decorative Gardening in Containers* (Doubleday, 1978)

Disabled Howard D. Brooks and Charles J. Oppenheim, *Horticulture as a Therapeutic Aid,* Rehabilitation Monograph No. 49 (Institute of Rehabilitation Medicine, New York University Medical Center, 1973). Mary Chaplin, *Gardening for the Physically Handicapped and Elderly* (Batsford, 1978). *Equipment for the Disabled, Leisure and Gardening* (Oxford Regional Authority, 1978). The last two are English publications

Ferns Jack Kramer, *Ferns and Palms for Interior Decoration* (Scribner, 1972)

Geraniums Helen Van Pelt Wilson, *The Joy of Geraniums* (Morrow, 1972)

Hydroculture Frans de Bruijn, *Hydroculture* (W. Foulsham, 1978)

Light gardening George A. Elbert, *The Indoor Light Garden Book* (Crown, 1975). *The Facts of Light About Indoor Gardening* (Ortho Books, 1976)

Orchids Alex D. Hawkes, *Orchids: Their Botany and Culture* (Harper, 1961). Jack Kramer, *Growing Orchids in Your Window* (Van Nostrand, 1976) Rebecca Tyson Northern, *Home Orchid Growing,* 3rd ed. (Van Nostrand Reinhold, 1970). Gloria Jean Sessler, *Orchids and How to Grow Them* (Prentice-Hall, 1978)

Window Gardening Dorothy H. Jenkins and Helen Van Pelt Wilson, *House Plants for Every Window* (Morrow, 1975)

Useful addresses

Most of the listed companies publish catalogs which you can write for. Many of them are free; others are available for a small fee. Remember that strict regulations govern the import and export of plants. Contact the U.S. Department of Agriculture, Plant Quarantine Department, regarding a permit for the importation of plants.

Indoor plants

Alberts & Merkel Bros., Box 537, Boynton Beach, Fla. 33435 (orchids, anthuriums, and other tropical plants)

Buell's, Box 218 Weeks Road, Eastford, Conn. 06242 (gesneriad specialists; catalog 25¢)

Cornelison Bromeliad Nursery, 225 San Bernardino Street, North Fort Myers, Fla. 33903 (bromeliads)

Davis Cactus Garden, 1522 Jefferson Street, Kerrville, Texas 78028 (cacti)

Edelweiss Gardens, 54 Robbinsville-Allentown Road, Robbinsville, N.J. 08691 (ferns, begonias, and other indoor plants; price list 35¢)

Fischer Greenhouses, Linwood, N.J. 08221 (African violets and other gesneriads)

Hausermann's Orchids, Box 363, Elmhurst, Ill. 60128 (unusual species orchids)

House Plant Corner, Box 810, Oxford, Md. 21654 (plants and equipment; catalog)

Jones & Scully, 2200 N.W. 33rd Avenue, Miami, Fla. 33142 (wide variety of orchids suited to growing indoors)

Kavutz Greenhouses, 92H Chestnut Street, Wilmington, Mass. 01887 (unusual houseplants)

Logee's Greenhouses, 55 North Street, Danielson, Conn. 06239 (catalog $1)

McComb Greenhouses, Route 1, New Straitsville, Ohio 43766 (unusual variety of exotic houseplants; catalog 35¢)

Merry Gardens, Camden, Maine (catalog 25¢)

Putney Nursery, Inc., Putney, Vt. 05346 (terrarium plants)

Rod McLellan Co., 1450 El Camino Real, South San Francisco, Calif. 94080 (color catalog $1)

Roehrs Exotic Nurseries, RFD, Box 144, Farmingdale, N.J. 07727 (wide tropical selection)

Seaborn Del Dios Nursery, Route 3, Box 455, Escondido, Calif. 92925 (wide variety of bromeliads)

Wilson Bros., Roachdale, Ind. 46172 (geranium specialists — including dwarfs and miniatures)

Unusual outdoor plants

Carroll Gardens, Westminster, Md. 21157 (herbs, dwarf trees, and shrubs)

Far North Gardens, 15621 Auburndale Avenue, Livonia, Mich. 48154 (primroses and primulas)

Gardens of the Blue Ridge, P.O. Box 10, Route 221, Pinola, N.C. 28662 (native species)

Gossler Farms Nursery, 1200 Weaver Road, Springfield, Ore. 97477 (magnolias, rare trees and shrubs)

A. H. Hazzard, 510 Grand Pre Avenue, Kalamazoo, Mich. 49007 (Japanese iris)

International Growers Exchange, Box 397U, Farmington, Mich. 48024 (extensive selection; catalog $2, deductible from order)

Iron Gate Gardens, Route 3, Box 101, Kings Mountain, N.C. 28086 (hostas, day lilies)

Miniature Gardens, Box 757, Stony Plain, Alberta TOE 2GE, Canada (dwarf plants, including conifers)

Nuccio's Nurseries, 3555 Chaney Trail, Altadena, Calif. 91001 (unusual varieties of azaleas and camellias)

Oakhill Gardens, Route 3, Box 87, Dallas, Ore. 97338 (sempervivums and sedums)

Pacific Bamboo Gardens, Box 16145, San Diego, Calif. 92116 (great variety of hardy and tender bamboo; price list 40¢)

Palette Gardens, 26 W. Zion Hill Road, Quakertown, Pa. 18951 (Alpine plants)

Siskiyou Rare Plant Nursery, 522 Franquette Street, Medford, Ore. 97501 (rock plants)

Louis Smirnow, 85 Linden Lane, Brookville, Glen Head P.O., N.Y. 11545 (peonies)

Sylvan Nursery, 1028 Horseneck Road, South Westport, Mass. 02790 (heathers)

Tillotson's Roses, Brown's Valley Road, Watsonville, Calif. 95076 (rare and old varieties; catalog $1)

White Flower Farm, Route 63, Litchfield, Conn. 06759 (perennials, bulbs, trees, and shrubs)

Seeds

John Brudy's Rare Plant House, Box 1348, Cocoa Beach, Fla. 32931 (rare seeds, also some plants; catalog 50¢)

W. Atlee Burpee Co., 300 Park Avenue, Wamminster, Pa. 18974 (full range of seeds plus fruit trees and berry bushes as well as nursery stock; catalog)

Comstock Ferre and Co., 263 Main Street, Wethersfield, Conn. 06109

De Giorgi Co., 1411 3rd Street, Council Bluffs, Iowa 51504 (flower and vegetable seeds; catalog 35¢)

De Sylva Seed Co., 21994 Tanager Street, Colton, Calif. 92324 (exotic seeds)

George W. Park Seed Co., Greenswood, S.C. 29647 (full range of seeds — annuals, perennials, vegetables, tropicals, etc.; catalog)

Stokes Seeds, Box 548, Buffalo, N.Y. 14240 (vegetable and flower seeds; catalog)

Suttons Seeds Ltd., Torquay, Devon, England (general; catalog)

Thompson & Morgan, Inc., 401 Kennedy Boulevard, Box 24, Somerdale, N.J. 08083 (general and botanical seedsmen; catalog)

Bulbs

Cooley's Gardens, Silverton, Ore. 97381 (iris specialist; catalog)

P. de Jaeger & Sons, 118 Ashbury Street, S. Hamilton, Mass. 01982

Alexander Heimlich, 71 Burlington Street, Woburn, Mass. 01801

McCormick Lilies, Box 700, Canby, Ore. 97013 (lilies and cyclamen; catalog)

Walter Marx Gardens, Boring, Ore. 97009 (all varieties of iris; catalog)

John Scheepers, 63 Wall Street, N.Y. 10005 (all types of flowering bulbs; catalog)

Van Bourgondien Bros., Box A, Babylon, N.Y. 11702

Wayside Gardens, Hodges, S.C. 29695

Aquatic plants and supplies

Paradise Gardens, 14 May Street, Whitman, Mass. 01382 (water lilies and other aquatics; pools, fountains, and accessories; catalog $1)

Slocum Water Gardens, 1101 Cypress Garden Road, Winter Haven, Fla. 33880

William Tricker, 174 Allendale Avenue, Saddle River, N.J. 07458; also located at 7125 Tinglewood Drive, Independence, Ohio 44131 (one of the widest selection of plants and supplies; catalog)

Van Ness Water Gardens, 2460 North Euclid Avenue, Upland, Calif. 71986 (tropicals and other aquatics — full range of supplies; catalog 25¢)

Bonsai

Allgrove Bonsai Farm and Nursery, 281 Woburn, Wilmington, Mass. 01887

Heirob Bonsai Nursery, Willowemoc Road, Livingston Manor, N.Y. 12758

Hortica Garden, Box 300, Placerville, Calif. 95667 (catalog 25¢)

Suzu-En Bonsai Co., 326 W. 31st Street, Erie, Pa. 16508

University Nursery, 1132 University Avenue, Berkeley, Calif. 94702

Western Arboretum, 435 North Lake Avenue, Pasadena, Calif. 91101 (catalog 25¢)

Herbs

Cedarbrook Herb Farm, Route 1, Box 1047, Sequim, Wash. 98382 (price list 10¢)

Greene Herb Gardens, Greene, R.I. 02827 (booklet including price list $1)

Hemlock Hill Herb Farm, Litchfield, Conn. 06759 (catalog 25¢)

Sunnybrook Farms Nursery, 9448 Mayfield Road, Chesterfield, Ohio 44026

Taylor's Garden, 2649 Stingle Avenue, Rosemead, Calif. 91770

Equipment, etc.

American Science Center, 5700 Northwest Highway, Chicago, Ill. 60644 (soil test kits, electronic timers, and other growth light products; catalog 50¢)

Aqua-Pots, 7602 30th Street West, Tacoma, Wash. 98466 (self-watering pots; brochure)

Atlas Fish Emulsion Co., 1015 O'Brian Drive, Menlo Park, Calif. 94025 (fertilizers)

Bernard J. Greeson, 3548 N. Cramer Street, Milwaukee, Wis. 53211

Grower's Supply Co., Box 1132, 33 N. Staebler Road, Ann Arbor, Mich. 48106 (timers, indoor greenhouses, light stands; brochure)

A. H. Hummert Co., 2746 Chouteau Avenue, St. Louis, Mo. 63103 (watering, spraying, and dusting devices; catalog)

Lilly's Garden, 510 South Fulton Avenue, Mount Vernon, N.Y. 10550 (hanging containers, brackets, and decorative flower pots)

Lord & Burnham, Irvington-on-Hudson, N.Y. 10533 (fluorescent-light garden units, heaters, thermometers, humidifiers, etc., catalog)

Shoplite Co., 566 Franklin Avenue, Nutley, N.J. 07110 (wide range of supplies for growing plants under artificial light; catalog 25¢)

General index

247

Index of plant names

This index lists all the plants mentioned in the book, with the exception of fruit, herbs and vegetables, under their botanical names. As explained in the Introduction, genus names are abbreviated after the first mention in an entry. The abbreviation *spp* means *species* in general; thus *Ficus* spp indicates the various species of the genus *Ficus*. The sign x indicates a hybrid.

In most cases, the names of individual varieties are not indexed. Common names, both English and American, are cross-referred to the botanical names.

Page numbers in **bold-face** type indicate major entries, principally descriptions of plants or how to grow them, while those in *italics* refer to illustrations. Passing references are in ordinary light-face type. An indication of plants' hardiness and longevity – intended as a general guide only, and not always applying to every species or variety – is given in brackets after the name. Where alternatives are given, separated by an oblique stroke (/), this means either that particular species or varieties can differ in characteristics, or that the plant can be treated in various ways – eg, either as a half-hardy annual or as a tender perennial.

Abbreviations are as follows:

T: Tender; to be grown indoors except in warm weather or subtropical areas
HH: Half-hardy; can be grown outdoors in most places, but will not tolerate frost
H: Hardy; tolerates all normal outdoor conditions
*H: Hardy, but not reliably so; needs winter protection in very cold areas
A: Annual
B: Biennial
P: Perennial (including trees and shrubs)
Q: Aquatic

Index of plant names (continued)

Index of plant names (continued)

Acknowledgements

The writers, artists and photographers who contributed the text and illustrations on each two-page spread of this book are listed below. In some cases, credit is given to the designer and/or owner of the setting after the name of the photographer.

Where more than one artist or photographer contributed the illustrations to a spread, these are listed from A to Z, starting with the picture farthest to the left and nearest the top of the page, and working down each column in turn.

Text

14–15: Michael Wright
16–19: Tessa Clark
20–21: William Davidson
22–27: R. H. Menage
28–29: William Davidson
30–33: Michael Wright
36–41: William Davidson
42–43: Michael Wright
44–45: William Davidson
56–59: Anne Ashberry
60–67: Thomas C. Rochford
68–74: William Davidson
75: Michael Wright
76–77: William Davidson
78–81: R. H. Menage
82–89: William Davidson
90–91: R. H. Menage
92–99: Peter Black
102–103: William Davidson
104–105: Harold Bagust
106–115: Frances Perry
116–117: Brian Langdon
120–121: Frances Perry
122–123: Tessa Clark
124–125: Frances Perry
126–127: Frances Perry and Michael Wright
128–137: Frances Perry
138–139: William Spink; John Ainsworth and Helen Varley
140–141: Tessa Clark and Michael Miller
144–167: Frances Perry
170–177: Frances Perry
178–187: John Ainsworth
188–195: Anne Ashberry
198–203: Michael Wright
204–205: Neil Ardley
206–207: R. H. Menage
208–213: Neil Ardley
216–217: Rosalie Vicars-Harris
218–237: R. H. Menage
238–239: Helen Varley
240–241: Neil Ardley; Helen Varley

Illustrations

2–3: Julie Styles
4–5: Julie Styles
6–7: A: Colin Gray; B: R. Guillemot/ Agence Top/Marc Held
8–9: Rod Shone
10–11: A: Spectrum Picture Library; B: Harry Smith
12-13: A: Julie Styles; B: Lyn Gray
14–15: A: J. Guillot/Agence Top/Gérard Gallet; B, C, F, G: Harry Smith; D: Rod Shone; E: R. Guillemot/ Agence Top/John Stefanidis
16–17: A: Angela Downing; B: M. Desjardins/Agence Top/François Catroux
18–19: A: R. Guillemot/Agence Top/ Jean Dubuisson/Serge Royaux; B: Harry Smith; C, E: A-Z Botanical Collection; D: M. Desjardins/Agence Top/François Catroux; F: Rod Shone
20–21: A, C, D, E, G: Rod Shone; B: A-Z Botanical Collection; F: Grosfillex
22–23: A, F: Colin Gray; B: Julie Styles; C, D: Bob Martin; E: R. Guillemot/ Agence Top/Hvisträk
24–25: Rod Shone
26–27: A, B: D. Wright/W. Richardson Ltd; C: A-Z Botanical Collection; D, E: Harry Smith
28–29: A: M. Desjardins/Agence Top/ François Catroux; B, C: Ove Arup & Partners; D: Rod Shone; E: Grosfillex

30–31: A: Gary Hincks; B: Harry Smith; C: Michael Ricketts; D, E: Rod Shone
32–33: A, C, E, F, H: Gary Hincks; B, D, G: Rod Shone
34–35: A: Julie Styles; B: Lyn Gray
36–37: Rod Shone
38–39: Rod Shone
40–41: A, C, D, E, F, G, H: Rod Shone; B: Hortico
42–43: A: Rod Shone; B: Ian Garrard
44–45: Rod Shone
46–47: Rod Shone
48–49: Rod Shone
50–51: Rod Shone
52–53: A, C: Rod Shone; B: Vana Haggerty
54–55: Rod Shone
56–57: Rod Shone
58–59: A, B: Gary Hincks; C, D: Creina Glegg
60–61: A: Harry Auger; B: Michael Wright; C: Ian Garrard; D, F: Milan Svanderlik; E: Harry Smith
62–63: Milan Svanderlik
64–65: Milan Svanderlik
66–67: A, B, C, D, E: Milan Svanderlik; F, G: Harry Auger
68–69: Rod Shone
70–71: A: Suttons Seeds; B, C, E: Milan Svanderlik; D, F: Rod Shone
72–73: A, B, C, D, E, F, G: Rod Shone; H: Harry Smith; I: Jim Bulman
74–75: A, B: Rod Shone; C: Suttons Seeds; D, E: Harry Smith; F: Hortico
76–77: A, B: Rod Shone; C: Suttons Seeds; D: Hortico; E: R. H. Menage
78–79: A, B, C, D: Suttons Seeds; E, G: Rod Shone; F: R. H. Menage; H, I: Unwins Seeds
80–81: A, F, G: Unwins Seeds; B: Harry Smith; C, D: Michael Wright; E, H: R. H. Menage
82–83: A, B, D, E: Rod Shone; C: Unwins Seeds; F: Thompson & Morgan; G: R. H. Menage; H: Suttons Seeds
84–85: A, D: Rod Shone; B: Frances Perry; C: Michael Wright; E: Suttons Seeds
86–87: A: Unwins Seeds; B: Suttons Seeds
88–89: A, D, E: Rod Shone; B: Michael Wright; C: R. H. Menage
90–91: A, C, D, E, H: Harry Smith; B: Hortico; F: Rod Shone; G: Thompson & Morgan
92–93: B: Michael Ricketts; E, F, G: Peter Black
94–95: A: Harry Titcombe; B: Michael Wright; C: Peter Black; D: Michael Ricketts
96–97: Peter Black
98–99: Peter Black
100–101: A: Julie Styles; B: Lyn Gray
102–103: A: Hortico; C, D, F, G, H: Harry Smith; B: Rod Shone; E: Unwins Seeds; I: Thompson & Morgan
104–105: A, E, F, G: Harold Bagust; B, C: Michael Wright; D: Unwins Seeds
106–107: Gary Hincks
108–109: A, D: Bulb Information Desk; B, C, G, H, I: Harry Smith; E: Hortico; F: Unwins Seeds
110–111: A, G: Hortico; B, D, E, F, H, I: Harry Smith; C: Broadleigh Gardens
112–113: A, C: Harry Smith; B: Bulb Information Desk; D, G: Hortico; F: Dobies Seeds
114–115: A, B, D, F: Harry Smith; C: Unwins Seeds; E: R. H. Menage
116–117: A, C, D: Brian Langdon; B, E: Suttons Seeds; F: Michael Wright; G: Rod Shone; H: Annabel Milne
118–119: A: Julie Styles; B: Lyn Gray
120–121: Harry Smith
122–123: A, C, D, E, F: Harry Smith; B, G: Bob Martin
124–125: A, B, D, F: Harry Smith; C, E: Bob Martin
126–127: A: A-Z Botanical Collection; B, C: Harry Smith; D: Mike Ricketts; E: Vana Haggerty
128–129: A: Bob Martin; B: Rod Shone; C: Gary Hincks; D: Norman Barber
130–131: A, B, D, E: Norman Barber; C: Bob Martin; F: Harry Smith
132–133: A: Phillip Ingram; B, C, D: Harry Smith
134–137: Harry Smith

138–139: A: Gary Hincks; B: Colin Gray
140–141: A: Colin Gray; B, C, D: May Warburg; E: Harry Smith
142–143: A: Julie Styles; B: Lyn Gray
144–145: A, B, E: Harry Smith; C, D, H: Hortico; F, G: Michael Wright
146–147: A, C: Hortico; B, D, E, F, G, H: Frances Perry
148–149: A: Harry Smith; B: Frances Perry; C: Hortico; D, G, H: Unwins Seeds; E: Rod Shone; F: Suttons Seeds
150–151: A, C, D, H: Suttons Seeds; B, F: Unwins Seeds; E, G: Rod Shone
152–153: A, D, E, F: Suttons Seeds; B, C: Unwins Seeds
154–155: A, G: Rod Shone; B, D, E, F, H: Unwins Seeds; C, I, J: Suttons Seeds
156–157: A, F: Thompson & Morgan; B, D, I: Suttons Seeds; C, E, H: Unwins Seeds; G: Rod Shone
158–159: A: Michael Warren; B, C, D, G, H: Hortico; E: Harry Smith; F: Unwins Seeds
160–161: A, H: Harry Smith; B: Unwins Seeds; C: Suttons Seeds; D, E, G: Hortico; F: Rod Shone; I: Frances Perry
162–163: A, C, D: Frances Perry; B: Bulb Information Desk; E, F, G: Suttons Seeds; H: Michael Wright
164–165: A, F: Alan Bloom; B, C, D: Frances Perry; E: Thompson & Morgan; G: Suttons Seeds
166–167: A, B, C, F, G, I: Frances Perry; D: Michael Wright; E: Thompson & Morgan; H: Roy Elliott
168–169: A: Julie Styles; B: Lyn Gray
170–171: A, C, E: Harry Smith; B: A-Z Botanical Collection; F: Frances Perry
172–173: A: A-Z Botanical Collection; B, C: Bob Martin
174–175: Frances Perry
176–177: A: Bob Martin; B: Rod Shone; C: Michael Ricketts; D: Frances Perry; E: Harry Smith; F: Eagle Alexander/National Coal Board
178–179: A: Harry Smith; B, D, E: Rod Shone; C: Harry Titcombe
180–181: A, C: Rod Shone; B: Colin Gray; D: Harry Titcombe
182–183: A: Rod Shone; B, C, D: Colin Gray
184–185: A, B: Rod Shone; C, D, E: Colin Gray
186–187: A, D: Colin Gray; B, C: Rod Shone
188–189: A, B: Rod Shone; C: Dateline Graphics
190–191: A, C, D, F: Rod Shone; B, E: Creina Glegg
192–193: A, B, C, D, E, F, G: Rod Shone; H: Vana Haggerty
194–195: A, B, D, E, F: Rod Shone; C: Dateline Graphics; G: Creina Glegg
196–197: Rod Shone
198–199: A, C, D, G: Gary Hincks; B: Rod Shone; E: Harry Smith; F: Michael Wright
200–201: Rod Shone & Gary Hincks
202–203: A, C, D, E, F, G: Bob Martin; B: Harry Smith; H: Michael Ricketts
204–205: A, C, D, E, F, G: Vana Haggerty; B: Julie Styles
206–207: A, C, F, I: David Cook; B, D: Suttons Seeds; E, G, H: Unwins Seeds
208–209: A, C, D, E, F: David Cook; B: Rod Shone
210–213: Vana Haggerty
214–215: Rod Shone
216–217: Richard Lewis
218–221: Andrew Farmer
222–223: A, B, C, D, E: Andrew Farmer; F: Mike Ricketts
224–225: Andrew Farmer
226–227: A, B, C, E, F: Andrew Restall; D: Autogrow
228–229: Andrew Restall
230–231: A: Bob Martin; B: Victoria Goaman
232–233: A: Richard Lewington; B: Dateline Graphics; C: Ken Lilly; D: Victoria Goaman
234–235: A: Harry Smith; B, D: Gary Hincks; C: Sylvania
236–237: Andrew Farmer
238–239: Colin Gray
240–241: A: Harry Smith; B, D: Dateline Graphics; C: Harry Titcombe
244–245: Vana Haggerty

The COMPLETE INDOOR GARDENER

The complete answer for everyone who loves growing plants
but has no garden. Whether you are a beginner or an expert,
whether you live in a penthouse or a single room, it shows
you how easy it is to grow all kinds of plants both indoors
and on patios and terraces, window ledges and balconies,
roof gardens and back yards. With 110 sections by 14 expert
writers and over 600 illustrations, most of them in color,
this revision of the million-copy best seller includes additional
plants, a brand-new section on hydroculture, many more
color photos and artwork, and a complete update of sources
for supplies and further information. This is, without
question, the ideal companion for the gardener
without a garden.

Houseplants and indoor gardening
Plants and interior design…grouping and displaying… window gardens… conservatories and garden rooms… terrariums…bottle gardens…palms… ferns…African violets…cacti… orchids…and hundreds more plants for indoors

Outdoor gardening without a garden
Patios…terraces …tub and pot gardens…balconies …window boxes… roof gardens… rockeries and raised beds…hanging baskets…and full details of numerous plants to grow in these places… shrubs…small trees …rock plants… easy annuals and perennials

Dual-purpose plants
Plants that you can grow indoors and also on a terrace or patio…more than 100 kinds of bulbs… geraniums… flowering begonias …flowering indoor shrubs to stand outside in summer

Exciting special features
Planting projects that will fascinate enthusiasts and beginners alike… terrace pools and water gardens… miniature landscapes in troughs…the ancient art of bonsai …and special fun ideas for children and adults…plants from pips and scraps …fruit, herbs and vegetables without a garden

Techniques and technicalities
Guidance on how to grow and care for plants…pots and potting…feeding and watering…heat and light…growing plants from seed and cuttings…plant health…pests and diseases…artificial light gardening… tools…gardening for the disabled

"*The Complete Indoor Gardener* is so all-inclusive that it overflows outdoors into
patios and small walled gardens. There's almost nothing you can't find presto and in
clear, concise form with the help of the best index I've ever seen in an instructional book."

—John Canaday
New York Times Book Review